DICTIONARY OF
BRITISH POLITICS

MANCHESTER
1824

Manchester University Press

This MUP series has been running successfully for nearly 30 years. We aim to provide excellent, clear analyses of aspects of British government, political ideas, single-country studies or international relations. These can be aimed at the student or teacher market but we also have major research-based works – like Arter's *Scandinavian Politics Today* – which would count as REF-recognised books.

We are constantly looking for new books on topics like: the media (including UK media), US government and politics, single-country studies of China, India, Australia, South Africa and Latin American countries. Anyone with a proposal or an idea for a proposal should contact me via the contact details below:

Bill Jones
Editor, Politics Today Series
Professor of Politics
Department of Politics and History
Liverpool Hope University
jonesb@hope.ac.uk
0151 291 3392

Ideology and politics in Britain today
  Ian Adams

Political ideology today, 2nd edition
  Ian Adams

Scandinavian politics today, 2nd edition
  David Arter

American society today
  Edward Ashbee

The US economy today
  Edward Ashbee

US politics today, 2nd edition
  Edward Ashbee

French politics today, new edition
  David S. Bell

Local government today, 4th edition
  J. A. Chandler

Irish politics today, 4th edition
  Neil Collins and Terry Cradden

Political issues in Ireland today, 3rd edition
  Neil Collins and Terry Cradden (editors)

US elections today (Elections USA, 2nd edition)
  Philip John Davies

Political issues in America today
  Philip John Davies and Fredric A. Waldstein (editors)

Devolution in Britain today, 2nd edition
  Russell Deacon

Spanish politics today
  John Gibbons

The Politics Today companion to American government
  Alan Grant and Edward Ashbee

European politics today, 2nd edition
  Patricia Hogwood and Geoffrey K. Roberts

Political issues in Britain today, 5th edition
  Bill Jones (editor)

British politics today: the essentials
  Bill Jones

Political issues in the world today
  Don MacIver

Italian politics today
  Hilary Partridge

The Politics Today companion to the British Constitution
  Colin Pilkington

German politics today, 2nd edition
  Geoffrey Roberts

The Politics Today companion to West European politics
  Geoffrey K. Roberts and Patricia Hogwood

Debates in British politics today
  Lynton Robins and Bill Jones (editors)

Parliament today
  Michael Rush

Russian politics today
  Michael Waller

Britain in the European Union today, 3rd edition
  Duncan Watts and Colin Pilkington

DICTIONARY OF BRITISH POLITICS

Second edition

Bill Jones

Manchester University Press

Manchester and New York

distributed in the United States exclusively by Palgrave Macmillan

The right of Bill Jones to be identified as the author of this work
has been asserted by him in accordance with the Copyright, Designs
and Patents Act 1988.

Published by Manchester University Press
Oxford Road, Manchester M13 9NR, UK
and Room 400, 175 Fifth Avenue, New York, NY 10010, USA
www.manchesteruniversitypress.co.uk

Distributed exclusively in the United States by
Palgrave Macmillan, 175 Fifth Avenue, New York,
NY 10010, USA

Distributed exclusively in Canada by
UBC Press, University of British Columbia, 2029 West Mall,
Vancouver, BC, Canada V6T 1Z2

British Library Cataloguing-in-Publication Data
A catalogue record for this book is available from the British Library

Library of Congress Cataloging-in-Publication Data applied for

ISBN   978 0 7190 7940 5 *paperback*

First edition published 2004
Second edition published 2010

The publisher has no responsibility for the persistence or accuracy of URLs
for any external or third-party Internet websites referred to in this book,
and does not guarantee that any content on such websites is, or will remain,
accurate or appropriate.

Typeset by R. J. Footring Ltd, Derby
Printed in Great Britain
by Bell & Bain Ltd, Glasgow

This book is dedicated to the many members of the Extra-Mural Wednesday Current Affairs Discussion Group from 1977 onwards, especially its two original members, Mrs Hilda Turner and Mrs Sheila Gardner.

For this second edition I extend the dedication to those members of the group – including Sheila – who have joined its separate continuation outside the university following the final (and very regrettable) extinction of any adult education provision by the University of Manchester.

About the author

Bill Jones was born on the Welsh border in Oswestry and educated at the Priory Grammar School for Boys, Shrewsbury, before studying international politics at University College of Wales, Aberystwyth, where he was awarded his doctorate in 1975. He was an administrative-class civil servant for two years at the Ministry of Defence in Whitehall before he joined the University of Manchester as its staff tutor in politics. He was made Director of Extra-Mural Studies 1986–91 but was forced to retire after a stroke, incurred while jogging, in 1992. He continued to teach at the university and to write books and articles on British politics, several for Manchester University Press but also including *Politics UK* (now in its seventh edition) for Pearson Education. He was Vice Chairman and Chairman of the Politics Association 1979–83 and was made a Life Fellow in 2001. When the PA ceased to exist in 2006, he was a founder member of the Political Education Forum, which went on to perform similar functions. He started teaching at Liverpool Hope University in 2006–07 and in 2009 was made a Professor in the Department of Politics and History. He has been twice married, has two children and lives in Stockport, Greater Manchester.

Contents

Preface to the first edition   page ix

Preface to the second edition   x

Acknowledgements   xi

Part I   Politics   1

Part II People   357

Bibliography   485

Preface to the first edition

There are plenty of dictionaries of politics on the market that deal with definitions or analytical terms, but very few reference books that focus squarely on the subject of British politics itself. Students, teachers and members of the public are often mystified by some term, event or personality they have read or heard about, and it seemed me that a ready source of reference would be very useful. I am aware that the Internet offers a rival service with which it is hard to compete but it is my belief that a need exists for students, teachers, journalists and the like for a comprehensive easy reference book on the British political scene. There is another, personal source for the book's provenance: my mother always used to scold me for asking questions which should have been looked up in dictionaries or other reference books. I realise that, in consequence, I have become that somewhat pedantic 'anorak' type of person who always likes to nail down the query.

The *Politics Today* series is dedicated to the publication of accessible books that are good value for money, on a wide range of political topics. As the series includes some reference volumes, Manchester University Press thought it a good idea to produce within it a reference work on the broad subject of British politics. As my choices of entry appeared, on occasions, to be a little eccentric, my publishers thought Graham Thomas and Adrian Sackman would bring some welcome objectivity as well as fresh perspectives and accuracy. I am pleased to say that they have both done so, as well as contributed helpfully to the text.

As the *Politics Today* series has a volume on the constitution, written by the late Colin Pilkington, constitutional matters are not covered here in great detail. Otherwise, I have tried to include every entry that is likely to be of interest and importance to both the teacher and the student of British politics, as well as those many people who have a thirst for the details of public life and current affairs. Ultimately, however, the selection has reflected personal choices. And, as Colin Pilkington wearily agreed, 'even though there are lots more entries one could add, one *has* to stop somewhere'. I must apologise in advance to any readers who have failed to find the reference they were sure they would find in this book. Please forward to the publisher any suggestions for entries in a future edition.

In essence the book aims to cover:

1 the most memorable political events since 1945;
2 the most important political institutions and offices;
3 in the biographical section, those people – politicians, journalists, academics, civil servants and others – who have had a formative influence on British politics since 1945 and, more selectively, before that too.

I have tended not to include entries on political concepts unless they have an especial relevance to British politics.

The structure of this book is simple. It is divided into two principal sections, 'Politics' – for events, institutions, concepts, places and so on – and 'People'. Within each, entries appear in alphabetical order and numbers appear where they would be if spelt out as words. A bibliography is provided for those who wish to follow up entries with more in-depth reading.

Bill Jones
Manchester, summer 2004

Preface to the second edition

For this second edition, six years after the publication of the first, I have tried to include all the major events and new players on the political stage. Entries are up to date as of early summer 2010. I am very grateful to Duncan Watts for the very generous time he gave to reviewing and correcting certain entries and suggesting new ones.

Bill Jones
Stockport, June 2010

Acknowledgements

Part of my impulse to write this book came from the Extra-Mural Wednesday Current Affairs Discussion Group which I initiated in the 1970s as a Staff Tutor in Politics for Manchester University, in the days when it – together with the Department of Education – had the excellent sense to fund extra-mural departments in British universities. Tragically, this provision has been terminated at Manchester University and many others too. These classes have been among the best and most interesting I have taught in a working lifetime of university teaching. Adult students bring their experience, intellectual energy and special knowledge to such forums and make them chock full of humour, friendly disputation and the lust for more knowledge. It is to this changing, dynamic group over 25 years or more that I dedicate this book; they have nourished my own love of the subject and have activated the part of my brain 'ordinary' teaching (with no disrespect to undergraduates) fails to stimulate. Thankfully, through our collective enthusiasm, the group has survived outside the university, by running it privately, and so far this has proved a great success.

More particularly, I would like to thank a number of people for their help with this enjoyable project. The late Colin Pilkington wrote a reference book on the British constitution in the *Politics Today* series and helped me considerably, as well as sharing with me the intractabilities of trying to include everything within a strictly finite space. My friend Andrew McLaughlin, who was with me when the idea of the book first dawned, has been very helpful and imaginative in identifying entries.

I must also thank: Nicola Viinikka, formerly at Manchester University Press, who encouraged me warmly and wisely on this project from the outset; Tony Mason, her successor – ably assisted by Lucy Nicholson – who nursed the project through to completion; and Richard Delahunty, who, while at the Press, was also endlessly supportive. I would in addition thank Philip Norton (or Professor the Lord Norton of Louth, to give him his full title) for his typically generous responses to my many queries. I thank Jon Tonge for his help on Northern Ireland items and Duncan Watts for his thoughtful and helpful suggestions on several matters. But most of all among colleagues, I must thank Graham Thomas, my friend and fellow textbook author for Manchester University Press, who has been a tower of strength in editing early drafts so meticulously and accurately. Also engaged in similar labour was my friend David Hesp, a long-time teacher of politics and someone blessed with a much better memory than I.

Copy-editors are seldom given the credit they deserve for the meticulous line-by-line work they do in preparing a manuscript for publication. In this case the contribution to the book made by Ralph Footring was immense and I mention it with gratitude. His careful attentions led to the rectification of many errors of fact and grammar in the drafts.

I owe all of the above a considerable debt. Any mistakes, misinterpretations or omissions are not their responsibility but mine. Also helpful have been Bob Franklyn, Jim Chandler, Philip Norton, Kate Morrison, Richard Kelly and Simon Bulmer. My son Markus kindly assisted with the bibliography.

For this second edition I warmly thank Tony Mason and Jenny Howard, who have smoothed out any wrinkles on the production side. Once again I owe a huge debt to Ralph Footring, the exceptional copy-editor whom I had the good fortune to be allocated by

Manchester University Press. His endlessly careful monitoring of the drafts and his many creative inputs into the text in truth merit a place for his name on the book's cover. Thanks also to Christine Spooner for her varied and much valued assistance.

abdication crisis, 1936

Edward VIII acceded to the throne in January 1936. By November he had decided to marry an American divorcee, Mrs Wallis Simpson. Given his role as spiritual head of the Church of England, his marriage to a divorcee was widely seen as inappropriate. A crisis ensued which culminated in the king's abdication on 10 December 1936. He was succeeded by his brother (who became George VI) and was made Duke of Windsor. In June 1937 he married Mrs Simpson. He was governor of the Bahamas from 1940 to 1945. Some 60 years later there was speculation that Elizabeth II might abdicate in favour of her son Charles, but it seemed that she was (and still is) determined to carry on as monarch.

abortion

Aborting foetuses before their full term used to be illegal but, following a long campaign focusing on the dangers of back-street abortionists, it was legalised in 1967 after a private member's bill, moved by David Steel and then supported by government, became law. The Abortion Act 1967 made abortion legal provided certain specified medical conditions were met and the pregnancy was less than 28 weeks. The period was reduced to 24 weeks in 2005 provided other conditions were met. The act does not apply to Northern Ireland, where abortion is allowed only when there is a 'serious risk' to the health of the mother. While the issue continues to be debated in the UK, especially by the Roman Catholic Church, which bitterly opposes legalised abortion, the issue is nowhere near as controversial as in the USA.

absolutism

Form of government characterised by one-person rule, unrestricted by law, institution or constitution. Britain has probably not seen such a ruler since King John was forced to accede to the restrictive demands of his nobles in 1215, when he signed the Magna Carta. In the 16th century Thomas Hobbes elaborated arguments in favour of absolute monarchical power, using the justification that only such a 'Leviathan' could prevent human beings becoming lawless.

See also Magna Carta; Hobbes, Thomas.

abstention

The decision not to vote in an election. Commentators have been worried at times about Britain's civic culture, as it reveals a high degree of apathy. This is most clearly expressed in low turnout at election times. While general election turnout used to be well over 70 per cent, in 2001 it slumped to under 60 per cent, the lowest since universal franchise was introduced in 1918. Even worse, the figure has been as low as 30–40 per cent for local elections, with some wards polling as few as 10 per cent of eligible voters. For European elections in 1999, the UK figure was the lowest in the European Union, at a mere 24 per cent; one ward in Sunderland registered only 1.5 per cent of voters turning out. In 2009, the EU average turnout was down to 43 per cent, from 62 per cent in 1979, with UK turnout in 2009 only 34.7 per cent.

In September 1998, the House of Commons Home Affairs Committee urged a debate on the low level of participation in elections, and called for weekend voting and easier voter registration. Critics, though, argue that devices like postal and weekend voting merely treat the symptoms and not the cause.

In the 2001 general election the question of apathy achieved front-page importance when only 59.1 per cent turned out to vote. Labour won the election easily but only one in four of the electorate voted for the party. A BBC/ICM recall poll produced some interesting reasons for choosing not to vote: 53 per cent said they thought the result was a foregone conclusion; 77 per cent said there was no point in voting as 'it would not change anything'; and 65 per cent said they did not trust politicians. On 12 June 2001 Professor Patrick Dunleavy in the *Guardian* pointed out that the 2001 general election turnout was even worse than the low of 1918, as the latter election involved 'around 60 per cent completely unused to voting'. The 2001 election, he opined, represented the 'nadir in our history as a liberal democracy'. Based on recent research he judged that 'the public do not believe they possess the power they want through conventional politics and are increasingly sympathetic to direct action'.

Turnout at the 2005 general election was slightly higher, at 62 per cent, and at the 2010 election slightly higher again, at 65 per cent. Some observers were disappointed that in 2010 a much closer three-way contest and the innovation of televised debates for party leaders had not produced a turnout in line with the post-war decades, when it averaged over 70 per cent.

See also civic culture; political apathy; political participation.

academy
A form of secondary school designed to replace failing comprehensives. They were brought in by the Labour government after 2002 in an effort to improve educational performance in deprived areas. They usually specialise in some broad part of the curriculum such as science or technology. They are 'independent' of local authority control and are mostly state maintained and controlled. In their early days they involved

an element of private sponsorship, and the sponsors had some influence over the running of the school. Some of the early ones were briefly known as 'city academies'. In February 2007, the National Audit Office reported on their performance; it concluded that, academically, their results were a substantial improvement on those of their predecessor schools. Some 200 academies were planned to be built by 2010, at a cost of £5 billion.

accountability
The requirement to take responsibility for one's actions and make redress when appropriate. In British politics five forms of accountability apply:

1 *Electoral accountability*. National governments are accountable at general elections, which must take place at least once every five years. Moreover, individual MPs are also accountable to their constituents at election time (and to their parliamentary party through the system of whips). Local councillors are elected for four-year terms.

2 *Administrative accountability*. Hierarchies exist in which civil servants are answerable to their political masters. In turn, government ministers must account for their actions to parliament through such procedures as debates and question time. The government is answerable to the electorate at general elections, thus creating the chain of democratic accountability and legitimacy on which British government rests. Within parliament, the accountability of the executive was enhanced by the extension of select committees in 1979.

3 *Public accountability*. Newspapers and broadcasters investigate and question government actions and contribute to public debate on the issues of the day. Leading interviewers like John Humphrys of BBC Radio 4's *Today* programme and Jeremy Paxman of BBC2's *Newsnight* use their robust forensic skills to penetrate politicians' evasions.

4 *Judicial accountability*. The government is not above the law and can be held

accountable in court for actions which exceed the powers granted to it by statute law, or if it fails to fulfil obligations laid upon it by parliamentary statute or international treaty.

5 *Service standards.* Professionals in the public services, such as the National Health Service and education, must now demonstrate to the consumer the effective use of public money and quality of service through transparent systems of accountability, including independent inspection regimes, performance league tables, and the 'naming and shaming' of poorly performing services.

act of parliament

Otherwise known as a statute – a legislative proposal, or bill, which has passed all stages of the parliamentary procedure. Most bills can be introduced in either house (the first reading), although those involving finance must start their life in the House of Commons.

1 The first reading is little more than an announcement of an intention to pass the bill.

2 The second reading is a full-scale debate on underlying principles, as well as the detail.

3 It then passes on to its committee stage, where a standing committee considers every clause and proposes amendments.

4 Any changes are announced at the report stage, when the amendments are voted on.

5 Next comes the third reading, in which the amended bill is again subject to a full debate.

A similar procedure takes place in the House of Lords. After the bill has cleared both chambers, it receives royal assent and becomes law.

The stages usually take several months, enough to allow time for debate and amendment, although, if necessary, for example in time of national crisis or war, the legislative process can be telescoped into a few hours. By virtue of the Parliament Acts of 1911 and 1949, the House of Lords cannot delay legislation for more than 12 months. Money

bills – that is, those concerned with taxation or public expenditure – always start their passage in the House of Commons and cannot be delayed or amended by the House of Lords (although the Lords nonetheless may influence the government as a result of its debate). The Parliament Act can be invoked in cases of disagreement between the two chambers to ensure the will of the elected house prevails.

See also legislative process; money bill.

Act of Settlement 1701

Act which provided that a Protestant (not a Catholic) must accede to the throne. It stipulated that the monarch must take communion with the Church of England (and to this day the sovereign must be a member of that church). A change in the constitution would be required to permit a Roman Catholic to become king or queen. The act meant that, in the event of William III or Anne dying without a surviving heir, the succession would pass to Sophia, Electress of Hanover (granddaughter of James I of England), or her Protestant descendants. Further, under the act heirs lose their right to succession if they marry a Catholic.

The act also required the sovereign to seek the consent of parliament before making war or protecting foreign possessions, and barred foreigners from office or parliament. It ensured the Hanoverian succession, thus neutralising the claims of the Stuarts. On the death of Anne in 1714 George I of Hanover succeeded her to the throne of Great Britain.

Act of Union 1536 (Wales)

Merged all Welsh territory with that of England when Henry VIII was on the throne, who was himself descended from the Welsh house of Tudor. Wales was given parliamentary representation and English was made the language of legal and administrative affairs.

Act of Union 1707 (Scotland)

When James VI of Scotland succeeded Elizabeth to become James I of England in

1603, the crowns of the two countries were unified. However, the kingdoms remained legally separate for another century. In 1707 it became strategically necessary to effect a legal union with Scotland because of the danger that France might re-establish an alliance with Scotland, which was a major concern due to the war between France and England at that time. Scotland was not as fully absorbed into the Union as Wales had been and retained distinctive legal and educational features as well as its Presbyterian church.

Act of Union 1800 (Ireland)

This last act of union joined Ireland to Great Britain, creating the United Kingdom of Great Britain and Ireland, on 1 January 1801. The reason once again was defensive, with Britain fearing that France would exploit a disaffected Ireland in the Napoleonic wars. The act was revoked in 1922 with the setting up of the Irish Free State.

Adam Smith Institute (ASI)

www.adamsmith.org

An independent, non-profit-making think-tank which explores new ways of 'extending choice and competition into public service'. It was founded in 1977 by two graduates of St Andrews University, Madsen Pirie and Eamonn Butler. The ASI designs 'practical policy strategies' and introduces 'innovative ideas into the public policy debate'. It is claimed to have inspired: the Education Reform Act 1988; the reduction of higher levels of tax; the policy of contracting out services in the public sector; and the citizens' charter. Following the political demise of Margaret Thatcher, not to mention the victory of New Labour in 1997, most commentators believe the ASI lost much of its influence. In the autumn of 1997 it produced a highly flattering assessment of New Labour's first 200 days. Since then it has tried to influence both Conservative thinking and that of the Labour Party, which has moved closer to it on a number of issues, including privatisation.

additional member system (AMS)

A hybrid electoral system combining proportional representation with first past the post. It is most notably used in Germany, where voters have two votes: one to elect half the members of the Bundestag as constituency representatives and another to elect the other half from regional party lists. It is the proportion of the vote won by a party in the latter vote which determines its overall seat entitlement, its constituency seats being 'topped up' from the regional list pool. AMS is also used, in an amended form in the UK, for elections to the Welsh assembly and Scottish parliament and for the Greater London Authority.

adjournment debate

A debate in the House of Commons prompted by the motion that 'This house do now adjourn'. There are four types of adjournment debate.

1 In the main house, there are those proposed by a back-bench MP (who is chosen by ballot) at the close of business for the day. A government whip moves the motion and then the MP speaks for 15 minutes, usually on a topic close to the heart, and a government minister replies.

2 In Westminster Hall on a Thursday afternoon, either a report of a select committee (selected by the Liaison Committee) or a government motion is debated. The debate which led to Winston Churchill replacing Neville Chamberlain was of this latter type – and is attractive to the government because no amendments to the motion can be tabled, no decision can be made except to adjourn and usually there is no vote.

3 Adjournment debates in Westminster Hall also occur on Tuesday and Wednesday mornings, when MPs are again selected by a speaker's ballot the week before.

4 Emergency adjournment debates are held under standing order 24 on matters of great moment. Few applications are successful under this standing order – perhaps only one a session. Usually 24 hours' notice is given but the debate can

take place on the evening of the day on which it is requested.

Some 25 per cent of the time of the House is taken up by debating adjournment motions.

See also half-hour adjournment; Westminster Hall Chamber.

administration

A term with a number of meanings. It can refer to the civil service or bureaucracy which advises ministers and coordinates and implements government policy. It can also refer to elected politicians who hold government office (the executive), or to the period of government led by a particular person, as in 'the Thatcher administration'.

administrative class

The elite stream of the civil service, recruited mostly from the best university graduates to provide the 'intellectual' leadership recommended by the Northcote–Trevelyan report of 1854. The 'executive' and 'clerical' classes were intended to provide lesser support. In theory, the administrative class was open to all applicants, but Oxbridge graduates have in practice dominated its ranks. In 1968 the Fulton report urged broader recruitment, more professionalisation and training, and a removal of 'class' barriers to promotion. The somewhat broader 'administration group' resulted, open to people with a first or upper second degree. In the 1980s the majority of recruits still came from Oxbridge. The term is no longer used but a similar group, 4,000 strong, still advises ministers on policy options and the like.

See also civil service; Fulton report; Northcote–Trevelyan report.

administrative court

See administrative law.

administrative law

The rules governing relations between the individual and the state. If a government agency acts in a way that is not sanctioned by the law, a court may judge it to be ultra vires. This may not be easy, as government

has a fairly wide degree of discretion. The scope of administrative law widened with the extension of government activity, especially with the emergence of the welfare state. The Queen's Bench Division of the High Court acts as the administrative court, which considers, for example, cases arising from immigration and tribunal judgements. Compared with that of the USA or France, the UK's administrative law is poorly developed.

See also ultra vires.

Admiralty

Body responsible for the Royal Navy from 1832 to 1964, when the Admiralty Board was merged into the Ministry of Defence.

adversarial politics

A bipolar system of politics where an incoming government, after unceasing attack in opposition, allegedly reverses the major policies of its predecessor. A two-party system plus a simple majority voting system encourages adversarial politics. However, in practice, reversals by Conservatives in the 1950s of Labour's measures were few, although in the 1980s the Thatcher governments used privatisation to reverse Labour's postwar nationalisations. After its 1997 victory, Labour, in keeping, perhaps, with a 'third way' pragmatism, reversed remarkably few of the Conservative measures it had bitterly attacked during the previous 18 years, such as privatisation and restrictive trade union legislation. Advocates of proportional representation argue that it would end dangerous swings in government policies by encouraging the formation of more cooperative coalition governments.

advisor

See political advisor.

Advisory, Conciliation and Arbitration Service (ACAS)

www.acas.co.uk

Body founded in 1975 by the Employment Protection Act of that year. ACAS seeks to 'promote the improvement of industrial relations'. In practice, it

POLITICS

engages substantially in the conciliation of industrial disputes and the provision of arbitration and mediation facilities, as well as giving advice to employers and employees. In the 1970s it was very much in the headlines, but once the Conservatives came to power in 1979 ACAS assumed a much lower profile.

Afghanistan
After the terrorist attacks on the USA on 11 September 2001, US president George Bush Jr attacked Afghanistan after its Taliban regime refused to hand over the Saudi Arabian dissident Osama Bin Laden, the man behind the attacks. Tony Blair declared he was standing 'shoulder to shoulder' with his US ally and travelled the globe doing his best to construct a worldwide coalition in favour of Bush's anti-terrorist action. As further justification for this support, he told the Labour Party conference in October 2001 that 90 per cent of the heroin on British streets originated in Afghanistan. British troops were available but were used sparingly during the successful military action; they assumed a more prominent role in the wake of the war as a peacekeeping force in Kabul.

From January 2006, NATO forces in the form of ISAF (International Security Assistance Force) gradually replaced US forces in southern Afghanistan as part of Operation Enduring Freedom. British forces comprised the 16th Air Assault Brigade and the Royal Marines, deployed for the most part in southern Afghanistan. In the same area were troops and helicopters from Australia, Canada and the Netherlands. Air support was provided by US, British, Dutch, Norwegian and French combat aircraft and helicopters.

While the war in Iraq was judged to be intractable and British troops were steadily withdrawn during 2007–08, the Afghanistan theatre was reckoned by the British military to be still 'winnable'. Critics doubted such optimism, pointing out that successive invaders, from Genghis Khan to the USSR, had all been eventually defeated and expelled. After Barack Obama was elected US president in 2008 he tried to encourage his European allies to contribute more troops, but only the UK was responsive and that to a limited extent: the 8,300 troops then fighting in the country were supplemented by a further 1,500.

See also Al-Qaeda.

Age Concern
www.ageconcern.org.uk
A classic sectional interest group representing older people, founded in 1940. In April 2009, the national member of the Age Concern federation, Age Concern England, joined with Help the Aged to create a new charity, Age UK, which continues to work closely with the 350 local Age Concerns to deliver support and services to older people, and to liaise with government departments and agencies.

ageing population
When the proportion of older people in a society is increasing. On 28 July 2004 the Office for National Statistics announced that the number of people aged over 80 years would grow from 2.5 million in 2002 to 4.9 million in 2031, peaking at 7 million by 2050. The number of those over state pension age would increase from 10.9 million in 2002 to 12.2 million in 2011. By the middle of the century older people will outnumber children by a large margin and the rise in the number of those who are of working age will not match the rise in the number of those who are older.

In August 2008 it was announced that, for the first time, there were more people over 65 in the UK than under 16. This reflects a world situation in which people over 65 now outnumber children under 5 for the first time. In 2010, the old age dependency ratio (the number of people over 65 for every 100 people of working age) was 16.4 per cent in the UK, compared with 19.3 per cent for Sweden, 20.4 per cent for Germany, 13.0 per cent for the USA and 5.4 per cent for China. However, the UK is relatively fortunate in that it attracts many immigrants and has tended to pay low rates for pensions, thus keeping expenditure relatively low.

agency
See executive agency.

agenda setting
Media selection of news stories. News organisations select their stories on the basis of a set of news values. These prioritise some issues, events and personalities over others. Although it does not determine what people think, agenda setting can influence what people think about, that is, the 'important' issues of the time. For example, throughout 2000 the news media gave extensive coverage to 'mad' or 'bad' doctors, thus setting the agenda for increased regulation of the medical profession, and in the spring of 2009 the *Daily Telegraph* published examples of questionable expense claims by MPs, which led to calls for reform. Political parties and government now make extensive use of spin doctors and public relations advisors, who attempt to influence the process of agenda setting. It was also alleged that during the 1980s the tabloid newspapers succeeded in determining the topics debated during election campaigns.

See also mass media; news values; political agenda; power.

Agenda 21
A 2005 United Nations sustainable development programme. Local councils are required to establish their own local programmes as part of the initiative.

agent
Candidates in an election employ an agent to organise their campaign, who will be legally responsible for it. Candidates can, however, act as their own agents. Given their greater financial resources, the Conservatives have tended to have more agents than Labour.

agriculture
See Department for Environment, Food and Rural Affairs; Ministry of Agriculture, Fisheries and Food.

Aims of Industry
A corporate lobbying group set up by business leaders in 1942 to resist wartime nationalisation of enterprises and then the postwar nationalisations by Labour, as well as aspects of the welfare state like the National Health Service. While in theory independent of the Conservative Party, it does have close links. It claims around 800 members.

Al-Qaeda
Loose alliance of Sunni Islamic militant organisations generally believed to have been founded by founded by Abdullah Yusuf Azzam in 1988, who was later replaced by the Saudi-originating Osama Bin Laden. Al-Qaeda is an Arabic term that translates as 'The Base'. The body emerged out of the fight against the USSR in Afghanistan and is founded upon the fundamentalist Islamist notion of 'jihad' or holy war against non-Muslims. The organisation attacked a number of targets associated with the leaders of 'western' civilisation, by far the most important being the Twin Towers of the World Trade Center in New York on 11 September 2001.

Connections with Britain are hard to specify but as a nation closely associated with the leader of the western world, the USA, Al-Qaeda has frequently identified Britain as a prime target. The home-grown London bombers of 7 July 2005, as well as others convicted for planned or actual attacks, were thought to have some kind of connection to the international movement, if only through training received in Pakistan and Afghanistan. The problem with identifying connections is that the organisation has no formal structure and exists mostly in the form of cells, which can be set up spontaneously and are not controlled from anything resembling a centre of operations.

POLITICS

POLITICS

alcohol

The Scottish government, in the spring of 2009, was considering imposing a minimum price for each unit of alcohol sold in a can or bottle, to discourage binge drinking (which had reached epidemic proportions in that country). Lager was being sold in off-licences for as little as £1 a litre and cider for £2.73 for three litres. Deaths from alcohol were twice as high in Scotland than elsewhere in the UK. Scots drink the equivalent of 11.8 litres of pure alcohol a year on average, although this is less than in Luxembourg, where the figure is 15.6 litres per person. A survey by a Swedish institute revealed that while 9 per cent of French people said a drink turned into a binge (i.e. a whole bottle drunk), compared with 13 per cent of Italians and 14 per cent of Germans, the figure for Scotland was a whopping 40 per cent.

alderman

Senior councillor who was elected by fellow councillors to serve six years. The aldermanic system of representation applied to county and county boroughs before the 1974 reorganisation of local government. The office was established in 1835. The system fell into disrepute due to corruption and the fact that local citizens were excluded from the process. The Local Government Act 1972 abolished it.

See also local government.

all-party group

Type of parliamentary body established to address an issue of interest. In 2010 there were nearly 450 such groups, in addition to 145 country groups. The disability group is especially effective as, allegedly, are the parliamentary reform and scientific groups; the football group has over 100 members. Many of the groups have links with relevant bodies outside parliament but they seldom exert much influence within parliament.

all-women short-lists

Practice whereby a party's short-list of parliamentary candidates for a constituency comprises only women, in order to increase the number of women MPs in that party. It was introduced by Labour in 1993 for winnable seats. However, in December 1995 two men challenged the rule under the Sex Discrimination Act 1975 and an industrial tribunal found in their favour. The 34 candidates already selected did not lose their candidacies but otherwise the process was suspended. Tony Blair described all-women short-lists as 'not ideal' but was prevailed upon to support new legislation, and the Sex Discrimination (Election Candidates) Act 2002 made them legal.

Alliance

Name given to the collaboration in September 1981 between the Social Democratic Party (SDP) and the Liberal Party. The Alliance fought the 1983 election on a joint manifesto, with Roy Jenkins as 'prime minister designate'. It garnered just over a quarter of the vote (25.4 per cent) but, because of the first past the post voting system, only 23 seats (3.5 per cent). In 1987 it fought under the joint leadership of David Owen and David Steel, when it gained a smaller share of the vote (20.6 per cent) and only 22 seats. In January 1988 the two parties formally merged to form the Social and Liberal Democratic Party.

See also gang of four; Liberal Democrats.

Alliance Party of Northern Ireland

www.allianceparty.org

One of the smaller Northern Ireland parties, historically important since it bridges the sectarian and thus political divide between Catholics and Protestants. It supports the unionist line on the constitution but attracts some Catholic support, especially among middle-class voters. The party has regularly gained 5–10 per cent of the vote in elections and strongly supports the power-sharing arrangements established by the Good Friday agreement in 1998. In 2007 it gained seven members of the Northern Ireland legislative assembly and in the 2010 general election one Westminster MP.

alternative vote

Majoritarian electoral system in which voters rank order their preferences from a list of candidates. If no candidate gains half of the first preferences, the one with the least votes is eliminated and the second-preference votes on those ballot papers are distributed. If no candidate has reached the 50 per cent threshold, then the next weakest is eliminated, the second preferences redistributed and so on until a winner is achieved. The Australian system of alternative vote has some support in Britain, where over half of MPs are elected on minorities of the votes cast. In February 2010 Gordon Brown offered MPs a referendum on scrapping first past the post for the alternative vote system, and the same promise was made by the coalition government after the general election in May that year.

See also alternative vote 'top-up'; Jenkins report; proportional representation.

alternative vote 'top-up' (also known as 'AV plus')

Sometimes referred to as 'limited AMS' (additional member system). Alternative vote 'top-up' was the system recommended by the Jenkins report in 1998. This operates on the principle whereby 80–85 per cent of seats are decided via the alternative vote, with the remaining 15–20 per cent providing a 'top-up' pool to be decided by a second vote for parties, which is used to achieve a degree of proportionality. Its supporters claim the system is fairer and more demo-cratic. However, the Labour government, which commissioned the report, buoyed up by its landslides in 1997 and 2001, sidelined discussion about electoral reform. Critics argued that to introduce forms of proportional representation for the devolved assemblies yet leave Westminster elections untouched was illogical and undemocratic.

Amalgamated Engineering Union (AEU)

See Unite.

amendment

See legislative process.

Amicus

See Unite.

anarchism

An approach to politics which rejects the need for the state and its coercive institutions. The view can be traced back to the Frenchman Pierre-Joseph Proudhon and the Englishman William Godwin, who suggested that governments would disappear as human beings acquired reason and judgement – a prediction that has not acquired any credibility with the passage of time.

Unsurprisingly, there are different forms of anarchist theory; for example, anarcho-syndicalism proposes that trade unions should replace the state. Some major anarchist thinkers include Max Stirner, Michael Bakunin, Peter Kropotkin and Leo Tolstoy. There are also elements of anarchist thinking in the writings of Karl Marx, who argued that the state would 'wither away' after the overthrow of capitalism and the establishment of socialism. Despite the occasional outbreaks of anarchist activity at demonstrations, sometimes peaceful, sometimes not, Britain has generally been free from this form of politics. However, the Anarchist Federation organised against the poll tax and an element of anarchistic activity was apparent in the May Day anti-capitalist protests of 2001. Anarchist groups issued leaflets in advance of those protests which identified stores like Tesco in the Old Kent Road and gave comments like 'encourages intensive monocrop agriculture', 'upsets eco-systems' and 'forces third world peasants to grow for export'.

See also political culture.

Anglo-Irish agreement, 1985

Agreement between Margaret Thatcher and Garret FitzGerald (the Irish taoiseach, or prime minister) signed at Hillsborough in 1985. The agreement represented yet another attempt to find a solution to the problems of Northern Ireland. Its main pro-visions were: that there should be no change in the constitutional status of Northern

Ireland without majority consent; that no majority for change existed in the province; and that the Republic of Ireland was to be given a consultative role in Northern Ireland via a permanent intergovernmental conference. Unionists and republicans both opposed the agreement at the time, but did not succeed in destroying it.

Animal Liberation Front (ALF)
See animal rights protest.

animal rights protest
Campaigns on behalf of suffering animals, and in particular those used for scientific research. The Animal Liberation Front (ALF) is the most high profile and argu-ably the most radical of such organisations. Its methods include picketing university laboratories, forcible entry into premises and, on occasion, violence against individu-als. In July 1998 activists released 6,000 mink into the New Forest area but the ploy backfired as the mink then killed many native animals. In the autumn of 2000 the home secretary, Jack Straw, announced plans to curb the unacceptable tactics of such groups, including intimidation and other activity which the police find difficult to prosecute. In January 2001 the govern-ment announced that it would introduce tougher powers to deal with violent animal rights protestors, such as those who were demonstrating outside the Cambridgeshire animal-testing firm Huntingdon Life Sciences and who violently attacked some of its staff. In October 2004 activists stole the body of Gladys Hammond from Darley Farm in Staffordshire, which bred guinea pigs for scientific experimentation. In 2005 Jon Ablewhite and others belonging to the Animal Rights Militia were jailed for 12 years each.
See also political violence.

Anti-Corn Law League (19th century)
Usually cited as one of the first effective pressure groups in British politics. It was established by radical factory owners under the leadership of future radical Liberals

Richard Cobden and John Bright, to oppose the laws which protected landed interests by levying charges on imported grain. Robert Peel was eventually persuaded by the League's arguments and repealed the Corn Laws in June 1846, thus ending his career – albeit honourably – and splitting the Conservative Party.

anti-globalisation protests
The movement against the 'globalisation' of capitalism attracts support from various sources, including: 'international socialist' varieties of Marxists; 'third world' sup-porters who criticise trade agreements weighted towards the 'first world'; green protesters who see constant economic growth as fatal to the planet; and any number of other groups, such as anarchists. The annual meeting of the International Monetary Fund in 1988, for example, attracted demonstrations, as did the similar meeting in 1994 in Madrid. In 1999 there was a major protest in Seattle where the World Trade Organization was meeting; and in April 2009 a wholly innocent newspaper vendor, Ian Tomlinson, was killed following police action at the G20 meeting in London.
See also globalisation.

Anti-Nazi League (ANL)
Body set up to resist the growth of Nazism in Europe in the 1970s. It was established mainly by far-left socialists, especially members of the Socialist Workers' Party, but re-launched in 1992 at a time when the far right was seen to be making inroads in eastern Europe, Germany, Belgium, Norway and Austria. The ANL sought to campaign by demonstrating against the British National Party (BNP) and events like the visit of the French far-right leader Jean-Marie Le Pen in April 2004. Sometimes the clashes became violent as the ANL argued that such threats had to be met in kind. It merged with the National Assembly Against Racism to form Unite Against Fascism in 2004. The latter organ-ised the 1,000-strong rally when BNP leader Nick Griffin and holocaust denier

David Irving spoke at the Oxford Union in November 2007.

anti-Semitism

It is hard to identify the sources of hostility to those of the Jewish race but it has possibly been connected to the visible difference of religious clothing and appearance and the cohesive family life, which has fostered high achievement in finance, business and the arts. There can be no doubt that it has existed in Britain from very early times. Robert Winder, in his book *Bloody Foreigners* (Little, Brown, 2004), provides the details. For example, 400 Jews were massacred in 1263 in London. In 1275 Jews were banned from lending money at interest, thereby ruining this aspect of their financial activities; in addition, all Jews over seven years old were required to wear a brand – a patch of yellow cloth – to identify them. In 1282 Jewish religious activities were banned. And so it proceeded, often in sudden surges, throughout most of Britain's history. However, Britain has a reputation for being less anti-Semitic than many other European countries. Cromwell in 1665 permitted Jews to enter the country and, during subsequent centuries, Britain became a haven for Jews persecuted in countries like Russia, Poland and, especially, Nazi Germany during the 1930s. Yet anti-Semitism survived in the UK, often covertly within the upper and middle classes and more obviously among the working classes, who provided recruits for Britain's fringe fascist movement. George Orwell wrote an essay on this subject in 1945 in which he noted that, if anything, anti-Semitism seemed to have grown during the war. Despite these irrational sentiments, Jewish people have managed to achieve prominent positions in British society, especially in their traditional fields of finance, business and the arts.

antisocial behaviour order (ASBO)

One of the principal elements of home secretary Jack Straw's Crime and Disorder Act 1998, which gave local agencies the power to prohibit for a period of two years violent or racist behaviour in local communities. Breach of an ASBO can result in a custodial sentence. Developed by Straw in liaison with police on housing estates in his Blackburn constituency, the order is targeted at, among others, the 'neighbours from hell' who make life a misery for those who live near them. At first, few ASBOs were issued but slowly cities like Manchester and Liverpool began to use them and by 2004 they were perceived as a useful weapon against yobbish behaviour. Critics argue that the orders have been overused, lead to young people being sent to prison without due process of law and are used by some antisocial youngsters as a 'badge of honour'.

By the spring of 2008 the Home Office evinced less enthusiasm. Figures showed the numbers applied for had dropped from over 4,000 in 2006 to 2,706 by 2007 and of the latter figure 61 per cent had been breached by teenagers. The Home Office began to look for alternative approaches and on 8 May 2008 home secretary Jacqui Smith announced a battery of new measures, including a 'constant surveillance' policy directed at trouble-makers, which had produced good results in Essex.

anti-terrorism legislation

Many acts outlaw murder, destruction of property and acts perceived as terrorism and in 1974 a renewable Prevention of Terrorism Act was passed designed to counter the threat of the IRA. However, the threat of radical Islam provoked new legislation, in the form of the Terrorism Act 2000, which made illegal any 'incitement of terrorism', providing training for it or training in any form of weaponry. In the wake of the attacks of 11 September 2001, some legislation was strengthened, as was also the case after the London bombings of July 2005. In December of that year a new Prevention of Terrorism Act was passed which made it possible for terrorist suspects to be held under 'control orders' rather than in prison, which had been judged unlawful by the High Court in relation to human rights legislation.

POLITICS

11

appeasement

The policy adopted in the late 1930s by the national government of Neville Chamberlain, and supported by much of the press and public, in an attempt to defuse Hitler's aggression in eastern Europe. It reached its climax at the signing of the Munich agreement on 30 September 1938, when Chamberlain, the French leader Daladier, Hitler and Mussolini agreed to the handing over to Germany of the Sudetenland, the German-speaking part of Czechoslovakia. Chamberlain returned to Britain with a 'piece of paper signed by Herr Hitler' to pronounce 'Peace with honour … peace in our time'. By March 1939 Hitler had marched into and occupied the rest of Czechoslovakia, making the Munich agreement forever the symbol of pusillanimity in the face of aggression. The term 'appeasement' has since become part of the vocabulary of political abuse, used to upbraid opponents who, in the eye of the accuser, lack moral courage. An example of this was just before the outbreak of the Falklands war in 1982, when Margaret Thatcher answered critics with 'Britain does not appease dictators'.

Appellate Committee of the House of Lords

See Supreme Court.

Appointments Office

Part of the machinery of the prime minister's office. It deals with those appointments, especially to the Church of England and universities, which are the premier's responsibility.

aristocracy

In his classification of constitutions, Aristotle (c. 383–322 BC) defined 'aristocracy' as 'rule by the best citizens'. In practice, however, in Britain it meant rule by the landed nobility, who dominated government up until the late 19th century, when they were challenged by the emergent upper middle classes. The reforms to the House of Lords in 1911 symbolised the decline of the aristocracy, but their influence continued

nevertheless. Between 1884 and 1924 they filled 43 per cent of cabinet posts and during 1933–64 they sustained 26 per cent of its membership. In 1999 the hereditary element in the House of Lords was reduced to a rump of 92. However, the influence of the aristocracy lingers on, especially in the Conservative Party, where, for example, Michael Ancram, heir to the Marquis of Lothian, served as MP and minister as well as party chair and who stood in the leadership election following the Conservatives' 2001 general election defeat. He declined to use his honorary title the Earl of Ancram while sitting in the Commons. He inherited the title on his father's death in 2004, but eschewed its use in public life. The House of Lords Act 1999 enabled him to accept his title without being disqualified from sitting in the Commons.

See also House of Lords reform.

armed forces

Term that covers the Army, Royal Navy and Royal Air Force (RAF). The UK's main armoury includes four Vanguard-class submarines carrying Trident nuclear weapons, which are on constant patrol. Before the conflicts in Afghanistan and Iraq, the biggest military deployment was an armoured division in Germany. From 109,144 personnel garrisoned overseas in 1975, the number fell to 48,841 in 1997. The defence budget in 2010 was £37 billion, 11 per cent higher than in 1997. By 2011/12, personnel were planned to be 35,380 Royal Navy, 101,510 Army and 40,170 RAF. In addition, there are 86,970 civilian personnel and 3,400 Gurkhas.

The RAF was formed in 1918 when the Royal Air Naval Service merged with the Royal Flying Corps. It was central to the country's survival in the Second World War, especially through its role in the Battle of Britain (1940), when it resisted the German aerial onslaught known as the Blitz. It is run by the Air Force Board, which is chaired by the secretary of state for defence. The RAF is organised into three commands: Strike (operational), Personnel, and Training and Logistics.

The Royal Navy was founded in the 9th century by Alfred the Great. In the 19th century it was the most powerful navy in the world and helped make Britain briefly (1815–70) the most powerful country. In the Second World War the Navy was essential in helping the country survive the attacks of the German U-boats and maintaining lifelines to the USA and to the USSR. After the war the Navy was over-shadowed by those of the two superpowers but its force of nuclear submarines carried Britain's nuclear deterrent in the form of the Trident missiles already mentioned. The Navy is run by the Admiralty Board and its chief officer is called the first lord of the Admiralty. The Royal Navy in 2010 had 12 submarines, 3 carriers, 2 assault ships, 24 surface combat ships, 16 minesweepers and 23 patrol craft. The replacement of the ageing Trident system is much debated, as its cost is likely to be some £60 billion (2009 figure).

The Army has five mechanised brigades, eight tank regiments and six armoured brigades.

In 2009 the Ministry of Defence an-nounced funding would allow it to proceed with two aircraft carriers (the *Queen Elizabeth* and the *Prince of Wales*). More armoured vehicles for the Army would be ordered, plus a sixth C17 Globemaster for the RAF, to increase its strategic lift capacity.

Given Britain's involvement in so many wars since Tony Blair's period in power (1997–2007), not least in Iraq and Afghanistan, defence experts have complained of severe 'overstretch'.

'arms to Iraq' affair
See Matrix Churchill case; Scott report.

Army
See armed forces.

Arthur Andersen Accounting
Worldwide accountancy firm. It first attracted attention in British politics in 1982, when the Conservative government blamed the company for enabling US

businessman John De Lorean to extract £70 million from taxpayers to fund a poorly implemented plan to establish a sports car production plant in Northern Ireland. In November 1997 the Labour government abandoned legal proceedings against the firm in exchange for £21 million, a fraction of what the government had claimed. Questions were asked regarding 'cash for access' in January 2002, when it transpired that Andersen had audited the faulty ac-counts of the defunct energy conglomerate Enron. It was pointed out that the company had provided advice and staff to New Labour free of charge and, it was claimed, in exchange it had received government contracts worth millions of pounds.

Arts Council
www.artscouncil.org.uk
(Arts Council England)
www.scottisharts.org.uk
(Scottish Arts Council)
www.artswales.org
(Arts Council of Wales)
www.artscouncil-ni.org
(Arts Council of Northern Ireland)
Body responsible for the allocation of public funding for the arts. There are separate Councils for England (with nine regional offices), Scotland, Wales and Northern Ireland. The Arts Council of Great Britain was founded in 1945 but was reconstituted in 1994 as the separate councils, and the devolved assemblies now take care of arts funding in their areas. The function of the Councils is to use an annual grant to develop and improve knowledge, understanding and practice of the arts and to increase public accessibility to them. The budget includes substantial funding from the National Lottery.

assassination
Murder for political cause. Britain has not been noted for assassinations; certainly, it is less dangerous for politicians than the USA, although this has not always been so. In 1812, the prime minister, Spencer Perceval, was shot in the lobby of the House of Commons by a Liverpool broker,

John Bellingham, who was later hanged
for his crime. In 1920, Sir Henry Wilson
was shot in London by a Sinn Fein activist.
More recently, Conservative politicians and
other members of the British establishment
were targeted by the Provisional IRA and
other terrorist groups. Tory MP Airey
Neave was killed by a car bomb at the
Commons in 1979 by the Irish National
Liberation Army; Earl Mountbatten
was assassinated while on holiday in the
Republic of Ireland in 1979; and Ian Gow
(Conservative MP and former minister)
was killed when a bomb exploded at his
Sussex home in 1990. Margaret Thatcher
and her husband Dennis narrowly escaped
without physical injury when the IRA
tried to blow up the British cabinet at
the Grand Hotel in Brighton in 1984.
However, others were less lucky, including
Sir Anthony Berry, MP, who was killed,
and Norman Tebbit's wife Margaret, who,
among others, was badly injured by the
bomb blast.

assembly
See Northern Ireland assembly; regional
assembly; Scottish parliament; Welsh
assembly and government.

assisted-places scheme
Introduced by the Conservative government after 1979 to give financial support
to bright children from under-represented
socio-economic groups to attend private
schools. Labour opposed the policy in
opposition and phased out the scheme
when it came into office in 1997, using
the funds thereby freed to help reduce
class sizes.

assisted suicide
According to the terms of the Suicide Act
1961, it is illegal for anyone to help someone to commit suicide. However, by 2009
over 100 people (mostly with terminal
illnesses) had travelled to Switzerland,
where voluntary suicide is not illegal, to
end their lives at the Dignitas clinic. Those
helping with travel and the like have not
been prosecuted and opinion polls show a

majority in favour of such assisted suicides.
In July 2009 Debbie Purdy, who suffered
from multiple sclerosis, won a High Court
judgement allowing her husband to assist
her in this fashion when the time arrived
for her.

asylum seeker
A person applying to live in Britain in
order to escape persecution in the home
country. Britain has long been a home for
people fleeing from oppression in other
countries, notably the Huguenots in the
16th century, and the Jews in the 19th and
20th centuries in the face of pogroms in
Russia and anti-Semitism in Germany,
especially during the 1930s, when the
Nazis persecuted Jews. More recently, refugees have poured out of the trouble spots
in the world – in Africa, eastern Europe
and the Middle East – and have sought
political asylum in Britain. However, at the
same time thousands of poor people from
the third world have been keen to enter the
country to improve their economic prospects
and enjoy the benefits of a western lifestyle.
It is the latter group who have caused a
political problem. Britain is a favourite
target for asylum seekers, as the welfare
system is relatively generous, work as an
'illegal' is quite easy to acquire and most
big cities have a potentially welcoming
community of immigrants of just about
every variety.
    Britain has been relatively free of racial
tension and support for the British National
Party (BNP) has been scant compared,
for example, with France's Front National.
However, evidence of racial tension sometimes surfaces in the form of riots, beatings
and murders, and the government has been
keen to limit the number of immigrants,
whether economic migrants (many of whom
are in great demand, especially skilled
workers) or asylum seekers. Politically,
the Conservatives have been more willing
to identify 'bogus asylum seekers' and to
support the somewhat fevered exaggerations
of the tabloid newspapers about how much
the government spends on supporting
asylum seekers while their applications are

being considered. Labour tended to take a more liberal view in theory but to be just as strict as the Conservatives in practice. The problem with the asylum laws was that it was possible for people to arrive in the country, apply for asylum and then disappear into their minority ethnic havens: it was calculated that some 200,000 such 'illegals' (possibly more) had entered the country in this way by January 2003. It is true that Britain has proved the most popular destination for asylum seekers and there is evidence to suggest the less liberal a country's immigration laws and procedures, the less likely it is to be the desired destination.

In September 2002 Tony Blair, interviewed on BBC2's *Newsnight* programme, agreed that the number of applications, at nearly 9,000, was too great; he hoped new measures would reduce this figure by 30 per cent within a few months and by 50 per cent within a year. By October 2003 applications had reduced to 4,225. In the queen's speech for that year even tougher measures were announced, including: restrictions on the rapidly increasing bill for legal aid for asylum appeals; a more restricted appeals procedure; possible jail for immigrants who travelled by air and destroyed their passports upon landing to make it impossible to discover their country of departure; and the possible taking into care of the children of immigrants denied leave to stay but who refused to take advantage of free air tickets to their home country. The number of asylum seekers had fallen to a 13-year low in 2006 but official figures were widely distrusted and the subject of political argument.

Athenian democracy

The world's first direct democracy, which existed between c. 500 and 321 BC. In contrast to representative democracy, the political system of Athens made use of an assembly of all citizens, which excluded women, slaves and foreigners, and council and citizen juries, which were in charge of the day-to-day government of the city. The membership of the assembly and

juries was decided by selection through a 'lottery' of all the citizens. In general terms, any Athenian male citizen could become directly involved in the political system of the city state. Clearly, Britain is too highly populated to allow an Athenian form of direct democracy, but advocates of more democracy, notably Tony Benn, urge its introduction into all forms of national and social life.

attorney general
www.lslo.gov.uk
The government's principal legal advisor. The attorney general, along with other law officers (for example the solicitor general), is part of the government and has the following functions:

1 to represent the government in civil and criminal proceedings, as either plaintiff (for example in relation to alleged breaches of the Official Secrets Act) or defendant;
2 to head the Crown Prosecution Service and the Serious Fraud Office, which play a major role in the criminal justice system;
3 to refer cases to the Court of Appeal if, in the eyes of the prosecution, a sentence is deemed too lenient (a function acquired in 1989).

The attorney general is accountable to parliament, as is any minister; however, according to received wisdom, the legal function is exercised independently of government.

When he became prime minister in June 2007, Gordon Brown foreshadowed some constitutional changes he thought necessary, including the office of the attorney general. In March 2008 Jack Straw announced the Constitutional Renewal Bill, which was to include an adjustment to the attorney general's relationship with the prosecuting authorities, whereby:

> the Attorney will cease to have any power to give directions to prosecutors in individual cases, save in certain exceptional cases which give rise to issues of national security. The Attorney will have to report to Parliament on any exercise of that power.

POLITICS

Despite such promises, the Constitutional Renewal Bill, published in July 2009, contained no such clauses and the role of the attorney general was set to remain precisely the same, including a seat in the cabinet.

audit

The process whereby the purpose of government expenditure is measured against its end result. There has been a dramatic increase in such activity and most public services are now subject to external scrutiny and an audit culture.

See also National Audit Office.

Audit Commission

www.audit-commission.gov.uk

Examines local government and health expenditure to ensure it has taken place as intended. The Commission was set up under the Local Government Finance Act 1982; it also has a remit to improve the efficiency and effectiveness of local government.

Auld report, 2001

A report by Sir Robin Auld, an appeal court judge, into the criminal justice system. He suggested a new, unified, three-tier system: a crown division with a judge and jury to try serious cases; a district division for cases eligible for up to two years in prison; and the magistrates to deal with the lesser cases. A separate youth court would hear cases involving young defendants. His proposal to make juries more representative was welcomed but his suggestion that defendants should lose the right to choose a jury trial where this option currently exists was widely criticised and finally dropped as a serious government intention in 2002.

authoritarianism

A highly directive system of government where rulers make decisions without the explicit procedural consent of the popula-tion. This is not to say that authoritarian systems do not make use of popular sentiment, but rather that no extensive

consultation or dialogue exists between government and the governed as is the case with representative democracy. Authoritarian regimes often fill the gap when the social, political and economic conditions do not exist for full liberal democracy. British government has been perceived as 'liberal' rather than authoritarian. Individual politicians, however, have often been described as authoritarian in style and spirit, for example Oswald Mosley in the early years of the last century and in the latter part, most notably, Margaret Thatcher.

authority

The legitimate use of power. The term can be applied to an individual office holder (for example the authority of the prime minister or a police officer), a collective of individuals, or an institution (for example the authority granted to a government by the mandate obtained at a general election). A useful distinction is made between 'authority' and 'power' whereby someone with a gun can com-mand compliance and an unarmed police officer can do the same. The difference is that citizens of a country accept the right of the police officer to give orders, who consequently has 'authority', while they obey the person with the gun only through fear, who consequently has 'power'.

Max Weber, the German political economist, proposed three types of authority: charismatic, traditional and legal rational. The first is based upon some special characteristic, such as a great sporting, sexual or personal prowess (for example Adolf Hitler). Traditional author-ity is based upon custom and practice and often the hereditary principle applies (as in the case of the monarchy). Finally, Weber argues that legal rational authority is associated with the development of the modern state and the associated large bureaucracies (the civil service) who staff its key institutions.

Changes of government are effected by the application of abstract rules and procedures; for example, the authority of a governing party in Britain is based upon it having obtained – usually – a majority of seats in the House of Commons following a general election.

See also leadership.

'awkward squad'

Term used in 2004 to denote the leaders of the then big four unions (Transport and General Workers' Union, Unison, GMB and Amicus), who coordinated a campaign in that summer to 'reclaim the Labour Party' and return it to more traditional values of public ownership, strengthened employment rights and more building of council houses. With organised labour still commanding half of Labour Party conference votes, a united stand by the unions was not something Tony Blair could easily countenance, especially as his party was relying on the unions to donate £20 million over the years 2004–06 to fund election and other expenses. However, it cannot be said that this more militant stance amounted to much: Blair continued to keep the unions at arm's length, as did his successor after June 2007.

B

backbencher

Term that denotes MPs who do not hold ministerial office or have a shadow cabinet portfolio. Many such MPs seek greater influence as members and chairs of the 20 or so select committees. Failed, disgraced or politically rejected ministers are often consigned to the back benches, where they may seek rehabilitation or merely seethe with rebellious frustration. Others seek to maximise their influence; for example Tony Wright as the influential chair of the Public Administration Committee and Frank Field as a thoughtful influence on social policy plus his successful effort at

forcing Gordon Brown to compensate the 5.3 million poorly paid disadvantaged by Brown's budget abolition of the 10p tax band in April 2008.

backwoodsman

Name given to a member (usually hereditary) of the House of Lords who took little active part in the day-to-day proceedings of the upper chamber but who turned up to vote on key issues for the Conservative Party. (Many defenders of the hereditary principle nonetheless used to argue that the Lords acted as a safeguard of the constitution and was thus above party politics.) The abolition in 1999 of the right to sit of all but 92 hereditary peers means that the term 'backwoodsman' is now essentially a historical one.

Bains report, 1972

Report that attempted to bring an element of streamlined corporate management to the over-complex world of local government committees. The idea of this approach, borrowed from the business world, was to weaken the heads of departments in favour of a collective approach. This centred on a form of local government 'cabinet', to be called the policy and resources committee, which coordinated council policies and priorities; there would also be a chief executive to head a chief officer's management team. Over time, many of Bains' recommendations were adopted by a large number local authorities and the 'cabinet' model was preferred to the elected mayor by many local authorities.

balance of payments

The gap between the overall value of the country's imports and exports. During the 1960s this measure of the economy's performance was closely scrutinised and a bad set of figures, shortly before polling day, was believed to have damaged Labour's election results in 1970. However, it receded in importance during subsequent decades as other, more potent indexes superseded it, such as inflation, interest rates, the growth in gross domestic product

POLITICS

and the money supply. Nonetheless, in early 2001 concern was expressed by economic commentators that the balance of payments was beginning to widen excessively, especially that relating to the manufacturing sector, which fell into recession during that year, and it had reached record levels by 2004. However, Britain's trade in 'invisibles' – investment income, fees for financial services and so forth – usually serves to lessen the gap.

Balfour declaration, 1917
Important early statement on the formation of a Jewish state. Arthur Balfour, when foreign secretary, wrote to the Zionist leader Lord Rothschild in November 1917 stating his support for the establishment of a Jewish 'national home' in Palestine. He included the proviso, however, that non-Jewish people's civil and political rights should not be prejudiced. These terms were embodied in the League of Nations' 'mandate' for Palestine, which Britain undertook. Some saw the move as an attempt to win support from American Jews as part of Allied attempts to bring the USA closer to the anti-German effort in the First World War. The declaration was crucial in making Palestine the focus of Jewish resettlement during the interwar years and subsequently.

Balkan war, 1996–2000
This was in effect the Serbian/Yugoslav war against the Kosovo Liberation Army, a mostly Albanian guerrilla force that sought separation from Yugoslavia. Tony Blair, appalled by the human rights violations of the Serbian leader Milosevic, adopted a clear leadership role regarding western intervention in the crisis and was able to persuade an initially reluctant president Clinton to use the weight of US armed forces under the aegis of NATO. Eventually the Serbian leader was forced to back down; some say Blair's success in this limited intervention encouraged him to contemplate bigger interventions, like the 2003 invasion of Iraq.
See also Kosovo crisis.

ballot
An election in which secret votes are cast for two or more candidates. The ballot box is the receptacle into which votes are placed before counting. Ballot rigging is the attempt to interfere with the voting process by fraudulent means. The Ballot Act 1872 introduced measures to counter corruption and intimidation; one of the most important of these measures was the requirement that voting was to take place in secret.
See also Reform Act; voting behaviour.

Bank of England
www.bankofengland.co.uk
Britain's central bank. Incorporated by statute in 1694 to provide finance for William III's French wars, the Bank of England was forbidden to lend money to the government without parliamentary approval, but was given the right to issue notes against the security of its loan to the government. It became the principal banker to government departments when it took over the administration of the national debt in 1750. In 1833 its notes became legal tender and it assumed a monopoly over the issue of English bank notes in 1844. From 1928 the Bank was no longer obliged to redeem bank notes in the form of gold coin. The Bank was nationalised in 1946, since when it has acted as an agent of and advisor to government on financial policies. Chancellor Nigel Lawson wanted to set the Bank free of government controls and allow it to set interest rates to control inflation, but Margaret Thatcher believed this would be 'abdicating responsibility'. When Gordon Brown became chancellor in 1997 he did give the Bank autonomy to set interest rates. A team of professional economists in the Monetary Policy Committee is now responsible for interest rates, which it must set to meet an inflation target stipulated by government; minutes of its monthly meetings are made public. However, Brown also stripped the Bank of certain of its regulatory powers over financial institutions. The role of the Bank became the subject of discussion in 2007–08 when the so-called 'credit crunch', caused by the

USA's 'sub-prime mortgage' crisis, crossed the Atlantic and affected British banks and building societies.

See also Monetary Policy Committee; Northern Rock.

bankers
The banking crisis of 2007–09 led to the summoning of the major bankers on 11 February 2009 to face the irreverent questioning of John McFall's Parliamentary Treasury Select Committee. This was seen as part of the blood sport associated with the crisis. All six of the banking supremos who had led their banks into the meltdown had clearly had some coaching from public relations experts. They outdid each other in trying to say sorry in the most extravagant and sincere fashion but none accepted any real responsibility for what had happened. On 27 February Sir Fred Goodwin's pension of some £700,000 a year was heavily criticised by those who pointed out that the Royal Bank of Scotland, virtually ruined under Sir Fred's stewardship, had made a record loss, also under his watch. Sir Fred, initially at least, refused to be cowed and insisted he was going to hang on to his pension, to which he was legally entitled.

Barnett formula
Formula devised by Joel Barnett, chief secretary to the Treasury under James Callaghan, for distributing central government funds to Scotland and Wales. The aim of the formula was to allow for the fact that both countries had lower incomes per head than England. So, for every £85 by which public expenditure on England rose, it would rise by an additional £10 in Scotland and £5 in Wales. Despite the fact that gross domestic product per capita has risen in these areas to not much less than England's, the Barnett formula still provides the basis for financial distribution, and spending per head still exceeds England's by up to 23 per cent in Scotland and 16 per cent in Wales. In 2004 Barnett expressed himself 'embarrassed' that his measure, intended only 'to last for a year', was being retained 'for fear of upsetting the Scots'.

barrister
Unlike other countries where lawyers advise clients and represent them in court, in the UK the legal profession was traditionally divided between solicitors, who advised, and barristers, who represented in court. This division has been eroded in that 'solicitor advocates' are now allowed to appear in court, although clients still usually employ barristers via their solicitor. While solicitors combine into partnerships, barristers form chambers as their economic units. Barrister is regarded as a high-paying elite occupation and as such is typically dominated by privately educated Oxbridge graduates. The profession is often an appropriate launching pad for a political career, as in the cases of Tony Blair and Michael Howard.

In May 2008 the lord chief justice, Lord Phillips, modelled a new form of attire for judges, which dispensed with their traditional 300-year-old horsehair wigs in all but a few legal settings; the new rules applied as of October 2008. However, a majority of barristers, according to a consultation by their professional body, the Bar Council, were in favour of retaining their characteristic head-wear, together with their gowns.

Battle of the Boyne
Battle fought on 12 July 1690 that was decisive in the aftermath of the Glorious Revolution, 1688–89. The problem of Northern Ireland has its roots deep in history, the Battle of the Boyne being one of the more notable dates in the calendar of sectarianism. The Battle is still celebrated on 12 July in Northern Ireland by Protestants as symbolic of the crushing of the Irish Catholics. In the battle, the army of the Protestant William III (William of Orange) crossed the River Boyne near Drogheda to outflank and defeat the army of the exiled James II. James thereafter fled to France and resistance in the rest of Ireland soon crumbled.

See also Orange Order.

BBC
See British Broadcasting Corporation.

POLITICS

beacon (authorities, schools, etc.)
Adjective used by New Labour to describe
outstanding local authorities and schools
which have demonstrated excellence in the
provision of public services. Such bodies
usually receive additional resources and
increased autonomy from central government control.

Belgrano
See *General Belgrano*.

best value
New Labour's approach to local government finance and service provision. Enacted
in the Local Government Act 1999, best
value replaced the Conservative policy of
compulsory competitive tendering (CCT).
Its advocates claim that, unlike CCT's
reliance on the operation of crude free
market forces in local government services,
best value provides a locally based set of
priorities which more properly meet local
needs. In particular, it has the following
four elements: service targets based on the
Thatcherite three 'E's (economy, efficiency
and effectiveness); annual plans which take
into account past performance and future
targets; new external audit and inspection
mechanisms; and procedures for public
consultation.
    See also compulsory competitive tender-
ing; market testing.

Beveridge report, 1942
The *Report on Social Insurance and Allied
Services*. This historic work by William
Beveridge established the basis for Labour's
welfare state legislation after the Second
World War. It identified five 'giants' to be
slain: illness, ignorance, disease, squalor
and want. It proposed a scheme of social
security together with a national health
service, family allowances and a policy of
full employment.

bicameral system
A two-chamber parliament. Britain has an
'unbalanced' bicameral legislative system,
in that the House of Commons (the lower
chamber) is much more powerful than

the House of Lords (the upper chamber).
British politicians tend to believe the second
(upper) chamber is useful and merely
needs to be reformed. The US Congress
provides the contrasting example of a
balanced bicameralism, where the House
of Representatives and Senate play more or
less equal parts in the legislative process.

'Big Society'
The theme of the Conservative's election
campaign in 2010, whereby voters were
'invited' to join in the government of their
own country. The manifesto was based on
this idea – that individuals would 'seize
back' control of their lives from the government and help run services like education
and benefits. Critics pointed out that, while
this sounded attractive in theory, in practice
it was difficult to explain to voters on the
doorstep. It was significant that David
Cameron chose to ignore the theme during
the televised party leaders' debates, which
covered all aspects of policy during the
campaign. Once the Tories were in power
after the election, some reference to it was
made in the early weeks but it remained to
be seen if this was a serious, radical new
direction or just a radical-sounding piece
of rhetoric to exploit an 'anti-politics' mood
caused by, among other things, the MPs'
expenses scandal. Some Conservatives
argued an alternative, more traditional
menu of policy proposals would have
appealed much more and won for the party
the overall majority which eluded it on
7 May. Cameron's advisor, Steve Hilton,
the chief author of the approach, was
singled out by some Tories for criticism.

bill
Name given to a legislative proposal before
it has passed through its stages in parliament and receives the royal assent, after
which it becomes law.
    See also act of parliament; hybrid bill;
money bill; private bill; public bill.

Bill of Rights, 1689
One of the most important documents of
the British constitution. It resulted from

the Glorious Revolution, 1688–89, when William III and Mary II were installed as monarchs to take the place of James II. It is a statute limiting the power of the sovereign but was called a bill as it was originally passed by a convention. It was only after that convention had been converted into the first parliament of William and Mary that it was possible to enact it as a statute but it has remained ever since 'the Bill of Rights'.

It limited the authority of monarchs so that they could not rule without the consent of parliament. It also established free and regular elections to parliament, as well as freedom of speech for those speaking in parliament. The consent of parliament was required for any changes in taxation. The Bill also forbade the maintenance of a standing army in peacetime without parliament's consent. The Bill of Rights is often described as the nearest thing to the written constitution which Britain (famously) does not have.

Constitutional reformers believe Britain's dependence on common law as a substitute for a modern bill of rights is insufficient in a time when the power of government has increased to the extent where, according to many critics, it now represents a serious threat to civil liberties. Proponents of reform suggest that basic rights should be entrenched in such a way that no government with a parliamentary majority can remove them. The Labour government incorporated the European Convention on Human Rights into British law in 1998, and thus provided the citizen with an easier form of redress of grievance against the state than was previously the case. The measure provided, in the eyes of some experts, another written element of the uncodified British constitution.

bipartisanship
Consensus within two-party politics. British party politics is based on the principle of conflict between opposing 'camps' of supporters; however, on some issues political differences give way to a united or 'bipartisan' approach. For example, on Northern Ireland the major parties tend to

respect a consensus regarding policy, and on foreign affairs, too, there is a general (though by no means invariable) tendency to ignore party differences, especially when ministers are travelling abroad.

Birmingham Six
Infamous instance of a miscarriage of justice, in which six suspected IRA terrorists were tried at Lancaster Castle and convicted in 1974 of placing a bomb in a Birmingham pub. After a long campaign, led by MP Chris Mullin and journalist Paul Foot, their convictions were found to be unsafe and were quashed by the Court of Appeal in 1991. The behaviour of the police in helping to obtain the original flawed convictions was roundly criticised.
See also Guildford Four.

bishop (Anglican)
The two Anglican archbishops of Canterbury and York sit in the House of Lords together with the 24 senior bishops of the Church of England, making up the 'lords spiritual' in that chamber. They tend to confine themselves to ethical and moral issues and generally refrain from party political debate.

black economy
Undeclared, unofficial and therefore un-taxed earnings, sometimes illegal and often in cash. A 2004 study in the *Economic Journal* suggested blue-collar self-employed people report only 46 per cent of their earnings, while white-collar self-employed people report 61 per cent. Using this and other measures, the study calculated that 'black economy' activities by self-employed people represented 10.6 per cent of annual gross domestic product. Benefit claimants who also do undeclared work are likely to represent a further element.

Black report, 1980
Report on inequalities in health published in April 1980. It was deliberately given a low profile by the then Thatcher Conservative government, which viewed with suspicion its emphasis on the social

21

causes of ill-health. Inevitably this exercise in 'under-promotion' backfired and the findings achieved wide publicity. They were that the lower down the social scale one is: the less likely one is to derive sufficient benefit from the National Health Service; the less healthy one is likely to be; the less likely one is to survive into old age; the more likely one's children are to suffer injury, sickness and death. Most disturbing was the conclusion that this effect begins in the womb: twice as many babies born to mothers in social class 5 (working class) were found to die compared with those born in social class 1 (professional class). The inquiry which led to the report was chaired by Sir Douglas Black.

Black Rod (Gentleman Usher of the)

Officer of the House of Lords. The post dates back to 1350. His duties include the maintenance of order in the Lords as well as security, and he also has some responsibility for ceremonial events. He is known chiefly for his annual duty of summoning the Commons to the Lords to hear the queen's speech. On this occasion he knocks three times on the door of the Commons with his ebony staff of office, which is topped with a gold lion's head. After his first knock the door is slammed in his face, which symbolises the Commons' right to be free from interference. In March 2002, in the wake of the queen mother's funeral, it was alleged by a number of publications – principally the *Spectator* – that the holder of the post, Sir Michael Willcocks (a former UK representative to NATO), was approached by a member of the staff at Number 10 seeking to enhance the role to be played by Tony Blair in the funeral ceremonies. Number 10 complained to the Press Complaints Commission but in June dropped the matter, claiming it had been 'resolved', although Boris Johnson MP, then editor of the *Spectator*, described this as a 'humiliating climb-down'.

black section

Special unit of the Labour Party for black members. Calls for special representation in the Labour Party for members of ethnic minorities surfaced at the annual conferences in 1983, 1984 and 1985. This was in response to the low levels of participation in the party, which resulted in the election of only one black candidate in the 1983 general election. However, most members of the parliamentary party opposed the idea, as did the Labour leader, Neil Kinnock. Ironically, Diane Abbott, a black Oxford-educated woman, who was one of the most enthusiastic supporters of the idea, defeated the sitting MP Ernie Roberts in the standard selection procedure for the safe seat of Hackney and Stoke Newington.

Black Wednesday

Wednesday 16 September 1992. On that day, international speculators, most notably George Soros, began to sell the pound relentlessly on the foreign exchange markets. Despite the Bank of England raising interest rates to 15 per cent and buying sterling massively in attempts to maintain the value of the currency within the European Exchange Rate Mechanism (ERM), Chancellor Norman Lamont was forced to take the pound out of the ERM. This was a huge reverse, as membership of the ERM was then the foundation of prime minister John Major's economic policy. Leaving the ERM effectively devalued the pound by 20 per cent. After this debacle, a 'black hole' appeared in the government's macroeconomic policy and serious damage was done to the reputation of the Conservative Party as a competent manager of the nation's finances. Major was unsure whether he could continue in government after such a reverse but did so, although this event, along with splits over Europe, marked the start of a period of apparently terminal decline of the Conservative government – the party's position in the polls failed to recover after this economic policy disaster until after the election of David Cameron as leader in December 2005. The sharp devaluation following Black Wednesday, however, helped the economy to begin a slow recovery, from which Labour was the main political beneficiary.

Blairism
See third way.

Blitz
Short for *Blitzkrieg* (lightning war). This was the all-out bombing attack on London from autumn 1940 to spring 1941. It is calculated 40,000 civilians were killed during this period plus 46,000 injured and 1 million homes destroyed or damaged. As well as London other cities were attacked, including Coventry, Liverpool, Southampton and Birmingham.

block grant
The name given to central government funding of local government services. Originally such funding was specific to each local authority service, but after the Second World War it was brought together into a single rate support grant or block grant, which the local authority could spend according to its needs. These grants were replaced by the more tightly controlled revenue support grant in 1980.

See also local government finance; rate support grant.

block vote
The casting of a large number of votes by a single delegate at a conference. At the Labour Party annual conference, trade union leaders once cast the votes of all members who paid a political levy, itself a somewhat negotiable figure for some large unions. This meant, in practice, that the four or five largest unions were able to determine the outcome of important policy debates. Many both inside and outside the party were uneasy about this lack of democracy for individual party members; moreover, it provided Conservative opponents with an easy target. Therefore, at the 1993 party conference, John Smith, as party leader, carried the proposal to introduce one member one vote (OMOV), accompanied by a reduction of the union vote from 70 per cent to 50 per cent of those cast. Tony Blair was the first Labour leader to be elected on the principle of OMOV.

blog
Short for 'weblog', a form of online diary which became popular during the late 1990s, initially in the USA. 'Bloggers' can write on any subject and some are essentially personal diaries, of little interest outside their families. 'Political bloggers', however, began to have an impact in the USA, especially the Drudge Report blog (www.drudgereport.com) and, more recently, the Huffington Post (www.huffingtonpost.com), as well as www.thedailybeast.com, which have broken important stories and influenced elections.

In Britain blogging is less advanced but there is a lively 'political blogoshere' with a tendency for right-leaning blogs – Iain Dale's Diary (http://iaindale.blogspot.com), Guido Fawkes (http://order-order.com) – to be the more popular, though neither exerts any regular discernible influence, and both deal mostly in political gossip. The author of this book runs a blog which readers can find at www.skipper59.blogspot.com.

Bloody Sunday
Sunday 30 January 1972. On that day, a banned civil rights demonstration in Londonderry (or 'Derry' to those from a Catholic or republican tradition) was fired upon by British soldiers. As a result, 13 civilians were killed and 17 wounded, creating a dramatically symbolic injustice which still causes immense ill-feeling against the British. It provoked intense sectarian violence and consequently direct rule was imposed on Northern Ireland in March 1972. The Widgery report (April 1972) into the tragedy cleared the British soldiers of wrongdoing but the issue would not go away and from 2000 the long-running Saville inquiry expended huge efforts to find the truth. In 2002 an influential film, *Bloody Sunday*, pointed the finger of blame at the military commanders on the spot.

See also Saville inquiry.

Blundell–Gosschalk classification
System used to classify the political persuasions of members of the public. In December 1997 a report by the Institute

of Economic Affairs, resulting from a collaboration between pollsters MORI and authors Blundell and Gosschalk, offered a new classification of political positions. The new classification did not attract much support, however. The following groups were identified (with percentages of respondents indicated):

1 conservative (pro free market but with ethical controls), 36 per cent;
2 libertarian (maximum personal freedom), 19 per cent;
3 socialist (big government with controls on market), 18 per cent;
4 authoritarian (anti-personal/anti-economic freedom), 13 per cent;
5 centrist (some economic and social freedom), 15 per cent.
See also left–right continuum; third way.

'boom and bust'

A phrase used to describe the tendency of the British economy to experience a cycle of rapid inflationary growth, often triggered by governments in advance of an election (for example Nigel Lawson's 1986 budget), followed by a recession, after interest rates have been increased to bring inflation under control, as occurred under the chancellorship of Norman Lamont in the early 1990s. Gordon Brown, New Labour's first chancellor, claimed he was breaking out of this tendency by letting the Monetary Policy Committee of the Bank of England set interest rates on purely economic criteria. Evidence in 2001, an election year, suggested that this policy had been successful, albeit with a temporary rise in rates to 7.5 per cent in 1998. However, rates declined subsequently and Labour was able to claim it had halved mortgage rates since 1997. During the 2001 general election campaign Labour made great play of how the economy had remained stable under its stewardship. Interest rates remained low after 2001 but began to rise in 2004 in an attempt to curb the housing boom which such rates had initiated. By 2008, the long slow 'boom' since the early 1990s seemed to be crumbling into 'bust' under the malign influence of the US-caused credit crisis. By 2009 'bust' was definitely back as western governments desperately sought to inject funds back into banks, to kick start their economies. Rapidly rising unemployment figures worldwide in 2009 confirmed that 'bust' was definitely back as the corollary of 'boom'.

See also political business cycle.

Border Agency

See UK Border Agency.

borough

Term originating from the Saxon *burh*, meaning settlement, but in British history a town awarded a charter endowing it with certain legal privileges. In the Middle Ages it denoted a town that elected a member of parliament. In the late 19th century boroughs became important units of local government and were run by elected councils. In 1972 boroughs outside Greater London were abolished, although the status may still be conferred by royal charter upon a district.

Boundary Commission

www.boundarycommissionforengland.org.uk (Boundary Commission for England)
www.boundarycommission.org.uk (Boundary Commission for Northern Ireland)
www.bcomm-scotland.gov.uk (Boundary Commission for Scotland)
www.bcomm-wales.gov.uk (Boundary Commission for Wales)
A body that draws up constituency boundaries and revises them regularly (at least every 15 years). There are separate Commissions for England, Northern Ireland, Scotland and Wales. The Commissions aim to produce constituencies of roughly equal size – about 65,000 voters, which follow existing county and natural boundaries as far as possible. Three of the four Commissions are based in London and the Scottish one is based in Edinburgh. They also drew up the boundaries for the European elections of June 1999, a task made more complex by the need to create

larger constituencies for the regional list system introduced in that year.

Most recent revisions of constituency boundaries have reflected a general movement of people from the inner-city areas out to the suburbs, to the disadvantage of the Labour Party, as its vote tended to be less in suburban areas than the Conservatives' vote. The number of MPs was increased from 651 to 659 for the 1997 general election.

The Commissions are chaired formally by the speaker of the House of Commons, although in practice by a High Court judge, who acts as deputy chair. The two other members of the English Boundary Commission are nominated by the home secretary and the environment secretary. On 6 February 2002 the Scottish Boundary Commission announced that Scottish Westminster seats would be reduced from 72 to 59 in the wake of devolution, which had given Scotland authority over its domestic affairs and thus reduced the need for Westminster representation. The changes affected Labour seats for the most part and initiated a rush among Scottish Labour MPs for new seats in the redrawn political map of their country.

See also Boundary Committee for England.

Boundary Committee for England
www.electoralcommission.org.uk/boundary-reviews/boundary _ committee
Successor to the Boundary Commission for Local Government. This body regularly reviews ward boundaries under the Political Parties, Elections and Referendums Act 2000. Boundaries are drawn up by an official of the Committee after consultation with interested parties, who may include political parties, community groups, the local authority and individuals. There are two rounds of consultation but no public inquiry: the first round produces a draft plan after consultation; the second round involves further consultation on the draft before decisions are made and boundaries are set for the next 10–15 years.

bourgeoisie
Name given by Karl Marx to the property-owning creators of capitalism who extracted surplus labour value from workers and in so doing 'exploited' members of that class. Those adopting the concept have reckoned it to comprise the middle or especially upper middle classes – basically those running all the economic and political institutions of the state and almost always voting Conservative. The 'petit bourgeois' were, accordingly, the small shopkeepers and those who aspired to full membership of the upper middle classes. The term was never popular with middle-of-the-road Labour MPs and was generally used only by those on the Marxist left.

See also class.

bovine spongiform encephalopathy (BSE)
'Mad cow disease'. An outbreak of bovine spongiform encephalopathy (BSE) occurred in Britain during the late 1980s. Its danger lay in the ability of the incredibly resistant infecting agent to transfer from cows to humans, when it would take the form of the terminal Creutzfeldt–Jakob disease (CJD). The first officially documented case of BSE was in 1986 but it was not until 1996 that it was confirmed that BSE could cause CJD. The disease is caused by giving cows feed containing the spine and brain of infected animals, thought to have originally been sheep with scrapie. Initially the government was reassuring but when the scale and severity of the problem became clear it introduced the following in 1989: a policy of slaughtering all potentially infected animals, numbered in millions (and for which farmers received only 50 per cent compensation); restrictions on the composition of animal feed; and measures to protect people from eating contaminated meat. Some studies suggest the incubation period for CJD might be as high as 50 years so the full extent of the disease may not have been yet experienced.

Despite costing a total of £4 billion, this initially failed to reassure Britain's trading partners, many of which, especially in the

POLITICS

European Union (EU), banned British beef. Slowly confidence was renewed and the EU bans were lifted in November 1998 but, given the ignorance over the incubation period for the disease, the full extent of the problem was still unclear, even when the ban was lifted. In July 2000 a report indicated that British beef exports, especially to France, were only a fraction of what they were before the crisis began. In October 2000, a report accused former Conservative ministers of not acting with sufficient speed or candour on the issue.

Bow Group
www.bowgroup.org
A centre-right think-tank formed in 1951 and with close links to the Conservative Party. The Group urges the acceptance of the postwar consensus on the welfare state and a mixed economy. It convenes a number of policy groups and publishes the journal *Crossbow*. It boasted a membership of 1,000 in the mid-1990s.

boycott
A form of direct action by people who wish to protest by withdrawing support from a product, service or gathering. For example, in the 1970s many students boycotted Barclays Bank because of its investments in apartheid South Africa; less successfully, in August 2000 an action group opposed to the high levels of excise duty on petrol organised a boycott of filling stations.

Bradford
See Ouseley report.

'briefing wars'
Name given by the press to attempts by politicians to undermine each other via spin doctors' briefings. The most intense period of such conflict was between Tony Blair and Gordon Brown, with Charlie Whelan for Brown and Alastair Campbell for Blair. But other senior politicians, for example Peter Mandelson, regularly indulged in briefing wars when seeking to accrue some advantage for themselves or to deliver disadvantage to others.

Brighton bomb, 1984
The IRA bombing of the Grand Hotel, Brighton, in 1984, during the Conservative Party conference. Patrick Magee, an IRA member, stayed in the hotel a month before the conference and concealed a time bomb weighing 20–30 pounds in a bathroom wall. It exploded at 2.45 a.m. on 12 October 1984, killing five (including Sir Anthony Berry, MP for Enfield Southgate) and injuring 34. Margaret Thatcher and her husband narrowly missed being affected by the blast, as did most of her cabinet, but Norman Tebbit was injured and his wife paralysed. Magee was sentenced to eight life sentences, was transferred to the Maze Prison in 1994 and then released under the Good Friday agreement in 1999 after serving only a third of his sentence. Michael Howard, former home secretary, called it a 'disgrace'; Tony Blair said it was 'very hard to stomach' but the manager of the Grand Hotel said he would forgive and forget and Magee would be welcome to stay as a paying guest. Anthony Berry's daughter, Jo Tufnell, met with Magee in November 2000 in an attempt to effect reconciliation.

British Broadcasting Corporation (BBC)
Established by royal charter in 1927 out of a company set up in 1922 by a group of radio manufacturers. It was eventually granted a monopoly over radio broadcasting in Britain and became financed through an annual licence fee. Another landmark in the Corporation's history arrived in 1936, when the world's first television service was introduced, in the London area. Its first director general was John (later Lord) Reith, a high-minded moralist who wanted the Corporation to 'inform, educate and entertain', a formula which was later to become known as the 'public service' tradition in broadcasting. During the 1960s the BBC shed its grey image and began to express some of the energy and rebellion characteristic of that decade, most famously perhaps in the form of the late Saturday night programme *That Was the Week That Was*, which transfixed the country

for a while before it was discontinued for stretching too far the boundaries of morality and censorship.

The BBC is given a royal charter which is renewed every 10 years – the current one runs 2007–16 – and tasks the Corporation to 'inform, educate and entertain' as always.

The BBC Trust came into being in January 2007, replacing the BBC Board of Governors. This holds accountable the executive board, which is in charge of day-to-day running. The director general chairs the Board. In October 2009 Ben Bradshaw, a former employee of the BBC and then culture secretary, criticised the BBC Trust for not being a 'sustainable model' and implying he would like to disband it.

The BBC is often accused by politicians of media bias in the reporting of political issues, especially those affecting the government; Winston Churchill thought it was full of communists, Margaret Thatcher that it contained 1960s liberals and advocates of permissiveness. Labour ridiculed such accusations but tended to replicate them when in power, especially with criticism of the *Today* programme. In recent years politicians have also accused the Corporation of 'dumbing down' in an attempt to attract audiences.

British constitution

According to Philip Norton – the foremost modern expert on this subject – a constitution is a set of rules which defines the 'composition and powers of organs of the state and regulates the relations of the various state organs to one another and those of the state organs to the private citizen'. Some constitutions are very long and include exhortations as to how citizens should behave.

The British constitution is famously unwritten. This is not strictly correct, however, in that large parts of it comprise written statutes. It is *uncodified* but has written and unwritten elements. There are four of these:

1 *Common law*. This comprises those legal principles which have evolved since Saxon times regarding the powers of the monarch and parliament.

2 *Conventions*. These are not legally binding laws but are rules of behaviour considered binding by those in authority.

3 *Works of authority*. There are a number of such works (for example those by A. V. Dicey), which are extremely influential in the interpretation of the constitution.

4 *Statute law*. This is the most authoritative element of the constitution, as a direct result of the doctrine of the sovereignty of parliament. The English Bill of Rights in 1689 defined the powers of parliament and the crown such that parliament had the sole source of authority or power to make or alter any law. The corollary of this is that parliament cannot bind itself but can rescind any law that it passes. In practice, given the fading of royal power at the end of the 17th century, 'sovereign power' passed to the executive (i.e. the government of the day).

There is no special procedure whereby the constitution is amended – the standard legislative stages that are required for any law apply also to constitutional ones. Consequently, all the following major constitutional amendments were passed in the normal way:

1 In 1972 Britain joined the European Economic Community and thereby made its laws subject to the superior law of that organisation.

2 The European Convention on Human Rights was embodied in British law in 1998 and came into effect on 2 October 2000. This provides in effect the kind of bill of rights for which reformers have long argued.

3 After 1997 separate assemblies were established for Wales and Scotland and later a new elected authority for Greater London plus an elected mayor.

4 In 2000 all but 92 of the hereditary members of the House of Lords were expelled from the legislature.

In 2009 Professor Vernon Bogdanor of Oxford University published a book

POLITICS

entitled *The New British Constitution*, which argued that, in effect, Britain had evolved a 'new' constitution, in the place of the old one. The old one was basically quite simple: as parliament was sovereign, according to the great 19th-century theorist A. V. Dicey, so the British constitution, says Bogdanor, 'can be summed up in just eight words – what the Queen in Parliament enacts is law'. He goes on, however, to argue that so many developments have happened since 1997 as to undermine the old certainties and provide an 'essential prologue' to an emergent new constitution. He lists 15 such developments, the most important of which are: the Scotland Act 1998, which set up the Scottish parliament; the Government of Wales Act 1998, which did the same thing for the Welsh assembly; the Northern Ireland Act 1998, which provided for devolution in that province; the establishment of an elected mayor for London and the related assembly; the Human Rights Act 1998, which affected public bodies at all levels; the use of proportional representation for European elections since 1998; the House of Lords Act 1999, which abolished all but 92 hereditary peerages from the Lords; the Freedom of Information Act 2000, which provided access to government information; the Political Parties, Elections and Referendums Act 2000, which regulates parties; and the Constitutional Reform Act 2005, which reformed the office of lord chancellor and set up the Supreme Court. There can be little doubt that Bogdanor is justified in saying that 'the new constitution is being created before our eyes'.

British Gas

www.britishgas.co.uk
Formerly the British Gas Board and made a nationalised industry after the Second World War. It then became a candidate for privatisation by Margaret Thatcher. Its chair, Sir Dennis Rooke, fought the transition but the Thatcher government had too much political will. The privatisation raised £7.3 billion in 1987. In March 1995, the reputation of the company was

damaged by the huge personal salary received by its chair, Cedric Brown, whose name was given to a live pig mascot used by protestors who demonstrated against the alleged greed of the chair and the company. Centrica is now the parent company of British Gas.

British Medical Association

www.bma.org.uk
The professional body for over 100,000 doctors in Britain. It has some 30 committees representing the various 'crafts' or clinical specialties and is run by a 57-strong elected council, which operates via a finance and general purposes committee and an executive committee. The Association meets annually to debate motions concerned with professional matters like conditions of work and pay but also ethical matters like genetic engineering and euthanasia. After the war it fought hard to resist the establishment of the National Health Service but has become its ardent supporter in subsequent decades.

See also General Medical Council.

British National Party

http://bnp.org.uk
Either of two postwar far-right parties. The first was formed in 1960 under the leadership of Colin Jordan. The grouping had anti-Semitism and anti-immigration as basic tenets. By 1967 there were 1,000 members but, in common with left-wing political fringe groups, the British National Party (BNP) was rife with personality feuds, especially between Jordan, John Tyndall and Martin Webster.

The second BNP formed out of a then declining National Front in 1982. It displayed a more fanatical approach and was rumoured to have contacts with neo-Nazi groups abroad. John Tyndall was its autocratic leader, until he was challenged and succeeded by Nick Griffin, a Cambridge graduate, in 1999.

Halting immigration by non-white people has always been central to the beliefs of the BNP and often disguises other kinds of underlying racialism, like anti-Semitism and the idea of a 'Zionist conspiracy'.

The party made little headway in electoral terms; in 1997 its 57 candidates mustered less than 2 per cent of the vote in all constituencies in which they stood. However, a major revival occurred in 2001, when it cleverly exploited racial tension in Oldham. Here riots occurred during the May–June general election campaign, partly stirred by incoming right-wing activists. In the election Nick Griffin stood in Oldham West and mustered 6,552 votes (16 per cent). In the neighbouring Oldham East constituency the BNP candidate, Michael Treacy, received 5,091 votes (11 per cent) and in Burnley the BNP also did well, polling over 4,000 votes (over 11 per cent). At an average of 3.9 per cent of the vote where candidates stood, 2001 saw the best performance to date by the party in general elections and was a worrying result for those who value toleration and a liberal political culture. To put the result in context, though, right-wing parties did negligibly compared with similar parties in Austria, Italy and France.

Griffin aimed to attract the 'neglected and oppressed white working class', possibly former Conservative voters. One of the slogans of the party was 'Defend Rights for Whites'. It subsequently won council seats in Burnley and, in January 2003, a 'sink' estate close to Halifax. For the May 2003 local elections the party fielded 221 candidates. It managed to win eight seats in Burnley, thereby becoming the second largest party on the council, and five others nationwide, including in Stoke-on-Trent. In the 2005 general election the party quadrupled its vote but still won none of its 119 contests. After the 2006 local elections the BNP boasted 53 councillors but by the end of 2007, through resignations and expulsions this number had fallen to 42.

The crisis in trust caused by the MPs' expenses scandal in spring 2009 produced a situation in which substantial support switched to fringe parties like the UK Independence Party and the BNP. In the 2010 general election the party polled 1.9 per cent overall (with around half a million votes) but still won no seats.

> The British National Party stands for the preservation of the national and ethnic character of the British people and is wholly opposed to any form of racial integration between British and non-European peoples. It is therefore committed to stemming and reversing the tide of non-white immigration and to restoring, by legal changes, negotiation and consent the overwhelmingly white makeup of the British population that existed in Britain prior to 1948. (BNP constitution, 11th edition, August 2009, section 1.2.b)

See also National Front.

British Rail
See Network Rail.

British Telecom
See BT.

British Union of Fascists
Party founded in 1932 by Oswald Mosley. Its provenance lay in Mosley's attempts to inject dynamism into British socialism after his own Labour government post and his brief flirtation with the 'New Party' failed. It sought to offer a mixture of fascism and racism to the British voter, particularly anti-Semitism. It organised the paramilitary Blackshirts, who participated in violent street demonstrations in the East End of London. The Public Order Act 1936 placed legal limits on its activities and it was banned in 1940, when Mosley was imprisoned. In retrospect the party was probably merely a vehicle for Mosley, who was seeking to emulate continental fascist leaders and to achieve political power. When the British voter proved unmoved, the attempt unravelled.

Broadcasting Act 1990
Act that changed the regulation of independent broadcasting. It was concerned with opening up the 'cosy' world of commercial franchises to market forces, which, according to Margaret Thatcher, one of the act's chief supporters, increase choice and quality. Under the act the Independent

Broadcasting Authority was replaced by the Independent Television Commission (which included cable in its jurisdiction) and the Radio Authority; these bodies awarded broadcasting licences to bidders – usually to the highest bidders but with some quality controls. Channel 5 was set up, along with three national commercial radio stations and new local radio stations. After the act, according to many critics, there was a concentration of ownership in fewer hands, and television companies fought to attract audiences and advertisers by offering mass market and in some cases down-market programming. This led to claims that, despite the act's intentions, audiences for independent television, and by extension audiences for the BBC, which must compete to justify the licence fee, were offered more of the same, and less real choice. The act was superseded in some respects by the creation of Ofcom in 2003.

See also Office of Communications (Ofcom).

broadsheets
Name given to 'quality' newspapers, which traditionally came in this larger sheet size, as distinct from the more popular 'tabloids'. They include the *Guardian*, the *Times*, the *Daily Telegraph*, the *Independent* and the *Financial Times*. In addition Sunday titles include the Sunday equivalents of the above-mentioned second, third and fourth titles plus the *Observer*, connected to the Guardian group of newspapers. The description 'broadsheet' became somewhat obsolete in that the *Independent* since 2003 has been available in tabloid format and the *Guardian* and *Observer* since 2005 have used the *Berliner* format, which is slightly smaller than the traditional size. Readership of the 'quality' papers is much more skewed to the middle classes than is the case for the tabloids.

Bruges Group
www.brugesgroup.com
Anti-European group of Conservative MPs set up in 1989 after the speech made by Margaret Thatcher in that city in September 1988 in which she outlined her doubts about European integration. Thatcher was its original president and it attracted much support from Eurosceptics in the early and mid-1990s.

Bruges speech, September 1988
A speech made to the College of Europe by Margaret Thatcher in which she expressed her anger and frustration at the creeping encroachments of European integration, as envisaged (especially) by Jacques Delors, president of the European Commission. The speech was heavily modified by Foreign Office senior officials to make it less offensive to partner countries. It contained the key sentence which summed up Thatcher's objections to the European idea: 'We have not rolled back the frontiers of the state in Britain only to see them re-imposed at a European level with a European super-state exercising a new dominance from Brussels'. The speech also invoked the 'Atlantic Community – our noblest inheritance and our greatest strength'.

BSE
See bovine spongiform encephalopathy.

BT
www.bt.com
Originally part of the General Post Office (GPO), but came into being after an act separated the postal side of the GPO from the telephone operation. The bill to privatise British Telecom (BT) lapsed in 1983 at the end of the parliament but Margaret Thatcher reintroduced it in changed form after the election and it became law in April 1984. BT was thus the first big privatisation undertaken by the Conservatives after 1979. The outcome of the process was somewhat different to the intended aim of reintroducing competition.

The flotation on the stock market produced £4 billion but within two years the value of its shares had doubled and most of the individual shareholders had sold their stock at a profit. BT shares ultimately reached around £15 each but during 2000, in common with other information technology stocks, they crashed to one-third of that figure, the principal reason being the high level of debt the company had incurred in trying to invest in new technologies. Chairman Sir Ian Vallance was forced to retire and a former chairman of the BBC, Sir Christopher Bland, took his place.

budget
The most well known part of the budgetary process, by which the spending plans of government departments and taxation are adjusted each year. The budget is an announcement of the result of this process and is presented to the House of Commons each March or April. Originally it was simply a statement of how revenue was to be raised but now it is a major economic instrument and is much analysed, although in recent years the chancellor's autumn statement has reduced the importance of the spring announcements. It is prepared with great secrecy and the Commons is supposed to be the first to hear its contents, although it is often the case that the government leaks proposals as a way of trailing them and gauging public reaction. The chancellor's statement – during which he sometimes sips, by tradition, from a glass of whisky and water – lasts about an hour or more and is followed by an extempore comment by the leader of the opposition. The government's taxation proposals usually come into effect immediately, although the legislative authority comes only with the passing of the subsequent Finance Act, usually in the early summer. Some measures are delayed by up to a year or more.

Bulger case
In 1993 a two-year-old boy from Liverpool was tortured and killed by two 10-year-olds, Robert Thompson and Jon Venables. The crime shocked the nation and helped shift the emphasis in penal policy further to the right. Michael Howard, the home secretary, declared they should serve a minimum of 15 years but the European Court of Human Rights over-ruled this decision and the boys were released on parole after serving eight and a half years.

The mother of James Bulger was outraged and many in her native city supported her attempts to rescind the Parole Board's decision. Labour's home secretary David Blunkett agreed with the Parole Board's decision. The two boys were given new identities and locations, although many fear they will be hunted down and harmed by vigilantes sympathetic to the Bulger family.

bureaucracy
A term (first used in 1818) used to refer collectively to the civil servants who assist and advise ministers. It is often used in a pejorative sense to suggest officials are inefficient. The Duke of Wellington captured this sense when he referred to officials as 'malevolent quill drivers'. The German sociologist Max Weber saw bureaucracy as a characteristic of modern society, based on rational rules, as opposed to his other identified sources of legitimacy – tradition or charisma.

See also civil service.

Business for Sterling
A group, formed out of several smaller ones, that opposes Britain's adoption of the euro. It was set up in June 1998, in the House of Lords. Its aim is to attract funds and support from businesses that may have been repelled by some of the more radical Eurosceptics in the past. Headed by ex Labour minister turned crossbencher Lord (Richard) Marsh, it also has the support of the electronics magnate Sir Stanley Kalms, the retired chairman of the Dixons group. Other corporate supporters include McAlpine, Matheson, Forte and Great Universal Stores, as well as Paul Sykes, the maverick millionaire who funded anti-European MPs in the 1997 election. The Institute of Directors also favours the anti-euro camp, as well as the Federation of Small Businesses. The *Sun* newspaper supports the 'anti' camp in accordance with the views of its owner, Rupert Murdoch.

Butler report, 2004
The Review of Intelligence on Weapons of Mass Destruction, resulting from the Butler inquiry. In the wake of the Hutton inquiry

and report into the death of David Kelly, Tony Blair opposed any formal inquiry into the much criticised intelligence upon which the decision to invade Iraq in 2003 was made. He changed his mind, however, after US president George Bush set up such an investigation in early February 2004. Blair chose former cabinet secretary Lord Robin Butler as the chair of the inquiry team; many immediately criticised the choice of such an impeccably establishment (though undeniably able) figure. Similar criticisms were made of the other members of the inquiry team: Ann Taylor, former Labour chief whip; Lord Inge, former chief of the defence staff; Sir John Chilcot, former permanent secretary to the Northern Ireland Office; and Michael Mates, former Conservative junior minister and before that an army officer. The Liberal Democrats refused to serve in the team, as they claimed its terms of reference were too narrow and should have addressed all the possible reasons for going to war. The Conservatives also withdrew but Mates insisted that he remain a member.

Lord Butler's eagerly awaited report was couched in polite and calm language but contained some substantial criticisms of the intelligence services, the infamous September 2002 dossier and Blair's informal style of decision making. Its key findings were as follows:

1 Intelligence on Iraq was thin and unreliable; the September dossier nevertheless was based upon it.
2 The claim that Saddam could attack the British forces within 45 minutes was wrong and was included only because of 'its eye-catching character'.
3 The separation between intelligence and policy had not been maintained.
4 The dossier and the intelligence were laid out side by side, showing how the qualifiers and caveats were removed in a dossier which rang with certainties.
5 The prime minister's style of government was based on unminuted oral briefings and not on pre-circulated papers.
6 The shift in policy on Iraq followed policy in Washington.

However, no single person was identified as responsible:

1 The shortcomings of the dossier were attributed to collective failures, a 'group think' which reflected a prevailing view that Saddam had stockpiles of weapons of mass destruction.
2 John Scarlett, chair of the Joint Intelligence Committee (JIC), had been too close to the policy process. He was not criticised but rather praised and his appointment to head MI6 defended. However, it was recommended that, in future, chairs of the JIC should not be vulnerable to career pressure and should preferably be in their final post.
3 No cabinet member was singled out, nor any of Blair's aides, who had seemed so active in creating the debacle when giving evidence to the Hutton inquiry. Nor was the good faith of any such people questioned.

In the following debate in the House of Commons Blair was able to declare he was responsible for the errors while appearing not to be to blame for them.

> I have been briefed in detail on the intelligence and am satisfied as to its authority. (Blair's foreword to the dossier, 24 September 2002)

> Intelligence on Iraq's weapons of mass destruction and ballistic missiles programmes is sporadic and patchy. (JIC assessment, 15 March 2002)

> I am in no doubt that the threat is serious and current. (Blair's foreword to the dossier)

> Intelligence remains limited and Saddam's own unpredictability complicates matters. (JIC assessment, September 2002)

See also Chilcot inquiry; Hutton report.

'Butskellism'

This was a term invented by the *Economist* to offer a satirical slant on the closeness of the economic policies of chancellor R. A. Butler and Labour's shadow, Hugh Gaitskell. It became a word signifying the postwar consensus between the two main parties on the need for a mixed economy and a welfare state.

POLITICS

by-election
Single-constituency election held when a vacancy arises in the House of Commons through the death or retirement or elevation of the sitting MP to the Lords. If the government is unpopular, by-elections can provide a partial snapshot of how the public perceives it. They often also include a number of frivolous candidates attracted by the high media profile such elections command. These tests of public opinion can often give a misleading picture because many supporters of a party use them as an opportunity to chastise a government for unpopular policies but then return to the fold during a general election campaign.

A little-known practice, until 1921, was the convention that cabinet ministers recontest their constituencies upon being appointed. Usually such contests were formalities but Winston Churchill actually lost his Oldham seat (albeit narrowly) in 1908 to William ('Jix') Joynson-Hicks.

Tony Blair finally began to lose by-elections in 2003, when Brent East was lost to the Liberal Democrats, followed in July 2004 by Leicester South, which went the same way, on a 21 per cent swing, and a 27 per cent swing nearly delivered Birmingham Hodge Hill. In all three cases the Conservatives came third. Gordon Brown's by-election problems began in 2008:

1 The Crewe and Nantwich by-election in May 2008 was caused by the death of the long-serving Gwyneth Dunwoody, whose daughter, Tamsin, stood for Labour in the seat. Labour chose to take a 'Tories are toffs' line, with activists dressed up like old Etonians. However, this had no traction with voters, who registered a swing of over 17 per cent against Labour and the Conservatives won with a majority of 7,680.

2 The Conservatives also won the Henley by-election in June 2008 with a majority of not far off 20,000. They managed to increase their vote; the Liberal Democrats were disappointed not to do better and Labour fell from third to fifth.

3 The Glasgow East by-election in June 2008 was caused by the retirement of the sitting MP, David Marshall. With a majority of over 13,000 it was Labour's third safest seat in Scotland, in a disadvantaged heartland of a disadvantaged city. In the event the Scottish National Party (SNP) romped home with a majority of 13,560, causing a sensation for the nationalists and, for Labour, humiliation.

4 Close to Gordon Brown's backyard, the Glenrothes by-election in November 2008 was regarded as highly vulnerable to the SNP, which controlled the Fife council. In the event Labour held it with a majority of nearly 7,000. Gordon Brown's wife, Sarah, had done some useful canvassing work in the constituency.

5 The Norwich North by-election in July 2009 was caused by the expenses scandal. Ian Gibson, the incumbent Labour MP, had been exposed as having sold his London flat – purchased with help from parliamentary expenses – to his daughter at below the market price. Gibson was summoned to a Labour inquiry and told he must stand down at the next election. He decided to resign there and then, thus triggering the contest. Gibson had been a popular MP and it was felt he had been badly treated. Chloe Smith, the 27-year-old Tory candidate, won handsomely, with a majority of 7,348.

by-law
See delegated legislation.

C

cabinet
The supreme committee of government, chaired by the prime minister. This body originated in the time of Charles II, when he consulted only a few of his over-large Privy Council in his private rooms: his 'cabinet'. As parliament increased its power at the expense of the monarchy,

senior ministers became more important and their forum, the cabinet, accordingly grew in importance. Majorities had to be organised in parliament to ensure the flow of taxation to sustain the armed forces. Under Queen Anne the term 'cabinet' became the official title for this committee. With King George I, whose English was very poor, the monarch stopped attending cabinet meetings and the first lord of the Treasury became the intermediary and hence, effectively, the 'prime minister'. Further restrictions of royal power in subsequent centuries delivered effective power to the prime minister and cabinet.

The prime minister decides the composition of the cabinet. This usually entails a judicious blend of: ideology (left/right, wet/dry, Europhile/sceptic); administrative experience; regional balance; and gender. The cabinet, usually 20–24 in number, comprises the main departmental ministers – chancellor, home and foreign secretaries – as well as the chief whip, lord chancellor and party chair. In addition there are a few individuals with non-departmental portfolios, like chancellor of the Duchy of Lancaster, who tend to chair cabinet committees and do the prime minister's bidding. Lesser departmental ministers are generally outside cabinet but may be invited to attend on specific issues.

In theory, the cabinet is the supreme committee of government, coordinating policy, deciding the big policy questions and resolving disputes between departments. Doubtless all these functions are performed in the present day but the nature of cabinet government has undeniably changed. Some commentators have discerned a process whereby the cabinet has lost real power to its committees and to the prime minister, and have concluded that we now have 'prime ministerial' or 'quasi-presidential' government. There is much to support this view. However, opponents argue that this depends on the personal style of individual premiers; in the case of the most powerful postwar example, Margaret Thatcher, her resignation followed a virtual vote of no confidence by members of her own cabinet.

Premiers have varied according to how they have run cabinets. Winston Churchill used to talk to the cabinet eloquently during the war but it was his deputy, Clement Attlee, who managed to work the cabinet through the agenda during the great man's absences. Most prime ministers listened to colleagues before signalling the taking of collective decisions but Thatcher seemed so concerned to advance her own agenda that she often led the discussion as well as summing up. She also 'fixed' the agreement of small groups in advance, thus tending to reduce the role of cabinet. Tony Blair was somewhat similar in style to Thatcher, preferring small ad hoc meetings outside cabinet with ministers, plus advisors (notably Alastair Campbell before his resignation). Some commentators suggest that Blair's full cabinets were as brief as half an hour, when he merely reported decisions made elsewhere. In the wake of the Butler report Peter Hennessy described the Labour cabinet of that time as 'The weakest since the Second World War'.

See also cabinet committee; prime minister; Privy Council.

cabinet committee

Any subcommittee of the cabinet. Because of the volume of work in cabinet, much is delegated to committees. These have the authority of cabinet decisions when their members are in agreement; if they fail to agree, the matter – at least in theory – will go to the full cabinet. The precise extent of cabinet committees and their remits used to be kept secret but the veil has been raised in recent years. There are standing committees, which are given a code letter, and ad hoc ones to deal with specific problems (these are not given a code letter but the records are filed as 'miscellaneous'). The prime minister usually chairs the most important ones, on the economy and defence and overseas policy. There were over 400 cabinet committees in the early 1970s but they were halved under James Callaghan and reduced still further, to 135, under Margaret Thatcher (25 standing and 110 ad hoc committees).

Cabinet Office
www.cabinetoffice.gov.uk
Civil service body that coordinates cabinet
briefings on matters of highest policy:
the security and intelligence services;
international meetings; appointments in
Whitehall; and honours. It also informs
departments of decisions taken and ensures
that appropriate action has been taken. It
was established by Lloyd George in 1916.
It is not merely bureaucratic in its function:
as Bernard Donoughue (a prime ministerial
advisor to Harold Wilson and later junior
minister) commented, it 'establishes the
agenda for policy discussion … thus shaping the structure, balance and timetable of
policy debate'.

The Office has three main sections:
Policy and Coordination; Civil Service;
and Intelligence Assessment. The Social
Exclusion Unit was set up after 1997 with
the cross-departmental task of monitoring
the extent of poverty and seeking ways of
alleviating its effects. In addition a Policy
and Innovation Unit was set up to fight
'departmentalism' and to promote government objectives.

In July 1998 the Office was strengthened
further when it absorbed the Office of
Public Service and its head was given a
wide-ranging brief across Whitehall to
ensure policy objectives were achieved.
This 'enforcing' job was initially performed
by Jack Cunningham, but it soon declined
in importance. When Mo Mowlam did it
she described herself as 'minister for paper
clips'. After Tony Blair's victory reshuffle
in June 2001, John Prescott was assigned
to it, assisted by Lord (Gus) MacDonald
('progress chaser in chief' according to
David Walker in the *Guardian*, 18 June
2001), Charles Clarke, junior minister
Barbara Roche and Blair's former political
secretary (raised to peerage) Sally Morgan.
In June 2007 Gordon Brown appointed
Hilary Armstrong, MP, to be minister for
the Cabinet Office and social exclusion,
thus allying the minister with the most
important unit in the Cabinet Office.

The Strategy Unit was set up in 2002
(when it was initially called the Future
Strategy Unit), headed by Geoff Mulgan
and including Lord (John) Birt, formerly
director general of the BBC, who was
asked by Blair to produce a study on
long-term transport policy.

Most commentators have concluded that,
under Blair, the Cabinet Office developed
into a de facto prime minister's department.
Some observers, unsurprisingly, criticised
the proliferation of special units and
diagnosed a lack of coordination.

cabinet secretary
Head of the Cabinet Office and head of
the civil service. 'The prime minister's
permanent secretary' is how Sir Burke
Trend described his office to Harold
Wilson in 1964 but, as the Labour prime
minister observed, he owed an equal loyalty
to the cabinet as a whole. The office was
founded in 1916 and the first incumbent
was Sir Maurice Hankey, during the First
World War; the job proved so useful it was
continued into peacetime and is now the
most powerful civil service appointment.
The cabinet secretary is in essence the
prime minister's principal advisor. However,
Sir John Hunt, though he saw himself in
this light under both Wilson and James
Callaghan, did not have constant access
to the prime minister but had to ring the
parliamentary private secretary to receive
clearance to come through the locked door
between the Cabinet Office (on Whitehall)
and Number 10. In 2002 Sir Richard
Wilson, the retiring cabinet secretary,
told the Commons Public Administration
Committee that new incumbents would be
interviewed by trained psychologists and a
report submitted to the prime minister. Sir
Andrew Turnbull, formerly of the Treasury
and Margaret Thatcher's private office, was
given the job in 2002; in June 2005 Sir
Gus McDonnell moved from the Treasury
to occupy this key role; he went on to serve
his former boss when Brown took over as
prime minister in June 2007.

Calcutt reports, 1990 and 1993
Reports from an inquiry by Sir David
Calcutt, QC, set up following deep

POLITICS

concern that the press, and especially the tabloid press, was too intrusive and irresponsible. Calcutt recommended that the industry-dominated Press Council be converted into the Press Complaints Commission, with stronger lay representation. The warning was given that this was the last chance the industry would have for self-regulation. However, the subsequent Calcutt review of the Commission in 1993 recommended a statutory framework to enforce responsibility. Andrew Neil, then editor of the *Sunday Times*, complained this would make the press the 'poodle of the establishment'; this received further support from Lord Wakeham, the then chair of the Commission, and the proposals were rejected by government. The tabloids still break the rules of the Commission and self-regulation clearly does not work; however, government control is fraught with problems and, arguably, is not consistent with British political culture.

Calman commission
www.commissiononscottishdevolution.org.uk
Study group set up by the Scottish parliament in December 2007, officially the Commission on Scottish Devolution. Its terms of reference were:

> to review the provisions of the Scotland Act 1998 in the light of experience and to recommend any changes to the present constitutional arrangements that would enable the Scottish Parliament to serve the people of Scotland better, improve the financial accountability of the Scottish Parliament and continue to secure the position of Scotland within the United Kingdom.

The Scottish executive receives £31.3 billion as a block grant from the Treasury, but the Calman report stated that Scotland's politicians were not accountable for their spending. The country raised less than it spent. The Commission judged that: devolution had been a success; while the Barnett formula will apply for the time being, the Scottish parliament should be given greater control over the raising of revenue from taxation; it should be given new powers in relation to capital projects;

and other sundry powers should be added to those of the devolved Scottish government. In November 2009 the government announced measures reflecting the major recommendations of the Commission. The Scottish National Party administration in Edinburgh criticised these as inadequate and promised more substantive proposals.

Campaign for Nuclear Disarmament (CND)
www.cnduk.org
Anti-nuclear movement formed in 1958 by a number of intellectuals, including Bertrand Russell, Michael Foot and Canon John Collins. Its aim was the unilateral abandonment by Britain of its nuclear weapons. While including many pacifists among its membership, the organisation has never itself been pacifistic. Its annual march from Aldermaston to London, culminating in a Trafalgar Square rally, attracted huge numbers of sympathisers in the 1960s. In 1960 CND effectively captured the Labour Party conference, which passed a unilateralist resolution, but this was reversed the following year when the party adopted a policy of multilateralism (i.e. disarmament via collective negotiations with other nuclear powers). The partial test ban treaty in 1963 took away some of CND's momentum but it gathered huge support again in the 1980s when NATO decided to site a new generation of nuclear weapons in Europe. Membership rose from 10,000 to 100,000 at the time of the women's protest against cruise missiles at Greenham Common. By the end of the 1990s, however, in the wake of the fall of the communist bloc, the movement became a shadow of its former self. Since 2003 its elected chair has been Kate Hudson.

Campaign Group
Left-wing Labour group set up in 1982 by 23 Labour MPs, many of them supporters of Tony Benn. It is sometimes called the Socialist Campaign Group. It advocated familiar left-wing themes such as more spending on welfare services and more government control of the economy, plus

constitutional changes such as the abolition of the House of Lords and the abolition of the exercise of the royal prerogative by 'proxy' by the prime minister. It eventually attracted 40 members and was very active early on, under the Thatcher Conservative governments, but has kept relatively quiet since. Its decline is yet another sign of New Labour's success in damping down ideological debate within the party.

Its chair is John McDonnell MP, someone who initially declared himself a candidate for the leadership in June 2007 but who could not attract the requisite number of MPs to nominate him. Members include Dianne Abbott, Jeremy Corbyn, Dennis Skinner, Anne Cryer, Alan Simpson and Bob Wareing.

campaign strategist

An umbrella term for an advisor, usually an unelected media, marketing and public relations professional, who provides information, analysis and guidance on how a political party should present itself to the electorate. Well known strategists include Tim Bell of Saatchi and Saatchi, Gordon Reece and Christopher Lawson, who were closely associated with the Conservative campaigns of the 1980s, and Philip Gould and Peter Mandelson, who were key figures in the reconstruction of the Labour Party's image after the 1983 defeat.

A number of political scientists have argued that the practice of employing campaign strategists who embrace a political marketing perspective can be dated back to the Representation of the People Act 1918, which trebled the electorate to 21 million. For example, Sidney Webb, joint author of the Labour Party's 1918 constitution, argued in 1922 that Labour should use 'stratified electioneering', an early form of dividing up the electorate into separate groups which could be targeted by political propaganda. In the 1990s and early 2000s campaign strategists made themselves an indispensable part of the political scene, communicating with key groups in the electorate, which raised questions about a democratic deficit created by their

lack of individual accountability to voters. Some more traditional politicians criticise the construction of political strategies on the basis of opinion-consulting techniques; they argue that the role of politicians is to lead public opinion, not merely follow it.

See also Campbell, Alastair; Mandelson, Peter; Reece, Gordon.

campaigning

The concentrated efforts party activists make at election time to persuade people to vote their way and to encourage their supporters to turn out on the day. At the local level, campaigns take the form of face-to-face encouragement (canvassing), leafleting and local meetings. Such activities have, though, become less common as national campaigns have assumed higher prominence and meetings have been changed to all-ticket party rallies along US lines. Access to the national media – especially television – has become critical in modern campaigns and parties do their best to intrude symbolic photo-calls of their leaders into news bulletins. Such images include the leader driving a tank (tough on defence), visiting hospital patients (caring about the National Health Service) or kissing babies (genuinely 'normal and nice' person). Similarly, they seek to win airtime for pithy one-line statements (sound bites). However, some experts point out that campaigns do not always have a large effect: in 1983 and 1987 the Labour Party under Neil Kinnock ran superb campaigns but managed to increase its vote by only 3.0 and 3.6 percentage points, respectively.

candidate for parliamentary election

Person standing for election as a member of parliament. To be eligible to stand for parliament a prospective candidate has to be a British citizen, a resident citizen of another Commonwealth country or of the Irish Republic, and be aged 21 or over. Candidates must be nominated by 10 voters and pay a deposit of £500, which is forfeited if less than 5 per cent of the vote is polled. In order to succeed, it is generally necessary to be nominated by a political party, and preferably one which has a chance of attracting a substantial number of votes, as the British electoral system (first past the post) does not favour independents or small parties with thin support. Those not allowed to stand include: members of the House of Lords who remain peers, bankrupts, ordained priests (though not nonconformist or non-Christian priests), holders of certain public offices, those suffering from severe mental illness and those serving prison sentences.

There were 3,000 candidates in the 1992 election, nearly all affiliated to political parties. However, in 1997 Martin Bell, an independent, unseated Neil Hamilton, in the safe Conservative constituency of Tatton. In 2001 Dr Richard Taylor was returned as an independent for Wyre Forest, after standing on the issue of the retention of a hospital in Kidderminster.

The parties select candidates in different ways. Labour begins its process by circulating a list of candidates approved by its National Executive Committee to all nominating bodies, including ward and branch parties, affiliated trade unions, socialist societies and the constituency Labour party (CLP) executive committee, all of which can nominate one candidate. The CLP makes up the short-list and since 1993 selection has been decided by one member one vote (OMOV). At least one woman has to be on the short-list. The NEC then has to endorse the candidate; in theory it can intervene at this point but such power is used sparingly, as it provokes so much local dissent.

For the Conservatives, a central list of approved candidates is kept, from which constituencies can select. A subcommittee of the constituency association executive draws up a short-list of about 20; after interviews, this is reduced to a list of no less than three. The executive then interviews the candidates and recommends two to the general meeting of the association – comprising paid-up members – which makes the final choice. Central Office would like to intervene from time to time to increase the number of ethnic and women candidates

as well as to exclude those of whom it does not approve but local associations jealously guard their independence. David Cameron brought in an 'A list' of desirable candidates, which includes women and members of ethnic minorities; the list has not met with total approval, especially on the part of those aspiring candidates not included.

The Liberal Democrats' procedure is similar to the Conservatives', with the addition of at least one woman on the short-list.

cannabis (legalisation of)

Calls for the legalisation of cannabis have been made since the 1960s but both main parties have shied away from even discussing it, for fear of offending a voting public alarmed at the spread of drug taking, principally among young people. Jack Straw when home secretary was determined to preserve the status quo, even when a strong case was made for the legalisation of cannabis for medical purposes. At the Conservative conference in 2000 Ann Widdecombe called for 'zero tolerance' but when the police condemned this as unenforceable she lost credibility. Influential elements of the police – especially the Met – have favoured a relaxation of the laws on smoking 'pot', as it tends currently to be seen as a relatively harmless recreational drug, possibly less harmful than alcohol. In July 2001 Mo Mowlam, former cabinet minister, called for the decriminalisation of cannabis. She advocated that it be controlled by the government like alcohol and tobacco and the proceeds used to fund public services. Surprisingly Peter Lilley, former deputy leader of the Conservatives and cabinet minister, called for the legalisation of cannabis in July 2001 on the grounds that this would remove the 'gateway' from soft to hard drugs which the dealers of cannabis represent. Prohibition had become unenforceable, he claimed, and so should be replaced by government-controlled off-licences selling the substance. In 2001 several peers came out in support of reform, including Roy Jenkins and Kenneth Baker. However, Melanie Phillips, in a well argued piece in the *Sunday Times* (8 July 2001), insisted the medical evidence was against cannabis and that foreign experience warned against legalisation – she cited the Netherlands and Sweden in support of her arguments. In 2001 the government marked the possible liberalisation of the law by deciding to give only cautions to those in possession of cannabis for personal use, though technically possession remained an offence. In 2002 David Blunkett, home secretary, downgraded cannabis to a 'class C' drug but increased penalties for dealers. Some criticised the change for giving a mixed message and the Conservatives attacked the policy as wrongheaded. The aim of the declassification was to give police time and resources to focus on class A drugs such as heroin and crack cocaine. However, the situation changed in April 2008, when the Advisory Council on the Misuse of Drugs (ACMD) recommended that cannabis should remain a class C drug. On 7 May 2008 home secretary Jacqui Smith defied this advice by reclassifying it as a class B drug, to avoid 'risking the future health of young people'. This decision followed some research work which had suggested cannabis smoking – especially the stronger 'skunk' variety – has a causal link with mental illness.

Cantle report, 2001

Report entitled *Community Cohesion* produced by the Home Office Independent Review Team chaired by Ted Cantle. The approach to race relations in Britain, which had embraced a degree of separate identity for different cultures, was shaken in the summer of 2001 by riots in northern inner cities. The report called into question the practice of allowing single ethnic groups to dominate schools in areas of high immigrant settlement. The report, published in December 2001, recorded the team's shock at the 'depth of polarisation' in housing, education, community and voluntary bodies, places of worship, languages and social networks. The team also suggested that the government practice of 'pump-priming' money into specific projects had

exacerbated these polarising tendencies. The review called for a 'national debate' and an end to the non-discussion of sensitive matters involving race and ethnicity.

capital punishment

See death penalty.

capitalism

Term used by Karl Marx to describe an economic system comprising a relatively unregulated market, private property, investment in projects and a workforce who produce profit for the owner in return for wages. Britain had the archetypal capitalist economy in the 19th century as the home of the industrial revolution and the so-called 'workshop of the world'. Marx argued that the private ownership of capital exploited workers ('wage slaves'), who would eventually rise up and overthrow the system that oppressed them. However, capitalism, rather than being destroyed, has prospered, albeit in a different form, and has been adopted by a number of previously communist states. Some commentators argue that 'globalisation' represents the final or 'monopoly capitalism' stage predicted by Marx. Francis Fukuyama, the US writer and theorist, argued in his controversial 'end of history' thesis that liberal capitalism had emerged victorious from the conflict with communism and as the template for the indefinite future.

See also Marxism.

'cash for influence' scandal

In March 2010 a Channel 4 *Dispatches* programme caught members of the Commons and Lords in a sting operation. Fifteen out the 20 approached agreed to be interviewed by a fake agency, including former Labour cabinet members Patricia Hewitt, Stephen Byers and Geoff Hoon. Byers suggested that his daily fee for lobbying would be £3,000–£5,000 and that he was no more than 'a cab for hire'. This series of events, vividly reported in the press and broadcasting outlets, did nothing for Labour's chances in the imminent general election.

POLITICS

'cash for questions' scandal

Concern over the payment of money to
Conservative MPs to ask parliamentary
questions in 1994. On 20 October of that
year the *Guardian* newspaper accused Neil
Hamilton, a junior trade minister, of accepting cash from Harrods owner Mohamed al
Fayed in exchange for asking questions in
the House of Commons. His co-accused,
Tim Smith, admitted the offence and
resigned, but Hamilton fought it, together
with lobbyist Ian Greer. Five days later
Lord Nolan's Committee on Standards in
Public Life was set up, which was destined
to change British politics in a number of
profound ways. Hamilton dropped his
libel case against the *Guardian* a year later,
citing lack of cash as the reason. The newspaper responded with a banner headline
above Hamilton's photograph branding
him 'A Liar and a Cheat'. The BBC news
reporter Martin Bell stood against him in
the Tatton constituency in May 1997 and
won by a huge majority. However, true to
his pledge to serve only one term Bell did
not contest it again and in 2001 Tatton was
won by George Osborne, once again for
the Conservatives.

See also Committee on Standards in
Public Life; sleaze; Hamilton, Neil.

Catalyst

Left-wing think-tank established in 1998
by former Labour Party director of policy
Roland Wales. It sought to stimulate
new thinking on such issues as forms of
government and political processes but
talked of 'policies of redistribution of
wealth, power and opportunity' – very Old
Labour ideas – and it was not surprising to
see Lord Hattersley as its editorial chair. In
2006 it merged with Compass.

catch-all party

Term associated with political scientist
Otto Kircheimer, who pointed to the
transformation of mass ideological parties
into political organisations which assembled
coalitions of support from a disparate
range of voters. It is likely his models were
American but it is arguably the case that

New Labour's 'third way' and 'big tent'
approach to politics marked Labour's move
towards this catch-all type of party.

Catholic emancipation

Catholics suffered discrimination from the
16th century onwards. The situation eased
in the late 18th century, when many of the
penal laws were repealed, but they were still
barred from sitting in parliament (though
not from standing as a candidate) until
1829 as a consequence of the anti-Catholic
oaths MPs were required to take. In 1828
Daniel O'Connell was elected to represent
County Clare and the strength of his support led to a fear of civil disturbance such
that even the (Iron) Duke of Wellington
decided to give way to the pressure and
accept that Catholics could now stand for
all public offices. It still remains a fact, however, that despite the repeal of anti-Catholic
measures the British monarch, according to
the Act of Settlement 1701, must not be a
Catholic or marry one.

cause group

A subdivision of pressure groups. The term
is used by political scientists to indicate
either: sectional groups, which defend and
promote specific social groups (for example
Age Concern, now Age UK, for the
elderly, Shelter for the homeless and Child
Poverty Action for the children of poor
families); or attitude groups, which share
common views on a particular issue and
seek to change social attitudes (for example
the Howard League for Penal Reform and
the Lord's Day Observance Society).

'celebrity' prime ministers

Peter Oborne, writing in the *Guardian* in
June 2009, observed how New Labour had
employed spin doctors to enthrone a highly
publicised version of the nation's senior
politician. Drawing support from fictional
presentations of British politics – Francis
Urquhart in Michael Dobbs' book *House
of Cards* (1990) and Armando Iannucci's
film *In the Loop* (2009) – he regretted how
the chief whip's advice had been usurped by
that of the chief spin doctor.

Oborne recalled Brown's promises:

He pledged to bring back cabinet government, respect civil service impartiality,
restore the primacy of parliament and to
abandon the dark political arts at which the
team of political assassins around Blair had
so excelled.

He went on to complain that Brown had
done none of these things and that spin
doctors remained essential instruments of
the prime ministerial will. To describe this
modern tendency, Oborne cited Anthony
Barnett's phrase 'manipulative populism'.

central–local relations

Relations between Westminster and local
government. Local government has always
operated by virtue of laws passed in
parliament and so its powers and to varying
extents its funding originate at the centre.
This means relations between the centre
and local authorities have traditionally
been problematic. When the Conservatives
were elected in 1979 they wanted to curb
public spending and reduce the powers of
what soon became Labour-dominated local
government. In 1986 the Greater London
Council and the metropolitan counties, set
up by the Local Government Act 1972,
were abolished. Attempts by local authorities to raise more funds from the rates were
countered first by 'rate capping' and then
by imposition of the ill fated 'poll tax'.
Further reforms ensured tension between
centre and periphery continued long into
the 1990s. Devolution for Wales, Scotland
and Northern Ireland, together with plans
for elected heads of city authorities (for
example Ken Livingstone in London
2000–08), suggest that the domination of
the centre may not be as powerful now as
in the past.

See also community charge; local government; rates.

Central Office

Headquarters of the Conservative Party,
previously based in Smith Square, then
in Victoria Street, but now in Millbank
Square, London. The party's bureaucracy
proved instrumental in the fall of Iain

Duncan Smith in November 2003, when
squabbles fuelled discontent with the
soon to be deposed leader. Once Michael
Howard became leader it was announced
that the Smith Square building was to be
sold in order to save money. In March 2007
Central Office moved from Victoria Street
to 30 Millbank Tower, close to the houses
of parliament.

See also Smith Square.

Central Policy Review Staff (CPRS)

Civil service body popularly known as
the Think-Tank. It was set up by Edward
Heath in 1970 to assist the cabinet with
strategic policy making. Its task was
generally to 'think the unthinkable', but
more particularly: to present briefing
papers on issues free from departmental
bias; to research 'horizontal issues' – those
for which responsibility ran across several
departments; and to assess how well
government objectives were being achieved.
Headed by the eminently suitable Lord
Rothschild, it drew its youthful personnel
half from 'outsiders' such as business
people, academics and members of the
professions, and half from 'insiders' – civil
service high-fliers. It considered a number
of subjects over the years, for example
airships, computers, Concorde, low-energy
cars, the coal industry and worker participation. In its first two years the CPRS was
influential, largely because of its charismatic
head, but after that it began to decline
until Margaret Thatcher, convinced she
knew the way forward without lengthy
discussion documents, put an end to it
in 1983. However, her Policy Unit was
similar to the defunct Think-Tank. Some
also saw resemblances to the Think-Tank in
Tony Blair's Strategy Futures Group in the
Cabinet Office, headed by Geoff Mulgan.

See also Policy Unit (Downing Street).

centralisation

The concentration of power and authority
in a single place. Critics of the unitary
state, with its headquarters in London,
have been vocal for many decades and have
two main criticisms: first, local decisions

are made away from the areas with which they are concerned (though devolution of powers to Scotland and Wales partially answered this); and second, power is overly concentrated in the hands of the executive, particularly the prime minister and a small group of key ministers and advisors. An example of centralisation was when Michael Heseltine, as deputy prime minister (1995–97), contrived to centralise a great many of the controlling threads of government in his own oversized office (he was given the chairmanship of four major cabinet committees and membership of all the others and he was in charge of industrial strategy as well as having a wide-ranging remit to promote competitiveness).

Despite constitutional changes such as Scottish and Welsh devolution, many commentators pointed to increased centralisation under Tony Blair's govern-ment, for example in education and health, although efforts to regionalise National Health Service administration were announced in spring 2001. In succeeding years few would claim that this happened.

An enduring problem of government seems to be the tension between the need for a democracy to devolve power yet the tendency for politicians to keep the reins of power in their own hands.

Centre for Management and Policy Studies (CMPS)
www.nationalschool.gov.uk
This body was set up in 1999 and incor-porated the Civil Service College, which had been set up in the wake of the Fulton report in 1970 and which had established a good name for itself as a provider of courses for senior civil servants – its course for assistant under-secretaries had been particularly well regarded and recognised as part of the transition to promotion. In 1995 the College narrowly missed being privatised and its ethos became more akin to the private sector, in keeping with the new managerialism of the civil service. In 1999 the Labour government set up the CMPS to 'be responsible for corporate civil service training and development'. It is now called

the National School of Government, and has a base at Sunningdale Park (Ascot) and centres in Edinburgh and London.

Centre for Policy Studies
www.cps.org.uk
One of the most influential right-wing think-tanks. It was founded by Margaret Thatcher in the 1970s, and it formulated or elaborated many of the constituent elements of 'Thatcherism'. However, by the early 1990s, with John Major in Number 10, like similar bodies, it was all but silent and, according to the *Economist*, had 'moved to a drabber address'.

centre party
Term used to describe political parties in the middle of the accepted left–right political continuum. On this continuum, parties on the right favour free enterprise, low public spending and tough law-and-order policies, while those on the left favour higher public spending, public sector activities and policies more sympathetic to offenders' rights. Centre parties, for example the Liberal Democrats, tend to advocate a judicious blend of free enterprise and public sector policies. However, Tony Blair claimed that his government's 'third way' politics broke out of this false dichotomy. By 2001 many commentators saw the Liberal Democrats as a centre party which had staked out a position to the left of Labour.

chancellor of the Duchy of Lancaster
Title created by Henry III in 1267 for his son Edmund. The crown continues to hold the Duchy's revenues and its chancellor sits in the cabinet with this title held in an honorary capacity; the assigned duties are ceremonial and the office holder usually performs a specific task for the prime minister. For example, in 1998 Jack Cunningham as chancellor was in charge of the Cabinet Office and was responsible for coordinating government policy (the media dubbed him Tony Blair's 'enforcer'). In May 2008 the title was held by Ed Miliband, who combined it with his job as minister for the Cabinet Office. From

May 2010 the post holder in the coalition government was Thomas Galbraith, Lord Strathclyde, who was also the leader of the House of Lords.

chancellor of the exchequer

Title that originated in the time of Edward the Confessor as the name for the king's chief secretary, who kept the great seal and presided over the Chancery. In the modern day the chancellor is the chief finance minister of the government, presenting budgets and controlling the nation's overall financial strategy, as well as having responsibility for expenditure and the raising of revenue from taxation. After the prime minister, the chancellor is the most important figure in the cabinet and is often seen as a likely successor to the prime minister. Two recent examples demonstrate the central role of this office. When Nigel Lawson resigned from the cabinet in 1989, it was seen as a disaster for Margaret Thatcher and was the beginning of the end for her tenure in power. Gordon Brown quickly assumed the role of a political colossus after 1997, master of the all-controlling Treasury and architect of New Labour's reputation for economic competence.

The chancellor relies upon the political support of the prime minister and vice versa, and the relationship between the two often decides the fate of a government. Examples include Lawson's 1986 budget, which laid the economic foundations for Thatcher's 1987 general election victory. Brown eventually took over from Tony Blair as prime minister in June 2007 but, ironically, his chancellor, Alistair Darling, was initially seen rather as Brown's mouthpiece. This soon changed as Darling grew in stature during the 2007–09 economic crisis, proving calm and clear headed under intense pressure. In June 2009 he successfully resisted Brown's attempts to replace him with his own favourite, Ed Balls. In May 2010 George Osborne became the new Conservative chancellor.

Chancery

See High Court.

Channel 5

www.five.tv

Television channel established by the Independent Television Commission in 1995 when it handed the Channel 5 Broadcasting Consortium the right to broadcast on a fifth terrestrial channel. It began doing so in January 1997 and quickly acquired a reputation for a decidedly down-market style of programming, adding fuel to the debate about the 'dumbing down' of terrestrial broadcasting as a result of the Broadcasting Act 1990. Some media watchers for a while feared the Labour government might be trying to free the channel for purchase by Blair supporter Rupert Murdoch.

Channel 4

www.channel4.com

Television channel set up in 1982 with a brief to encourage innovation and cater for minority interests. Initially it was funded by contributions from other television companies but in the late 1980s it became a public corporation funded by its own advertising. It was especially successful, under the executive leadership of Michael Grade, in collaborating with film companies, and this helped to initiate a new wave of creativity in British film. Some programmes proved too avant garde for some tastes and they attracted protest from those wishing to keep television suitable for 'family viewing', while others criticised it for 'dumbing down'. In 2001 arts and media commentators reacted with horror to William Hague's suggestion that a future Conservative government would privatise Channel 4. *Channel 4 News* has established itself as an authoritative source of news and comment.

Channel Islands

Crown dependencies close to the French coast. They were occupied by Germany during the Second World War. Jersey has 150,000 inhabitants; St Helier is its capital. Along with Guernsey it has been part of England since 1106. Alderney and Great and Little Sark are also part of the same group of islands. They are legally part of the UK and, though not represented in Westminster, they are ruled directly by the crown. British acts of parliament do not affect the islands unless specifically indicated, although the British government is responsible for external affairs. The Channel Islands are not part of the European Union de jure.

Channel Tunnel

Rail tunnel 31.4 miles long which links England to France. Mooted since the time of Napoleon, a tunnel under the English Channel (one was started in 1906 but discontinued for security reasons) was not constructed until the time of Margaret Thatcher, a famously Eurosceptic politician. Ironically, the tunnel joining Britain to the European continent has become a kind of monument to her years in power. She insisted it should not be built from public funds, so mostly private finance was sought for it. It opened in 1996. Britain, it could be argued, is now physically as well as politically part of Europe. The Eurostar rail service from London to Paris is well established.

charisma

Natural leadership quality which commands attention or even obedience. British politicians have seldom had such qualities, although Winston Churchill and possibly David Lloyd George can be said to fall into this category. The charisma alleged to have been possessed by Margaret Thatcher and Tony Blair probably owed as much to clever public relations as to the genuine quality.

See also authority.

Charter 88

www.charter88.org.uk

Pressure group for constitutional change. It was set up in 1988 to commemorate the Glorious Revolution 300 years earlier, which had inaugurated the emergence of parliamentary government out of monarchical rule. The organisation captured the support of the leading left-leaning

intellectuals of the day and its agenda of devolution, reform of the House of Lords and the voting system was virtually taken over by the Labour government in 1997. Much of it was implemented, with the notable exception of reform of the voting system. In March 2007 it combined with the New Politics Network to form a new campaigning body, Unlock Democracy.

charter mark

www.cabinetoffice.gov.uk/chartermark

A means of rewarding outstanding service in the public sector and fostering the consumer approach to public service provision. Recipients achieved 'a national standard of excellence in consumer service'. It was introduced by John Major in 1993. The charter mark was supplementary to the citizens' charters introduced at the same time but, like these, never really made a deep impression on the public consciousness. Following the introduction of the government's 'customer service excellence' standard, charter mark was closed to new applications.

See also citizens' charter.

Charter Movement

Conservative Party group that has as its aim the democratisation of the party. It was set up by party activists in the early 1980s and it aims to replace the hegemony of the leader with more member votes. For example, it called for a new Policy Committee answerable to the Central Council and a fusion of the National Union of Party Activists with Central Office by giving activists the right to vote for a party chair in a postal ballot. In 1997 William Hague introduced some of the reforms long called for by Charter members. By 2010, however, the group seemed barely extant.

See also Conservative Party.

Chartist

A supporter of the popular movement for political reform in the 19th century. The People's Charter, drafted by William Lovett, demanded: annual parliaments, universal male suffrage, equal electoral districts, an end to property qualifications for MPs, voting by ballot and payment of MPs. Fergus O'Connor and James O'Brien were the demagogic leaders of the movement. In July 1839 parliament rejected a petition bearing over a million signatures and did the same to one with 3 million signatures in May 1842. The Chartists became disunited over strategy after these setbacks and failed to agree a general strike. When the government reacted with the threat of military action to the attempted third petition in 1848 the movement crumbled and faded away, although most of its objectives were achieved within the next century.

Chicago School of Economics

Associated chiefly with the name and ideas of Milton Friedman, though close also to the ideas of Friedrich von Hayek. Two key ideas lie at the heart of the School's approach: that government should be as much as possible non-interventionist; and that it should restrict its activities to controlling the supply of money in the economy, on the grounds that an uncontrolled money supply leads inevitably to inflation. All else would be looked after by the 'hidden hand' of an unfettered market. Friedman's brand of monetarism influenced both Margaret Thatcher and Nigel Lawson, although its predicted remedial effects were hard to discern during the 1980s.

chief scientific advisor

See government chief scientific advisor.

chief secretary to the Treasury

The most important Treasury brief after the chancellor of the exchequer. It is a high-profile job because the chief secretary is the 'scrooge' of the nation's finances since he or she (Yvette Cooper in January 2008 was the first female holder of the office) is responsible for controlling public spending (especially monies granted to local government), ensuring public services deliver value for money and scrutinising and controlling pay in the public sector. The post holder also chairs cabinet committees on public

expenditure and future legislation. All these functions come together in the annual spending round, when the chief secretary manages negotiations between the Treasury and spending departments and chairs the PX and QFL cabinet committees. John Major was a successful chief secretary before becoming chancellor in 1989: none of his negotiations had to be referred to the informal 'Star Chamber' which adjudicated on such matters.

See also Star Chamber.

chief whip

Appointed by all parties to manage the teams of whips. Whips are an important mechanism of intra-party control and communication in both houses of parliament. In particular, the chief whip's greatest power comes through the role of advising the party leader on appointments to front-bench jobs and thus career advancement. Equally, the chief whip can advise on demotion, perhaps as a punishment for failing to follow the party line on a compulsory party vote ('three-line whip'). The government chief whip (or 'parliamentary secretary to the Treasury' to use the official terminology) is close to the centre of power, with a seat at the cabinet table. The office at Number 12 Downing Street, however, is no more, having been taken over by prime ministerial functions, and the chief whip now resides at 9 Downing Street. The parties (though more the Conservatives than Labour) have traditionally seen the whips' office as a 'nursery' of future ministerial talent and some chief whips – such as Edward Heath – have gone on to become prime minister.

See also whip.

Chilcot inquiry

www.iraqinquiry.org.uk
Established in June 2009 to consider British involvement in Iraq from 2001 to 2009. Its terms of reference covered the run-up to the war in March 2003, the course of the military action and the manner in which decisions were made, as well as to learn lessons for the future. Sir John Chilcot, a former civil servant,

chairs the inquiry and he is assisted by: Sir Lawrence Freedman, professor of war studies, King's College, London; historian Martin Gilbert; former diplomat Sir Roderick Lyne; and Baroness Prashar, chair of the Judicial Appointments Commission.

child benefit
Established by the Child Benefits Act 1975 to replace family allowances.

Child Poverty Action Group (CPAG)
www.cpag.org.uk
Pressure group founded in 1963 which exists for the 'relief, directly or indirectly, of poverty among children and families with children'. It 'works to ensure that those on low incomes get their full entitlements to welfare benefits' and campaigns via public education, lobbying and demonstrations. One of its former directors, Frank Field, became a Labour minister for social security in 1997, but resigned shortly afterwards, claiming his ideas were being ignored.

Child Support Agency (CSA)
www.csa.gov.uk
A government agency set up in 1993 in order to implement the Child Support Act 1991, and now part of the Child Maintenance and Enforcement Commission. It calculates and collects child maintenance from parents (generally fathers) who have left their families. The Agency epitomises the Conservative idea that people should be responsible for their actions. The huge growth in the proportion of children born outside the traditional two-parent family (over a quarter in the mid-1990s), plus the related problem of increasingly large welfare demands on the agencies of the state, all combined to support the creation of the CSA. However, the practice was not in line with the theory and the CSA soon became exceptionally unpopular, not only for delays and other administrative failings, but also for the fact that fathers willing to pay were allegedly charged crippling rates while those who

prevaricated seemed to get away with it as before. Press stories abounded of fathers driven to nervous breakdown or even suicide. The government, in line with the 'naming and shaming' of civil servants, responded by changing the chief executive from Ros Hepplewhite to Ann Chant in 1994. The CSA continued its work as part of the Department for Work and Pensions but not without continuing criticisms of its competence and excessive expenditure on administration. In December 2006 John Hutton announced its absorption by the Child Maintenance and Enforcement Commission.

child trust fund
Government donations to individual child savings. It was ended in 2010 by the Conservative–Liberal Democrat government as an economy measure. It had been initiated in 2005. Each newborn child received a sum of £250 followed by another £250 on their seventh birthday; the fund could not be accessed until the child was 18. More than £4 million tax-free funds of this type were opened after 2005 – a 75 per cent take-up rate. Supporters of the scheme mourned a genuinely successful initiative to encourage the habit of saving for every family and every child.

> Whilst everyone accepts the need for spending reductions, the abolition of child trust funds is a disappointing and retrograde decision. While prosperous parents will continue to make financial provision for their children's future, children from modest and low income families will miss out – starting adult life with yet another disadvantage. (Anne Longfield, chief executive of 4Children, 24 May 2010)

Chiltern Hundreds
An Anglo-Saxon unit of local government. If MPs wish to resign a seat, they must apply for one of two stewardships: of the Chiltern Hundreds (the better known) or of the Manor of Northstead, in Yorkshire. The arcane constitutional reason is that since 1707 any paid officer of the crown may not sit in parliament. There are three

Chiltern Hundreds: Stoke, Desborough and Burnham. Tony Blair resigned in this way on 27 June 2007.

Christian socialism

An important strand within British church history, especially Methodism, and the Labour Party. Many Labour politicians claim that Christ and his teachings represent a more powerful element of party doctrine than does Marx and dialectical materialism. In essence, it stresses the importance of social responsibility, especially towards the poor, and the duties of employers towards their workers. State education holds a special place in this strand of thought. Some have suggested that this is a form of 'gentle capitalism' or capitalism with a caring face, although it must be said that Christian socialism does point towards alternatives such as cooperatives and other voluntary associations. Tony Blair, among others in the Labour Party, could claim a link with this tradition, and stated in a speech before the 1997 election that he was his 'brother's keeper'. Gordon Brown's passion for relieving poverty probably owed something to his upbringing as the son of a pastor of the Church of Scotland.

Church of England

www.cofe.anglican.org
The 'official' or national church of the United Kingdom, established in the 16th century during the Reformation (as a breakaway from the Church of Rome occasioned by the Pope's refusal to sanction Henry VIII's divorce from Catherine of Aragon). In 1563 the Articles of Religion laid out the basic doctrines of the Church, at the behest of Elizabeth I, which are still in force today. During the Civil War the Church was suspended until the Restoration in 1660. The attempts by James II to introduce pro-Catholic reforms contributed to the Glorious Revolution of 1688. 'Low Church' practices, closer to Presbyterian thinking, and 'High Church', closer to Catholicism, became a feature of religious life. The monarch is the supreme

governor of the Church of England and the Archbishop of Canterbury traditionally performs coronations in Westminster Abbey. Some bishops of the Church of England – the 'lords spiritual' – are entitled to sit in the House of Lords.

It is also the 'mother church' of the worldwide Anglican communion, which claims 77 million Christians as members – the third largest church in the world. Each national member is independent and there have been intense disagreements in recent years over the ordination of gay priests and the legitimacy of gay marriages, with some African churches opposed and Archbishop Dr Ronan Williams struggling to control similar arguments within his own national church.

Compared with many Christian countries, especially the USA, Britain is a relatively secular country with only 1.7 million people attending church every month in 2003 and 1.2 million every week.

It is thought to be an advantage politically to profess Christianity and many politicians attempt to identify themselves with the Church; Tony Blair was a high-profile and active member of the Church of England, though was careful to insist his beliefs were separate from his politics. In December 2007 he became a Catholic, the religion of his wife, Cherie.

See also bishop; Glorious Revolution.

citizen

Term referring originally to an inhabitant of a city, later applied to a native or naturalised member of a state who has certain rights and reciprocal obligations. Citizenship has been a potent idea behind political education: that people need to learn something of the workings of a democratic system in order to participate effectively. (Sir) Bernard Crick has been a leading thinker in this field and chaired a working party on citizenship after Labour won the 1997 election.

In formal or legal terms British citizenship has changed markedly as a result of the British Nationality Act 1981, the Immigration Act 1988 and the British

Nationality (Hong Kong) Act 1990. Further changes occurred when Britain signed the 1992 treaty on European Union, which granted UK citizens a number of rights (residence, work, voting and freedom of travel) in European Union countries and reciprocal ones for European Union nationals in Britain. Citizenship teaching has now entered the national school curriculum.

citizens' charter

An attempt by John Major in November 1991 to combat bureaucratic inefficiency and indifference. The idea was to provide standards of service across the public sector and then measure how the various agencies were performing. Some 38 charters were published, including British Rail's Passenger Charter and the National Health Service's Patients' Charter. Charter mark awards were given to those agencies judged to have performed especially well. Cynics observed that the idea involved no extra resources and others claimed that this, the only 'big idea' from the Major government, failed to capture the public imagination.
    See also charter mark.

citizenship

See citizen.

citizenship education

Citizenship was introduced as a statutory subject in the English national curriculum in 2002. This followed the recommendations of Sir Bernard Crick's 1998 report and affects all children aged 11–16 years taught in state schools.

citizenship test

Officially the 'Life in the UK Test', now required for settlement (indefinite leave to remain) in the UK or British citizenship. It is run by the Home Office UK Border Agency. Introduced in November 2005, the test requires 'sufficient knowledge' of the English language and wider knowledge of life in the UK. The test lasts 45 minutes, in which 24 multiple choice questions must be answered and a 75 per cent pass mark

achieved. Successful applicants attend a ceremony in which an oath of allegiance must be made.

City (the)

The area of London where the most important financial transactions take place. Often called 'the square mile', this ancient area of the capital city is located on the north bank of the Thames between Tower Bridge and London Bridge. It includes the Bank of England, the London Stock Exchange, Lloyds Insurance and the headquarters of most of the important banks, insurance companies and other financial institutions. 'The City' is often used as a catch-all term for foreign markets and for large corporate interests.

'civic culture'

Term originating in Almond and Verba's study of political culture that appeared in 1963. It defined civic culture as a majority acceptance of the authority of the state and a commitment to participation in public duties. The authors saw Britain as having the ideal political culture, in which citizens trusted their ruling elites, believed in a degree of participation and accepted the validity of the laws of the land. This moderate, non-ideological culture is believed to have protected the country from extremist ideas, whether of the fascist right or the Marxist left. Margaret Thatcher sought passionately to change the British culture, to be more self-reliant, more opposed to high levels of taxation and more entrepreneurial. Survey evidence suggests she was unsuccessful and that the majority of respondents still believed in higher social expenditure, even if this meant higher taxes. However, high poll responses for such measures did not prevent the voters electing Conservative governments in 1987 and 1992. The civic culture thesis has been subject to much criticism, especially the view that it is based on data collected during the late 1950s, a particularly quiescent period of British political and social history. Since then there has been a marked decline in deference and respect for politicians, not to mention the political system itself, as evidenced by declining turnout at elections, especially the 59.2 per cent in 2001.

See also civil society.

Civil Contingencies Committee
See COBRA.

Civil Contingencies Secretariat
www.cabinetoffice.gov.uk/ukresilience/ccs.aspx
Civil service body set up in 2001 to provide early warning of impending problems. The secretariat is staffed by 100 civil servants based in the Cabinet Office, where it reports to the prime minister through the cabinet secretary. Its remit is to 'scan the horizon' as an early warning system and then to coordinate departments to ensure their response is effective. This initiative emerged from the debacle involving foot and mouth disease, when it was widely perceived that the Ministry of Agriculture, Fisheries and Food had not performed these jobs properly. Bruce Mann became head of the Secretariat in 2004.

civil law
Law that governs the rights of individuals and organisations and their dealings with each other. It is also called 'private' as opposed to 'public' and 'criminal' law and stipulates, for example, the principles of commercial transactions, family, property and inheritance. Civil disputes are heard in civil courts and the police are not involved. One of the key legal differences between the two kinds of law is that the civil courts require a lower standard of evidence: in criminal law the case against the accused has to be 'beyond reasonable doubt' while in civil courts it has to be on 'the balance of probabilities'.

civil liberties
Those rights and freedoms so precious they are thought to underlie liberal democratic government. Most of the freedoms focus on the protection of the individual from the coercive power of the state executed by political or legal authorities. The rights include: freedom of speech; freedom of

religion and thought; freedom of movement; freedom of association; right to a fair trial; and freedom of the person. Economic freedom – the right to buy, sell and make a profit – is central to the liberal democratic tradition of Britain and the USA.

In Britain civil liberties do not receive any special constitutional protection and many have argued that they have been eroded in recent times. For example, the right to remain silent when arrested and not have this held against you was abolished by the Criminal Justice and Public Order Act 1994, and ethnic minorities believe that they suffer disproportionately from the police power to stop and search people.

The pressure group Liberty is an enthusiastic campaigner for the protection of civil liberties in Britain. The Human Rights Act 1998 provided for the first time statutory defence of basic human rights in British courts. The terrorist outrages of 11 September 2001 and 7 July 2005 swung government towards more stringent controls at the expense of civil liberties. For example, Tony Blair wanted to extend the courts' right to hold a suspect without trial for 90 days but this was defeated in the Commons in November 2005; it ended up being set at 28 days. In 2008 an attempt was made to extend this limit to 42 days. Critics argued that this would be counter-productive, in that it would make British Muslims less likely to supply intelligence to the authorities about indigenous terrorism. Shadow home secretary David Davis resigned over the issue and stood for re-election in his Yorkshire constituency on 10 July 2008. The major parties did not stand against him and his victory was predict-able. Critics asserted that he had raised awareness of the issue only marginally and had forfeited his chance to do anything about the problem, as David Cameron had refused to keep his shadow portfolio open while he fought his by-election.

civil list
The annual grant given by parliament to the royal family to run the royal households. It was distinguished from other public

POLITICS

monies in 1698, when parliament decided to limit the monarch's ability to control public funds by exerting control itself over all funds except for those required by the monarch for day-to-day expenses. By the early 20th century the sum was £700,000 and over 2000–10 it was fixed at £7.9 million. Prince Charles is excluded from the list as he has income from estates owned from his position as Duke of Cornwall. In 1993 the queen announced she was willing to pay income tax for the first time and removed all members of the royal family from the civil list except for herself, the Duke of Edinburgh and, until her death, the late Queen Mother. Upkeep of royal castles and the royal train are met from the relevant departments but the royal yacht, *Britannia*, was decommissioned in 1997 after Labour (in opposition) refused to support a government scheme to build a £60 million replacement. The *Daily Mail* in May 2003 ran a story that John Major had not been made a member of the Order of the Garter, as is traditional for former prime ministers, because of royal anger at his 'mishandling' of the replacement issue.

civil rights

An umbrella term for the rights of a disadvantaged group, usually suffering racial or religious discrimination, which is campaigning for equal treatment in economic, political and social life. Although mainly associated with the US civil rights movements of the 1960s, the Northern Ireland Civil Rights Association campaigned against the religious discrimination practised against Catholics in Ulster before the troubles. Civil rights movements traditionally use non-violent methods of protest, such as marches and civil disobedience. Legislation has since outlawed many forms of discrimination on the grounds of sex, race or religion and the incorporation of the European Convention on Human Rights into UK law provides extra protection for individuals and minority groups.

civil servant

See civil service.

civil service

www.civilservice.gov.uk

All those employed by central government to run its administration. The civil service is the workhorse of central government and is responsible for carrying out the wishes of the legislature as interpreted by the ministers who head up departments of state. In the early 1980s there were over 700,000 civil servants but by 1996 this figure had shrunk – as a result of privatisation and the Next Steps reforms – to under 500,000. This reduction was both an attempt to decentralise the administration and to reduce the workforce, as well as to relieve overload on Whitehall by hiving off the routine aspects of government to executive agencies. Policy was still to be formulated by ministers, who in turn were to be advised by some 4,000 elite ('administrative class') civil servants. In 1968 the Civil Service Department was set up to run the public service but this was abolished in 1981 and its functions were replaced by the Office of Public Service in 1995, which in turn was later absorbed by the Cabinet Office.

One of the abiding debates in the study of British politics is the extent of civil servants' influence on the formation of policy. The comic *Yes, Minister* and *Yes, Prime Minister* series on television and radio suggested that the clever Sir Humphrey Appleby almost always outwitted the somewhat dim minister Jim Hacker, although expert commentators assert that decisive ministers will usually prevail if they know their subject and their own minds.

One of the most important developments since 1979 has been a decline in the traditional formula that civil servants should be anonymous, neutral and permanent. Margaret Thatcher put up Sir William Armstrong to defend the government in the attempt to prevent the book *Spycatcher* by Peter Wright from being published, for example. Civil servant Clive Ponting, on the other hand, decided to ignore the conventions of Whitehall and in July 1984 sent confidential information regarding the *General Belgrano* affair to MP Tam Dalyell. Other civil servants have been 'named and shamed' by senior politicians, arguably trying to escape their responsibilities, as in the case of Ros Heppelwhite of the Child Support Agency or Derek Lewis of the Prisons Agency in 1996.

Tony Blair's government also left its mark on the service. Not only were traditional higher-flying bureaucrats joined by media-savvy special advisors, but all government departments began to adopt a customer-friendly approach to their client groups, similar to the customer service ethos now common in retailing and other service industries. In addition, the civil service was redirected to be more focused on 'delivery': the priority Blair faced once it became clear voters were dissatisfied with the state of the public services. In the autumn of 2001 Lord Birt was appointed part-time to the new Forward Strategy Unit (FSU) in Number 10 to help reform the civil service, which was widely perceived as failing to deliver the results required by government. In July 2004 chancellor Gordon Brown, as part of that year's comprehensive spending review, announced planned 'efficiency' cuts of 84,000 in the civil service to save over £20 billion in expenditure.

> As I learnt very early on in my life in Whitehall, the acid test of any political question is: what is the alternative? (Lord (Burke) Trend, secretary to the cabinet, 1975)

See also administrative class; executive agency.

Civil Service College
See Centre for Management and Policy Studies; Office of Public Service.

Civil Service Department
See Office of Public Service.

civil service pay
On 1 June 2010 the *Guardian* revealed that 170 top civil servants earned over £150,000 a year. This was 10 times the average national income and £8,000 more than the prime minister. The head of the Office of Fair Trading received £275,000;

the chief executive of the National Health Service £255,000; the director general of the Department for Work and Pensions £249,000; the chief of the defence staff £245,000; and the cabinet secretary, Sir Gus O'Donnell, £240,000. Several others received six-figure salaries for working part time, for example Sir Michael Scholar, chair of the UK Statistics Authority, took home £150,000 for a three-day week. In a time of economic recession the government found itself vulnerable to critical press accounts of high public sector pay.

civil society
The non-political relationships in society – those of family, business and, especially, voluntary organisations. These relationships, it is argued, provide the 'glue' which cements society together and instruct people in the arts of compromise, responsibility, self-discipline and leadership. The concept was originally related to the 17th-century notion of the 'state of nature' which humans supposedly inhabited before entering the 'civilised' confines of the state. The idea was crucial in that it enabled thinkers like John Locke to argue that citizens had the right to overthrow a government which failed to live up to its 'contract' with citizens. It has been suggested that the lack of strong or 'thick' civil society in eastern Europe hindered its transition to democracy after the collapse of communism.

Studies have found substantial group membership in Britain: 16 per cent church; 14 per cent trade unions; 17 per cent sporting bodies; and 5 per cent environmental groups. However, the poor turnouts in national, local and European elections suggest civil society in Britain is 'thinner' than is healthy for the body politic as a whole. Some social observers believe the *Bowling Alone* thesis of Robert Putnam (1995) applies to Britain as well as to the USA. He argues that the dramatic decreases in citizen participation rates in social and voluntary activity represent a worrying decline of civil society. Data collected in 1999 by the US scholar Peter Hall, however, suggested British civic culture or 'social capital' is healthier than the US one. Sheffield University's social audit seemed to reinforce Hall's findings, despite the poor turnout in the 2001 general election.

See also civic culture.

Civil War
See English Civil War.

Clarendon schools
Term originating from the nine schools studied by the Clarendon commission in 1861 to ascertain their state of repair, management and finances. These nine are still regarded as the leading private schools in the country: Eton, Harrow, Westminster, Charterhouse, St Paul's, Merchant Taylors, Rugby, Shrewsbury and Winchester.

class
A combination of economic, occupational and social status and identity. Class is an emotive question in Britain, which is famously obsessed with it. Interestingly, the subjective perception of class in Britain differs markedly from the objective: a survey published in the Daily Telegraph (25 September 1998), for example, revealed that 70 per cent of respondents saw themselves as 'working class', even though at least half of them would be classified as middle class.

Generally speaking, definitions of class fall into two broad categories: the two-class model developed by Karl Marx; and the multi-class system associated with Max Weber. Marx saw society as stratified into two major and antagonistic classes based on their relationship to the productive process: the proletariat (working class) and the bourgeoisie (middle-class owners of means of production). He believed the proletariat would eventually realise the bourgeoisie was exploiting it and rise up to establish a new classless socialist society. History has suggested that such a revolution is far from the inevitable conclusion of social interaction which Marx believed it would be.

Political scientists prefer more specific classifications, developed from Max

Weber's distinction between class and occupational or status groups. A number of different classifications are in use in Britain, three of the most common being the ABC scale of the British Market Research Association (BMRA), John Goldthorpe's salariat system and the eight-point classification used by the Office for National Statistics (ONS). In November 1998 the ONS issued a report based upon an Economic and Social Research Council (ESRC) study into class categories. Existing class categories were based on a six-fold division: professional, managerial and technical, skilled non-manual, skilled manual, partly skilled and unskilled. The report argued that changes in 'the nature and structure of both industry and occupations have rendered [current classifications] both outmoded and misleading'. The new system is based to a greater extent upon job security and career prospects.

The ABC scale
A   Upper middle – professional, higher managerial (3 per cent of households)
B   Middle – middle managers (16 per cent)
C1 Lower middle – junior managers, routine white collar (26 per cent)
C2 Skilled – plumbers, carpenters, mechanics (26 per cent)
D   Semi-skilled and unskilled – manual workers (17 per cent)
E   Residual – dependent on long-term benefit (13 per cent)

The salariat scale
Higher salariat (12 per cent)
Lower salariat (16 per cent)
Routine clerical (24 per cent)
Petty bourgeoisie (7 per cent)
Foremen and technicians (5 per cent)
Skilled manual (11 per cent)
Unskilled manual (25 per cent)

ONS scale
1   Higher managerial and professional
1a Employers and managers in large organisations

1b High professionals – lawyers, doctors, dentists, civil servants, professors, teachers and airline pilots
2   Lower managerial and associate professionals – police sergeants and constables, prison officers, fire-fighters, journalists, nurses and professional sports people
3   Intermediate occupations – computer engineers, dental technicians, secretaries, flight attendants, driving instructors
4   Small employers and own account workers – self-employed non-professionals
5   Lower supervisory, craft and related occupations – electricians, car mechanics and engine drivers
6   Semi-routine occupations – drivers, shop assistants, traffic wardens and postal workers
7   Routine occupations – car park attendants, cleaners, road workers, refuse collectors, labourers, road sweepers
8   Never worked and long-term unemployed

classical liberalism

One of the most important traditions of political thought of the last 200 years. These ideas can be traced back to the writings of John Locke and Adam Smith, among others, and evolved into the laissez faire or free enterprise economics of the 19th century. Adam Smith was a key early economic theorist; he believed that the government should eschew all subsidies and anything likely to distort markets, that is, he advocated the free play of the forces of supply and demand in the market. He also advocated that business people should be allowed to produce goods to meet market demand, employ labour to produce goods at the rate that the market dictates, take profit in accordance with their efficiency and competitiveness, and invest profits in other enterprises. According to Smith, this capitalist system would, if left unaided, prove to be the most efficient means of producing goods possible. In the 19th century the Liberals espoused this doctrine while the embryonic labour movement

became increasingly hostile to its inegalitarian tendencies. Socialist critics maintained that free enterprise inevitably created huge disparities of wealth and poverty, destroyed the idea of craftsmanship and created an alienated urban population.

Allied to Adam Smith's economics were the philosophical ideas of Jeremy Bentham, James Mill and John Stuart Mill. Bentham inaugurated the idea of utilitarianism. James Mill and his son went on to add to classical liberalism the basic arguments for representative government. Richard Cobden and John Bright completed what is usually perceived as classical liberalism with the idea that the extension of trade worldwide would naturally incline nations towards peace rather than war.

In the 20th century the Conservative Party under Margaret Thatcher rediscovered classical liberalism and, also influenced by the 'Chicago School of Economics', absorbed it into party policy. Labour was in turn influenced by these developments and adapted them, albeit with special reference to 'globalisation'. This has led some to claim, with some justification, the long-term triumph of classical liberalism's advocacy of capitalism.

clause 4

The 'nationalisation' clause of the Labour Party's constitution. The constitution was drafted by Arthur Henderson and Sidney Webb in 1918 and clause 4 established as a benchmark of British socialism that it was the party's intention to achieve the 'common ownership of the means of production, distribution and exchange'. However, in practice the party never attempted to achieve a comprehensive 'common ownership' and tacitly accepted a capitalistic private sector as the engine of the economy. Anthony Crosland's widely accepted revisionist reformulation (*The Future of Socialism*, 1956) arguably made the clause unnecessary in any case. Hugh Gaitskell tried to change it formally in 1959 but was defeated by indignant left-wingers. Tony Blair used its reform, however, as a sign that he meant business in modernising

Labour. His campaign was supremely successful and a special conference in April 1995 accepted a reformulation which spoke of 'a dynamic economy' in which the 'enterprise of the market' is joined with the 'forces of partnership and cooperation'. Veteran Old Labourites like Arthur Scargill protested in vain: clause 4, as traditionally understood, was no more.

cleavage

Term used to denote major divisions in society. Britain is generally believed to lack many of the cleavages which cause problems in other societies, like religion (apart from in Northern Ireland). The main cleavage in British society is normally thought to be class, but even class divisions have become blurred over the past half century.

See also class; voting behaviour.

Cliveden set

A upper-class group of British right-wingers who used to meet in Nancy Astor's stately home (Cliveden) in Buckinghamshire during the 1930s. The group were fervent supporters of appease-ment and, being Germanophile, encouraged better relations with Nazi Germany. Some claim the 'set' was an invention of left-wing journalist Claud Cockburn, but most accept there was a basis of fact behind the identification of such a group. Astor is seen as the leader of the group, which also included Geoffrey Dawson, editor of the *Times*, and Edward Wood, Lord Halifax, foreign secretary at the time of the Munich agreement.

closed shop

The system whereby all employees in an enterprise are obliged to join a specified union or unions. Usually in such circum-stances the employer is in agreement, as it is advantageous to deal with as few bodies as possible that represent workers. However, such agreements prevent the employment of workers who do not wish to join unions and the Conservative government passed legislation in the early 1980s to weaken the closed shop by insisting that such

agreements receive in a secret ballot the support of 80 per cent of those covered by them. This measure was moderated by the Employment Relations Act 2000, which obliges employers to recognise unions for negotiation purposes, provided a majority of workplace members are in favour.

coalition government

When two or more political parties combine to form a joint government, usually (in Britain's case) in the face of war or some other crisis. In the 20th century there were a number of occasions when such governments were formed. In 1915 Herbert Asquith formed one to conduct the war. David Lloyd George took over as its leader in 1916 and its mandate was reaffirmed in 1918 until it fell in 1922. The next example was in 1931, when Ramsay MacDonald split the Labour Party and was elected as head of the national government, which was re-elected and was technically still in office in 1940 when the Conservatives, under Winston Churchill, formed his wartime coalition government with Labour and the Liberals. After 1945 governments were always single-party ones, although between 1976 and 1978 Labour needed Liberal MPs to support it in votes in order to survive (the 'Lib–Lab pact'). Close electoral contests, as in 1992, often encour-aged speculation that either Labour or the Conservatives might do a deal with the smaller third party and govern in coalition. The possible reform of the voting system to a system of proportional representation would certainly make such arrangements more likely. Despite Liberal Democrat hopes of a referendum on this topic after 1997, Labour hostility to the idea led to it being shelved.

The 2010 election produced the first hung parliament since 1974. Initially it was thought Labour's greater willingness to compromise with the Liberal Democrats over voting reform would produce linkage with them, but their combined seats would still have required the inclusion of smaller parties. The Liberal Democrats eventually reached an agreement with David Cameron's

Conservatives in coalition, with whom they produced a good working majority. Nick Clegg became deputy prime minister and his colleagues Vince Cable, Chris Huhne and David Laws were given cabinet jobs.

See also general election; national government.

COBRA

Name given to the Civil Contingencies Committee which meets in a windowless underground Whitehall corridor in times of emergency threatening the nation's health, safety and security. The name, in fact, stands for Cabinet Office Briefing Room A. Membership varies according to the nature of the crisis but the home secretary or prime minister usually chairs the meeting, which includes senior figures from the military, police, intelligence services and other specialists. Former anti-terror senior officer Andy Hayman criticised COBRA in his 2009 book (with Margaret Gilmore) *The Terrorist Hunters* for slowing up remedial action and providing a forum for petty political competition between rival agencies.

code of conduct for MPs

Drawn up by the Standards and Privileges Committee in 1995 in the wake of the 'cash for questions' scandal and approved by the House of Commons in July 1995. It laid out the duties of MPs to serve their constituents, obey the law and observe the principles of 'selflessness, integrity, objectivity, accountability, openness, honesty and leadership'. Observance of the code is monitored by the parliamentary commissioner on standards and the Standards and Privileges Committee.

See also Committee on Standards in Public Life; ministerial code of conduct; parliamentary commissioner for standards; parliamentary privilege; Standards and Privileges Committee.

Cold War

The name given to the period of tension after the Second World War when the USSR began to impose its influence upon eastern Europe, especially Poland, Bulgaria, Romania, Hungary and Czechoslovakia. The degree of tension and armed preparedness between the great powers was akin to a real war but the fear of nuclear exchange prevented outright conflict. The USA decided to support western Europe after 1946, when Winston Churchill made his speech at Fulton, Missouri, when he said 'From Stettin in the Baltic to Trieste in the Adriatic, an iron curtain has descended across the continent'. Once Britain pulled out from supporting the pro-west side in the Greek civil war, the USA moved in and after Marshall aid was introduced, was persuaded, partly by the British foreign secretary Ernest Bevin, to participate in a permanent security alliance: the North Atlantic Treaty Organisation (NATO). The Cold War continued throughout the 1950s and 1960s and after the 1962 Cuban missile crisis. In the 1980s US president Ronald Reagan began embarking on an anti-ballistic missile system known as 'Star Wars', designed to destroy incoming missiles from the communist east. The USSR was unable, ultimately, to afford the arms race which resulted from the Cold War and it essentially ended once the USSR collapsed in 1991. However, tension between Russia and the USA and its allies was partially revived by the attempts of Russian president Vladimir Putin to assert his country's power and influence in the world.

collective ownership

See clause 4.

collective responsibility

A principle of British government that key decisions should be taken only after full discussion in cabinet and that, once taken, all ministers are obliged to support the decision, despite any individual reservations that they may have had. The convention is codified in the document *Questions of Procedure*, which sets out ministerial rules of behaviour: 'Decisions reached by the Cabinet or Cabinet Committees are binding on all members of the government'. Anyone breaching this convention will normally be called upon to resign unless there is a special dispensation, as with the Labour cabinet over the question of continued membership of the European Economic Community in 1975, when ministers were allowed publicly to oppose continued membership.

collectivism

The assertion of the good of society as a whole, as opposed to the good of the individual. It is usually associated with the idea of equality within that society. Further, it is often associated with state intervention on behalf of the greater whole and, related to this by its critics, with bureaucracy and inefficiency. In Britain Labour has been the natural home of collectivist ideas, although in the decades before and after the Second World War both the Liberals and moderate Conservatives embodied elements of it in their own philosophies, while 'New' Labour shed much of the collectivism associated with traditional views of the party.

College Green

A green and grassy area outside the houses of parliament where television interviews are often done. The area is sometimes called 'St Stephen's Green' or 'Abingdon Green' or just 'the Green'.

Combat 18

www.combat18.org

Hitler-revering far-right grouping espousing neo-Nazi ideas. Combat 18 is named after the alphabet positions of Adolf Hitler's initials. It is connected to the organisation Blood and Honour, which promotes skinhead and other right-wing groups. According to its website Combat 18 used to be 'a brigade of fearless storm troopers' which provided security at meetings of the British National Party (BNP), but when the BNP leadership decided to 'play the game of democracy' Combat 18 was 'promptly given the boot'. The group openly accepts violence as a policy (or 'constructive Aryan militancy' as the

website has it). The group was active in the north-west towns of Oldham and Burnley during the race trouble in 2001.

Combined Online Information System (COINS)

The government's central accounting system. This online system shows what each government department is spending, together with its spending programme. The *Guardian* on 5 June 2010 reported the Treasury was resisting any release of data from its detailed archives, on the basis that it would provoke a 'disruptive' amount of follow-up requests. However, on that day a huge amount of financial information was released about every aspect of government spending.

> The data has gone from being jealously guarded ... to being a public asset for free use. (*Guardian*, 5 June 2010)

commercial radio and television

Before 1973 radio broadcasting was the preserve of the BBC, although large numbers of young people tuned in to listen to pop music broadcast from illegal pirate radio stations such as Radio Caroline. However, in 1973 the Conservative government allowed applications for commercial franchises. They now operate in most parts of the country, financed by advertising. The BBC's television broadcasting monopoly was broken in 1955, when commercial television was introduced, with over a dozen companies operating all over the country. The system was policed by the Independent Television Authority (superseded by the Independent Television Commission in 1990), the chair of which was appointed by the government. In 1982 Channel 4 was launched and in spring 1997 Channel 5. Cable television and satellite stations also provide a variety of different channels for the viewer.

See also Broadcasting Act 1990; Independent Television Commission; Office of Communications.

Commission for Local Democracy

Independent think-tank on local government. In 1995 it judged 'the present system of local government in Britain as seriously inadequate to meet the requirements of a mature democracy'.

Commissioner for Public Appointments

www.publicappointmentscommissioner.org
Office created in 1995 (as the Commissioner for Public Appointments) by the Major government as one of the recommendations of the Nolan report. The aim was to monitor some 12,000 appointments made by ministers to public bodies, many of them quangos. The first commissioner was Sir Leonard Peach. On 17 July 2002 the second commissioner to be appointed (in 1999), Dame Rennie Fritchie, accused a number of departments, including the Treasury, Health and Culture, of failing to get independent assessors to sit on appointment boards. In addition, she criticised them for failing to ensure that jobs up for reappointment were made open to competition and for ignoring her own code of conduct for filling posts on merit. Janet Gaymer was appointed in January 2006 to serve a fixed five-year term.

Commission for Racial Equality

www.cre.gov.uk
Set up in 1976 to encourage racial equality and investigate racial discrimination in employment and other areas. It was incorporated into the new Equality and Human Rights Commission in 2007.

See also Equality and Human Rights Commission.

Committee of the Whole House

The House of Commons meets as a whole in such a 'committee' when a matter of particular importance is being considered. For several centuries any bills concerning taxation or expenditure were so treated and in 1993 the contentious Maastricht bill was considered in the same way.

Committee of Ways and Means

A Committee of the Whole House, when the house meets as such to discuss the budget, presided over by the chair of ways

and means (i.e. the deputy speaker). The Committee was abolished in 1967, but 'supply' (i.e. relating to taxation) is still raised on ways and means resolutions and it is still the chair of ways and means who chairs the budget debate.

Committee on Standards in Public Life

www.public-standards.gov.uk
A standing body constituted in 1994, in the wake of 'sleaze' allegations relating to parliament. The Committee's members are appointed for up to three years. It has been successively chaired to date by Lord Nolan, Lord Neill, Sir Alistair Graham, Sir Nigel Wicks and Sir Christopher Kelly. Its work covers MPs and ministers, civil servants and members of key executive agencies, as well as party funding, for example.

See also Neill committee; Nolan committee; parliamentary commissioner for standards; Standards and Privileges Committee.

committee stage

See act of parliament; standing committee.

Common Agricultural Policy (CAP)

Possibly the most contentious of all European Union (EU) policies. The two key undertakings behind the CAP were the agreement to guarantee prices for agricultural commodities and the guarantee that all surpluses would be bought by the European Community; in addition, quotas are placed upon imports of certain goods from outside the EU. This proved an open invitation to farmers to produce more than was needed, to receive the benefits of a captive market; and it also subsidised inefficient production methods. The results included the infamous butter 'mountains' and wine 'lakes'. Two-thirds of the Community budget was spent on the CAP in the 1980s, which almost resulted in bankruptcy. In 1986 a five-year reform programme was introduced whereby farmers were asked to limit production and were compensated for land 'set aside'. By 1992 the proportion of the budget spent on the CAP had been reduced to 55 per cent. In January 2003 Tony Blair rowed with Jacques Chirac when it became known to him that France and Germany had collaborated on changes to the CAP without informing Britain. The addition of 10 more countries to the EU in May 2004 – some of them relatively poor and dependent on agriculture – had implications for the CAP. By 2005 CAP represented 44 per cent of EU spending, or €43 billion.

common law
Derived from court decisions rather than statute, this type of law has been developed by judges from 'custom and precedent'. Much of it developed after the Norman conquest and is based on legal interpretations of local customs to create a law 'common' to all the kingdom.

Common Market
See European Union.

Commoners' Register
In Bristol a pensions consultant, John Oliver, runs a Commoners' Register, to which he invites members of the House of Lords to declare they do not wish to be known by their titles. The first member was Lord Noel Annan in the early 1990s and the Register now has 120 members signed up; they include Roy Hattersley, former Labour cabinet minister, David Steel and Shirley Williams. The *Guardian* on 27 April 2001 gave the Register its blessing and announced its policy henceforward was not to use titles in its letter page.

Commons
See House of Commons.

Commonwealth (British)
www.thecommonwealth.org
The organisation which emerged from the chequered history of the British Empire. Most of the former colonies are members. In 1926, at the Imperial Conference, the 'white' dominions were established as independent states, although with 'common allegiance to the Crown

and freely associated as members of the British Commonwealth of Nations'. The Statute of Westminster in 1931 gave legal force to this independent status. After the Second World War most of the countries achieving independence from Britain joined the Commonwealth so that in 2010 there were 54 member states and a total population of 1,900 million. The queen is head of state in 16 countries, while most of the others 32 are republics (a few have their own monarchs). Australia has been ambivalent for some time about the queen being head of state and seeks to make alternative arrangements. Burma withdrew in 1947, the Republic of Ireland in 1949 and Fiji in 1987. (Fiji was readmitted but was then suspended in September 2009 as the interim prime minister, Frank Bainimarama, had not held democratic elections.) Pakistan left in 1972 but rejoined in 1989. South Africa left in 1961 over disputes surrounding its racist internal policies; it was readmitted in 1995. Nigeria was suspended in 1995 because of its abuse of human rights but surprisingly in 1997 Mozambique was adopted as the 54th member even though its former colonial country was Portugal. As a result of illiberal actions by president Musharaff, Pakistan was suspended in November 2007 but was welcomed back to the organisation in May 2008.

High commissioners represent Commonwealth members in London and the organisation meets once every two years via the Commonwealth Secretariat, which was founded in London in 1960. Kamalesh Sharma, an Indian diplomat, became Commonwealth Secretary-General in 2008.

See also Empire (British).

communication
See political communications.

Communist Party of Great Britain (CPGB)
www.cpgb.org.uk
Founded in 1920 by a combination of left-wing socialist groups but largely the

Socialist Party of Great Britain. From the outset it followed the teachings and became a slavish supporter of international communism based in Moscow. As such it was seen as alien to the British tradition and attempts to affiliate to the Labour Party were smartly rejected. The party attracted little electoral support and in 1932 had only 6,000 members. However, the identification of the USSR as an emergent 'utopia' encouraged membership and CPGB members infiltrated other organisations (for example the Popular Front and the National Unemployed Workers Movement) in order to capture them for their movement. Once the USSR joined the Second World War there was widespread enthusiasm for the party and membership exceeded 40,000, but after the war Stalin's incursions into eastern Europe and the start of the Cold War returned the party to the periphery, with little influence except in certain trade unions. During the 1970s the party split as the more independent 'Eurocommunism' became popular. In 1991, in the wake of the USSR's collapse, the party declined to a few thousand members, dissolved and renamed itself the Democratic Left, though retaining the *Morning Star* as its newspaper. One splinter group named the Communist Party of Britain claimed continuity with the original CPGB.

communitarianism
A social philosophy which can be traced back to the ideas of the German philosopher G. W. F. Hegel and the work of T. H. Green, among others. It argues that individuals achieve their identities only through the communities that raise and nurture them; in return these individuals have an obligation to support and contribute towards their communities.

community charge (poll tax)
Form of taxation to raise revenue for local government. In the wake of the Hundred Years War in 1377 parliament levied a flat charge per head of 4 pence for everyone aged over 14 – a poll tax. When a poll

tax was introduced in 1380, it triggered the Peasants' Revolt, and the device lay unused until a Conservative government exhumed it in the late 1980s, though the official name given to it at the time was 'community charge'. Margaret Thatcher came into power looking for an alternative to the rates system, which was paid by only a proportion of householders. Her answer was the community charge, which she believed was fair in that: it was a flat charge on every elector; it gave an incentive to all voters to keep the charge as low as possible; and it increased the accountability of local government to voters. It was introduced in Scotland in 1988 and in England and Wales in 1989. However, it was deemed unfair by many because: it taxed a duke as much as a labourer; it was expensive to collect and was easily evaded; and central government still determined much of local spending, thus eroding the idea of accountability. It was dubbed the 'poll tax' as it was a per capita charge and, though the government tried, it never shook the popular derisive name for the ill-fated local tax.

Opposition was intense and in April 1990 there were riots in central London against the tax. Some commentators assert it was the major reason why Margaret Thatcher fell from power in November 1990. Despite the ostensible issue of Europe, too many Conservative MPs calculated she had lost an unacceptable degree of popular support over her stubborn insistence on pushing through the poll tax. The incoming John Major appointed Thatcher's long-term opponent Michael Heseltine to be in charge of a replacement and in 1993 he introduced the council tax, a means of raising finance not dissimilar to the old rates but this time based on houses according to bands of value so that owners of larger houses paid more than those living in smaller ones.

See also council tax.

community politics
The concentration upon 'grass roots' issues like pavements, litter and dog fouling, adopted by the Liberal Party in the 1970s

as its way of raising the political awareness of people, and thus winning acceptance at local level. The Liberal Democrats adopted the concept when the Liberals fused with the Social Democratic Party in 1988.

Compass
www.compassonline.org.uk
Left-of-centre think-tank founded in 2003. It was unhappy with the direction Labour had taken under Tony Blair's leadership. It was also widely seen as a faction within the party. Its founding document was *A Vision for the Democratic Left* but several documents have followed, including *A New Political Economy* and *The Public Realm*. Compass also considered supporting moves to remove Gordon Brown in November 2009. Its chair is Neal Lawson and its secretary Gavin Hayes.

Competition Commission
www.competition-commission.org.uk
Independent public body set up in April 1999 by the Competition Act 1998. It replaced the Monopolies and Mergers Commission, which had been set up in 1973 under the Fair Trading Act by government to investigate and report on possible monopolies following from mergers and takeovers, as well as the transfer of newspaper assets. The Competition Commission similarly inquires into those matters referred to it by other competition authorities concerning monopolies, mergers and the regulation of utility companies. Tribunals hear appeals against the decisions of the director general of fair trading and the regulators of utilities.
See also Office of Fair Trading.

competitiveness
Ability to compete in the international economy. In April 1998 the *World Competitiveness Yearbook*, produced by the Institute for Management Development based in Switzerland, calculated Britain was declining on this crucial index. In 1997 Britain had been shown to have leapt from 19th to 11th place, but in 1998 had fallen back to 12th. In 2009 it was in 21st

position, behind Ireland and China. The USA was top of the index, followed by Singapore and Hong Kong. The *Yearbook* judged that the change of government in 1997 did not appear to have altered the generally favourable conditions caused, as in the USA, by privatisation, deregulation, flexibility in the labour market and massive investment. The Department of Trade and Industry in 2008 reported that the productivity gap with France on a per worker basis had been halved since 1995 and the gap with Germany closed. The gap with USA, however, remained the same.
See also productivity.

comprehensive school
The model of education adopted by Labour, under the influence of Anthony Crosland, to counteract the socially adverse effects of elitism in education resulting from fee-paying 'public schools' and the selective grammar schools. During the 1970s Labour did its best to remove grammar schools although Harold Wilson, an ex-grammar school pupil himself, had earlier claimed that 'it would be over my dead body'. The public schools were left untouched. Comprehensive schools are generally thought to have been a failure in terms of making education more egalitarian, as the children of middle-class families still dominate those who go on to higher education. Moreover, as schools recruited from geographical catchment areas, those in rundown working-class districts tended to be of poor quality, dubbed 'sink schools', and those in middle-class areas much more successful. The substitution of comprehensive for grammar schools, therefore, according to their critics, denied the bright working-class child the chance of 'escaping' from an unsupportive culture. Moreover, many comprehensives suffer from poor behaviour, which creates inadequate learning environments for the children who do want to study, thus strengthening the appeal of private education. The Labour government in the years after 2000 sought to replace comprehensives with 'academies'. While they have

improved GCSE results substantially, they have not removed the main body of underachievers who leave school with few if any qualifications.

See also academy; education policy; 11-plus test; grammar school; public school.

comprehensive spending review (CSR)

A 'rolling programme' whereby a three-year expenditure plan is updated each year. The 2004 review continued the pattern of generous spending on public services (figures per annum increases for three years): 7.1 per cent on health; 4 per cent on education; about 4 per cent to the Home Office in an effort to cut crime by 15 per cent 2004–07; 10 per cent for the security services to prosecute the war on terror, though less than 2 per cent for defence.

The 2007 CSR revealed that £551 billion was to be raised (2007–08) in taxation (including £154 billion from income tax, £97 billion from national insurance, £81 billion from VAT and £47 billion from corporation tax) while £589 billion would be spent by government, including: £159 billion on social security; £105 billion on health; £78 billion on education; £20 billion on transport; £26 billion on personal social services; and £32 billion on defence. The increases in expenditure which character-ised Labour's second and third terms were planned to ease from thereon, according to the Treasury: £617 billion in 2008–09; £647 billion in 2009–10 and £678 billion in 2010–11. Another CSR was due in 2009 but the *Observer* reported on 22 March 2009 that it had been postponed as it would reveal the need for sweeping cuts and thus neutralise Labour's planned attack on Conservatives in the forthcoming election. Following the establishment of the coalition government in May 2010, spend-ing totals are expected to be reduced over future years as cuts to reduce government debt are made.

comptroller and auditor general

See National Audit Office.

compulsory competitive tendering (CCT)

Part of the Conservative 'market testing' approach to government whereby specific functions should be tested against the kind of competitive bids outside agencies can offer, uncushioned by monopoly provision and strongly protective public sector unions. CCT was introduced during the Thatcher regime, initially for refuse collection and hospital catering. However, the 1991 white paper *Competing for Quality* asserted that 'Public services will increasingly move to a culture where relationships are contractual rather than bureaucratic'. By 1995 it was claimed by government that staff numbers had been cut by some 30,000 in this way and £750,000,000 saved. New Labour replaced CCT with 'best value' in the provision of local government services.

See also best value; market testing.

Confederation of British Industry (CBI)

www.cbi.org.uk

The 'peak' organisation of business interests, formed in 1965 out of three employers' bodies. The CBI seeks to defend and represent its 15,000 members' interests. It employs over 400 staff and offers members a range of services. It holds an annual conference and has regular access to government. In 1971 a number of smaller firms withdrew to form the Smaller Business Association and the tension between the large companies, which domin-ate, and the smaller ones still underlies the CBI and inhibits its effectiveness as a lobbying instrument. After 1979 it had less influence with government as Margaret Thatcher tended to see it as part of the 'consensual culture' she opposed. Tensions surfaced when director general Sir Terence Beckett promised a 'bare knuckle fight' with her government in 1983 over the sharp decline in manufacturing industry (after meeting her, he emerged chastened and she unmoved). Technically apolitical, the CBI has many more links with the Conservatives than with Labour, although Tony Blair and Gordon Brown did much to lean their party towards the business community. Richard Lambert took over as director general in spring 2006.

confidence and supply agreement
An agreement by a party in parliament to support a minority government on motions of confidence (in its ability to govern) and supply (the provision of funds to finance itself). If lost, either motion would require the government to resign but such an agreement with another party or parties enables it to continue. In May 2010 the Conservatives discussed such an arrangement with the Liberal Democrats but both eventually decided the stronger relationship of a formal coalition was preferable. Critics of the Liberal Democrats suggested their leaders had been lured by the offer of being in power for the first time but they insisted their concern was with the effective government of the country in parlous economic times.

congestion charge
A fee charged to motorists entering the central area of the capital. It was introduced, at £5, in February 2003 by London mayor Ken Livingstone. The aim was to reduce traffic flow by 15 per cent and ease conditions which often approached gridlock. Exemptions for certain groups – minicabs, taxis, school buses, motorbikes – proved controversial as others, especially public sector workers, made the case for similar treatment. The income was to be used for improving public transport. The scheme is policed electronically and fines are set for non-payment. The scheme was extended to parts of west London in February 2007. Each vehicle has to pay a fee of £8 (as of 2010) every time it enters the zone between 7 a.m. and 6 p.m.

By the summer of 2004 the charge was deemed such a success – with an 18 per cent reduction in traffic flow – that even the Conservatives had ceased to oppose it. Livingstone rode on its success on 10 June 2004 to re-election as mayor of London. The new mayor, Boris Johnson, elected in May 2008, favoured a reconsideration

of the western extension of the scheme. In the autumn of 2008 he announced the extended zone would be removed by 2010.

In the summer of 2008 it was proposed that Manchester should adopt such a scheme though one involving an outer and an inner zone. In exchange government funding of £3 billion would be forthcoming for improvement of the Metrolink tram system to other parts of the city. In the vote in December 2008, all 10 districts of Greater Manchester voted against the proposal: 78.2 per cent in total votes against, 21.2 per cent in favour.

consensus
See postwar consensus.

conservatism
This tradition of political thought, at least as it is understood in Britain, can be traced back to Edmund Burke's *Reflections on the Revolution in France* (1790). While there are various strands of conservative thinking, and guises in which it presents itself, it is possible to identify some essential features:
1 a reluctance to theorise or engage in social engineering or attempts to change human nature;
2 an acceptance of human imperfectibility and that, contrary to liberal notions, there are limits to human reason and the degree of progress possible in society;
3 an acceptance of market forces as a natural consequence of human behaviour (but otherwise conservatism has no distinctive economic theory);
4 an acceptance of the inevitability of social inequality and the organic nature of human society;
5 a belief in the need for leadership and the maintenance of law and order through the established institutions of church, family and political authority;
6 a suspicion of radical change, or change for its own sake;
7 a belief in a community of faith, often interpreted as a commitment to the established church, that is, the Church of England.
See also Conservative Party.

Conservative Future

www.conservativefuture.com

Youth organisation of the Conservative
Party, formed in 1998. It claims 15,000
members, with an upper age limit of 30.
It has an elected executive based on the
party's 43 regions, each with a chairperson,
and separate university branches. Its
forerunner, the Federation of Conservative
Students, was deemed too libertarian and
poorly behaved; Norman Tebbit wound it
up in 1987.

Conservative Mainstream

http://conservativemainstream.org.uk

Centre-right umbrella body for individuals
and groupings in the Conservative Party.
It has been led by former ministers, such
as David Curry, Ian Taylor and Stephen
Dorrell. Its chair is Damian Green, MP.

Conservative Party

www.conservatives.com

Arguably the traditional party of
government in Britain, as it governed for
two-thirds of the 20th century; it was out
of office for only 17 years between 1945
and 1997. The political scientist Samuel
Beer argues that its roots can be traced
back to the early Tudor period. There was
certainly a Tory grouping of aristocrats in
the 17th and 18th centuries who supported
the monarchy, Empire and Church, as well
as aristocratic privileges and agricultural
interests. In the wake of the Great Reform
Act of 1832, which established a new
expanded franchise, the Tories quickly took
advantage of the new environment and,
under Robert Peel, organised the embryo
of the modern party by registering voters
and developing a programme based on his
Tamworth manifesto. Benjamin Disraeli
contributed a vital element to modern
Conservatism with his vision of a united
nation based on an alliance between the
aristocracy and the working class. As the
franchise extended, the party succeeded in
winning the support of a significant portion
of the new voters. Initially the party tended
to speak for the landed interests but soon
came to represent business, as the Liberals
began to favour more interventionist policies
to restrain the excesses of capitalism and
(later) Labour to advocate the imposition of
socialism. The extension of the franchise in
1867 caused the formation of the National
Union of Conservative and Constitutional
Associations in the same year.

During the 1930s, a section of the
Conservatives were influenced by the
emergent economic ideas of the Liberal John
Maynard Keynes, and after the Second
World War subscribed to a consensus on
the mixed economy and the welfare state.
However, the relative economic decline of
Britain in the 1960s and 1970s produced
a strong reaction against consensus politics
and under the influence of Enoch Powell,
Keith Joseph and Margaret Thatcher the
party 'rediscovered' classical liberal thinking
on economics, as elaborated by the Chicago
School of Economics. Under the leadership
of the charismatic Thatcher, the party won
three elections, in 1979, 1983 and 1987,
and, after her downfall in 1990, another
under John Major, in 1992. However, when
Tony Blair repositioned New Labour in the
centre ground, and with the Conservatives
now divided over Europe and weakened
by growing evidence of 'sleaze', the party's
credibility collapsed and it crashed to defeat
in the 1997 election.

The youthful William Hague was
elected leader and set about reforming
the party's internal structure to compete
more effectively with the remodelled New
Labour machine. A further problem was
the Conservative Party's large decline in
membership since the 1950s; in addition,
the membership had a markedly high
average age, of over 60. Hague attempted
to emulate Blair by reforming his party,
which he did by unifying the parliamentary
party with the wider one in the country
and establishing a controlling board (see
below). He also sought to defuse the
debate over Europe in the autumn of 1998
by issuing a questionnaire to the party's
members asking them to say whether they
agreed that the single currency should not
be introduced for at least 10 years. He
won the vote handsomely, but the debate

continued (not without acrimony) at the party conference of that year. In 1999, Hague sought to move his party away from his initial 'caring Conservatism' direction and towards the right. In the spring of 2000 this appeared to be meeting with some success, as the Conservatives adopted populist policies opposing the arrival of asylum seekers and supporting the rights of householders to defend their property from intruders. However, Hague's poll position failed to improve and he entered the June 2001 election on a somewhat incoherent right-wing platform, for example advocating policies to 'save the pound' (i.e. opposing Britain joining the single European currency), to address the problem of bogus asylum seekers and to make cuts in planned Labour spending while still increasing spending on public services. Faced with Labour's emphasis on public services the party crashed to its second successive defeat, mustering only 166 seats – one more than four years earlier. Hague resigned and plunged the party into an unseemly fight to elect a new leader. After a long process, Ken Clarke and Iain Duncan Smith emerged as the two short-listed for the vote by over 300,000 party members in August 2001, with the latter winning the ballot of members a month later.

Ironically, Duncan Smith swung his party towards the very policies he was seen as opposing at his party's 2002 spring conference. Now it seemed his party favoured a shift towards public services and the 'vulnerable' in society. On 30 April 2003 a report by the think-tank Conservatives for Change concluded the party lacked a sense of identity and pointed out that its average poll figure between 2001 and 2003 was 30.4 per cent. Discontent festered throughout the year and came to a head with the party's third place in the Brent East by-election. Duncan Smith's speech at the Blackpool conference was consequently billed as 'career defining' but, despite assiduous coaching and the assistance of young aides, who prompted 19 standing ovations, the speech was generally seen as a failure. Once it was suggested that his

wife, Betsy, had been paid improperly for acting as her husband's secretary, letters requesting a vote of confidence in the leader began to reach Sir Michael Spicer, chair of the 1922 Committee. By 27 October the required 25 letters from MPs – representing 15 per cent of the parliamentary party – had been received and the next day the vote took place. Duncan Smith polled a creditable 75 votes but there were 90 against. Possible candidates like David Davis, Michael Ancram and Theresa May stood down to allow Michael Howard a free run at the top job. The 'coronation' took place on 6 November, when Howard pledged to continue with the social justice thrust of the previous leader's policies, although zero tolerance on crime and opposition to the European Union were also stressed.

Membership of the party had fallen from around 1,000,000 in the 1950s to a third of that by 2001, but in August 2004, at 320,000, it still exceeded that of Labour, with, it was claimed, a membership surge in progress.

The Conservatives under Howard fared little better than they had under his predecessors. When it came to the May 2005 election, an unpopular government was re-elected with a majority of 67, largely because the alternative was seen as even worse. Howard appointed two able young backbenchers to the shadow portfolios of education – David Cameron – and Treasury – George Osborne. This enabled the former to raise his profile for a leadership bid in the wake of Howard's retirement as leader. At the 2005 party conference, candidates for the leadership strutted their stuff before the membership. None was more successful than Cameron, who 'acted' his speech, without notes, to great acclaim. In the eventual membership vote on the remaining two candidates Cameron defeated Davis by 2–1. A new era now began for the Tories, who shifted into the centre ground on public services, tax, social policy and cultural issues like gay marriage. On all these things Cameron, or 'Dave' as he wished to be called, was relentlessly liberal, to the extent that on some issues he appeared to be well to the left of Labour. Cameron succeeded in lifting the poll standing of the party to equal with and then above that of Labour – the first time this had happened since the early 1990s. Surrounded by advisors with similar old Etonian backgrounds, Cameron continued to prosper during 2007. He encountered a blip in the late summer of that year when the incoming Gordon Brown achieved a temporary level of popularity which tempted him to give the impression an election might be called. But when poll standings changed Brown lost heart and Cameron capitalised during a year in which his party rose to a 20-point lead in the polls, hammered Labour in the 2008 local elections, won the London mayoralty via Boris Johnson and won the Crewe and Nantwich by-election: a sign that at last the Conservatives were beginning to make inroads into traditional Labour strongholds in the midlands and the north. From then on the Conservatives went from strength to strength, assisted by Brown's lacklustre leadership of the government. In the autumn of 2009 the Conservatives were 20 points ahead in the polls but this lead narrowed as the election approached on 6 May 2010. The result was a hung parliament, with Conservatives 307, Labour 258, Liberal Democrats 57 and others 28. Cameron negotiated a coalition with the Liberal Democrats and formed a government; Liberal Democrat leader Nick Clegg gained the deputy premiership plus four seats in the cabinet.

See also Conservative Party annual conference; Conservative Party leadership contest; 1922 Committee; Tory.

Conservative Party annual conference

An annual event of some four days, held usually at a seaside location. Conference involves up to 9,000 'representatives' – they are not elected delegates. It is not organised as a policy-making event (unlike for the Labour Party), at least in theory, but is more a rally of the faithful and a morale-

boosting activity for party workers. Arthur Balfour, Conservative prime minister at the start of the 20th century, famously said he would sooner take advice from his valet and this indifference was reflected until 1965, as the leader rarely attended until the final afternoon. However, the political writer Richard Kelly questioned the view that the conference was of marginal importance and suggested that the gathering is best understood within the context of the 60 or so regional and sectional conferences which occur during the year. He maintained that grass-roots concerns 'bubble up' from these conferences, creating a 'mood' which informs policy makers. For example, in the 1980s trade union reform was a powerful theme in Conservative trade unionist conferences, as was the reform of married women's taxation in Conservative women's conferences. In both cases action eventually flowed from this articulation at conferences.

Conservative Party leadership contest

New leaders used to 'emerge' from a huddle of senior party figures but, following the 'emergence' of Lord Home in 1963, this was held to be undemocratic and a new system was introduced whereby annual challenges were made possible. New leaders were to be chosen via a series of ballots, in the first of which a candidate required 65 per cent of the vote (i.e. Conservative MPs) to obtain victory. Edward Heath was the first leader to be chosen via this procedure. Margaret Thatcher missed the required percentage by a mere four votes in 1990, when she was deposed, and when William Hague became leader he (helped by Lord Parkinson) changed the system yet again to make it more democratic. The parliamentary party now votes on declared candidates – the candidate with the lowest number of votes dropping out until only two remain, at which time the national membership of the party is enabled to vote to select the new leader. Hague resigned in June 2001 and five candidates fought for the parliamentary party's choice. Michael Portillo was the shock casualty after the second ballot, leaving Kenneth Clarke and Iain Duncan Smith to fight for the votes of party members. In September 2001 the latter, a Eurosceptic right-winger, triumphed over the Europhile moderate Clarke.

In 2003 the challenge element in the rules was activated against Duncan Smith. This required 15 per cent of Conservative MPs to write to the chair of the 1922 Committee (at the time Sir Michael Spicer) to trigger a vote of confidence. By 26 October 2003 this had occurred, and Duncan Smith was then voted out by 90 votes to 75.

The problem with the democratic Hague system was that it enabled a leader to be selected by party members whom only a minority of MPs supported. Moreover, the ageing membership was biased against any candidate embracing the centrist or centre-left ideas needed to win elections. It was therefore of interest that possible candidates stood down to enable Michael Howard to have a free run at the leadership, and the rank and file membership was not allowed any input into the process. Howard was officially 'crowned' on 6 November 2003. But his nemesis awaited in the 2005 election, which Blair comfortably won for Labour. At the 2005 party conference several candidates for office addressed the faithful, none more successfully than the old Etonian David Cameron, who 'acted' his speech without notes. He went on to win the party ballot 2–1 over his rival David Davis.

Conservative Party reforms, 1998

In 1998 William Hague introduced more far-reaching reforms of his party than any British party had adopted since the 19th century.

1 The party became a single entity – for the first time the parliamentary party, the professional and voluntary parties were unified, and a board was established to manage it.
2 The National Conservative Convention now meets twice a year to link members with leadership.

3 The Conservative Policy Forum was established, through which members can influence policy.
4 A centrally held national membership list was drawn up for the first time. This enables the leadership to know who is in the party and how many members there are.
5 The Ethics and Integrity Committee was established. It was set up to prevent situations like that involving Neil Hamilton and the cash for questions scandal recurring. It expelled Lord Archer from the party for five years.
6 The leadership election rules were changed to enable members to vote on a short-list of two, decided upon by the parliamentary party.
7 The Young Conservatives were wound up.
8 Foreign donations were banned.

Conservative Way Forward

www.conwayfor.org

Group established in 1991 by Thatcherites to keep alive the flame of the departed but still revered leader. It is not dissimilar to the No Turning Back Group. Its first chair was Cecil Parkinson and other members included such luminaries as Norman Tebbit and Keith Joseph. In 2008 it campaigned in favour of car drivers, advocating the ending of speed cameras and the building of more roads to free up traffic.

Conservatives for Change (C change)

www.cchange.org.uk

Conservative think-tank set up in 2002. Conservatives for Change argues that the 'ability to adapt to an evolving society has been the key to Tory success for more than two hundred years'. Its aim is to modernise the party and ensure its policies are in line with the realities and complexities of modern Britain.

constituency

The name given to electoral registration and voting districts in Britain. In 1997 there were 659 constituencies. At the

May 2005 general election there were 646 across the UK. For the 2010 general election this had increased to 650, and in the process only 138 of the constituencies had no boundary change. Both the Liberal Democrats and the Conservatives in the post-2010 coalition favoured reducing the overall number of MPs – to 585 for the Tories and to 500 for the Liberal Democrats, which will require redrawing of boundaries.

The Boundary Commissions (one each for England, Scotland, Wales and Northern Ireland) are required to undertake a general review every 8–12 years in order to ensure that the sizes of the electorates in each constituency are as similar as possible (currently about 70,000 electors, typically reflecting a total population of 90,000). The Commissions also carry out local interim reviews.

Constituency boundaries will be substantially altered if Britain adopts a system of proportional representation for parliamentary elections, a number of versions of which require the introduction of multi-member constituencies.

Ross, Skye and Lochaber is the geographically biggest constituency, at 12,000 square miles.

See also Boundary Commission.

constitution
See British constitution.

constitutional approach to politics
The approach to the study of politics which concentrates on the formal institutions of parliament, the cabinet, ministers and departments of state. This legalistic approach was dominant in Britain until the 1960s, when it was judged to be too dry and failed properly to reflect the nature of political processes. Instead, new approaches have been developed, which focus on issues, political behaviour, psephology and political psychology, for example.

constitutional checks and balances
See separation of powers.

Constitutional Commission
The title for the Conservatives' unofficial commission on reforming the House of Lords. On 17 September 1998 it suggested the voting rights of hereditary peers should not be abolished until after the next election. It also suggested the upper chamber could become more effective as a scrutiniser of legislation, giving up its legislative rights in exchange for the enhancement of such a role. Its chair was Lord Mackay, the former Conservative lord chancellor. Most of these suggestions were rendered irrelevant by the ending of the hereditary element by Labour in 2000 and its winning of the 2001 election by a huge majority. The commission was one of three set up by the shadow cabinet in order to contribute to the debate and was disbanded after reporting.

Another constitutional commission was set up in March 2008 under Sir Kenneth Calman to examine Scottish devolution 10 years on.

See also Calman commission.

constitutional law
Britain is unusual in that it does not have a special body of statutes governing state and citizen, sometimes referred to as constitutional or fundamental law. The constitution is the result of the ordinary law of the land as laid down by parliament, the courts and more recently (and controversially) the European Union. After Labour entered office in 1997, a draft constitution for the UK was developed by reformers, although it is difficult to see a full-blown written constitution emerging in the near future.

See also British constitution.

constitutional monarchy
See monarchy.

constitutional reform
Like any long-standing institution, the British government has been resistant to reform. In 1828 the Duke of Wellington denied it required any reform, as it was already perfect. Traditional Conservatives argue that an organic constitution adjusts 'naturally' to changing social and political

conditions. Many of a more radical frame of mind disagree and a constant pressure for change has characterised British government over the last two centuries. Towards the end of the 20th century Labour allied itself with the Liberal Democrats and the campaigning Charter 88 organisation. Initially the raft of proposed reforms, like devolution and change to the House of Lords, were opposed by the Conservatives, but as the measures passed into fact they too began to accept their validity.

In June 2007, the new prime minister, Gordon Brown, spoke boldly of constitutional reform but little came of it. More was spoken of in the wake of the MPs' expenses scandal in the spring of 2009 as a means of 'cleansing' and renewing the political system.

constitutionalism

An aspect of 18th-century liberal thinking which, while supporting the need for government, was also mindful of the danger it might pose to liberty through a concentration of power. To guard against this eventuality liberal philosophers argued for constitutionalism, which includes the following key elements:

1 the diffusion of power into different parts of the state;
2 the creation of checks and balances to ensure no single branch of government becomes over-mighty;
3 the establishment of a codified written constitution, to clarify the powers, rights and duties of each part of government in relation to the citizen.

Continuity IRA

Dissident republican terrorist group, sometimes linked to the Real IRA. It is said to have support in South Down and Fermanagh in Northern Ireland and to have been responsible for many incidents following the Good Friday agreement when the IRA agreed to a cease-fire. In February 2003 the group threatened to kill Catholic police officers if Sinn Fein joined a new policing board and in March 2007 it claimed it shot dead a policeman.

See also Irish Republican Army.

control freak

Someone who feels the need to exercise total control. 'Are you a pluralist or control freak?' asked Paddy Ashdown of Tony Blair, but the answer was never given definitively. The implication in the tag, attached regularly to Blair when he was in power, was that despite outward appearances of giving power away, he still wanted to control things personally. Moreover, it is often asserted, he sought to control Labour MPs through party headquarters, and for example issued pagers to MPs to keep them informed of policy at the centre and to keep an eye on what they were up to. Evidence cited in support of the claim includes the suggestion that he gave power via new assemblies to Scotland, Wales, Northern Ireland and London but then sought to nominate the politicians in charge. Further items on the charge sheet include neutering the Freedom of Information Act and trying to prevent a reformed House of Lords becoming an elected chamber. Finally, he seemed to turn his back on reforming the voting system in the wake of the 1997 election when he noted that proportional representation tends to give disproportionate power to small parties (*Economist*, 9 June 2001).

control order

An order, signed by a minister, to restrict the freedom of a person suspected of terrorist activities. Control orders were introduced under 2005 anti-terrorism legislation, when existing legal rules for detaining terrorist suspects were held to be in breach of human rights by the then law lords. The government insisted it could not prosecute such suspects as this would expose too much information about the use of secret intelligence processes. Someone under a control order is not allowed to use telephones outside their house; their passport may be confiscated and their travel on public transport disallowed. In January 2010 there were 10 control orders in force; six of the foreign nationals held under the orders had been deported.

convention

Unwritten rule or understanding based upon past practice. Britain does not have a fully written or codified constitution and therefore large areas of government practice are governed by convention. For example, it is a convention that the monarch will call upon the leader who can command a majority in the House of Commons to form a government, although there is no formal law which embodies such a procedure.

'core executive'

Term used to describe the apex of the decision-making pyramid, that involving the prime minister and cabinet, as well as a network of related personnel, including the permanent under-secretaries of the Whitehall departments, the Cabinet Office and the Downing Street Policy Unit. The utility of the term lies in its inclusion of officials: a recognition that their contributions are as important as those of the elected politicians who in theory (only) run the country.

corporatism

Traditionally the intermediary role played by corporations and professional associations, or unions, between the public and the state. In the postwar period, it has become a pejorative term used by both left and right. The right point to the over-cosy relationship between trade union leaders and the Labour government of the mid to late 1970s, while those on the left criticise the close relationship between corporate business and government during the periods of Conservative government in the 1980s. Such a close conclave between peak organisations and government was thought to be anti-democratic 'high-level fixing', which sidelined parliament and thus the electorate. The term tends not to be used extensively these days but most governments seek to use the approach to some extent in practice.

See also tripartism.

council housing

Subsidised local authority housing. The Housing and Town Planning Act 1919 established council housing on a large scale.

During the interwar years over a million houses were built by local councils for rent, many on the outskirts of large towns and cities. After the Second World War even more effort was channelled into this sector – over 3 million such houses were built in the period 1945–85. By 1979 one in three houses was council owned. However, by the 1980s council estates had become identified with social problems and this, together with the 1.7 million houses sold under Margaret Thatcher's 'right to buy' policy and the growing preference for Britons to live in their own houses, helped reduce the public sector in housing to under a quarter of the total. By 1998 local authorities in the north were finding it hard to find tenants for houses which had traditionally been highly sought after. The sale of council houses, often the best stock, left 3.4 million homes of variable quality and many families preferred to buy a cheap terraced house. This led to a situation in which councils were having to advertise for tenants to move in and occupy a huge redundant housing stock. However, in the south of England waiting lists persisted. By 2000 virtually no new council houses were being built, as the government put more emphasis on new housing association properties instead.

Over half of those of working age living in social housing are without paid work – twice the national average. Moreover, nearly three-quarters of social tenants aged under 25 are unemployed. Partly in consequence, the image of council house estates has progressively assumed that of poorly maintained, grey, lawless urban wildernesses. Notwithstanding, in 2009 over a third of the nation's housing stock was still council owned. In July of that year, the Homes and Communities Agency announced 139,000 council houses would be built over the next decade, the biggest increase for over 20 years. They will all be needed, as it is calculated that the waiting list for social housing will have reached 5 million by 2012. The government favours small groups of 30–40 homes instead of the massive estates of earlier decades.

See also right to buy.

POLITICS

Council of Europe
www.coe.int
European body (though not part of the
European Union) concerned with human
rights, culture and the environment. It was
established in 1949 by a resolution passed
at the 1948 Congress of Europe and is
based in Strasbourg. Founding members
were the UK, France, the Netherlands,
Belgium, Luxembourg, Denmark, Sweden
Norway, Ireland, Italy and Greece. As
of 2010 it had 47 members. The Council
has: a Committee of Ministers (foreign
ministers); a parliamentary assembly
(comprising 286 members divided into
five political groups); and the Congress of
Local and Regional Authorities of Europe.
The Council has its own secretariat of
over 1,000 officials, headed by a secretary
general elected by the assembly. The
Council cannot make laws but issues
conventions or charters or codes. Initially
the Council was the main forum for
discussion about European integration but
its advice was largely ignored by member
states as the emergent European Economic
Community – later the European Union –
became the leading force in Europe.
The Norwegian Thorbjørn Jagland was
appointed secretary general in October
2009.

Council of Ireland
Part of the power-sharing Sunningdale
agreement in 1973. The Council was set up
to accommodate the 'Irish dimension' and
allowed delegates from the north and south
of Ireland to discuss common problems.
It collapsed along with the Sunningdale
agreement: yet another false dawn.
    See also Sunningdale agreement.

Council of Ministers
The main decision-making part of the
European Union (EU), comprising
ministers from all member states. It is to
be distinguished from the Council of the
European Union. It meets over 100 times
a year, with relevant ministers attending to
deal with the issue under discussion, illus-
trating how wide the impact of the EU now

is upon the politics of member states. The
Committee of Permanent Representatives
(COREPER) undertakes most of the
preparation for these important meetings.
This body, in tandem with the Council, is
chaired by the country currently holding the
six-monthly presidency according to a rota.
    Council decisions are issued in a number
of forms, two of the most important being:
regulations, which have immediate force as
EU law; and directives, which are binding
on members, but national governments have
discretion on how to implement policies,
an example being the UK's decision to use
the simple plurality method of elections for
the European parliament until 1999, when
it was changed to the regional list system
of proportional representation. On some
nominated issues, decisions are taken via a
qualified majority voting system, whereby
members' votes are 'weighted' according to
population size; on other issues unanimity is
required. This move away from unanimity
has been controversial and has been
criticised by the Eurosceptics as undermining the sovereignty of member states.
    See also qualified majority voting
(QMV).

Council of the European Union
www.consilium.europa.eu
Body that comprises heads of government.
It was set up in 1974. In France's case the
president attends. Also included are the
foreign ministers and two commissioners. It
meets twice a year and has been responsible
for some of the major initiatives in the
development of the European Union,
like the European Monetary System and
the Maastricht treaty. However, Council
meetings sometimes become a matter more
of appearance and media events than of
substantive discussion.

council tax
Form of local taxation introduced by
John Major's government in 1991 which
replaced the hated poll tax. The council
tax represented a return to something
approaching the rates, in that it is based
on property values. However, unlike the

old system there are bands based upon the market value, with a 25 per cent reduction for single-person occupancy. Compared with the poll tax the new system was accepted with minimal dissent. However, steep rises, above inflation, in 2004 caused widespread protests and the government moved to cap spending by some local authorities. In July 2004 proposals were made to reform the council tax by introducing more complex banding that takes more account of property values. On 18 July 2004 the government denied claims that the forthcoming review of the council tax would lead to threefold increases; rather, it would clarify problems and issues for further analysis. In 2008 the average annual amount levied was £1,146.

See also community charge; rates.

councillor

Elected member of local government. To qualify to stand for election, candidates must: be over 18; be registered voters; have no undischarged criminal sentence; not be insane; and be either resident in the local authority concerned or own property or work within its borders. They must not be an employee of the authority for which they seek election nor a senior employee of any other local authority. Councillors, in common with MPs, are unrepresentative of the socio-economic profile of the people they represent. The 2008 census of council-lors revealed: 31 per cent were female (up from 28 per cent in 1997); 96.6 per cent were white (i.e. 3.4 per cent were from an ethnic minority background); the average age of councillors was up from 55.4 in 1997 to 58.8 years; 88.4 per cent claimed a desire to serve their local community as their motivation; and on average they spent 22 hours a week on council/political business.

Country Land and Business Association

www.cla.org.uk

Organisation (formerly known as the Country Landowners Association) with 50,000 members, which promotes the interests of those who own property and land in England and Wales. This body, founded in 1907, speaks for those closely involved in the rural economy from the owner's point of view.

Countryside Agency

A body set up in 1999 to extend access and recreational opportunities to people who enjoy the countryside. Its remit extended to issues of conservation and landscape beauty. It advised the government on national parks, areas of outstanding natural beauty and nature trails. It replaced the Countryside Commission, which had originally been set up in 1949 as the National Park Commission. Following the Natural Environment and Rural Communities Act 2004, the Agency was partly merged with English Nature and the Rural Development Service, to form Natural England. The remaining part of the Countryside Agency was reborn as the Commission for Rural Communities.

Countryside Alliance

www.countryside-alliance.org.uk

A loose coalition of lobby groups concerned with the countryside, some of which hold conflicting views. The Alliance opposed the private member's bill on banning fox-hunting and in the spring of 1998 mounted a very successful demonstration in London, when it mustered over 300,000 protestors. In May 2009 it claimed over 107,000 members.

county

Local government unit in Britain. Counties date back to Saxon times. Since the Local Government Act 1888, they have been run by councils elected every four years. The Local Government Act 1972 drastically reduced the number of counties and rationalised structures in England and Wales. As a result there were 47 'shire' county councils containing 333 district ones, as well as six metropolitan counties with 36 elected district councils. In the mid-1980s, the Conservative government controversially scrapped the metropolitan

POLITICS

county councils and transferred their functions to the districts or to joint boards. The same government then abandoned the 'two tier' pattern of local government for the 'unitary', single-area model, performing all the functions within its borders. There are now 56 unitary authorities in England and 27 shire counties with a total of 201 district councils.

See also Local Government Act 1972; unitary authority.

county court
Court that hears most cases arising under civil law within each county. County courts deal with claims for up to £5,000 damages and cases that involve, for example, landlord and tenant disputes, mortgage claims, equity trusts and probate, bankruptcies, undefended divorces and injunctions against domestic violence. Cases are heard by either a judge or a registrar (a junior judge). There are over 340 county courts in England and Wales.

See also civil law; High Court.

Court of Appeal
Court that hears appeals from lower-level courts. People dissatisfied with a verdict in a criminal or civil court can apply to the Court of Appeal, which was set up in 1968 and comprises a criminal and civil division. It is staffed by 16 lord justices of appeal plus a number of ex-officio judges. Appeals are not reruns of trials, as the court listens only to arguments put by lawyers and witnesses are not heard again. Rather, the court listens to legal argument with reference to the original trial record. Most appeals are heard by three judges; however, their decisions need not be unanimous. The head of the Civil Division is the master of the rolls. The Criminal Division is headed by of the lord chief justice and it hears cases from lower courts and can give judgements on the safety of a decision, quash or confirm the conviction, and vary the sentence. Since October 2009 the Court of Appeal has been the second most senior court, after the Supreme Court.

See also Supreme Court.

credit crunch
Crisis in the banking world beginning around 2007. This worldwide phenomenon was caused by the excessively available credit occasioned by very low interest rates from the 1990s onwards. The USA was the first to get caught. When interest rates began to increase, mortgages were not so easy to come by and so house prices fell. This meant the many 'sub-prime' mortgage holders with no resources – 'NINJA' borrowers, that is, those who had no jobs, no income and no assets – were no longer insulated by rising house prices and were forced to default on their payments in their hundreds of thousands. This hit US banks but the way these debts had been packaged up as mortgage-backed 'securities' and sold on international markets as dividend-paying investments contaminated the world's banking system with huge amounts of 'toxic' debts which would never be repaid. Once defaulters reached a high level, banks realised they were in trouble and either went bust or refused to accept or issue loans, thus causing an extraordinary crisis all over the world, especially in those countries where banks had ingested large amounts of toxic debts. This meant that mortgages dried up, business was starved of funds, bankruptcies caused unemployment and the world sank into the biggest recession since the 1930s.

British banks had taken on dangerous amounts of such debt, notably Northern Rock and the Royal Bank of Scotland, and once Lehmans investment bank, the biggest in the world, failed in September 2008, these and other banks faced ruin, as did, by implication, the whole British banking system. Prime minister Gordon Brown decided that the loss of any major bank would be potentially disastrous and so the government moved quickly to provide emergency funding (taxpayers' money) to prevent failure. It took some time but after a few months and a precarious, recessionary 2009, the economy inched its way out of recession into a fragile, still vulnerable recovery.

Crichel Down case

Case that concerned land taken over by the Ministry of Defence during the Second World War and resold improperly. It is a crucial case in any discussion of ministerial responsibility. The minister of agriculture, Sir Thomas Dugdale, knew nothing about the sale but resigned in 1954 as a result of the supposed rule that ministers are always responsible for the actions of civil servants in their departments. However, subsequent analyses suggest that he was forced to resign through lack of back-bench support rather than rigorous adherence to the rules governing resignations and ministerial responsibility.

crime

Britain is usually held to be a relatively peaceful country but crime levels, as in most developed countries, have rocketed since the Second World War. In 1979, for example, there were 2.5 million notifiable offences but by 1990 the figure had doubled. The Conservatives pride themselves on being the party of 'law and order'. Senior party members, especially home secretaries, were encouraged by the annual conferences to legislate for harsher sentences, including the reintroduction of capital punishment. But the vast increases in crime during their term in office (1979–97) lost the Conservatives their advantage. The public's disaffection was exploited by Labour, traditionally the party which tended to speak up for the civil rights of the accused and which argued for wider social answers to rising crime levels. This position changed when Tony Blair, as shadow home secretary, decided to take a tougher line on crime and coined the slogan 'tough on crime, tough on the causes of crime'. This proved an effective blend of the old approach and a more populist, tougher new one; it was to become part of Blair's repositioning strategy for the party when he became leader.

Despite criticism from the Conservatives and voter unease, crime figures reduced during the first term of Labour rule. British Crime Survey (BCS) figures (based on interviews with a random sample of 40,000 citizens and hence judged to be more reliable than police figures) issued in July 2004 revealed that the risk of being a victim of crime had fallen from 40 per cent in 1995 to 26 per cent in March 2004. Four years on, in 2008 the drop in crime since the mid-1990s, as measured by the BCS, was 40 per cent, with a 9 per cent fall in crime from the previous six months.

Figures released on 16 July 2009 revealed that the recession had not had the expected effect of increasing rates of acquisitive crime; for example, domestic burglary was expected to increase by 4 per cent but did so by only 1 per cent.

Under the arrangements for statistics supervised by the new UK Statistical Authority, the risk of being a crime victim fell to 22 per cent, the lowest level recorded since the BCS was established in 1981. However, media concern in the summer of that year focused on the alleged surge in knife crime, though statistics suggested even this aspect of criminal activity had remained stable for the past decade. Distinguished criminologist Robert Reiner of the London School of Economics argues that the sudden increase in crime during the 1980s was the result of 'neo-liberal' economic policies. In 2009, in the book *The Spirit Level*, Richard Wilkinson and Kate Pickett argued that countries with high levels of social and economic inequality, like the USA, the UK, Australia and Canada, were likely to suffer high levels of crime and other social dysfunctions.

See also Crime and Disorder Act 1998; crime statistics; murder rate; penal policy; vigilante movement.

Crime and Disorder Act 1998

Since the late 1970s law and order has been a key issue in British politics. During the 1980s and early 1990s successive Conservative governments passed a raft of legislation which strengthened the powers of the police and courts and allowed the party to claim that it, and not Labour, was the trustee of the nation's tranquillity and the enemy of the criminal. However, rising crime figures during the 1980s and early 1990s gave Tony Blair (then shadow home secretary) the opportunity to develop a new approach to the Labour Party's law and order policies. Once elected to office, Labour's home secretary, Jack Straw, introduced the Crime and Disorder Bill (the first of many crime bills) as the centrepiece of the party's law and order policies. Enacted in 1998, it contains the following provisions:

1 fast tracking of persistent young offenders;
2 a final police warning to replace the discredited repeat caution system;
3 new compulsory parenting orders and counselling sessions;
4 reparation orders designed to make the offender pay compensation for damage done to victims;
5 local curfew schemes to keep disorderly youngsters at home;
6 local authorities to set up partnerships with voluntary and statutory agencies to tackle crime prevention;
7 the police given powers to apprehend school truants;
8 antisocial behaviour orders introduced to control disorderly or aggressive people in the local community;
9 compulsory testing and treatment of drug offenders;
10 special orders for sex offenders, including the provision that the police monitor the movements of rapists and similar offenders when released from prison;
11 a new offence of racially aggravated assault introduced to deal with racially motivated violence.

See also antisocial behaviour order; crime; Macpherson report.

crime statistics

Voters are highly interested in crime statistics as they bear so closely on their daily lives. Conservative research produced a figure of 277 stabbings for 2007–08, suggesting a one-third rise since 1997. The British Crime Survey, in contrast, suggested a fall of 10 per cent in all crime in 2008 and 50 per cent since 1995. But two-thirds of people, when asked, think

crime is rising, not falling, and that official figures are false. Government spin and counter-spin have made the public distrustful of such figures and they are ready to judge by gut instinct on things such as crime. The Home Office responded in October 2008 by releasing figures which seemed to prove that measures to curb knife crime in 10 areas had been successful. Sir Michael Scholar, however, chair of the UK Statistics Authority, stated that these figures were selective and misleading and should not have been published at all. Jacqui Smith, the then home secretary, was forced to apologise for the government.

criminal law

Applies to a vast area of social and public life, ranging from relatively minor offences such as breaking the speed limit (covered by the Road Traffic Acts) to the taking of life. A crime is an act (or failure to act) defined by statute or common law to be a public wrong and therefore punishable by the state in a criminal court. For a wrong to count as a crime, the person must actually commit it (actus reus) and have a guilty mind (mens rea). Ministers of the crown and MPs are subject to criminal law as private individuals. However, MPs do enjoy parliamentary privilege and ministers are protected for actions carried out as part of their official role.

See also parliamentary privilege.

'cronyism'

Form of favouritism. An accusation frequently made against New Labour was that it moved friends into top jobs. Tony Blair was reckoned to have been the chief culprit, with his former flatmate Charles Falconer given ministerial office; his former boss, Lord Irvine, made lord chancellor; and his tennis partner Lord Levy made an unofficial envoy to the Middle East. Irvine, too, when in office, was accused of the same tendency, with former colleagues given roles as government advisors and senior appointments to the judiciary made from among his friends and those connected to government. Blair's opposition to an elected upper house

drew the criticism that he, personally, wanted to fill a whole legislative chamber with 'Tony's cronies'.

crossbencher
A member of the House of Lords who decides not to take up the party whip and sits instead on the 'cross benches'. After the expulsion of most hereditary peers in 1999 the crossbenchers held the balance of power in the upper chamber.

Crossman reforms
Proposals to reform the House of Lords and set up departmental select committees put forward by Richard Crossman in 1968–69. He suggested a two-tier solution to the problem of the upper chamber, involving 250 voting peers with the remainder participating but not voting. Hereditary peers would be abolished; the Lords' power of delay would be reduced to six months and peers would lose the right to vote from the age of 72. The proposals were defeated by a combination of the left, led by Michael Foot, who thought them too mild, and from the right, led by Enoch Powell, who thought them too extreme.

crown
See monarchy.

Crown Appointments Commission
Body that appoints archbishops and bishops. It was set up in 1976 by the Callaghan Labour government. A 12-strong committee including representatives of the Synod, the House of Laity and the relevant diocese meets to decide on two names to pass on to the prime minister, who chooses one and recommends it to the queen.

crown court
A court that hears the more serious criminal cases. Crown courts involve the full majesty of the law and are staffed by a judge and jury, with barristers (and soliticor advocates) representing both prosecution and defence. They were set up by the Courts Act 1971. Judges can pass sentences up to the maximum set by parliament

and hear appeals against convictions in magistrates' courts. The Criminal Justice Act 2003 came into force on 24 July 2006, part 7 of which makes it possible for a non-jury trial to be held in cases where it is believed there is danger of jury tampering or where jury tampering has taken place.

crown dependency
See Channel Islands; Isle of Man.

Crown Estate
www.crownestate.co.uk
Body charged with administering royal properties. In 1761 the crown gave up revenues from its estates and an office was established to arrange the sale, purchase and management of the crown estates. In 1927 it became embodied in the Commissioners of the Crown Lands. The Crown Estate was formed in 1956.

Crown Prosecution Service (CPS)
www.cps.gov.uk
The agency which decides whether or not a case should be pursued in a criminal court. The CPS was set up in 1986 for England and Wales. Before its establishment such decisions were taken by the police and police solicitors alone, an arrangement which attracted criticism as it was thought the police were often biased. The CPS is staffed by 2,000 lawyers – solicitors and barristers – operating through 15 regional groups via 42 prosecution areas, each with its own chief crown prosecutor. The head of the CPS is the director of public prosecutions (Keir Starmer, QC, was appointed in November 2008), who reports to the attorney general.

The CPS has attracted more than its fair share of controversy and in 1998 the National Audit Office accused it of being over-bureaucratic, slow and inefficient. The CPS's director, Barbara Mills, resigned before the report was published. In October of the same year it was disclosed that a secret list of police informants had been leaked from the CPS to the criminal underworld, placing informers' lives at risk.

See also director of public prosecutions.

cube law
Statistical 'law' of voting adduced originally by David Butler, one of the first British psephologists. It posits that in a two-party majoritarian voting system a mathematical relationship exists between a party's share of the seats in a legislative chamber and the proportion of the vote it receives. Baldly stated, the 'law' predicts that where parties A and B contest an election and the votes are divided in the ratio of y:x, the seats won will reflect the ratio x^3:y^3. However, the applicability of the cube law began to decline with the development of a three-party system in the 1970s and 1980s and is now rarely cited.

cultural governance
Norman Fairclough argued in *New Labour, New Language?* (2000) that part of the Labour government's approach to dealing with social exclusion was to change the culture of public services and those they serve, in particular the attitudes of welfare claimants and the general population. A key element in this process was the use of a new language to encourage a new way of thinking about social welfare and social exclusion, something which Margaret Thatcher and 'new right' activists did in their enthusiasm for the entrepreneurial culture in the 1980s. He quoted from an official press release:

> The Social Security Secretary stressed that as part of the fight against poverty a radical change of culture-confronting attitudes and long-term dependency is needed.... This is the poverty of expectation that we must tackle by changing attitudes, and making sure that people know what help and opportunities are available to them.

See also ideology; new right; political language.

curia regis
The royal court of the Norman monarchs. Originally it embodied all the functions of government: making, interpreting and implementing laws. It declined as the functions of the monarchy became more complex and its duties were transferred to other specific bodies. Nevertheless, it is one of the founding 'embryonic' institutions of British government.

Curry report, 2002
Report of the Policy Commission on the Future of Farming and Food, chaired by Sir Donald Curry. Many factors suggested that farming was in crisis in the early years of the 21st century: farmers earned on average only £5,200 a year and that for working a week which for 60 per cent of farmers was over 66 hours long. The Curry commission studied food and farming policy in early 2002. It recommended: better cooperation between farmers; a relaxation of competition rules to enable farmers to negotiate collectively with the food industry; encouragement for farmers to sell their food locally; the scrapping of production subsidies by the European Union, as they tend to make production inefficient; and creating higher food prices.

Cymru Annibynnol
See Welsh Republican Movement.

D

D notice
Document sent by the Ministry of Defence's D Notice Committee to journalists to prevent the publishing of information deemed harmful to the national interest. D notices were introduced in 1912 in an atmosphere of concern over the risk of German spies. They have not been used very often since the 1960s. In 1993 they were renamed 'defence advisory notices'. On 8 April 2009 the government issued a D notice relating to anti-terror documents photographed when assistant commissioner Bob Quick arrived at Downing Street for talks. He did not realise the papers he was carrying could be photographed and enlarged.

Daily Express

www.express.co.uk
Daily popular newspaper, founded in 1900 and taken over by Lord Beaverbrook in 1916. For many decades it was the leading popular newspaper; its circulation exceeded 4 million during the 1960s but fell dramatically during the next two decades to just over 1 million. Its political stance used to be loyally right-wing Conservative but when sold to Labour-supporting Lord Hollick it changed camps and became 'Blairite'. Northern and Shell became the owner of Express newspapers after they were sold by Lord Hollick. The group is headed by Richard Desmond, who also has an assortment of pornographic publications in his portfolio, which was the reason why his donation to the Labour Party became controversial. As of May 2009, the *Daily Express* had a circulation of 726,000; the *Daily Star* 822,000; and the *Sunday Express* 637,000, giving Northern and Shell a share of around 13 per cent of the national newspaper circulation.

See also Beaverbrook, Max.

Daily Herald

Newspaper that was relaunched in 1964 as the *Sun*. It first appeared in 1911 as a strike sheet for the London print unions. The *Daily Herald* was officially founded in 1912 and owned partly by Odhams Press and the Trades Union Congress (TUC). The TUC sold its 49 per cent holding in 1961 to the International Publishing Corporation (which owned the *Daily Mirror*). Through-out its life the *Herald* supported the labour movement and the policies of the Labour Party; ironically, its successor was bought by Rupert Murdoch in 1969 and turned into a raucously right-wing newspaper, the *Sun*.

See also Sun; Murdoch, Rupert.

Daily Mail

www.dailymail.co.uk
Newspaper founded in 1896. It was one of the new kind of popular news-paper invented by Alfred Harmsworth (Lord Northcliffe), which adapted certain American features of design and presentation. It favoured a right-wing political stance and gave much publicity to the forged Zinoviev letter in 1924. It accordingly criticised left-wing protests against unemployment as communist inspired and sympathised with the anti-Semitism of Nazism in the 1930s. It suffered a decline in the 1960s and 1970s but was overhauled in the early 1980s under David English, who was knighted by Margaret Thatcher for his loyal support. Its editor, Paul Dacre, appointed in 1992, was successful in making it 'the housewife's favourite' and added three-quarters of a million readers within five years. In the run-up to the 1997 election the paper nudged closer to New Labour. However, after a few years it returned to opposing the Labour government and during the second term fiercely attacked many aspects of New Labour, including the prime minister's wife. Tony Blair was said to be influenced by the newspaper as the 'voice of middle-class England'. In May 2009 its circulation was 2.2 million.

See also Zinoviev letter; Harmsworth, Alfred.

Daily Mirror

www.mirror.co.uk
Newspaper founded in 1903. The *Daily Mirror* was owned by Lord Rothermere, brother of Lord Northcliffe. It appeared to be dying in the 1930s, as advertisers did not like its tabloid style, and Lord Rothermere abandoned it, but it was relaunched successfully, aimed at a young working-class audience. It reached a circulation of 1.5 million by 1939. During the war Herbert Morrison defended its right to be critical of the government but its director, Cecil King, was in any case difficult to silence. After the war, under its famous editor High Cudlipp, the *Daily Mirror* became the classic and dominant paper of the working class and Labour in its sympathies. However, it had to give way to a new and brasher competitor, the *Sun*, which came to prominence in the 1970s and pre-eminence in the 1980s. The *Mirror* has maintained a pro-Labour stance but by 2002 its editor,

Piers Morgan, was increasingly critical of Tony Blair and all his works. Morgan was sacked in May 2004 after publishing pictures of Iraqi prisoners being mistreated which later proved to be fake. In May 2009 its circulation was 1.3 million.

Daily Sport
Newspaper founded in 1992 as a soft porn publication by David Sullivan. Its political stance is irrelevant as it virtually eschews news and politics for sex and trivia; indeed, it scarcely passes muster as a newspaper at all and is excluded from most circulation statistics.

Daily Telegraph
www.telegraph.co.uk
Newspaper founded in 1855. The *Telegraph* was the first of the 'penny' papers to be published in London. It merged with the Conservative *Morning Post* in 1937, and has since offered staunch support to the Conservative Party up to the present day. Its circulation was 817,000 in May 2009.

Daily Worker
See *Morning Star*.

de Chastelain commission
See Independent International Commission on Decommissioning.

death penalty
For many years the punishment for murder in Britain, but the subject of much soul searching whenever it was implemented. The Murder (Abolition of Death Penalty) Act 1965 replaced the death penalty with a mandatory life sentence. The punishment was retained, at least in principle, for 'treason' and 'piracy with violence', but these, too, were dropped with the passing of the Crime and Disorder Act 1998. In 1999 the home secretary signed the sixth protocol of the European Convention on Human Rights, which ensured the death penalty could not readily be revived.

Traditionally, the parliamentary votes on this subject were free of party control and subject to 'conscience'. In every

parliamentary session during the 1980s a vote was held and lost; in 1988 the majority opposing reintroduction was 123, in 1994 even bigger. It seemed Conservative MPs who won support in their constituencies for supporting the death penalty changed their minds when they heard the rational arguments against its reintroduction. These included: there was no increase in Britain's low level of murders, about 650 per annum, in the years after abolition (though it was closer to 900 by the end of the millennium); it would put more pressure on judges and juries; it would remove the possibility of reversing wrong judgements; it would be a retrogressive step for a civilised society; finally, it would cast a shadow over the criminal justice system, which is one of the central institutions of a civilised society. Nevertheless, many Conservative MPs advocated a return of a punishment routinely applied in the USA. Surveys show that two-thirds of the British people tend to agree.

debate
The principal means whereby conflicts of ideas or policy are examined in democracies. In Britain they occur in the media, for example newspaper articles and current affairs programmes, but more importantly in the House of Commons.

Commons debates take many forms: a substantive motion allowing a wide-ranging discussion; an adjournment motion at the end of a day's business; and second and third readings or the report stage of the legislative process through which a bill progresses. Many debates are initiated by the opposition, which has some 20 days of parliamentary time at its disposal, or by private members (i.e. MPs), who have most Fridays devoted to their proposals. Debates are controlled by the speaker, who calls contributors alternately from the parties. Similar procedures are followed in the House of Lords.

Critics claim the quality of debate in the House of Commons has declined since the golden years of the 19th century and the brilliance of more modern orators like

POLITICS

Aneurin Bevan and Winston Churchill. Debates, however, are very lively compared with those in some other legislatures, for example in Scandinavia. In the Commons members can speak from where they sit, interruptions are very frequent and the cut and thrust of debate is often supplemented by heckling. This means the speaker of the house has a special responsibility for maintaining order and preventing debates degenerating into chaos. The televising of parliament has done nothing to reduce this tendency, but neither has it led to the predicted excesses by those who opposed its introduction. Televised extracts from Commons debates tend to be well received in the USA, although not as well as the reliably eventful prime minister's questions (PMQs). Tony Blair was criticised for not participating in parliamentary debates and for seldom turning up to vote, thus demonstrating an alleged contempt for parliament, though few would dispute his mastery of it at PMQs and in debate. His successor, Gordon Brown, enjoyed a reputation as an effective debater during the 1990s when in opposition but once in power he tended to rely too much on citing statistics. When prime minister his performances in debate and PMQs were unexceptional and few judged that David Cameron failed to better him.

See also act of parliament.

decentralisation
The opposite of centralisation, an affliction believed to affect British government with its focus on decision making by London-based institutions. Devolution to Scotland and Wales undertaken by the Labour government after 1997 was one form of decentralisation. Another was the hiving off of routine central government functions to agencies following the Ibbs report. Parallel with this tendency, however, was a continuing drift towards centralisation: a desire by Tony Blair, when in office, not to 'let go' of power and to seek to control appointments/elections to devolved bodies. Peter Hennessy was sufficiently concerned about this trend in July 1998 to speak of

the dangers of 'court government' and a 'command premiership', a view echoed by Andrew Rawnsley in his book *Servants of the People* (2000).

See also devolution; Ibbs report.

decolonisation
The process whereby Britain surrendered its imperial possessions, often reluctantly and in the face of armed nationalist demands. By the 1931 Statute of Westminster, Canada, South Africa, Australia and New Zealand as well as Newfoundland gained formal independence as part of the British Commonwealth. The process of succumbing to armed pressure effectively started in the 1930s when Iraq (1932) and Egypt (1936) gained independence. It continued after the war when India, Pakistan and Burma were given independence by Attlee's Labour government in 1947. During the 1950s the Conservatives strove to hang on to the Empire and fought uprisings in Kenya and Malaya, but the debacle of Suez, pressures of nationalist movements and the expense of resisting them produced a change in policy. In 1960 Harold Macmillan delivered his 'wind of change' speech in South Africa, which, on the heels of independence for Ghana (1957) and Nigeria (1960), heralded another bout of decolonisation.

The Empire was virtually gone by the 1980s, with only a few far-flung possessions left, the major one of which, Hong Kong, was transferred back to China in 1997. In 1982 Britain went to war with Argentina over the Falkland Islands, which remain British, a situation still contested by Argentina. Gibraltar is another colony in dispute, with Spain claiming it. Only a 14 islands remain as crown possessions, including Bermuda, Tristan da Cunha, the Pitcairn Islands and the Cayman Islands.

See also Commonwealth (British); Empire (British); Statute of Westminster.

decommissioning
Term used to describe disarming by paramilitaries in Northern Ireland. The surrender of its arms by the Irish

Republican Army (IRA) was a crucial point in the negotiation of the Good Friday agreement (1998). In its aftermath, the unionists complained that the IRA was showing no signs of movement on an issue which was crucial to the agreement and in January 2000 the power-sharing executive in Northern Ireland was suspended by the then secretary of state, Peter Mandelson, for the lack of progress. However, the executive had been re-established by the early summer of that year when the IRA agreed to put its arms 'beyond use'. The issue remained, however, and David Trimble, under pressure from within his own Ulster Unionist Party, threatened to resign if the IRA failed to begin meaningful decom-missioning by the beginning of July 2001. However, when the IRA offered two acts of disarmament the unionists were not satisfied and demanded the disbandment of the IRA; Tony Blair backed this up in October 2002 by requiring republicans to give up paramilitarism.

defence forces
See armed forces; Ministry of Defence.

defence policy
The government's direction of the armed forces in promotion and defence of the nation's interests. After the Second World War a key aspect of British defence policy was to maintain a role as a world power. The development of nuclear weapons and the maintenance of overseas commitments were both part of this. Relative economic decline, however, and the costs of colonial commitments made this progressively difficult and defence policy was suc-cessively scaled down. In the 1960s Denis Healey decided to withdraw the British presence from east of Suez and British entry into the European Community led to a reordering of defence priorities. During the 1980s defence expenditure was further reduced, though the Falklands war delayed the full implementation of this. During the financial year 1998–99 defence expenditure was £22.2 billion, out of a

total government expenditure of £332.5 billion (6.6 per cent).

The emphasis of defence policy is now firmly tied to the North Atlantic Treaty Organisation (NATO), in particular to react rapidly to overseas trouble-spots, especially terrorist-inspired problems, with flexible airborne armed forces. British armed forces were sent to Bosnia to assist peacekeeping efforts in November 1992; in 1999 to Kosovo to prevent Serbian persecution of mostly Albanian Kosovars; to Afghanistan in October 2001; and in March 2003 to Iraq, where some 10,000 troops supported the US-led action against the Saddam Hussein regime. In July 2004 a series of cuts in the armed forces were announced but in 2008 annual defence spending was still £44.5 billion, second only to the USA's massive £391 billion. As the Iraq situation eased British troops were pulled out in 2009, though increased in Afghanistan, where it was planned for 10,000 British troops to be in place by 2010.

See also armed forces; Ministry of Defence.

deference
Term usually used in two senses in relation to British political culture: 'political deference', meaning respect for government and a willingness to obey the laws of the land; and 'social deference', meaning the preference of some people for a political elite drawn from the upper and middle classes. Both forms have declined, some of the reasons being the revelations of 'sleaze' during the time of the Major government (1990–97) and the MPs' expenses scandal of 2009, both of which brought all poli-ticians into disrepute, and the decline of a 'superior' political class in the Conservative Party, which preferred grammar school products like Edward Heath, Margaret Thatcher, John Major and William Hague as leaders, rather than those educated at private schools such as Eton and Harrow. However, the election of old Etonian David Cameron in December 2005 and his subsequent success suggest a privileged

background is no longer an impediment to achieving high political office via the Conservative Party.

See also political culture; sleaze.

de-industrialisation

A phenomenon caused by the recessions of the 1980s, when whole tranches of heavy and manufacturing industry, for example shipbuilding, coalmining and textiles, found it difficult to compete against foreign producers. Low levels of productivity and profitability were some of the more important reasons for this decline, together with Britain's poor record for industrial relations. By the mid-1980s many firms had gone bankrupt, putting hundreds of thousands out of work. Less than one-fifth of employees were now engaged in manufacturing, and vast areas of the midlands and the north were reduced to industrial wastelands. During the 1990s many areas began to revive with the arrival of service and 'sunrise' industries and overseas capital investment, especially from Japan and the USA. In 2008 manufacturing represented only 16 per cent of the national product.

delegate

A person who is authorised to act on behalf of another or group. The term is most usually associated in British politics with delegates who attend party conferences to vote on policies and elections of officials. 'Mandated delegates' to the Labour conference have specific instructions to perform certain tasks or vote a specific way; their degree of autonomy is strictly limited. Representatives at Conservative conferences do not expect to help formulate policy, although they will press their views when given the chance.

See also representative.

delegated legislation

'Secondary' legislation or a statutory instrument (SI) that is formed on the authority of 'primary' or 'parent' legislation. Legislation often contains authority for regulations to be made by ministers,

agencies and sub-national levels of government. An example would be the Baking and Sausage Making (Christmas and New Year) Regulation 1985. This owed its existence to the Health and Safety at Work Act 1974, and comes under the aegis of the Health and Safety Executive, which has authority over working conditions. There are various methods for introducing delegated legislation but typically a 'commencement order' is laid before parliament, and if there are no objections from either house it becomes law within 40 days. The Statutory Instruments Committee has the job of sifting through the SIs and investigating any which take their interest. Few do. In 1996, 1,832 SIs were passed, half of which were concerned with local government and not subject to parliamentary control. Orders in Council, issued by the Privy Council, and local authority by-laws are other forms of delegated legislation.

See also Delegated Powers and Deregulation Scrutiny Committee.

Delegated Powers and Deregulation Scrutiny Committee

Permanent committee of the House of Lords that examines delegated legislation in order to determine whether the powers so delegated are justified and necessary. It makes recommendations to parliament accordingly.

See also delegated legislation.

Delors plan, 1989

Plan that advocated economic and monetary union between member states of the European Community, named after Jacques Delors, president of the European Commission 1985–88. The plan envisaged a three-stage process of union: increased coordination of economic policies, through the Exchange Rate Mechanism; the establishment of a European Central Bank; and finally the introduction of a single currency. Margaret Thatcher said 'The Delors proposal would not command the support of the British cabinet', although Geoffrey Howe (foreign secretary) and Nigel Lawson (chancellor) did support it.

She grudgingly agreed at Madrid in June 1989 to the first stage, provided the second and third were left open. John Major eventually took Britain into the Exchange Rate Mechanism in October 1989, a decision which he and others would later come to regret.

See also Black Wednesday.

demand management
See Keynesianism.

democracy
A term derived from the Greek words *demos* (people) and *kratos* (strength). It originally referred to the method of rule whereby citizens of the Greek city states participated in public affairs, the essential idea being that ultimate sovereignty or authority lies with those sections of the population eligible to vote. In most truly democratic countries this is supplemented by respect for opposition parties, free speech and regular free elections so that the people are able to exercise their ultimate power and possibly change those who rule them. Britain's democracy has an unusual provenance as the country began with a traditional monarchy but adjusted over time to the demands of an emergent parliament. Almost seamlessly, democratic institutions developed to the extent that the monarch was displaced and replaced by a prime minister as chief executive who dominated the legislature by virtue of leadership of the majority party in that branch of government. 'Democracy' is a word that means far more when it is qualified by another, like 'liberal' or 'representative'.

> No word in the vocabulary has been more debased and abused than democracy.
> (Lord Shawcross, 1977)

See also direct democracy; liberal democracy; political participation; representative democracy.

Democracy Movement
www.democracy-movement.com
Group founded in autumn 1998 from a merger between a fledgling organisation

run by Paul Sykes, the Yorkshire millionaire businessman, and the Referendum Movement, a successor to James Goldsmith's Referendum Party. The Movement campaigns – on what it claims is a non-party basis – against what it sees as the encroachment of the European Union. In 2001 Sykes rejoined the Conservative Party. The Movement campaigned in the general election of that year but in 2004 was not active in the European elections.

Democracy Party
Eurosceptic political party launched on 21 November 1998 by Worcester businessman Geoff Southall. Commentators and other 'sceptics' observed the relatively large number of such organisations and perceived the danger that they might be dividing the potential opposition to a European single currency rather than strengthening it. By 2008 it appeared to be inactive.

democratic control
Control of the executive by the legislature. One of the basic tenets of democracy is that government works best within the context of scrutiny, control and accountability. This is achieved via an active legislature which scrutinises government and a vigorous media that is not easily manipulated or coerced.

In Britain there is some discussion as to whether parliament exercises sufficient control over an executive which has traditionally been strong, but few question the ability of the House of Commons to deny legislation it finds unacceptable, or ultimately (via loss of support in the governing party) to dismiss governments. Following the MPs' expenses scandal in 2009 there was much talk of strengthening the legislature at the expense of the executive.

democratic deficit
A lack of democratic control with the consequent danger of power being abused. One example relates to the European Community during the 1980s, when the European parliament had few instruments

whereby control could be exerted over the powerful European Commission and Council of Ministers.

Democratic Left
The successor to the Communist Party of Great Britain, formed in 1991 and committed to democratic pluralism. It was no more successful at the polls than its predecessor.

democratic pluralism
See pluralism.

democratic socialism
Term applied to those who pursue a socialist agenda through democratic institutions, such as free elections and parliament. Democratic socialists oppose political violence and the subversion of state institutions for political ends.

Democratic Unionist Party (DUP)
www.dup.org.uk
Ulster political party formed in 1971 and led by the fiery Reverend Dr Ian Paisley, a militant Protestant. The party, unlike the Ulster Unionist Party (UUP), was hotly opposed to the Anglo-Irish agreement, the Downing Street declaration and the Good Friday agreement, as well as Sinn Fein, the Irish Republic, and Catholicism and all its works. It consistently appealed to working-class Protestant voters and in the 1997 UK general election won two seats. Paisley seemed at that time to express all that is intractable and uncompromising in Ulster, as epitomised in the slogan 'No Surrender'.

In elections for the Northern Ireland assembly on 25 June 1998 the DUP won 20 seats. In the 2001 the UUP suffered reversals at the hands of Paisley's party in both the Westminster and local elections. In delayed elections to the assembly in November 2003 the DUP gained 10 seats and eclipsed the leadership of the loyalist community formerly occupied by the weakened UUP. On 8 May 2007 the two extremes of Sinn Fein and the DUP were able to settle their differences and establish a new Northern Ireland executive, with Paisley as first minister and Martin McGuinness as his deputy – an astonishing turn-around given the province's troubled history. Paisley resigned in June 2008 and was succeeded by Peter Robinson.

democratisation
In general terms, the transition of a state from an authoritarian to a democratic form of rule, such as took place in many of the former eastern bloc countries in the last decade of the twentieth century. Democratisation involves political institutions, but also economic and cultural ones. It also requires the development of a self-sustaining civil society. In Britain, the expansion of the franchise between 1832 and 1918 was a clear example of democratisation, where elite participation was transformed into mass democracy.

See also civil society.

Demos
www.demos.co.uk
Leftward-leaning think-tank set up in 1993 to encourage long-term non-partisan thinking by drawing ideas from outside the political mainstream (for example from industrialists, scientists and community activists). Specifically, it seeks to 'modernise the political culture, to make it more relevant, more international and more at ease with the future'. In addition, it aims to target new forms of governance and democracy for the 21st century. Its founder, Geoff Mulgan, joined the Number 10 Policy Unit after 1997 and its report on the reform of the monarchy in September 1998 attracted considerable publicity and discussion. Demos's senior project officer, David Ashworth, caused some bewilderment by changing his name to Perri 6; he is now professor of social policy at Nottingham Trent University.

Department for Children, Schools and Families
Government department established in 2007 as the successor to the Department for Education and Skills, with Ed Balls

POLITICS

appointed secretary of state. The department never ran schools and colleges directly but only indirectly via agencies like the inspectorate. After May 2010, under the new coalition government, it again became the Department for Education.

Department for Culture, Media and Sport
www.culture.gov.uk
Government department that began in 1992 as the Department of National Heritage. It has been regarded as having a somewhat uneasy collection of responsibilities. Its first minister was the Conservative David Mellor and under Labour Chris Smith in 1997 took over the renamed portfolio, which also included responsibility for the ill-fated Millennium Dome. After the 2001 election, Labour's Tessa Jowell took over as culture secretary, with increased responsibility for gambling, licensing, censorship and horse-racing, plus planning for the Golden Jubilee. The new minister described her department as the 'ministry of free time', the title given to its French equivalent. Ben Bradshaw briefly served as secretary of state from June 2009 before the Conservative MP Jeremy Hunt took over in May 2010.

Department for Education
www.education.gov.uk
Government department responsible for education and children's services. It had briefly been the Department for Children, Schools and Families towards the end of Labour's term office, but reverted to Education in May 2010, under the new coalition government, with Michael Gove as secretary of state.
See also education policy.

Department for Environment, Food and Rural Affairs (DEFRA)
www.defra.gov.uk
Government department created in 2001, partly to take over the role of Ministry of Agriculture, Fisheries and Food (MAFF). MAFF was in charge of the foot-and-mouth crisis in 2001 and was widely seen as having handled it ineffectively.

As a result of these perceived failures the ministry was reformulated in June 2001, with Margaret Becket taking charge of a new Department for Environment, Food and Rural Affairs.

The Department of the Environment was created in 1971 from the merger of the older departments of Housing and Local Government, and the Ministry of Works. It was concerned with housing, town and country planning, pollution, and management of a large portion of the government's 'estate'. Michael Heseltine gave the department a high profile when he was placed at its head in 1979 and introduced MINIS, a new management information system.

Hilary Benn was placed in charge of DEFRA in June 2007 and Caroline Spelman took over in May 2010 after the general election.

Department for Transport
www.dft.gov.uk
Department responsible for transport policy on road, rail, sea and air. It dates from 1919. The department has had some notable successes, like the bridge at Dartford, the second Severn crossing and the extension to the Jubilee Line of the London Underground, all privately financed. The department is responsible for the country's 2,700 km of motorways and 7,800 km of trunk roads. Strategic planning is undertaken by the department but maintenance and construction are undertaken by the Highways Agency. In 1997 it was included in deputy prime minister John Prescott's Department of Environment, Transport and the Regions. After the 2001 general election this area of government was reorganised to create a Department of Transport, Local Government and the Regions. It was given additional responsibilities for electoral law and the fire service but lost regional development to the Department for Trade and Industry.

Lord Andrew Adonis was appointed secretary of state in June 2009. The Conservative MP Philip Hammond took over from May 2010.
See also transport policy.

POLITICS

Department for Work and Pensions
www.dwp.gov.uk
Although pensions appeared early in the
20th century, central administration was
put in place only after the Second World
War, with the Ministry of Pensions, the
National Assistance Board and the Ministry
of Labour. From 1968 these functions
were combined with health within the
Department for Health and Social Security
(DHSS). These were split in 1988, and the
Department for Social Security itself became
the Department for Work and Pensions in
June 2001, with some responsibility for what
formerly came under the Department for
Education and Employment. It is a small
department, as much of its work is performed
by large executive agencies like the Benefits
Agency and the Child Support Agency.
The department is, however, the biggest
spender of any government department –
social security amounted to 28 per cent of
government spending in the mid-1990s. Iain
Duncan Smith was appointed secretary of
state for work and pensions in May 2010.

Department of Health
www.dh.gov.uk
Originally the Department of Health had
responsibility for housing programmes and
sanitary measures. This connection was lost
in the years after the union of health with
social security. As well as overseeing the
work of the National Health Service, the
department also supervises local authority
community care, as well as social work
provision. The NHS Policy Board is
chaired by the secretary of state for health
and lays down overall policy but the Blair
government introduced a new regional
structure in the summer of 2001 to achieve
more decentralisation of responsibility.
Andy Burnham was appointed secretary
of state for health in June 2009. Andrew
Lansley took over in May 2010.

Department of Trade and Industry (DTI)
www.dti.gov.uk
Originally set up in 1621 as the Board of
Trade, the DTI has undergone constant
reincarnations and mergers. It dates in its
modern form from 1970, when it was given
responsibility for fostering the competitiveness of British industry, especially in
relation to the European Community.
It is also charged with regulating the
privatised industries and consumer
protection, encouraging technology transfer
and reducing red tape. Under Margaret
Thatcher the DTI was viewed as an
'intervener' in the economy and therefore
was not her favourite department. Michael
Heseltine injected spice into the office when
appointed in 1992; he insisted on using
the old title of 'President of the Board of
Trade', a practice continued by Margaret
Beckett after 1997, but not by Peter
Mandelson when he was promoted to the
office in July 1998. In 2007 the department was renamed Business, Enterprise
and Regulatory Reform and headed up
by John Hutton; in October 2008, in a
surprise move, Gordon Brown invited
back into this role his former colleague and
one time friend, Peter Mandeslon. The
department was renamed, yet again, as
Business, Innovation and Skills, though
'Board of Trade' is retained as a secondary
title. After the May 2010 general election
Liberal Democrat Vince Cable was given
the post in the coalition government.

departmental select committee
Parliamentary scrutiny committee
which shadows the work of a government department. Departmental select
committees are therefore, in principle,
instruments of the legislature to scrutinise
the executive. During the first half of
the 20th century there were only two
select committees, the Public Accounts
Committee and the Estimates Committee.
The former examined whether expenditure
had been disbursed legitimately, while the
latter examined the legitimacy of future
expenditure. In the 1940s and 1950s
two more were created, concerned with
statutory instruments and nationalised
industries, and in the 1960s the Crossman
reforms introduced new ones on science
and technology, agriculture, education,

race relations, overseas development and Scottish affairs. Their efficacy, however, was limited because of their scarce resources and powers.

In 1979 Norman St John Stevas, as leader of the House of Commons, introduced 12 new committees, which shadowed departmental activities. By 2010 there were 19 committees:

1 Business, Innovation and Skills
2 Children, Schools and Families
3 Communities and Local Government
4 Culture, Media and Sport
5 Defence
6 Energy and Climate Change
7 Environment, Food and Rural Affairs
8 Foreign Affairs
9 Health
10 Home Affairs
11 International Development
12 Justice
13 Northern Ireland Affairs
14 Science and Technology
15 Scottish Affairs
16 Transport
17 Treasury
18 Welsh Affairs
19 Work and Pensions.

Most have a remit to examine the expenditure, administration and policy of the department concerned. Committees decide what to investigate and their ability to interrogate ministers and civil servants in public has made them ideal for television. Their deliberations are consequently now taken seriously, although the government does not necessarily accept all of the recommendations produced by the committees. Furthermore, it has no obligation to act on a report produced by one, although there is an obligation to respond in written form – usually within two months. Critics complain the committees have too few resources and powers which are too limited.

In March 2000, the chairs of the select committees banded together to form the Select Committee on Liaison, which issued *Shifting the Balance*, a report on the balance of power between the executive and legislature. It called for bigger budgets, more staff, more time for debates and

acceptance by ministers that MPs should have a role in making laws. However, the leader of the House of Commons, Margaret Beckett, and chief whip, Ann Taylor, gave away nothing. The government whips continued to appoint members to committees. Beckett praised their output (175 reports in 1998–99) but refused to let committees follow through policy, as it would involve too many civil servants having to give evidence.

See also Crossman reforms; nondepartmental select committee.

'dependency' culture

A term employed by the 'new right' to describe the alleged passive state of dependency of those surviving on government benefits. According to this thinking, large sections of the population, but especially the so-called 'underclass', have become so dependent on state welfare benefits they have lost the will to find work for themselves or to take responsibility for themselves and their own families.

See also entrepreneurial culture; social exclusion.

dependent territories

Territories for which Britain still remains responsible. They comprise: Anguilla, Bermuda, British Virgin Islands, Cayman Islands, Falklands Islands, Gibraltar, Montserrat, Pitcairn Islands, St Helena, South Georgia, South Sandwich Islands and the Turks and Caicos Islands. There are also two dependencies offshore in the form of the Channel Islands and the Isle of Man.

deposit

See candidate for parliamentary election; lost deposit.

deputy prime minister

Constitutionally there is no such office but prime ministers have found it expedient at times to invent one. It had become almost a regular feature of government, although in 2007 Gordon Brown did not appoint one when he became prime minister. Geoffrey

Howe was elevated to the position following one of Margaret Thatcher's reshuffles; Michael Heseltine was also given the title, plus coordinating powers, in exchange for supporting John Major in his re-election as party leader in July 1995. John Prescott was made Tony Blair's deputy and was given a major department portfolio in recognition of his influence with more traditional Labour voters and his role as deputy leader of the Labour Party.

The precise duties of deputy prime ministers vary according to the prime minister. Most deputise for the prime minister at question time, for example, but there is no established department for him or her to lead. In the event of a prime minister dying the deputy would take over until a new party leader was elected. Only one deputy prime minister went on to become the premier and that was Anthony Eden; he had been seen as Churchill's heir apparent for many years.

deputy speaker

In the 19th century the speaker had no deputies but by the middle of that century it became obvious that assistance was needed and so three were created by election from sitting MPs. The deputy's official title is the 'chairman of ways and means'; the holder is elected at the beginning of each parliament and, like the speaker, does not vote or act in partisan fashion. The budget debate is always presided over by the chairman of ways and means, as is the Commons when sitting as a Committee of the Whole House.

See also speaker.

deregulation

A tenet of right-wing economic thinking based on the premise that the economy functions best when it is left to market forces and free from government intervention. Accordingly, sectors of the economy were deregulated by the Conservatives in the 1980s, for example the operation of buses and the Stock Exchange. The philosophy of deregulation came under severe attack following the banking crisis of 2008–09, when it was widely believed that more, not less, regulation would have been necessary to prevent the contamination of international financial dealings by 'toxic' securities embodying worthless loans.

deregulation order

A means of repealing or amending primary legislation. Deregulation orders originate from the Deregulation and Contracting Out Act 1994; they allow for the repeal of primary legislation which has become burdensome to anyone carrying on a trade or profession. The department concerned has to draft a proposal for a deregulation order and then consult those affected, after which the appropriate action is taken.

deselection

The decision of a constituency organisation to reject its sitting MP. If deselected, MPs sit in the house until the end of the parliament, when they can decide whether to stand again – possibly as an independent. In 1980 Labour left-wing activists changed the rules of nomination which required sitting MPs to undergo mandatory reselection within the lifetime of a parliament. In practice, this meant right-wing Labour MPs could be deselected and left-wingers substituted. Nearly a dozen were deselected before the 1983 election, and others who joined the Social Democratic Party would probably have gone the same way had they stayed in the party. In 1987 six more were treated in this way, but by then certain left-wingers had come under pressure too. In 1990 it was decided to limit such inquisitions to occasions when the membership in the constituency decides via a ballot to order the deselection process. Following the MPs' expenses scandal in 2009, a number of MPs were threatened with deselection and a number opted to stand down to avoid such an embarrassment.

See also reselection.

despatch box

Boxes in each of the houses of parliament placed on the table separating the government and opposition benches. They were originally donated by New Zealand to mark the rebuilding of parliament after the Second World War. Speakers tend to lean on the boxes and, when roused, to thump them with fists to emphasise points. The boxes do not hold items for 'despatch' but instead contain Bibles.

detention without trial

The holding of suspects in detention until such time as a case can be created against them. This has been a product of the times, in that terrorist suspects are often elusive people who have covered their tracks. Security forces insist they need to hold dangerous suspects securely until a case has been put together. In 2005 Tony Blair placed his authority on the line by demanding a 90-day period of detention without trial, but that November Labour rebels voted with Conservatives and Liberal Democrats to reject the measure, contained in the Terrorism Bill. It was replaced by a 28-day period but the government was still unhappy and Jacqui Smith, home secretary under Gordon Brown, set her sights on a 42-day period. Again, a wide range of influential figures, including Lord Goldsmith and a former director of public prosecutions, Ken Macdonald, opposed the measure. During the summer of 2008 the measure passed through the Commons but it was torpedoed in the Lords that October, where it was soundly rejected, 309 to 118. Opponents pointed out that no other country had imposed such a draconian period of detention, even countries like Spain, which had suffered from terrorist attacks.

devolution

The transfer of governmental authority from the centre to the regions. Over-centralisation has long been recognised as a weakness of British government and, in an attempt to assuage nationalist sentiment, in 1979 the Labour government planned regional assemblies for Scotland and Wales but failed to attract sufficient support in the referendums held. Under Margaret Thatcher the issue died for a while but not

for the nationalists, who increasingly felt they were ruled by an 'alien' government. Labour promised them devolution and in September 1997 the Scottish referendum returned a two to one majority for a separate assembly, plus endorsement of tax-varying powers. The 'No' campaign in Wales was even less well funded than in Scotland and the result was again a victory for the 'Yes' camp, although only by the narrowest of margins: less than 1 per cent. In 1999 the assemblies were elected and they have been operating ever since, but there are substantial problems regarding funding and authority which still remain to be resolved. The first problem arose in January 2000, when the Scottish parliament voted to abolish tuition fees for Scottish university students. Eventually the coalition Liberal Democrat–Labour Scottish administration agreed to rescind this measure.

At the Conservative conference in 1998 William Hague made a speech in which he held out the possibility that England would soon seek a separate parliament if Scotland had its own assembly plus the ability to influence English politics via representation at Westminster. In June 2003 Tony Blair reorganised government responsibility for the residual secretaries of state for Wales and Scotland by subsuming them into the new Department for Constitutional Affairs. However, the spokespeople for Wales and Scotland in the House of Commons were to be the leader of the house, Peter Hain, and the transport secretary, Alistair Darling, and this 'part-time' arrangement was condemned by critics as disrespectful to Scotland and Wales.

In 2007 the Scottish National Party (SNP) became the biggest party in the Scottish parliament and formed a minority government under Alex Salmond, raising the possibility that Scotland might eventually opt for independence, though polls in 2008 showed majorities against such a course.

Regional government for England became a problem during the second half of the first Blair administration when it became obvious the Celtic assemblies were strengthening the Scottish and Welsh bids for resources. Gordon Brown had appeared to join John Prescott in championing regional assemblies but the queen's speech in June 2001 contained no commitment to such an objective. Eventually a white paper appeared in June 2003 and Prescott announced plans to hold referendums for regional assemblies in the north-east, the north-west and Yorkshire and Humberside. By late summer 2004 the three referendums had been reduced to one, in the north-east, held in November 2004; despite vigorous campaigning by Prescott, there was a three to one vote against a regional assembly.

See also Northern Ireland assembly; Scotland; Scottish parliament; Wales; Welsh assembly and government.

d'Hondt method (of seat allocation in regional list systems)

This system, invented by Belgian mathematician and lawyer Victor d'Hondt (1841–1901), comes into play in regional list proportional voting systems. It is the mathematical means whereby the number of votes cast is translated into the number of seats to which the participating parties are entitled. It is widely used in Europe, including the UK, where regional list systems are employed (e.g. election to the European parliament).

dignified/efficient (constitution)

A term first used by Walter Bagehot, who made a distinction between those dignified elements of the British constitution, which represent the symbols of power (for example the monarchy, the Privy Council, Her Majesty's state opening of parliament), and the efficient parts, such as Her Majesty's government, which actually has the political muscle to bring about change (for example the prime minister's office and cabinet committees). Commentators regularly suggest new items of the constitution have joined the 'dignified' parts, most notably the cabinet, although some have even added the House of Commons, the influence of which allegedly declined as a result of the

large government majorities after the 1997 and 2001 general elections, together with the effects of Tony Blair's more personal, presidential style. Some would contest that it had declined, however, given the acute problems Blair had in winning parliamentary support for both foundation hospitals and top-up fees in January 2004.

direct action

A generic term for peaceful political demonstrations or an activity compatible with democratic politics but often pushed to the limits of the law, especially in the case of trade union industrial action (for example the miners' strike in 1984–85). Since the 1990s the main proponents of direct action have been environmentalists, who have taken their lead, to a degree, from the US environmental grouping Earth First! These protests have represented an alliance between local and national activists and middle-class sympathisers. The actions against road building at Twyford Down in the early 1990s as well as Manchester Airport's second runway in the late 1990s were unusual in that they involved protestors living in trees and tunnels, thereby risking their lives. It seems the embrace of some radical campaigns by middle-class 'respectable' people has given the notion of direct action (as opposed to political violence) a degree of respectability.

direct democracy

A form of government where the people have direct control over policy making and the institutions of the state. It is a type of rule where representatives are not used, but committees, citizen juries and people's assemblies are instead. Direct democracy first appeared in Athens. The new millennium has witnessed its growth in some restricted respects – for example with the introduction of a type of 'virtual' democracy where telecommunications and computers allow instant or 'real-time' feedback from citizens and consumers. Direct democracy is not really appropriate for a country of Britain's size.

See also Athenian democracy.

direct rule

The term usually employed to describe the decision in 1972 to replace the elected Stormont government in Northern Ireland and rule directly from Westminster. It was hoped the beginnings of local democratic rule had been initiated in June 1998 when the new Northern Ireland assembly was elected and an executive committee was established under David Trimble as first minister. Direct rule was reinstated following yet another crisis in the autumn of 2002. It took until 2007 before the Northern Ireland executive finally resumed, under with Ian Paisley as first minister.

See also Northern Ireland assembly; Stormont.

Directgov

http://direct.gov.uk

Government website that opened in August 2004. It offers a huge amount of information on a variety of activities (e.g. finding jobs, educational opportunities) as well as a massive A–Z facility on British government and links to a myriad of related matters. Worth consulting by every citizen.

directive (EU)

See Council of Ministers.

directly elected mayor

See elected mayor; mayor.

director of public prosecutions

The person in charge of the Crown Prosecution Service (CPS), which decides whether an alleged offence justifies a court case. The director of public prosecutions (Keir Starmer, QC, was appointed in November 2008) is responsible to the attorney general.

See also attorney general; Crown Prosecution Service.

discrimination

The process whereby certain groups of people, usually minorities, are treated badly and often given unequal legal rights. Centuries ago such minorities were often religious groups but in the modern day they are more often distinguished by race and sexual orientation. Advocates of a written constitution believe an incorporated bill of rights would protect such groups more effectively and some protection has been afforded by the incorporation into British law of the European Convention on Human Rights. Perhaps the biggest group feeling on the receiving end of discrimination is the elderly, especially when, as now, there are more people aged over 65 than there are under 16: a situation which can only become more acute.

See also civil rights.

dissident republican group

Any of the terrorist groups still committed to violent struggle for a united Ireland after Sinn Fein and the Provisional IRA agreed to the terms of the Good Friday agreement. On 7 March 2009 two young soldiers were murdered in the Massereene army barracks when they stepped outside to collect a pizza. On 9 March 2009 a police constable was shot in the head when answering a call from Craigavon. Dissident republican groups claimed responsibility for the killings: the Continuity IRA for the latter and the Real IRA (also responsible for the Omagh bombing in 1998) for the former. These deaths (the first since 1998) brought out thousands in protest. Peter Robinson, the then first minister, condemned the killers as 'evil'. Gerry Adams and Martin McGuinness also condemned them, the latter using the word 'traitors'. Both former IRA leaders flanked police chief Sir Hugh Orde to ask for information leading to the capture of the gunmen.

dissolution of parliament

The act by which the sovereign closes a session of parliament and sets in motion the process for a general election and the start of a new parliament. Dissolutions are nearly always requested by the prime minister, usually before the five-year expiry date set by the Parliament Act 1911 (before then, parliaments ran for a maximum of seven years). Constitutionally, a prime minister will be obliged to seek a dissolution if his or her party loses a vote of no confidence, or the government has been defeated on the passage of a finance act. Finally, the House of Lords can immediately call for a dissolution if the House of Commons attempts to stay in power longer than five years. It is sometimes thought that the threat of dissolution can be used to counter rebellion within the governing party but in practice it is rarely credible, as few prime ministers would risk losing a general election for the sake of party unity.

See also parliament.

divine right of kings
The idea that a monarch had a holy right to succeed to the throne. Developed in the middle ages, it was used to reinforce the moral position of monarchs. After the defeat of the Royalists in the Civil War the doctrine faded away in Britain. The origin of the royal 'we' is thought to refer to the monarch plus God.

division lobby
Corridor running alongside the debating chamber of the House of Commons, used by MPs in the process of voting. The voting by MPs is sometimes therefore called a 'division'. The House of Commons is unusual in maintaining a physical rather than an electronic means of voting. When it comes to the vote, MPs walk through either the 'ayes' (right-hand) or 'noes' (left-hand) 'lobby' and are counted by 'tellers' as they re-enter at the speaker's end of the chamber. Defenders of the archaic system point out that this is one of the few occasions when back-bench members can meet with ministers and raise urgent matters with them. Moreover, while electronic systems might be vulnerable to external interference, it is hard to fake votes when people are being physically counted. Most reform proposals have tried to maintain this feature of the house's workings.

divisional court
The part of the High Court which hears appeals. It is divided into:

1 the Queen's Bench, which hears points of law from criminal cases in magistrates' courts;
2 the Chancery, which hears appeals from county courts on bankruptcy matters;
3 the Family Division, which hears domestic and matrimonial cases.

When sitting as divisional courts, three High Court judges need to preside.

divorce
The legal severing of a marriage contract. Its constitutional importance lies in the fact that the monarch, as head of the Church of England, has traditionally supported the institution of marriage but its authority was eroded by the decision of Edward VIII to abdicate in order to marry a twice divorced woman in 1936. Later, several members of the royal family, including Princesses Margaret and Anne, as well as Prince Andrew and Prince Charles, obtained divorces.

The broader social importance of divorce in Britain is that the divorce rate has continued to rise since the Second World War, aided by easing of the relevant laws, in particular the Divorce Reform Act 1967. Concern regarding the social fabric has been expressed by church leaders, and Conservative politicians, because divorce is associated with the increasing number of single-parent families and the fact that Britain has one of the highest rates of births outside marriage in the European Union.

'dodgy dossiers'
In September 2002 the government published a dossier on Iraq's weapons of mass destruction that reported substantial intelligence information. In February 2003 another dossier was published focusing on the Iraqi regime's concealment of such weapons. Neither dossier was judged convincing at the time – especially when the latter was damagingly revealed to include a plagiarised section of a PhD thesis – but in the wake of the war critical scrutiny intensified. It was alleged by journalists that senior intelligence officers were accusing New Labour's Alastair Campbell, the

POLITICS

Downing Street press secretary, of adding his own material to the dossiers to 'sex' them up, that is, to make more compelling the case for a war his master favoured. In the ensuing furious row many observed that the intelligence services had been involved closely (and unhealthily) in the presentation of political arguments.

See also Campbell, Alastair.

dominant class

The owners of property and capital. The concept is based upon the social analyses of Karl Marx, who perceived the creation in society of social groups according to their relationship to the means of production. He believed such groups were inevitably in conflict and would continue to be so until the working classes finally overthrew the 'ruling' or 'dominant' class. In Britain such a class would be perceived in the mostly privately educated leaders of the main institutions of the country: the civil service, business, parliament, the church, the military, the judiciary and so forth. It followed, according to Marx, that the dominant class would permeate society with its own ideas and values.

See also dominant values; establishment.

dominant values

Concept associated with the Marxian belief that the ruling ideas of any era are those of the ruling class. According to this perspective the owners of capital dominate all the key positions in society and infiltrate their values into them and the media. Neo-Marxists like Antonio Gramsci argued that the control of the media was the means whereby the working classes were induced to accept dominant values and submit to a class subservience. Only left-wing members of the Labour Party subscribe to such ideas and they worry that New Labour's enthusiasm for business leaders signifies support for or absorption of such dominant values.

Downing Street declaration

Declaration made in December 1993 by John Major and Irish prime minister Albert Reynolds on the issue of Ulster. Effectively it expressed agreement between the two governments that there would be no change in the status of the province without majority agreement, something which pleased the Ulster unionists, although it did not remove their suspicions of the Irish republicans.

Downing Street Press Office

Office that controls the prime minister's relationship with the media. Since the Second World War it has become gradually more important, so much so that some believe the power of the premier's press secretary rivals that of senior ministers through access to the prime minister and proximity to crucial discussions. This follows from the close relationship Sir Bernard Ingham established with Margaret Thatcher, when he not only interpreted her mind for the media at his daily press conferences but also advised her on a range of important issues. Alastair Campbell occupied a similar, even closer, role in relation to Tony Blair and was regarded as one of his closest aides; some jokingly referred to him as the 'deputy prime minister'. Gordon Brown suggested he would be less interested in presentation than his predecessor, though by the summer of 2008, when he was 20 points down on the Conservatives in the polls, some critics argued his government's presentation record had been poor.

See also prime minister's department.

E

early day motion (EDM)

A motion submitted by an MP for an 'early day' debate in the Commons. The debate rarely occurs but the motion is printed and others may add their names. EDMs therefore are like parliamentary petitions and act as barometers of back-bench opinion. Sometimes a large number of names have been thought to have initiated action, such as the Conservative EDM in the 1980s to abolish compulsory membership of student unions. In the 1970s and 1980s some 300–400 EDMs were tabled each year. By the 1990s the annual figure had reached 1,000. In May 2009 Douglas Carswell MP moved an EDM proposing to remove speaker Martin following what was regarded as an inadequate response to the MPs' expenses issue. He later changed this to a 'substantive motion' to enable a vote to be taken.

'east of Suez' (policy)

British foreign policy relating to the Middle East and Far East. When the Suez Canal was built in 1869 it became enormously successful as a means of avoiding the huge journey around the Cape of Good Hope. For the British Empire it was vital, given that India was its 'jewel in the crown' and the multiple interests of Britain in Malaya, China and elsewhere in the Far East. After the Second World War Britain was forced to withdraw from exposed parts of the Empire, including India and Burma in 1947–48. Macmillan's 1960 'wind of change' speech in Africa was matched in 1967 by Harold Wilson's endorsement of the decision of his defence secretary, Denis Healey, to withdraw troops from Malaya and Singapore. Since that time 'east of Suez' policy has entered into mainstream usage.

> Ship me somewheres east of Suez, where the
>   best is like the worst,
> Where there aren't no Ten Commandments
>   an' a man can raise a thirst
> (Rudyard Kipling, 'Mandalay')

Ecclestone affair

Allegation of sleaze early after Labour's 1997 election victory. In its 1997 manifesto Labour stated that smoking was the greatest cause of preventable illness and that it would ban tobacco advertising if elected. Health secretary Frank Dobson repeated the pledge in June 1997 but said it was not intended to damage sports that benefited from the backing of the tobacco industry. In November the government

stated it would exempt Formula One motor racing from the ban. Then it transpired that Bernie Ecclestone, the billionaire figure behind Formula One in Britain, had visited Tony Blair in October and insisted such a ban would lead to 50,000 full-time jobs and 150,000 part-time jobs being lost. It then became public knowledge that Ecclestone – previously a donor to the Conservatives – had made a £1 million donation to Labour and the spectre of sleaze arose for Labour, very early into its first term. Eventually Ecclestone was given back his donation, and Blair appeared on television to apologise for his mistake.

See also sleaze.

Ecology Party

See Green Party.

economic and monetary union

See European economic and monetary union.

Economic and Social Committee (ESC)

www.eesc.europa.eu
Institution of the European Union which considers a wide range of legislation. It was originally set up by the treaty of Rome to supplement the European assembly (now the European parliament) as a forum for employers, employees and other interests to consult, cooperate and advise on policy. While the assembly has evolved into the European parliament, the ESC remains a purely consultative body. National governments appoint members to the committee via the Council of Ministers.

economic competition

The idea central to (Thatcherite) neo-liberal economic thinking. It is held that if businesses are ranged against each other in the marketplace, they seek efficiency married to quality, to gain the advantage which will enable them to make profits, maintain employment and reinvest in more modern equipment. At the same time consumers are served well as they receive the best possible product at the lowest possible price. Competition therefore is the central requirement for economic efficiency. The Conservatives maintained that the public monopolies created by nationalisation after 1945 created inefficiency, which led to their annual losses, for which the taxpayer had to pay. They also pointed to those countries in eastern Europe with 'command' economies (based on monopoly production and provision of goods) as proof that the communist project had failed to provide prosperity for their citizens. These countries eventually collapsed from economic failure and corruption in the late 1980s. However, the Conservatives did not always practise their ideology, in that privatised industries, including British Telecom and British Gas, were allowed to operate as private monopolies for a while. The privatised water companies still enjoy such a privileged position in the marketplace and it is hard to see how any effective competition, in any case, could be introduced.

See also privatisation.

economic crisis, 2007–09
This was triggered by the 'sub-prime' mortgage crisis in the USA which caused the acute banking crisis of summer/autumn 2008. The UK (and international) banking system required huge amounts of public money to save it from collapse, which put great strains on government expenditure. Lack of credit led to a contraction of the economy – by about 5 per cent in 2008–09 – which reduced tax revenue and raised the public sector borrowing requirement (PSBR) to stratospheric levels. Prime minister Gordon Brown put his faith in Keynesian policies of channelling vast amounts of money into the economy, either by selling government bonds, or by 'printing' money ('quantitative easing' as the Bank of England called it). The Conservatives responded – more traditionally – by insisting the government should initiate deep cuts in public spending. By the summer of 2009 the economy was showing a few 'green shoots' of recovery but the wiser economic pundits, including the

Bank of England itself, warned there was much further to go.

See also credit crunch; quantitative easing; sub-prime mortgage crisis

economic decline
Term used to describe the British economy's postwar lacklustre performance. In 1939 Britain's economy was second only to that of the USA in terms of gross domestic product (GDP) per capita. After the war Britain began a decline which continued until the late 1980s. Although the economy grew in absolute terms, it declined relative to its competitors. The reasons are contentious but agreement tends to centre on six factors.

1 *History*. Competitors had the advantage of the latest technology while world war had exhausted Britain and left it in debt, and the ending of 'imperial preference' removed Britain's cushion from the real economic world.

2 *Geography*. Britain was hit harder by world recessions because its island nature make it more dependent on exports.

3 *Culture*. Class divisions fuelled poor industrial relations, the education system tended to discriminate against vocationally useful subjects like engineering and foreign languages, and the emphasis on home ownership blocked the mobility of the workforce.

4 *Politics*. Labour policies after the war encouraged an unhealthily large public sector. Moreover, all parties criticised the lack of continuity in economic policy making caused by changes of government.

5 *Finance*. Low industrial investment starved research and development of much needed funds.

6 *Economics*. Britain had low levels of productivity and investment, and endemic inflation, which developed into the so-called 'stagflation' of the mid-1970s. This signalled the breakdown of Keynesian demand management and left a gap in macro-economics that was quickly filled by the new right and monetarism.

See also imperial preference.

economic interest group

Pressure or interest group concerned with the economy that seeks to influence government policy. A range of groups represent and promote the interests of business producers like multinational companies; the 'peak' organisation is the Confederation of British Industry (CBI). The trade unions also represent producer interests, from an employee perspective, their peak organisation being the Trades Union Congress (TUC). In recent years governments have attempted to promote the interests of consumers, not so much through formal pressure group involvement in policy making but through the creation of public sector consumer watchdogs.

economic management

Government management of the economy. The government is able to manage the economy, if only to a degree, through the following:
1 fiscal measures – adjusting direct and indirect taxation;
2 monetary measures – controlling the money supply by adjusting interest rates;
3 stimulating trade via diplomatic means, for example through the Department for Business, Innovation and Skills (formerly Trade and Industry) and the Foreign and Commonwealth Office;
4 providing support and subsidies for economic activity (again via the Department for Business, Innovation and Skills, though less so under the Conservative governments of the 1980s);
5 providing a national infrastructure of transport and public services.

The Conservatives have tended to view genuine economic growth as best achieved when industry and markets are left alone by government. Labour, before Tony Blair became the party's leader, favoured nationalisation of the commanding heights of the economy (although it never attempted this in practice) and a policy of Keynesian demand management. Under Blair and Gordon Brown, Labour governments pursued economic policies not dissimilar to those of Margaret Thatcher and John Major, although there were a number of New Labour or 'third way' innovations, such as an independent Bank of England, the promotion of public and private sector partnerships in the delivery of central and local government services, and a more supportive position on membership of the European single currency.

economic policy making

Possibly the most important function of modern British government. Economic policy making involves a 'community' of individuals in and around the core executive, some of the most important being: the chancellor, the chancellor's personal advisors, the chief secretary to the Treasury, the senior civil servants at the Treasury, the governor of the Bank of England (charged with setting interest rates since May 1997), the Monetary Policy Committee (charged with advising the Bank on interest rates), and other economic ministers, such as the minister for business, innovation and skills.

Since Britain joined the European Economic Community (now the European Union) the 'Europeanisation' of policy making has taken place, where key civil service committees are now meshed into the European Union structure. For example, policy making on regional economic development requires collaboration between national and supranational bodies in London and Brussels. Gordon Brown, appointed chancellor in 1997, proved a dominant minister who controlled policy in a very personal fashion. Some tension was discerned between Brown and Tony Blair after the 2001 victory regarding entry into the euro. Brown was seen as cautious and insistent upon his 'five conditions' being met while Blair was seen as more enthusiastic about entry.

See also five tests; Keynesianism; monetarism.

Economist

www.economist.com
Weekly journal of news, comment and analysis. It was founded in 1843. The

POLITICS

Economist has established a respected position in British politics as an authoritative journal which is widely read by the elites. It sells well worldwide, especially in the USA. It tends to take an orthodox monetarist line on economic policy but is generally liberal on human rights and always independent in its views. Known to employ brilliant young people from Oxbridge, it is occasionally criticised for being arrogant in its lofty prescriptions for the world.

economy (British)

The British economy was the first to benefit from the industrial revolution and Britain became the 'workshop of the world' in the 19th century. The British Empire provided huge benefits in terms of cheap raw materials and closed markets. However, other countries caught up, benefiting from the latest plant and machinery while Britain laboured with out-of-date equipment. The Empire broke up as countries achieved independence and set up their own indigenous industries. Traditional industries like shipbuilding, steel, coalmining and textiles began to decline rapidly – almost to extinction – during the postwar period. However, new industries based on new technology emerged, many in the service sector: information technology, advertising, financial services and the assembly of mechanical and electrical goods (financed mostly by overseas investment). In absolute terms Britain is almost three times better off in the early years of the new millennium than in 1945. Inflation has increased prices 20-fold but income has increased 50-fold. In relative terms Britain has fallen from its peak as the USA, Germany and Japan now have bigger economies. But as the sixth biggest economy, Britain is still a wealthy country. Its economic problems include:

1 poor competitiveness compared with the USA;
2 poor manufacturing output;
3 a balance-of-trade deficit;
4 a pound which has tended to be overvalued, making exports more difficult to sell.

Labour's perceived safe stewardship of the economy helped it to win a second victory in 2001. In 2003 economic output was in decline as the world economy was damaged by plummeting share prices and the war in Iraq. Chancellor Gordon Brown was able to claim throughout the period of his incumbency, however, that the British economy had outperformed the economies of other member states of the European Union and of many other advanced industrial countries in terms of growth, inflation and employment levels. Brown's prognosis for the British economy in July 2004 was a continuation of steady growth for the foreseeable future. These optimistic prospects were shattered in 2007–08 when the 'sub-prime' mortgage crisis occurred in the USA, caused by loans being given to people who could not repay them but which were then turned into complex securities traded internationally. Once their 'toxicity' became apparent, US investment banks like Lehman Brothers went bust and UK banks like Northern Rock had to be saved by the British taxpayer via the government. In 2009 the British economy was still reeling and in the middle of a deep recession.

Education Act 1944

The act that established the principle of free state education for all children from the age of 5 to 15 (and 16 when deemed practical). It left it to local education authorities to determine their own systems of ensuring that a child's education was appropriate to age, aptitude and ability, which in most cases meant the use of the 11-plus test and selection for secondary school.

education action zone

See education policy.

education policy

The Labour Party manifesto of 1997 stated: 'Education will be our number one priority, and we will increase the share of national income spent on education as we decrease it on bills of economic and social failure'. The electorate were promised: class sizes reduced to 30 for children under seven years of age; nursery places for all four-year-olds; an attack on low standards in schools; increased access to computer technology; the development of lifelong learning through a new University for Industry; and more spending on education. Philosophically, the policy commitments, along with ambitious literacy and numeracy targets, originated from two areas of thinking: the 'third way', in particular the need to create informed citizens; and 'new growth' theory, which views education as a tool governments need to use to produce skilled, flexible workers who can enable the nation to compete effectively in the global marketplace.

In electoral terms, Labour's education policy was part of a catch-all approach to winning elections. For this reason, Labour carried forward the tough approach of previous governments regarding poor teachers and failing schools. The Labour government gave itself powers to close down schools and reopen them with a new management team and staff ('Fresh Start' schools), or establish education action zones, to set up local partnerships (a key New Labour word) of businesses, voluntary groups, parents, local education authorities and other interested parties. The education action zone represented one of the most radical solutions to the challenge of local service provision and went beyond the simple public versus private alternative of 'old style' politics, at least according to 'third way' theorists. The tough chief inspector of schools, Chris Woodhead, was retained by Labour for some time, despite intense criticism of him by the teaching unions. Despite its ambitious rhetoric, Labour's record on education was mixed: standards did rise, but a large number of pupils still left school ill equipped for the world of work.

The Conservative approach to education tends to favour the private sector together with selection of pupils by schools. The party has argued for 'education vouchers', whereby parents would be allowed a financial entitlement to education, which they could supplement to send their

children to private schools should they wish. Michael Gove, Conservative spokesman on education, favoured giving schools more freedom and parents more power, as in the case of Sweden's 'free' schools. In May 2010 Gove came into office and declared he would introduce widespread changes, including potentially every secondary school converting into academies, as well as his 'Swedish'-style innovations.

Education Reform Act 1988
One of the most important pieces of education legislation since the 1944 act. The Great Education Reform Bill or 'Gerbil': introduced central government control of learning (the national curriculum); increased parental choice by allowing schools to compete with each other for pupils; allowed some schools to opt out of local authority control and receive their funds from central government (termed grant-maintained schools); and established local management of school budgets and staff. Finally, the act made regular pupil testing via 'SATs' (standard assessment tests) an obligatory part of the education process, along with league tables of performance to help parents evaluate schools. New Labour continued with this consumer focus, although the party abandoned the grant-maintained schools in favour of specialist schools.

educational theories
The *Economist* of 13 December 2008 reflected on the fact that many people brought up in the 1960s apparently suffered a poor education as a result of certain schools of thought regarding how subjects should be taught, in particular spelling and handwriting. The national curriculum ended this in 1988 but at the cost of imposing an unwieldy bureaucratic blueprint which is often too broad brush to be effective. A report to the Department for Children, Schools and Families by Sir Jim Rose in April 2009 (*Independent Review of the Primary Curriculum: Final Report*) suggested six 'teaching areas', merging history and geography, reading, writing and

foreign languages, physical education with
some science and so forth. Rose believed
this would combine flexibility with more
focus on priorities but learned societies for
history, geography and others protested.
Nonetheless, slimming down the curriculum
was bound to exclude some elements,
according to the *Economist*, which went
on to suggest that Rose, judging from his
previous major reports, seemed too keen to
tell his political bosses what they wanted to
hear. The report's proposals were described
by opponents as a 'mish-mash' which did
not capture any distinctive national theme.

Efficiency Unit
Unit set up by Margaret Thatcher
shortly after her 1979 election victory
in order to improve management within
the civil service. It was headed by Derek
(later Lord) Raynor, formerly of Marks
and Spencer, who had established his
reputation advising the Ministry of Defence
(1970–72). Raynor was greatly trusted
by Thatcher and he was given a free rein
to introduce economies and more efficient
procedures and enhance the importance of
management in the public sector. Raynor's
successor, Sir Robin Ibbs, went on to
introduce the far-reaching reform of the
civil service, the 'Next Steps' programme.
See also Ibbs report.

egalitarianism
See equality.

elected mayor
An idea, based on US models, originally
proposed by Michael Heseltine and then
taken up by New Labour as part of its
'modernising' agenda in its first term. The
office of mayor for London was established
by the Greater London Authority Act
1999; the Local Government Act 2000
provided the means for mayors to be
directly elected for other cities as well. In
London, a referendum approved the idea
and a protracted election campaign led up
to a poll in May 2000. Ken Livingstone
won the election despite the opposition
of Tony Blair. The government hoped

the idea would prove popular and renew
interest in local politics but many councillors objected to it as it diminished the role
of the ordinary member of the council. In
referendums held on elected mayors up and
down the country in 2001–02, less than
a dozen out of over 30 council areas voted
to move to such a system. In 2008 Boris
Johnson beat Livingstone in the election
for London mayor but the notion of elected
mayors remained a minority taste in the
UK as a whole.

elected second chamber
A popular proposal to replace the
hereditary House of Lords. Another is
the representation of specific sections of
society, such as the regions, business and
academe. Also popular is the idea of
using proportional representation to elect
members to what has often been called a
new 'Senate' rather than Lords. However,
the major problem with such a scheme is
that if it is given a real job to do in order to
attract high-quality candidates, its authority
will challenge the presently all-powerful
House of Commons and trigger a constitutional crisis. For this and other reasons
Tony Blair made it known in January
2003 that he was against an elected second
chamber and preferred an appointed one.
See also House of Lords; House of
Lords reform.

election
A means by which representatives (for
example MPs, councillors and MEPs) are
appointed to political office by the people.
The most important are general elections,
whereby governments are selected in the
British political system. Elections for
parliament occur at least once every five
years, and are based on the first past the
post (FPTP) system. Elections are held
on Thursdays, the (alleged) logic being
that this allows the maximum number
of days campaigning in the last week of
the campaign without extending into the
weekend. Voting is from 7 a.m. to 10 p.m.
Candidates' names are placed in alphabetical order on the voting slip and each

elector must indicate a preference by writing a cross opposite the person chosen. The completed slips are placed in ballot boxes, which are sealed and taken away for the counting of votes. The frequency of local elections depends on the council concerned.

See also electoral system.

election campaign
See campaigning.

election campaign costs
The costs incurred by political parties during election campaigns. In 1997 the cost of holding the election was £52 million to the government; and that was in addition to the £50 million it costs annually to maintain the electoral register. In constituency elections agents are required to show that expenditure has been under the limit of a basic £7,150 plus 5p or 7p per elector depending on whether it is a borough or county constituency. Given this cap, local candidates can do little more than print out leaflets, although they are entitled to free postage for their election addresses plus free hire of school halls for meetings. Until 2001 there was no legal limit, however, to spending nationally by parties or any obligation to publish their election accounts. Modern parties spend huge amounts on advertising, opinion polling, travel and meetings. In 1997 the Conservatives spent £13 million with the Saatchi agency and Labour £7 million with the BMP agency. Such heavy spending, combined with falling membership receipts, has made parties dependent on big donations; the concern is that such a reliance is traded for political influence. Following the Neill committee's report on funding for political parties in 1998, a cap for national election spending was imposed by the Political Parties, Elections and Referendums Act 2000. The cap applied to those parties contesting all 659 parliamentary constituencies. Lower limits applied to elections to other bodies, such as the devolved assemblies. Limits were also introduced for referendums, of between £0.5 and £5 million for a registered political party. The registered treasurer of a party is required after an election to submit accounts to the Electoral Commission, and these must cover the previous 365 days in the case of Westminster elections or four months before the poll in the case of other elections.

election court
Court that hears disputes over the validity of the election of an MP or a local councillor. The case is raised via an election petition and is decided by an election court that comprises two High Court judges.

elective dictatorship
A term first used by Lord Hailsham in 1976 and now part of the lexicon of British politics. Hailsham criticised the British constitution's ability to make the majority (or indeed the largest minority) party, once elected, an effective dictatorship until the next election, even though, like the Labour government of that time, it might be elected on a minority of the national vote. Once the Conservatives were back in office after 1979, Hailsham lost his enthusiasm for attacking this aspect of the constitution.

electoral college
Usually associated with the US presidential elections but also an occasional feature of British politics, especially in the Labour Party. In 1981 it was introduced to elect Labour's leader. Trade unions, Labour MPs and party members all have a share of the vote, initially in the proportions 40:30:30 but later changed to one-third each. In May 1999 Labour used an electoral college to elect its candidate – eventually the reluctant Frank Dobson – for London mayor. A similar ploy was used to elect Alun Michael (and keep out the popular choice, Rhodri Morgan) as leader of the Welsh Labour Party in the wake of Ron Davies's enforced resignation.

Electoral Commission
www.electoralcommission.org.uk
Set up under terms of Political Parties, Elections and Referendums Act 2000 in November of the same year. Its remit is to

'increase public confidence in the democratic process ... and encourage people to take part by modernising the electoral process'. It also reviews the administration and law of elections, encourages greater participation and oversees the activities of the Boundary Committee for England (formerly the Local Government Commission).

electoral reform

The alleged injustice of the electoral system has given rise to a movement for reform. Initially it was mainly an obsession of the Liberal Party and its successors, and clearly in their interests, but others became convinced of the case for reform in other parties; for example, Labour's Robin Cook and Charter 88 took up the cause in the 1980s and 1990s. Despite the scepticism of Jack Straw, home secretary, and the agnosticism of Tony Blair, Labour in 1997 set up the Jenkins commission to recommend a more proportional system; it reported in 1998. It recommended an amended version of the German electoral system, with 500 seats elected by the alternative vote from constituencies and the remainder from a regional list which would provide 'top-up' seats to reflect more properly the proportion of votes cast between the parties. A referendum was to determine whether the commission's recommendations were to be adopted, as it would be a decision with momentous implications for the political life of the country. However, the experience of proportional representation in the devolved assemblies of Scotland and Wales reduced Labour's enthusiasm for reform and talk of a referendum faded, although the Liberal Democrats continued to press for it. In 2008–09, anger at the MPs' expenses scandal fuelled talk of when radical constitutional reform. After the May 2010 general election the new coalition government promised a referendum on the alternative vote system.

See also electoral system; Jenkins report.

electoral register (alternatively 'roll')

A list of names of all those entitled to vote in each constituency. Electoral registers are drawn up by local registration officers (employees of local authorities). To be included a person must be resident in the constituency, be over 18 years old and be a British or Commonwealth subject. Irish nationals can vote if they have lived continuously for three months in the UK. Aliens and those judged insane cannot vote (though the latter may do so in periods of mental lucidity), nor can those found guilty of corrupt electoral practices and certain categories of prison inmates. Approximately 43.7 million people are eligible to vote in Britain, although not all appear on the electoral register, through negligence or design. In the wake of the community charge ('poll tax') it was believed thousands – one estimate in 1992 put it at over a million – neglected to register to vote in order to disguise their presence from the authorities charged with collection of the new tax. Registers used to be updated annually, with checks being sent out in the autumn for publication on 16 February each year. However, this annual procedure has now been changed so that the register is constantly updated on a 'rolling' basis. Failing to register as a voter is a criminal offence punishable by a fine of up to £2,000. In September 2001 Brian Robertson, a retired accountant from Pontefract, launched a High Court challenge to his local authority for selling on details of his name to direct-marketing enterprises, something which most local authorities, it transpired, did as a matter of course. The judge found that the government had breached the European Convention on Human Rights in that the interference with Mr Robertson's private life was disproportionate.

electoral system

The electoral system in Britain is the first past the post (FPTP) or the single member, simple plurality (SMSP) system. The 650 constituencies for the 2010 general election drawn up by the Boundary Commission elect one member to the Commons at each general election, which occurs at least once every five years, or in by-elections. The person gaining the most votes is the winner, irrespective of the number of candidates and no matter how small the majority. Britain is the only country in Europe to use this system, and even beyond Europe there are few other examples (India, the USA and Canada). The system is straightforward but it produces extravagant anomalies: parties with thin national support can receive disproportionate numbers of seats. This was shown especially in 1983, when the Alliance won 26 per cent of the votes yet only 3 per cent of the seats. Psephologists have also shown how the system at present works to the advantage of the Labour Party (for example even if both parties had polled the same number of votes in the 1997 election, Labour would still have won 79 more seats than the Conservatives). For obvious reasons the two major parties, with some exceptions, favour the existing system. The 'hung parliament' of May 2010 reinforced the case for a change to the electoral system as the Liberal Democrats, though gaining 23 per cent of the vote, received less than 10 per cent of the seats. Moreover, polls during the campaign had suggested Labour could have had the lowest number of votes yet the highest number of seats. As part of the coalition deal, a prospective referendum on the alternative vote system was agreed.

See also electoral reform; first past the post.

electricity industry

British electricity generation (by the Central Electricity Generating Board) was formerly a public utility. However, in 1990 it was divided into three companies (Powergen, National Power, and Nuclear Electric, plus a transmission company, National Grid) and sold off to the private sector. Nuclear power, which then produced one-fifth of the nation's electricity, was kept in public hands in the form of Nuclear Electric. National Power, one of the privatised companies, produces half the country's power, from both fossil fuels and renewable sources. Twelve electricity distribution companies were sold off in 1990, for £5.2 billion. The National Grid was sold off in 1996 for £5 billion.

electricity shortfall

The *Economist* on 8 August 2009 directed attention to the prospect of selective blackouts in the UK within a few years unless the government could prevent the 'energy gap' growing. In 2009 the UK consumed 59 gigawatts: 45 per cent from North Sea gas; 35 per cent from coal; 15 per cent from nuclear power; and the rest from renewables and other sources. By 2115, the journal reckoned, 64 gigawatts will be required. Coal is the dirtiest type of fuel and runs counter to climate change policies. North Sea oil peaked in 2000 and is falling away rapidly. Nuclear energy seems to be an alternative but has its own band of resolute environmental critics and severe financial constraints too. To make matters even worse, some 20 gigawatts of capacity will disappear by 2015, meaning that, too, will need to be replaced. EDF, the nuclear power producer, talks up its product by predicting a gap of 32 gigawatts, and the possibility of electricity having to be rationed (as in a third world country) cannot be ruled out. The irony is that wave and wind power is amazingly plentiful in this windswept island but the technology to harness it has proved elusive. Britain's future uninterrupted supplies might very well depend on some sort of technological breakthrough being made.

11-plus test

Set up by the Education Act 1944, the examination determined which children would go to grammar, technical or secondary modern schools. Although inspired by good intentions, for example to identify those working-class children who would benefit from an academic secondary education as a preliminary for university entrance, the test resulted in injustices. Virtually all children took the examination, with regional variations, of whom about one-third passed. Studies showed working-class children tended not to pass while middle-class ones did. Moreover, the pass mark was adjusted upwards for girls in certain authorities that needed to ensure a gender balance in schools. The system was deemed to be unfair, especially as the future lives of the school population were decided at such a young age. After Labour was returned to power in 1964 the examination was phased out and comprehensive schools gradually introduced. Despite this, pockets of selection remained, such as Kent, Trafford and Tameside.

See also grammar school.

11 September 2001 terrorist attacks
See 9/11, 2001.

elite
Small group of people who have influence and power out of all proportion to their number. Vilfredo Pareto and Gaetano Mosca argued in the early 20th century that democracy was a sham, as the many are ruled by the few. In Britain the traditional ruling elite was the aristocracy, mainly comprising large landowners, but the industrial revolution added a new group: prominent industrialists. Moreover, with the expansion of the franchise in the 19th century and the growth of higher education, meritocratic virtues substituted new provenances for the elites of Britain. Thus, the social/educational background of MPs is heavily skewed towards independent school and Oxbridge. For example, in 1992 three-quarters of Conservative MPs were privately educated, 10 per cent at Eton alone, and just under half had been to Oxbridge; the figures for Labour were 15 per cent privately educated and 16 per cent Oxbridge. Even higher percentages of such politicians go on to serve in the cabinets of both parties and similar concentrations of upper-middle-class products, upwards of 50 per cent, go on to dominate all the main centres of power in Britain. These include ambassadors, High Court judges, senior military officers, civil servants and directors of major companies; sometimes these elites are joined together by marriage or blood ties. However, Budge et al. (in The New British Politics, fourth edition, 2004) questioned the existence of a consolidated elite; instead they suggested a series of 'fragmented' elites, for example media and

opinion formers, who may act independently of political leaders. In December 2002, however, the Economist published its list of the 100 most important British decision makers, and this showed that since 1992 the percentage who were educated at public schools had fallen from 66 to 46 and those who were Oxbridge educated from 54 to 35.

Some have questioned the whole notion of elite power. Karl Marx argued that political power is derived wholly from the ownership of the means of production; Robert Dahl suggested that it is one thing for an elite to have the potential to exercise power but it is another for it to ride roughshod over opposition to get its own way.

See also establishment; power elite; social mobility.

emergency debate
Debate allowed under standing order number 10 of the Commons. Some two or three emergency debates are allowed each year by the speaker. In applying for one, MPs are given a platform of sorts as they are allowed to make a three-minute speech to present their case for such a debate.

emergency powers
Special powers available to government in the event of a national emergency, or when the civil authorities are unable to deal with a threat to life, property and civil order. Historically significant are the Defence of the Realm Acts 1914, 1915, and the Emergency Powers Acts 1939, 1940, which were used in time of war and gave sweeping powers to government to act in whatever way the circumstances required, including seizure of private property, billeting of troops and other persons, and detention without trial. Although repealed, the authorities can use powers under later acts to deal with civil emergencies, the most important example being terrorist violence in Northern Ireland. Between 1973 and 1976, the Prevention of Terrorism (Temporary Provisions) Acts and Northern Ireland (Emergency Provisions) Act provided a legal basis for the military to 'aid the civil power when requested by

the latter to do so', and for the government to detain suspects without charge for seven days (later reduced to three days with the agreement of a court of law) and to exclude undesirable persons from the UK. More recently the Official Secrets Act 1989 and the Criminal Justice (Terrorism and Conspiracy) Act 1998 gave further legal powers to the authorities in dealing with emergencies and national security.

See also Security Commission; Terrorism Act 2000.

Empire (British)

The foundations for the British Empire were laid in 100 years from the middle of the 18th century, when India, Australia, Canada, New Zealand, Cape Colony and other territories, including Hong Kong, were colonised. In the late 18th century however, the 13 colonies on the eastern American seaboard became engaged in a revolutionary war against the mother country, resulting in the establishment of a separate United States of America in 1787, when its constitution was adopted. During the next phase of empire making Britain was less driven by purely commercial factors and more by a sense of mission, for example abolishing the slave trade and talking of the 'white man's burden' to civilise primitive races and spread Christianity.

In the second half of the 19th century Britain won more colonies through the so-called 'scramble for Africa'. Early in the 20th century the Empire covered over one-fifth of the world's landmass, nearly 12 billion square miles, and contained 410 million people. It used to be said, with pride, that the 'sun never set' on the British Empire. However, the acquisition of more territories after the First World War occurred just when Britain's economic power was beginning to wane and nationalist movements were beginning to flex their muscles. The transfer of power to the Dominions (Canada, Australia, New Zealand and South Africa) was orderly and peaceful, but otherwise the move to independence often involved bitter conflicts, with the imperial power struggling to

hold back the unstoppable tide. India and Burma gained independence in 1947 and decolonisation followed very quickly during the 1950s and 1960s. In 1998 Hong Kong was handed back to China.

See also Commonwealth (British).

Employment Acts 1980, 1982

The basis of the Conservative government's attack on what it believed to be excessive union power. These acts, together with the Trade Union Act 1984, weakened the closed shop; curtailed industrial action by outlawing secondary picketing; and imposed balloting requirements for union officials and for donations to political parties from trade unions (the political levy). Further acts followed in 1988 and 1990. The Labour government elected in 1997 retained many of these, thus signalling a break with Old Labour and the continuation of the Thatcherite restrictive agenda of labour relations, albeit with some 'third way' fine-tuning.

employment tribunal

See tribunal.

enabling authority

Description of a local authority. The 'enabling' model of local public service provision suggests that as many functions as possible should be contracted out to private companies, in order to achieve efficiency and thereby keep local taxes to a minimum. According to this approach, local government plays a strictly limited role, namely contracting out functions and ensuring they are performed correctly and at the lowest possible cost. The Conservative-controlled London borough of Wandsworth is often cited as the classic exemplar of such an authority. The New Labour government of 1997 was committed to substituting the somewhat similar (although allegedly more bureaucratic) 'best value' approach.

energy

Britain in recent years has had an annual increase of 0.5 per cent in its energy consumption and faces a future as a net importer of gas; it is already a net importer of oil. Cost factors make this possibility problematic. In 2001 the percentages of energy sources were: natural gas, 37 per cent; coal, 33 per cent; nuclear, 22 per cent; imports, 3 per cent; oil, 1 per cent; hydro-electricity, 1 per cent; renewable sources, 2 per cent. By 2020, it is estimated the figures will be as follows: gas, 49 per cent; oil, 38 per cent; coal, 6 per cent; renewable sources 4 per cent; and nuclear 3 per cent. The supporters of nuclear power believe it will help fill the gap but there are both safety and cost concerns. There is a prospect that tide-driven turbines – more reliable than wind power and ecologically friendly – could provide more than enough electricity for Britain if developed sufficiently. But the hope that renewable energy will expand to take on a substantial share of energy needs is still highly speculative.

English Civil War, 1642–51

Conflict between supporters of the crown – the Cavaliers – and those of parliament – the Roundheads – under their leader Oliver Cromwell. Its provenance lay in the differences between Charles I and the so-called Long Parliament. Religious differences were especially important, as Archbishop Laud had sought to impose a common liturgy, which had alienated large sections of the populace. The king also tried to impose taxes without the approval of parliament, thereby alienating many of its members. When parliament raised an army led by Cromwell, the king lost the ensuing battle at Edgehill in 1642. He then lost at Marston Moor in 1644. The Roundheads' improved military capacity, reflected in the New Model Army, was confirmed at Naseby in 1645, where Charles was crushed. In 1647 he surrendered. He was beheaded in 1649. Subsequent Cavalier risings in different parts of the country culminated in a more final defeat at Worcester in 1651. Cromwell became lord protector from 1653 to his death in 1658. The Civil War helped settle the long-running conflict between the British crown and parliament, in the latter's favour. From then on

parliament became the final arbiter of how the country was to be governed, culminating in the Glorious Revolution of 1688.

enlargement of the European Union

The 'European Community', as it was once called, originated with the 1957 treaty of Rome and had six signatories. It added three more in 1972 when Britain, Ireland and Denmark joined. Greece, Spain and Portugal joined in the 1980s and then Austria, Sweden and Finland in the wake of the end of the Cold War. In 2004 a whole raft of eastern European states joined and in 2007 Bulgaria and Romania. A number of other states are keen to join, including Turkey and other countries like Ukraine and Georgia, though political problems surround all these possibilities.

Enron

US energy conglomerate. In January 2002 the company crashed, ruining the lives of thousands of its workers. It seemed some of its activities had been facilitated by favours granted in exchange for plentiful cash handouts to key people in the US Congress and government. Some critics pointed to the money donated to New Labour and the subsequent change in policy on gas-fired power stations (which was to Enron's advantage). The government denied undue influence, claiming the change was won by argument, not purchased influence. It was also the case that Enron had given money to the Conservative Party when it had been in power.

entrepreneurial culture

National cultural environment conducive to business. An aspect of Margaret Thatcher's self-appointed mission was to reject the culture of the 'nanny' state in favour of a willingness to invest time and money in launching new money-making projects and individuals standing on their own feet. Most surveys of public attitudes suggested her crusade was not especially successful, as many people still believed that the state had a big part to play in health and social welfare provision. These findings were noted by Tony Blair and his political strategists in their attempt to forge a new consensus on the proper balance between public and private provision. The legacy of this crusade lives on, not least in the language of New Labour, and the plethora of words imported from the business world and now part of everyday language, for example: 'partnerships' for long-term human relationships, and 'delivering' as a serviceable synonym for 'providing'.

See also paternalism; political language.

entryism

A strategy, used by fringe parties, of gaining power and influence by invading a mainstream democratic party. This method was used by the far left in the 1970s to infiltrate the Labour Party and take over its constituency organisations. The Militant Tendency, a Trotskyist grouping, was the most notorious user of the tactic, which was facilitated by an exodus of members from the Labour Party in the wake of the Wilson governments of the 1960s and 1970s. Entryism caused major problems to Labour's public image and provoked bitter internal conflicts, for example in the mid-1980s when Militant-controlled Liverpool City Council (led by Derek Hatton) confronted Neil Kinnock, who was committed to rebuilding the party as a mainstream electoral force. Labour's National Executive Committee expelled a number of prominent militants during this decade. Critics, especially from the left, later suggested that 'right-wing entryism' had taken place in the Labour Party, media professionals and London elites having played a central role in the take-over of the party at national level and the creation of New Labour.

See also far left; Hayward report; Militant Tendency; Whitty report.

Environment Agency

www.environment-agency.gov.uk
All-embracing agency set up in 1996 with a wide range of functions, including: flood de-fence, water resource management, pollution control, fisheries protection (freshwater),

navigation of inland waterways, recreational use of water and land, and conservation of the landscape and archaeological heritage. Ever since the 1970s there had been calls for an integrated body to protect the environment; this involved the unification of several disparate bodies, notably the Pollution Inspectorate, the National Rivers Authority and the waste regulatory authorities. The Environment Agency has been active in initiatives to promote waste minimisation in business. It has not been afraid to prosecute even high-profile offenders, including ICI three times in relation to its plant in Runcorn, Cheshire.

environmental group

Pressure group promoting green issues. Traditionally Britain has a well developed environmental lobby and some estimates place membership of such groups at 4.5 million or 8 per cent of the population. Prominent groups include Friends of the Earth (formed in 1969), Greenpeace (in 1972) and Sustrans (in 1977). As well as these there are bodies like the National Trust and National Heritage. Interest in the environment has burgeoned since the 1970s and has given birth to a new kind of direct action politics. However, the radical potency of the movement has been blunted, to some extent, by mainstream parties, which have developed their own 'light green', consumer-friendly environmental policies.

Equal Opportunities Commission

Body founded in 1975 by the then Labour government to implement the Sex Discrimination Act 1975. Its function was: to promote equality of opportunity; to strive to eliminate discrimination; and to review sex discrimination legislation. Many criticised it for being toothless. In 2007 its role and functions were taken over by the Equality and Human Rights Commission.

equality

A social or political relationship in which no special privilege, benefit or status is bestowed on individuals or groups other than those that are morally or logically justified. Two types of equality can be identified: equality of opportunity and equality in outcomes.

First, equality of *opportunity* refers to a 'level playing field' of rules and conditions between individuals and groups who are in competition for valued social, economic or political rewards. For example, all candidates should be treated equally in the conduct of an examination and the marking of their papers. The British legal system makes use of the associated principle of even-handed treatment, which dictates that people should all be treated alike, regardless of social (or other) status. However, certain categories of persons, for example the police, ministers of the crown and the sovereign do have powers not enjoyed by the 'ordinary' citizen. As far as ideology is concerned, all mainstream parties accept the principle of equality of opportunity, although socialist movements such as Labour have tended to emphasise the socially and morally damaging effects of unrestrained individual liberty, especially with regard to property rights within a capitalist economic system.

Second, equality in *outcomes* is achieved by taking into account differences between individuals or groups in order for people to be placed in the same situation. For example, socialists and civil rights campaigners have promoted the idea of positive discrimination or quotas for disadvantaged groups (such as ethnic minorities, women, the poor) in the world of work. In this case the principle of equal opportunity is suspended in order to achieve a fairer outcome.

Equality Act 2006

The act that set up the Equality and Human Rights Commission (EHRC), which took on the former remits of the Equal Opportunities Commission (EOC), the Commission for Racial Equality (CRE) and the Disability Rights Commission (DRC). It made illegal discrimination on the basis of religion, belief or sexual orientation. It also imposed

an obligation on public bodies to encourage equality of opportunity and discourage discrimination and harassment in the exercise of public functions.

Equality and Human Rights Commission (EHRC)

www.equalityhumanrights.com
Non-departmental public body set up by the Equality Act 2006. The chair is Trevor Phillips, who was previously chair of the Equal Opportunities Commission. The EHRC combined the responsibilities of three former commissions: the Commission for Racial Equality, the Equal Opportunities Commission and the Disability Rights Commission. Some criticised the new body as unwieldy and the appointment of Phillips proved controversial. After supporting the idea of multiculturalism he later condemned it as sleepwalking 'towards segregation'. During July 2009 he came under heavy fire for his managerial style, despite being appointed for a further three-year period by Harriet Harman. However, six of his fellow commissioners resigned that same month and calls were made for his resignation.

established Church

See Church of England.

establishment

A pejorative term for the administrative, professional, business and academic elites who have key positions of influence in the British state. This was first used in recent times, according to historian Peter Hennessy, by journalist Henry Fairlie in his *Spectator* column in September 1955, but more truly entered the language after a well known collection of critical essays edited by the then young historian Hugh Thomas which was entitled *The Establishment* (1959). It contained chapters by, among others, John Vaizey on the class system; Thomas Balogh on the senior civil service; and Fairlie himself on the 'most powerful voice of the establishment', the BBC. Ironically Vaizey and Thomas ended up with peerages and as disciples of Margaret

Thatcher; Hennessy quotes Rose Macauley, who said that 'the moderns of one day become the Establishment of the next'.

ethical foreign policy

When Robin Cook was made foreign secretary in May 1997 he declared there would henceforth be an 'ethical dimension' to the Foreign Office's mission statement, by placing human rights at the heart of the work of his department. A year later critics rounded on policies which seemed to cast doubt on this mission, citing: his approval of arms sales to Sandline International, a mercenary company which assisted General Kabbah in his illegal attempt to regain office in Sierra Leone; and his approval of 64 arms export licences to Indonesia as well as 86 to Turkey for arms which could be used for internal repression. On the other hand, Cook had achieved a new agreement on landmines, a new code on arms exports, and the establishment of the International Criminal Court; he had also promoted the military action which liberated Kosovo. Neal Ascherson, writing in the *Observer* (2 August 1998), judged that other foreign ministers recognised that 'the British, especially during their presidency of the EU, have shown vigour and at times leadership in forcing a human rights dimension into international agreements and institutions'. However, by January 2000 the 'ethical' theme to Foreign Office statements had been toned down, possibly in response to the doubts of officials. Tony Blair's later active support of the US war on terrorism and Iraq was sometimes presented as an extension of this ethical theme but in this case also supporting arguments seemed badly flawed.

See also foreign policy.

ethical socialism

The name given to the ideas of 19th-century socialist thinkers, for example Robert Owen and William Morris, who condemned capitalism as an evil system and advocated a socialist society in which private enterprise would be abolished and human nature changed for the better. This was a noble

vision, if a somewhat vague approach, which offered no answers to several key questions: How free would people be in a socialist society? How would wealth be created? Who would be in charge of the economy? Tony Blair attempted to reintroduce elements of ethical socialism into his approach to social problems, although critics pointed out that he was doing so just as he was burying traditional notions of the doctrine within the party.

See also Christian socialism.

ethnic minority

See immigration.

ethnicity

Refers to social groups who distinguish themselves from others, or are distinguished by others, by differences in cultural behaviour – which may include language and religion – or physical appearance. Sociologists often use this term to describe British citizens who can trace their origins to Commonwealth countries or émigrés fleeing persecution in eastern Europe in the first half of the 20th century. The term 'race' is seldom used as a sociological description owing to its direct association with the discredited eugenics movement and the bogus scientism of the Nazis in the 1930s.

In the 2001 census, the ethnic composition of the UK was 92.1 per cent white and 7.9 per cent ethnic minorities (the respective 1991 census figures had been 94.5 per cent and 5.5 per cent). The distribution of ethnic minorities is very uneven, with most being concentrated in the inner cities and very few in rural or semi-rural areas. This has favoured the Labour Party, which is perceived by many ethnic voters as close to meeting their economic and social concerns. However, there is evidence that second- and third-generation ethnic Britons are now moving up the class ladder, securing jobs in the professions and adopting middle-class lifestyles. The full impact of this on British politics, and party allegiance in particular, has yet to become clear. It would seem, however, that all mainstream parties would need to broaden their appeal by increasing membership among ethnic minorities and placing their concerns on the political agenda. In 2003, Labour seemed to have the best opportunity of achieving this – for the reasons stated above and the fact that the Labour government was committed to tackling social exclusion – but the Iraq war lost the party support among Muslims. The Conservatives are less well placed, as they tend to be associated with harsh immigration controls and a lack of sympathy with ethnic groups, whether deserved or not. David Cameron, however, elected Tory leader in 2006, has tried hard to modify his party's attitude towards immigrant groups and to encourage more ethnic minority candidates.

eugenics
The 'science' of how the physical and mental attributes of a population can be enhanced through policies which improve the 'breeding stock'. It was popular across Europe in the latter part of the 19th and early part of the 20th century. Some British intellectuals flirted with the idea, including Sidney and Beatrice Webb and George Bernard Shaw. However, it is now more widely known for its adoption by the Nazi regime, which sought to engineer a dominant Aryan race and eliminate 'inferior' races.

euro
The European single currency. European economic and monetary union (EMU) was a dream of Europhiles for many years, although it was not officially mentioned until the Single European Act of 1986. The Delors plan included an inter-governmental conference on EMU and this in turn led to the 1992 Maastricht treaty, which called for the eventual creation of a single currency. A European Central Bank was set up to supervise the single currency and in January 1999 11 members of the European Union subscribed to the new currency; by 2010 this had increased to 16. Britain and three other member states decided to stay out and wait until the conditions were right for them to join. This 'wait and see' policy provided both John

Major and Tony Blair with their positions, although chancellor Gordon Brown insisted on five conditions being met before Britain could join the single currency. In January 2002 euro notes and coins were introduced in the then 12 'Euroland' countries and this applied more pressure to the Labour government to declare itself willing to risk a referendum on Britain joining. However, Brown stood firm, despite signs that opinion might be shifting slightly towards entry, with a majority believing it to be in any case inevitable.

See also European economic and monetary union; five tests.

Eurocommunism
Body of thought developed in the 1970s by Italian, French and Spanish communists. Essentially this new approach disengaged communism from the USSR as the sole model and argued that each party needed to adapt to national conditions. It also urged collaboration with other 'progressive' forces to transform society to the left. In Britain the emergence of a Eurocommunist faction helped bring about the demise of the Communist Party of Great Britain.

'Europe des patries'
'Europe of the nations' is a phrase associated with French president Charles de Gaulle in the 1960s when he insisted the emergent European Community should not be evolving towards any kind of federation but should remain an organisation in which states could retain their own character and express their own personalities. The difficult general, had he lived long enough, would have found many echoes of his ideas in the Euroscepticism of Margaret Thatcher and others in the British Conservative Party and other parties throughout Europe who favour a loose economic arrangement rather than a European 'super-state'.

European Atomic Energy Community (Euratom)
Organisation formed by the treaty of Rome (1957) to promote and develop

peaceful uses of atomic energy in Europe. In 1967 it merged with the European Coal and Steel Community (ECSC) and the European Economic Community (EEC) to become part of the European Community (EC).

European Commission
http://ec.europa.eu
The main administrative body of the European Union (EU), sometimes known as 'the College of Commissioners'. It is the most dynamic element of the EU and has responsibility for: proposing legislation and policies; implementing the decisions of the EU Council and parliament; enforcing European law (jointly with the Court of Justice); and representing the EU on the international stage.

Members of the Commission are supposed to uphold the interests of the EU as a whole and not to be bound by loyalty to their own home countries. Its president used often to be seen as the embodiment of the EU and its most important spokesperson and leader. However, following the 2009 Lisbon treaty a president of the European Council has partially taken over this role. Usually members of the Commission are distinguished politicians who have a commitment to the idea of Europe. Previously, the bigger countries nominated two each of the then 20 commissioners and the smaller countries one, but in 2010 27 commissioners were drawn from the 27 member states. The president of the Commission remains José Manuel Barroso, appointed in 2004. After Baroness Ashton's appointment as high representative for foreign and security policy, her role was judged to be the equivalent of a Commissioner portfolio, so there was no replacement.

European Conservatives and Reformist Group (ECR)
www.ecrgroup.eu
Set up in July 2009, this is one of seven political groupings in the European parliament. It is Eurosceptic and anti-federalist. It has 54 MEPs, including

the British Conservatives, who left the mainstream European People's Party (EPP) Group on the grounds that it was inherently federalist. The move was criticised by some Conservative MEPs and more widely by those who objected to the allegedly racist and homophobic attitudes of some ECR members.

European constitution
Proposed constitution for the European Union (EU). A European convention, chaired by former French president Giscard D'Estaing, was established to draw up a draft constitution for the EU by May 2004, when 10 new members joined. The aim was to reshape and simplify existing treaties. After several years of fairly intense discussion the resultant document was deemed, by most commentators, to favour the larger, more populous countries in the form of decision-making proposed. A charter of fundamental rights was resisted by some British experts on the grounds that this would cut across Britain's unwritten constitution. Similarly, a proposed new foreign minister for the EU was controversial, as it appeared to undermine the sovereign rights of nations to conduct their own relations with others. Defence, too, was problematic, especially the idea favoured by France, Belgium and Germany for a new defence planning staff, to be set up in Tervuren in Belgium.

The British government initially argued that no referendum was necessary on the new constitution as it did not propose to alter the fundamental nature of Britain's relationship to the EU. The Conservatives vigorously disagreed and Michael Howard, once installed as leader in November 2003, threw his weight behind the campaign to hold a referendum, in line with certain other member states. In the spring of 2004 Tony Blair performed a *volte face* on the issue (and was consequently much criticised by supporters of the EU) and declared a referendum would be held. In the event, no referendum was held, much to the anger of Eurosceptics.

See also Lisbon treaty; red lines.

European Convention on Human Rights (ECHR)

Convention of the Council of Europe, established in Rome in 1950 and signed by Britain in 1951. It spells out those rights which should be protected – for example the rights to life and freedom of thought and speech – and lays down the procedures for determining infringements. If necessary, cases can be referred to the European Court of Human Rights. Following a pledge in the 1997 Labour manifesto, the Convention was incorporated into British domestic law via the Human Rights Act 1998. This had the effect of adding another written element to the British constitution, as well as giving a more political, more interpretive role to senior judges. From October 2000 British courts began to hear cases brought by British citizens under the Convention. Tony Blair's wife, Cherie, was involved in new chambers, Matrix, formed to specialise in human rights cases. In August 2001 several inmates of a detention centre for asylum seekers at Oakhampton took legal action under the new human rights legislation. They claimed their rights had been violated through their physical detention in the centre when they offered no threat to the community. The judge upheld their claim, angering the Home Office and leading to some calls for new legislation to make detention of asylum seekers legal: a difficult measure as it would require the recasting of the ECHR itself and the agreement of all signatories.

See also European Court of Human Rights.

European Council

See Council of the European Union.

European Court of Human Rights

www.echr.coe.int

The court established in Strasbourg by the 1950 European Convention on Human Rights. It hears cases referred to it from the European Commission of Human Rights when a satisfactory resolution has not been found to a case where an individual

has complained of a violation of rights by the government of a member state. Court rulings have had far-reaching effects, for example forcing Ireland to drop its constitutional clauses against homosexuals. By the early 1990s Britain had appeared before the court some 200 times and was found guilty of violations in two-thirds of cases. In 1998 the European Convention on Human Rights was incorporated into British domestic law; the major advantage of this for claimants is that is they can now have their cases heard in British courts, thus saving time and not an inconsiderable amount of money.

See also European Convention on Human Rights.

European Court of Justice

http://europa.eu/institutions/inst/justice

Body that deals with alleged breaches of European Union law. It is based in Luxembourg and is formally entitled the Court of Justice of the European Communities (it should not be confused with the European Court of Human Rights at Strasbourg). It ensures that European treaties are observed and their terms are interpreted fairly. It is the highest court in the EU. It comprises one judge from each member state – currently 27 – who are assisted by eight advocates general. Cases can be brought before the court by member states or institutions of the EU or by the Commission against non-complying members. Individuals who feel European laws have been breached to their disadvantage can also bring cases against national governments. Most of the court's work, however, arises from requests from member states for clarification of aspects of European Community law. Only the most important cases are heard in plenary sessions of seven judges; mostly panels of three sit in hearings, which vary from rulings on treaties to rulings on decisions made by the Commission. Because of the weight of cases, a Court of First Instance has been set up to deal with minor cases; it is now known as the General Court.

European economic and monetary union (EMU)

A key element of the development of the European Union (EU), involving the creation of the single currency for member states. Supporters believe it will deliver prosperity and long-term peace, while opponents point to the erosion of national sovereignty, especially in domestic economic policy making (public expenditure planning and taxation). In particular, they fear it could never serve the heterogeneous needs of so many different economies; for example, some will require high interest rates to control inflationary pressures, whereas others will not need such monetary constraint. Some suggest that the tensions will be such that economic disaster for millions of Europeans will result.

EMU was launched in the summer of 1998, when 11 countries joined the scheme; the other four member states of the EU at the time, including Britain, withheld judgement and membership until it had got under way after January 1999. By January 2000 the euro was trading badly on the foreign exchanges and sections of the British political and economic class were signalling at best a cooling of interest in the scheme. The crisis caused by the acute indebtedness of eurozone countries in 2010 ruled out any chance of UK membership for the foreseeable future.

European Economic Area (EAA)

Free trade area formed through collaboration between members of the European Free Trade Association (EFTA) and the European Union (EU). It enables member states to participate in the European Union's single market without actually joining the EU. It was set up in 1993 by a treaty signed in Oporto and now embraces the 27 EU members plus Iceland, Liechtenstein and Norway. The EEA Council meets twice a year at ministerial level; the Joint Committee, comprising senior officials, meets monthly and takes decisions by consensus. The EEA Joint Parliamentary Committee meets twice a year for discussions on general matters, with the EEA Joint Consultative Committee performing a similar role.

European Economic Community (EEC)

One of the three institutions that merged in 1967 to become the European Community and in turn the European Union. After the Second World War a number of idealists, including the two French statesmen Jean Monnet and Robert Schuman, set up the European movement. Monnet believed the problem of national sovereignty would have to be tackled on one 'front' at a time. The strategy began with heavy industry – coal and steel – but Monnet made it clear this was only a 'narrow front' and the ultimate objective was political integration. After the formation of a number of European organisations the core countries of France, Germany, Belgium, Italy, the Netherlands and Luxembourg came together to form the European Economic Community, more popularly known as the Common Market, by signing the treaty of Rome in 1957. This had the eventual aim of furthering economic efficiency and consumer choice by removing trade tariffs, facilitating the free movement of goods, services, persons and capital, and the necessary harmonisation of the legislation of each member state. Thus economic logic would demand a degree of political union. Britain, which had shown little warmth towards the idea in its early days, changed its mind once the experiment proved economically successful. It tried unsuccessfully to join twice in the 1960s – French president Charles de Gaulle vetoed the 'Anglo-Saxon' application – but was admitted in 1973 when the application made by Edward Heath's government was accepted. In 1993 the term EEC was superseded by 'European Union' (EU).

See also European Atomic Energy Community; European Union.

European election

The means whereby membership of the European parliament is determined. Elections take place every five years. There are 736 members. The UK presently elects 72 MEPs. In 1999 the system was changed to the regional list; the UK then still managed a turnout of only 24 per cent, compared with an EU average of some 50 per cent. The Conservatives, who fought a Eurosceptical campaign, won the most seats (36 out of 87) based on this pitifully low turnout. On 10 June 2004 postal voting in the European elections helped raise turnout to a still woefully low 37 per cent (compared with an EU-wide average of 45 per cent). At 52 per cent Northern Ireland had the highest turnout, but the south-west only 31 per cent. Both the main parties, competing for the lower total of 75 seats (following the entry of 10 new EU members in May 2004), lost votes and seats: Conservatives 27 per cent of the vote and 27 seats (down 9) and Labour 23 per cent of the vote and 19 seats (down 6). The Liberal Democrats gained 15 per cent of the vote and 12 seats (down 2) and the Greens gained 2 seats from 6.3 per cent of the vote. The British National Party garnered 5 per cent but no seats. However, the spectacular success of these elections belonged to the UK Independence Party (UKIP), campaigning on a platform of withdrawal from the EU: it gained 16 per cent of the vote and 12 seats (up 2 from 1999). In June 2009, 72 UK MEPs were elected: Conservatives 25, UKIP 13, Labour 13, Liberal Democrats 11, Greens 2, British National Party 2, Scottish National Party 2 and Plaid Cymru 1, with the other three seats in Northern Ireland.

See also European parliament.

European Free Trade Association (EFTA)

www.efta.int

Set up in 1960 as a low-tariff agreement to counter the European Economic Community. It originally comprised Britain, Denmark, Portugal, Austria, Norway, Sweden and Switzerland. Some countries left EFTA to join the European Union (EU) but other countries later joined EFTA. In 1994 the diminished EFTA and the EU established the European Economic Area as a common market.

European idea

Enthusiasts for the ideal of a federal Europe originally helped to launch the idea of a united continent from previously warring countries. In a poll taken in 1994, the populations of eight out of the then 12 member states of the European Union (EU) registered a minority of supporters for the federal ideal. In Britain, enthusiasm for all things European tends to be lower than in most other member states, with opposition concentrating in the Conservative Party, where the Eurosceptics caused John Major's government so much trouble. Advocates of the European idea are often accused by 'sceptics' of being a small elite who wield great power from positions of authority within the governing classes of EU countries and impose their integrationist policies on populations who often object when they learn the facts or are consulted in referendums.

European Monetary System (EMS)

An arrangement whereby the members of the European Union fixed the exchange rates of their currencies to guard against large fluctuations. It began in 1979 with the aim of countering inflation and encouraging steady economic growth. The main instrument used was the adjustment of interest rates to keep variations within a narrow range, called the Exchange Rate Mechanism. In 1994 the European Monetary Institute was set up as a transitional step towards the European Central Bank (ECB) and a common currency. The ECB was created in 1998 and in 1999 the single currency, the euro, was introduced, though Britain, Denmark and Sweden opted to stay outside the 11-nation 'euro-zone', while Greece joined it in 2001, and later Cyprus, Malta, Slovakia and Slovenia.

European parliament

www.europarl.europa.eu

The 'legislature' of the European Union (EU) but for many years seen merely as a 'talking shop', with scant powers in relation to the European Commission and Council of Ministers. However, since the 1980s it has acquired considerable powers and its prestige has grown accordingly. Plenary sessions take place in Strasbourg yet, awkwardly, committee meetings take place in Brussels and nonsensically its secretariat is based in Luxembourg. The parliament used to be a feeble democratic instrument but in the 1970s it gained influence over the Community budget and with the Single European Act in 1987 it gained more legislative power. At Maastricht in 1992 it also gained 'co-decision' powers, which gave it ultimate power to reject legislation altogether. In addition it has the ability to veto the accession of new member states. MEPs sit according to compatible ideological groups, which include: Greens, Socialists, Liberals and the European Conservatives and Reformist Group (which includes the British Conservatives). Britain initially refused to use proportional representation for elections to the European parliament, unlike the other member states, as the Conservatives in particular felt it would be the thin end of the wedge for similar changes for Westminster elections. However, the change was made when Labour came to power in 1997 and the first elections using proportional representation, based on 11 electoral districts nationwide, were held in 1999.

Results in the 1999 election reflected a very low turnout – 24 per cent – and some sympathy for the Conservatives' Eurosceptic manifesto: 36 Conservative, 29 Labour, 10 Liberal Democrat, 3 UK Independence Party, 2 Green, 2 Plaid Cymru, 2 SNP, 3 others. Criticism was made of the way in which the regional lists and the order of candidates were drawn up, even though all parties claimed members were consulted as much as possible.

In June 2004 the Conservatives won 27 seats, Labour 19, the Liberal Democrats 12, the UK Independence Party (UKIP) 12, the Scottish National Party 3, the Greens 2 and Plaid Cymru 2.

In 2009 the results were: Conservatives 27 per cent and 25 seats; UKIP 17 per cent and 13 seats; Labour 16 per cent and 13 seats; Liberal Democrats 14 per cent and 11 seats; Greens 9 per cent and 2 seats; British National Party (BNP) 6 per cent and 2 seats; Scottish National Party 2 per cent and 2 seats; Plaid Cymru 1 per cent and 1 seat. These results were regarded as disastrous for Labour, both for coming behind UKIP and for the BNP result.

The 2009 Lisbon treaty gave the European parliament legislative powers equal to the Council's in most areas, including powers over the entire EU budget.

See also European Union decision making; regional party list.

European rebate to Britain
Money refunded to Britain from its contribution to the European budget. The question of a rebate arose upon the accession to power of Margaret Thatcher in 1979. Her advisors noted that Britain received only a tenth of Community agricultural expenditure, which comprised two-thirds of the total budget, while it contributed a fifth of the Community's revenue. They argued that Britain's contribution was higher than was merited by its gross domestic product (ranked seventh in the European Community); indeed, Britain and Germany were the only net contributors, while all the others were recipients. Thatcher refused an initial offer of £350 million, despite Foreign Office advice to settle, and she held out stubbornly for more. She eventually won £2 billion for the years 1981–82 plus a formula for annual rebates. Her stance convinced her that intransigence was the best way to deal with the Community.

In July 2004 it was argued by EU partners that Britain's revived economy now made the rebates unnecessary but Tony Blair emphatically refused to accept this.

European Regional Development Fund (ERDF)
Set up in 1975 to help poorer areas within the European Community. The ERDF and European Social Fund (ESF) demonstrate that the European institution now fills the gap left by the nation state, since many economically distressed regions

across Europe have common interests best served by a supranational organisation. The UK has benefited from regional aid in areas like Northern Ireland and Merseyside. Enlargement of the EU means that available funds are spread more thinly, especially as many of the new members are relatively poor.

European Social Fund (ESF)

Used by the European Union to feed resources into social policy programmes connected, for example, with employment training or retraining. Both this and the European Regional Development Fund benefited from the desire in the 1980s to achieve 'cohesion' and to avoid any disadvantage being suffered by member states as a result of the internal market. Enlargement of the EU means that available funds are spread more thinly, especially as many of the new members are relatively poor.

European Union (EU)

http://europa.eu

Intergovernmental and supranational organisation that can be traced back to the treaty of Paris, signed in 1951, when France and Germany established, under the Schuman plan, the European Coal and Steel Community (ECSC). Since then, the organisation has deepened in terms of integration and enlarged in terms of membership. In 1957 the treaty of Rome established the European Economic Community (EEC) and Euratom and was signed by the then six member states. In 1986, the Single European Act (SEA) put into effect the idea of a Europe open to trade, qualifications, movement of workers and important aspects of regional and social policy. In 1992 the Maastricht treaty accelerated the processes of integration, though prime minister John Major negotiated an opt-out from the provisions of the Social Chapter. With Maastricht came a formal change of name to reflect more properly the unifying nature of the organisation: European Union. By 1992, the EU had a number of institutions: the

European Commission, the Council of Ministers, the European parliament and the European Court of Justice.

The stated objective of the EU is to move towards greater economic and political union, but members differ in their enthusiasm for such a goal. Britain was initially kept out of the EEC by French president Charles de Gaulle, who was suspicious of Britain's 'special relationship' with the USA, but after his death France withdrew its veto and Britain joined in 1972, premier Edward Heath signing the treaty of accession.

In 2004 10 new members joined the EU, taking total membership up to 25; in 2007 Bulgaria and Romania joined, making it 27 in all.

European Union constitution

See European constitution.

European Union decision making

Complex process involving a number of separate procedures. Very generally the process can be seen to originate in the European Commission, which has always consulted widely before putting forward a policy proposal. The proposal is then forwarded to the Council of Ministers, where it is considered by specialist officials of member states. At the same time it is sent to the European parliament and the Economic and Social Committee, which submit reactions to the Council. The so-called 'co-decision' and 'consultation' reactions are the most frequent. During this phase extensive lobbying takes place before a decision is reached. The 2009 Lisbon treaty increased the number of policy areas where the European parliament has to approve European legislation, together with the European Council of Ministers (the co-decision procedure).

See also Council of Ministers; European Commission; European parliament.

Europhile

Person or party enthusiastic about the European idea and the European Union (EU). Early Europhiles included Winston

Churchill and Ernest Bevin, though there were limits to their enthusiasm. The most enthusiastic Conservatives after Churchill included Harold Macmillan, Edward Heath (who negotiated Britain's entry in 1972), Michael Heseltine and Kenneth Clarke. On the Labour side Roy Jenkins – a president of the Commission – was prominently pro-Europe, as was Tony Blair. The Liberal Democrats are the most pro-EU of the mainstream parties; the *Guardian*, *Independent* and *Observer* are the most Europhile of the major newspapers.

Eurosceptic

A word popularly used to describe a person or party opposed to further economic or more especially political integration within the European Union (EU). Some believe such integration will erode British sovereignty and lose the country valuable national symbols, like the pound. Others argue for complete withdrawal from the EU. Opposition has existed ever since Britain proposed to join the European Community and used to characterise the approach of Labour's left wing in the late 1960s and early 1970s. However, this faded and by the 1980s the Conservatives became the chief Eurosceptic party. A small group of recalcitrant MPs, led by William Cash (not to mention a group in the Lords led by Norman Tebbit), eventually had the whip withdrawn in 1994 for their open hostility to John Major's attempt to get the Maastricht treaty through parliament, although it was soon restored. In April and June 1996 two anti-European motions attracted the support of one-third of back-bench Conservative MPs. During the 1997 general election the split between the Eurosceptics and the leadership, especially over Britain's putative membership of the European single currency, contributed to the party's and leader's difficulties. Divided parties lose elections and the Conservatives were deeply divided over Europe; they suffered one of their worst defeats in 1997. Leading Eurosceptics included: John Biffen

(who saw himself almost as a mentor to the sceptics), Teddy Taylor, Nicholas Budgen, George Gardiner, John Wilkinson, Lord (Woodrow) Wyatt, Lord Beloff, Lord MacAlpine and, of course, Margaret Thatcher. Labour Eurosceptics included Dennis Skinner and Austin Mitchell, though the best known was probably the late Peter Shore and Tony Benn. There are also many Eurosceptics in the rank and file of both the Labour Party and the Conservative Party.

The UK Independence Party (UKIP) won 16 per cent of the vote in the June 2004 European elections; nearly half of these votes came from former Conservatives but a fifth were drawn from Labour voters.

Some rich business people are prepared to fund Eurosceptic parties: for example the late James Goldsmith and the Yorkshire businessman Paul Sykes.

The British press is characterised by a number of broadsheets and tabloids hostile to the idea of closer integration, most notably the *Sun* and the other Murdoch-owned papers, the *Times* and *Sunday Times*. The *Daily Mail*, the *Express* and the *Daily Telegraph* have been hostile to a greater or lesser degree.

An *Economist* poll on 30 May 2009 revealed that UK enthusiasm for the EU has been declining for a number of years. Over the past quarter century: the proportion of people thinking the EU is a 'good thing' had declined from 43 per cent to 31 per cent; those thinking it a 'bad thing' had risen from 30 per cent to 37 per cent.

e-voting

Voting by electronic means. In July 2002 a consultation paper was released on e-voting that suggested it had a bright future. According to the proposals the existing system of ballot papers and voting booths would be scrapped and all voters offered four voting options: online from home or work, by post, by telephone, or at polling stations equipped with online terminals. The hope is that such new accessibility will increase voter turnout and help reverse evidence of voter apathy. The proposal was to set up the new system by 2006 and to have the electoral register maintained electronically. A total of £30 million was allocated to develop e-voting over the years 2002–05. By 2009 little progress had been made to introduce such innovations.

Exchange Rate Mechanism (ERM)

The part of the European Monetary System of the European Union (EU) which attempted to maintain exchange rates within a narrow band. Nigel Lawson and Geoffrey Howe, the British chancellor and foreign secretary respectively, were in favour of joining but succeeded in persuading Margaret Thatcher only in late 1990 and then at a rate to the Deutschmark of £2.95, which would be hard to sustain. In the autumn of 1992 currency speculators targeted the weaker EU currencies in the ERM. Given fears about the future of European integration, there was a huge exodus of currency out of the weaker ones – the lire, pound and franc – into the Deutschmark. Britain was unable to persuade Germany, scarred by unhappy memories of inflation, to reduce interest rates, and on 16 September 1992 ('Black Wednesday') Britain became the subject of a concerted attempt by speculators to exploit the weakness of the pound. Two increases in interest rates had no effect, nor did huge sums transferred from Britain's foreign exchange reserves, and the chancellor, Norman Lamont, had to withdraw Britain from the ERM and effectively devalue the pound. The value of the pound fell quickly, aided by sharp cuts in interest rates. Ironically, the economy began to recover from recession but the impression of economic incompetence was very damaging to Conservative fortunes and some commentators date their loss in 1997 and subsequent decline to this single catastrophic event.

See also Black Wednesday; European Monetary System.

exclusion

See social exclusion.

executive

Often used to describe the institutions tasked with the job of day-to-day government or the execution of policy. In Britain this would include the cabinet, departments of state, the civil service and other agencies of government. The other two branches of government usually cited are the legislature (law-making bodies) and the judiciary (law enforcement and interpretation).

executive agency

A generic term for any government body but given specific sense by the Ibbs report in 1988, which led to the so-called 'Next Steps' agencies. These represent the hiving off of certain of the more routine government functions to new organisations, which are given substantial management and financial autonomy under a director, who reports to the permanent secretary of the department involved. The idea is to relieve the workload and responsibility falling upon ministers. Examples include the Driver and Vehicle Licensing Agency, the Central Office of Information and the Ordnance Survey. By the spring of 1997 nearly 80 per cent of all civil servants were employed in some 200 agencies. Tony Blair fully accepted that the agencies were part of Britain's system of public administration and went further with plans to privatise National Air Traffic Services (NATS) and a number of other public services. However, major concerns have been expressed by many observers at the lack of accountability of the agencies, which are run at arm's length from the minister, away from direct parliamentary scrutiny.

exit poll

An opinion poll commissioned either by a party or by a media organisation which takes place immediately after people have voted at a polling station. Such polls are said to be more reliable, for a number of technical and psychological reasons. However, in the 1992 general election the technique was questioned, along with the polling industry generally, when, together with late campaign polls, exit polls overestimated Labour support and resulted in a gross underestimate of the Conservative vote during the coverage of the event on television; instead of the expected neck-and-neck race, the Conservatives won by 7 percentage points. The problem was circumvented in revised methods of polling used for the 1997 general election.

exploitation

In general terms, the unfair extraction of benefit or an advantage taken from another person or group. Although a feature of many societies, though not necessarily of all, the term is closely associated with Karl Marx's analysis of power in a capitalist society based on his studies of 19th-century Britain. He argued that the owners of the production process receive unfairly the value created from the work of their employees (termed surplus labour value) and who thus 'exploit' them. The concept was based on the labour theory of value first adduced by John Locke, who stated: 'whoever created things from nature by their own labours had joined to it something that is his own, and thereby makes it his Property'. Marx developed this idea that the exchange value of a good was determined by the quantity of labour that had gone into producing it. The worker was entitled to this value but received only enough to continue living. The capitalist extracted the 'surplus value' and the workers were thus 'exploited'. Clause four of the Labour Party constitution, abandoned after Tony Blair became leader in 1994, referred to these arguments when it stated its objective of securing for the 'workers ... the full fruits of their industry'.

extra-parliamentary party

Political party that is not represented in parliament. There are a number of these in Britain, especially on the far left and far right. The first past the post electoral system discriminates against smaller parties in that those with thin national support find it difficult to win any seats. Being excluded from parliament means effectively being excluded from shaping the political agenda

and most extra-parliamentary parties have short, unhappy lives.

Some Marxist parties have condemned the parliamentary struggle as a diversion, as part of the mystification used by the ruling class to disguise their dominance. Instead, they urge action on the streets and the mobilisation of the workers for some form of revolution. To date, workers have tended to ignore such injunctions, preferring to earn enough to keep themselves and their families rather than risk everything in a speculative revolutionary process. Modern Marxists argue that this is an important feature of capitalist democracies, where formal or procedural rights, such as the freedom to vote, obscure powerful economic forces, which make 'citizens' prisoners of their material circumstances.

F

Fabian Society

www.fabian-society.org.uk
Left-of-centre membership-based think-tank, founded in 1884 by such socialist intellectuals as Sidney and Beatrice Webb, George Bernard Shaw and H. G. Wells. The Fabians followed the cautious strategies of the Roman general Fabius Maximus and favoured a gradual, reformist path to socialism. It was a founding member of the Labour Representation Committee in 1900 and did much to encourage development of early policies via pamphlets, books and discussion events like summer schools. These roles continue to the present day; the Society has several thousand members, including some half of the Parliamentary Labour Party. Few would claim, however, that the Fabians now exert as much influence as they did during the early days of the labour movement.

See also Labour Representation Committee.

POLITICS

Factortame case, 1990

Landmark case brought by the Spanish company Factortame against the British government. It illustrated the impact of membership of the European Union on British law. The case originated when Spanish trawler owners challenged the British Merchant Shipping Act 1988, which had sought to prevent 'quota-hopping', on the grounds that it was contrary to European law regarding the registration of shipping. Eventually the European Court of Justice found for the trawler owners, and this emphasised the superiority of European law over domestic law and the fact that Britain was no longer supreme as it once was over its own laws: a higher European authority had proved it could overrule statute law.

Falklands war

The Falkland Islands form an archipelago (with two main islands) in the South Atlantic of some 12,000 square miles and a population just over 3,000 in 2008. They were invaded on 2 April 1982 by the right-wing military government of Argentina. The Falklands had been claimed for Britain in 1690 and became a colony in 1833. Sheep farming is the main occupation and the islands were known as a telecommunications relay station. Once they were occupied by Argentina, Margaret Thatcher's government sent a naval task force to recapture them. Shuttle diplomacy by the US secretary of state and intervention by the United Nations failed to prevent a short but vicious conflict in which several ships were sunk on both sides, the most controversial being the British sinking of the General Belgrano, an Argentinean battle cruiser which was heading away from the battle zone when torpedoed. The war and the fortunes of the task force on these inhospitable islands transfixed public opinion. Thatcher, then unpopular at home, won plaudits for her coolness of nerve and determination to repel the enemy. Argentinean forces on the islands surrendered on 14 June 1982. The war succeeded in strengthening the political position of Thatcher's government and she gained a huge win in the 1983 general election, albeit over a divided opposition. The Argentinean government fell and was replaced by a democratically elected one. The islands continue to be occupied by a British force and agreement over their future is still to be reached between the two countries.

See also General Belgrano.

family

Most people live in families and accordingly families have long been the concern of governments. Margaret Thatcher famously said 'There is no such thing as society. There are individual men and women and there are their families'. This tended to stress individualism at the expense of the collective, which has been a Labour theme. The Office for National Statistics calculated in 2007 that there were 17.1 million families in the country, averaging 1.8 children each. Seventy-one per cent were headed by a married couple (a disproportionate percentage of whom lived in London), with an average income of £32,779, with 90 per cent of men going out to work and 68 per cent of women. Seventy-nine per cent lived in a house that was mortgaged; 65 per cent had a computer, 52 per cent a pet and 79 per cent a mobile phone. Figures show that a fair number people aged 20–24 still live with their families: 58 per cent of men and 39 per cent of women. Inevitably, family concerns – income, employment, prices, schools, health care, benefits, pensions – are all major political issues. Conservatives tend to stress in addition that the family is the basic 'building block' of society, which deserves support, along with the institution of marriage; Labour reflects many similar concerns, though perhaps gives more recognition to co-habiting families with children. Persuaded that the early years are crucial to later intellectual and emotional development, Labour initiated the Sure Start programme, something which the Conservatives came also to support in the 2010 general election.

POLITICS

far left

Parties centring on Marxist or Trotskyist ideas. There are several such parties in Britain. In both cases emphasis is placed upon a 'vanguard party' of hardened revolutionaries who will lead the masses when the time is right and resist the inevitable counter-revolution of capitalism. Trotsky was a renegade communist to followers of the orthodox Moscow line but his vision of worldwide revolution was attractive to western activists on the left, and a number of factions supported his views. The originally Moscow-leaning Communist Party of Great Britain folded in 1991 to become the more pluralist and gradualist Democratic Left. The Revolutionary Socialist League spawned a number of followers, among them Militant Tendency, formed under the influence of Pat Taafe and Ted Grant on Merseyside. Militant used entryism to influence the Labour Party but this tactic was rebuffed by Labour in the 1980s and the influence of the far left declined once Tony Blair became Labour's electoral saviour after 1994. Other left-wing parties include the Socialist Workers Party, the Workers Revolutionary Party and a host of others, almost all with small memberships and minimal electoral support.

far right

Parties centring on fascist and racist ideas. The British Union of Fascists was established by Oswald Mosley in the 1930s. His violent rallies in the East End of London were curbed by legislation and Mosley was interned during the war in case he aided the enemy. After the war he attempted to revive his party but to no avail. In the late 1960s the National Front emerged from a coalescence of right-wing groups and fought some elections with scant success. After 1979 Margaret Thatcher's tough line on immigration tended to attract back right-wing members for mainstream Conservatism and the National Front's fortunes slumped yet again. Combat 18 overtly uses violence and infiltration to achieve an impact; it targets football hooligans for recruitment and support.

The British National Party (BNP) is the closest to a successor to the National Front in recent years. In 1993 the BNP won a council seat in Tower Hamlets and in 2001 two BNP candidates polled over 10 per cent in the two Oldham constituencies. The BNP also won a council seat in early 2003 near Halifax. In June 2009 the BNP enjoyed its greatest success to date when it managed to elect two candidates as MEPs in Brussels; the election of its leader Nick Griffin in the north-west resulted from the dramatic decline in the Labour vote.

Although small in number, far-right groups contribute to the shaping of the political agenda by exploiting popular concerns of the day, such as capital punishment, child abuse or alleged bogus asylum seekers. A recent development has been a change in language, evident in groups' websites, where a more reasonable, quasi-intellectual tone has replaced the crude and overtly offensive 'rants' of former years, but which nevertheless promote a thesis of 'white tribe' separateness.

fascism

Right-wing ideology based on authoritarian nationalism. The term, based on the Latin symbol of the state, a bundle of rods or *fasces*, was usurped by Mussolini's movement, which came to power in Italy in 1922. Subsequently it has been used as a generic term for similar ideologies. Fascism is based on: xenophobic nationalism; worship of a unified state; a revered and charismatic leader; a fundamentalist vision of society; a struggle to achieve these objectives both domestically and internationally; and a hostility to social pluralism and liberal democracy. These ideas were put into practice in Mussolini's Italy and influenced, along with other factors, the development of National Socialism or Nazism in Germany. However, Italian fascism lacked the highly systematised and terrorist elements of German National Socialism, and did not have the latter's single-minded obsession with racial purity.

Generally speaking, British people have tended to steer away from extremist nationalistic ideologies, especially any containing overt hatred of others, despite a recognisable xenophobic tendency which surfaces periodically, as in the growth of Mosley's British Union of Fascists in the 1930s, support for the National Front in the 1970s, Enoch Powell's ideas and those of the BNP.

fat cat
Derogatory name given to executives of big companies who receive excessive salaries. It became an issue in the autumn of 2001 when Lord Simpson, the head of Marconi, received a £2 million payoff after presiding over a catastrophic slump in share price from £20.50 per share to a mere 29 pence: effectively a loss of 98 per cent of the multinational's value. The company had to lay off 10,000 employees. This followed the award of £1.3 million to Gerald Corbett, former head of Railtrack, who failed to turn the ailing service around but who nevertheless benefited hugely and went on to another lucrative job with Woolworths. Such rewards were hard to justify at any time (the usual argument is that huge salaries are necessary to prevent able managers from being 'poached' by US companies) but even more so when the recipients have clearly failed to make their companies more profitable. Patricia Hewitt at the Department of Trade and Industry introduced measures to enable shareholders to vote down pay increases more easily and to make companies more accountable to shareholders generally (*Observer*, 9 September 2001). Fat cats in the banking business were even more reviled in 2008–09 for causing a crisis, allegedly through their own greed-fuelled risk taking. Sir Fred Goodwin, former chair of the Royal Bank of Scotland, for instance, initially insisted on receiving his £700,000 pension despite having presided over a £28 billion loss the previous year (a record for any company).

father of the house
Title given to the MP who has served for the longest unbroken period. The title came

to be used in the 19th century and holders have included former prime ministers like Winston Churchill and Edward Heath. Duties are minimal and seem to be limited to chairing the election of a new speaker. The holder of the title in 2004 was Tam Dalyell, veteran MP for Linlithgow and an MP since 1962. In 2009 the holder was Alan Williams, MP for Swansea West, first elected in 1964. The second longest serving MP is sometimes called 'uncle of the house'; in 2009 it was Sir Peter Tapsell (MP for Louth and Horncastle), first elected in 1966.

fatwa
The binding legal decision of a Shiite Islamic court. Unlike the nations of the European Union, North America and other secular states, Islamic fundamentalist countries such as Iran fuse state law with religious or ecclesiastical law. An example of this is the fatwa. In February 1989, the author Salman Rushdie was accused of blasphemy against the prophet Mohammed in his book *The Satanic Verses*. Demonstrations by British Muslims took place in many cities. However, a more sinister turn of events took place when a court in Iran issued the fatwa against Rushdie and offered a reward for the 'execution' of the author. He went into hiding under the protection of armed officers, though he emerged from 'exile' as the threat receded; it was formally withdrawn in 2000. However, despite changes in the domestic politics of Iran and a thawing in British relations with that country it will be some time before Rushdie can be assured of his personal security from freelance assassination squads. The significance of the case is to point up the political linkages between 'sovereign' states and the different interpretations of freedom of expression within a democratic multicultural society.

federalism
An arrangement whereby power is constitutionally divided between a central government and other units. The USA is often taken as the example whereby states

retain authority over discrete, mostly local functions while the federal government takes care of country-wide ones such as defence, economic management and diplomatic relations. In the UK there are two aspects to this debate. First, there are those who advocate a federal structure, with Scotland and Wales and Northern Ireland, though not usually the English regions, having legislatures and powers analogous to American states. Second, there are those who urge a similar constitutional setting for Europe, with increased integration towards such an ideal. Supporters of the latter vision are more likely to be found among the ranks of the Liberal Democrats than in the Labour Party, and less likely still among the Conservatives, who may be more generally characterised by a visceral hostility to a concept which would dilute and deny national sovereignty.

Federation of Young Conservatives
See Conservative Future.

feminism
A set of perspectives on the damaging effects of the social power of men (patriarchy) in modern politics and society. It contains strands of thought which range from broadly social reformist measures to Marxist and radical feminist solutions to patriarchy. Britain was influenced strongly by the feminist movement of the 1960s and 1970s in response to the subordinate roles performed by women in many walks of life, including work, central and local government and the law. Since then significant strides have been made, particularly with the provision of equal opportunities legislation for pay and conditions at work. There has also been greater representation at many levels within public and private sector organisations. For example, 106 women Labour MPs were elected in 1997 and several were given government office by Tony Blair, including Margaret Beckett (Board of Trade) and Harriet Harman (Social Security).

In their book *Contemporary Feminist Politics* (1993), Joni Lovenduski and

Vicky Randall discerned a falling off of activism during the Conservative years of the 1980s and a 'deradicalisation' as activists retired or died. Even though huge tasks remain, the authors argue, allied with this decline has been a greater permeation of feminist ideas within most important areas of society but especially: political representation; work; health and reproductive rights; motherhood and child-care; and male violence. One of the earliest British feminist writers was Mary Wollstonecraft, who wrote arguably the first feminist tract, *Vindication of the Rights of Women* (1792); a more recent contributor has been the Australian academic and media personality Germaine Greer, whose most celebrated work is *The Female Eunuch* (1970).

feudalism
A medieval system of land tenure whereby tenants paid rent in terms of services and received protection in return. Feudalism is believed to have started in France and to have been imported into Britain by the Normans, though it did exist in an earlier form under the Anglo-Saxons. Pledges of allegiance were made by both sides (tenant and landowner) and upwards ultimately to the monarch. In the modern day the term is used to describe any aspect of government or society which harkens back to medieval times and so, for example, may be used to describe working-class deference and the House of Lords.

filibuster
An American term, used also in Britain, for an attempt by a politician to oppose a measure by talking on it at excessive length. In the Commons this takes the form of a concerted effort by an opposition, hotly opposed to a measure, to pressure the restricted legislative timetable and thereby prevent its passing. It is also used in debates on private members' bills, where a strict time limit is enforced. The government can respond by setting its own limits to debate in the form of a guillotine motion.

See also guillotine motion.

Finance Act
See budget.

Financial Management Initiative (FMI)
A series of efficiency drives in central government departments. It was launched in 1982, in the wake of Number 10's Efficiency Unit. The FMIs were led mostly by business people. The essence of the changes it has promulgated are: a delegation of budgets; the setting up of effective information systems; and accountable management – managers are allowed freedom within set limits as long as they meet resource and performance targets. The evaluation of FMI changes in 1988 led to the report by Sir Robin Ibbs which set up the 'Next Steps' reforms leading to executive agencies.

See also Efficiency Unit; executive agency; Ibbs report.

financial market
Margaret Thatcher once said 'you cannot buck the markets', meaning the laws of supply and demand throughout the world would ultimately determine economic choices, and success or failure. What the national and global markets will or not accept circumscribes much economic policy. An illustration of market power overruling government policy was Black Wednesday, when speculators drove Britain out of the Exchange Rate Mechanism, causing huge losses to the Bank of England and huge gains for speculators such as George Soros. However, the banking crisis 2007–09 revealed that unregulated markets can become destabilised, causing widespread bankruptcies.

Financial Services Authority (FSA)
www.fsa.gov.uk
Body that regulates a number of financial activities, including banking, insurance and financial advice, as well as the mortgage industry. It started life as the Securities and Investments Board in 1985 but was changed to the FSA in 1997. It exercises statutory powers under the Financial

Services and Markets Act 2000. It aims to sustain confidence in the financial system, encourage public awareness and restrict financial crime. It reports to Treasury ministers who are answerable to parliament but it maintains a fair degree of independence. In addition to regulating banks, insurance companies and financial advisors, the FSA has regulated mortgage business since 2004 and general insurance since 2005. During the banking crisis of 2007–09 it was widely criticised for being weak and ineffective; even the FSA itself had to admit its 'light touch' regulation had not worked. Its chair is Lord (Adair) Turner and its chief executive officer Hector Sants.

Financial Times
www.ft.com
Newspaper founded in 1888 and controlled by the Pearson Group since 1957. The 'FT', as it is sometimes called, pursues an independent line dictated more by financial than by political considerations. It usually backs the Conservatives, but surprisingly advised readers to vote Labour in 1992 and then, less surprisingly, advised them similarly in 1997 and 2001.

First Division Association (FDA)
www.fda.org.uk
The professional association, or effectively trade union, of the administrative (elite) class of the civil service and government professionals (diplomats, economists, solicitors and so forth) which is consulted over pay as well as terms and conditions of service. The FDA has over 18,000 members, including most of the permanent secretaries.

first Gulf war
War between Iraq, led by Saddam Hussein, and a coalition of 40 powers led by the USA, 2 August 1990 to 28 February 1991. US forces provided the major element, with, notably, UK, Egyptian and Saudi Arabian forces involved also. The war had been caused by Iraq invading Kuwait, in an apparent grab

at oil reserves. A coalition of resistance was soon organised and the United Nations validated the military action named Desert Storm. The fighting was undertaken chiefly from the air and Iraqi army units were destroyed with embarrassing and inhumane ease. Saddam had named it 'the Mother of all Battles' and refused to accept he had been defeated, which set up the conditions for the 2003 Iraq war (second Gulf war).

first lord of the Treasury
The formal title of the prime minister. In the 17th century the first lord was in charge of the commissioners who ran the nation's finances on behalf of the monarch. Given the relative unavailability of Queen Anne and then George I, the first lord became the person virtually in charge of government. Robert Walpole was the first politician to realise fully the potential of the office and became the first prime minister as a result. The term 'prime minister' was originally used in a satirical or derisive sense until it entered mainstream usage. Once prime minister, the first lord tended not to attend meetings of the Treasury commissioners and it was the chancellor of the exchequer who substituted, thus creating the second most important political position in government.

See also prime minister; Walpole, Robert.

first minister
The name given to the head of the executive committee set up after the elections to the Northern Ireland assembly, Welsh assembly and the Scottish executive; effectively prime minister of the province.

David Trimble, head of the Ulster Unionist Party, was the first incumbent in Northern Ireland, with Seamus Mallon of the Social Democratic and Labour Party as his deputy. He was under great pressure in 2001 to resign or to threaten to do so unless the IRA agreed to disarm. He resumed his office when the IRA agreed to compromise on the issue. Subsequently the executive spent some years in abeyance but came into being again in 2007 when Dr Ian Paisley, surprisingly, became first

minister with Martin McGuinness his deputy. Since June 2008 it has been Peter Robinson.

In Scotland, the first first minister was Donald Dewar; in the summer of 2009 it was Alex Salmond, leader of the Scottish National Party, in a minority administration since May 2007.

In Wales, Rhodri Morgan has been the first minister since February 2000.

first past the post
Popular name given to the voting system used in Britain and the USA. According to this the candidate receiving the most votes is elected, whatever proportion of the popular vote the candidate receives. This has led to many candidates (over half) being returned on less than 50 per cent of votes cast. The system is also criticised for penalising small parties with thin national support; for example, the Alliance in 1983 won 26 per cent of the vote but received only 3.5 per cent of the seats. It can produce other anomalies; for instance, in the 2001 general election Labour won a majority of 167 or 63 per cent of the seats on 42 per cent of the votes, while the Conservatives won 25 per cent of the seats on 33 per cent of votes cast. In 2005 the figures were Labour 55 per cent of seats on 35 per cent of votes; Tories 30 per cent seats on 33 per cent of votes. A commission chaired by Lord (Roy) Jenkins reported in 1998 and advised the adoption of a modified version of the German electoral system. It was never seriously considered though it did receive some additional attention in 2009 when some senior Labour figures suggested it might help close the gap of trust and understanding between government and voters.

The outcome of the 2010 general election saw the Liberal Democrats poll 23 per cent of the vote but receive under 10 per cent of seats, thus strengthening the case for reform. The party managed to extract a promise from its Conservative coalition partners of a referendum on voting reform but only to the non-proportional alternative vote system.

fiscal policy
See taxation.

five tests (for Britain's membership of the euro)
The conditions which have to be met before Britain can safely join the European single currency, the euro, as set out by chancellor Gordon Brown in October 1997.

1 Is our business cycle compatible with that of the euro zone so that Britain can live comfortably with European interest rates? This is probably the most important test. Despite some apparent convergence, the British economy is qualitatively different to that of the rest of Europe in certain respects, such as the proportion of the population who have mortgages and are thus sensitive to changes in interest rates. Further, some people worry that a 'one size fits all' single interest rate across Europe would not always be the optimal one for Britain.
2 Would there be sufficient flexibility to deal with problems as they emerge? For example, interest rates which are too high could inhibit growth and wage cuts would have to replace the device of adjusting the exchange rate, which has made exports cheaper in the past.
3 Would entry have an adverse effect on the competitive position of Britain's financial services industry? Finance is a major sector of the British economy.
4 Would entry create better conditions for inward investment in Britain? Britain has been the prime destination for foreign capital investment in Europe for a number of years.
5 Will joining help promote higher economic growth, stability and employment? If the other four tests are met then this final one would automatically be met also.

Critics maintain that these five tests were so vague that Brown could interpret them more or less as he pleased, thus retaining control over the nation's economic future and the key to the most important political decision the nation then faced.

See also euro; European economic and monetary union.

floating voter
One of the unaligned group of voters who determine the outcome of elections by shifting their support to the party which wins their approval. It was at one time believed that it was this group in British politics which decided general elections. The argument ran that the two main parties drew on class constituencies and that it was those detached from regular class fidelities who could prove decisive. Many floating voters were attracted by the policies of the Liberal Party, but in more modern elections class attachments have weakened and psephologists have discerned a greater volatility. In other words, a huge segment of the electorate is now 'floating' at election time; they are open to persuasion as to how they will vote. This phenomenon also helps explain sudden volatile changes in poll ratings of political parties.

See also partisan dealignment.

focus group
A small group (usually 8–12 or so) of socially representative people who are questioned in depth on particular subjects to ascertain their views and, by extension, those of the electorate. Focus groups are an import into politics from the world of marketing and advertising. They are sometimes used as an alternative, or in addition, to opinion polls as indices of opinion. They can be ad hoc or part of a series addressing a number of topics. Following the failure of polls to predict the 1992 Conservative victory, Labour placed more faith in focus groups. Philip Gould, a former marketing expert and one of Tony Blair's close advisors, was the man who championed the use of focus groups and who had observed their use in the USA. In the summer of 2000 focus groups became the subject of attack as the impression grew that the Blair government used this technique to respond to public opinion rather than to lead it. Ironically, the complaint in 2003 was that he had ignored public opinion and gone ahead with the Iraq war, notwithstanding widespread opposition.

See also opinion poll.

Food Standards Agency (FSA)

www.food.gov.uk

Government body set up in April 2000 in the wake of the BSE crisis to 'protect people's health and the interests of consumers in relation to food'. It is based in London but also has offices in Scotland, Wales and Northern Ireland. The Agency can commission research and make its recommendations public. The FSA employs 2,200 staff throughout the UK, most in the Meat Hygiene Service, an executive agency of the FSA.

foot-and-mouth disease

Contagious disease affecting sheep, pigs and cows. Outbreaks of foot-and-mouth disease in February 2001 soon spread from Heddon on the Wall in Northumberland to most parts of Britain, facilitated by the rapid and widespread movements of sheep and cattle around the country. By April the number of outbreaks had risen to over 40 a day and the customary solution of slaughtering infected animals followed by their incineration caused great anguish to farmers and to the country as a whole. The tourist industry was also heavily hit by the closures enforced by the Ministry of Agriculture, Fisheries and Food (MAFF) under its then minister, Nick Brown. Some critics pointed out that the value to the national economy of meat exports was only £0.5 billion annually, while tourism earnt over £12 billion. Others argued that vaccination rather than slaughter is a better solution to the disease on economic as well as moral grounds. As the number of outbreaks continued to rise during April 2001, Tony Blair decided to postpone the forthcoming general election, widely expected on 3 May, to June. By this time outbreaks had fallen to single figures per day – on 15 May there were no outbreaks reported, for the first time since the problem arose – but the disease was not beaten and continued to afflict the farming community for several months afterwards.

Some 2,030 cases of the disease occurred – making it worse than the last such crisis in Britain, in 1967–68 – and some 6 million animals were slaughtered and incinerated, representing 10 per cent of Britain's livestock. Some calculations put the total cost of the crisis in excess of £20 billion and 60,000 jobs were lost as a result of the outbreak. The reputation of MAFF was destroyed by the outbreak and its poor response to it. Nick Brown paid with his job in the post-election reshuffle, when he was demoted out of the cabinet and the ministry itself was merged into the new Department for Environment, Food and Rural Affairs, under Margaret Beckett. MAFF was criticised for its assumption – reinforced by the National Farmers' Union – that agriculture is the backbone of the rural economy when in fact tourism is much more important in the present day; in consequence tourism was neglected and food production was given priority, causing bigger losses than should have been the case. A report by the Council for the Protection of Rural England declared on 24 September 2001 that the 'cure was worse than the disease'.

Foreign and Commonwealth Office (FCO)

www.fco.gov.uk

Government department headed by the foreign secretary, whose purpose is to enhance the security and prosperity of the country and its citizens overseas, by providing them with a consular service. It was formed in 1782, when it was decided to deal with political matters for home and abroad separately. Despite Britain's reduced international role, the FCO is still of key importance and, in the view of former foreign secretary Douglas Hurd, enables the country to 'punch above its weight'. Some 215 overseas posts are funded by the FCO and funds for the World Service of the BBC also come out of its budget. Most effort is focused on the European Union, NATO and the United Nations, and much more emphasis is now placed on promoting British exports and attracting inward investment. Altogether the FCO employs 9,700 civil servants.

POLITICS

foreign policy

Traditionally British foreign policy entails three interlocking circles, namely Europe, North America and the Commonwealth. Until the 1950s the Empire still exerted an influence and the wartime alliance with the USA was a powerful cultural and historical bond. But the Suez alienation from the USA, Britain's faltering economy and the European Community's economic success encouraged politicians to overcome their sense of superiority to the Continent. In 1972 the die was cast and – despite rearguard actions by Eurosceptics – Britain has become ever more deeply involved in the European Union, both economically and politically.

On becoming foreign secretary in 1997, Robin Cook announced that Britain would henceforth pursue a foreign policy with 'an ethical dimension', although three years into government the term 'ethical' was quietly dropped from public statements.

In 2009 an inquiry was announced into the decision to enter the Iraq war as the period of arguably slavish adherence to US leadership under George Bush came under critical scrutiny.

See also ethical foreign policy.

foreign secretary

The minister responsible for Britain's diplomatic relations with the rest of the world. This post is especially high profile, both internationally and domestically, with the post holder usually being a senior politician and a possible candidate for the prime minister's job. Many distinguished politicians have held this office, from Lord Castlereagh and Viscount Palmerston to Ernest Bevin, Anthony Eden and Lord Carrington. In recent times both James Callaghan and John Major went on to Number 10 following a period as foreign secretary. On coming to power in 1997 Tony Blair appointed Robin Cook as foreign secretary, who attempted to pursue an 'ethical foreign policy' with mixed results; in 2001 Jack Straw took over. When Gordon Brown took over in 2007 he appointed David Miliband as holder of this

position. In May 2010 William Hague took over the portfolio for the Conservative–Liberal Democrat coalition.

See also ethical foreign policy; foreign policy.

foreign trade

Trade patterns have changed radically over the past 50 years, with Commonwealth trade declining and European trade growing vigorously. In 2009 UK exports chiefly went to the USA (13.8 per cent), Germany (11.5 per cent), the Netherlands (7.8 per cent), France (7.6 per cent), Ireland (7.5 per cent), Belgium (5.3 per cent) and Spain (4.1 per cent). Imports mainly came from Germany (13.0 per cent), the USA (8.7 per cent), China (7.5 per cent), the Netherlands (7.4 per cent), France (6.8 per cent), Belgium (4.7 per cent) and Italy (4.1 per cent). The emphasis of modern trade on Europe is clear.

foundation hospital

Hospital run by a board representative of the local community, with the right to opt out of government guidelines and to set its own clinical and financial priorities, and possibly set its own pay levels. At the 2002 Labour Party conference in Blackpool, Tony Blair argued that 'foundation hospitals would put power in the hands of patients and NHS staff'. The idea was to let good hospitals develop but many feared such a move would create a 'two tier' hospital service. 'Old Labour' voices, like that of former health minister Frank Dobson, were hotly raised in opposition and chancellor Gordon Brown was said to oppose it as it would give the National Health Service a blank cheque to spend more money. The Conservatives supported the idea, which made it even more difficult for Blair to sell it to his own party. In July 2003 the necessary legislation was passed with a majority of only 35.

14-day rule

Rule in force after the Second World War which forbade the mention on television of anything of topical political interest that was likely to be discussed in parliament during the next 14 days. This stemmed from suspicion by the political class of this new medium with such a massive potential for influencing people. Winston Churchill, for example, saw the BBC as a 'red conspiracy' and supported the rule. It was broken by Granada Television, which covered the Rochdale by-election in 1957 in defiance of the rule and suffered no repercussions. After that breach the rule was ignored.

foxhunting
See hunting.

franchise
The right or eligibility to vote. Political scientists also use the term as an indicator of political modernisation. Thus, at the start of the 19th century Britain was a kind of 'elite democracy' with a tiny electorate, where the right to vote was determined by property ownership and being male. Furthermore, before the Great Reform Act of 1832 the franchise was a patchwork affair with some constituencies returning MPs on the basis of a handful of voters or, as in the case of Old Sarum, no voters at all. The Reform Acts in the 19th century widened the franchise successively in 1867 and 1884, until women were given the right to vote on a limited basis in 1918 and then generally in 1928. In 1969 people aged 18 and over were granted the vote. Britain had become a mass democracy.
See also Reform Act.

free vote
Parliamentary vote for which the whip is removed to allow MPs to vote freely on matters of personal conscience or inclination. The most well known example concerns capital punishment, but others have been allowed, for example on foxhunting in the autumn of 1997.

Free Wales Army (FWA)
Tiny militant faction active in the late 1960s. The FWA was founded by 'Cayo' Evans, a public school boy and former serving soldier. It was dedicated to freeing Wales from 'English rule' and provided a colourful but unimportant accompaniment to events in Wales. Evans died in 1995 but earned the compliments of a biography and a Cardiff pub in his name.

> The only thing the English understand, boy, is … bullets! (Cayo Evans to author, in an Aberystwyth pub, 1969)

freedom
Alternatively known as 'liberty' and having two important senses. Negative freedom, championed by thinkers such as Adam Smith and John Stuart Mill and, more recently, Friedrich Hayek and Robert Nozick, is interpreted as the absence of interference from others. However, political philosophers have pointed to the fact that capacity or resources are important prerequisites for exercising freedom and this leads to the second sense of freedom: positive freedom. This is the capacity to do things to improve one's lot, and in this sense T. H. Green argued in the 19th century that anyone prevented from realising personal potential, perhaps due to poverty, was not a free person. This dichotomy of meaning has characterised the two main parties in Britain, with the Conservatives championing negative freedom as the only legitimate form and Labour the positive variety.
See also equality; libertarianism.

freedom of information
The open and unrestricted access of the public to information held by government and its agencies. This applies not only to the workings of government and policies pursued under particular administrations, but also to information which government may have on individual citizens. In the USA there is a Freedom of Information Act which enables the public and journalists to examine government papers. In Britain there is a culture of secrecy, sustained by the Official Secrets Act, which many argue acts as a cloak for what governments do not want the public to know. Conservatives tend to ignore calls for

more information and argue that government needs secrecy in order to function efficiently. In opposition in the 1980s and 1990s Labour argued strongly for a Freedom of Information Act and it was a regular feature in the party's manifestos. However, in office Labour's freedom of information measures (the Data Protection Act 1998 and Freedom of Information Act 2000), introduced by Jack Straw when home secretary, were much criticised for being half-hearted and arguably restrictive.

See also freedom of speech; Official Secrets Act.

Freedom of Information Act 2000

The promise of such an act along US lines appeared in Labour Party general election manifestos but the promised legislation was not forthcoming. The original minister charged with piloting the measure through, David Clark, was replaced by the home secretary, Jack Straw, in 1998, but he was a sceptic on freedom of information. The Select Committee on Administration, chaired by a Labour MP, tried to insist that the measure appeared in the queen's speech for 1998–99 but was unable to secure this. Large exemptions were agreed during 1997 to such a bill, should it ever begin its journey through parliament, including: the police, immigration and security services, privatised utilities and civil service policy advice to ministers. The act was passed in 2000 but in October 2001 the Guardian reported that Tony Blair was keen to delay the implementation of the act until 2004, shortly before the next election. Straw supported such a move but Lord Irvine, the lord chancellor, favoured an earlier, phased introduction. Some weeks later the paper announced that Blair had won his argument and that the new legislation would not come into effect until January 2005. Lord McNally of the Liberal Democrats described this as a 'betrayal of the agreement we negotiated with the government with the aim of getting the act passed and implemented rapidly'. Labour MP Mark Fisher said there was 'no reason why this should be delayed for so long after

parliament has examined it at such length'. The information commissioner, Elizabeth France, sided with Lord Irvine's objections.

Despite its alleged shortcomings, the act was partially responsible for helping to extract data relating to MPs' expenses in 2009, which later developed into a huge national scandal which broke several political careers.

The Economist in February 2009 reported that it took two months for an application it had made to be answered in the negative, and three further months for this to be confirmed on appeal. In theory public bodies must respond within 20 working days unless one of 23 approved reasons apply. Some 400,000 requests had been made over four years, 'but noncompliance is endemic'.

Richard Thomas, the information commissioner, criticised the Department of Communities for taking up to 400 days to process enquiries. The commissioner argued that he would be able to process more complaints if the office was properly funded.

See also freedom of information.

freedom of speech

The liberal thinker John Stuart Mill argued that freedom of expression and its concomitant, freedom of thought, are important qualities of a free person. Moreover, freedom of speech and the free interchange of ideas have long been perceived as key liberties in the British political system, and a basic condition for democratic government. However, there are limits laid down regarding what can be said about people (for example the libel laws and laws against incitement to racial hatred). The Official Secrets Act in its various guises makes it a criminal offence for a person to communicate classified information to an unauthorised person.

See also freedom of information; Freedom of Information Act; Official Secrets Act.

Friends of the Earth (FOE)

www.foe.co.uk
Environmental pressure group founded in the USA in 1969 and in Britain in 1971.

It has 250 groups in the UK, which target environmental issues at central and local government level, and support various other groups and occasionally direct action concerning motorways and similar developments. It is now a respected group which government regularly consults. Along with the Green Party it played a significant role in drafting the Road Traffic Reduction Act 1997. In 2001 FOE's membership was just over 110,000.

fuel protest, September 2000

Action by consumers which plunged the country into near paralysis for a number of days. With fuel costs and taxes continually going up, British consumers copied French road hauliers and used direct action to advance their protest. Farmers for Action, with links to North Wales, were joined by taxi drivers, lorry drivers, fishermen and others in blockading petrol refineries and thus preventing the distribution of fuel nationwide. Panic buying soon emptied the petrol stations and the nation ground to a halt. Polls showed that a huge majority supported the protestors and that the Conservatives had taken a lead over Labour. After some undignified manoeuvring the government conceded some ground on fuel tax despite the harmful environmental side-effects of petrol and diesel and the protest fell away.

full employment

A notion introduced as an achievable objective by the Beveridge report during the Second World War. Buttressed by Keynesian economic theory, this objective was pursued by both major parties during the 1950s and 1960s. It was also the official policy of the Labour Party as late as 1983. This changed in the late 1980s as full employment no longer seemed achievable, as government spending was held to create inflation and undermine competitiveness. Under Neil Kinnock the Labour Party eventually adopted a position similar to that of the Conservatives in seeking merely to minimise unemployment, though when in office under Tony Blair

New Labour showed considerable vigour in pursuing its New Deal programme, designed to get people off benefit and into work. Given the numbers of people who cannot work for various reasons, an unemployment rate of 5 per cent, which was the level in the summer of 2004, effectively represented 'full employment'.

See also New Deal.

Fulton report, 1968

A report on the recruitment and structure of the civil service. It made a number of criticisms of British public administration, which had not changed since the Northcotte–Trevelyan reforms of the 19th century. In particular, it pointed to the fact that senior civil servants came from a narrow and unrepresentative social background, their education reflected an Oxbridge elitism, there were too few representatives from other walks of life such as business and the law, and there was a somewhat amateurish faith in the generalist all-rounder instead of the trained specialist (as would be found in France). The report made a number of recommendations, some of which were implemented, for example the establishment of the Civil Service College. However, the report is more remembered for what it did not do, rather than the changes it introduced, as many of its suggested reforms were blocked by civil service mandarins.

See also civil service; executive agency; Northcotte–Trevelyan report.

functional representation

The idea that groups in society can be represented in legislative chambers as well as by constituency members. There is a long tradition of individual representation in the British political system, with MPs being elected by individual members of a constituency. However, some reformers have argued that the British political system does little to represent specific groups in society and they suggest a reformed House of Lords might rectify this if it comprised elected representatives of groups in society, such as academics, doctors, business people, lawyers and so forth. Others argue pressure group activity serves this purpose, although these groups lack the formal status which functional representation would provide.

G

G8

An intergovernmental organisation comprising the eight richest industrial nations: Italy, Canada, the USA, Britain, Germany, France, Japan and, from July 2001 (before which it met as G7), Russia. Since the 1950s they have met once a year to discuss questions of international finance. British ministers regard membership as an important symbol of Britain's continuing status as a major economic and political power, a fact borne out by the G7's involvement, along with Russia, in the attempt to end the 1998 Kosovo crisis in the former Yugoslavia. In July 2001 the group met in Genoa and the growing international opposition to globalisation resulted in major riots which left one demonstrator dead and much property damaged. Following the financial crisis of 2008–09 an extended gathering of world leaders – the G20 – met in London.

G20

Group of major advanced and emerging economies set up in 1999, in the wake of the 1997 Asian financial crisis, to stabilise the global financial market. The G20 holds annual meetings of finance ministers and central bank governors. There are 19 member states (Argentina, Australia, Brazil, Canada, China, France, Germany, India, Indonesia, Italy, Japan, Mexico, Russia, Saudi Arabia, South Africa, South Korea, Turkey, the UK, the USA), with the 20th member being the European Union.

The G20 meeting convened by Gordon Brown to consider the banking crisis of 2008–09, held in London on 1–2 April 2009, was a huge event for Brown in that he hoped it would show him striding the world as a trusted statesman, seeking to mend the world's economy. The results were better than expected – not just empty rhetoric but: a full turnout of world leaders; £1.1 trillion for the International Monetary Fund; the establishment of the Financial Stability Board; and an agreement to control hedge funds. The Keynesian principles urged by Brown were substantially endorsed by the leaders present. However, there were street protests during the meeting and Ian Tomlinson, an innocent newspaper vendor, unconnected with the demonstrations, was knocked down by a policeman and later died.

Gallup
www.gallup.com
Polling organisation established by George Gallup in the USA in 1935. There is now a branch in Britain. Gallup polls initially appeared in the *News Chronicle*, but since the 1960s the *Daily Telegraph* and *Sunday Telegraph* have become their regular home, where Professor Anthony King used to provide academic analysis of them.
See also opinion poll.

gang of four
The pejorative/ironic term given to the original group of Labour Party defectors who established the Social Democratic Party (SDP) in 1981. Shirley Williams, David Owen and Bill Rodgers were soon joined by Roy Jenkins, making the group congruent with the Chinese 'gang of four' who briefly led the country in the 1970s after the death of Mao Tse-tung.
See also Social Democratic Party.

garbage-gate
See Mittal affair.

gender gap
Difference in the percentages of men and of women voting for a party. For the Labour

Party it was around 17 per cent in the 1950s but it gradually fell thereafter, so that by 1997 it had virtually disappeared. Some polls in the early years of the new millennium, however, showed that women were less likely than men to be satisfied with the Labour government. This was possible because, in the view of some, 'women's issues' had languished and 'Blair's babes' – the 106 female Labour MPs elected in 1997 – had failed to make much of an impression. In June 2009 Caroline Flint, Europe minister, resigned, apparently angry at not being offered a promotion; she complained Gordon Brown had women in his government merely as 'window dressing'.

General and Municipal Workers' Union
See GMB.

General Belgrano
The name of a battle cruiser of the Argentinean navy that was torpedoed and sunk by the submarine HMS *Conqueror* on 3 May 1982 in the Falklands war. The sinking caused much debate, as the loss of life was heavy and evidence suggested the ship had been heading away from the 'exclusion zone' and not towards it, as claimed by the government at the time. Margaret Thatcher was at the peak of her power and the allegation that the ship had been sunk for political reasons, namely to pre-empt the possibility of peace negotiations, attracted much attention. Her defence of the decision to sink the ship was that the *General Belgrano* was a threat to British ships and service personnel. The issue gained further notoriety when a Ministry of Defence official, Clive Ponting, leaked secret material to the Labour MP Tam Dalyell. In the summer of 2004 support for Thatcher's decision arrived from an unlikely source: the former captain of the *Belgrano* claimed he would have done the same thing had he been the *Conqueror*'s captain.

General Court
See European Court of Justice.

general election
The Septennial Act 1716 increased the life of parliaments from three to seven years. This move was designed to bolster the power of the Whigs but historians judge it had more effect in underpinning the stability of the House of Commons. The Chartists' demands in the mid-19th century included one for annual parliaments, but few others seriously wanted this, as it would be likely to introduce too much instability. The Parliament Act 1911 reduced the maximum term to five years. Critics of the system focused on the right of the prime minister to choose the election date, to party advantage. This, though, was set to be removed in May 2010 when the coalition government announced there would henceforward be fixed five-year parliamentary terms.

In recent times prime ministers have tended to go to the polls after four rather than five years, to avoid being boxed in by unpredictable events as the deadline approaches. The 2001 general election was held on 7 June, after Tony Blair's preferred date, 3 May, was deemed unsuitable because of the intensity of foot-and-mouth disease, which was ravaging the countryside. The campaign was relatively short (four weeks) but failed to engage the public to any significant degree. Blair ran on his record and the promise to improve public services. William Hague for the Conservatives hoped hostility to Europe would deliver seats but he was disappointed. The result was a second landslide for Labour: 413 (down 6) to 166 (up 1) for the Conservatives, with the Liberal Democrats on 52 (up 6). Labour gained only 10.7 million votes (41 per cent), fewer votes than any winning party since 1929. The turnout was a mere 59.2 per cent.

The 2005 election took place in the middle of the Iraq war and Blair was forced to overcome the unpopularity this caused. But he hung on to win with a 67 majority. Labour won 356 seats, the Conservatives 198 and the Liberal Democrats 62. Turnout was fractionally higher than in 2001, at 61.3 per cent.

POLITICS

The 2010 general election was held on 6 May, after a four-week campaign which had itself been preceded by much anticipatory campaigning. In the autumn of 2009 the Conservatives were some 20 points ahead in the polls but their policy of deep cuts to correct the national finances proved unpopular and their lead was in single figures from December onwards. The campaign itself was transformed by the televised party leaders' debates, held weekly for three weeks from 15 April. The first one exposed Nick Clegg to many voters for the first time; he was held to have 'won' and support for the Liberal Democrats soared to equal that of Labour and in some cases the Tories too. However, this development favoured the outcome, predicted by many polls, of a hung parliament. This duly came to pass on 7 May, with the Conservatives on 307 seats, Labour 258, Liberal Democrats 57 and others 28. Turnout was 65 per cent, a big advance on the previous two elections but still well down on average figures for elections 1945–97. All the major parties were disappointed: Labour because it had lost nearly 100 seats; the Tories because they had failed to gain the overall majority they fully expected to win; and the Liberal Democrats because their poll success after the first televised debate had not been converted into more seats; in fact they lost five seats compared with 2005. Nevertheless, Clegg found himself at the centre of a bidding war from Gordon Brown and David Cameron. Cameron seemed to be heading for an agreement on 9 May but his offer was suddenly 'trumped' by Brown and negotiations proceeded with Labour for a while. These were undermined by leading Labour figures – John Reid, Lord Falconer, Andy Burnham – who argued such a 'rainbow coalition' (nationalists and others would have had to be included) would be unstable and appear to be a 'coalition of the losers'. On 10 May the Conservative–Liberal Democrat negotiations resumed and after extensive consultations concluded in a historic agreement whereby the Conservatives formed a coalition with the Liberal Democrats, with

Cameron as prime minister, Clegg as his deputy, and with four Liberal Democrats in the cabinet. Labour was left to reflect that it had lost massive support among its core vote and faced the prospect of a realignment in British politics which could keep the party out of power for some time.

general management committee (GMC)
The decision-making body of each Labour constituency party. It used to select candidates in most instances (a short-list for such candidates was drawn up and the GMC would make the final decision). However, infiltration of GMCs by Militant Tendency supporters in the 1970s and 1980s led to changes. Now open meetings for selection are held and the selection is according to votes by all constituency members following presentations by each aspirant candidate.

General Medical Council (GMC)
www.gmc-uk.org
The professional body which regulates entry to and conduct of the British medical profession. Traditionally doctors, and in particular hospital consultants, who can earn over £175,000 per year, have enjoyed social esteem and autonomy unrivalled by any other profession. However, in recent years there has been increasing media attention on medical errors and the failure of the GMC to act decisively to deal with medical incompetence. Politicians have locked on to this public concern as a way of tightening control over the profession and the British Medical Association and General Medical Council have reacted by trying to tighten up supervision and disciplinary procedures, in an attempt to avoid state control.

General Strike, 1926
Strike that took place between 3 and 13 May 1926, called by the Trades Union Congress (TUC) in an attempt to support coalminers already on strike against pay cuts. It was not strictly 'general' as only key industries were targeted, like railways, docks and the power industries, but with over 2 million men on strike it worried the

government considerably once in progress. Considering this was the closest Britain came to a left-wing revolution in the interwar years, the strikers and the authorities were remarkably civil to each other. The government under Stanley Baldwin kept basic services going throughout the 10 days and the TUC eventually called off the action – allegedly in response to the Astbury judgement, which empowered government to sequester union funds – and the miners were left to fight on alone until they too gave up the unequal struggle in October 1926. The failure of the strike reinforced the moderate trade unions and relegated a worker-led revolution in Britain to a very remote possibility.

genetically modified (GM) food

This debate took off in the late 1990s, when there was public opposition to the introduction of GM crops, something which had not raised much comment in the USA when they had been introduced there on a commercial basis. The government was generally in favour of GM food, as it predicted large financial and other advantages, but environmental pressure groups were hotly opposed and sabotaged crop trials in various parts of Britain. Opinion polls showed public concern and opposition, and their stance seemed vindicated by the October 2003 results of three major trials of GM crops, begun in 1998, which revealed that in two cases damage to wildlife had been recorded, with long-term effects on the bee, butterfly and bird populations. The case against GM foods seemed to have been proved but the government refused to confirm that this was so.

gerrymandering

The drawing of constituency boundaries in such a way that one party benefits. The name originates with that of a governor of Massachusetts in the early 19th century who was guilty of such practices. In Britain the Boundary Commissions are supposed to eliminate the risk of such outcomes but in Protestant-dominated Northern Ireland gerrymandering became an established part

of the political culture. The practice spread to mainland Britain in the 1980s, and both major parties have been accused of gerrymandering. Labour has been accused of the practice in Newcastle, Liverpool and, in Scotland, Monklands. However, the most notorious case was in Westminster, where the council was accused of a kind of gerrymandering by seeking to sell its council properties only to more affluent, Conservative-voting buyers. The Audit Office report of 1996 named both councillors and officials, including the leader of the council, Tesco heiress Dame Shirley Porter, who was later cleared on appeal but this appeal was itself overturned in 2001 and she was forced to settle by paying over £12 million in 2004.

See also 'homes for votes' scandal.

Gershon report, 2004

Report proposing reform of the civil service by Sir Peter Gershon, a former senior executive with BAE who became head of the Office of Government Commerce. His recommendations amounted to a virtual revolution in Whitehall – cutting bureaucracy and 'back office' functions, to save a total of £14.5 billion by 2007. His suggestions included: central procurement agencies to replace the myriad buying arrangements; shared human resources services; centralised information technology for groups of departments; reformulated retail networks; and the use of insurance companies and banks as collecting agencies for taxes and fines. Overall, his programme planned huge savings, but at the cost of 80,000 jobs. Oliver Letwin, the shadow chancellor, tried to exploit the report, which was leaked at the same time as his spending proposals, by suggesting that a 'consensus' already existed between the parties over cuts in the bureaucracy. However, while the government wished to plough back savings into spending, Letwin proposed to use them for tax cuts. In his statement on future spending in July 2004, chancellor Gordon Brown drew upon the report when he proposed savings involving the abolition of over 80,000 civil service jobs.

GfK NOP (National Opinion Polls)
www.gfknop.com
Global market research organisation.
National Opinion Polls (NOP) was
established in the UK by Associated
Newspapers in 1957 as a polling organisation used mostly by the *Daily Mail*. In
1979 MAI, owned by the Labour peer
Lord Hollick, bought NOP, and merged it
with another body but continued to use the
NOP rubric. In 2005 NOP was acquired
by the German-based agency GfK.

Ghurkas
A brigade of Nepalese soldiers in the
British army, famous for their curved
knife, called a *kukri*, and for their fighting
prowess. At the beginning of the 19th
century Nepalese soldiers were encouraged
by British officers to join East India
Company forces. During the Indian Mutiny
Ghurka troops remained loyal and were
incorporated into the British Indian Army.
Following Indian independence the Brigade
of Ghurkas was formed, based in Malaya.
The brigade proved useful in different
parts of Asia as well as in the Falklands
and later in Afghanistan. The settlement
rights of retired Ghurkas became an issue
in the early years of the 21st century, with
a vigorous campaign being waged to gain
improvements. Some 2000 retirees were
denied settlement rights in 2008, when they
were said not to have proved 'strong ties' to
Britain. The actress Joanna Lumley, whose
father had been an officer in the brigade,
took up the cause with great passion and in
April 2009 won a decision amounting to
complete victory regarding Ghurka settlement rights. In July 2009, Lumley visited
Nepal and received a heroine's welcome.

Gibraltar
A British dependency off the southern
tip of Spain, with a population of 30,000
(area 2.5 square miles). The Moors ceded
the rock to Spain in 1462 but the English
admiral George Rooke captured it from
Spain in 1704 and the treaty of Utrecht
made it a British possession in 1713.
Inhabitants strongly wish to remain British

but Spain is keen to regain this promontory.
The British military garrison was halved in
1989 and removed in 1991, though air and
naval units remained. Talks in late 2001
indicated a joint sovereignty arrangement
had been negotiated by Jack Straw with his
Spanish counterpart but the Gibaltarians
were stoutly opposed and began a vigorous
campaign, including a referendum, which it
overwhelmingly won to frustrate the plan.

Glasgow University Media Group
www.gla.ac.uk/centres/mediagroup
Research-based grouping of academics
within the sociology department of Glasgow
University. These media researchers (for
example Greg Philo) argue that broadcast
news on television is characterised by
systematic, if unconscious, bias against trade
unions and their activists. Thus in industrial
relations disputes, union representatives
tend to be presented as scruffy, somewhat
irresponsible men on picket lines while the
management are seen pronouncing reassur-
ingly from behind desks and wearing suits.
The Group's work on the Falklands war
suggested that television and press journalists uncritically recycled Ministry of Defence
propaganda on the bombing of the Port
Stanley airfield, and reported it as objective
fact. The Group's methods of analysis have
received much criticism. However, it has
stimulated useful discussion and opened up
an important area of debate on the supposed
objectivity of news broadcasting.

globalisation
Term that refers to the many ways in which
countries are connected by transactions
beyond the nation state boundary, for
example new communications technology;
growth of trade (increased at least 10-fold
since 1913); the foreign exchange markets;
and multinational companies (for example
Microsoft). Britain has seen globalisation
affect it in many ways, for example: the
speed at which the financial world turned
against the pound on Black Wednesday
in September 1992; the need to keep
workforce levels to a minimum in order to
compete; the 'outsourcing' of call centres to

cheaper providers in the developing world; and the worldwide television audience which watched the funeral of Diana Princess of Wales in 1997.

A particularly menacing manifestation of the world's interconnectedness was the global economic recession of 2007–09, triggered by the 'sub-prime' mortgage crisis in the USA caused by finance companies lending to people unable to repay their loans. Mortgage debt had been 'bundled' to create securities traded on the international exchanges. When sound, these virtual IOUs provided good returns for investors but when sliced up and added to complex financial products they proved fatal, creating a banking crisis which saw the collapse of major investment banks like Lehman Brothers in September 2008.

> Tony Blair embraces globalisation with almost evangelical zeal, as opportunity rather than threat. (Blairite Labour MP Tony Wright)

See also anti-globalisation protests.

Glorious Revolution, 1688–89

The events leading to the removal of James II from the throne and the installation of his daughter Mary and her husband William of Orange. James's injudicious rule had led seven prominent statesmen to invite William to invade Britain. When he did so, James disappeared to France. William and Mary both accepted the Bill of Rights in February 1689 and were then declared sovereigns. The document stated that parliaments must be held regularly and must be free, and that there should be freedom of speech and other safeguards. It is usually held to be the point at which the British crown accepted the supremacy of parliament and began its journey to a respected but ceremonial role in the constitution.

See also Bill of Rights; British constitution.

GMB

www.gmb.org.uk
Union originating in 1889 as the General and Municipal Workers' Union with the

legendary trade unionist Will Thorne. It joined with two other unions in 1924 to provide one of the biggest unions in the postwar period. In 1982 it merged with the Amalgamated Society of Boilermakers, Shipwrights, Blacksmiths and Structural Workers to form the General, Municipal, Boilermakers and Allied Trade Union. In 1989 it became simply the GMB. Its membership, mainly distributive industries and local government personnel, fell drastically after 1979 but it still boasted 700,000 members in 2003 (down to 600,000 in 2009). The union has tended to be on the centre or right of the political spectrum and generally supportive of the Labour leadership.

On 8 July 2004 the union's general secretary, Kevin Curran, met with MPs sponsored by the union. The latter criticised the union's policy of withholding financial support from those MPs not 'loyal to GMB policies and values'. Curran warned in a *Guardian* article (9 July 2004) that total disaffiliation of the union from Labour remained a 'real option'. Curran was replaced in 2005 by Paul Kenny. In 2008 the union withdrew financial support from over a third of its 100 sponsored Labour MPs but did not carry out its earlier threat of disaffiliation.

'goats'

The name given to the outside experts Gordon Brown appointed as ministers when he came to power in June 2007. By July 2009 three lords – Digby Jones, Mark Malloch Brown and Ara Darzi – had resigned for various reasons, leaving only security minister Lord West in post. Such 'outsider' experiments – trade unionist Frank Cousins was appointed by Wilson in the late 1960s – generally end in similar fashion.

golden triangle

Term possibly invented by historian Peter Hennessy and used by others to describe the select group of cabinet secretary, prime minister's principal private secretary and the queen's private secretary, who sit at the

POLITICS

'heart of the constitution' when problems arise and decisions need to be taken. Such weighty matters are usually anticipated in the event of a hung parliament. The 2010 election produced the first hung parliament since 1974 and the three key figures were called into play. However, the queen was not involved in any unusual political role as the leaders of the Conservatives and the Liberal Democrats managed to agree to form a coalition within a few days of polling day.

Good Friday agreement, 1998

The peace negotiations in Northern Ireland initiated by John Major but which reached a climax at Easter 1998, under Tony Blair. To avert an impasse, Blair flew to Stormont on 10 April along with Irish premier Bertie Aherne. After 36 hours of non-stop negotiations the agreement was announced. It had the following provisions:

1 a recognition that a majority of the people of Northern Ireland at present wished to remain part of the UK;
2 amendment of articles 2 and 3 of the Irish constitution, to remove its territorial claims over Northern Ireland;
3 a 108-member assembly elected by single transferable vote;
4 a Northern Ireland executive;
5 a North–South Ministerial Council designed to foster consultation, co-operation and action within the island of Ireland;
6 a British–Irish Council, incorporating the British and Irish governments and representatives of the devolved assemblies of Northern Ireland, Scotland and Wales;
7 a British–Irish intergovernmental conference, which would facilitate cooperation on non-devolved matters;
8 the secretary of state for Northern Ireland would remain responsible for matters not devolved to the assembly.

The agreement was implemented in autumn 1999 but initially failed to become fully operational through lack of trust between the two sides and the refusal of the more militant unionists to accept it. After a number of suspensions of the Northern Ireland executive, the Democratic Unionist Party agreed to power share with Sinn Fein, with Ian Paisley becoming first minister and Martin McGuinness his deputy.

See also Northern Ireland.

governance

The exercise of power and authority in governing. It is a term that is increasingly used in political debate and academic study of politics generally. It broadens greatly the more traditional ways of analysing political processes. Questions relating to power and authority can no longer be answered by reference to the British state and its formal institutions alone, but must include consideration of non-state institutions and agencies. In modern Britain, power is increasingly shared between state, community, business and voluntary groups. Moreover, in the age of globalisation the institutions of the British nation state can no longer be assured of control or influence over the people but must share power with international market forces and global media.

See also cultural governance; government; ideology; political language.

'Governance of Britain' green paper, July 2007

Document produced by Gordon Brown's government shortly after he took office as prime minister in June 2007. It envisaged a constitutional renewal of Britain, invigorating democracy, clarifying the role of government, rebalancing the power of parliament with that of government and rebuilding the sense of what it is to be British. Specifically, the green paper proposed:

1 to limit the prerogative power to deploy troops abroad;
2 to streamline the process of public appointments;
3 to reform the role of the attorney general;
4 to strengthen the role of regional ministers;
5 to complete reform of the House of Lords.

Reform enthusiasts were subsequently bitterly disappointed with Brown's almost total lack of progress on these matters.

POLITICS

government
The authoritative decision-making arrangements of the state at central and local level (distinct from governance). Its provenance covers the whole machinery of administration, including the civil service and other official agencies. It is also used to describe the particular party controlling the administration of the state at any given time: for example, 'the Labour government' elected in 1997.

government chief scientific advisor
Principal advisor to the prime minister and cabinet, working from the Government Office for Science, located in the Department of Business, Innovation and Skills. Professor John Beddington became holder of the post in January 2008.

Government Communications Headquarters (GCHQ)
www.gchq.gov.uk
One of the three British intelligence agencies (along with the Security Service, MI5, and the Secret Intelligence Service, MI6), originating in the code-breaking body founded after the First World War and which became based in Bletchley Park during the Second World War. The modern incarnation is based at Cheltenham and is responsible for the gathering and analysis of intelligence signals from British 'listening' stations across the world. A civil service strike in 1981 interrupted the flow of information and angered the US intelligence service, with which information was pooled. The director of the agency recommended de-unionisation, but the Permanent Secretaries Intelligence Steering Committee advised against it. When Frank Cooper (permanent secretary at the Ministry of Defence) and Douglas Wass (permanent secretary at the Treasury) retired, however, Margaret Thatcher proceeded to ban the unions, even though a no-strike agreement seemed achievable. Trade union rights were restored under Tony Blair's incoming Labour government after 1997. In 2003 GCHQ moved to a new building nicknamed the 'Doughnut'.

Since 1994, Parliament's Intelligence and Security Committee has exercised a general oversight of GCHQ activities while the Intelligence Services Act 1994 established its aims and objectives.

Government of Ireland Act 1920
A landmark in the development of the 'troubles' in Northern Ireland. The act attempted to strike a compromise between the competing claims of Protestants and Catholics by splitting Ireland (then a constituent state of the UK) in two. A 26-county, predominantly Catholic, state was carved out in the south and ruled by a devolved Dublin parliament – the region did not become an independent state until 1949. The remaining six counties, predominantly Protestant, though with substantial Catholic minorities, became the new administrative unit of Northern Ireland, and still remain part of the UK. Thus was established an arrangement which preserved some autonomy for the protestant Irish minority but only at the cost of some thousands of lives and intercommunal tensions which persist to the present day.

See also Good Friday agreement; Irish Republican Army (IRA); Ireland; paramilitary.

grammar school
Type of school established by the (Butler) Education Act 1944. The term derives from schools set up to teach Latin, for example King's School, Canterbury, in 597. Modern grammars were selective educational establishments which pursued an academic curriculum for the fortunate one-third or so of pupils who passed the 11-plus test. Their products often went on to do well at university and in later life. However, many educationalists and other observers, including many in the Labour Party, felt that the problems of the 11-plus test and the domination of the grammar schools by the middle classes were undermining the principle of parity of esteem between the grammars and other secondary schools which the 1944 Act had tried to establish.

From the mid-1960s, many local authorities started to replace the grammars with non-selective 'comprehensive' schools. The Conservative government of Edward Health (1970–74) continued the process, with, ironically, Margaret Thatcher as education secretary. However, some grammars survived in a few education authorities (for example Kent and Tameside) or were converted to grant-maintained schools. The New Labour government elected in 1997 decided not to pursue the full abolition of grammar schools, but introduced the option of parental ballots to decide each school's future. There are still over 160 state-funded grammar schools; they tend to be concentrated in particular areas like Trafford, the Wirral, Kent and Medway.

In 2002 Sinn Fein abolished grammar schools in Northern Ireland and when direct rule was reintroduced this was not reversed, despite unionist opposition. However, the latter won the promise in advance of power sharing in 2006 that in future a non-selective system would not be imposed without cross-community consent. But while polls show support for selective systems, there is no agreement on whether it should be based on the 11-plus. Supporters cite the high numbers of A levels passed and the absence of private schools in the province; opponents cite the high levels of children with no qualifications and the fact that few poor children pass the 11-plus. It seemed in 2009 that the 69 grammar schools would establish their own tests for selection.

See also comprehensive school; 11-plus test; grant-maintained school.

grant-maintained school
Term used to refer to a school, usually a grammar, which received a grant to supplement its funding from local authority sources. Grant-maintained schools mostly became independent in the 1970s (the Manchester Grammar School, for example). The term took on a new meaning in the 1980s when Conservative education ministers freed certain schools from local authority control and funded them directly from the centre. It was generally recognised

that such schools tended to be better funded than if they had not applied for such status. The most famous example of such a school was the Oratory in London, where Tony Blair sent his son Euan, despite opposition from the left of the party and unease from the rest.

Grassroots Alliance
Group that contested the elections to the Labour Party's National Executive Committee in autumn 1998. Former party leader Neil Kinnock lambasted these 'Trotskyists, sectarians and other selfish parasites' (*Guardian*, 18 September 1998). However, four of the six members of the Grassroots Alliance were elected in September 1998, including Liz Davies, who had been banned as a candidate in 1997 for allegedly Trotskyite political views – allegations she dismissed as rubbish and a smear by the leadership to stifle criticism.

See also Militant Tendency.

great and the good
A somewhat ironic term to describe the list of worthy people whom the government and key opinion formers think fit to chair or sit on public bodies. The list is slightly mysterious but was kept by the Treasury when it was responsible for the civil service as a whole. Politicians have been sufficiently frank to admit that the membership of royal commissions is often 'rigged' through the appointment of people who will come up with the recommendations the government thinks are appropriate. Peter Hennessy in his book *Whitehall* (1991) reported a 1954 minute on discussions relating to membership of the Independent Television Authority, which classically states: 'The qualities required in the chairman and members [are] tact and sound judgement rather than energy and administrative ability'.

See also establishment.

great power
Britain was a 'great power' in the world for only a brief period, c. 1815–72, when it

commanded the British Empire, comprising around a quarter of the world's landmass and population. Then the USA and Germany began to catch up and overhaul the 'workshop of the world' (as Britain was known) and by the 20th century Britain's superiority was virtually nonexistent. After the two World Wars the country was effectively bankrupt, having spent imperial assets in defeating Hitler, and was unable to prevent the huge empire just melting away through a combination of military and economic weakness. When US pressure enforced the abandonment of the Suez Canal venture, it was clear Britain was no longer a 'great power' but only a medium-sized one, dependent on the USA for its nuclear capacity and much of its diplomatic clout.

Great Reform Act 1832
Usually seen as the Act which marked the death of the old political system, when the aristocracy could influence the composition of the House of Commons. It was passed as a result of widespread political unrest. The act was passed only because William IV was willing to create enough peers to vote it through the House of Lords. It removed 56 'rotten' and 'pocket' boroughs, redistributed 143 seats to under-represented county and urban areas, and extended the franchise to include a wider range of property holders (to borough householders paying an annual rent of £10 and to leaseholders paying £50 a year). The act increased the electorate from 435,000 to 652,000. Effectively it enfranchised the middle class but still excluded the working class, who nonetheless refused to be forgotten. Pressure from the working class and from radical reformers helped bring about the Reform Acts of 1867 and 1884 and led the way to the development mass democracy in the 20th century. In late May 2010 Liberal Democrat leader Nick Clegg described his role in the new coalition government as one of ushering in the biggest shake-up of the British political system 'since the 1832 Great Reform Act'. Sceptics dismissed this as an exaggeration.

Greater London Authority (GLA)
www.london.gov.uk/who-runs-london/greater-london-authority
A strategic authority that supports both the work of the mayor of London and the London assembly. While the mayor and the assembly members are elected, the GLA has a permanent staff headed by an executive team. Leo Boland was appointed chief executive in January 2009. The GLA was created by the GLA Act of 1999 and was established in July 2000. Its areas of responsibility include economic development, social development and environmental improvement. It shares local government responsibilities with the 32 borough councils of London and the City of London Corporation.

Greater London Council (GLC)
The body that replaced the London County Council in 1965. When it became the centre of left-wing activism, especially during the tenure of Ken Livingstone as leader in the early 1980s, the Conservatives reacted by abolishing it in 1986, along with the Inner London Education Authority, by placing the powers released with the boroughs and various joint boards. After 1997, the Labour government introduced an elected mayor and a small council called the Greater London Authority.

green paper
Statement of proposed policy by government. This type of statement is usually consultative and aims to elicit comment from interested parties so that a more definite statement in the form of a white paper can be produced.

Green Party
www.greenparty.org.uk
Began life as an environmental pressure group in 1973, became the Ecology Party in 1975 and changed its name to the Green Party in 1985, in line with continental groupings. In the 1983 general election the party's 108 candidates polled only 1 per cent of the vote, but in 1989 it gained some of the protest votes which had previously

gone to the Alliance and registered an astonishing 15 per cent in the European elections. However, its amateurish approach to politics and the greater 'green' emphasis of the main parties saw its support subsequently collapse back to its 1983 levels. The claim of one of its spokespeople, David Icke, in 1991 that he was 'an aspect of the godhead' damaged the party's credibility. In the 1997 general election the Greens contested only 80 seats. However, membership of the party grew from 3,500 in 1996 to 5,000 in 2002. In the 2001 general election the Greens won an average of 2.45 per cent in the 145 constituencies it contested. Brighton Pavilion, however, saw it poll a respectable 9.3 per cent and in Bradford West the party received more votes than the Liberal Democrats. In June 2004 the Green showing of 6.3 per cent in the European elections marked a slight improvement and in the local elections it won nine extra seats plus 2 per cent of the vote for the London assembly. In the 2009 European elections the Greens polled 8.6 per cent and won two seats. In the 2009 local elections 124 Green councillors were elected, an increase of four. In May 2010 the Greens finally gained a Westminster seat, in Brighton Pavilion, won by their leader, Caroline Lucas.

green thinking

An umbrella term for a constellation of different environmental perspectives, which share a commitment to 'reintegrating' humans back into the natural ecosystem, and to protect the natural environment for future generations. Its basic standpoint is that the world's resources are finite and the planet should be preserved for future generations. Green thinking can range from 'light green' or consumer-friendly environmentalism, where the market is used to internalise the costs of pollution for example, while at the same time maintaining high-technology economic growth, through to 'dark green', where there is a fundamental rejection of economic growth and modern industrialism and a wish to return to a form of small-scale cooperatives.

All major parties have recognised the potency of these ideas and sought to embody their less radical elements into mainstream political programmes. Extremist parties, in particular those on the far right, use environmental messages to 'hook' on to the concerns of potential supporters.

Greenham Common

Former US air base which became the scene for a long-running women's demonstration against Cruise missiles (carrying nuclear warheads). In September 1981 a march by Women for Life on Earth reached Greenham Common to protest at NATO's decision to site Cruise missiles at the base. In March the following year 250 women blockaded the base and arrests were made. In November 1983 some 70,000 members of the Campaign for Nuclear Disarmament linked arms to create a 14-mile demonstration against the missiles. By this time a camp had been set up by a number of women, who gave it as their postal address. In 1987 Ronald Reagan and Mikhail Gorbachev signed the Intermediate Nuclear Forces (INF) treaty and Cruise missiles began to be withdrawn. By 1992 US forces had left the base and by 2010 it was being dismantled.

Greenpeace

www.greenpeace.org.uk
One of the world's largest environmental pressure groups. Greenpeace was founded in 1971 by a small group of US campaigners concerned about the environment. By 2008 its membership had increased to 2.8 million people from all over the world. In Britain its membership was 200,000 in 2010. In addition to normal pressure group methods such as lobbying decision makers, it also uses high-profile techniques, sometimes involving its own ocean-going vessels, to protest against nuclear tests, nuclear power, commercial whaling and sealing. Its most active campaigners risk their lives in pursuit of a cleaner world, not only through accidents at sea, but through human malice, as demonstrated by the

sinking of the Greenpeace vessel *Rainbow Warrior* by agents of the French government in 1985.

grey power
The political power of those aged over 65 years. This constituency has long been recognised but is growing as a result of demographic change. The over-65s constitute one-fifth of the electorate but one-quarter of the vote, as they are much more likely to turn out. They tend to be poorer, perceive themselves as poorer and thus care more about welfare issues. In 1997, 38 per cent voted Labour and 29 per cent Conservative but by 2001 polls showed the gap was much smaller, possibly influenced by the chancellor's award of a mere 75 pence per week pension increase in 2000 – something for which he subsequently apologised. As the 2010 election approached, both major parties wooed those aged over 55, though with final-salary company pension schemes on the way out and severe public spending limits there was little available to win any votes. Social care for the elderly and how it can be funded also featured in the parties' election campaigns.

See also ageing population.

gross domestic product (GDP)
The value of all goods and services produced within a country. Usually the figure given is for the year as a whole but it is often expressed per capita. In 2009 the GDP of the UK was $2,149 billion – the sixth largest in the world – and per capita it was $35,200 – 34th in the world.

gross national product (GNP)
This is measured as GDP plus the total value of goods and services produced by companies owned by a country (income from abroad minus income earned by foreign investors).

Guardian
www.guardian.co.uk
Originally the *Manchester Guardian* when the newspaper was founded in 1821 and the mouthpiece of Manchester radical liberalism. It is now owned by the independent Scott Trust. Its editors have included some distinguished journalists, such as C. P. Scott and A. P. Wadsworth. It traditionally took a liberal line and still does. It tends to have a pro-Labour stance when the party is in opposition but is often less supportive when Labour is in power. Its columnists are quite eclectic, with the left-wing Polly Toynbee and Jackie Ashley balanced by the more centrist Simon Jenkins and Max Hastings.

Guildford Four
Infamous case of a miscarriage of injustice relating to alleged Irish republican terrorists. In 1975, four Irish people, Gerard Conlon, Carole Richardson, Patrick Armstrong and Paul Hill, were found guilty of placing bombs in Guildford and Woolwich public houses. They served 14 years in prison but after a hard-fought campaign on their behalf from supporters, and procrastination on the part of the authorities, their convictions were found to be unsafe and they were released in 1989.

See also Birmingham Six.

guillotine motion
A procedural device used in the House of Commons. More formally called an 'allocation of time motion', this is a device which speeds up the passage of contentious legislation. It was introduced in the 1880s to prevent Irish MPs from obstructing legislation. A strict time limit is placed upon the debate of any clause and when it expires a vote is taken. This device effectively counters the filibuster technique used by politicians opposed to a measure, but is introduced only after a considerable time has already been spent discussing it. Debate can also be curtailed by an informal agreement between the party whips or by a programme motion, which amounts to an agreed timetable for a measure.

See also filibuster; programme motion.

Gulf war
See first Gulf war; Iraq war.

H

habeas corpus
An ancient constitutional rule, dating back to Edward I (1239–1307), whereby a person cannot be detained without due cause. The Habeas Corpus Act 1679 laid down that a prisoner must be brought before a court without delay. This rule is the citizen's guarantee against arbitrary arrest and detention, hallmarks of a civilised society. In practice it takes the form of a writ challenging the validity of someone's detention, issued by the Divisional Court of the Queen's Bench Division. Parliament has suspended the act in times of emergency, as in 1715, 1794 and 1817. There was much controversy over the Anti-Terrorism, Crime and Security Act 2001, which allowed terrorist suspects to be held without trial for an indefinite period if they were foreign nationals, and also over government attempts to set a legally sanctioned period of detention without trial, first for 90 days, by Tony Blair in November 2006, and then for 42 days, by Gordon Brown in October 2008. Both attempts failed through lack of political support.

See also detention without trial.

half-hour adjournment
Most well known form of Commons adjournment debate. It takes the form of a motion tabled at the end of the day's proceedings when an MP, selected by ballot, can use it to air any issue he or she chooses. Competition is fierce as the debate is for 30 minutes. The final adjournment debate before recess is longer and the motion is chosen by the government.

See also adjournment debate; early day motion; private notice question.

Hansard
www.publications.parliament.uk/pa/pahansard.htm
The official record of parliamentary proceedings. It includes all speeches, questions asked and answered and statements made in both houses of parliament. It started life in 1803 as a set of informal notes taken by William Cobbet. Luke Hansard succeeded him and, using a team of skilled shorthand writers, he produced a verbatim account which could be published. His family continued to be associated with the work until late into the 19th century, when the government took over the job. In 1943 the name *Hansard's Parliamentary Debates* was restored to the title page. Each reporter works only for a short time as such intensive shorthand is exhausting. Members can review their speeches before final publication in *Hansard* to amend simple errors and grammar is almost always corrected by the official record takers.

Harris Research Centre (HRC)
www.harrisinteractive.com
Opinion polling organisation. HRC was set up by the *Daily Express* and Louis Harris, an American pollster. It took over the ORC polling organisation in 1983. It continues polling for the Conservatives and publishes its findings in the *Observer* and via several television current affairs programmes.

Hayward report, 1982
Labour Party report into the Militant Tendency. Hayward exposed the determined entryist tactics of the organisation and persuaded the leadership to take decisive action. It advised the compilation of a 'register of recognised groups allowed to operate within the party'. In practice, however, this proposal had little effect and it was left to the Whitty report (1985) to initiate tougher and more effective action.

head of state
The official personification of a nation state and its people. Heads of state may be purely symbolic or ceremonial, carrying out duties at home and abroad. They may also be functional, as head of a government. The British head of state, Her Majesty Elizabeth II, is a hereditary monarch and was crowned at Westminster Abbey in 1953. She has a

wide range of official and ceremonial duties, including the state opening of parliament, the queen's speech, giving the royal assent to parliamentary bills, dissolving parliament and appointing a prime minister. In theory she could exert political power in the event of a hung parliament through her ability to invite a likely person to form a government. However, in practice few constitutional experts believe she could intervene decisively in the political process as she acts on the 'advice' of her ministers.

Health and Safety Commission
Body that was responsible for overseeing the Health and Safety Executive (HSE), with which it was merged in April 2008.

Health and Safety Executive (HSE)
www.hse.gov.uk
Body responsible for the protection of health, safety and the welfare of employees and for safeguarding those who may be exposed to risks from industrial activities. It was set up by the Health and Safety at Work Act 1974.

hegemony
Antonio Gramsci's term for the values of the ruling capitalist class which condition the thinking of all other groups and institutions. In so doing, the system is perceived as 'natural' and appeals to common-sense assumptions and therefore exercises a persuasive power over its victims which brute force could never do. Some commentators believed Margaret Thatcher's period in office during the 1980s demonstrated such control, although others dispute this.

A second meaning is associated with the worldwide influence of Britain during the 19th century and the USA since 1945.

Her Majesty's Revenue and Customs (HMRC)
www.hmrc.gov.uk
Government department formed in April 2005 with the merger of the Inland Revenue and HM Customs and Excise. It collects both direct taxes (income tax, inheritance tax, national insurance

contributions, capital gains tax, corporation tax) and indirect taxes (e.g. VAT, excise duties, stamp duty) and also administers child benefit and tax credits. It is also involved in enforcing the national minimum wage and recovering student loans. In 2008–09 it collected £439 billion.

Herbert report, 1960
Report on the local government of London that led to the replacement of the London County Council by the Greater London Council, which itself was abolished in 1986 by Margaret Thatcher's government.

hereditary peerage
A title conferred originally by the monarch and then handed down through the generations via inheritance. Because the aristocracy were major owners of property they tended, naturally, to support the Conservatives and so the House of Lords represented a stronghold of Conservative political power until 1998, when all but 92 hereditary peers were abolished by the Labour government. Some peerages (mostly life but also some hereditary ones) were created by Labour prime ministers and there were Liberal peers as well as crossbenchers, with no party affiliation, but the Conservative dominance was never broken. In the 1950s Lord Stansgate, or Anthony Wedgwood Benn as he was then called (later Tony Benn), sought to disclaim his title in order to sit in the Commons; the eventual result of his efforts was the passing of the Peerages Act 1963, which made this possible. Following the House of Lords Act 1999, hereditary peers were able to sit in the House of Commons (for example Douglas Hogg, Viscount Hailsham).

The order of seniority among the peers is: duke, marquess, earl, viscount and baron.
See also House of Lords reform.

High Court
Court that hears all the more important civil cases and some criminal appeals. In the hierarchy of courts, the High Court comes between the Court of Appeal and the crown and county courts. It has three divisions:

POLITICS

1 Chancery hears contract cases, tort claims and claims for the recovery of land. Seventeen judges work in this division, which has a vice chancellor at its head. It deals with huge sums of money and such cases as the aftermath of Robert Maxwell's death or the Lloyds insurance crisis in the late 1990s.

2 Queen's Bench hears equity matters such as mortgage repossessions. It has 69 judges and deals with cases too complex for county courts or which involve large sums of money. The division also includes a commercial court and an admiralty one dealing with shipping cases. The Divisional Court of the Queen's Bench can issue writs of habeus corpus regarding unlawful imprisonment. It is also the destination for appeals against government actions which may have exceeded statutory authority. The court dealing with such cases is called the Administrative Court.

3 The Family Division hears disputes over adoptions and defended divorces, for example; it also dealt with Diane Blood's request to receive insemination from her dead husband's sperm. This division has 16 judges.

high Tory

Originally a group of Tories in the early 18th century who were devoted to the Church of England and who opposed most constitutional changes, including union with Scotland. Today it is used as a term to describe old-fashioned Conservatives who are sceptical about any radical reform. For example, high Tories see the constitution as an organic thing which is best left alone to develop 'naturally' over time. They tend to be against reform, almost on principle. Thus, Douglas Hurd while foreign secretary (1989–95) cautioned against pushing the tide of reform too far and too fast in the Thatcherite revolution.

Hillsborough agreement, 1985

Treaty between Britain and Ireland signed in November 1985 which allowed the latter a consultative role in the government of

Northern Ireland in exchange for a pledge that the province would remain part of the UK as long as a majority of its population wished it. In the short term the agreement caused bitterness on the part of unionists and did not stimulate the round-table negotiations the two governments desired. However, in a historical context, it marked a degree of collaboration between London and Dublin which foreshadowed the more successful talks of the mid to late 1990s.

Hinduja brothers

Three wealthy Indian businessmen who were accused of various improprieties in their own country and who donated £1 million to the struggling Millennium Dome. When a citizenship application for one of the bothers was dealt with much more quickly (in six months) than normal, accusations were made of improper favours being granted in exchange for the brothers' donation to a New Labour project. Peter Mandelson was the minister (without portfolio) in charge of the Dome when the donation was made and it was alleged that he rang up the Home Office to apply pressure on behalf of his Dome 'sponsor' in 2001, when he was secretary of state for Northern Ireland. A small group of ministers, including Derry Irvine, Tony Blair and Jack Straw, eventually asked Mandelson to resign in January 2001, and he did so, albeit reluctantly. The Hammond report into the matter appeared to clear Mandelson.

Holyrood

The seat of the Scottish parliament. Controversy broke out regarding the new site for the parliament building when the original cost of £40 million rose to £195 million by 2001. Removal of the spending cap in that year opened the prospect of the cost rising well over the £200 million mark. Some critics claimed the new building was becoming Scotland's 'Dome'. By the spring of 2004 predicted costs had been 'held' to £431 million. In September 2004 it finally opened for use by the Scottish parliament.

Home Affairs Committee
See departmental select committee.

Home Office
www.homeoffice.gov.uk
Government department responsible for
home affairs. It was formed in 1782, when
it was decided to deal with political matters
for home and abroad separately. Something
of a 'catch-all' department, it covers a vast
area of public policy including: passports,
immigration and race relations, broadcasting, prisons, sentencing policy, betting,
gaming and liquor licensing, administration
of justice and the police. In March 2007,
home secretary John Reid (who accused
the Home Office of being 'not fit for
purpose') pushed through – against
some internal opposition – a hiving off
of probation, prisons and prevention of
reoffending in England and Wales into a
new Department of Constitutional Affairs,
which was then renamed the Ministry of
Justice in May 2007.

The Home Office is usually recognised
as fourth in the ministerial hierarchy, after
Downing Street, the Treasury and the
Foreign Office. In common with other
government departments, it now has its
own mission statement and corps of special
advisors who deal with marketing and
public relations issues. In June 2009 Alan
Johnson was appointed home secretary.
Theresa May was his Conservative
successor after the 2010 general election.

Home Policy Committee
One of key the committees of Labour's
National Executive Committee (NEC)
in the 1980s. In the late 1970s and early
1980s Tony Benn was its chair and
did much to move official policy to the
left, with arguably disastrous electoral
consequences for the party. After 1983
Neil Kinnock as party leader concentrated
on strengthening his position on the NEC
and Benn's power waned. After Labour's
1987 general election defeat Kinnock
authorised a comprehensive review of
policy to be undertaken not by the Home
Policy Committee but by seven other

policy groups. The reports of these groups
moved the party decisively to the centre
and right and paved the way for Tony Blair
to accelerate the move after 1994. New
Labour ensured the NEC could no longer
hope to exercise any real power or influence
in determining party policy.

home secretary
The cabinet minister in charge of the
Home Office, a key spokesperson on law
and order issues and a major 'player' in
the race for the prime minister's job. The
home secretary also used to be directly
responsible for the Metropolitan Police
Force (now rechristened 'Service') but
this responsibility has passed to the
Greater London Authority. Notable recent
Conservative holders of the office have
included William Whitelaw, Douglas Hurd
and Kenneth Clarke. Under New Labour,
Jack Straw took a robust and proactive line
on racism in society and public bodies,
in particular the police force. In common
with previous incumbents, he steadfastly
refused to consider the decriminalisation
of so-called 'soft drugs' such as cannabis.
His successor, David Blunkett, however,
did relax the laws on cannabis to a small
degree. Other Labour home secretaries
were Charles Clarke, John Reid, Jaqui
Smith and Alan Johnson. Theresa May
took over after the May 2010 election.

homelessness
The most visible symptom of poverty.
Homelessness was especially visible in
the big cities during the 1980s, often in
the form of young people sleeping in shop
doorways or in 'cardboard cities' under
railway arches (16–17-year-olds had had
their right to state benefits withdrawn). In
theory local authorities have a duty to house
anyone without shelter. However, partly
because of the decline of council house
stock (a result of the 'right to buy' policy of
the early 1980s) local authorities have not
been able to house everyone. Figures from
the charity Shelter show a decline in the
number of homeless people, from 223,860
in 1991, to 179,610 in 1996 and 172,760

POLITICS

in 2000. Similarly, on 3 August 2001 the government's Rough Sleepers Unit, headed by Louise Casey, reported a drop in homelessness. According to its report there were 703 people sleeping rough in England each night, down from 1,180 in 2000. In London, too, the number had nearly halved: down from 621 to 357.

In spring 2009 the Office for National Statistics revealed a reduction in homelessness from over 25,000 in 1998 to just over 15,000 in 2009.

See also council housing; Shelter.

'homes for votes' scandal

Scandal involving Westminster council. The district auditor John Magill investigated the accounts of the council in 1994 and revealed that housing had been preferentially sold to people deemed likely to vote Conservative. The council – especially its leader, Dame Shirley Porter – was condemned by the report and she was ordered to repay some £35 million. Those accused vehemently denied the charges and Porter was cleared on appeal in May 1999. However, in December 2001 the House of Lords reimposed a £26.5 million surcharge. In August 2002 the council won a High Court judgement to help it recover the sum but Porter claimed that her net assets were now only £300,000 rather than the estimated £70 million she was reputed to be worth. In April 2004 a £12.3 million settlement was reached between the council and Dame Shirley.

homosexuality

In medieval times, ecclesiastical or Church law designated homosexual acts a sin, though not too serious a crime. The first law against homosexuality was passed in 1534. In 1885 buggery was made a criminal offence, even if performed in private between consenting adults. The most famous person convicted for homosexual activity was Oscar Wilde, in 1895, who was given two years in Reading prison. In that same year homosexual importuning was made illegal; however, attempts to extend the law to lesbianism in

1921 failed. In 1957 the Wolfenden report recommended repeal of laws pertaining to homosexuality and in 1967 homosexual acts between consenting males over 18 were no longer a criminal offence in England and Wales. However, Scotland, the Republic of Ireland and Northern Ireland had to wait much later for decriminalisation. In 2000, the Labour government embarked on repealing section 28 (of the Local Government Act 1988), which had made it an offence for local authorities to 'promote' (the precise meaning of which is unclear) homosexuality, for example in schools. These changes reflect a more tolerant moral climate towards alternative sexual orientation in Britain. The climate of acceptance improved markedly during the early years of the present century, with both major parties elevating openly gay politicians to high office and seeking to present themselves as appealing to the 2.5 per cent of the population deemed to be gay.

See also section 28; Wolfenden report.

honourable

See parliamentary terms of address.

Honours Scrutiny Committee

Committee of parliament which checks whether nominees for honours are a security risk or have a criminal record. It allegedly was responsible for turning down Margaret Thatcher's attempt to elevate Jeffrey Archer in 1990. In 2000 the Neill Committee on Standards in Public Life recommended the committee be given responsibility for checking whether honours were connected to political donations.

honours system

The system whereby the crown, advised by the government, hands out peerages, knighthoods and sundry medals to those thought to be deserving of them. Opponents claim this is a feudal relic which should be abolished as it adds even more power to the incumbent of Number 10 Downing Street. Defenders say it is a means of rewarding citizens for services to the life of the nation. It comprises a whole hierarchy of awards, from the MBE, CBE and OBE to knighthoods and peerages. Life peers are entitled to sit in the Lords. There have been accusations that governments have been prepared to give honours in exchange for contributions to party funds and there is some evidence to support this, despite the filtering work of the Honours Scrutiny Committee. The Labour government introduced in January 2001 a new category of honour called 'people's peers', whereby individuals could nominate themselves or others. The first such list was much mocked, as it included a number of professors and successful business people.

In February 2004 the Commons Public Administration Committee, chaired by Dr Tony Wright MP, announced it would hold an inquiry into reform of the honours system, declaring reform was a matter of 'when, not if'. This followed revelations in December 2003 of a system which was: too secretive; dominated by civil servants; and characterised by a surprising number of people who chose to refuse acceptance of any proffered honour. In July 2004 the committee urged a drastic reduction in the honours given; for example, dames and knights should go as well as the Order of Bath, and the name 'Empire' should be changed to 'Excellence'. Despite the praise which the report attracted, nothing substantive resulted by way of reform.

> Members of the civil service orders rise from CMG (known sometimes in Whitehall as Call Me God) to the KCMG (Kindly Call Me God) to – for a select few governors and super ambassadors – the GCMG (God Calls Me God). (Anthony Sampson, *Anatomy of Britain*, 1962)

House of Commons
www.parliament.uk/commons
The so-called 'lower' chamber of parliament – the Lords is the 'upper' – and effectively the forum for democratic government of the country. It can be traced back to the gathering of representatives from local communities. In 1295 Edward I summoned two knights from each of the shires, two citizens to represent each of

the cities and two others to represent each of the boroughs. This assembly came to be known as the Commons and in time sat separately from the House of Lords. Over time it was the Commons which agreed to grant taxation to the monarch and its support was also sought in respect of certain royal policies. In exchange for such support the crown agreed to redress grievances from the citizenry and from this foothold the Commons came to exert its right to help formulate new laws. In 1547 the Commons were allowed a permanent location in the chapel of St Stephen in Westminster. During the English Civil War the Commons became the seat of rebellion against the crown and by the end of the 17th century its importance was entrenched by the Glorious Revolution (1688–89). The decision to invite Mary and William of Orange to accede to the throne in place of James II was made on certain conditions. Parliament was to entrench its control over the supply of finance to the crown and to insist the crown could govern only with the 'consent' of parliament. The 1694 Triennial Act removed the crown's ability to extend the life of supportive parliaments indefinitely. The Lords, however, still held the important national debates and extensive patronage enabled the aristocracy to dominate membership of the lower chamber. However, the Great Reform Act 1832 ended such control and elections to the Commons came to provide the legitimate government. The right to vote was extended in 1867 and 1884 and the number of MPs rose to 707 in 1918, though fell to 619 in 1920 after the creation of the Irish Free State. In 1997 there were 659 MPs elected, all representing single-member constituencies; in 2010 there were 650. The Parliament Act 1911 marked the end of the hegemony of the Lords and the beginning of the modern era in which the election of candidates to the Commons determines the party which is to form the government of the day. In 1997 the Commons cost a total of £202 million to run. The cost of the House of Commons in 2008–09 had increased by some £12 million from the previous year, to

£392 million, £157 million of which went on MPs' salaries and pensions.

In the wake of the MP's expenses scandal, which reached its height in May–June 2009, various constitutional remedies were suggested, including: giving more power to the Commons to check an over-powerful executive; fixed-term parliaments; reform of the voting system to make MPs more representative and accountable to voters; open primaries; and a recall mechanism to enable voters to replace an MP who had not proved acceptable.

See also House of Commons reform; MPs' expenses scandal; Westminster Hall Chamber.

House of Commons reform

Reform of the Commons was a concern of many MPs and activists before New Labour came to power in 1997 – the chief complaint being that the legislature was too weak in relation to the executive. Labour did not greatly change that imbalance but did introduce a number of reforms after 1997, including the dropping of the use of a top hat for points of order (members previously had to place a top hat on their head to indicate they had a point of order to make) and the speaker's wig, extra debates in Westminster Hall, more pre-legislation consultation, Thursday morning sittings, early finishes on Thursday evening, fewer Friday sittings and better staff and facilities. In the autumn of 1998 the Jenkins commission reported on the reform of the voting system which elects MPs to the Commons but no action was taken as a result.

In the summer of 2000 the chairs of select committees wrote a report recommending more power to the legislature but the then leader of the house, Margaret Beckett, was unimpressed. After June 2001 the same group of MPs hoped to convince the new leader of the house, Robin Cook, that such a shift of power was necessary in a chamber with such a massive government majority and a premier who tended to ignore it. On 21 June 2001 Robin Cook gave heart to reformers by promising to bring parliament's procedures into the 21st

century and act as an effective democratic check on the executive. He introduced a raft of reforms in the autumn of 2002, including an earlier finishing time for debates, but critics insisted he had done little to improve the overall balance between the government and the legislature.

Before the 2010 election the chair of the Public Administration Select Committee, Dr Tony Wright, compiled a package of reforms designed to strengthen the legislature against the executive which attracted much cross-party support. It remains to be seen if the coalition government will implement any or all of them.

> Being an MP feeds the vanity and starves the self-respect. (Matthew Parris, 1997)

> The earlier parliament can get in on the act of drafting bills, the better the chance of MPs of influencing the shape of bills. (Robin Cook, 7 January 2002)

House of Lords

www.parliament.uk/lords

The upper chamber of parliament. Originally the Lords comprised those senior nobles, usually substantial landowners and clergy, who advised the monarch. Despite the fact that the representatives of local communities (the Commons) became powerful through their control of granting taxation revenues to the monarch, the Lords provided the most important personnel of government right up until the late 19th century. However, the changing balance of economic power from the landed aristocracy to industrial middle class was slowly becoming reflected in the highest circles and at the end of the first decade of the 20th century a great conflict occurred in which there could be only one winner. David Lloyd George's people's budget of 1909 contained social reforms and dared the Lords to refuse a money bill – something which by convention it had always passed. Eventually it was passed but the reforming government of Herbert Asquith was determined to curb the undemocratic upper chamber. The Parliament Act 1911 restricted its powers to delaying money bills by one month and other public bills by up to two years; the Parliament Act 1949 reduced the latter to one year. The Labour Party resolved early on its history to abolish the chamber but then softened its position to one of reform as it basically accepted that the Lords' functions of debating, amending and revising were worthwhile and necessary.

In March 2010 the Lords had 704 members, of whom 25 were lords spiritual (bishops); there were 211 Labour peers; 188 Conservatives; 72 Liberal Democrats; 2 UK Independence Party; 182 cross-benchers; and 24 'others'. Of the total, 587 were life peers and 92 hereditary peers. A reported in 2007 stated that the average daily attendance was around 408. In 2008–09 the cost of running the Lords was £106.5 million.

A study in reported in the *Economist* in September 2008 revealed that membership of the Lords was very much skewed to the south, with 23 per cent living in London, 18 per cent in the south-east and only 2 per cent in the north-east, with similar percentages in other provincial regions. Whereas the US Congress ensures representation of rural backwaters by giving two Senate seats to each state, the Lords offers no protection. Moreover, getting rid of the hereditary peers has accentuated the effect as so many of them dwelt in rural areas. It is expected that plans to reform the Lords may see it converted into a wholly elected body with the voting system based on 'regional or sub-regional constituencies'. Ironically, peers living in London had voted on only one-third of motions. Even the eight who lived abroad had better voting records.

> I went to the House of Lords because I had nowhere else to go. (Emmanuel Shinwell, 1977)

> A big cat detained for a period in a poodle parlour, sharpening her claws on the velvet. (Matthew Parris on Lady Thatcher in the Lords, 1993)

House of Lords Appointments Commission (HLAP)

http://lordsappointments.independent.gov.uk
Non-departmental public body, set up in May 2000, sponsored by the prime minister. It recommends appointments of all non-party political life peers and vets all nominations for the chamber. This body took on a role previously undertaken by the prime minister, who now informs the Commission of the number of nominations required for non-party political peers. The premier then puts the Commission's recommendations to the queen in the same way as nominations made by political parties. In addition, the Commission vets nominations to the Lords 'to ensure the highest standards of propriety'. The government's consultation paper on reforming the Lords, published September 2003, envisaged a statutory appointments commission to take over the work of the HLAP.

House of Lords reform

This has been a source of much debate and conflict since Labour announced it would reform the chamber in its 1997 manifesto. Some reformers even argue that the upper chamber is redundant and that only one is necessary for good government, as shown by Sweden, which abandoned its second chamber in 1970. The hereditary peers were virtually abolished in 1999, although 92 were retained as part of a compromise until the nature of the new chamber had been resolved. Then the Wakeham royal commission proposed a new chamber, for which 20 per cent of the members would be elected. The resultant white paper built on these proposals but they were savaged by party critics and a joint Lords–Commons committee proposed a number of options for reform, which were debated in February 2003. Tony Blair, together with the Lords themselves, favoured an all-appointed house but all the options for a new house were voted down. In September 2003 Lord Falconer, the lord chancellor, announced the imminent abolition of the residual 92 hereditary peers and declared the house would be filled by appointment, an outcome which was denounced as contrary to Labour's 2001 manifesto and to a specific vote in January 2003. In July 2007, Jack Straw, Gordon Brown's new lord chancellor, declared that: 'The Government is determined to proceed with this programme of reform with a view to its completion'. In July 2008 a white paper on the subject was issued which suggested: an 80–100 per cent elected chamber; confirmation of continuing Commons supremacy; a single, non-renewable term of 12–15 years; members to be elected in thirds coinciding with general elections; a significantly smaller chamber, though with Church of England bishops retained; the ending of any residual hereditary peers' presence; and the establishment of an appointments commission in the event of there being an appointed element in the membership.

See also Wakeham report.

houses of parliament
www.parliament.uk
Also known as the Palace of Westminster. Most of the medieval royal palace was burnt down in 1834, but it was rebuilt over two decades (1840–60) by Charles Barry and A. W. Pugin in a distinctive Gothic style. In 1940 the debating chamber was burnt down following an attack by incendiary bombs during the Blitz. It was rebuilt in its original form by G. G. Scott and opened in 1950. The palace is often perceived as the foremost symbol of British democracy and is one of the best-known buildings in the world.

housing association
An association of tenants independent of a local authority. Housing associations were encouraged by the Conservative governments of the 1980s and increased their share of dwellings from 1 per cent in 1979 to 4 per cent in 1995.

See also housing policy.

housing policy
This effectively began after the First World War, when the government decided to subsidise local authority housing with contributions from local government and tenant rents. In 1972 a rent rebate was introduced to give means-tested assistance to some tenants. By 1980 councils owned 32 per cent of all dwellings. Margaret Thatcher's

government was in favour of helping people to buy their own homes. In 1980 the right to buy policy enabled tenants to buy their own council houses at a discount. In 1982 housing benefit was introduced by local authorities. During the 1980s housing subsidies were drastically slashed and housing was subject to more cuts than any other form of public spending. By the end of the decade over 65 per cent of people owned their own homes and only 18 per cent of the population resided in council housing. John Major's government reduced the proportion of mortgage interest payments eligible for tax relief, a process completed by Labour chancellor Gordon Brown after 1997.

The 2001 queen's speech revealed that two new reforms were in the pipeline. First, conveyancing would be brought up to date – a practice hitherto based on an 1875 Act. New procedures would be based on electronic methods, to speed up the process of house purchase. Measures to reform leasehold tenure were also unveiled; these were aimed at ending the activities of unscrupulous landlords and giving tenants a say in the management of the property they rent.

The Guardian on 21 June 2001 reported that council housing appeared to be in terminal decline as a local authority responsibility. In 1988 the Conservatives gave permission for councils to sell off all of their council house stock but in recent years it has been Labour and Liberal Democrat councils which have taken advantage of the measure. Mostly the houses are sold to housing associations, as they are subject to fewer financial constraints than are local authorities. By 2015, the Guardian calculated, there would be 5 million houses owned by housing associations and only a handful of council houses would be left.

In March 2002 the Joseph Rowntree Foundation produced a report which predicted that Britain needed to build 4 million houses by 2012 if house price inflation was to be curtailed. The authors were concerned that large numbers of public sector workers could no longer afford to buy homes.

In his comprehensive spending review in July 2004 chancellor Gordon Brown announced a 4.1 per cent increase in spending on housing for the three years from 2005. In money terms this amounted to a pledge of £1.3 billion, enough to build an extra 10,000 homes a year for renting by 2008. In late June 2009 prime minister Brown announced a programme of trebling spending on housing to £2.1 billion over the next two years, funding 110,000 affordable houses to buy or rent.

Human Rights Act 1998

Human rights are basic entitlements which a person can expect to receive from the state and power holders, such as the rights to life and freedom from unlawful imprisonment and torture. More recently claims have been made to include such entitlements as economic and social resources as a basic human right. All civilised societies claim to respect human rights. Britain, a signatory of the United Nations' Universal Declaration of Human Rights (1948) and the European Convention on Human Rights (1950), generally has a good record on humanitarian treatment of its citizens as well as aliens, although Britain has a poor record in terms of judgements in the European Court of Human Rights. In October 2000, the European Convention was incorporated into British law by the Human Rights Act 1998, thus fulfilling a pledge made by New Labour in its election manifesto of 1997. British closeness to US policy in Iraq and some of the related abuses at Guantanamo Bay prison and the flying by the CIA of suspects to countries where torture would be used as an interrogation technique (the so-called 'extraordinary rendition' process) have harmed the country's reputation for upholding human rights.

hung parliament

A situation when no single party commands an overall majority in the House of Commons. The end result is most likely to be the formation of a coalition or minority government, at least in the short term, until a new election is called by the prime minister. Precisely whom the monarch should invite to form a government is the subject of debate, though in the first instance it would almost certainly be the leader of the largest party in the Commons. If no pact could be established to create a working majority the monarch would be advised to dissolve parliament and call another election.

Hung parliaments occurred in February 1974 and in May 2010; in the former, a minority Labour government emerged and in the latter a coalition government between the Conservatives and Liberal Democrats.

See also 'golden triangle'; head of state; Lib–Lab pact.

hunting

Labour promised to ban hunting with dogs in its 1997 manifesto but was influenced by the outcry this caused in the countryside, as expressed by the Countryside Alliance, which mobilised marches in London and other demonstrations. In September 2004 Tony Blair fulfilled his 2000 promise to push through a hunting ban. This sop to his party was not won without violent demonstrations outside and within the Commons. The ban came into effect in July 2006 in England (in Scotland it was already banned). Should they wish to organise a hunt, hunting associations have to lay an artificial trail, though the League Against Cruel Sports alleges that many hunts are breaking the law. Supporters claim 320,00 turned up to hunt on Boxing Day 2008; the Master of Foxhounds Association claimed 184 functioning hunts in November of that same year.

hustings

Place of electoral debate. Before the Ballot Act 1872, parliamentary candidates would be nominated at open public meetings, and would make speeches to the electorate from a platform. The term is still used to describe the debates during election campaigns, although live public meetings have, since the 1960s, tended to die out as elections have increasingly been fought via the media. As a result of this many politicians have not troubled to acquire the art of public oratory, and now rely upon the professional speech writer and media advisor or spin doctor to burnish their performance.

Hutton report, 2004

www.the-hutton-inquiry.org.uk
Report of the Investigation into the Circumstances Surrounding the Death of Dr David Kelly. The inquiry was set up in July 2003, under Lord Justice Hutton, to investigate the circumstances of the death of Dr David Kelly, a Ministry of Defence (MoD) weapons advisor who committed suicide after it became known he had spoken to BBC reporter Andrew Gilligan earlier in the year. Gilligan had claimed, in a May 2003 report on the *Today* programme on Radio 4, that a 'senior intelligence source' had told him that the September dossier (on Iraq's weapons of mass destruction) had 'sexed up' the material provided by the security services. The name of Alastair Campbell, the Downing Street press secretary, was specifically mentioned. The resulting row between the government and the media was volcanic. The key issues which witnesses were pressed upon were:

1 The decision by the MoD to make Kelly's name public. It transpired that senior civil servants and ministers, including Tony Blair (prime minister) and Geoff Hoon (secretary of state for defence), were involved in the decision and the methodology whereby the MoD virtually encouraged the press to identify him.

2 Whether the claim that Iraq could mount an attack with weapons of mass destruction in 45 minutes was correct or a wilful exaggeration. Evidence revealed that the claim referred only to 'battlefield' and not long-range weapons.

3 Whether staff in Blair's office manipulated intelligence material to help persuade a doubting country that war was justified. It seemed clear, from evidence submitted to the inquiry, that

some elaboration of the dossier did take place at the behest of Number 10.

Lord Hutton announced the conclusions of his report on 28 January 2004. He astonished the political class by finding almost wholly for the government and clearing politicians (Blair, Hoon), senior civil servants (Sir David Omand, Sir Kevin Tebbit) and senior intelligence staff (John Scarlett). It was the BBC which bore the brunt of the criticism: he found fault with its editorial control of Andrew Gilligan and with its governors for backing a flawed story without checking the facts. The next day the BBC chairman, Gavyn Davies, the director general, Greg Dyke, and Gilligan himself all resigned. Press and public reactions were generally adverse, with loud accusations of a 'whitewash' by an establishment figure; one poll suggested the public did not believe Hutton had achieved the right balance.

See also weapons of mass destruction (WMD).

hybrid bill

Bill with the characteristics of both a private and public bill; that is, while it may be of general interest it may also have significance for certain individuals or organisations. The procedure to be followed in respect of such bills includes elements of the procedures for both public and private. Backbenchers may introduce bills which come to be judged as hybrid, but this is rare – a recent example being the Crossrail project for central London in October 2007.

hypothecated tax

A tax raised by a particular means for a specific purpose. The Liberal Democrats regularly declare such 'ring-fencing' in their manifestos (for example a penny on income tax for education). Other parties have considered the idea but, despite some evidence that the public favours it, the Treasury resists any weakening of its control over how the general tax take should be disbursed.

I

Ibbs report, 1988

Improving Management in Government: The Next Steps, by Sir Robin Ibbs. The report recommended the separation of the routine from the policy-advising functions of the civil service. This meant in practice the hiving off of routine government functions into executive agencies – good examples of which are the Benefits Agency and the Driver and Vehicle Licensing Agency, at Swansea. Some 80 per cent of civil servants now work in such agencies, with the general conclusion being that they represent an improvement on previous practice.

See also executive agency.

ICM

www.icmresearch.co.uk

Polling organisation which began life as Marplan and whose polls were usually reported in the *Guardian*. In 1989 the chief researcher left Marplan and set up ICM. The *Guardian* is still its regular customer for political polls.

identity card

A means of identifying every citizen in a country. Home secretary David Blunkett announced a consultation exercise on compulsory identity cards on 5 February 2002. The idea was to make them 'entitlement cards', which would help to prevent fraudulent use of public services and help the police to combat terrorism and credit card fraud, for example. Opponents claimed it would cost over £1 billion and would violate civil liberties. Blunkett made clear, however, that the police would not be able to demand sight of the card and not having one would not be an offence. In July 2002 over 100 MPs plus a battery of pressure groups declared their opposition to the scheme. Peter Lilley, former social security secretary, condemned the idea as unworkable and an affront to civil liberty. In September 2003, however, Blunkett

insisted the plan was worth introducing, despite the cost and the scathing opposition of civil libertarians. After a battle in cabinet Blunkett overcame opposition from chancellor Gordon Brown to the idea in November 2003 but the plan now was to introduce the scheme gradually, in the following stages: a six-month pilot of the new face and fingerprint 'biometric' security features involving 10,000 volunteers; legislation to authorise identity cards by 2004; introduction of a biometric 'credit card' passport in 2006; full identity cards to be introduced by 2007; and a final decision to proceed with a compulsory scheme in 2013. On 29 July 2004 the Home Affairs Select Committee gave qualified backing to the scheme. In July 2009 home secretary Alan Johnson declared he was 'accelerating their introduction', despite his earlier cancellation of a compulsory trial for 30,000 pilots and airport workers. There had always been much debate over the efficacy and cost of the proposition, with the Conservatives and Liberal Democrats opposing it on these grounds as well as on civil rights grounds, and in June 2010 the new coalition government abolished the scheme.

ideology

One of the most hotly debated and used terms in politics. Generally speaking, there are two meanings: a 'relaxed' definition, which sees ideologies as necessary intellectual constructs by which people make sense of the world around them; and a 'restricted' definition, which argues that a ruling group sustains its position and privileges in society not by force alone, but through a set of ideas which act with great intellectual and psychological force upon individuals and groups within society. An example of the latter usage is the Marxist analysis of liberal democracy (sometimes called capitalist democracy), which argues that people have formal political power through the vote but that real power is located deep down in the economic relations of capitalist society: governments may come and go but the economic order remains largely unchanged.

POLITICS

In the British context this would translate into a view which asserts that the establishment is always in control; and, indeed, the general lack of difference between the agendas of the two main parties in the early years of the new millennium might be seen as reinforcement for such a view.

British politics has always tended to be non-ideological, in the sense that parties avoid extreme beliefs and values, but there have been coherent sets of political ideas informing political parties since the 18th and 19th centuries: conservatism, socialism and liberalism. Marxism and fascism never made much headway, though 'green thinking' won converts towards the end of the 20th century. The British tradition is essentially pragmatic within the context of a system which reflects, and is underpinned by, liberal assumptions. Some political scientists argue that British political culture is rather non-intellectual compared with, say, the French, and indeed suspicious of grand systems of thought such as Marxism. After the Second World War, sharp disagreements in ideology tended to diminish as the postwar consensus on the Keynesian mixed economy and welfare state became established. But the relative economic decline during the 1960s and the appearance of 'stagflation' in the 1970s caused the fracture of the cross-party agreements and ideology re-emerged in the form of the new right in the Conservative Party led by Margaret Thatcher and Keith Joseph. Thatcher championed classical liberal ideas on the economy and favoured a minimal role for the government, at least in terms of the economy and social provision. Labour experienced a similar radicalisation but leftwards, the party producing one of the most socialist manifestos in its postwar history for the 1983 general election. However, the rout of the party at the polls gave credence to Gerald Kaufman's quip that the manifesto was the 'longest suicide note in history'.

After this debacle, the Labour Party was reconstructed, first by Neil Kinnock, then John Smith and Tony Blair, the result being the repositioning of Labour into a centrist position which was closer to Thatcherism

than socialism in a number of key respects, especially: an anti-inflationary economic strategy, a tough line on crime and the acceptance of privatisation in the public services. After its landslide victory in 1997, Labour continued the macro-economic policies of Margaret Thatcher and John Major in a number of ways, though chancellor Gordon Brown did substantially increase public spending. Political scientists are divided, however, on whether the party developed an authentic ideological position, especially Blair's vaunted 'third way'. Some argue that the position was essentially Thatcherite with a socialist 'spin' via distinctive New Labour language. Others argue it responded to events and reacted to focus groups in particular, as part of a strategy of maintaining popularity at all costs. Indeed, Robert Worcester, chairman of MORI and former advisor to Harold Wilson, suggested that political parties in 2001 were mainly concerned with winning elections, rather than developing any distinctive ideological position, an argument reinforced by students of political marketing like Jennifer Lees-Marchment.

The accession to power of David Cameron as Conservative leader in December 2005 marked a switch of direction for this traditional right-wing party. By degrees he nudged it towards a more liberal agenda, less opposed to spending and the European Union and more liberal in attitude to gays and ethnic minorities. Some compare his political rise to that of Tony Blair, and the easy charm, good televisual skills and good Commons debating are certainly redolent of New Labour's long-time leader. The result was an initial blurring of identity between the two main parties but the 2007–09 financial crisis saw Brown championing a Keynesian policy of continued borrowing and spending while Cameron urged curbs on spending and an end to any more borrowing.

See also hegemony; postwar consensus.

illegal immigrant

An immigrant who has managed to avoid the legal processes required to reside legally within the UK. Illegal migrants may be failed asylum seekers, the children of illegal immigrants, visa over-stayers, or people smuggled in via various means of transport. In March 2009 a study by the London School of Economics estimated there were close on a million such immigrants but other estimates exceed even that figure, much to the indignation of those who oppose what they regard as excessive immigration. Such people often manage to stay with relatives and find work, usually at very low wages in the 'black economy', in restaurants, cleaning companies and the like.

image
The perceptions of party, leader and policies formed in the minds of voters and opinion formers. In this political sense, at least, appearances make reality and in the media-dominated world of modern politics the presentation of ideas is as important as content, if not more so. One expert commentator (B. Bruce, *Images of Power*, 1992) reported that 'the impact we make on others [on the television] depends on ... how we look and behave (55 per cent); how we speak (38 per cent); and what we say (only 7 per cent)'. Despite the media skills of Harold Macmillan and Harold Wilson, not to mention James Callaghan, Margaret Thatcher was the first modern British politician fully to embrace the implications of the media for politics. Her advisor, Gordon Reece, encouraged her to take great care with her image: her appearance was transformed from frumpy housewife to warrior queen, and her voice was lowered to avoid its disconcerting tendency to be shrill. In addition, her speeches were studded with sound bites to catch the attention of the news bulletins. Under the tutelage of spin doctors like Peter Mandelson and Alastair Campbell, the Labour leadership followed suit and soon bettered the Conservatives at projecting the best possible image of party and leader. It is widely believed the political career of Labour's Robin Cook would have flourished more had he been born with a face which looked attractive on television and Ming Campbell's had he not looked

older than his 65 years when elected leader of the Liberal Democrats – a sad comment on our times perhaps.

See also campaigning; political marketing; spin; spin doctor.

immigration
The movement of people into the country for residence, for whatever reason but often to seek asylum or refuge or for economic betterment. Immigration has climbed up the list of voter concerns, with polls showing 68 per cent think Britain has too many immigrants. Reducing immigration, however, is constrained by: membership of the European Union, from whence arrive 30 per cent of the net inflow; legitimate asylum seekers; and inter-ethnic marriages. Students make up a large slice of immigrants but their study fees are valued; skilled workers, comprising 20 per cent of immigrants, often compensate for indigenous skill shortages.

Before 1945 immigration controls were minimal and waves of refugees from overseas regularly arrived, including Jews, socialists and other political creeds. They were all attracted by the reputation Britain had built up as a welcoming refuge for such persecuted groups. Around the Second World War migrant Jews and Poles were assimilated with relative ease. Shortly thereafter, the government encouraged economic migration from Commonwealth countries to meet shortages in service industries like the National Health Service and London Transport. It did this by introducing the British Nationality Act 1948, which gave British citizenship to all Commonwealth citizens and so provided the legal basis for the influx of workers, initially from the Caribbean. Later India and Pakistan were the source of thousands of emigrants, who generally found employment in low-paid, traditional sectors like textiles. Many immigrants lived in inner-city areas of the big conurbations like London, Manchester, Leeds and Bradford.

By the 1960s some problems integrating the newcomers into British culture were being experienced and the government decided to place curbs on future immigration. The Commonwealth Immigration Act 1962 was consequently passed. It limited entry to holders of passports issued in Britain itself and required immigrants to hold 'work vouchers'. The Race Relations Act 1965 outlawed discrimination on the grounds of race. The Race Relations Act 1976 set up the Commission for Racial Equality. From 1968 immigration became a volatile political issue after Enoch Powell, a Conservative front-bench figure, forecast 'rivers of blood' if immigration were not drastically reduced (he later called for it to be ended). In 1978 Margaret Thatcher expressed her opposition to unlimited immigration by saying Britain did not wish to be 'swamped' by new cultures. This confirmed her party as the main opponent of immigration, apart from the overtly racist far-right parties. The British Nationality Act 1981 and the Immigration Act 1988 sought to restrict immigration.

There are often suggestions that poorer white people in immigrant areas feel that immigrants and asylum seekers receive too many favours and hand-outs. Some commentators argue that Britain has been hypocritical over immigration, encouraging it in the 1950s when cheap labour was required but closing the door in the 1970s once economic problems had put a squeeze on employment. However, population projections suggest more rather than less immigration will be needed again, as a result of the declining birth rate.

Immigration minister Liam Byrne, in the autumn of 2008, reckoned the advantage to the British economy of immigration was as high as £6 billion in 2006, and this was seen as a reason for accepting the social costs of such inflows. But the Lords Economic Committee begged to differ in its report of 1 April of that year. It argued that, with a net immigration of 190,000 each year, the overall economic benefit is negligible. Gross domestic product might be boosted by more people living and working in the country but the per capita share is unaffected. The report argued that such large numbers coming into Britain

depressed wages for the lowest paid and tended to push up house prices, but had helped reduce the unemployment rate, as these incomers were more willing than British workers to accept certain jobs. The *Economist* did not see this as a 'bad news' report but recognised that the government's defence of immigration in the coin of national economic advantage was devalued by the evidence that the effect is, in fact, 'merely neutral'.

The 2001 census revealed that there were 4.6 million people of ethnic minority in the UK: 7.9 per cent of the total, increased from 6 per cent in 1991. Half of these were Asian, with mixed-race people accounting for 15 per cent. Half of all minorities live in the London area, where they comprise one-third of the whole. Leicester's proportion of white residents fell from 70.1 per cent in 1991 to 59.5 per cent in 2008; by 2026, calculates Sheffield University, it will be 44.5 per cent. In 2007, some 591,000 immigrants arrived – the largest groups from Pakistan, Bangladesh and Sri Lanka – but 400,000 long-term migrants left.

The introduction of a new points-based system for skilled workers seeking entry to the UK began in autumn 2008. Under it, immigrants need to speak English to a 'basic user standard'. Immigration minister Liam Byrne reckoned if the system had been in place during 2007, it would have excluded 20,000 people. The principle behind the scheme is that British workers are allowed first chance at UK vacancies and then applicants from overseas, with sufficient points, are allowed to compete. 'By moving points up and down we can make sure the numbers we allow into the UK are in line with the needs of British business and the country as a whole', said Byrne (*Guardian*, 7 May 2008).

See also asylum seeker; citizenship test; imperialism.

impeachment
Form of criminal trial initiated by the House of Commons with the Lords acting as judge. It emerged in the 14th century

but then fell into disuse until the 17th century, when the Indian administrator Warren Hastings was impeached; his trial lasted seven years, after which he was found innocent but by then he had been financially ruined. Its last employment in Britain was in 1848 but in August 2004 Adam Price MP (Plaid Cymru) attempted to impeach Tony Blair for misleading the country over the war in Iraq. The process requires an MP to make the accusation and present the case to the house. If a majority agrees, a committee draws up articles of impeachment and then the case is heard before the Lords.

imperial preference

A system of defensive tariffs designed to advantage the British Empire. The author of the idea was Joseph Chamberlain and the aim was to offset Britain's relative economic decline. The national government adopted the policy in 1931; the Ottowa conference in 1932 added the dominions; crown colonies were included in 1933. The postwar preference for Commonwealth goods was gradually phased out and ended when Britain entered the European Community in 1973.

imperialism

The policy of developing an empire, which Britain did partly for economic reasons and partly for the glory. Britain began building its empire in the 16th century; the process gathered pace through to the 19th century and then declined in the 20th. Some historians argue that the empire was acquired almost accidentally; for example, once the Suez Canal had been bought by Disraeli it followed that the countries bordering it needed to be friendly to Britain, hence the need to extend British influence in North Africa and the Middle East. The imperialist idea was sustained and overlaid by a belief (or at least assertion) that Britain was fulfilling a mission to civilise and improve backward peoples. This nourished a defensive attitude towards colonial subjects, usually accompanied by a feeling of superiority.

A nostalgic atavism regarding the Empire helps to explain some of the hostility of the Conservative Party towards the Europe Union. The availability of cheap labour in the Empire led to waves of immigration, which was often encouraged by British governments in the 1950s and 1960s to meet Britain's labour shortages, a situation sharply curtailed by Immigration Acts when economic problems emerged in the early 1970s and Britain no longer needed its imperial mobile labour force.

A related term, 'cultural imperialism', developed in the 1960s and 1970s, is used to describe the impact of a dominant western culture, usually associated with the USA, on other countries. This is manifested in music, film, clothes and language. In Britain and many other countries, both inside and outside Europe, the baseball cap and Coca-Cola have become icons of a US-inspired style.

Improvement and Development Agency for Local Government

www.idea.gov.uk
Agency devoted to improving the delivery of public services by local government. It was set up in 1999 with the aims of: offering practical solutions to performance problems; developing innovative approaches (for example e-government) to ensure internal knowledge transfer; and acting on behalf of local government as a whole.

'In Place of Strife', 1968

Title of a white paper on industrial relations written by Barbara Castle in 1968. At the time, Britain's economy was being damaged by a wave of unofficial strikes and the white paper was an attempt to bring some order to the apparent anarchy. It ignored the voluntary regulation urged by the 1968 Donovan report on labour relations and instead advocated legal sanctions. There was to be a 28-day 'cooling off' period before strikes could legally take place. Workers who ignored this condition could be prosecuted, and fined or imprisoned if found guilty. In addition, it proposed government-imposed strike ballots and settlements to inter-union disputes. British unions, at that time, opposed government or legal interference in their concerns as an article of faith and the bulk of them angrily rejected these ideas. In the early months of 1969 Castle was supported by her prime minister, Harold Wilson, and the chancellor, Roy Jenkins, but was opposed most notably by the home secretary, James Callaghan, plus a majority of the parliamentary party, not to mention the incensed ranks of the trade unions. The proposals fell and along with them the prospects both for Castle's long-term political success and for trouble-free industrial relations during the coming decade.

incentive

The key to right-wing ideas about the economy and founded on an assumption about human nature. Conservatives have always argued that human beings are motivated by the anticipation of personal gain and that this is no bad thing, as it creates enterprise, employment and wealth in society. They have opposed the gradual equalisation of incomes favoured by Labour with its redistributive welfare programmes and have argued that workers need to be given the opportunity to become rich, as restrictions only inhibit the working of the market and reduce efficiency and prosperity. Consequently they have argued for increased incentives for high earners through a reduction of taxation levels; they delivered this during the 1980s, especially through the reduction of the top rate of income tax to 40 per cent.

income tax

First introduced in 1799 at two shillings in the pound to help finance William Pitt's war against Revolutionary France. The measure was briefly repealed in 1802, was then reintroduced from 1803 to 1816 and then abolished, with all records destroyed, until Robert Peel reintroduced it again in 1842. Peel reimposed it to compensate for cuts in customs duties and by the end of the century it was a reluctantly accepted feature of life and a major source of government

funding. David Lloyd George recognised the need for allowances for pensioners and, at the other end of the scale, introduced a 'surtax' on the very rich. Since the Second World War (during which the standard rate was over 50 per cent of earnings) manifold allowances were introduced to take account of people's needs and government health and welfare priorities. By the 1970s income tax was thought to be too high by the Conservative Party and Margaret Thatcher resolved to bring it down to provide incentives for people in work. In 1987 chancellor Nigel Lawson reduced the top rate from over 80 pence in the pound to 40 per cent. The incoming Labour government in 1997 retained income tax at this level and relied on indirect taxes to raise more revenue. After 2001 Tony Blair still opposed any increase in income tax, on the grounds that it would be unacceptable to 'middle England'. This appeared to contradict Labour's preference for progressive taxation (taxing the rich proportionately more) but was to some extent offset by chancellor Gordon Brown's redistributive budgets after 1997.

Britain's levels of income tax are lower than those of most of its European neighbours, although, in a dramatic break with earlier policy, in April 2009 Labour announced a future top rate of 50p in the pound for people earning over £150,000 a year.

See also indirect taxation.

incomes policy

Government regulation of wage increases across the whole economy. John Maynard Keynes argued for full employment, although he was aware that in a free market workers have the power, through free collective bargaining, to negotiate higher wages, which are then passed on to the market in higher prices, which then stimulate further demands for wage increases – in other words a price spiral or inflation. Governments after the war tried all kinds of incomes policies to deal with this problem, for example pay freezes and pay norms, but they all, eventually, broke down.

In the 1970s the collapse of the Conservatives' prices and incomes policy was disastrous and set off an inflationary price spiral which Labour, in power after February 1974, initially could not control. After inflation reached 30 per cent per annum the Social Contract was agreed between unions and the government, which gave the unions a say in certain areas of policy in exchange for a pay norm for the year. This approach brought inflation down to single figures, but in 1979 the Trades Union Congress refused to accept a 5 per cent norm and there was an outbreak of strikes by the lower paid, resulting in the so-called 'winter of discontent'. This eventually helped bring down the Labour government of James Callaghan, and the incoming prime minister, Margaret Thatcher, emphatically rejected an incomes policy. Instead she insisted on tight control of the money supply via interest rates to reduce inflation. This was intended to demonstrate to the unions that there was no money available, and thus inhibit wage demands, but in practice it pushed up the value of the pound and made business more difficult. The resulting unemployment, which exceeded 3 million, was one of the reasons why wage claims reduced and inflation came down.

In the wake of the 2009 recession some voices were raised calling for a public sector wage freeze as a means of restricting spending.

incrementalism

The theory that decisions are made by governments through minor adjustments to existing policy. Charles Lindblom suggests that policy makers are not so much rational in their choices but rather build on the status quo and then 'muddle through', making incremental adjustments where appropriate. The theory may be useful in explaining British policy making, which is notorious for 'muddling through'. For example, the policy of privatisation in the 1980s was not prepared by the Conservatives in opposition and did not appear in their 1979 manifesto. Instead

it was adopted incrementally and, once it became popular with the electorate, was developed and extended to become possibly the Conservatives' major policy platform by the end of the decade. In keeping with this theory, the New Labour government of Tony Blair, elected in 1997, did not reverse significantly any of the privatisations; indeed, Labour built upon them with further sales of public utilities such as the National Air Traffic Services (2001).

One of the problems of the theory is that it fails properly to explain sharp and radical changes in policy, perhaps as evidenced by the abandonment of demand-side Keynesianism in the 1970s and the adoption of a monetarist-inspired approach to the economy from the late 1970s. Another example might be the railways, which were privatised in the mid-1990s but, in view of their failure, effectively taken back into government hands by 2002.

Independent Broadcasting Authority (IBA)

Body set up by statute in 1954 to regulate the 15 independent broadcasting companies. The chair was appointed by the prime minister but the source of revenue from advertising made independent television freer from government pressure. It oversaw the setting up Channel 4 in 1982 and approved satellite broadcasting some years later. The IBA was replaced by the Independent Television Commission under the Broadcasting Act 1990 (itself replaced by Ofcom in 2003).

See also Broadcasting Act 1990; Independent Television Commission.

Independent International Commission on Decommissioning

Set up in 1995 to assist the disarming of the paramilitaries in Northern Ireland. The Commission has been headed since its inception by the Canadian general John de Chastelain. The general's patience was sorely tried for several years until May 2000, when the IRA offered to give up its weapons. Two arms inspectors, Marti Ahtisaari and Cyril Ramaphosa, visited

POLITICS

a number of arms dumps and declared the arms could not be used without their knowledge. After much toing and froing the Commission oversaw a fourth and final act of decommissioning in September 2005 and declared 'We are satisfied that arms decommissioning represents the totality of the IRA's arsenal'.

Independent Labour Party (ILP)

Founded in 1893 (i.e. before the Labour Party) by Keir Hardie as a vehicle for working-class representation in parliament. It was one of the organisations affiliated to the Labour Representation Committee in 1900 and thus was instrumental in the setting up of the modern Labour Party. For the next 46 years it ran alongside Labour, usually as a left-wing gadfly under the leadership of the likes of Fenner Brockway and James Maxton. When the latter died in 1946 the influence of the three-man party was at an end. The ILP ceased to exist in 1975, although it reconstituted itself as a political pressure group.

independent MP

An MP with no party affiliation. Entry into the Commons is now mainly dependent on membership of a party, but there were more independent MPs in the interwar and war years: some two dozen represented university seats; nearly a dozen were elected as a result of wartime exigencies; nearly another two dozen were maverick Conservatives (including Oswald Mosley 1922 and 1923); ten were dissident Liberals; eight were dissident Labour; and six were elected by virtue of support from the left (including Vernon Bartlett, who served as an MP from 1938 to 1950). D. N. Pritt was returned as an independent in 1945 but lost in 1950. In 1970 S. O. Davies, already in his 80s, fought and won as an independent.

In the 2005 election 166 independents stood but only two succeeded. In 2010 the total was nearer 300, most notably, perhaps, Esther Rantzen in Luton South, although she lost her deposit.

Candidates can now rarely secure a seat without the support of a political party.

The few recent examples of independents include Martin Bell, the former BBC foreign correspondent who in the general election of 1997 took the Cheshire seat of Tatton from the Conservative MP Neil Hamilton (who had become engulfed in accusations of sleaze) and, in the 2001 election, a retired consultant, Richard Taylor, who was sensationally returned for Wyre Forest on a campaign against the removal of emergency treatment facilities from Kidderminster Hospital. Following his ejection from the Labour Party in October 2003, George Galloway became an independent MP, though he also stood (unsuccessfully) as a candidate for the European parliament in the June 2004 elections for the anti-Iraq war Respect party. In May 2005, however, he narrowly won a sensational victory in Bethnal Green, where he beat the sitting MP, Oona King. After winning the seat, records show he was not assiduous in attending debates or speaking in the Commons.

> You need three conditions to win [as an independent]. A vulnerable incumbent – there are still too many crooks in Parliament – a well known independent and a good cause. (Martin Bell)

Independent Network

www.independentnetwork.org.uk
Organisation set up in 2005 to support independent candidates who are not attached to established political parties. Supporters include Martin Bell, the former BBC correspondent and independent MP for Tatton 1997–2001, and Dr Richard Taylor, who was elected as an independent for Wyre Forest on the issue of the retention of Kidderminister's hospital. To be members it is necessary to adhere to seven principles drawn up by Martin Bell in 2009 centred upon democratically representing constituents.

Independent Parliamentary Standards Authority

www.parliamentarystandards.org.uk
Independent body set up under the Parliamentary Standards Act 2009. It

replaced the Parliamentary Fees Office and is in charge of the Register of Members' Interests. It has powers to fine MPs who break the rules and oversees the code of conduct for peers. It is also able to implement recommendations from the Committee on Standards in Public Life. The parliamentary standards regulator oversees financial matters, investigates abuses and enforces sanctions. The chair of the authority is Sir Ian Kennedy.

Independent Police Complaints Commission (IPCC)

www.ipcc.gov.uk

Independent commission, set up in April 2004 under the Police Reform Act 2002, tasked with initiating, investigating and monitoring complaints against misconduct by the police. There are 12 commissioners and a chair. The IPCC's remit was extended in 2006 to include serious complaints relating to staff at the Serious Organised Crime Agency (SOCA) and at Her Majesty's Revenue and Customs (HMRC), and again in February 2008 to include serious complaints and conduct matters relating to officers and officials at the UK Border Agency (UKBA).

independent school

Any privately funded school. The private sector, including most boarding schools, accounts for about 7 per cent of all children in education. The more established and exclusive, not to mention expensive, private schools are confusingly called 'public schools'. School fees vary widely but usually exceed £10,000 per pupil per annum.

See also assisted-places scheme; public school.

Independent Television Commission (ITC)

Established in 1990 as the successor organisation to the Independent Broadcasting Authority but itself subsumed within Ofcom (the Office of Communications) in December 2003. The ITC was an attempt to introduce market forces into the cosy world of independent television. In 1990 it decided on applications for the new franchises. The ITC was charged with selecting companies on the basis of who would pay the largest annual fee to the government each year, subject to a quality threshold. As a result of the auction Thames TV, TVAM, TVS and TSW lost their franchises and were replaced by new contractors. The Commission also had a quality remit and in the early 1990s reprimanded Carlton Television for the standard of its programming. It also laid down regulations on questions of decency in advertising and programming. In 1997 it oversaw the introduction of Channel 5 broadcasting.

See also Broadcasting Act 1990; Independent Broadcasting Authority; Office of Communications (Ofcom).

indirect taxation

Taxes upon spending on retail products and services. When most people think of tax they think of direct taxation: the proportion of total income deducted at source by their employer and sent straight to Her Majesty's Revenue and Customs. However, taxes upon retail products such as alcoholic beverages, tobacco and petroleum produce huge amounts of money for the Treasury. Value added tax (VAT) amounted to about £80–100 billion in 2008–09.

Conservative economists tend to favour indirect taxes, as a consumer can choose not to pay the tax by not buying that particular product. This was one of the reasons why Geoffrey Howe increased VAT substantially, in contradiction to pre-election statements, soon after the Conservatives came to power in 1979. However, consumers will continue to buy certain types of product irrespective of price increases, for example petrol, which is a necessity for motorists in rural areas ill served by public transport. In 1999/2000, Conservative politicians, among others, started to use the term 'stealth taxes' to describe the increased level of indirect taxation under New Labour.

industrial democracy
The view that workers should have active participation in the running of their work organisations. Apart from a number of minor and isolated examples, full industrial democracy is unknown in Britain, and even under Labour the nationalised industries did not develop democratic structures for workplace management in anything like the way they did in countries such as postwar Germany. Under New Labour no radical changes were introduced to the management of private or public organisations.

industrial relations
Relations between workers and employers. In Britain these have traditionally been fraught because of 'us and them' attitudes based on class antagonisms. Moreover, compared with other European Union countries there is no strong framework of law to regulate this area in Britain. Indeed, traditionally unions enjoyed legal immunities, though not rights, protecting them from being sued for industrial action. Free collective bargaining was extensively practised, with no central machinery for national wage bargaining.

Governments have tried with varying degrees of success to introduce a framework for industrial relations: Harold Wilson's 'In Place of Strife' policy was destroyed by union and Labour opposition inside cabinet; Edward Heath's statutory approach (including an industrial relations court) came to nothing and ended with his election defeat in 1974; and James Callaghan's Social Contract was destroyed by the 'winter of discontent' of 1978–79. Riding on public dissatisfaction with Labour's closeness to the unions, Margaret Thatcher won the 1979 general election, and passed legislation curtailing union power and letting market forces decide wages and employee–employer relations. The miners' strike of 1984–85 was a watershed in that it marked the breaking of the industrial muscle of organised labour; power then passed away from the unions and to the employers, and unemployment further weakened the unions through its ability to

reduce the willingness of workers to take industrial action. Consequently the number of days lost through strike action fell to record low levels in the 1980s and 1990s. After 1997, the New Labour government did not repeal Conservative trade union legislation; however, it did pass legislation to make employers recognise trade unions if more than half the employees want one. It signed the Social Chapter of the 1992 Maastricht treaty (which John Major's government had declined to do at the time), which grants workers certain basic rights and regulates working times.

See also 'In Place of Strife'; Industrial Relations Act 1971; Information and Consultation Directive; Social Chapter; Social Contract.

Industrial Relations Act 1971
An ill-fated piece of legislation, introduced by the Heath government, intended to solve intractable industrial relations disputes in Britain. It provided a framework of law for unions and established a national industrial relations court. Its legal terms allowed for compulsory recognition of unions, a registration system for unions, legally binding contracts between unions and employers, strike ballots, and cooling off periods during a dispute. The Trades Union Congress condemned the act and unions simply refused to register. Lord Donaldson's Industrial Relations Court was little used and many questioned whether the law could adjudicate over wages and conditions of work. The Wilson government of 1974 repealed the act.

industrial revolution
Term applied to the period 1750–1850 and usually associated with Arnold Toynbee's lectures in the 1880s. Historians still debate the precise causes but the symptoms began with a move of labour away from the land, as it underwent enclosure and a drive for agricultural efficiency, into the towns. Combined with this a series of inventions, for example Arkwright's 'spinning jenny' and Crompton's 'mule', made textile manufacturing more efficient

and profitable. Moreover, the availability of accumulated capital in the hands of merchants and aristocrats enabled these inventions and others, such as the steam engine, to be disseminated throughout the British economy. Other important factors include the availability of economic markets for textiles and the rapidly improving infrastructure of roads and canals. There is no single or even multiple group of reasons to explain the industrial revolution, except perhaps for the fact that all these factors happened simultaneously and interacted. The effect of this economic revolution was to move the balance of economic, and hence political, power from the landed gentry to the industrialist middle classes. The creation of a huge urban proletariat also provided concentrated masses of population, who responded to calls for greater democracy which followed from the French and American Revolutions.

By 2000 many economic historians spoke of a post-industrial age, where, in the west, manufacturing had given way to new 'sunrise' industries in the service sector – computers and telecommunications being two of the most important.

industrialism

A term used by Jonathan Porritt in his book *Seeing Green* (1984) to describe the consensus between the major parties on the need for economic growth. The ecologist sees such development as injurious to humankind's interests, in that it encourages the over-consumption of resources. 'Industrialism' continues unabated in the 2000s, with pollution and environmental destruction. Green thinking, in all its guises, urges the adoption of an alternative set of policies, including sustainable economic growth, with low-energy, low-consumption strategies and the decentralisation of decision making.

See also Green Party; green thinking.

inequality (economic)

When the share of national income earned by the richest 20 per cent of the population is divided by that of the poorest 20 per

cent, an index of inequality is achieved: the higher the figure, the greater the inequality. According to this, Britain, in 1996, managed a figure of 9.6, higher than the USA (8.9), Germany (5.8), Denmark (7.1) and Sweden (4.5). In 1997, 24 per cent of all workers in Britain earned less than £4 per hour and 8 per cent less than £3. Compared with other countries Britain was second only to New Zealand in the growth of economic inequality during the period 1977–90. Some have suggested that one of the results of this development was the growth in Britain of an underclass. Figures from the Department of Social Security's Family Expenditure Survey (15 October 1998) revealed that the proportion of people living on less than half the average income, a widely accepted measure of poverty, had increased to 24 per cent. During the Thatcher administrations numbers below the line tripled but these fell back after John Major came to power. The gulf began to reopen, however, after 1995, despite the improvement in the nation's economic performance. From 1979 to 1997 average incomes grew 44 per cent in real terms after allowing for housing costs. However, the top tenth of earners gained a 70 per cent increase, while the poorest tenth suffered a drop in real income by 9 per cent.

In 2008, half the population had an income below £393 and half above this (median) figure. The top 10th of income earners received four times the poorest 10th. The top 1 per cent enjoyed incomes five times the median. In terms of wealth, the top 10th of households had wealth above £853,000 and the poorest 10th less than £8,810.

Debate exists over absolute poverty and relative poverty: the Conservatives stress that, in absolute terms, poverty as known in the 19th century has been abolished. However, those on the left, and many sociologists who specialise in this area, point out that relative poverty is the more realistic index, since it draws attention to people being excluded from participation in activities which many in society enjoy,

POLITICS

for example going on an annual holiday, or having a balanced and varied diet. In 2009 a book written by Richard Wilkinson and Kate Pickett, *The Spirit Level*, revealed astonishingly positive correlations between countries with high inequality and symptoms of extreme social dysfunction, like drug taking, crime rates, poor health and low life expectancy.

See also poverty; social exclusion; *Spirit Level*.

inequality (gender)
Differences of wealth and opportunity which disadvantage women. Reports in February 2000 and January 2001 from the London School of Economics claimed that women in Britain earned on average £250,000 less than men during their lifetimes. This is because women tend to be concentrated in low-paid jobs and are often paid less than men for doing the same work. Women working full-time earned 84 per cent of male earnings for the same jobs, while part-timers earned only 58 per cent. The Equal Opportunities Commission also reported that women are routinely denied access to bonus and pension schemes.

inflation
Defined by most economists as continuous rises in prices across the whole economy over a relatively short period. In addition to economic problems such as uncertainty for business and investors, inflation can, as the German Weimar Republic demonstrated, erode democratic institutions and lead to extremist politics. In Britain after the Second World War inflation was generally low but the growth of union power in the 1970s, the maintenance of full employment and the oil price rises of the early 1970s created pressures which pushed up wages as well as prices. The result was a rate of inflation which exceeded 25 per cent per annum in 1975. The Social Contract agreement between government and the unions brought this down to below 10 per cent by 1978 but by then faith in Labour had evaporated and the Conservatives came into power in 1979.

Margaret Thatcher attacked inflation through confronting the unions and the imposition of high interest rates but it still hit double figures in 1980 and 1990 and ran ahead of that of other European economies. Since the early 1990s it has levelled out at below 4 per cent per annum. The credibility of a government rests on the electorate perceiving it as a sound economic manager and thus it is no surprise that New Labour was assiduous in fostering an image of a sound manager of the nation's finances, with Gordon Brown being characterised as the 'iron chancellor'. Indeed, his stewardship of the economy – aided by the Monetary Policy Committee's control of interest rates – produced for Britain the lowest inflation rate in the European Union, at around 2 per cent per annum. His huge borrowing as prime minister following the banking crisis in 2007–09 raised fears that excessive credit could fuel inflation.

Information and Consultation Directive, 2001
A directive issued by the European Union. Writing in the *Observer* (17 June 2001) Will Hutton described the introduction of this directive as an 'earthquake'. It means that British employers now have to consult workers, not just on redundancies but on 'every strategic and financial development of their organisations'. Similar attempts to introduce consultation were rejected by union leaders in the 1970s as a 'sell-out' to capitalism. Hutton reflected that the unions had lost their 'negative, oppositional power; what they have won is integrated positive power'. The Confederation of British Industry proved wary of the directive and criticised it, though its own survey of 673 firms in the summer 2001 revealed that 40 per cent had adopted some form of consultation already.

information commissioner
www.ico.gov.uk
The official given responsibility for implementing the Freedom of Information Act 2000, the Data Protection Act 1998 and

the Environmental Information Regulations 2004. The commissioner is responsible, broadly, for the freedom of information and the privacy of personal information. In June 2009 Christopher Graham took over as commissioner from Richard Thomas.

inheritance tax

Tax paid on the value of an inherited of an estate, over a certain threshold. In 2010 this was payable at 40 per cent and the threshold was £325,000. Many people on ordinary salaries complained that this threshold was too low, given the rapid rise in house prices during the boom years of the 1990s and the first decade of the new century. The Conservatives had promised to raise the threshold to £1 million but this was dropped during the May 2010 post-election coalition negotiations.

Inland Revenue

See Her Majesty's Revenues and Customs.

'inner' cabinet

Small group of ministerial colleagues who offer the prime minister advice. Every premier, records show, since Robert Walpole has developed one. After 1945, Clement Attlee relied on Ernest Bevin, Herbert Morrison and Stafford Cripps. Margaret Thatcher in the early 1980s looked to John Biffen, John Nott, Geoffrey Howe and Keith Joseph. Tony Blair, unsurprisingly, included Gordon Brown and John Prescott in his inner cabinet. Gordon Brown also had his favourite advisors, including Ed Balls and, to an even greater extent, after his return to the cabinet in 2008, Peter Mandelson.

inner city

Urban residential area often characterised by poverty and crime. In the early years of the industrial revolution, much economic activity developed close to centres of settle-ment, especially in northern industrial areas of England. As the economy grew, factories moved further afield from what had become cities, with the original centres taking on administrative and shopping functions.

The cheap housing originally used by industrial workers became run down and occupied by lower income earners and immigrant groups. Consequently these areas became characterised by poverty, poor housing and racial tension. In the 1980s unemployment exacerbated such problems and riots broke out in major cities like Manchester, Liverpool and Leeds, as well as London. After her 1987 election victory Margaret Thatcher declared she would solve the problems of the inner cities, but they were only marginally ameliorated and difficulties remained well into the new millennium, despite strenuous attempts at urban regeneration by local authorities and central government, even with European Union funds.

inquiry

Investigation carried out under the aegis of government. Tony Blair's New Labour government seemed to specialise in inquiries into virtually everything. Such activities are useful to politicians in that: they can genuinely identify good policy options; they can buy time; and they can take the heat out of an issue by providing the appearance of action plus the excuse not to comment while the inquiry is doing its work. The Saville inquiry into Bloody Sunday was set up in 2000 but the report was not delivered until June 2010, at an estimated cost of £400 million. Blair's government preferred shorter, more focused inquiries, like those chaired by Hutton and Macpherson. However, such initiatives carry risks: reports can criticise, like Macpherson's claim that the police were guilty of 'institutional racism', something about which the government could do little. In February 2004 the Public Administration Committee decided to make a study of inquiries, so numerous had they become. One possible reason was that the Hutton inquiry had been able to obtain many more documents than the Foreign Affairs Select Committee, which actually had superior legal powers.

See also royal commission; select committee.

POLITICS

insider group

A term invented by Wyn Grant of Warwick University to describe pressure group proximity to government decision making. Insider groups have been drawn into the process of government itself and a classic example is the link established during the Second World War between the National Farmers' Union and the Ministry of Agriculture, Fisheries and Food.

See also outsider group; pressure group.

Institute for Fiscal Studies (IFS)

www.ifs.org.uk

Financial think-tank set up in 1968 focusing on taxation. Its aims are: to change the climate of opinion within which the tax system operates; to improve the procedures whereby changes are made in the tax system; and to help create a more rational tax system. Professor Richard Blundell has been research director of the IFS since 1986.

Institute for Government

www.instituteforgovernment.org.uk

Politically neutral think-tank set up by the Gatsby Charitable Foundation, funded by the Sainsbury family. It aims to improve the efficacy of government and works with all political parties as well as civil servants. It undertakes research to this end, 'providing evidence based advice that draws on best practice from around the world'. It also organises seminars and events for senior decision makers plus an inspirational learning and development programme. Former permanent secretary at Employment, Michael Bichard, is executive director and its senior fellows include that doyen of commentators, Peter Riddell of the *Times*.

Institute for Public Policy Research (IPPR)

www.ippr.org.uk

Think-tank founded in 1986 by 'leading figures in the academic, business and trade union community to provide an alternative to free market think-tanks'. It has produced blueprints for New Labour policy but has also trodden on previously forbidden ground, for example by suggesting in 1992

that universal welfare benefits might be profitably replaced with targeted ones. Its one-time director was Patricia Hewitt, a former advisor to Neil Kinnock and later a government minister.

Institute of Directors

www.iod.co.uk

Right-wing think-tank with campaigning tendencies. It opposed prices and incomes restraints when the Confederation of British Industry (CBI) was prepared to accept them. It enthusiastically supported Conservative policies of privatisation, reducing public spending and freeing up economic markets. In fact it still holds true to a Thatcherite set of economic policies, although the influence of all think-tanks declined towards the end of the Conservative period of rule, largely because most of their aims had been achieved and partly because of spectacular failures like the poll tax, which originated in think-tank deliberations.

Institute of Economic Affairs (IEA)

www.iea.org.uk

Think-tank set up in 1955 to advance then unfashionable right-wing economic ideas. It has been a bitter critic of the public sector, seen as the child of vote-courting politicians and sectional interests. The IEA was especially important in giving a wider audience to the ideas of Friedrich von Hayek and Milton Friedman. It has argued that the role of government should be limited to providing essential services like defence and clean air; all else can be provided by market forces. Some of its more controversial policies have included the wholesale privatisation of health and education.

institutional racism

See Macpherson report.

Intelligence and Security Committee

www.cabinetoffice.gov.uk/intelligence

Body established by the Intelligence Services Act 1994 to examine the 'expenditure, administration and policy of the Security Service, SIS and GCHQ'. The Committee comprises nine members drawn from both houses. They are appointed by the prime minister in association with the leader of the opposition. It reports annually to the prime minister, who then lays the report before parliament. In May 2003 the Committee was tasked with investigating the intelligence on which Tony Blair based his case to make war on Iraq. Critics complained the Committee was too much in the gift of the prime minister and therefore not sufficiently independent. As of February 2010 its chair was Dr Kim Howells MP; other members included Michael Mates MP, Michael Ancram and Sir Ming Campbell.

See also security services.

intelligence services
See security services.

intelligence services commissioner
https://www.mi5.gov.uk/output/intelligence-services-commissioner.html
Official tasked with authorising intrusive surveillance and interference with property. The post was established under section 59(1) of the Regulation of Investigatory Powers Act 2000. The commissioner – a person who has held high judicial office – has the job of ensuring warrants issued by the secretary of state to undertake intrusive surveillance are done so on a proper basis. The commissioner submits a report to the prime minister once a year, which is also laid before parliament. Sir Peter Gibson was reappointed from April 2009 for a further three-year term.

interest group
See pressure group.

interest rate
A key instrument in economic management, since the interest rate influences the speed of economic growth and the rate of inflation. Businesses rely on borrowing money to purchase new machinery, set up new enterprises and to survive downturns in economic activity. Most economists accept that increasing interest rates tends to lower inflation by reducing the amount of money in circulation, as this makes borrowing more expensive. However, sharp increases also push businesses into debt and sometimes bankruptcy. This happened on a massive scale in the early 1980s, when the Conservative government pushed up rates to counteract inflation. One of the side-effects of high rates is that the pound becomes more attractive to foreign investors. This in turn pushes up the exchange rate of sterling, with the result that exports become more expensive to overseas buyers, making British goods less competitive. High interest rates also caused a deep recession in the early 1990s when chancellor Norman Lamont used them to bring down inflation and maintain sterling's exchange rate in the European Monetary System (EMS); this was successful eventually in quelling inflation but only at a high economic cost in terms of business failures and mortgage repossessions. When Labour won its 1997 victory one of the first actions of chancellor Gordon Brown was to give control over interest rates to the Monetary Policy Committee (MPC) of the Bank of England, in the hope that purely economic (as opposed to political) criteria would be applied, thus ensuring long-term low inflation. Brown was successful, through such devices, in keeping the British rate of inflation either under or close to 2.5 per cent after 1997. The correct interest rate for the British economy is a crucial factor in relation to the debate over the country joining the single European currency. The banking crisis in 2007–09 produced a situation in which interest rates were slashed to less than 1 per cent but this was much less important than the fact that banks were nervous about lending to anyone, and lending was severely restricted for some time.

See also euro; European Monetary System; inflation; Monetary Policy Committee.

international law
System of agreements between states and supranational organisations, such as treaties and conventions. This kind of law

POLITICS

is not binding in the sense that domestic law is, as enforcement procedures are lacking. However, there are a vast range of agreements between states which in effect have the force of law and some argue are becoming more akin to domestic law as time goes by. There are three main types of international law:

1 *Public*. This deals with relationships between states and international organisations, like the law of the sea and international criminal law.
2 *Private*. This deals with the location of jurisdictions and which type of law applies in particular cases.
3 *Supranational*. This applies when a state is held to be in conflict with the laws of a supranational organisation.

Despite lack of enforcement procedures, most countries strive very hard to keep within the confines of international law. For example Tony Blair – though ultimately unsuccessful – was determined to acquire United Nations support for the 2003 invasion of Iraq to ensure it was endorsed by this kind of law.

International Monetary Fund (IMF)
www.imf.org
Organisation established by the 1944 Bretton Woods agreement as part of the United Nations. It aims to facilitate world trade and payments between nations. The IMF also provides standby loans for members who face problems with a balance of payments deficit but they usually have to implement remedial measures as the *quid pro quo*. In 1976 chancellor Denis Healey was forced to seek a substantial loan from the IMF to tide the country through a bad economic period; he had to accept conditions including cuts in public expenditure, limits on incomes and monetary growth. Economists point to this date as one of the first uses of monetarism.

internationalism
A view of international politics which claims its major problems can be solved through cooperative action by states. Radical Liberals like

J. A. Hobson, Norman Angel, E. D. Morel, H. N. Brailsford and Charles Trevelyan elaborated a critique of the international system in the early part of the 20th century which focused on secret diplomacy, imperialist competition for markets, balance-of-power policies and the arms trade. The antidote offered to such shortcomings was often couched in terms of strong international institutions. Such ideas helped to form the League of Nations in 1919 but it was seen as feeble indeed by the mid-1930s and it failed to prevent the rise of Hitler. The United Nations, which was formed in 1945, was a more carefully constructed body but has been only marginally more successful than its predecessor. However, many commentators on international affairs still insist that the only hope for the world is through greater cooperation by all states.

Internet
A worldwide network of computers linked together. Generally thought to have been invented by a British professor at the Massachusetts Institute of Technology, Timothy Berners-Lee, its origins lay in the US defence community's need for computers to talk to each other. The Internet has become of increasing importance as a source of information and exchange, not least because it has no central source or controlling authority, although service providers are legally liable for breeches of criminal or civil law. British political parties have not been slow to try to exploit the 'net' for communicating with members of the public and supporters. Government departments and Number 10 have their own web pages, which provide information for the general public and students of politics. The Internet has also given birth to a worldwide 'political blogosphere' whereby 'bloggers' express their views and interact with readers worldwide.

See also mass media; virtual politics.

internment
The confinement of a person regarded as a security threat. During the Second World

War some foreign nationals, not to mention the British fascist leader Sir Oswald Mosley, suspected of loyalty to Germany, were held in internment camps. The device was used again in the early 1970s in Northern Ireland when IRA suspects were held without trial, but the backlash against it in the nationalist community was such that it was deemed to have been unsuccessful. In the wake of the Good Friday agreement, a bomb explosion in Omagh in August 1998 awakened calls for internment to be reintroduced.

inward investment
Capital investment by overseas companies. Attracting such investment from the likes of Japan and the USA has been a policy successfully pursued by both Conservative and Labour governments. Such activity benefits employment substantially and also has the effect of improving the productivity of business elsewhere, as foreign-owned firms produce 40 per cent more per worker than native businesses. According to the *Economist* (14 July 2001), inward investment was not damaged by Britain's absence from the euro: for the two years after the currency's creation in 1999, inward investment was buoyant, at £86 billion in 2000, and the stock of inward investment was worth about a fifth of gross domestic product. In June 2009 the government announced increased inward investment for 2008–09, with a third coming the USA.

Iraq war (or second Gulf war)
Initiated when a US-led coalition invaded Iraq in March 2003. The war had many causes but was to some extent based on the first Gulf war, of 1990, when Saddam Hussein invaded Kuwait and was expelled by a similar coalition led by US president George Bush senior. Saddam's continuing challenging behaviour during the 1990s had produced calls for an invasion among some Republicans and, after the Al-Qaeda attacks on the World Trade Center in New York in September 2001, George Bush junior acceded to their advice and opted to invade Iraq, once the Taliban had been driven out of power in Afghanistan. The

British prime minister, Tony Blair, ignored entreaties within his own party and insisted on lining up British troops alongside the Americans. His argument was that Saddam had weapons of mass destruction (WMD) which he was likely to use against other countries – a government publication in the autumn of 2002 even claimed that such weapons could reach British territory within 45 minutes. The United Nations despatched weapons inspectors to Iraq under Hans Blix, but his team were unable to find any such weapons.

The initial progress of the war was comparatively straightforward and Saddam was soon overthrown but there were insufficient troop numbers to ensure order and a huge error was made when the army and police in Iraq were disbanded and Saddam's civil administration cast out. This left the vanquished country wide open to looting and disorder and into this vacuum moved a number of armed religious groups as well as units of Al-Qaeda. US expectations that a grateful liberated country would garland US troops in flowers proved the thinnest of hopes as Iraqis merely saw brutal invaders to be resisted. The result was a tragic immolation of innocent Iraqis as the two wings of Islam – Sunni and Shia – fought murderous tit-for-tat campaigns in the streets of the capital and elsewhere in the country. With great difficulty and no little incompetence the US constructed a democratic system of government for the country it had invaded but even after the capture and execution of the former president, the country remained a battleground and the war proved deeply unpopular all over the world, including the USA. Ignoring the advice of those who advised withdrawal, Bush authorised a 'surge' of troops in 2007–08, and it had some good effect in terms of reducing conflict. US president Barack Obama was elected in 2008 with a mandate to withdraw and this has taken place in the form of US troops returning home in phases. Some Republicans argued the relative calm which followed the 'surge' showed that the invasion had produced a good outcome but

POLITICS

critics pointed to: the 4–5 million refugees; the upwards of 100,000 civilians killed; the 4,400 US service people killed (179 for the UK); not to mention the devastation of the whole country and an astronomical military budget. In the UK the Chilcot inquiry still sits, seeking to unravel the mysteries of why Britain became involved in the conflict.

See also Chilcot inquiry; first Gulf war; Hutton report; Iraq war decision; weapons of mass destruction.

Iraq war decision
Decision of the Blair government to support the USA militarily in the invasion of Iraq on 20 March 2003. Opponents of the war have long sought to discover how the cabinet decision was made and have tried to elicit the relevant cabinet papers via the Freedom of Information Act (2000 and 2005). However, on 24 February 2009, Jack Straw, for the government, vetoed a ruling by the information commissioner that the papers should be released. The attorney general produced two pieces of advice on the legality of the war 10 days apart, with the second much more pro-war than the first. Jack Straw argued the public interest was opposed to release – he was a partici-pant in these discussions – as it could deter members of cabinet from speaking freely in a future crisis. However, most of the people present had since given their account of the cabinet meeting at the heart of the issue and it was unlikely much new could have been gained by the release.

In July 2009 Gordon Brown announced that an inquiry into the decision to invade Iraq would take place after all, chaired by former senior civil servant Sir John Chilcot. Initially it was to be held in private but after furious protests Brown agreed parts could be held in public. Chilcot said at the launch of the inquiry on 30 July 2009 that hearings would be held in private only in exceptional circumstances and that it might well continue until 2011.

Ireland
England's first involvement with Ireland began in 1171, when Henry II invaded the island. Thereafter it became a country substantially owned by absentee landlords living in England. English settlement occurred in the prosperous parts of the country and the Irish were forced to live in the less fertile regions, such as upland and bog areas. For centuries Ireland remained a land simmering with conflict and rebellion and became more so after the plantation policies in which Catholic Irish tenants were replaced with those of English or Scottish descent, usually Protestant. Disaffected Gaelic leadership threw in their lot with the enemies of England and this led to several invasions and repressive measures. There was a rebellion in 1641, savagely put down by Oliver Cromwell, especially at Drogheda and Wexford, where thousands were put to the sword. Catholic landowners were dispossessed and expelled and excluded from sitting in the Irish parliament. In 1800 the Act of Union was passed, which united Britain and Ireland from January 1801. In the 19th century the decision of Irish MPs sitting in the Commons to campaign for home rule dominated much domestic debate. Gladstone decided to give home rule to Ireland but the plan was never implemented as the First World War intervened. After the war the Protestant minority demanded and received six northern counties as their own homeland, thus creating the province of Northern Ireland, while the 26 southern counties achieved independence. In 1949 Ireland became a republic and left the Commonwealth.

See also Northern Ireland.

Irish National Liberation Army (INLA)
Militant nationalist paramilitary organisa-tion. In 1975 after the IRA declared a cease-fire a third of the membership of the official IRA broke away to form the INLA. Its first high-profile victim was Airey Neave in 1979. The splinter group proved vulnerable to internal disputes and several members died in bloody reprisal killings. In 1980 it killed 17 people in Derry in the Drop In Well disco; in 1981

three INLA prisoners were among the
10 who starved themselves to death in
the Maze Prison; in 1982 it killed more
people than the IRA itself; in 1995 its
former chief, Hugh Turney, declared a
cease-fire from the dock of a Dublin court;
in December 1997 its members shot Billy
Wright, leader of the Loyalist Volunteer
Force, inside the Maze; finally, in August
1998 the INLA declared a cease-fire in
recognition of the changed situation in the
province as evidenced by the referendum in
favour of peace.

See also Irish Republican Army.

Irish Republican Army (IRA)

Militant nationalist paramilitary
organisation. The IRA is a body of the
political party Sinn Fein, both of which
are dedicated to a united Ireland and were
long prepared to use violence to achieve
this. Founded in 1919 by Michael Collins,
it prosecuted a successful war against
the occupying power in 1919–21. It took
a back seat for several decades and was
militarily inactive between 1962 and 1969,
although it did pursue a programme of
Marxist-inspired social agitation. The more
radical Provisional IRA split away from
the Official IRA in 1970 and henceforth
pursued an aggressive military campaign
against the Royal Ulster Constabulary
(RUC) and the British army; it also engaged in some 'policing' of Catholic areas.
Violence reached a climax in 1972 with a
brutal campaign of bombing on the British
mainland. In the 1980s violence declined
and but there was another mainland
campaign in London and Manchester in
the mid-1990s. The IRA and Sinn Fein
signed up to the Good Friday agreement in
April 1998. The IRA remained, however,
and insisted on retaining its weapons,
albeit 'putting them beyond use' in arms
dumps that were subject to inspection
by the de Chastelain commission (the
Independent International Commission on
Decommissioning).

See also dissident republican group;
Irish National Liberation Army;
Provisional IRA; Real IRA.

iron law of oligarchy

A theory developed by the German
sociologist Robert Michels, who argued
that socialist political parties would be
controlled by a small powerful elite who
were dedicated to retaining power despite
the existence of democratic structures and
claims of internal democracy. Although
based upon the self-evident truths of
classical elite theory, the 'law' raises
questions about the degree of internal party
democracy which has existed in various
periods of Labour Party history.

iron triangle

The US phenomenon of mutually beneficial
relationships between corporations,
Congressional oversight committees and
federal agencies.

Islamic Party of Britain

www.islamicparty.com
Political party founded by David Musa
Pidcock in 1989 to help campaign against
Salman Rushdie's novel *Satanic Verses*.
It also campaigned for state funding
for Muslim schools. The party fielded
candidates in the 1992 general election but
has not had any major electoral impact.

Islamophobia

The characterisation of Islam as an alien,
aggressive, misogynistic creed which offers
a threat to peace and domestic harmony.
This has long been an element in the racist
attitudes to people from Pakistan and other
Asian countries, like those propagated by
the British National Party. It has become
much more intense and widespread in
recent years in consequence of terrorist
atrocities like 9-11 and the London bombings of 2005. Islamist scholars for the most
part insist their religion is wholly peaceful
and that it is radical misinterpretations of
it which create the variety responsible for
terrorism.

Isle of Man

Crown dependency off the coast of north-
western England. It remained Norwegian
until 1266, then was Scottish until it was

POLITICS

ceded to Britain in 1765. It has a legislative council, a lieutenant governor and
the representative House of Keys, which
together make up the Court of Tynwald.
It passes laws subject to the royal assent.
Westminster laws affect it only if specifically
so stated in the statute.

issue network

Alliance of pressure groups that try to
influence a particular government policy.
They often operate on the Internet,
for example on the environment. They
can include academics, journalists, civil
servants, management consultants and
the like.

issue voting

Voting for candidates on the basis of
their stance on particular issues. In the
postwar period, British voters traditionally
reflected class loyalties, but from the
1960s onwards psephologists noted that
the degree of class loyalty was declining
and that people were voting more and
more on the basis of key issues. The rise of
issue voting is associated with a number of
developments, including the fragmentation
of the electorate into 'market segments'
based on housing tenure and consumption
patterns, the growing impact of the mass
media on voters' decision making and the
decline of the ideological or class party.
Furthermore, the political scientist Ivor
Crewe has delineated 'salience' – the
extent to which people are aware of an
issue – and 'party preferred' in terms of
policies on that issue.

Issues vary according to elections; in
October 1974 it was mainly prices but
in 1983 it was unemployment. Defence
has seldom been a key issue but was in
the post-Falklands 1983 election. In
August 2004 the *Guardian*'s ICM poll
showed that, of the 10 most important
issues facing voters, health and education
were close to the top, while Iraq and the
European Union were 8th and 10th,
respectively.

See also catch-all party; political
marketing.

J

Jenkins report, 1998

*Report of the Independent Commission on
the Voting System.* Lord (Roy) Jenkins of
Hillhead was asked by Tony Blair to chair
the Commission, to find an alternative
which achieved proportionality, stability,
extension of voter choice and maintained
the link between MP and constituency.
Studies calculated that there were long
periods when the voting system worked
strongly against one side or the other.
Between 1945 and 1970, it worked for
the Conservatives: Labour piled up votes
in safe constituencies but failed to muster
enough votes in the decisive marginal
constituencies. However, the bias moved in
favour of Labour, with a vengeance, in the
1990s. In 1992 the Conservatives received
a similar percentage of the vote to Labour
in 1997, yet enjoyed a majority of only 21
compared with Labour's 179. Indeed, if the
two parties had received an equal number
of votes in 1992, Labour would have had a
majority of over 80. Jenkins explained the
reasons for this bias: Labour benefited from
the over-representation of seats in Scotland
and Wales; Liberal Democrat electors
voted tactically to keep the Tories out; some
constituencies were unequally populated in
England and the Boundary Commission
always runs a few years behind such shifts;
and Labour traditionally won a high
proportion of low-polling inner-city seats,
which gave it a higher ratio of seats to votes
than the Tories. An alternative voting
system would have much to offer the Tories,
but they prefer to stick with the existing
system of first past the post.

Jenkins recommended the alternative vote
(AV) 'top-up' – a system combining the
German additional member system with
the existing first past the post system. The
Commission suggested that 85–90 per cent
of seats should be elected in single-member
constituencies via the alternative vote and
the rest to act as top-up seats drawn from

80 special constituencies, to be used to make the overall result more proportional. Initially it seemed a referendum would be held to discover whether the country wanted to change its voting system and the Liberal Democrats became optimistic about finally gaining a regular place in government. But Labour's landslide in 1997 convinced many of the party's MPs that they could continue to win majorities, and experience of coalition government in Scotland and Wales highlighted some of the problems which proportional representation can usher in. In the brief enthusiasm for constitutional reform which followed the MPs' expenses scandal in 2009, the Jenkins report was again brought up but, while the alternative vote proposal was not rejected, both major parties drew back from the proportional element. The Liberal Democrats then gained the promise of a referendum on the alternative vote system in their coalition negotiations with the Conservatives after the May 2010 election.

jerrymandering
See gerrymandering.

'joined up' government
Phrase introduced by the New Labour government after 1997 to describe governing in a way which showed regard and awareness for what was being done by other parts of the government machine. Naturally, New Labour argued that it achieved this ideal in practice.

Joint Intelligence Committee (JIC)
The committee which coordinates intelligence from Government Communications Headquarters (GCHQ) and other agencies, such as MI5. It decides what the national requirements of the intelligence services are and then sets about meeting them via the agencies concerned; this work also involves liaison with foreign intelligence services, for example the US Central Intelligence Agency (CIA). The person who takes the lead on this is the intelligence coordinator. The JIC and its head, John Scarlett, were forced out of the shadows of

national life in the summer of 2003 when the Hutton inquiry summoned Scarlett to give evidence on the circumstances leading to the death of Dr David Kelly. The role of the JIC in the production of the intelligence-based dossier on Iraq's weapons of mass destruction published in September 2002 was investigated in detail. Hutton's report cleared Scarlett but some suspicions remained that he had been over-accommodating of the political priorities of Number 10. Significantly, in the wake of the Hutton report, another inquiry – this time into the intelligence services themselves – was set in train under the chairmanship of the former cabinet secretary Lord (Robin) Butler.

joint select committee
Set up by the two houses of parliament on particular subjects. For instance, in July 2002 a joint committee was appointed to consider the future of the House of Lords. Members of a joint committee are usually chosen in equal numbers by the respective houses.

Jopling report, 1992
Report (*Sittings in the House*) of a committee chaired by a former Conservative cabinet member. It recommended for the Commons a reduction of late-night and Friday sessions and that morning sessions take place on Wednesdays. These changes were introduced in 1994 and, according to political scientist Philip Norton, 'provided a somewhat more rational timetable for plenary sessions and reduced pressure on the floor'.

judge
There are more than 11,000 full-time and 2,000 part-time judges, with the lord chief justice being the most senior. Since the passing of the Constitutional Reform Act 2005 the lord chief justice has been chosen by a specially convened committee of the Judicial Appointments Commission (JAP). The hierarchy from this office downwards entails: lord of appeal in ordinary (House of Lords); lord justice of appeal (Court

of Appeal); High Court judge (High Court); circuit judge (crown or county court); recorder (crown court). Judges are drawn almost exclusively from the ranks of barristers of at least 10 years' standing, though more recently solicitors can also become High Court judges. Appointments are advertised publicly and made from the relatively small pool of senior barristers. Information on likely candidates used to be stored in the Lord Chancellor's Department but this subjective system had its critics and since the 2005 Act it is the JAP which takes care of such selections.

The distinguished law professor J. A. G. Griffith alleged that judges were drawn from an overly exclusive social background and were predominantly male and elderly (judges do not have to retire until aged 70). In 1998 only 8 out of 143 senior judges were female and only one was not white. Over 80 per cent went to public school and a majority went to Oxford or Cambridge. Critics claim judges are out of touch with the rest of society and their occasional expressions of ignorance in court causes them to lose public respect. Defenders of the system dismiss this critique as a caricature. They argue that the best legal brains tend to rise to the top and should take senior places irrespective of background, and that a public school/ Oxbridge background in no way precludes the ability to reach balanced judgements.

In July 2004 the new JAP reported on its first investigation of senior judicial appointments made under the old system during 2003. It found 'substantial inequalities in the treatment of the candidates', with a 'substantial inbuilt bias' in favour of QCs and against solicitors and circuit judges seeking promotion to the High Court bench.

Judicial Appointments Commission (JAC)

www.judicialappointments.gov.uk
Independent body that selects candidates for judicial office in courts and tribunals. In December 1999 Sir Leonard Peach reported on his Independent Scrutiny of Appointment Processes for Judges and QCs. He recommended the introduction of a commissioner for judicial appointments to advise on appointments and audit the process. This was set up in 2001 with a brief to handle complaints arising from judicial appointments. A Judicial Appointments Commission was proposed in the Constitutional Reform Bill which was passed in 2005. Its composition is such that: five must be judicial members; two must be professional members (one barrister and one solicitor); five must be lay members; one must be a tribunal member; and one must be a lay justice member. The chair must always be a lay member, the current one being Baroness Usha Prashar. The idea of the JAC was that it would help redress certain imbalances but in 2008 it was revealed that appointments of women and ethnic minorities to the bench had actually reduced from the year before the JAC began work. Marcel Berlins in the *Guardian* suggested it could be because these groups were not applying for judgeships, as they might still believe that they had no chance of preferment.

judicial review

The ability of judges to call government and other statutory authorities to account if they exceed their statutory powers. This is also sometimes called 'judicial activism'. The cases are heard by the Administrative Court of the Divisional Court of the Queen's Bench Division. During the 1970s there were four cases where the courts found Labour ministers had exceeded their powers. Equally, they found against several Conservative ministers in the 1980s and early 1990s, especially Michael Howard as home secretary (1993–97). This willingness has encouraged individuals to apply for judicial review. In 1980 there were 491 cases and by 1994 there were nearly 4,000. Increasingly the courts have taken on an assertive role in relation to the executive, insisting on interpreting the law in a way which defends the rights of the individual and enhances the role of the judiciary. The government can, if it so wishes, overrule the courts by changing the law but there are penalties attached to this course of action, not least the signal that it is 'moving the goalposts'. In most cases it accepts the judgement with the best grace it can muster.

judiciary

Perhaps a neglected aspect of British government in that it has always been seen as subordinate to parliament. Judges have been appointed by the Judicial Appointments Commission since 2005. Parliament has sovereign authority in terms of what it may pass into law; however, the judiciary has a degree of independence in terms of security of tenure in appointments and judicial review. This has opened a new area in which the courts find themselves 'checking' the executive and providing new interpretations of the law, although to nothing like to the extent possible in the constitutionally entrenched US Supreme Court. The embodiment of the European Convention on Human Rights into British law in October 2000 was a major development, because although judges cannot strike down parliamentary statutes, senior British judges now have a power of legal interpretation hitherto unknown in the British political system. The legal hierarchy begins with the magistrates at the bottom, then up to the county and crown courts, followed by the High Court with its three divisions of Family, Chancery and Queen's Bench. From there the next tier up is the Court of Appeal with its Criminal and Civil Divisions, topped off, since 2008, by the Supreme Court (before that date, by the House of Lords Appellate Committee).

See also judge; judicial review.

jury

Introduced by the Normans as a means of determining the guilt or innocence of the accused. The jury was developed, mainly in English-speaking countries, into a panel of usually 12 citizens chosen at random from the electoral register. In an English or Welsh court a jury can reach a verdict by a 10–2 majority. In Scotland a jury has 15

members and can return a verdict of 'not proven'. From the late 1990s moves were made to remove the option of a jury trial for certain types of crime. This was proposed in the Auld report into the criminal justice system in 2001. Many senior judicial figures spoke out against this proposal and eventually it was dropped in January 2002, though it was reintroduced for certain categories of criminal charge by the Criminal Justice Act 2003. The Criminal Justice Act 2003 came into force on 24 July 2006, part 7 of which makes it possible for a non-jury trial to be held in cases where it is believed there is danger of jury tampering or where jury tampering has taken place.

See also Auld report.

Justice and Home Affairs

One of the three 'pillars' of the European Union (EU). It covers such areas as asylum, immigration, drug addiction, international fraud and terrorism. The other two 'pillars' of the EU are the European Community and the Common Foreign and Security Policy.

justice of the peace (JP)

See magistrates' court.

K

Keep Left

Group on the left wing of the Parliamentary Labour Party which formed in 1947, led by Michael Foot, Richard Crossman and Ian Mikardo. It urged a more independent foreign policy from the USA and favoured an alternative approach based on social democracy rather than US capitalism or Soviet communism. Elements of this group and its near successor, Keeping Left, went on to support Aneurin Bevan's unsuccessful bid for the party's leadership in the 1950s.

Keynesianism

Theory of macro-economics developed by the British economist John Maynard Keynes and set out in *The General Theory of Employment, Interest and Money* (1936). This overthrew economic orthodoxy by arguing that, when the economy was in recession, the government ought to spend or invest money to stimulate the economy and boost demand. Similarly it suggested that governments should use the instruments of taxation (fiscal policy) and interest rates (monetary policy) to manipulate demand within the economy to sustain growth and deter recession. In one of his most memorable phrases he called for a 'comprehensive socialisation of investment' as a prerequisite for full employment. However, he was no socialist, since he argued that full employment could be achieved by a partnership between the public and the private sector, a phrase echoed in the language of the New Labour government elected in 1997.

On 24 November 2008, chancellor Alistair Darling announced his proposed measures to deliver a 'fiscal stimulus' to the economy in response to the banking crisis. This approach owed everything to the Keynesian idea that, in a recession, when the economy has slowed down, it requires a government-inspired stimulus to deliver a 'kick-start'. For example, a series of public works would employ hundreds of thousands of people; their wages would be spent buying food, travel and the necessities of life, thus providing work for others, whose consumption in turn would generate more activity and so on. Such an approach succeeded in the case of Roosevelt's New Deal in the 1930s. Darling's thinking, not to mention that of most other western finance ministers, was along similar lines.

See also Keynes, John Maynard; monetarism.

Kilmuir guidelines

Advice to judges issued in 1955 by Lord Kilmuir that they should not make any overt political or partisan comment, in recognition of their sensitive position as members of the judiciary. Kilmuir was a distinguished Conservative lord chancellor. The guidelines were relaxed in 1970 but reimposed by Lord Hailsham as the lord chancellor in 1980, as he felt politicians and judges should stick to their own spheres. Some judges (notably Judge Pickles of the northern circuit in the 1980s) become short-term notorious celebrities by airing their views in the media.

kitchen cabinet

Name popularly given to the small group of advisors based in 10 Downing Street. It originated with the advisors to Harold Wilson in the 1960s, most notably Joe Haines (press secretary) and Marcia Williams (personal secretary). Today it is usually considered to include the press secretary, the chief of staff and in addition, possibly, the Policy Unit, which can include over a dozen advisors (nearly 30 special advisors are based in Number 10). By this definition, Tony Blair's corps of unelected advisors required somewhat more accommodation than is afforded by the normal-sized kitchen.

See also cabinet; 'inner' cabinet.

Kosovo crisis, 1999–2000

Balkan war in which Britain became a prominent player through its NATO role. Kosovo is the southern section of the former Yugoslavia Federation and includes a majority of people with Albanian origins. This majority was keen to win independence from the Federation and the Kosovo Liberation Army (KLA) had sprung up by 1999. Slobodan Milosevic, the Serbian leader, used the KLA as an excuse to use armed force to quell Kosovo, a region with special resonance to most Serbs. Regular army units were augmented by irregulars, some of whom had seen service in Bosnia. Atrocities soon began to happen as the Kosovan Albanians were driven from their homes. British politicians began to call for NATO troops to defend the Kosovans. Eventually a NATO force was assembled and air strikes began to be made against Serb targets in Kosovo and Serbia. The conflict seemed to be interminable but when Russia withdrew support for Milosevic he was persuaded to back down. Tony Blair, Robin Cook (foreign secretary) and George Robertson (secretary of state for defence), the British politicians most involved, received considerable credit for their resolution during a conflict which seemed not to advance significant British interests.

Kosovo is currently a self-declared independent state, although Serbia does not recognise it but prefers to see it as territory governed by the United Nations.

Kyoto protocol, 1997

Agreement reached by industrialised nations to reduce emissions of carbon dioxide to below 1990 levels by the year 2012. Britain was one of the prime movers in this agreement, via Labour's deputy prime minister, John Prescott. He was less successful at making the agreement stick when another summit on global warming, convened by the European Union at The Hague in 2000, foundered on US reluctance to be bound by Kyoto. US president George W. Bush refused to accept the phenomenon of global warming while campaigning for the presidency but in 2001 reversed his position when scientific reports proved it beyond any doubt. Critics argued he was merely defending the interests of the oil industry. When visiting Britain in July 2001 he said that the USA could not support any agreement which harmed its economy and threatened employment. In July 2001 an attempt was made to save Kyoto at a meeting in Bonn convened by the United Nations. After several days of non-stop negotiating, an agreement was reached which was legally binding. Despite rejection by the USA, the Kyoto protocol had been resuscitated and endorsed by many of the world's nations. The Bonn agreement was a triumph for the European Union and a slap in the face for the USA, whose delegate was booed as she read out a statement. Michael Meacher for Britain hailed a 'historic day'.

The protocol needed to be ratified by 55 nations – together accounting for 55 per cent of the world's carbon dioxide emissions – to come into force. Without the participation of the USA this target is impossible to reach. Britain has 1 per cent of the world's population but produces 2.3 per cent of its carbon dioxide emissions. The USA has 4 per cent of world's population yet produces 36 per cent of its emissions (*Times*, 23 July 2001). The election of Barack Obama in November 2008 raised hopes that the USA might take a more active role in making the agreement work but so far, despite joining the 2009 Copenhagen climate change conference, the USA has not ratified the agreement.

L

Labour Coordinating Committee

Group which led the party's move to the left in the 1970s and created, along with other factors, the conditions for the intra-party conflict of the early 1980s. However, in the mid-1980s the grouping helped Neil Kinnock start the process of moving the party into the centre and ceased to be such an important player in left-wing politics.

'Labour Isn't Working'

Slogan on a billboard poster designed in August 1978 by Saatchi and Saatchi, depicting a dole queue. It was later used in the 1979 election campaign to communicate the idea that the Labour government of 1974–79 was responsible for rising unemployment. Its significance lies in the fact that it is an early example of the Conservatives' use of commercially inspired techniques of election campaigning. The people used in the photograph of a long, snaking queue were all employees of the Conservative Party. In March 2009 the Conservatives re-ran the poster, amended to read 'Labour Still Isn't Working'.

labour movement

Groups of the skilled and unskilled working class, who since the 19th century have advanced their economic, social and political interests through trade union organisation. The principal vehicle for political action has been through the Labour Representation Committee (1900) and the Labour Party (1906) and as such the movement has been committed to a non-violent, social reformist approach to change, rather than the revolutionary one seen at times elsewhere in Europe. The movement has undergone significant change in recent years, including a decline in trade union membership since 1979 and the fragmentation of the working class, most notably the development of, according to political scientist Ivor Crewe, a new working class, who work in the private sector, are non-union members, live in the south of England and who do not have a 'natural' loyalty to the Labour Party. Under Tony Blair, New Labour distanced itself from the trade unions, and thus the labour movement, but many institutional and emotional connections remain, notwithstanding.

Labour Party

www.labour.org.uk
Formed in 1906, when the Labour Representation Committee was renamed. The party was given a constitution in 1918, drafted by Sidney Webb, which committed it to socialism, effectively via some form of nationalisation. An electoral pact with the Liberals in 1903 gave the embryonic party 29 seats in 1906. In 1918 it gained 63 seats and in 1923 191 seats, when Ramsay MacDonald formed a 10-month minority government. In 1929 MacDonald was returned again as a minority leader but he was unable to find a solution to the acute economic depression and when he made a deal with the Conservatives his party split and he became prime minister in the national government; the majority of the remaining Labour MPs went into opposition. In the ensuing 1931 general election Labour won only 52 seats, and remained in opposition for a decade, when

it supported opposition to fascism in Spain and Germany. George Lansbury was leader until 1935 but Clement Attlee took over soon afterwards. During the Second World War Labour and the Conservatives formed the national government led by Winston Churchill and, as his deputy, Clement Attlee. In 1945 Labour won by a landslide of 393 to 213 and implemented a programme of nationalisation of the main utilities and the development of social services, including the National Health Service in 1948. The government faced shortages and introduced austerity measures to combat them but the nation's enthusiasm for socialism waned and Labour scraped home by a thin margin in 1950. By 1951 the leadership was exhausted and the election in 1951 saw the party defeated, although it obtained its highest ever number of votes, at 13.9 million. Thirteen years of opposition followed, during which the party suffered internal conflicts over defence, with Aneurin Bevan mounting a divisive challenge to the leadership of Hugh Gaitskell. In 1964 Harold Wilson won a narrow general election victory over Alec Douglas-Home and in 1966 a much larger one over Edward Heath – by over 100 seats. During this period the Labour government was dogged by economic problems of devaluation, balance of payments and strikes. Left-wing dissenters harried it over its support for US involvement in Vietnam and prevented reform of the unions taking place in the later part of the decade. In 1970 Heath won a surprise victory. In opposition Wilson adopted a cooler position over Britain's membership of the European Economic Community and Europe as a whole, which he reversed once back in office in 1974. However, in 1976 he resigned as prime minister and James Callaghan took over. Despite his assured leadership the country was forced to borrow heavily from the International Monetary Fund and reduced inflation only via wage deals with the unions and huge cuts in public spending. When the unions refused to accept a 5 per cent pay norm in 1978 the stage was set for the 'winter of discontent', which destroyed Labour's credibility and opened the door for 18 years of Conservative rule. Margaret Thatcher won in 1979 and then again in 1983, arguably with the help of the successful Falklands war. Michael Foot was elected leader in 1980 and presided over one of the party's gravest electoral defeats in 1983, when it was lucky not to have been beaten into third place, behind the Alliance. In 1983 Neil Kinnock became leader and is credited with starting the party's slow climb back to electability. He introduced, via Peter Mandelson and Philip Gould, significant innovations in election campaigning, which made the party more electorally credible. Although the party lost in 1987 and 1992, the shift to the centre initiated by Kinnock was decisive in advancing the cause of the 'modernisers'. John Smith became leader after 1994 and introduced the one member one vote system (OMOV) into party elections, partially replacing the trade union 'block' vote, whereby union leaders could cast a vote representing their whole membership. After his untimely death in 1994, he was succeeded by Tony Blair, who made a major step towards electoral success by persuading the party to abandon clause 4 of its constitution. He was also successful in repositioning the party as 'New Labour', in order to widen its electoral appeal to include middle-class and skilled working-class voters. He was arguably one of the most effective Labour leaders since Attlee and, along with Peter Mandelson, engineered the landslide victory of 1997. With Mandelson lost through various misadventures, Blair succeeded in winning another landslide victory in 2001: Labour 413 seats (42 per cent of the vote); Conservatives 166 seats (33 per cent of the vote); Liberal Democrats 52 seats (19 per cent of the vote). However, the gloss was taken off the victory by a record low turnout of only 59 per cent, and a mere one in four of the electorate actually voted for New Labour.

Most commentators did not perceive substantial improvements in public services during this period and from 2003 onwards there was the running sore that was the Iraq war. However, Blair succeeded in winning his third election victory in May 2005, with 356 seats (to the Conservatives' 198 and the Liberal Democrats' 62), a majority of 67. A succession of political reverses in the spring and summer of 2006 was behind a plot to dislodge Blair in the autumn of that year. He had already announced his intention to stand down before the end of the session, to allow his successor 'ample time' to bed himself in before the election expected in 2009–10. But this decision turned him into a 'lame duck' prime minister and his opponents eagerly sought to drive him from office even earlier than his stated intention. The Manchester party conference managed to smooth over the widening divisions but Blair was forced to declare he would go within a year of it. Many believed the organising force behind these events was Blair's rival since the 1990s, Gordon Brown, his brooding chancellor. Brown eventually took over, unchallenged, in June 2007 and showed himself to be much more uncertain in the top job than he had been as chancellor. In the summer of 2009 most political commentators, aware of the double-figure Tory lead in the polls, did not give Labour much chance of winning the next election. In the event, Labour was beaten in May 2010, though not demolished, as polls had suggested the party might be. Labour's 258 seats was a big reduction but no 'meltdown'. Studies showed the major group of voters who deserted the party were the skilled working class, or C2s.

See also Labour Representation Committee; modernisation; National Executive Committee; Parliamentary Labour Party.

Labour Party leadership contest
Whether in opposition or the party of government, a challenger needs to command 20 per cent of the votes of the Parliamentary Labour Party (PLP) and the contest needs to be approved by two-thirds of the annual conference. Once approved, the electoral college is activated, in which trade unions (political levy payers only), constituency parties and the PLP

vote separately and have one-third of the vote each. If no candidate receives more than half of the accumulated votes on the first ballot a second is held, with the second preferences being redistributed.

Labour Party shadow cabinet election

Elections by the Parliamentary Labour Party (PLP) of those people it would like to see in the shadow cabinet. When in opposition the PLP elects a shadow cabinet. Each member casts 19 votes; since 1992 four of these must be for women candidates. These elections are something of a popularity contest for Labour MPs. The leader, deputy leader, chief whip and chair of the party select the shadow cabinet from those elected. Since 1980 the leader is obliged, after a general election victory, to form the first cabinet from those who served in the preceding shadow cabinet, but the leader is not bound in any way in subsequent reshuffles.

Labour Representation Committee (LRC)

The committee out of which the Labour Party emerged. It was established following a conference in 1900 of trade unionists and socialist societies, including the Indepen-dent Labour Party, the Marxist Social Democratic Federation and the Fabian Society. The conference decided to sponsor candidates for election and the LRC won two seats in 1900. In 1906 the LRC was renamed the Labour Party but it did not receive a proper constitution until 1918.

laissez faire economics

See classical liberalism.

law and order

See crime.

law lord

Type of life peer. They are the lords of appeal in ordinary who sit in the House of Lords. They are limited to a maximum of 12 in number, must have at least two years' high judicial office and are appointed by the queen on the advice of the prime minister. Those sitting in the Lords in July 2009 became the first justices of the new Supreme Court and were thus excluded from sitting or voting in the Lords. When they retire they can return as full members but new members of the Supreme Court will not have seats in the House of Lords.

See also Supreme Court.

Law Society

www.lawsociety.org.uk

Professional body which ensures solicitors do their jobs properly. It provides training for solicitors; anyone wishing to join the profession must receive the required train-ing and education. They are then 'admitted to the rolls' and allowed to practise. For this they need a 'practising certificate' issued by the Society. In 2002 there were 90,000 solicitors holding such certificates. The Society also lays down rules regarding the management of clients' money and assets. It also has disciplinary powers and investigates complaints against members.

Layfield report, 1976

Report of a committee set up in response to a perceived crisis in local government finance in 1974. It criticised the lack of responsibility for spending levels and urged greater accountability, at either central or local level. The majority of the committee favoured more local fund-raising instruments, especially local income tax. The Labour government of the time was unimpressed and decided to continue with the status quo, although it signalled it favoured 'greater central control over local government spending', something which the Thatcher government provided in abundance during the following decade.

leader of the House of Commons

Cabinet post concerned with the parlia-mentary timetable and the management of government legislative business. In addition, the incumbent is in charge of the select committee network and any reforms of the House of Commons. The post is not of key importance but usually requires a senior

politician who is familiar with the ways
of the house. John Biffen was a respected
holder of the office and it became the
consolation prize for Robin Cook when
he was sacked as foreign secretary in June
2001. He declared he was in favour of
strengthening the house in relation to the
executive; some refused to believe this would
ever happen, so great is the government's
desire to move business smoothly through
the legislative process. In February 2003 he
suffered a rebuff when his hopes of reforming the Lords to become at least partially
elected was contradicted by Tony Blair
and all the options were voted down. The
government also has a leader of the House
of Lords, often a cabinet post as well.

See also House of Lords reform; lord
president of the Council.

leaders' debates

See party leaders' televised debates.

leadership

A role or office in organisations, political or otherwise, associated with the
exercise of authority. Max Weber, the
German political economist, pointed to
the legitimate basis of leadership, namely
charismatic, traditional and legal rational
authority. The procedures for selecting a
party leader in the British system of government have varied over time and between
parties. However, in the new millennium
all mainstream parties operate, in various
forms, a system of internal party democracy
for the selection of leaders. In terms of
leadership style, British party leaders
have been, with a few exceptions, safe and
cautious: for the Conservatives Stanley
Baldwin and Arthur Balfour; for Labour
Clement Attlee, Harold Wilson and James
Callaghan. There have been charismatic
premiers, however, like the war leaderships
of David Lloyd George and Winston
Churchill and the dynamic reformer
Margaret Thatcher. On the Labour side,
too, there have been charismatic leaders
such as Ramsey MacDonald and latterly
Tony Blair; the former, however, proved
unreliable and a 'traitor' to the party,

though the latter proved electorally highly
successful, despite accusations of betrayal
by some party activists.

Philip Norton distinguishes a number
of different types of premier: innovators
(Churchill, Heath, Thatcher); reformers
(Campbell-Bannerman, Asquith, Attlee);
egoists (Lloyd George, MacDonald, Eden,
Wilson); and balancers (Bonar Law,
Douglas-Home).

> I learned that a great leader is a man who
> has the ability to get other people to do what
> they don't want to do and like it. (Harry S.
> Truman, US president)

See also authority.

leadership team (Conservative Party)

Title given to Michael Howard's shadow
cabinet, selected on 11 November 2003.
He decided to reduce the shadow cabinet
from 22 members to a mere 12, to increase
focus and improve the degree to which
his main players would be recognised.
Some members, like Tim Yeo, were given
wide-ranging jobs, in his case covering the
whole of the public services; deputies were
appointed to cover individual ministries.
Howard sought to cover all sections of
the party – including the Europhiles and
modernisers – in his team, though the
reduced number of the main portfolios must
have bruised a few egos. Howard showed
additional skill in keeping former leaders
onside by setting up an advisory group
comprising John Major, William Hague
and Iain Duncan Smith, plus the talented
Europhile Ken Clarke. The idea was to
call upon their expertise and experience
and occasionally to ask them to speak for
the party from the front bench. David
Cameron, elected December 2005, chose
not to continue such an arrangement.

League Against Cruel Sports

www.league.org.uk
Organisation founded in 1924 which
believes 'that it is iniquitous to inflict
suffering, either directly or indirectly, upon
sentient animals for the purpose of Sport'.

It opposes any kind of animal hunting. It prospered partly because the RSPCA refused to oppose hunting. The League increased its pressure during the time of New Labour, when it passionately supported those MPs wishing to outlaw such activities. The Hunting Act was passed in 2004, and outlawed hunting with dogs. Its supporters have often sought to advance their arguments by trying to prevent hunts taking place.

leak

Release of information via informal channels (usually illicit). Leaks are a familiar characteristic of modern government. They are sometimes unofficial and deliberate, for example Clive Ponting's leaking of confidential material on the sinking of the *General Belgrano* to a Labour MP, or officially sanctioned, like the leaks of intended budget measures designed to test public reaction before final decisions are made. Because of the tradition of secrecy in British government, leaks have a news value they would not otherwise have. Every effort is made to trace the source of leaks within departments; they often come from officials opposed to the measures concerned. The price paid by the source of the leak may be the loss of his/her job or, worse still, prosecution under the Official Secrets Act. Some ministers deny that something they have told a journalist constitutes a leak: James Callaghan once said to a questioner, 'You leak, I brief'.

> I don't want a leak inquiry. I want to find out who did it. (Jim Hacker in the *Yes, Prime Minister* series, when told the civil service would spare no effort to discover the source of a leak in his department)

left–right continuum

The traditional classification of political stance. It derives from the seating arrangements in the French Estates-General in 1789, where the popular movements sat to the left of the king and the aristocrats on his right. Left-wingers in Britain, typically socialists in the Labour Party, have come to represent the values of equality, collectivism

and collective or social ownership (formerly called nationalisation), while the Conservative right has been characterised by freedom, individualism and free enterprise. Centre parties like the Liberals have adopted various syntheses of both left and right. However, a more sophisticated way of mapping ideological positions can be found by using, in addition, the authoritarian–libertarian continuum, as is done by the Blundell–Gosschalk classification. New Labour sought to transcend the left–right dichotomy by asserting the 'third way': a so-called synthesis of the socialist and Conservative traditions.

See also Blundell–Gosschalk classification; third way.

legislative process

How a bill becomes an act. A governing party has the lion's share of parliamentary time to pass public bills, which are the principal means of implementing manifesto pledges. Each year civil servants and senior ministers decide on the legislative programme, as announced in the queen's speech. A drafting and consultation process then follows, where the sponsoring department and minister issue a green paper and sometimes a white paper. The final form of the bill is then introduced in either of the houses of parliament. If all the stages are complete the bill goes to the queen for the royal assent and then becomes law.

See also act of parliament.

legislature

The law-making assembly of a political system. In the case of Britain, the legislature developed from the councils of nobles assembled to advise the monarch and substantially to provide the revenue to run the monarch's court and conduct wars. Over a period of a thousand years these assemblies used their control of finance to accumulate the right to pass and scrutinise new legislation. Eventually the monarch tried to rule without their help and the 17th-century Civil War resulted, after which parliament was in the ascendant and the monarchy became purely constitutional,

presiding over a system of an elected
Commons and a cabinet led by a prime
minister. Once political parties developed
in the 19th century the leader of the
biggest party elected at a general election
generally became the person invited by
the monarch to become prime minister.
Parliament comprises the monarch, the
Commons and the Lords. Britain has an
unbalanced bicameral legislature, meaning there are two chambers of unequal
power: the House of Commons and the
(reformed) House of Lords.

legitimacy
The justified exercise of power or authority.
A political regime is unlikely to last long
without some form of justification and
acceptance by citizens: *might* must be
turned into *right*. British government has
traditionally been perceived as having
high legitimacy, through its longevity
and sequential solving of great political
questions like relations between the church
and state, the crown and state, and the
extension of the suffrage. It is also suggested that the ceremony and salience of
the monarchy as a symbol help the British
people to feel comfortable with government
and part of a unified political entity.
See also authority; political culture.

Levellers
Reformist grouping at the time of Civil War.
The name, as so often, began as a term of
abuse but stuck. John Lilburne and others
wrote pamphlets advocating wide-ranging
reforms to the franchise and government.
Initially they received support from the
ranks of the army but senior officers eventually opposed them and they were repressed
after mutinies in 1649. The movement then
faded away but is still invoked by modern-
day radicals like Tony Benn.

Liaison Select Committee
www.parliament.uk/parliamentary_
committees/liaison_committee.cfm
Committee established in 1980 and
comprising, for the most part, chairs of the
other select committees. Its prime function

is to coordinate the work of select committees, which were also established in 1980.
Seats are shared between parties. There is
no formal requirement for the chair of the
committee to come from the government
side, although in practice this has always
been the case.

The 32-strong committee attracted
attention on 16 July 2002 when the then
prime minister, Tony Blair, appeared before
it to answer questions on Iraq, parliament
and his own special advisors. He was more
forthcoming than he might have been at
prime minister's questions but few judged
the questioning to have represented a
'grilling'. Given Blair's clear mastery of this
new format, few felt its continued use made
him more accountable.

> He has discovered that he is his own best
> spin doctor. (Simon Jenkins on the extended
> questioning session, *Times*, 17 July 2002)

Lib–Lab pact, 1977–78
The Labour government under James
Callaghan lost, through by-elections, its
thin overall majority in 1977 and, in order
to stay in office, when faced with a vote
of confidence on 23 March, made a deal
with David Steel's Liberals. The pact
was renewed in the autumn of 1977. In
practice this did not mean Liberals sitting
in the cabinet but merely some nominal
consultation with a named Liberal for
each important function of government; for
example, Denis Healey consulted with John
Pardoe over economic policy. Steel formally
ended the pact in June 1978, judging it to
be a vote loser in the run-up to the by then
imminent general election.

liberal democracy
Form of democracy (and there are others)
developed in Britain during the 18th and
19th centuries, and in many other parts of
the economically developed world, including North America and western Europe. It
is essentially an amalgam of liberalism with
a number of crucial political and individual
rights and characteristics, including:
1 there is freedom of speech, within the
   law;

2 there is freedom of the press, within the law;

3 there is freedom of thought and religion;

4 overall political authority lies with the electorate, who vote in periodic free elections;

5 elected representatives exercise authority and have the ability to remove the government;

6 there is respect for human rights and dissenting minority political rights;

7 there are economic freedoms, associated with free market capitalism.

Since the collapse of the Soviet Union and its satellites in eastern Europe in the late 1980s and early 1990s, liberal democracy has extended its reach, with varying degrees of success. For this reason, Francis Fukuyama, the US political philosopher, argued that western liberal democracy had in effect 'won' the battle of ideas and that we face the 'end of history', whereby liberal democracy would preside indefinitely – a challenging thesis which provoked much discussion but little agreement. However, the fierce demonstrations mounted by those opposing corporate capitalism at various world and European summits over the past decade, together with the challenge to the west mounted by militant Islam, suggest Fukuyama's predictions may be overly complacent and naive.

Liberal Democrats

www.libdems.org.uk

Formed out of a merger between the Liberal Party and the breakaway Social Democratic Party in 1988. The 1987 election campaign had revealed the problems of an 'alliance' between the two paries, with two leaders, David Steel (Liberals) and David Owen (Social Democrats), and it seemed logical to formalise what had in any case taken place on the local level between activists in the two political groupings. However, despite his party's acceptance of the merger and the launch of the Social and Liberal Democratic Party (SLD), Owen insisted on leading a small rump party into the political wilderness. In the 1990 Bootle by-election it famously came

seventh, behind Screaming Lord Sutch's Monster Raving Loony Party, and was wound up shortly afterwards. When Steel stood down Paddy Ashdown took over as leader in March 1988, defeating Alan Beith in the leadership election, with 72 per cent of the vote. In 1990 the party became known as the 'Liberal Democrats' after an all-member ballot agreed and the fuller title was dropped.

The party has a federal structure with autonomy given to regions for the selection of candidates and for conference and policy committees. In theory the two annual conferences have the power to make party policy but in practice the leadership has the decisive say.

In the 1997 general election the party increased its representation from 20 to 46 MPs. Ashdown steered a course of 'constructive opposition' to Tony Blair's government, advocating more spending on welfare services, a more ethical foreign policy and constitutional reform, especially of the voting system. Ashdown was given a seat on a cabinet committee on constitutional reform.

After Ashdown's resignation, Charles Kennedy was elected leader in 1999. He indicated he was going to eschew a drift to the left but he entered the 2001 election campaign committed to specified tax increases and increased spending on public services. His laid-back style worked and stilled criticism that he was lazy and lacking in leadership qualities. The Liberal Democrats increased their share of the vote to 19 per cent in 2001 and their number of seats to 52. However, the prize of a new voting system still eluded them. On 30 June 2001 the *Observer* carried a report that the Transport and General Workers' Union was considering backing the party because of the New Labour government's plans to increase the involvement of the private sector in the public services. In the autumn of 2001 dissident Labour MP Paul Marsden joined the Liberal Democrats after extended disputes with his party's whips; this increased the party's membership in the Commons to

53. Early in 2003 some polls showed
the party closing on the Conservatives as
Kennedy voiced widespread criticism of
Blair's support for the US military action
against Iraq. Soon after the war, when it
seemed to have been justified, the party
showed some decline in the polls but when
the occupation proved problematic and
opinion shifted against the rationale for the
war – and Charles Kennedy took a more
aggressive line against New Labour – the
Liberal Democrats began to pick up
support, most notably demonstrated in the
stunning by-election victory at Brent East
on 18 September 2003. Soon afterwards a
Guardian ICM poll showed the party on 28
per cent and nudging the Conservatives as
the most popular opposition party. In July
2004 the party won the Leicester South
by-election on a 20 per cent swing and narrowly failed to win the Birmingham Hodge
Hill one despite a 27 per cent swing.

In the 2005 election the Liberal
Democrats won 62 seats on 22 per cent of
the vote. Kennedy's laid-back style suited
the campaign for the 2005 election and
his party emerged with a record 62 seats.
However, soon after a whispering campaign
against him began criticising his low level
of activity and accusing the Scot of being
over-fond of the demon drink. By the end
of the year, several of his colleagues had
broken cover to make their criticisms public.
After denying the problem for so long,
Kennedy decided to admit he suffered
from alcohol dependence and on 7 January
was eventually forced to resign. Then
followed a farcical contest in which two
candidates – Mark Oaten and then Simon
Hughes – were both involved in scandals
regarding their sexuality. In the end, the
two candidates on whom the membership
voted were the veteran foreign affairs expert
Sir Ming Campbell and the untried but
lively Chris Huhne. Campbell's experience
and length of service in the party eventually
won through and he won by 30,000 votes
to 22,000. At first the new leader had difficulty finding his feet, especially at prime
minister's questions, but by the end of the
year he commanded a little respect, even if

a section of the membership still hankered
for Charles Kennedy, with or without a
drink problem. Critical voices, however,
eventually won the day against Ming, too,
and on 16 October 2007 he stood down.
Chris Huhne mounted another challenge
but Nick Clegg won the vote in December
2007. Clegg was something of a sensation
in the televised party leaders' debates in the
run-up to the May 2010 election and his
party's poll ratings soared but managed to
disappear by the time polling day arrived.
Instead of polling 30 per cent or more, the
Liberal Democrats managed only 23 per
cent – one point more than in 2005 – and
57 seats – five less than in 2005. However,
his MPs were sufficient to make a coalition
with the Conservatives seem like a good
idea and Clegg duly became deputy
premier to David Cameron, with four
colleagues also in the cabinet.

liberal elite
Group of influential people in society
regarded as espousing and representing
progressive views. In the summer of 2000
the Centre for Policy Studies published a
pamphlet called *The Great and the Good:
The Rise of the New Class*. It argued that
Tony Blair had brought about the rise of a
new 'establishment' or liberal elite, which
included the likes of David Putnam, Greg
Dyke and Helena Kennedy. Allegedly
they all believed in social engineering, state
regulation and political correctness. In support it pointed out that Blair had ennobled
176 peers – some would say many were his
'cronies' – in just over three years compared
with Thatcher's 216 over 11 years.

Liberal National Party
Formed when 23 Liberal MPs led by Lord
Simon split from their party to join the
national government in 1931. However, in
1932 supporters of Herbert Samuel left in
opposition to the protectionist policies of the
government. Supporters of Lord Simon won
33 seats in 1935. By 1945, however, they
could muster only 13 seats. In 1948 they
changed their name to the National Liberal
Party, a label abandoned finally in 1966.

POLITICS

Liberal Party

Party that emerged from an amalgam of the Whigs, Radicals and supporters of Robert Peel in the middle of the 19th century. It advocated laissez faire economics, international trade, political freedom and constitutional reform. After the Reform Act 1867 the party appealed effectively to the enlarged electorate and held office in 1868–74, 1880–85, 1886, 1892–95 and 1905–16. Gladstone dominated the middle of the century with his preference for gradual reform and free trade but his decision to support Irish home rule split the party and kept it out of office until 1905, when Henry Campbell-Bannerman won a massive landslide. His reforming administration effectively represented working-class interests, and social and trade union reform resulted in a programme reflecting a more interventionist role by the state. Herbert Asquith, prime minister from 1908, gave his dynamic colleague David Lloyd George a role in government which led to his wartime premiership and provided a launching pad for the coup which the Welshman made, with Conservative support, to become prime minister himself. However, in the process the party was yet again split, with a large group remaining loyal to Asquith. This division helped Labour to become the natural opposition party and marked the end of the Liberals' possession of political power in the 20th century. In 1924 the party gained only 40 seats and in 1929 just 59; a small group around Lord Simon thereafter became indistinguishable from the Conservatives. In 1935 the reduced party gained 20 seats and this figure dropped to 12 in 1945; in 1951, 1955 and 1959 the party won only 6 seats.

Jo Grimond stimulated a revival in the 1950s but, even though Liberal votes increased, the party failed to make the threshold required in a first past the post system. Reform of the voting system became probably the chief objective of the party after 1945, as the vote it received was never proportionally represented in parliamentary seats. It also sustained its tradition of internationalism by championing the cause of European integration, a platform which the Liberal Democrats fully absorbed. Jeremy Thorpe was an effective leader but the scandal which engulfed him damaged his party and it was left to David Steel to pick up the pieces and lead the party into the Lib–Lab pact in 1977. After the Alliance with the Social Democratic Party, the Liberals merged with the latter in 1988 to form the Social and Liberal Democrat Party, the forerunner of the Liberal Democrats.

Liberal Unionists

Party created in 1886 when the Liberal Party split over home rule for Ireland. The Liberal Unionists, led by Joseph Chamberlain, opposed home rule. In the 1895 election 70 Liberal Unionists were elected; they became absorbed into the Conservative Party and went on to help constitute its liberal, social reforming wing.

Liberal Youth

http://liberalyouth.org
Youth and student organisation of the Liberal Democrats. It represents the interests within the party of members aged up to 26, and students of any age. It campaigns on issues affecting young people.

liberalism

Essentially, a belief in the freedom of the individual and human improvement. It is one of the major traditions of political thought in Britain, along with conservatism, socialism and Marxism. It is associated with the social and economic forces of the industrial revolution and the intellectual speculations of the Enlightenment, although traces of liberal thinking were present in John Lilburne's tracts and his Levellers during the time of the English Civil War. Prominent thinkers from this tradition include John Locke, Tom Paine, John Stuart Mill, Jeremy Bentham and the political economist Adam Smith. In British political history 'liberalism' is the doctrine of the Liberal Party and initially comprised a commitment to: individual rights, laissez faire economics, minimal government, representative government, a utilitarian approach to legislation and peace through trade. To an extent this 'liberalism' established the basic values of the British constitution but it also emerged, via the Liberal Party, as a creed in the marketplace of political ideas as well. By the end of the 19th century that party's appeal to the newly enfranchised working class led it to embark on a path towards emphasising a more paternalistic, protective approach, by which the brutal excesses of capitalism were to be curbed. Moreover, the state was looked upon as a necessary agent for social reform, taking on responsibility for the welfare of the poor and old in order to reduce inequality in society. Later the Liberal economists William Beveridge and John Maynard Keynes elaborated the more interventionist approach which was adopted by Labour as its own. The 1970s witnessed a renewed interest in classical liberal ideas of the free market, which the new right took up and which were personified by Margaret Thatcher, who was sometimes described as a 'classical liberal'. Liberalism has thus been one of the most powerful political doctrines of the last 200 years.

See also classical liberalism; communitarianism; new right.

libertarianism

In modern usage, the rights of the individual, unencumbered by moral, legal or political restraint. In essence individual liberties come before obligations to the state. However, there are different forms of libertarianism. One school, associated with the political philosopher Robert Nozick, argues that the rights of the individual should never be abrogated and that the state should act only to promote individual liberty, including economic freedoms. The economist Friedrich von Hayek moves beyond the individual to assert that the free market is beneficial to all and that the interventionist state can only be inefficient and a threat to the general good. Another stream of libertarian thought retains the state, but shrinks it to a minimum, whereby it provides only territorial defence against invasion, sound currency and a bare body

of civil and criminal law. The new right was influenced by some, though not all, of these ideas, and Margaret Thatcher went as far as to say that she wanted to 'roll back the state' and that there was 'no such thing as "society", only individual men, women and families'. The value of libertarianism to an understanding of modern British politics lies in its ability to throw into sharp relief the interdependent nature of modern social and political organisation, a phenomenon underlined by globalisation.

See also limited government.

liberty

See freedom.

Liberty

www.liberty-human-rights.org.uk
Group that campaigns for civil liberties and human rights. It was formerly known as the National Council for Civil Liberties, founded in 1934 by Ronald Kidd, who had been deeply affected by the police's use of agent provocateurs, or police agitators, during the 'hunger marches' of 1932. His solution was to encourage reliable people to attend public events and be independent witnesses to complaints of police misbehaviour. His activities widened to include other threats to civil liberties, such as the rise of fascism and government censorship.

Liberty is committed to the defence and extension of civil liberties in Britain and to the rights and liberties recognised by international law. Sister organisations are the Scottish Council of Civil Liberties and Northern Ireland's Committee for the Administration of Justice. Shami Chakrabarti was appointed Liberty's director in 2003.

life peerage

The Life Peerages Act 1958 introduced the creation of non-hereditary members of the House of Lords, including women for the first time. After the Act it was still possible to create hereditary peers, although this was not used again after 1964 until Margaret Thatcher so ennobled Harold Macmillan, Willie Whitelaw and George Thomas in

1983. Life peers have since constituted the most active element in the Lords and have been responsible for a renaissance in its activity and effectiveness. In 1999 Labour ended the hereditary element in the Lords except for 92 survivors, who would go once the reforms were complete. But Labour gave no indication of any overall reform of the chamber. Some critics observed that if only the 'lifers' remained, then the chamber would quickly become a giant quango, appointed by the prime minister and comprising, in the argot of the tabloids, 'Tony's cronies'.

See also House of Lords reform.

limited government

A crucial element of early liberal ideology and libertarian thinking, that government should be limited to the bare necessities of maintaining national security and a sound currency. The corollary of the idea is that citizens should be allowed to live their lives unimpeded by government as far as possible. Conservative theorists of the new right adopted the idea in reaction to the postwar consensus. However, despite Margaret Thatcher's often quoted wish to roll back the state and to promote economic deregulation, she presided over a substantial increase in central government power. This included: restrictions on local government finance, the introduction of a national curriculum in schools, increased powers for the police and the abolition of trade unions at Government Communications Headquarters (GCHQ).

See also consensus; libertarianism; new right.

Lisbon treaty, 2009

Treaty of the European Union (EU) that modified the EU's institutions, partly in response to EU enlargement. Also known as the reform treaty, it embodies a draft revised constitution which had been produced by G'Iscard D'Estaing but rejected in referendums by France and the Netherlands in 2005. It was signed by EU members in December 2007. For Britain, Gordon Brown arrived late and signed separately from other EU premiers. Changes to the running of the EU include:

1 more powers for the European parliament;
2 changes to qualified majority voting;
3 fewer commissioners, to reflect new total membership of 27 states;
4 the appointment of a new president of the European Council for a fixed term to represent the EU in a single person.

The treaty was well on the way to full ratification when Irish voters in June 2008 rejected it in a referendum. However, in October 2009 they said 'yes' by 67 per cent of the vote in a repeat referendum on the same treaty, though with some further EU commitments made to Ireland on specific issues. Britain ratified the treaty in July 2008 but William Hague for the Tories condemned this as a betrayal of Labour's election promise to offer a referendum on acceptance of the EU constitution.

> to complete the process started by the Treaty of Amsterdam [1997] and by the Treaty of Nice with a view to enhancing the efficiency and democratic legitimacy of the Union and to improving the coherence of its action. (Stated aim of the treaty)

lobby

Organisations that seek to influence government in the interests of the specific groups they represent. The term derives from the name given to the area close to a legislative chamber where it is possible to gain access to members. It is more American but in Britain it is also used, as are 'lobbying' or 'lobbyist', although 'pressure groups' or 'interest groups' are more frequent. This said, in recent years there has been a growth in companies and consultancies that offer professional services to those companies and groups which wish to gain access to key people in and around government.

See also 'cash for influence' scandal; 'cash for questions' scandal.

lobby system

The system that governs journalists' access to politicians in Westminster. In Victorian times William Gladstone used to commune with selected journalists and give them privileged information about his plans and thoughts. During the 20th century this practice became formalised, the numbers grew and aspirant members of the parliamentary lobby had to apply. Some 200 attend the twice-daily briefings from Downing Street and the Commons. They can also roam the corridors of Westminster and have access to most areas except for the floor of the chamber itself. The idea is that they receive information in briefings they would not otherwise learn but in exchange do not reveal the origin of their source. This led to code words being used like 'sources close to the prime minister' (the prime minister's press secretary) and the meetings and even meeting places were kept secret, unlike the on-the-record televised briefings used in Washington, DC. In the late 1980s the *Independent*, the *Guardian* and the *Scotsman* withdrew from the lobby for a while, arguing that it enabled government to control the agenda of discussion, to favour one section of the press over another, and to use the briefings to fly kites or rubbish other members of the government or otherwise manipulate the news agenda. In 1997 Alastair Campbell, Tony Blair's press secretary, decided to allow himself to be identified in stories as the 'prime minister's spokesman' in an attempt to make the system less secretive. As the 2001 general election approached Campbell withdrew from daily briefings to occupy a more strategic role. In May 2002 certain changes were made whereby morning lobby briefings would be open to all journalists and, when ministers attend, are both on the record and on camera. Edited versions of the briefings also now appear on the Number 10 website. On 20 June 2002 a lobby briefing was televised for the first time. Michael White, political editor of the *Guardian*, predicted that few briefings would be televised, as they were so 'boring'.

local government

A form of devolution whereby decisions about local services are placed nearest to the people who use them. The Municipal Corporations Act 1835 established rules for the election of councillors, their duties and the powers of councils. As the life of industrial Britain became more complex, local government took on additional duties in terms of education, health and planning, to the extent that more uniform and stronger structures were required. The Local Government Act 1888 established the procedures for elected county authorities, and in 1894 legislation created urban and rural district councils within those counties. This system survived into the next century but was found inadequate and many functions like health were lost to other bodies. The Local Government Act 1972 reformed the system quite drastically but further change was still to come. This included the abolition of the Greater London Council and other metropolitan counties in 1986 and the creation of unitary authorities in the early 1990s. This was achieved in Scotland and Wales, but only partly in England, for example York and the Isle of Wight. More significant have been the local government reforms since 1997 and devolution in Scotland and Wales.

In the local elections held on 1 May 2003, the Conservatives won back a big slice of control of English local government, with well over 500 gains. The Liberal Democrats also did well, with 150 gains, and Labour suffered over 700 losses. In the 2004 elections the usual mid-term swing against the government – this time aided by opposition to the Iraq war – produced 232 more seats for the Conservatives and 151 more for the Liberal Democrats, while Labour lost 468. This left Labour controlling only 39 councils compared with the Conservatives' 50, the Liberal Democrats' 9 plus 65 without overall control. Turnout was up, to average 40 per cent, partly as a result of the experiment with postal voting in three regions. But by May 2010, while Labour was losing the general election, it was doing much better at the local level, where both the Liberal Democrats and the Conservatives lost control of four councils each while Labour gained 17.

See also London government; regional assembly.

Local Government Act 1972

Act that introduced two tiers of government: county and district. It also introduced 6 metropolitan counties, 36 metropolitan districts, 53 shire counties and 369 shire districts, all performing different functions. The act took effect in 1974. To counteract the increased remoteness of local government, parish councils were retained but had little practical role. New shire counties were created in Avon, Cleveland and Humberside, while old counties such as Rutland disappeared. New names such as 'West Yorkshire' were introduced to replace the age-old West Riding of Yorkshire. Many of these changes provoked anger and resentment among local people, which lives on today.

Local Government Act 1988, section 28

See section 28.

Local Government Association

www.lga.gov.uk

Voluntary lobbying organisation that represents the interests of local government. It was formed in 1997 and represents some 500 local authorities – that is, virtually all – which cover around 50 million people and annually spend £78 billion. It is located near the centre of London within easy access of decision-making centres. Strategic objectives for 2001–06 included redressing the balance between the centre and local authorities, increasing the powers and flexibility of local authorities and improving their financial situation.

local government finance

The money raised by local authorities through local taxation (principally the council tax and uniform business rate); central government grants (principally the revenue support grant and other specific grants); fees and charges for services (for example rents); and borrowing from banks and the like. Capital can also be obtained from the European Union, the National Lottery, the private finance initiative and the sale of assets. Funds are also available from the Department for Environment,

Food and Rural Affairs for specific projects in transport, education and other areas.

Local government spends large sums of money, about a quarter of all public spending, via central government grants, council tax and business rates. It totalled £154 billion 2007–08.

It is subordinate to central government and can act only within the terms of statutes passed at Westminster and this constitutional fact determined the development of local government finance during the 1980s. In 1980, 1982 and 1984 Conservative governments passed a raft of legislation to control spending by local authorities. The measures included rate capping, grant-related expenditure assessments, compulsory competitive tendering, the introduction of the poll tax or community charge, the sale of council houses and the introduction of standard spending assessments. Supplementary rates were made illegal in 1981 when the High Court ruled that the Greater London Council (GLC) had acted ultra vires, or beyond its powers, in using an additional rate to subsidise London Transport buses and tubes. The abolition of the GLC and the metropolitan counties in 1986 further reduced the financial independence of local government. Despite further changes since 1997, the local authorities appear to have insufficient money to fund the services which many supporters of local government call for.

local government reform since 1997

After 1997 the Labour government's approach to local government was characterised by a change of emphasis, and some innovation, rather than wholesale reform, a theme very much in line with the party's eclectic policy making. Significant innovations included:

1 democratisation of councils, for example by means of directly elected mayors;
2 councils holding local referendums and introducing innovations in polling to increase participation rates;
3 crude council tax capping ended, though with reserve powers left with central government;

4 beacon councils established, which
   set standards of excellence for service
   delivery;
5 more consultation with local people and
   businesses on service provision;
6 compulsory competitive tendering
   replaced by 'best value'.

However, continuity with the Thatcher
and Major years was maintained by the
retention of the national business rate,
although with some latitude for variation,
and by the emphasis on efficiency, economy
and effectiveness (the three 'E's) in the
delivery of services. Overall, the Labour
government moved some way towards
recognising the value of local government,
albeit with continued centralisation from
Westminster.

local taxation
See community charge; council tax; local
government finance.

Lockerbie
Village (population 4,000) in Dumphries
in Scotland into which Pan Am flight 103
crashed on 21 December 1988, after a
bomb exploded in the plane's hold. There
were 270 fatalities: 11 were villagers and
the rest on the plane, from 21 different
nations. In 1991 two Libyans were charged
with the offence but were not brought to
trial for 10, years when Abdelbaset Ali
Mohmed Al Megrahi was found guilty
and sentenced to life imprisonment. His
co-accused, Amin Khalifa Fhimah, was
acquitted. There ensued much controversy
about the guilt of the man imprisoned and
many claimed an injustice had been done.
In the summer of 2009 he was released
on compassionate grounds by the Scottish
executive, much to the fury of the bereaved
US families, especially when Megrahi
returned to a hero's welcome in Libya.

London assembly
www.london.gov.uk/who-runs-london/
assembly
Body established in 2000 to scrutinise the
work of the London mayor. The assembly
is intended to hold the mayor to account,

to examines the mayor's spending (it
can amend the budget when two-thirds
of the members agree to do so) and to
investigate important issues concerning
the capital. Assembly members also have
representation on the Metropolitan Police
Authority (formerly the responsibility of
the home secretary), the London Fire and
Emergency Planning Authority and the
London Development Agency.

Assembly members are elected for
four-year terms. Four per cent of the vote
is needed to save a candidate's deposit. An
adapted additional member system (AMS)
is used, with 14 constituency members from
the boroughs (average electorate 350,000)
and 11 from London-wide party lists. In
the June 2004 election, Labour won seven
seats, the Conservatives nine, the Liberal
Democrats five, the Greens two and the
UK Independence Party two. George
Galloway's Respect party did not win a
seat but polled commendably well. In 2008,
the Conservatives increased their seats by
two to 11; Labour went down one to 8; the
Liberal Democrats lost two to go down to
2; the Greens held onto 2; and the British
National Party managed to gain one
elected member. Boris Johnson bested Ken
Livingstone in the mayoral election.

London bombings, 7 July 2005
See 7/7 bombings.

London government
The Local Government Act 1888 created
the London County Council but this was
replaced by the Greater London Council
in 1965, which looked after city-wide
functions like transport and planning which
the 32 London borough councils could not
easily deal with. When Margaret Thatcher
came to power she immediately encountered
conflict from Labour-controlled city
authorities, especially in London, where
Ken Livingstone led a high-profile left-wing
administration. While her abolition of other
metropolitan counties caused no outcry, the
loss of an area-wide council for the nation's
capital provoked heated criticism and not
just from Labour.

After 1997, Labour introduced plans for an elected mayor for the capital. The first elections took place in May 2000, amid controversy over nominations and candidates in both major parties. Ken Livingstone won, despite standing as an independent (Tony Blair had effectively vetoed his candidature for the Labour Party), leaving Frank Dobson, the official Labour candidate, humiliated and Tony Blair tainted with accusations of 'control freakery'. Labour's National Executive Committee voted to allow Livingstone back into the party in January 2004; he went on to be easily re-elected as London mayor in June of the same year. Boris Johnston became mayor in 2008.

London mayor
www.london.gov.uk/who-runs-london/mayor
Directly elected politician with responsibility for promoting the economic, social and environmental development of the capital. (In contrast, the lord mayor of London is a ceremonial role for the City of London.) The elections use the supplementary vote, in which electors can express a second preference. In the first elections Ken Livingstone stood as an independent against Labour's official candidate Frank Dobson. The latter had been 'steered' towards the election by Tony Blair, who was opposed to Livingstone standing as the official Labour candidate despite his popularity, because, allegedly, he was associated with the 'loony left' days of the defunct Greater London Council. For the Conservatives Jeffrey Archer defeated Steven Norris to become their candidate but was forced to stand down after the *News of the World* made allegations of libel, of which he was later convicted. The candidacy passed to Norris. Livingstone was victorious in the election and went on to win a second term, this time as the official Labour candidate. Boris Johnson for the Conservatives beat Livingstone in the 2008 election (53 per cent versus 47 per cent).

London Underground (the 'Tube')
A rapid-transit underground rail system covering most of Greater London, with

250 miles of track. Its future became an issue in the 2000 mayoral contest, with Ken Livingstone proposing to raise funds via the issue of public bonds and Gordon Brown, the Labour chancellor, via a public–private partnership. The issue festered unresolved during Livingstone's first term in office. Former CIA agent Bob Kiley (who had tackled New York's subway problems), brought in to resolve the problem, condemned Brown's plan as 'fatally flawed', as it fragmented the system into three services, for tracks, stations and signalling. In July 2001 Kiley was sacked by the minister for transport, Stephen Byers, allegedly on the instructions of prime minister Tony Blair, under pressure from his chancellor.

Modernisation of the Underground remains problematic. Modernisation of the infrastructure was handed over to two companies, Metronet and Tube Lines. Metronet entered administration in July 2007, although Tube Lines has continued to function. Some £16 billion of funding has been arranged over a 30-year period with improvements aimed for with special reference to the 2012 London Olympics.

Lonrho affair, 1973
Scandal involving excessive payments to Duncan Sandys, chair of the African mining company Lonrho. This company had been built up by the dynamic but controversial Tiny Rowland in the 1960s as a huge African enterprise. The scandal erupted at a time when prime minister Edward Heath was trying to 'create a national mood of restraint'. A group of directors was seeking to dislodge Rowland and during the course of the struggle it emerged that the chairman of the company, Duncan Sandys, a former cabinet colleague of Heath, had received $10,000, deposited in a Cayman Island account, apparently to avoid tax payments. Heath decided this was indefensible and denounced it as 'the unpleasant and unacceptable face of capitalism'. He denied, however, that the 'whole of British industry consists of practices of this kind'.

lord advocate

Government's principal law officer in Scotland, in charge of public prosecutions and who pleads in all cases that concern the crown. The lord advocate is the head of the system of public prosecutions and is aided by a solicitor general and by 'advocates depute'. The office was established early in the 16th century; the office holder is allowed to wear a hat in court. The officer oversees three offices:

1 the Lord Advocate's Department, which assists, among other things, in the drafting of Scottish legislation;
2 the Crown Office in Edinburgh, which deals with the administration of criminal law in Scotland;
3 the Scottish Courts Administration, which deals with civil law in Scotland.

lord chancellor

The oldest public office, dating back 1,400 years. It used to be cited as a constitutional anomaly, in that its holder was at once a member of: the judiciary, as its head; the executive, by virtue of being in the cabinet; and the legislature, by virtue of being a member of the House of Lords. The lord chancellor also acted as the speaker of the Lords (and so sat on the woolsack). Lord Irvine of Lairg was lord chancellor to Tony Blair for six years and was a staunch defender of the powers of his ancient office. However, he was forced to retire in June 2003 as the office was reformed into the Department for Constitutional Affairs, with an additional responsibility for the residual duties of the Scottish and Welsh secretaries. The Judicial Appointments Commission was also set up to appoint judges. Blair was criticised for lack of consultation, though few argued with the sense of separating the judiciary more clearly from politics. Ken Clarke became lord chancellor in May 2010.

Lord Chancellor's Department

Department created in 1885 but replaced in 2003 by the Department for Constitutional Affairs, which itself became the Ministry of Justice in 2007.

The Department was in charge of the administration of the courts but was also tasked from June 2003 with the residual responsibilities (after devolution) of the Welsh and Scottish secretaries.

lord president of the Council

The person charged with running the Privy Council and its office but the job is merely ceremonial. The office holder is usually the leader of the house and also a senior cabinet minister who chairs committees and reports back to cabinet.

lord privy seal

In the middle ages the officer who took charge of the privy seal but now, as with so many ancient posts, one of those 'dignified' constitutional roles which sound grand but have virtually no power. The office is often given to a senior politician, known to have good judgement, who chairs important cabinet committees. Occasionally the office is given to someone with a specific and important job to perform, like Edward Heath in 1960–63 when negotiating Britain's entry into the European Community.

lost deposit

Generally, a candidate in an election has to deposit a certain sum which is lost unless a certain proportion of the vote is mustered. Originally the Representation of the People Act 1918 set the deposit at £150 but this soon became outdated through inflation and failed to deter a plethora of joke candidates. In 1985 the sum was increased to £500 but the limit required was lowered from one-eighth to one-twentieth of the poll. The sum is also £500 for the Scottish parliament and Welsh assembly but deposits vary in other elections, from none in local elections to £5,000 for Euro-elections and £10,000 for the London mayoral elections.

Low Pay Commission

www.lowpay.gov.uk
Independent agency set up by the National Minimum Wage Act 1998 to advise the government on the minimum wage.

loyalist

The name often given to people who feel particular support for a certain cause but especially to members of Protestant groupings in Northern Ireland who are 'loyal' to the British crown.

Loyalist Volunteer Force (LVF)

Formed in 1996 from renegade elements of the Ulster Volunteer Force (UVF). This sect is opposed to the Northern Ireland peace process. Billy Wright was an early leader before being shot dead in Maze Prison by the Irish National Liberation Army (INLA) in 1997. It has around 500 members.

M

Maastricht treaty, 1992

The treaty on European Union. A meeting of the European Council at Maastricht in the Netherlands on 11 December 1991 agreed amendments to the founding treaties of the European Community necessary to achieve further economic and political union. European ministers met again in February 1992 at the same place to sign what became known as the treaty on European Union, which came into force on 1 January 1994, at which point the European Community became the European Union (EU). The treaty's main aim was to register, according to its article A, a 'new stage in the process of creating an ever closer union among the peoples of Europe'. Accordingly it provided, among other things, for extended majority voting rather than unanimity in the Council of Ministers and gave increased power to the European parliament. John Major, negotiating on behalf of Britain, insisted on the addition of two protocols which removed the requirement for Britain to move towards economic and monetary union and to accept the Social Chapter, which commits members to improve employment and working conditions. Initially the agreement was received calmly but when Denmark rejected the treaty in June 1992 internal opposition within the governing Conservative Party began to grow, encouraged by France's wafer thin referendum endorsement (a 2 per cent margin) in September. In December 1992, at Edinburgh, Maastricht was formally endorsed but Major was able to extract more concessions, especially on 'subsidiarity', which is the notion of decision making being made at more local levels wherever possible, and which was designed to assuage fears of a drift towards federalism or a European 'super-state'. A rider to article A was therefore added: 'in which decisions are taken as closely as possible to the citizen'. Even this addition was deemed insufficient by Conservative 'Eurosceptics' and the treaty took over 200 hours of passionate Commons debate and a government defeat before being ratified on 2 August 1993. The German chancellor Helmut Kohl alerted Eurosceptics to the implications of the treaty when he described it as the 'foundation-stone for the completion of the European Union ... the United States of Europe'.

Macpherson report, 1999

Report of an inquiry by Sir William Macpherson into the murder of a black student, Stephen Lawrence, and the failure of the Metropolitan Police to conduct the case properly and secure convictions. In particular, the police were condemned for failing to recognise that the crime was racially motivated and for their treatment of the Lawrence family plus his friend, Dwayne Brooks, who survived the attack. However, the inquiry went further and revealed that racism was not just a problem for individual police officers, but also for the culture of the Metropolitan Police and other public service organisations. Macpherson used the term 'institutional racism' to describe the collective failure of an organisation to provide appropriate and professional service to people because of their colour, culture or ethnic origin. It can be seen or detected in processes, attitudes and behaviour which amount to discrimination through unwitting prejudice, ignorance, thoughtlessness and racist stereotyping, which disadvantage minority ethnic people.

The report proposed a raft of recommendations, including the following:

1 All public service organisations should assess whether they are acting fairly, that they are meeting the needs of the communities they serve, and that professional standards are maintained in every situation.

2 Management structures and procedures should be in place that give effect to these tests.

3 The Race Relations Act 1976 should be amended to make it unlawful for the police to discriminate on racial grounds in the exercise of law enforcement.

4 Independent investigations should take place of serious complaints against the police.

5 Racially aggravated offences should receive stiffer sentences.

6 There should be increased recruitment of ethnic minority police officers, with targets established and monitoring of performance in this respect.

A report 10 years later (2009) by the Home Affairs Select Committee noted: the increased accountability of the police; progress on changing the culture of the police; and improved treatment of victims and witnesses, including the use of family liaison officers.

'magic circle'

Name given to describe the informal system of appointing Conservative leaders up to 1965, when Edward Heath became the first to be openly elected. Leaders emerged after extended internal soundings made by leading members of the party. The last leader to emerge in this way was Alec Douglas-Home, in 1963.

magistrates' court

The most junior court in the country. The 650 magistrates' courts hear the vast majority of cases brought forward – over 95 per cent. Most magistrates, or justices of the peace (JPs) to use the traditional title, apart for the 'stipendiary' ones in the big cities who are professional lawyers, are voluntary unpaid judges recruited from local people of good standing. They can hear both civil and criminal cases, although the latter provide the bulk. All criminal prosecutions must begin in a magistrates' court. On the civil side, magistrates have extensive powers to make maintenance, affiliation and adoption orders and to set restrictions on violent husbands' access to their families, for example. They also deal with juveniles, liquor laws and applications for betting licences. Magistrates receive some training but the source of much legal knowledge is the clerk to the court, by profession an experienced solicitor or barrister and often the real source of the decisions made by lay magistrates. There are also 130 professional magistrates, with several years' experience as a lawyer, who sit as district judges in magistrates' courts.

See also crown court; judiciary.

Magna Carta

The fundamental statement of British liberties, signed by King John at Runnymede in June 1215. It arose from the acute discontent of the king's barons with his heavy tax burden and was the product of there not being an adult member of the royal family to foment a rebellion, John being the last of the Plantagenet line. Consequently the barons had to lead their own revolt, behind a charter of reform. John decided to accept the charter when the rebels seized London. This did not stop the fighting, however, and modified charters were issued in 1217 and 1225, the latter text, with 63 chapters, being the one lying on the statute book as the most basic of British laws. The best-known clauses guarantee the citizen freedom from illegal interference with person or property and justice to everyone. The king was forbidden from raising certain taxes without the consent of the 'common council' of the realm. The original charter was to be enforced by a

POLITICS

council of 25 barons, who threatened war if the king went back on his promises. The four remaining copies of the charter are in Salisbury and Lincoln Cathedrals and the British Library (two copies).

maladministration
See ombudsman.

Managerial, Scientific and Financial Union
See Unite.

Manchester radicals
Mid-19th-century advocates of laissez faire economics, including Richard Cobden and John Bright. Regarded as extreme in their day, their ideas came to influence Thatcherism over a century later.

mandarin
Name given to a senior civil servant in the UK deriving from their similarity to officials in the Chinese Empire, who also were required to pass examinations before being employed.

mandate
The endorsement of policy proposals by victory in an election. There are intriguing questions on the use of the term: is the mandate a general authority to govern in the best interests of the people, or a specific instruction from the electorate on each and every promise made in a party's manifesto, or is it both? There are no definitive answers to these questions; history is a better guide. Some within the Labour Party, especially in the early part of the 20th century, interpreted it as a duty to fulfil promises given and therefore believed it was incumbent on all elected representatives to do this.

As a verb, again in the Labour Party, it indicates a duty to behave in a certain way, as when a union delegation is 'mandated' by the union's conference to vote a particular way at the Labour Party conference.

Another usage views the mandate as a rod with which to beat the House of Lords: an unelected chamber has no right to reject legislation promised in a party's manifesto and passed by elected representatives in the House of Commons. This argument, the Salisbury doctrine, was used by Margaret Thatcher a number of times in conflicts with the upper chamber in 1985.

See also manifesto; Salisbury doctrine.

Mandelson's return
In an extraordinary move, on 3 October 2008 Gordon Brown appointed Peter Mandelson, the twice sacked architect of New Labour, as secretary of state for business, with a seat in the Lords. Given that Alastair Campbell was also known to be advising Brown, this re-established something of the 'old guard' from prior successful times. In a major interview in the *Guardian* (29 November 2008) Mandelson admitted he was not sure why Brown had asked him back after their history of passionate enmity following Mandelson's swapping of sides to Tony Blair in 1994, but felt he had been welcomed back surprisingly warmly by his former party colleagues, maybe because he was no longer the 'chief courtier to the prime minister'. He commented:

> after a very difficult year New Labour and the party were approaching something akin to a political nervous breakdown and I felt my role was to bring people together.

He felt Brown had lost had way in his first year, but had become more at home with the economic crisis.

manifesto
The programme of government presented by parties to voters at election time. The first was the Tamworth manifesto in 1835, which Robert Peel drew up in response to the Great Reform Act of 1832.

In theory, Labour's manifesto is endorsed by the party conference and a two-thirds majority vote on a proposal guarantees its inclusion. Once elected into office the Parliamentary Labour Party is 'mandated' to carry it out.

In an age of television politics very few ordinary voters actually read the manifesto document; nevertheless, it is still important because it contains a party's programme for government. It is also an anchor point for a party's campaign, politicians referring to it or defending it from attack. The style of the document has changed from the dull 'wordy' tracts of the 1950s to the glossy, picture-rich policy statements headed up with catchy titles of today. For example, in 1997 the Labour Party's manifesto had a picture of Tony Blair on the front cover, with the words 'New Labour: Because Britain Deserves Better'. The Conservatives' 2010 manifesto, intriguingly, was published in the form of blue-covered booklet bearing the title 'Invitation to Join the Government of Britain'. The thrust of its message was that the party intended to provide the opportunity to voters to seize back control of their lives from the government.

See also mandate; Tamworth manifesto.

Manor of Northstead
See Chiltern Hundreds.

marching season
See Orange Order.

marginal seat
A parliamentary constituency where the margin of victory between the winner and runner-up is close, often no more than a few percentage points difference. In contrast to 'safe seats', where large majorities are secured by winners, the outcomes in marginal seats are difficult to predict. Factors which swing the balance may include tactical or negative voting, the impact of national issues, party or leader image, the personality or reputation of the candidate and the effectiveness of the local campaign. For these reasons, marginal seats often hold the key to victory in general elections and parties will therefore target their campaigning there. That said, in 1997, many safe seats, occupied by senior members of the government, fell to Labour in a surge of anti-Tory sentiment, altering the electoral map of Britain. In the 2001 general election the Conservatives did not generally perform well in the marginal seats, where often Labour managed to

improve on its small 1997 majority. One of the reasons was a continuous monitoring of voter opinions by Labour in these seats, whereby 'tailored' approaches could be made to the 1,000 or so voters who would decide the contest.

market
The mechanism in society whereby supply meets demand. In the process, society is changed profoundly and so markets are politically significant. In a free market, goods are offered to the public at prices which the producer thinks they are worth and which the public are prepared to pay. If they are successful, business flourishes, people are employed and profits are used for purchasing and reinvestment. However, if they are not a success, business failure follows, with unemployment and possibly misery until success in a new market can be achieved. In this way people come to be rich or poor, employers or employees and their chances in life, not to mention those of their families, are influenced accordingly. In Britain a market economy was established in the 19th century but the excesses of poverty were criticised and so socialism through the Labour Party became a popular option. After 1945 the economy was affected by nationalisation, whereby 20 per cent of it was taken into public ownership. In the 1970s the government intervened in the economy in many ways and provoked the neo-liberal reaction of Thatcherism, which led to privatisation in the 1980s and a determination to allow the market to proceed unfettered by government action so far as possible. New Labour, when it came to power in 1997, accepted this view of the market and more or less adopted the Conservative attitude towards the market.

market testing
A process of competitive tendering. Market testing was inspired by the privatisation policies of the 1980s and the success (in terms of cost savings) of compulsory competitive tendering (CCT) in local government and the National Health

Service. John Major went further and the 1991 white paper 'Competing for Quality' proposed the market testing of a number of central government functions, including secretarial, accountancy, statistical and information technology services. The aim was to allow competitive bids from the private sector to undertake the same work and to award a contract to those that could deliver quality and efficiency of service. Certainly the tendering process identified true costs and sharpened up operational practices, but the approach was criticised by some as bureaucratic, costly and inimical to the public service ethic of the civil service. By 1996, Major's government claimed to have saved £720 million per year and to have shed some 30,000 posts. The scheme was replaced in 1997 by 'best value', where there was increased emphasis on service quality and the dropping of the need to have a compulsory tendering process.

See also best value; compulsory competitive tendering.

Marshall aid

The US funds given as part of the Marshall plan or European Recovery Program. This was passed by the US Congress, not without doubts, in 1948. Its impulse was to bolster a weakened Europe against the threat of communism from the east. Secretary of state George Marshall was the author of the plan, under which European countries were invited to articulate their requirements for recovery. British foreign secretary Ernest Bevin was quick to react to the offer and helped to make it a reality for the whole of Europe. The Soviet Union refused to participate and tried to subvert the plan.

The Organisation for European Economic Cooperation was set up to administer the plan. Between 1948 and 1951 over $13.5 billion was disbursed via the plan, which is considered in the light of history to have been far-sighted and highly successful.

Marxism

One of the most significant political and intellectual movements of the 19th and 20th centuries, and named after the scholar and radical Karl Marx. Marx believed he had discovered the true motor of history in the relationship of people to the changing means of wealth production. He argued that those who controlled the means of production always became the dominant class of people in any society and went on to permeate that society with the ideas and values which underpinned their supremacy. He analysed history along these lines, declaring that, in the modern industrial era, 'bourgeois' owners of capital were the ruling class and the proletarian masses the subordinate one. The latter were exploited by the capitalist class to produce wealth, which only the ruling minority truly enjoyed. He predicted that the constant search by capitalists for bigger profits and lower prices to beat the competition would push down wages and create increasing poverty for the proletariat. Eventually the masses would rise up and throw off the controls of the dominant bourgeoisie and would go on, after a period of dictatorial control, to eliminate capitalism, and to introduce a socialist society in which ownership of property would be collective and not private. Once common ownership was introduced the benefits of social justice and equality would work their way through the economy and society and create a human fellowship based on trust and cooperation. Eventually, he predicted, the state would 'wither away' as an international commonwealth of communists came into being.

Marx did not have any doubts about his analysis and his predictions, which, he claimed, were based on the 'scientific' study of society and therefore inevitable. Lenin, a Russian intellectual and radical, reinterpreted Marx's original formulations and applied them to Russia in the revolution of 1917, but any hopes of a socialist utopia soon withered as Stalin took total and murderous control. Similar regimes were set up after 1945 as the USSR assumed a hegemony over eastern European countries.

All of the world's communist regimes, except China, North Korea and Cuba, collapsed in the late 1980s and early 1990s and were replaced by regimes sympathetic to capitalism if not always to liberal democracy. It is historical fact that Marxism as a political programme was a gigantic and costly failure for many of the people who lived in communist countries; it failed to protect minimum human rights and produced precious little material prosperity either.

Britain tended to be immune to any substantial Marxist influence, albeit the country had a tiny Communist Party and a few sympathetic trade unions, as well as Militants (following a Trotskyist version of Marxism) in the Labour Party, who were in any case by and large expelled in the late 1980s. This having been said, Marxism was and remains a formidable system of intellectual thought, which is still used by social scientists as a form of analysis, and is respected even by some of those hostile to its revolutionary prescriptions. There is some truth in the quip that 'Marx was right about what was wrong but wrong about what was right'.

See also capitalism; Marx, Karl.

mass media

Defined by Dennis McQuail (a political scientist) as 'The organised means for communicating openly and at a distance to many receivers within a relatively short space of time', and usually taken to mean the press, broadcasting (especially television), advertising, books and periodicals, cinema and, more recently, the Internet. In Britain there are 10 daily newspapers and nine Sundays. The BBC runs five national radio channels and two television ones, as well as digital radio and television channels. Independent television came into being in the 1950s and now runs three channels. Satellite television arrived in the 1990s and after a shaky start became successful. There is also a plethora of cable companies. Most people now derive their political information from television and tend to trust in its impartiality. On average people watch well over 20 hours of television a week and a fair proportion – some 20 per cent – covers news and current affairs. Since 1959 all elections have become television events,

with voters forming their opinions about politicians by seeing them interviewed or otherwise speaking on television. Since Richard Nixon's 'Checkers' speech in 1952, in which his crude sentimental appeal to voters to trust him proved spectacularly successful, and the same man's failure to best John Kennedy in the 1960 presidential debate, politicians have realised the image projected is vital, hence the importance of media advisors and 'spin doctors' such as Peter Mandelson and Alastair Campbell. Indeed, most political commentators argue that the mass media, and television in particular with its modern 24–7 coverage, have turned attention away from the content of a message and towards its presentation. In the run-up to the 2001 general election New Labour came in for much criticism for relying too much on 'spin' and presentation. Certainly Labour had tended to continue in government the focused management of the media which had characterised its years in opposition.

See also political marketing; spin; spin doctor.

master of the rolls

Originally the person who looked after the parchment records for the lord chancellor. In the 18th century the master of the rolls became the second judge in the Court of Chancery and in 1881 a member of the Court of Appeal. The office holder presides in the Civil Division of this court and has special responsibility for solicitors. The master of the rolls is one of the most important judges in the land and can influence the legal climate of the times on a wide range of issues. Legal records are now kept in the Public Record Office.

Matrix Churchill case, 1992

This originated when three businessmen were prosecuted for selling arms to the Middle East which ended up in Iraq, contrary to government guidelines. In court a government minister, Alan Clark, testified that the businessmen had been informally told their planned sale was acceptable. The huge row which resulted led to the Scott report into the affair and the identification of some officials and ministers who had acted less than properly. William Waldegrave was found to have misled the Commons over the government's policy in this area and wrongly advised ministers to sign public immunity certificates, which had the effect of allowing the government to withhold documents which the defence would have used to demonstrate that the businessmen were merely following the informal guidance given by government.

See also Scott report.

May Day

1 May and the most important holiday for workers on the continent of Europe. It has also been a day of demonstrations and celebrations by trade unionists in Britain. In recent years May Day has become an occasion of anti-capitalist demonstration.

mayor

Formal title given to the non-executive head of a district council granted borough status. In some cases, usually big cities, the chair of the council may be called lord mayor. In terms of power, the mayor is little more than a figurehead, opening fetes and presiding over council meetings, though the dignity of the office and the accompanying mayoral chain makes it an honour sought after by many councillors. In its first term the New Labour government introduced US-style directly elected mayors for London and (later) other cities as well.

See also elected mayor.

mayor of London

See London mayor.

Maze Prison

Symbolised the intractable conflicts of Northern Ireland. The prison, sited on a disused RAF airfield at Long Kesh, began as a prisoner of war camp in 1941. In the early 1970s it was used to intern IRA suspects without trial, who organised themselves along the lines of prisoners of war. In 1978 eight 'H blocks' were opened at the site, for the detention of paramilitaries,

and the prison was renamed the Maze. In 1981 Bobby Sands and nine others starved themselves to death. In 1998 Mo Mowlam, then Northern Ireland secretary, visited the Maze to assist the peace process. The prison closed in 2000.

means-testing

An assessment of wealth to determine a person's eligibility for a benefit, usually a state one. In the 1930s the poor were means-tested as a condition of benefit and sometimes had to sell items of a sparse household to qualify. Consequently the approach was discredited until more recent years, when universal benefits were judged to advantage the wealthy, who did not need them. The alternative to means-testing – targeting payments or benefits – received considerable attention after Labour came to power in 1997 and was applied in some areas, for example student loans.

Mebyon Kernow

www.mebyonkernow.org
The Party for Cornwall. Established in 1951, this small party celebrates Cornish language and culture and calls for home rule for Cornwall. In the 1970s the party won council seats and averaged 15 per cent in local elections. Its call for a separate seat for the county in European elections won it over 10,000 votes in 1980. However, in elections for Westminster candidates have mustered only a few hundred votes. In the 2009 Euro-elections the party won nearly 15,000 votes and did better than Labour. In the 2009 local elections it fielded three candidates and managed to get three elected. Its leader is Dick Cole.

media bias

While newspapers openly display their political opinions, which is a legacy of the development of the press in Britain, broadcast media are required by law to maintain political balance in their coverage of party political issues. However, politicians from Winston Churchill, Harold Wilson and Edward Heath to Margaret Thatcher and Tony Blair have accused the BBC of bias. On occasion politicians threaten, usually vaguely, to alter the basis of the Corporation's funding or attack particular programmes which they allege display the bias, for example (and especially) Radio 4's *Today* programme. After 1945 the press was usually pro-Conservative in its sympathies, but this changed in 1997 when many publications, most notably the *Sun*, owned by Rupert Murdoch, changed sides. Until this time Labour regarded the press as hostile and the radio and television as 'our' media.

Marxists and neo-Marxists like Antonio Gramsci assert that ruling-class values underpin most media output, which helps to indoctrinate the masses and blunt their ability to question such values. Others, like the Glasgow University Media Group, have suggested that working-class activists or striking trade unionists are generally represented as 'irresponsible extremists', whereas management or other authority figures are portrayed in a flatteringly 'responsible' light, thus legitimising an establishment agenda.

media cross-ownership

This is an issue which focuses largely on the role of media magnate Rupert Murdoch, who owns four daily newspapers in Britain as well as the television satellite broadcaster Sky. Rules were established to prevent newspaper proprietors also owning more than 20 per cent of a terrestrial television company. The Communications Act 2003 offered a number of changes. These included the possible merging of all independent television companies and it allowed Murdoch, in theory at least, to make a bid for Channel 5. Broadcasters were surprised at the latter measure and many concluded a deal had been done by the Australian-American with the Blair government. Certain key regulations remained, however, for example that national newspaper groups are not allowed to own a terrestrial television company and regional newspapers may not own a local television licence. The media ownership rules are reviewed by Ofcom every three years.

Meibion Glyndyr (Sons of Glyndyr)

Militant Welsh faction which objected to the English 'invasion' of Wales for holiday homes as this, it was claimed, caused high house prices for local people. Some 300 holiday homes were firebombed between 1974 and 1994. In 1989 the organisation declared 'every white settler is a target'. The group also placed incendiary bombs in estate agents' offices in London, Liverpool and Sutton Coldfield. In 1990 the Welsh poet R. S. Thomas called for a campaign to deface English-owned homes; in 1993 Sion Aubrey Roberts was jailed for three years for sending letter bombs to Conservative politicians. Since the mid-1990s the group has been inactive.

> Dal dy dir. [Stand your ground.] (Slogan of Cymuned, a pressure group dedicated to the defence of Welsh culture and language)

See also Free Wales Army.

member of parliament (MP)

Any member of either of the houses of parliament (though in the public mind usually the Commons). MPs used to be unpaid and drawn substantially from the landed gentry; however, after 1911 they started to receive salaries and expenses. In May 2010 an MP's annual pay was £64,766, with allowances for paying office staff, living in the constituency and London plus attendant travel. The prime minister received £142,500 p.a.; a cabinet minister £134,565 (Lords £101,038); a minister of state, £98,740 (Lords £78,891); and a parliamentary under-secretary £89,435 (Lords £68,710). In 2010 there were 650 MPs, although the Tory–Liberal Democrat coalition established in 2010 promised to reduce this number by around 150.

Fabian author Greg Power argues that MPs waste too much time on constituency problems and suggests that an ombudsman could take care of such matters, while MPs concentrate on holding the executive to account. He also argues for a proper career path for MPs to rival the lure of ministerial office, something which effectively neutralises up to a third of

POLITICS

them, and often the brightest, as effective parliamentarians.

Since the Second World War the House of Commons has become increasingly middle class. In 1951, 24 per cent of Conservative MPs had been to Eton, 65 per cent to university and 52 per cent (of the total) to Oxbridge, while the figures for Labour were 1 per cent to Eton, 41 per cent to university and 19 per cent to Oxbridge. By 1992 this had changed to 10 per cent to Eton, 73 per cent to university and 45 per cent to Oxbridge for the Conservatives, and for Labour it was 1 per cent to Eton once again, 61 per cent to university and 16 per cent to Oxbridge.

meritocracy

The idea that a ruling elite should be selected on the basis of ability rather than social origins. Often this is thought to be a concept favoured by those liberals working for a fairer society. However, Michael Young showed in *The Rise of the Meritocracy* (1958) that it can be just as harmful as a hereditary elite. New Labour under Tony Blair enthusiastically talked of making Britain a meritocracy, where opportunities existed for all who had the talent to succeed. However, Young's book had been a warning rather than a blueprint. As he wrote in the *Guardian* (29 June 2001), he was arguing that while it is sensible to give jobs to people on merit, it is the opposite 'when those who are judged to have merit harden into a new social class without room in it for others'. A free market in ability, in other words, can produce just as exclusive an elite as one based on birth or the accumulation of money. He pointed out that education had served to select a new kind of ruling elite based on ability, something which, like aristocratic credentials, is given by birth. These academically able children – predominantly born into the meritocratic class – are selected to shine at a young age while the rest are relegated to the bottom streams 'at the age of seven or before'. This large excluded group are destined to feel failures, to feel disconnected and to lapse into demoralised apathy, even failing to

vote. The result is that the masses become disenfranchised as their potential leaders are sucked into the meritocracy. Young points out that the giants of Clement Attlee's cabinet were working-class men like Ernest Bevin, Herbert Morrison and Aneurin Bevan. In contrast, Blair's cabinet members were all products of the educational meritocracy. The result, predicted Young's prescient book, is a polarised society which is becoming more so, even to the extent of selection being reconsidered for education. Lord Hattersley reasserted Young's thesis in articles in the *Guardian* during 2001 and attracted some support in the party for his more traditional line of argument.

metropolitan county

Administrative unit set up by the Local Government Act 1972. These were urban 'super-counties' with near regional functions regarding planning and transport. As well as Greater London (set up by an earlier act) there were Tyne and Wear, the West Midlands, West and South Yorkshire, Greater Manchester and Merseyside. In the 1980s they were all Labour controlled and Margaret Thatcher decided to abolish them in 1986. Labour warned that an outcry would result but there was none beyond complaints from sections of the political class and media. The counties passed away largely unlamented and unnoticed.

MI5

See security services.

MI6

See security services.

middle class

According to the British Market Research Association's six-category scheme, the middle classes are A (3 per cent of households) and B (16 per cent) and C1 (26 per cent) – the working class being C2 (26 per cent), D (17 per cent) and E (13 per cent). John Goldthorpe's alternative seven-point classification, of which the first four would qualify as middle class, runs through: higher salariat (12 per cent); lower salariat

(16 per cent); routine clerical (24 per cent); petty bourgeoisie (7 per cent); foremen and technicians (5 per cent); skilled manual (11 per cent); unskilled manual (25 per cent).

As traditional industries died out, new ones developed, in the service sector for example, which tended to employ more educated middle-class people. In 1914, 80 per cent of Britain's population was working class; by the 1980s, less than 50 per cent could be so described. The middle class has therefore swollen and become dominant, with consequent changes in aspirations and ways of life; for example, one in four children in 2008 proceeded to university, compared with only one in 20 in 1960. Significantly, Tony Blair, leader of the 'working class' party, had classic middle-class qualifications, and more importantly values, of the kind usually associated with Conservative leaders. And while the Conservatives were able to claim four-fifths of middle-class votes in the 1960s, by the 1990s their share had fallen to three-fifths; similarly, Labour received a diminishing share of a shrinking working-class vote until the landslide victory in 1997 reversed the trend, when some of the largest swings to the party were from the lower middle classes, or C1 groups, a result assiduously pursued by Blair via his appeal to 'middle England'. Significantly there was a drift away from Labour among working-class voters in the 2001 general election but a drift towards Labour among the middle-classes, which suggests Blair's appeal was more attractive to the latter than the former.

In the 2005 general election, the percentage polls by middle-class strata were as follows, with 2001 figures in parentheses: Conservative A, B, 37 (43); C1, 34 (35); Labour A, B, 32 (30); C1 35 (37).

See also class.

middle England
Term used to denote the group of middle-class voters who can allegedly swing elections. Certainly the Labour Party needed to woo this section of the populace as the size of its traditional working-class

constituency shrank along with manual occupations. Hence the emergence of 'typical' voters like 'Mondeo man' or 'Worcester woman', at whom parties would aim their messages. Both Tony Blair and Gordon Brown carefully read the *Daily Mail* and trimmed policy accordingly, as the paper was held to speak for the 'middle England' voters Labour needed.

Migration Watch
www.migrationwatchuk.org
An independent, non-political (self-styled) think-tank, established and chaired by Sir Andrew Green, a former ambassador to Saudi Arabia. It argues immigration has been excessive, quoting the Office for National Statistics that, of the 10 million expected increase in population over 2010–2034, 70 per cent will be the result of immigration. The many reports of the body on aspects of migration are eagerly publicised by newspapers on the right like the *Daily Telegraph* and the *Daily Mail*.

Militant
See Militant Tendency.

Militant Labour Party
Set up by Peter Taafe in 1993 in the wake of the Labour Party's successful campaign to expel members of the Militant Tendency, an extremist Trotskyite organisation that tried to infiltrate the party and influence its policy towards revolutionary goals.

Militant Tendency (Revolutionary Socialist League)
One of the most prominent Trotskyist political groupings in Britain since the Second World War. In political terms, militancy refers to aggressive, combative action, sometimes direct action, in pursuit of political or ideological objectives. A militant would see politics as warfare, a struggle against opposites, whether these are from the left or right. The Militant Tendency was founded around the *Militant* newspaper, started in 1964, and was led by the South African Ted Grant (1913–2006), formerly of the Militant Labour

POLITICS

League and the Revolutionary Communist Party before the two merged to form the Revolutionary Socialist League. Grant teamed up with Peter Taafe from Liverpool to set up the *Militant* newspaper and the League adopted the policy of 'entryism' to infiltrate the Labour Party. The League therefore took a covert role and members of Militant were in theory only supporters of a 'Tendency' or a newspaper and not a party within a party, which would have been against Labour Party rules. However, this 'nonexistent' organisation succeeded in taking over Liverpool council, with its member Derek Hatton becoming deputy leader and someone with a national profile. After 1983 Militant boasted two MPs: Terry Fields, a fireman from Liverpool, and Dave Nellist, who represented a Coventry Labour seat. Although numbering only some 5,000 members, its impact on Labour's public image was significant, as it provided ammunition for Labour's enemies in parliament and the press. The crunch came when Militant ran Leslie Mahood against Peter Kilfoyle in the Walton by-election following the death of Eric Heffer; Kilfoyle easily won and those who supported the Militant candidate revealed themselves as supporters of a party hostile to Labour and were therefore vulnerable to expulsion. Labour leader Neil Kinnock also won a huge moral victory at the party's 1985 conference by bitterly attacking Militant and its extremist policies, which in Liverpool had nearly brought the city to bankruptcy. Towards the end of the 1980s Militant suffered expulsions from Labour and lost support. In 1993 it re-emerged as the Militant Labour Party, a separate party with scant support. Its policies included nationalisation of the top 200 companies; extension of state control to the whole of the economy; workers' control; and the nationalisation of the media. Remnants of Militant joined the Socialist Alliance, an umbrella grouping on the left which fought some seats in the 2001 general election with no success.

See also entryism; Hayward report; Whitty report.

military
See Ministry of Defence.

Millbank Tower
Former headquarters of the Labour Party and, for mordant critics of the party's modernisation, the nerve centre for Labour's media machine. These smart offices were occupied for the 1997 election after the less salubrious accommodation of Walworth Road was left behind. Its high-tech resources and the proactive style of its staff became associated with the party's alleged 'control freak' tendencies, whereby MPs, members of the National Executive Committee and even ordinary members were coerced into toeing the New Labour line. On 20 March 2002 it was announced Labour would be moving again, this time to modern offices in Old Queen Street, behind the houses of parliament, at a cost estimated at £6 million: Labour's fifth home in 102 years.

See also on message.

Millennium Dome
Conceived by John Major's Conservative government in 1996 as a celebration of the forthcoming millennium celebrations, it was supported by Tony Blair's incoming Labour administration in 1997. Some suggested Blair saw the project as a symbol of a new 'inclusive' Britain. Richard Rogers, the architect, designed the building, which cost £750 million to erect. However, controversy developed early on, when the creative director resigned in January 1998 and the opening night was a disaster in that 3,000 guests were stuck in queues for hours, including journalists and other influential people. In February 2000 the chief executive was replaced by Pierre-Yves Gerbeau, recruited from Disneyland in Paris. Despite his colourful efforts, he failed to bring in the planned millions of visitors and the Dome was forced to go cap in hand for more money, first £29 million in May 2000, then £43 million in August and another £47 million in September, when it acquired yet another new management team. The Japanese company Nomura

considered buying the Dome in August 2000, planning to turn it into a theme park. Few supporters of the Dome remained and when Nomura pulled out during the latter part of the year the matter became even more of an embarrassment to the Blair government, both as a commercial venture and as a symbol of its 'big tent' inclusive philosophy. Responsibility for the debacle shifted ministerially around the Labour cabinet, ending up with Lord Falconer, who, despite frequent calls from the opposition, refused to resign following the Dome's failure.

In May 2002 the Dome was finally disposed of: it was given, for no charge, to a business syndicate, which planned to convert it into an entertainment complex. In exchange the government was to receive a share of the profits.

The O2 arena was constructed on some half of the original Dome structure and was completed in 2007.

I'm sorry, with the benefit of hindsight, we should have thrown in the towel. (Peter Mandelson, once minister in charge, on the Dome to GQ *Magazine*, July 2002)

See also Hinduja brothers.

miners' strike, 1984–85

A watershed event of the 1980s which confirmed Margaret Thatcher's political dominance and broke the power of unions to determine political events. The miners' strikes of 1972 and 1974 are widely understood to have brought down the Heath government in 1974. In 1981 Joe Gormley, president of the National Union of Mineworkers (NUM), won his confrontation with the government, but only because it felt unable to sustain a fight. In 1984 the situation was different. The union was now led by Arthur Scargill, an avowed revolutionary and charismatic leader who was convinced the miners could lead a political rising against the Conservatives. He was a clever tactician and skilful with the media but a poor long-term strategist and was too convinced that he knew best. Ostensibly the dispute focused on the

proposed closure of pits but Scargill had his own agenda. The stocks of coal available to power stations was plentiful and sufficient to last out the winter of 1984–85, at which time miners had already been without pay for six months. The Coal Board was led by someone unafraid of Scargill and unaffected by recent political history, Ian McGregor. The police took a much more militant approach to the strikers than had been taken in 1972. The cabinet remained united and Thatcher instructed McGregor not to settle. The Labour Party was noncommittal throughout, opposed to Thatcher but unsure about Scargill and the effect support would have upon voters as a whole. Scargill was possibly unnerved by two previous members' ballots which had refused to endorse strike action and declared a strike without any such reinforcement, now legally a requirement under the Employment Act 1982. The courts were able to declare the action illegal and sequester union assets, to the detriment of the union's ability to continue the struggle. Finally and decisively, miners in the midlands decided to go back to work and defy the NUM; they also set up their own breakaway union, the Union for Democratic Mineworkers. The NUM decided to go back to work at the delegate conference of 5 March 1985, a year after the miners had first gone out. It had been a defeat of massive proportions, leaving a residue of bitterness and weakening the trade union movement for a decade or more. Subsequent events proved Scargill's predictions regarding the closure of pits to be more than justified. The number of miners now working in Britain is a small fraction of what is was (over a million) in 1945. But his strategy regarding the strike, by any standards, was still risky and unwise.

miners' strikes, 1972 and 1974

Miners' strikes which weakened and finally helped destroy Edward Heath's Conservative government elected in 1970. The first centred on pay and began in January 1972. By February a state of emergency had been announced when coal supplies were low enough to threaten industrial production. The young Yorkshire miners' leader Arthur Scargill closed Saltley Power Station in Birmingham through the use of 'flying pickets', who outnumbered police 7,000–500. The Wilberforce report soon recommended a massive pay increase, which made a mockery of Heath's attempted industrial relations strategy.

The 1974 miners' pay claim and resultant strike occurred in the shadow of the massive increases in oil prices prompted by the Organization of Petroleum Exporting Countries. Given the support for the miners by other unions, together with the residual sympathy the miners were always able to provoke, the strike hit hard. In January 1974 Heath called a three-day week to conserve coal supplies. He then called an election with the theme of 'Who Governs Britain?' in a direct challenge to the unions' power. Sadly for Heath the voters were not ready to oppose union power and he was forced to give way to Wilson's third term of government.

See also three-day week.

minimum wage
Part of Labour's 1997 general election manifesto. The minimum wage was introduced after 1997 at £3.60 per hour; employers paying below that amount would be liable to legal action. A lower level was set for those aged 18–21 years. Contrary to warnings from the Conservatives and the Confederation of British Industry, its introduction had minimal impact on employment levels, as it was widely believed to have been set sufficiently low. The new measure had the effect of improving the pay of 1.7 million workers. The government's Low Pay Commission makes recommendations regarding the appropriate rate.

In October 2000 the rate was increased to £3.70 but the Trades Union Congress (TUC) campaigned for a flat rate of £5.00. John Monks, secretary general of the TUC, described the minimum wage as 'one of the government's greatest achievements'

in August 2000. In October 2001 it was increased from £3.70 to £4.10 and the lower rate for younger workers (18–21) from £3.20 to £3.50 per hour, rising to £3.60 by October 2002. It was estimated by the government that, as a result of the minimum wage, over 1 million people – mostly women – enjoyed an average increase in their wages of over 15 per cent. In the 2004 budget the minimum wage was increased to £4.85 per hour for workers over 22 and £4.10 for those aged 18–21. In October 2009 the rate rose to £5.80 per hour.

Fears that the new measure would cause widespread unemployment proved groundless and the Conservatives dropped their opposition to the measure.

MINIS
Management Information System for Ministers, invented by Michael Heseltine while he was secretary of state for the environment from 1979. According Michael Crick, it was 'knowing about whom in his [Heseltine's] department did what, and at what cost' (*Michael Heseltine: A Biography*, 1997, p. 206). The idea was that the minister could then make judgements about those activities that were worthwhile and those that were not. He claimed this would make officials more cost-conscious and help to keep bureaucratic growth in check. Each of the Department of the Environment's 65 directorates produced a long report on its activities in 1980, setting its priorities, expenditure and staff costs. The process became an annual one, with the minister passing responsibility over to officials after the first year. At first civil servants resisted the system as unjustifiably intrusive but eventually came to accept it as useful. Heseltine introduced it to the Ministry of Defence when he moved there, although less successfully. Crick (p. 209) judges it represented a lasting contribution to cost cutting across Whitehall.

minister
Person appointed to government by the prime minister on behalf of the queen. Ministers represent the 'front line' of

democratic control of the government machine on behalf of voters; they provide the connection with the voter in that they are drawn from the largest party elected at a general election. That said, it is not necessary for a minister to be a member of either house (a notable example was Patrick Gordon Walker). It is a convention that they do so, though the solicitor general for Scotland has variously not been an MP or peer. In theory ministers lay down the policy their department will pursue but in practice much of it will have been decided in opposition and much of this will be modified and interpreted by civil service advisors.

The most junior ministerial rank is that of parliamentary private secretary, a kind of parliamentary 'bag carrier' but nevertheless part of the team and, if promise is shown, likely to progress further. Next comes the parliamentary under-secretary, a junior minister who will speak for the department in the house and help usher through bills. The minister of state comes next, a middle-ranking position, followed by ministers who are heads of department but not in the cabinet. Finally come full cabinet ministers, usually known as secretaries of state.

It is possible for a minister to be head of a department but not to be given a place in the cabinet, and some ministers attend cabinet though not as members, the main one being the chief whip (a class of minister), though others occasionally do, like John Reid, who in 1998 was transport minister.

> You can read. It is a great happiness. I totally neglected it while I was in business, which has been the whole of my life, and to such a degree that I cannot now read a page – a warning to all Ministers. (Robert Walpole, the first prime minister, on seeing Henry Fox, Lord Holland, reading in a library at Houghton)

ministerial code of conduct

A substantial publication produced by the Cabinet Office. It was originally drawn up in 1945 but was kept confidential until 1992. Its purpose is to provide guidance and regulation of relationships between ministers, the prime minister and government departments. It was reissued in 1997 under the title 'A Code of Conduct and Guidance on Procedures for Ministers'. The code is advisory and there are no stated sanctions. Under Tony Blair it was seen as part of New Labour's concern to control ministers from the centre. The newly written paragraph 88 in particular was cited in support of this argument: it insists all new policy initiatives and proposed public interviews with ministers be cleared first with the Number 10 Press Office.

See also code of conduct for MPs.

ministerial direction

An occasion when civil servants disagree so strongly with a minister over a measure that they refuse to be accountable for it. On 18 May 2010 the *Guardian* ran a story that such written disavowals of policy had taken place under Labour five times in the four months leading up to the election in 2010. On all occasions the complaint had centred on the excessive costs of the project concerned.

ministerial resignation

Reasons for ministerial resignations include the following:

1 they feel unable to support government policy (for example Aneurin Bevan and Harold Wilson over cuts to the National Health Service in 1951, Michael Heseltine over Westland);

2 they are asked to do so by a prime minister who wishes to dispense with their services (for example David Mellor after the scandal involving his affair with the actress Antonia de Sancha);

3 they wish to run for the leadership (for example John Redwood in July 1995; it was also suggested this was Bevan's true motive when he resigned);

4 they feel they have to take responsibility for policy failure (for example Lord Carrington over the invasion of the Falklands Islands in 1982);

5 they are subject to intense public criticism (for example Nicholas Ridley after his anti-German comments in 1990);

6 like Estelle Morris in October 2002, they feel they are not 'as effective' as they should be.

Alan Milburn resigned as health minister in June 2003 because he wanted to spend more time with his young family.

Ministerial sackings are sometimes formally described as resignations, for example the departure of Peter Mandelson after his apparent lapse involving the Hinduja brothers. John Major's governments 1990–97 witnessed 12 ministerial resignations altogether: four as a result of sex scandals; three as a result of financial scandals; four from principle; and one because of public criticism.

See also ministerial responsibility.

ministerial responsibility

A constitutional principle that ministers are responsible to parliament, effectively the House of Commons, for what they and their departments do. In the 18th century ministers were still responsible to the monarch but as power shifted to parliament their accountability shifted accordingly. Ministers now became responsible to parliament individually and collectively, and would be required to resign if a policy or ministerial action proved impossible for the cabinet to support.

Ministers also resign occasionally from a sense of honour, as in the case of Lord Carrington over the Argentine attack on the Falklands Islands, although few of his colleagues felt he was personally responsible. He went after Conservative MPs saw fit to criticise his department as culpable; he believed it not to be, but felt could not carry on without the confidence of his party.

See also collective responsibility.

Ministry of Agriculture, Fisheries and Food (MAFF)

Name given to the ministry in charge of agriculture 1903–2001. Once the principal source of wealth in Britain, agriculture now employs less than 3 per cent of the workforce. However, its political importance should not be underestimated.

The Board of Agriculture was established in 1793 to stimulate agricultural improvement. In 1893 a ministry was set up and it encompassed fisheries from 1903. In 1955 it absorbed food to become the Ministry of Agriculture, Fisheries and Food (MAFF). The National Farmers' Union worked closely with the ministry and was regarded as exerting a less than healthy influence over its policy formation by some. MAFF was a cabinet ministry but was not regarded as being in the first rank of importance, although occasionally it became so for political reasons. In theory it was responsible for public consumption of food and those who produced it. The conflict was exposed during crises such as that which occurred over BSE (bovine spongiform encephalitis), where it was unclear whether MAFF's principal concern was with the consumers or the farmers. The Phillips report into the handling of the BSE crisis was highly critical of the ministry. MAFF negotiated with Brussels over payments under the Common Agricultural Policy (CAP) of the European Union. It also: looked after the countryside and the coast; licensed veterinary products; registered pesticides; and undertook necessary scientific research. MAFF was in charge of the foot-and-mouth crisis in 2001 and again was widely seen as having handled it ineffectively. As a result it was subsumed within the new Department for Environment, Food and Rural Affairs in 2001.

See also bovine spongiform encephalopathy; Curry report; Department for Environment, Food and Rural Affairs; foot-and-mouth disease; Phillips report.

Ministry of Defence (MoD)

www.mod.uk

Ministry in charge of armed forces. The three armed services used to boast a ministry each – the Admiralty, War Office and Air Ministry – but they were brought under one umbrella and in 1964 the MoD was established as a ministry in its own right. It was later led by Denis Healey, the powerful Labour politician.

According to the 2003 annual defence white paper the MoD's mission is:

> to provide, by the most effective means, armed forces of appropriate capacity, readiness and sustainability to implement our defence strategy through national, NATO, UN, WEU and other allied operations as necessary.

Since the amalgamation of the three services in the unified ministry the armed forces are treated more as a single unit than a tripartite one.

See also armed forces; defence policy.

minority government

A government that takes office or continues in office without the absolute majority needed to vote its measures through. This happened in the case of Labour governments in 1924 and 1929–31. In February 1974 Labour formed a government despite being in an overall minority, something which was corrected in the October 1974 general election, when the party managed to gain a majority of three. However, this thin advantage did not last and from 1976 to 1978 the Liberals supported Labour: the so-called Lib–Lab pact.

After the elections to the Welsh assembly in 1999 Labour failed to win a majority but decided to rule as a minority administration based on the calculation that the Liberal Democrats and Plaid Cymru had no reason to bring it down when the assembly was still in its early stages. Soon after, Labour entered a coalition with the Liberal Democrats, thus matching the arrangement in the Scottish parliament. In May 2007 the Scottish National Party became the largest party by just one in the Scottish parliament and Alex Salmond formed what proved to be a relatively popular minority administration.

mission statement

Strictly speaking, the purposes and scope of an organisation's activity. The term, usually associated with commercial organisations, has now spread to hitherto non-business operations such as charities and educational institutions. Mission statements have been introduced – to the derision of some commentators – into many government departments, an example being the Home Office, whose mission in 2004 was summed up as 'Building a Safe, Just and Tolerant Society'.

See also political marketing.

Mittal affair

The revelation in February 2002 that prime minister Tony Blair had signed a letter supporting the attempt of an Indian billionaire, Lakshmi Mittal, to buy Sidex, a Romanian state-owned steel company. The outcry was occasioned by the facts that Mittal had donated £125,000 to the Labour Party, his company, LNM, was not British, and he proved to be a lobbying champion of measures in the USA which disadvantaged the British steel industry. Blair derisively termed it 'garbage-gate'. On its own the issue was not especially important but, ranked together with the Ecclestone affair and the alleged ability of Rupert Murdoch to influence in Number 10, it seemed to be part of a pattern of 'cash for influence'.

mixed economy

A concept which effectively entered the language after 1945, when the Labour government nationalised 20 per cent of the economy. This produced a substantial public as well as private sector – hence a 'mixed' economy. Left-wing members of the Labour Party called for a bigger public sector from the 1950s onwards, while those on the 'revisionist' right believed the private sector was now 'tamed' and functioning in a more or less responsible fashion. The debate continued through the 1960s and 1970s but the size of the public sector shrunk drastically in the 1980s, when Margaret Thatcher pursued her privatisation policies. The Labour government under Tony Blair seemed happy with the 'mix' in the national economy inherited from John Major and indeed took a pragmatic approach to further privatisations if they seemed to offer the best means of delivering a service. Gordon Brown seemed not to cavil at such a settlement when he took over in June 2007.

modernisation (of the Labour Party)
Name given to the changes wrought in the Labour Party after its disastrous defeat in the 1983 general election. Neil Kinnock as Labour leader thereafter urged his party to rethink its structure, decision making and its policies, especially on Europe, unilateralism, nationalisation, the free enterprise economy and the unions. John Smith, Kinnock's successor, advanced the process still further, with reforms of the party's links with the unions and democratisation of the annual party conference. But the biggest changes were introduced by Tony Blair and Gordon Brown, assisted by 'modernisers' like Peter Mandelson (who had been appointed the party's communications director by Kinnock). They moved Labour policy both in opposition and government to be far more friendly to business and less radical in most policy areas except constitutional reform. For example, Blair's abolition of clause 4 removed the damaging fiction that Labour wished to impose state control over the whole of the economy. Part of the process was designed for political purposes – to demonstrate within the party what could be done nationally, that is, a modernised party would be a model for a modernised monarchy, business world, or indeed the whole country. The constitutional changes introduced in the early years of the Labour government after 1997 – such as devolution, elected mayors and the reform of the House of Lords – were all part of this modernising agenda. The term assumed the status of an article of faith for those committed to the 'project' of reinvigorating British society and institutions. The term surfaced in Labour's plans for changes in central government, as announced in the white paper 'Modernising Government', published in March 1999. This signalled a drive not only for efficient, integrated or 'joined up' government, but also open and citizen-focused administration.

Modernisation Committee
www.parliament.uk/
parliamentary_committees/
select_committee_on_modernisation_of_
the_house_of_commons.cfm
Select committee considering how the House of Commons might be modernised. This 15-member committee was set up in June 1997 by a standing order of the house, which was renewed in 2001. Its terms of reference tasked the committee to 'consider how the practice and procedures of the house should be modernised, and to make recommendations thereon'. The committee produced a number of reports and under the chairmanship of Robin Cook introduced substantial changes which became operative in January 2004.

monarchy
www.royal.gov.uk
A traditional form of government which held sway for over a thousand years since Britain emerged from the struggles among the seven kingdoms comprising Anglo-Saxon England. Early monarchs wielded supreme power but the monarch is strictly limited in the modern day to performing ceremonial functions, like opening parliament and meeting delegates from abroad. The monarch is, in theory, the supreme head of the country and can reject legislation but in practice the queen follows the instructions of the prime minister of the day. Some constitutional experts argue that the monarch's residual right to choose the prime minister when there is no clear winner after a general election is important and could be vital if, for example, the voting system were to be changed to one of proportional representation, when coalition government would become much more likely. Other experts disagree and argue that any such intervention would precipitate action to abolish these remaining powers.

The scandalous events surrounding the British monarchy during the 1980s and 1990s diminished its popularity but polls show the public still felt the country needs a monarch and a majority believed Prince Charles had done a good job of bringing up his two sons following the death of their mother in 1997. According to commentators, as the new millennium approached, the monarchy was ripe for 'modernising' reform. In 1994 the queen had met some of her critics by agreeing to pay tax on her private income. By early 2000 cuts in the civil list were predicted and the monarchy was urged to save money, as it proved it could do in respect of travel costs in the year 2000.

In February 2002 Kevin McNamara moved a 10-minute rule bill to repeal the law which bans Catholics from succession to the throne. The Act of Settlement in 1688 had enshrined this measure following the replacement of Catholic James II by William and Mary.

> Monarchy is something kept behind a curtain about which there is a great deal of hustle and fuss, and a wonderful air of seeming solemnity. But when by accident the curtain happens to be opened and the company see what it is, they burst into laughter. (Tom Paine)

See also civil list; golden triangle.

Monday Club
www.conservativeuk.com
Conservative group set up in 1962 in the wake of Harold Macmillan's 'wind of change' speech, which anticipated the country's withdrawal from its imperial possessions. It concerns itself with defence and foreign affairs and immigration and takes a militant right-wing stance, to the extent that it attracted accusations of being suspiciously close to neo-fascist groupings. The organisation comprises 'members and supporters of the Conservative Party and Conservative Associations' but is usually best known via its MP members, who have included, over the years, George Gardiner, Harvey Proctor and Neil Hamilton.

monetarism
The theory that the supply of money circulating in the economy has a direct relationship to price levels. The theory leads to the assertion that excessive money supply causes inflation; restricting money supply therefore brings it down. It was articulated in the 1970s by Milton Friedman and others at the Chicago School of Economics and influenced the Labour chancellor Denis Healey as well as the more ideologically sympathetic Conservatives, including Keith Joseph, Geoffrey Howe, Nigel Lawson and Margaret Thatcher. The Conservatives applied their brand of monetarism in the 1980s and their medium-term financial statement (MTFS) was designed as a way of limiting future money supply. Although the MTFS was never a good guide to rates of inflation or public spending, and the targets were regularly overshot, the basic tenets of monetarism have not been rejected; rather they have been absorbed into Treasury thinking to form a new orthodoxy.

See also Chicago School of Economics; new right.

Monetary Policy Committee (MPC) (of the Bank of England)
The body, set up in 1997, that sets the rate of interest for the British economy. The ability to set interest rates is possibly one of the most powerful tools a government possesses in controlling the national economy. Traditionally the Bank of England did this on the instructions of the chancellor. Many criticised the 'politicisation' of the process by which interest rates were raised or lowered according to political rather than economic criteria, the cost being to the long-term health of the national economy. To counter this and mark a break with the past Gordon Brown, the incoming Labour chancellor, announced in early May 1997 that he would be giving the Bank of England the power to set interest rates independently. The Monetary Policy Committee of the Bank was given responsibility to set interest rates in order to achieve price stability, as defined by the 2.0 per cent government inflation target. This was a momentous change to the role of the Bank and required legislation which amended the Bank of England Act 1946, a decision strongly influenced by Ed Balls, the chancellor's economic advisor.

The MPC is composed of the governor of the Bank, the two deputy governors, the Bank's chief economist and executive director for market operations, and four external members appointed by the chancellor. It meets once a month, when decisions are made on the basis of one person one vote (however, the governor has a deciding vote if there is no majority). In keeping with the principle of open government espoused by New Labour, minutes of the meetings are published, and the MPC is accountable to the House of Commons through the Treasury Committee. Brown signalled that British monetary policy would be attuned to the needs of the national economy and aligned Britain with the independent central banks of many other countries.

money bill

An item of legislation which concerns taxation or public expenditure. The Parliament Act 1911 provided that money bills passed by the Commons become law if not passed without amendment by the Lords within one month. Nonetheless, the House of Lords can and sometimes does debate money bills, as it is always possible that the government may be influenced. There is normally a short debate on second reading of the Finance Bill, for instance. Few bills are certified as money bills because they have to deal exclusively with money – if a bill has any non-supply provisions, then it cannot be so certified.

money supply

See monetarism.

Monopolies and Mergers Commission

See Competition Commission.

Monster Raving Loony Party

www.omrlp.com
Political party set up in the 1960s by ('Screaming') 'Lord' David Sutch, a pop singer, in part to replace Commander Bill Boackes, who used to turn up at the counts in his wellington boots and scruffy overcoat,

as the regular by-election 'joke' candidate. It proposes a nonsensical set of policies. It has fought over 40 by-election contests and never saved its deposit but once, in 1994, mustered 4.8 per cent of the vote. In 1989 it polled more than David Owen's rump Social Democratic Party at the Bootle by-election, an event that was rumoured to have persuaded Owen to wind up the organisation. It once had a councillor sitting under its banner in the West Country. 'Lord' Sutch died in 1998 but his party fought the 2001 general election, when it won some 6,000 votes in total; it promised smaller class sizes through the device of asking the children to stand closer together.
See also Sutch, David.

Mont Pelerin Society

www.montpelerin.org
International conference formed immediately after the war in which academics and politicians met to discuss the ideas of Friedrich von Hayek and Milton Friedman. It provided the inspiration for the formation in 1957 of the Institute of Economic Affairs, which did so much to introduce free enterprise and monetarist thinking into the Conservative Party.

Moore's email, 2001

Email sent to departmental press staff in the immediate wake of the 11 September 2001 terrorist attacks in the USA in which Jo Moore suggested this was an opportune moment to 'bury' sensitive announcements, for example on councillors' expenses. Jo Moore was an advisor to transport secretary Stephen Byers and her email caused outrage. Jonathan Freedland in the *Guardian* wrote that the message 'will remain forever the set text of the spin doctor's craft' and will be cited as 'evidence of New Labour cynicism for years to come'.

The case was further complicated when it emerged she was in conflict with the head of communications at the ministry, Martin Sixsmith. Jo Moore hung on for several months but was forced to resign in February 2002 when it was alleged she had issued a similar message regarding Princess

Margaret's funeral. Sixsmith's departure was more turbulent, as his resignation was originally announced by Sir Richard Mottram, the permanent secretary to the department, but Sixsmith then denied that he had resigned and a public row broke out in which Byers' veracity was prominently questioned. The whole saga placed the 'culture of spin' in New Labour in the spotlight and reflected very badly on the government.

moral hazard

This occurs when people who are immune to a risk act differently to how they would behave had they been exposed to it. The term was used frequently in relation to banks during the 2007–09 economic crisis, when their critics pointed out there were no restraints upon their actions if their financial failure was to be prevented by taxpayer-funded bail-outs.

MORI (Market and Opinion Research International)

www.ipsos-mori.com

Polling and market research organisation founded by the political scientist Robert Worcester. It is now part of Ipsos MORI. MORI used to provide private polls for the Labour Party and is one of the most respected names in British market research. It publishes its surveys in the *Times*, *Sunday Times*, *Daily Express*, *Daily Star* and *Economist*, among others. It also conducted the research work for the government's People's Panel, a 5,000-strong sounding board which was terminated in 2002.

Morning Star

www.morningstaronline.co.uk

Newspaper founded in 1930 as the *Daily Worker* by the Communist Party of Great Britain and an assiduous follower of the line set by Moscow, even during the Molotov–Ribbentrop pact in 1939. For a while in the early part of the Second World War it was suppressed, as Soviet neutrality at that time was felt to be friendly to Hitler. Once Hitler attacked the USSR in 1941 the ban was lifted and the newspaper

became part of the war effort. In 1966 the paper changed its name to the *Morning Star*. Circulation figures for the publication were regularly boosted by the extra copies bought by the USSR. The paper is no longer connected to the Communist Party but its former editor, John Haylett, claims its 'credo is based on the nonsectarian approach of Britain's Road to Socialism, the programme of the Communist Party of Britain which was set up in 1988 as the re-establishment of the party founded as the Communist Party of Great Britain (CPGB) in 1920'.

motion

The device used to initiate a debate in either house. A motion to 'take note' is often used to debate something specific like a report of a select committee. A motion 'calling for papers' is often used by backbenchers to direct attention to something they feel strongly about. At the end of the debate convention demands that the backbencher withdraws the motion.

MP

See member of parliament.

MPs' expenses scandal

Scandal that erupted in May–June 2009 when the *Daily Telegraph* acquired a record of all expense claims and payments given to MPs over recent years. Ever since Derek Conway MP claimed for a researcher's allowance for his sons when they did little or no work for him, the media and some activists had been seeking full disclosure of MPs' expenses. While some MPs had agreed this was justified, others opposed disclosure and the speaker of the house tended to take the side of the latter.

At the time, MPs receive a salary of £64,000 a year but a maximum of double that in allowances. Most controversial was the second homes allowance, paid to those having to maintain a second home in order to serve in the Commons. As some MPs chose to make their main home in London, MPs were required to designate one of their homes as 'main' in order to claim up to £24,000 in assistance with mortgages and furniture and such like. The revelations showed that some MPs had used the allowance to improve a property and then sold it on to make a profit. They also 'flipped' designations of 'main' and 'second' homes to maximise what they could claim. So Jacqui Smith, then home secretary, came in for much criticism for claiming her 'main' home was the room in her sister's London flat so she could claim allowances on her constituency home where her husband and children lived. Other excesses included: the plethora of claims for just under £250, as anything over that sum required a receipt; claims for gardening expenses; tree surgeons for an arboretum; the cost of a duck house in the middle of a pond; and sundry claims for expenditure on food. The public felt angry that their representatives, already on a salary over double the average, were getting for nothing things which everyone else had to pay themselves. Worse, and possibly fraudulent, were the cases of MPs who continued to claim mortgage payments for years after they had been paid off. The uproar was unprecedented and the speaker, Michael Martin, became its focus when he was judged to have shown a complacent disregard for full disclosure. He was forced to stand down in June 2009 and a new speaker was elected.

In November 2009 Sir Christopher Kelly's Committee on Standards in Public Life reported on the expenses issue and recommended, among other measures: no second-home allowance for MPs within 'reasonable' commuting distance of Westminster; the second-home allowance to continue for council tax, water, fuel and insurance but not for gardening, cleaning and furnishings; no payment of mortgages and only rental or hotel costs to reimbursed; any future capital gains in value of accommodation to be surrendered to the exchequer. Kelly also advised a ban on MPs employing members of their own family but in March 2010 it was conceded that they could employ one family member (only).

In the aftermath of the scandal, both main parties competed to be tougher on offenders and many MPs were forced to resign or stand down at the next election. Much was made of possible reform of the Commons, though this appeared to quieten down after only a few weeks.

multiculturalism

The assumption that people from different ethnic backgrounds can live side by side, accepting diversity and respecting other cultures. However, the riots in Oldham, Burnley and Bradford in 2001 revealed ethnic communities which were isolated and polarised, living 'parallel lives' and unable to relate to the host community. The Cantle report called for proactive measures to encourage social cohesion, including the need for better training in English and the confronting of practices at variance with British values, like forced marriages.

multilateralism

Consensus-based approach to problem solving in international relations. Elements of multilateralism can be discerned in the 19th-century 'Congress system'. It received full institutional expression in the form of the League of Nations in 1918, the United Nations in 1945 and the Bretton Woods agreement in 1945. Regional organisations like the European Union have undermined some of the consensus, and the determination of US president George W. Bush to disown agreements like the Kyoto protocol on global warming was a major setback to those who view this approach as the only hope for the world.

multi-party system

See party system.

Munich agreement, 30 September 1938

Signed by Neville Chamberlain, Mussolini (for Italy), Hitler (for Germany) and Daladier (for France). The German dictator had threatened to go to war in support of German-speaking Nazi supporters in the Sudetenland, part of Czechoslovakia. Chamberlain, who feared another world war, agreed to the transfer of the territory; the Czechs were neither present nor consulted. He returned home to announce 'peace in our time' to a relieved nation. Hitler marched in on 5 October and in March 1939 occupied the rest of the country. In retrospect Munich is seen as a betrayal and invitation to Hitler to continue until war was inevitable, but some argue 'appeasement' enabled Britain to prepare more effectively for the imminent war.

Municipal Corporations Act 1835
First attempt to reform local government in towns and cities in response to the vast economic and social changes of the industrial revolution. The act established councils elected by ratepayers and indirectly elected aldermen and mayors.

murder rate
In 1989 there were 622 murders in the UK but this figure rose steadily over the next decade until it peaked at over 1,000 in 2002–03 once Dr Harold Shipman's activities were counted in. After that, however, the figures rapidly decreased until the figure 2008–09 was only 648, the lowest for 20 years.

Muslim community
There were 1.8 million Muslims in Britain in 2002. Over 80 per cent of Muslims voted Labour in 1997. However, signs emerged by 2001 that Muslims were quite prepared to vote for another party if their candidate was also Muslim. In the 1997 general election the Labour majority in Bradford West was slashed after Labour adopted a Sikh candidate, Marsha Singh; the Conservatives fielded a Muslim candidate, Mohammed Riaz, who clearly persuaded substantial numbers of former Labour-voting Muslims to switch sides. However, Labour's share of the vote increased in the 2001 general election in that constituency. In seven constituencies – in the north and the midlands as well as London – the Muslim vote exceeds Labour majorities, so is clearly important.

Since the terrorist attacks of 11 September 2001 and in particular 7 July 2005, Britain has awoken to the threat posed by militant Muslim groups, including Al-Muhajiroun, Hizb-ut-Tahrir and Supporters of Sharia, as well as individuals like Asif Mohammed Hanif, who became a suicide bomber in Tel Aviv in April 2003. In July 2004 Muslim disaffection caused by the Iraq war helped create massive swings against the government in two by-elections in Leicester and Birmingham.

N

nanny state
See paternalism.

'Napoleonic system'
Phrase famously used in 1997 by Jonathan Powell, Tony Blair's chief of staff, to describe the way in which the 'feudal barons' of Whitehall would be bent to the government's will. Andrew Rawnsley in the *Observer* (18 February 2001) judged that this had not happened: 'The Civil Service has frustrated the PM subtly and sinuously'. He went on to argue that the civil service had managed to defend both the status quo and its own failings remarkably successfully.

nation state
The main unit of political and social organisation, and an organising concept in the study of history and international relations (a branch of political science). Nation states are characterised by territorial sovereignty and the sharing of features of history, language and cultural identity. However, very few states exhibit all these characteristics, in particular the quality of having a single cultural and linguistic identity. The idea of a nation also has ideological uses, for example in the building of political movements such as nationalism.

The United Kingdom is by definition a state which originated from the separate political units of England, Scotland, Wales and (Northern) Ireland. However, these 'provinces' (or 'nations') still retain strong cultural and, in the case of Wales, linguistic traditions, which symbolically challenge the idea of a United Kingdom. The force of this challenge is evidenced by the devolution measures introduced by Labour after 1997 to satisfy nationalist sentiment. The 'troubles' in Northern Ireland go beyond symbolic representations and bear witness to the fact that not all inhabitants of the United Kingdom consent to be part of that state. Moreover, the development of a British multicultural society further emphasises the mythical elements of a single British nation. This having been said, the concept is still important in the Conservative Party, as nationhood constitutes a central element in the party's traditions. The idea of a nation state also has value to those who claim that British sovereignty is threatened by supranational organisations such as the European Union.

See also devolution; sovereignty.

National Air Traffic Services (NATS)

www.nats.co.uk

The body that provides air traffic control services over UK airspace. During the run-up to the 1997 general election future Treasury minister Andrew Smith declared that 'our skies are not for sale' and criticised Conservative plans to privatise NATS. However, once in power Labour decided on a part privatisation of the system, allegedly in order to facilitate much-needed private investment. There was a great deal of criticism from within the party, especially as the privatisation of the railways was unravelling during this time. However, the measure was pushed through in 2000 in the form of a sale of a 51 per cent stake for £750 million to a consortium of seven airlines, led by British Airways, Virgin Atlantic and EasyJet. Some thought this price excessive given the volatile state of the industry and the beginnings of recession in

the US economy. Financial targets set by the new consortium – involving stringent cost and staff savings – were regarded as tough and on top of that came the reluctance of people to fly in such great numbers following the terrorist attacks in the USA on 11 September 2001. By February 2002 NATS was in difficulties and required more funding as well as a possible increase in its charges. In March 2002 the government fed in £30 billion of a planned £60 billion worth of aid. Two months later NATS suffered from computer breakdowns but after that has functioned without noticeable public complaint.

National Archives

www.nationalarchives.gov.uk

The Public Record Office merged with the Historical Manuscripts Commission in April 2003 to form the National Archives. This body, based in Kew, west London, looks after the records of central government and the law courts and makes them available to the public.

National Asset Register

A 900-page modern-day Domesday Book compiled by the Treasury in 2001, designed to inform government of what the state owns and to sell off anything which is superfluous to requirements. Number 10 Downing Street was priced at £20 million; a Trident submarine at £800 million; and the British Library at £400 million.

National Association of Schoolmasters and Union of Women Teachers (NASUWT)

www.nasuwt.org.uk

A rival to the National Union of Teachers. The union has over 200,000 members. It is not linked to any political party.

National Audit Office (NAO)

www.nao.org.uk

Originates from the office of the comptroller and auditor general (who now heads the NAO), which was established in 1866 to ensure money raised through taxation is used for the purpose parliament intended.

The staff has grown to around 800 and the NAO focuses its investigations on value for money and efficiency in the public services. The auditor general is responsible to the Public Accounts Commission (PAC, not to be confused with the Public Accounts Committee), which comprises nine senior MPs and was set up in 1984. In 1987–88 the NAO made 174 recommendations to achieve value for money; the PAC accepted 161 of them and passed them on to the government, which accepted 153. The comptroller and auditor general is forbidden from commenting on policy but inevitably the reports have clear policy implications. The NAO provides reports on all government spending, although shares government auditing with the Audit Commission and other agencies of public audit. Some NAO reports are not published and decisions to publish in sensitive areas can be controversial. In the *Guardian* (20 July 2001) David Walker commented that, for all the excellence of the job it does, savings from NAO activities amounted to a relatively miniscule £400 million in 2000–01, compared with a total public spending figure of over £600 billion.

See also audit; Audit Commission.

national debt

Sum of the funds which government borrows at home (internal debt) and from creditors abroad (external debt). The debt originated in 1692 to fund the war with France and was more formally established in 1694, when the Bank of England was set up, partly in order to deal with it. Robert Walpole set up a 'sinking fund' in 1717 to allocate money for the repayment of the debt but it was eventually hijacked by other spending objectives and external events like the Napoleonic wars.

The national debt rose from £33 billion in 1971 to £113 billion in 1981, though inflation was responsible for an element of this increase. In 2000 the national debt was £350 billion or about £5,900 per person. The higher the level of debt a government faces, the higher its interest charges and the less it can spend on, for example, public

services. The Blair governments were keen to repay elements of the debt to reduce the associated interest payments. All these plans came crashing down in 2007–09 with the world banking crisis. Gordon Brown sought a Keynesian solution through massive borrowing to shore up the banks and provide a 'fiscal stimulus' to economic activity. This produced huge indebtedness. The public borrowing requirement was around £175 billion in 2009–10, and led to increased rates for any further borrowing as international markets began to doubt Britain's ability to repay. Figures published by the Office for National Statistics in November 2009 showed that the UK's public sector net debt was £870 billion, or nearly 62 per cent of national gross domestic product.

National Economic Development Council (NEDC)

Set up in 1962 by the Macmillan government to advise government on economic policy. Its members were drawn from business, government and the unions. There were a number of smaller 'Neddy' committees that dealt with specific areas. The Conservative governments after 1979 did not support this approach to economic policy making as it smacked too much of 'corporatism' and intervention in market forces. The body limped through the Thatcher years but John Major finally abolished it in 1992.

National Enterprise Board

Set up in 1975 to promote economic efficiency. The board invested in a number of enterprises including the ill-fated British Leyland. In 1981 it merged with the National Research and Development Corporation.

National Executive Committee (NEC) (Labour Party)

www.labour.org.uk/National_Executive_Committee

The body which runs the Labour Party's organisation. The unions once dominated this governing committee of the party,

POLITICS

but changes in the 1990s reduced union influence. Now its 32 members are as follows: the leader, deputy leader and treasurer (all elected by conference); 12 trade union members (elected at the annual conference), 6 constituency party members (elected by all members of the party – not MPs); 3 government ministers (chosen by cabinet); 3 MPs or MEPs (elected by conference); 2 Labour councillors (elected by the Association of Labour Councillors); 1 Young Labour representative (elected by the youth conference); 1 representative of the socialist societies (elected at the annual conference); and the leader of the European Parliamentary Labour Party (elected by Labour MEPs). The NEC used to be influential in the days when Tony Benn chaired its Home Policy Committee but since Neil Kinnock and Tony Blair wrestled control of policy back to the leadership the body has been relatively peripheral.

National Farmers' Union (NFU)

www.nfuonline.com

Represents farmers and growers in Britain. It was founded in 1904 by nine Lincolnshire countrymen. Farming was so important during the Second World War that the NFU managed to win statutory rights of consultation with the Agriculture Act 1947. From being a key 'insider' group with the Ministry of Agriculture, Fisheries and Food (MAFF) it extended its lobbying activities to take on the European Community after 1973.

National Front (NF)

www.national-front.org.uk

Right-wing neo-fascist political party founded 1967 out of the League of Empire Loyalists, the British National Party, former members of the White Defence League and sundry ex-Mosleyites. It fought 10 seats in the February 1974 general election and 92 in the October 1974 one. During the 1970s it was rumoured that the NF was close to the Monday Club, especially over the issue of immigration. Ostensibly the NF opposed immigration and the alleged flexibility of the law that

allowed New Commonwealth citizens to enter the country and to find work. Its beliefs, however, are more accurately described as neo-fascist: anti-Semitic, imperialist and racist. It stimulated the formation of the Anti-Nazi League. In 1979 the NF's vote collapsed, possibly as a result of the Conservatives taking a much tougher line on immigration, and the grouping spawned several smaller units, including the British National Party, which won a council seat in 1993 in the East End of London and various other council seats in the north-west in 2002–03, not to mention two MEP seats in June 2009. In June 2001, 11 NF members drawn from all over the country were convicted of taunting Asians in Oldham during the general election campaign. NF members had travelled up to support two candidatures of the British National Party in Oldham.

> The National Assistance Board pays the blacks for the coffee coloured monstrosities they father.... Material rewards are given to semi-savages to mate with the women of one of the leading civilised nations of the world. (Colin Jordan, when leader of the White Defence League, a forerunner of the NF, 1958)

> In our democratic society the Jew is like a poisonous maggot feeding off the body in an advanced state of decay. (John Tyndall, later of the NF, 1962)

See also British National Party; Monday Club.

national government

Name given to the administrations governing from August 1930 to May 1940. The first was led by Ramsay MacDonald following the ending of the Labour government. MacDonald split his party by joining the Conservatives; Labour and Liberals formed the opposition. In October 1930 the general election saw the government returned with 554 Conservative seats to 54 Labour. In June 1935 Stanley Baldwin replaced MacDonald as prime minister, in a government which was essentially Conservative. He went on to win an election victory over Labour later in the year.

Neville Chamberlain replaced Baldwin in 1937 and his government survived until May 1940, when Winston Churchill's wartime coalition came into being. It is often forgotten that this government's mandate dated back to 1935 and was not succeeded until 1945.

National Health Service (NHS)
www.nhs.uk
Set up by the National Health Service Act 1946. The service, fully funded out of taxation, began in July 1948, and provided free medical, dental and optical treatment to citizens irrespective of income or status. After a few years of operation, partial charges were introduced for spectacles and later dental treatment and medical prescriptions. Its founder, Labour minister of health Aneurin Bevan, hoped the service would eventually cost less as the nation became healthier but an ageing population and more expensive treatments ensured this was a fallacy. Throughout its history the NHS has been short of funding but its popularity has ensured that all Conservative governments have sustained it as much as they felt able. In this respect Margaret Thatcher declared 'the NHS is safe in our hands', although internal reforms were introduced in the early 1990s to separate consumers from providers via an 'internal market'. Labour chancellor Gordon Brown announced substantial extra funding in July 1998. In the summer of 2000 still more funding was pledged – an average 6 per cent annual increase for the next five years – along with Tony Blair's announcement of a comprehensive modernisation of the service. More funds for the NHS was a main theme in the 2001 election campaign for Labour but was neglected by the Conservatives. In July 2001 former Labour leader and then vice president of the European Commission Neil Kinnock suggested the NHS required more money, raised through taxation but 'ring fenced' and used specifically for the health service. This contrasted with the public–private strategy favoured by Blair and chimed in with the hypothecation of taxes as advocated by the Liberal Democrats.

In his 2002 budget Gordon Brown announced increases in taxation to fund even more spending on the NHS. However, a survey in May of that year revealed that only a small minority believed the government would fulfil its pledges regarding the promised increased numbers of nurses and doctors as well as the reduction of waiting times for operations to a maximum of six months. However, the survey also showed that three out of four patients were either 'very satisfied' or 'quite satisfied' with their last visit to a general practitioner or local hospital. This seemed to confirm a tendency for consumers to think local provision good but national provision poor. Some on the left suggest the latter tendency could arise from media coverage, as the tabloids can sensationalise mistakes and incompetence. Funding levels came under close scrutiny after the economic crisis of 2007–09, when cuts in public expenditure came onto the political agenda, although, during the election campaign of 2010, both main parties promised to ring-fence health, education and the police.

national insurance
Form of direct taxation, paid by both employees and employers. National insurance payments lead to entitlement to certain welfare benefits, including the state pension. They are payable from age 16 if in employment and cease at retirement age, currently 60 for women and 65 for men (though these ages are liable to change).
　　See also retirement age.

National Labour Party
Formed in 1931 by the few supporters of Ramsay MacDonald's national government. In the 1931 election 13 of its 20 candidates were elected and in 1935 just 8 of its 20 candidates. In 1945 the party wound itself up.

National Lottery
www.national-lottery.co.uk
A government-approved national lottery which makes a profit for its private operator and contributes a proportion to sport, arts

and charities. John Major's government passed the National Lottery Act 1993 and set up Oflot (now the National Lottery Commission) to regulate it. It began in 1994. The company operating it is Camelot, though in the autumn of 2000 a rival company, the People's Lottery, chaired by Richard Branson, was awarded the new operating licence only for this to be rescinded and Camelot to regain its original role. Its average weekly sales are around £90 million; total sales between May 1999 to May 2004 were £22.4 billion. In January 2009 Camelot began its third licence period, and increased the money given to good causes and to retailers. To do so it cut costs by 25 per cent, including by shedding 45 of its staff at Aintree.

National Lottery Commission
www.natlotcomm.gov.uk
Body which in 1999 took over from Oflot (set up in 1993) the issuing of licences for the company running the lottery and the responsibility for monitoring its progress. The Commission re-awarded the licence to the company Camelot in 1999, to run until January 2009 and then for a third period beyond that.

National Policy Forum
Policy-making body of the Labour Party. Set up in the middle of the 1990s, the Forum has 184 members (trade unionists, MPs, MEPs, representatives of socialist societies and senior ministers). It meets in private – thus avoiding the public conference rows of the past – and (so it is claimed) makes party policy. The Forum debates new policy and, if approved, it becomes party policy. Critics claim it has usurped the role of conference but others claim the Forum is itself a 'farce'. Writing in the *Guardian* (11 July 2004) Roy Hattersley claimed education policy, about to be debated in the Forum, had already been decided: 'conceived in the back rooms of Downing St', then 'imposed' on education secretary Charles Clarke at a meeting with the prime minister and finally 'announced' to the Commons on 8 July.

National School of Government
See Centre for Management and Policy Studies.

national service
Conscription of civilians into armed forces or industry from 1947 to 1962. The perceived threat of the USSR after the war led to the retention of conscription after the Second World War. National service applied to men aged 18. It was initially two years' military training but was then reduced to 18 months. It has long been thought subsequently by some that this experience of military discipline was good for those involved and ought to be reintroduced.

National Socialism
See fascism.

National Statistics
See UK Statistics Authority.

National Union of Journalists (NUJ)
www.nuj.org.uk
Founded in 1907, it represents some 30,000 people working in print, television and radio journalism. It has no political affiliation.

National Union of Rail, Maritime and Transport Workers (RMT)
www.rmt.org.uk
Specialist transport trade union. A merger between the Seamen's Union and the Railway Workers' Union (both dating back to the 19th century) in 1990 established this 70,000-strong union, the general secretary of which, for many years, was the gravel-voiced Scotsman Jimmy Knapp. Under Bob Crow (from 2001) it increased membership by a third by 2006.

National Union of Teachers (NUT)
www.teachers.org.uk
Founded in 1870 to represent the interests of teachers, by the 1980s it had lost members to its less militant rivals. It orchestrated opposition to the introduction to school testing in the early 1990s. It had

292,000 members in 2009, making it the largest teacher's union in the UK.

nationalisation

The policy of taking whole enterprises into public ownership adopted by the Labour Party, especially after the Second World War. The original idea, based upon the party's clause 4, was to end private ownership, believed by Karl Marx to be the basis of capitalism's evils. However, it was also thought that nationalised industries would be more efficient than privately owned ones. The major public utilities like gas, electricity and water were nationalised by the postwar Labour government as well as the coal industry; nationalised industries then made up 20 per cent of the economy. In some cases during the 1970s ailing industries were taken over by the government to prevent their collapse, as in the case of part of Rolls-Royce in 1970. The policy was perceived to have failed as early as the 1950s in terms of efficiency and even the Labour Party leadership sought to distance itself from it. The left wing, however, remained true to the old ideal and refused to believe the policy had not been successful, despite the billions of pounds which were required by government to subsidise these loss-making enterprises.

The Conservative governments after 1979 introduced 'privatisation' to reverse nationalisation in most areas. The Labour Party urged more state control in its 1983 manifesto but after its catastrophic loss began to abandon the idea and Tony Blair had few problems in changing clause 4; this was endorsed by a large majority at a special conference in 1994. Only the more eccentric parts of the mainstream left now advocate the policy, though the railways were effectively taken back under government control in 2004. State control, however, does remain part of the programmes of numerous far-left minor parties.

nationalism

A love of one's nation that is distinguished from patriotism by elevating its virtues above those of others. The 19th century is often seen as the 'age of nationalism', when a variety of ethnic minorities, citing the principles of the French Revolution, asserted their right to run their own affairs. In some cases this applied to minorities within large political structures like the Austro-Hungarian Empire or to ethnic majorities covering large geographical areas, as in Germany and Italy. More nation building occurred after the First World War, such as Czechoslovakia being formed out of the Austro-Hungarian Empire in 1918, and after the Second World War many colonies of the British Empire spawned nationalist movements, which demanded self-rule. Nationalist parties also asserted themselves in Wales and Scotland after the war and gained representation in the Commons. To some extent the policy of devolution was designed to assuage nationalist sentiment in the UK but it is arguable whether it merely encouraged the movements to set their sights higher.

In Britain nationalism is seldom expressed openly except during international sporting events, notably cricket and football, where a form of sublimated patriotism may exist, but it runs deep nevertheless, as was evidenced during the Falklands war. It is also expressed indirectly through racism – and the National Front and the British National Party seek to make political capital out of fusing the two.

See also nation state.

nationalist party

See Plaid Cymru; Scottish National Party.

NATO

See North Atlantic Treaty Organization.

Natural Law Party

Party, founded in April 1992 by Geoffrey Clements, that sought to advance the meditation ideas of Marahishi Mahesh Yogi – that regular meditation can end world conflict and that 'yogic flying' has the same effect. Television coverage of such 'flying' proved singularly

POLITICS

unconvincing as exponents, from their determined lotus positions, strove mightily to become airborne. It fielded 310 candidates in the 1992 general election but failed to save a single deposit. The party ended in January 2001.

NEET
Acronym for a young person 'not in education, employment or training', also used, for reasons unclear, in China, Japan and South Korea. The age group in the UK for such a classification is 16–24. There are over 1 million NEETs in the UK, nearly 10 per cent of the age group and costing the economy an estimated £3.65 billion annually.

negative voting
See tactical voting.

Neighbourhood Watch
Scheme set up in the 1980s to help deter theft from a neighbourhood. Neighbours get together, usually with a representative from the police, and agree to keep an eye on each other's property, and to alert the police if anything suspicious occurs. Some 40,000 schemes had been established by the end of the decade and to a certain extent they have been successful.

Neill committee
The Committee on Standards in Public Life under its second chair, Lord (Patrick) Neill (of Bladen). Under its first chair, Lord Nolan, John Major had specifically excluded from the remit of the committee the subject of party finance. This, however, was taken up by Neill, who produced his report in October 1998. It made over 100 recommendations but the main ones were:
1 full disclosure of donations of more than £5,000 nationally and £1,000 locally;
2 a maximum of £20 million for each party's election expenditure;
3 'blind' trusts (when donors do not make their names public) to be abolished;
4 donations by people living abroad who are not British citizens to be banned;
5 no anonymous donations above £50;

6 a powerful parliamentary commissioner for standards to oversee party funding.
   See also Committee on Standards in Public Life; Nolan committee; parliamentary commissioner for standards.

neo-liberalism
See new right.

Network Rail
www.networkrail.co.uk
Non-profit-making company that maintains the railways. Railways were nationalised after the Second World War and public dissatisfaction with British Rail became a feature of Britain. Many hoped privatisation in the early 1990s might improve things. However, the service was so under-funded it had to receive substantial public injections of cash – over £1.5 billion – before the transition was possible and in the event was somewhat rushed. In 1996 Railtrack, which owned the infrastructure, was sold off separately for £1.8 billion and companies were awarded 25 franchises to provide services. The Public Accounts Committee in August 1998 condemned the failure to insert 'claw-back' provisions to prevent easy profits. The Strategic Rail Authority was set up as the body to run the industry.

The privatised rail service was much criticised, not least for its fragmentation. The public complained even more bitterly about punctuality and regularity of service after privatisation than they did when the industry was in public hands, the most notorious offender being Virgin, which runs the West Coast Line. Furthermore, the Health and Safety Executive in March 1998 argued that many parts of the network were unsafe. During the autumn of 1999 there were a number of railway accidents, most notably at Hatfield, where four passengers were killed, and Ladbroke Grove (Paddington), where 31 were killed. As a result, the network was forced to undergo repairs and delays became a national scandal. By the summer of 2001 repairs were virtually complete but Railtrack shares had plummeted in value.

Many urged the renationalisation of the railways but the New Labour government signalled it was disinclined to do so.

The *Economist* on 9 June 2001 published a poll which showed that 70 per cent of the public favoured renationalisation of the railways, with only a tiny percentage opposed.

On 19 June 2001 Lord Cullen published his report into the Paddington rail disaster. He condemned the industry for 'institutional paralysis'. He criticised Railtrack especially for its 'lamentable' failure to check faulty red signal lights. He also reserved harsh words for the railways inspectorate, which he said lacked resources, was too slack and placed too much faith in Railtrack. In all he made 88 recommendations, which he asked for the Health and Safety Executive to implement during the following two years.

In 2001 Stephen Byers was made transport secretary but his 10-year plan to revive transport was defeated by events. In the autumn of 2001 Railtrack applied to the government for another injection of cash – some £3.3 billion – but Byers refused. Railtrack shares continued to slide, which elicited complaints from those employees who had invested in their own company with retirement in mind. Byers declared the company effectively bankrupt and replaced it with a non-profit-making company, Network Rail, as a preliminary to further restructuring but, in early 2002, many believed renationalisation was effectively taking place. In January of that year Tony Blair, occupied with foreign affairs, asked former BBC head John (Lord) Birt to prepare a report on Britain's transport system. This move was widely perceived as a snub to Byers, who was sacked shortly afterwards and replaced by Alistair Darling.

The Strategic Rail Authority, which Byers set up in 2001 to oversee a 10-year plan for the railways, lasted less than four years. On 15 July 2004 Alistair Darling announced its demise, with most of its functions passing to Network Rail and to the Department of Transport. With punctuality still lagging behind targets and money still being poured in, the railway system faces a tough battle to achieve quality and credibility.

New Deal

A New Labour programme designed to move unemployed people from benefits into work. It used a windfall tax on the privatised utilities to help 460,000 young and 165,000 long-term unemployed people into jobs. In December 2003 chancellor Gordon Brown announced that the windfall tax would henceforward be used to contribute to enhance skills of the unemployed. The pilot schemes funded employers – usually small companies – to allow workers time off to upgrade their skills in such areas as literacy and numeracy. The scheme was to be extended to cover a third of the country and 80,000 employees, most of whom had left school early with no qualifications. The chancellor also announced that all claimants on job-seekers' allowance would be forced to attend a skills course or lose their benefit. Lone parents, of whom 225,000 had found jobs under the New Deal, would also be forced to attend work-focused interviews and courses.

New Labour

Name given to the Labour Party by Tony Blair and his media-savvy team after 15 years of opposition (from 1979 to 1994). Blair was seeking to present a party free of vote-losing ideological baggage and associations, and so the prefix 'New' was widely used, to rebrand a party that had shifted to the centre-ground. Given the ridicule heaped on the name it did quite well to survive into the new millennium.

new left

Political movement developed in reaction to the disillusion felt in the 1950s at the behaviour of the USSR, especially Khrushchev's revelations at the Twentieth Congress of the Communist Party in 1956 about the brutality of Stalinism and the invasion of Hungary. Elements of the new movements in left-wing thought included

POLITICS

Maoism, the Cuban revolution of 1959 and the anti-colonial movements in Asia and Africa. In the 1960s groups of women, black-power militants and anti-Vietnam war activists claimed to represent the interests of the proletariat and took to the streets. The high point was the May events in Paris in 1968 but the intellectual influence of new-left gurus like Herbert Marcuse and Antonio Gramsci, who were concerned with alienation and cultural transformation, continued into the 1970s and 1980s. The *New Left Review*, founded in 1960, became the journal of the grouping.

new liberalism

Brand of liberalism, sometimes referred to as reconstructed liberalism, that emerged at the end of the 19th century under the influence of writers such as T. H. Green and L. T. Hobhouse. In contrast to laissez faire or classical liberals, Green believed the state had an obligation to intervene in order to improve the living conditions of the less fortunate, such as the working class, the old and children. Later liberal thinkers like John Maynard Keynes and William Beveridge took Green's ideas forward and developed interventionist policies on the economy and social insurance.

New Politics Network (NPW)

www.new-politics.net
Think-tank which campaigned on democratic renewal and popular participation. Founded in 1999 following the winding up of the Democratic Left, the NPW was formed from the ashes of the Communist Party of Great Britain. However, it eschewed political bias and sought to 'encourage cooperation and the sharing of best practice between people and organisations involved in the modernisation of politics'. In November 2007 it merged with Charter 88 to form the constitutional reform group Unlock Democracy.

new right

Term applied to the political economy associated with the classical economic liberalism of Adam Smith, and thus sometimes called

neo-liberalism. Its ideas emerged during the late 1970s from the Chicago School of Economics. Proponents advocated the rigorous application of market forces and the withdrawal of the state from its interventionist stance adopted since the end of the Second World War. In particular, they argued for the denationalisation of state-run industries, letting 'lame-duck' companies fail and the application of monetarist economic policy. They also advocated the curtailing of trade union power, as it acted as a block on the operation of market forces, and the reduction of the welfare state, which, the new right argued, had a debilitating effect on individual responsibility and wealth creation. Deregulation was to take place in the operation of industry and flexibility in labour markets was to be encouraged. There was also an acceptance of capital mobility, not only within economies but also on a global scale. The movement came to influence Ronald Reagan and the Republicans in the USA and crossed the Atlantic where, in Britain, it was promoted by think-tanks such as the Institute of Economic Affairs, the Adam Smith Institute and the Centre for Policy Studies. Also influential were individual politicians like John Biffen, Keith Joseph, Nigel Lawson and, inevitably, Margaret Thatcher. She blended these liberal elements with her belief in strong political authority plus a traditional Conservative line on law and order. She often referred to herself as a 'neo-liberal' Conservative.

See also Chicago School of Economics; monetarism.

new social movement

One of the new pressure groupings, not primarily economic, associated with social campaigns like the women's movement, gay rights, ecology and peace movements.

New Statesman

www.newstatesman.com
Weekly journal of comment and analysis founded in 1913. It was always close to Fabian Society positions, independent but sympathetic to radical liberal policy on

international questions and Labour Party policy on domestic issues. Kingsley Martin was its long-serving editor from 1931 and other notable editors included Richard Crossman and Anthony Howard. It teetered on the brink of collapse in the late 1980s but was saved by a rich benefactor, the former Labour minister Geoffrey Robinson, who sold the journal on to Michael Danson in November 2008.

news
In a literal sense, that which is new, unexpected or different. In relation to mass media, it refers to the reporting of news-worthy events, understood by journalists as a story which is interesting to themselves or their audiences. This has led students of the media to argue the news is a wholly artificial construction based upon a number of professional values, which compresses complex events and ideas into a certain form and size. Furthermore, the Glasgow University Media Group has suggested that news creation includes a wide range of mainstream assumptions about social reality which often exclude more radical interpretations. In the world of politics the news is the means whereby the political system is driven forwards and therefore a controversial aspect of the media among political parties.

On average, British people watch well over 20 hours of television per week, 20 per cent of which is current affairs and news. How politicians appear on news broadcasts has become of key importance ever since the primacy of image in politics became fully appreciated. The news has also become the target of regular 'sound bites', which are short, self-contained messages, carefully crafted to be both memorable and sufficiently brief to fit easily into a news bulletin. Both the BBC and Independent Television News are required to be unbiased but they regularly are accused of bias by politicians and their spin doctors.

See also Glasgow University Media Group; image; news values; political marketing; sound bite; spin; spin doctor.

news values
Criteria employed by editors in the print and broadcast media in the selection of stories. Experience suggests that these values lead to the selection not of things like policy briefings or analyses of official reports – which arguably might inform a serious democracy – but of stories con-cerned with personalities, sexual scandal, financial wrongdoing and celebrity gossip. What makes the situation even worse from the point of view of informed democracy is that those newspapers that take the 'serious' route sell far less well than those that follow the 'popular' route. Television tends to follow trends in print journalism and critics claim that this is why television has been subject to a 'dumbing down' in recent years.

Next Steps agency
See executive agency.

'NICE' decade
The 'Non-Inflationary Consistently Expanding' first 10 years of New Labour's period in office. In June 2008 the governor of the Bank of England made a speech in which he declared that the good times, as defined by the acronym, were now over and that economic times would be considerably tougher from now on.

'nimby' ('not in my back yard')
A derogatory acronym normally applied to those whose self-interest is threatened by development plans which would damage the value of their property or quality of life. The term is often applied to those who may in other respects promote economic development, or be supporters of free market capitalism, and are thus guilty of hypocrisy. While no human being is perfect, politicians should be particularly careful to avoid nimbyism, exposed as they are to the glare of publicity in the media and political attack in parliament. There are some examples of political nimbies, one such being Nicholas Ridley, secretary of state for the environment in Margaret Thatcher's first government. In 1986 he had objected to a planning application for new homes

near his residence, despite his granting of permissions for other developments.

9/11, 2001

Day on which Muslim fundamentalist terrorists hijacked four domestic airliners flying out of Boston and flew two of them into the twin towers of the World Trade Center in New York. Of the other two one hit the Pentagon and the other crashed when passengers apparently overpowered the hijackers. The towers collapsed and over 3,000 people were killed, including over 100 British citizens. Tony Blair immediately announced his support for US president George W. Bush's declared war on terrorism and made a speech proposing an attempt at a new world order at the Labour Party conference on 2 October 2001.

See also terrorism.

1922 Committee

Name given to the committee which emerged from a famous meeting in the Carlton Club in 1922 of Conservative MPs unhappy at the continuation of the party in David Lloyd George's coalition government. The meeting ended both the coalition and the leadership of Austen Chamberlain; it thus established the independence of Conservative MPs and their strength when roused to express their discontent. The committee meets every week and acts as a conduit of opinion from the back benches to the leadership on general issues and in specific policy areas from its various subcommittees (which are attended by party whips).

It is maintained by some commentators that it was the questioning of Lord Carrington by the foreign affairs subcommittee of the 1922 Committee which forced him to resign after the Falklands war. Academics Martin Burch and Michael Moran argue (in an article in *Parliamentary Affairs*, winter 1985) that the tendency for Conservative MPs to come increasingly from state secondary schools and to have local government experience tends to make them less accepting of a single all-powerful leader.

No Turning Back Group

Group of Conservative MPs established in 1983 by some passionate Thatcherites, including Peter Lilley and Michael Fallon. The group calls for a whole package of right-wing measures, including extensive privatisation and the virtual abolition of the welfare state. Margaret Thatcher, unsurprisingly, was keen to attend its dinners and was generally supportive of its policy thrust but the group lost influence once John Major came to power in 1990. Since 2005 it has been chaired by John Redwood.

Nolan committee

The Committee on Standards in Public Life under its first chair, Lord Nolan. The committee was set up in response to a *Sunday Times* 'sting' operation whereby Graham Riddick MP and David Tredinnick MP were asked to put parliamentary questions in exchange for money. Their willingness to do so caused public outrage. Nolan reported in autumn 1995 and made a number of recommendations, including the need for MPs: to register their business interests with a new and powerful parliamentary commissioner for standards; to declare their income according to bands; and to be prevented from tabling questions and amendments on behalf of outside interests. In the ensuing parliamentary debate John Major opposed the recommendations but they were passed in any case.

See also Committee on Standards in Public Life; Neill committee; parliamentary commissioner for standards; Standards and Privileges Committee.

nomination of parliamentary candidate

See candidate for parliamentary election.

non-departmental public body

See quasi-autonomous non-governmental organisation (quango).

non-departmental select committee

Investigative committee of parliament not related to the work of a department. The best-known committee of this type is the Public Accounts Committee. The Public Administration Committee, chaired by Tony Wright, has carved out an enviable reputation for effective questioning of ministers and witnesses on often politically sensitive matters. Moreover, the Modernisation Committee has helped reform the practices of both chambers. Also in this category are the following: Broadcasting, Deregulation and Regulatory Reform, Environmental Audit, European Scrutiny, Information, Selection and Standing Orders. In addition there are a number of other useful 'domestic' committees concerned with parliament itself: Accommodation and Works, Catering, Finance and Services, Standards and Privileges, Procedure, and Liaison. Finally, there are non-departmental select committees on Human Rights and Statutory Instruments, both joint committees of both houses of parliament.

NOP (National Opinion Polls)
See GfK NOP.

North Atlantic Treaty Organization (NATO)
www.nato.int
A military and political alliance established in 1949. After the Second World War, the perceived threat of the USSR encouraged Britain and then the USA to take defensive measures. Marshall aid was designed by the USA to strengthen European economies against the internal threat of communism. NATO was designed to counter the external threat of the Red Army. With the growing tension after 1947 from the orchestrated communist take-overs in eastern Europe, culminating in the fall of Czechoslovakia and the Berlin blockade, the idea of a collective security organisation for the west took shape. On 4 April 1949, 12 countries (10 European, plus Canada and the USA) signed a treaty which laid down that 'an armed attack against one or more of them in Europe or North America shall be considered an attack against them all'. Despite the formation of a retaliatory Warsaw Pact, NATO kept the peace successfully for 40

years and after the fall of the communist regimes in 1989 NATO extended an invitation to establish contacts with the organisation. Full membership remained a contentious proposal for some of the former communist countries but a number joined, including Romania and Poland. By 2010 NATO had 28 member states.

Membership of NATO remains the bedrock of British defence policy and British forces are allocated to come under its command in certain crises. NATO found a role for itself in helping alleviate the crisis in the former area of Yugoslavia. Led by the USA, its forces saw active service in spring 1999, the first time since its formation, when its airforces, mainly US, bombed Serbian military units in Kosovo. In 2003 a crisis developed over NATO support for Turkey in relation to the anticipated attack on Iraq. In the same year it took command of western forces in Afghanistan, for the first time in an area outside Europe.

See also Cold War; Marshall aid.

north–south divide
The economic disparity between the generally more prosperous south of England and the less prosperous north, as well as Wales and Scotland. Certainly the south-east is more prosperous than the other areas of the UK, with higher salaries and higher house prices. The north tends to be more favourable to Labour and the south to the Conservatives, while the Liberal Democrats have strength in the south-west.

Northcote–Trevelyan report, 1854
One of the most important reports ever published on the British civil service. Written by an obsessive reformer who later became permanent secretary to the Treasury (Charles Trevelyan) and a future chancellor (Stafford Northcote), it was backed by the reformist prime minister William Gladstone. The report observed that 'Admission to the Civil Service' was 'eagerly sought after' by the 'indolent and incapable', whose 'abilities do not warrant an expectation they will succeed in the

POLITICS

open professions'. Instead, the report recommended entry through merit in open examinations and a separation of tasks into the 'intellectual' and the 'mechanical', which were to be undertaken by different classes of entrant. The report's recommendations were resisted initially but were eventually implemented. It took 50 years for the stratified system to form but it produced a durable model, which has arguably served the country well. It has introduced a powerful sense of public service for the able sons and daughters of the middle classes. In modern times this sense has been in marked decline as the products of Oxbridge have sought more financial rewards.

See also civil service; executive agency.

Northern Ireland (Ulster)

The English invaded Ireland in the 12th century, followed by the Scots in 1315. As a consequence, Ireland became a strife-torn land for many centuries. Originally Northern Ireland was predominantly Catholic; however, it became more equally Protestant as Scots immigrants, appointed by City of London companies, were given land to settle and farm. The province played a crucial role in the Glorious Revolution, when William besieged Londonderry and emerged victorious from the Battle of the Boyne.

Heavy industry developed in Belfast in the form of shipbuilding and also textiles. Loyalist Ulster Protestants opposed the home rule movement in the 19th century. As the negotiations for home rule proceeded, Ulster insisted on being treated separately under the effective advocacy of Sir Edward Carson. The Government of Ireland Act 1920 established a separate parliament at Stormont in Belfast for the six northern counties of Fermanagh, Armagh, Tyrone, Londonderry, Antrim and Down. In 1925 the Boundary Commission fixed the line between the north and south of Ireland. The 1937 Irish constitution embedded the notion of unification and Protestant northerners thereafter constantly feared these territorial claims, encouraged by IRA activity and

the nationalist sympathies of the large (40 per cent) Catholic minority. Consequently politics in the province was dominated by the Protestants, to the detriment in political and employment terms of the Catholics, who reacted in the late 1960s with a civil rights movement. Civil rights marches in 1968 turned into riots and troops were sent in. The Provisional IRA emerged and wrought havoc in the early 1970s. Internment proved ineffective, as did most other measures, and in 1972 direct rule from London was introduced. Attempts to introduce power-sharing executives failed in 1974 and 1975–76, because of loyalist strikes. Over 3,000 people died as a result of the violence from the late 1960s, until the Good Friday agreement in 1998 offered new hope that power sharing might work. After several delays, occasioned by the refusal of the IRA to 'decommission' or disarm, the two biggest parties in May 2007, the Democratic Unionist Party (DUP) and Sinn Fein, agreed to share power in a new Northern Ireland executive, with Ian Paisley as first minister. In January 2010 devolution was completed when the executive took responsibility for the police and the courts.

See also Good Friday agreement; Northern Ireland assembly.

Northern Ireland assembly

www.niassembly.gov.uk
Established with the Good Friday agreement of 1998. It has 108 seats and has powers over devolved matters (plus an Irish dimension). After the first elections to the assembly, on 25 June 1998, the Ulster Unionist Party (UUP) had the most seats and David Trimble (its leader) became first minister. Sinn Fein, led by Gerry Adams, was given two portfolios in the administration, including Martin McGuinness as education minister. However, problems persisted, with the Unionists demanding the IRA decommission its arms. Trimble used a threat of resignation to pursue his objectives. His most acute political problem lay with his own party, which was implacably opposed to cooperating

with partners who allegedly maintained strong terrorist links. In September 2002 the assembly was suspended. In May 2003 Tony Blair and Bertie Ahern, the Irish premier, sought to extract a definitive disavowal of violence from the IRA but Adams' form of words ultimately did not satisfy the British prime minister, aware as he was that Trimble's position would be vulnerable to a challenge from the Democratic Unionist Party (DUP), led by Ian Paisley, unless the renunciation was clear and absolute. Consequently elections were postponed from May to November 2003. These elections resulted in a squeezing of the centre in the form of the Social Democratic and Labour Party (SDLP) (lost 6 seats) and the UUP (lost one seat) and the strengthening of the extremes in the form of Sinn Fein (gained 6 seats) and the DUP (gained 10 seats). In 2007 the assembly finally was re-established when Sein Fein and the DUP agreed to cooperate. Ian Paisley became the first minister, with Martin McGuinness his deputy. Peter Robinson took over as first minister in June 2008.

Northern Ireland executive

www.northernireland.gov.uk
Set up by the Good Friday agreement in April 1998 as the executive arm of the Northern Ireland assembly. This body is composed of 12 members, including a first minister, deputy, and heads of department, including health, environment, education, economic development, agriculture and finance. David Trimble of the Ulster Unionist Party was elected first minister, with Seamus Mallon of the Democratic and Labour Party (SDLP) as his deputy. The education portfolio was given, controversially, to Martin McGuinness, of Sinn Fein, who, it is alleged, once commanded the Londonderry brigade of the Provisional IRA. The executive was suspended in autumn 2002 and direct rule reintroduced. Ian Paisley became first minister in June 2007, stepping down a year later to let Peter Robinson take over. McGuinness remained as deputy.

Northern Ireland peace process

See peace process.

Northern Rock

www.northernrock.co.uk
A Newcastle-based bank which had to be taken over by the government when it went bust in 2008. It started life as the Northern Rock Building Society, which floated as a bank on the Stock Exchange in 1997. Following the repercussions of the 'credit crunch' in 2007, caused by the US 'sub-prime mortgage' crisis, the bank was eventually nationalised in February 2008 when no other credible buyer could be found for it. In January 2010 Northern Rock was split into two parts: a bank and an asset company.

nuclear energy and waste

Nuclear power stations began to contribute to the National Grid in the 1960s but political opposition began to grow in the wake of worries that waste could not be processed satisfactorily and that genetic defects could be found in children living close to such plants. Following the Chernobyl accident in 1986 the industry was criticised bitterly by the environmental lobby as unsafe. Given Britain's need to bridge the energy gap as North Sea oil runs out, however, nuclear energy has become a candidate for expansion despite the fact that it is the most subsidised form of energy and still cannot compete in the marketplace.

In 1995 the eight nuclear power stations in Britain came under British Energy, which was taken over by the French company EDF (Electricité de France) in January 2009.

On 30 August 2004 it became known that, despite ministerial pledges that Britain would not become a dumping ground for nuclear waste, some 10 countries – including Germany, Japan and Italy – had been transporting nuclear waste to Britain for reprocessing by British Nuclear Fuels. The idea was to extract the uranium and plutonium and to send it back to the sender countries for reuse. However, the process did not produce the expected results and the waste ended up being stored in some 20 locations, including 10,000 tons in concrete bunkers in Drigg, Cumbria. The reasoning for this was that transporting it back to the originator countries was judged to be excessively expensive. Some environmental experts estimated a cost of £80 billion to maintain the waste over the next 100 years and that the high- and intermediate-level waste would not be safe for human contact for the next 200,000 years.

See also energy.

nuclear weaponry

Britain acquired nuclear weapons just after the Second World War, in a bid to equip the country with the most up-to-date weapons. In the 1950s the Campaign for Nuclear Disarmament urged the unilateral abandonment of such weapons and was influential in winning Labour to its cause. However, Conservative victories in the 1980s stimulated a rethink and Labour came to accept a multilateral approach to disarmament – that is, it would take place only when other states disarmed as well. Currently nuclear weapons are available to British defence forces, the most powerful being the submarine-launched ballistic missile system, Trident.

See also Campaign for Nuclear Disarmament.

Number 10, Downing Street

See 10 Downing Street.

oath of allegiance

The swearing of allegiance to the crown. There have been several oaths of allegiance required at different times in British history, the first being in 1534 to ensure loyalty to Henry VIII and Anne Boleyn.

A further oath of allegiance was required in statute form in 1606 to support the reign of James I. The Test Act 1673 required all office holders to take one. Today, such an oath is sworn by MPs on first taking their seat. The Sinn Fein MPs Gerry Adams and Martin McGuinness refuse to take their seats as they feel they cannot take the oath of allegiance. However, both decided to take advantage of their parliamentary allowances and offices in Westminster in January 2002.

The citizenship ceremonies introduced at Brent Town Hall in February 2004 involved an oath of allegiance to the queen. They continue to be held, if necessary in overseas locations, via diplomatic personnel.

Office for Budget Responsibility

A body providing independent economic forecasts as the basis for government budgets. This was unveiled by the Conservative–Liberal Democrat government in May 2010 as its answer to alleged failures by Labour to offer reliable forecasts during its time in government. Sir Alan Budd, prominent economist and former chief economic advisor to the Treasury, was made its head; he described his appointment as the 'most exciting challenge of my professional life'.

Office for National Statistics (ONS)

www.statistics.gov.uk

Established in 1996 in a merger of the Central Statistical Office and the Office for Population Censuses and Surveys. ONS provides the government's statistical service and regularly publishes reports on social and economic matters. It stands as the Office of the National Statistician, who functions as the chief executive of the National Statistics Institute.

See also UK Statistics Authority.

Office for Standards in Education, Children's Services and Skills (Ofsted)

www.ofsted.gov.uk

In charge of inspections of schools and tasked with raising standards. Its remit covers inspection of independent and state schools, as well as local education authorities, child day care and child minding in England.

Office of Communications (Ofcom)
www.ofcom.org.uk
Regulator for communications industries – television, radio, telecommunications and wireless communications services. Set up in 2002 this body replaced five media regulatory bodies: the Broadcasting Standards Commission, the Independent Television Commission, Oftel, the Radio Authority and the Radio Communications Agency. Ofcom employs over 1,000 people and has powers to control the behaviour and standards of media companies, including the BBC and Sky, as well as telecommunications companies such as BT. The BBC is not bound by Ofcom, though calls for it to be so were voiced after the David Kelly affair and the Hutton inquiry.

Office of Fair Trading (OFT)
www.oft.gov.uk
Body established by the Fair Trading Act 1973 to ensure market forces work in the consumer's interest. It enforces consumer protection and competition law to protect citizens from violations of both. It prohibits unfair trading, conspiracies and cartels among companies to fix prices. The Competition Act 1998, which came into force in March 2000, greatly strengthened the OFT, giving it the power to levy fines of up to 10 per cent of turnover on companies involved in uncompetitive practices. The act stipulates criminal penalties for those obstructing the OFT in its monitoring of mergers and takeovers. Despite some successes, the OFT has been criticised as less effective than its US 'anti-trust' equivalent. In 2009 the National Audit Office commented: 'so whilst the OFT has improved the value for money it provides, there remains scope for further improvement'. In spite of this very mixed judgement, its chief executive, John Fingleton, in 2010 was the highest-paid official in the public sector, receiving £275,000 p.a.

Office of Government Commerce (OGC)
www.ogc.gov.uk
Body formed in April 2000 as an independent office of the Treasury. It is responsible for much of the government's civil purchasing and project management previously offered by the Treasury Procurement Group, the Buying Agency, Property Advisers and Civil Estate, the Central Computer and Telecommunications Agency and the policy aspect of the Private Finance Initiative Taskforce. Its aim is to ease the process whereby business sells to government and to increase competition. The OGC has a chief executive appointed at permanent secretary level. It reports to the chief secretary to the Treasury.

Office of Public Service (OPS)
This evolved out of various successive bodies with responsibility for the civil service. Initially the personnel and training functions were the preserve of the Treasury and its principal official was also head of the civil service. In 1968 the Civil Service Department (CSD) was created, along with the Civil Service College for training purposes. Margaret Thatcher, however, saw the CSD as too incestuously protective of civil service interests and in 1981 it was abolished. Its functions were subsequently redistributed to various agencies, ending up in the new OPSS in 1992 (which lost 'science' to become the OPS in 1995). The OPS, with its responsibilities for the Efficiency Unit, the Next Steps programme and the citizens' charter came under the responsibility of the Cabinet Office and was headed by the secretary to the cabinet, who ensured a more centralised degree of control over the public service. In 1998 the OPS was formally merged with the Cabinet Office.

Office of the Commissioner for Public Appointments
See Commissioner for Public Appointments.

Office of Water Services (Ofwat)

www.ofwat.gov.uk
Set up by the Competition Services
(Utilities) Act 1992 to regulate the
privatised water companies.

official gift

Gift given to a minister of the crown in
the course of work. Ministers frequently
receive such gifts. However, there is often
a suspicion that they may be given in
respect of favours either already given or
anticipated. To guard against this, a limit of
£140 has been set (January 2010) for such
items and any gift worth more than that has
to be declared and, if the recipient wishes
to keep it, the balance of value paid. In July
2004 Tony Blair decided to give back the
guitar given to him by rock star Bono when
they met in May 2002 to discuss the AIDS
epidemic in Africa.

Official Secrets Act

Usually understood to refer to the two acts
of 1911 and 1936 which forbid anyone
to pass on secret information, including
information derived from being a servant of
the crown, whether or not that information
could be of any use to an enemy. Section I
of the 1911 act covered spying but section II
was broader and made it an offence for
a crown servant to communicate official
information to a person when it was not
'in the interests of the state or otherwise in
the public interest' to do so. This covers
all official documents and information. In
theory it would include, for example, the
staff directory of the Ministry for Work and
Pensions. Reformers have railed against
this illiberal statute but governments and
bureaucracies find it convenient to keep
secrecy wrapped more closely around the
workings of British government than is the
case in most similarly developed liberal
democracies.

The Official Secrets Act 1989
attempted to clear up some of the confused
areas of secrecy, but did not make the
situation any more liberal. Its remit covers
security, defence and international relations,
as well as crime and its investigation. Any
release of related information deemed
'harmful' to the public interest is a criminal
offence and it is no defence to claim the
information is in the public domain abroad.
Those covered by the act include members
of the security services, all civil servants,
government contractors and journalists.

New Labour came into office in 1997
committed to removing secrecy from British
government, but few believe radical or fundamental change took place, as evidenced
by a limited Freedom of Information Act
and the arrest in September 2000 of
David Shayler, a former employee of the
security services, who was charged under
the Official Secrets Act for revealing an
alleged plan to assassinate the Libyan head
of state, Colonel Gaddafi. The Freedom of
Information (Scotland) Act 2002 applies
to Scotland.

Ofsted

See Office for Standards in Education,
Children's Services and Skills.

oligarchy

See iron law of oligarchy.

ombudsman

www.ombudsman.org.uk
A person who investigates complaints about
government departments and their agencies.
Ombudsmen originate from Scandinavian
practice. In the UK this is done by
the parliamentary and health service
ombudsman (previously the parliamentary
commissioner for administration, PCA).
The office was established in 1967 to
investigate maladministration by government departments and certain other bodies,
including the Arts Council. Complaints
have to be referred to the ombudsman by
MPs but the ombudsman has no effective
powers of enforcement.

One survey found that more than 10
per cent of MPs never referred cases to
the ombudsman, while less than 10 per
cent often sent papers for consideration.
Most MPs prefer the direct approach to
a minister, as they can keep the matter
in their own hands and reap credit if

successful. Usually complaints number about 1,000 per year and about 10 per cent of these are upheld. If an upheld complaint is not remedied the ombudsman can report the case to parliament and the government will decide whether to act. In his annual report for 2001–02 Sir Michael Buckley, as ombudsman, said he had received 2,139 complaints, a 24 per cent increase on the previous year. The Department for Work and Pensions accounted for the largest number of complaints (693).

Since 1967, the idea has been extended to other areas of government, with an ombudsman established for Northern Ireland in 1969, for local government in England and Wales in 1974, for local government in Scotland in 1976, and also a special ombudsman who reports to the European parliament in 1994.

In 1993 the Health Service Commission (HSC) was created as the second element of the office. Ann Abraham was appointed to the post in 2002.

on message

Timely assertion of the official party line. Since the development of a mass electorate in the 19th century there has been a need for political parties to appear united, and for all their members to convey the same message, at least in public. However, the growth of electronic media, especially television, has increased both the speed of communication and the need for politicians to synchronise their messages, as determined by the leadership and corps of special (media) advisors. These people now dominate election campaigning and party communications, especially since the New Labour victory of 1997. For many, Labour's then headquarters, at Millbank Tower, came to symbolise the party's concern with media presentation, in particular that Labour politicians be on message at all times. Infamously, for a while after 1997, Labour MPs were required by their whips to carry a pager so that they could be kept in touch with party thinking and policy and consequently be 'on message'.

'one nation' Conservatism

Strand of Conservative thinking which stresses the need for social harmony and measures which will help achieve this, like enlightened state welfare and egalitarianism. It originated, for some, with Benjamin Disraeli's novel *Sybil*, which talks of 'two nations', the rich and the poor. Since Disraeli's day the question has been much debated inside the Conservative Party. The balance between individualism and collectivism in the Conservative Party has varied, but in the wake of the First World War a concern with national cohesiveness predominated and a raft of social legislation ensued in the 1920s and 1930s which anticipated the so-called postwar consensus. The thrust of the approach was to ensure the unity of the nation was sustained. Some historians argue that the basis of the Conservative manifesto in 1945 was almost as collectivist as Labour's, although the voters did not perceive this to be the case. Margaret Thatcher was more interested in asserting the individualist element in Conservatism, though some of her close advisors, like John Biffen, contrived (and succeeded) to be 'one nation' Conservatives as well as free market enthusiasts.

open government

The principle that all government information should be freely available to the public. Following the *Spycatcher* case of 1988 the Conservative government passed the Official Secrets Act 1989, which removed the 'public interest' defence for those in breach of the law. In practice the culture of secrecy was not changed by the new law, and large amounts of information were still either unavailable to the public or very costly to elicit: the *Economist* (20 January 1996) reported that one inquirer was charged £2,000 for the provision of information and another £100 for photocopying. The Freedom of Information Act 2000 passed by Labour disappointed some by its failure to allow disclosure of civil service advice to ministers but was lauded by others as a vital extension of democratic freedom.

open primary

System of selecting candidates whereby all voters are consulted. On 4 August 2009, the Conservatives in Totnes replaced Anthony Steen (the sitting MP who had announced he would retire at the next election) with Sarah Wollaston, a general practitioner, as their prospective candidate. It was done though an open primary system whereby every voter in the constituency has a say in selecting who represents each party in the general election. The system is widely used in the USA and Martin Bell and David Cameron have both expressed support for it. However, critics point out that: it is costly (£40,000 to contact the 69,000 voters in Totnes); opponents can vote tactically to distort the result; and producing a more acceptable candidate might have the effect of excluding radical voices from parliament.

opinion poll

Systematic questioning of a representative sample of respondents. The opinion polls industry started life in the USA as a market research exercise for consumer products, and then moved to politics during the 1930s when Dr George Gallup developed a scientific approach to opinion measurement. Opinion polls successfully predicted the Labour Party landslide in 1945 and were soon embraced by the British press, to the extent that polls have become an indispensable feature of every general election since. In particular, they are used by the press as barometers of government popularity, and the strength of leaders and their parties.

There are eight major polling organisations in Britain: Com Res, Ipsos-MORI, Yougov, R8 Your Politician, ICM, GfK NOP, Bpix and Populus. The British Institute of Public Opinion was founded in 1937 and its work was reported sparingly during the 1940s but increasingly thereafter as polling was seen to be an accurate predictor.

During the 1992 general election campaign it was calculated that 18 per cent of all newspaper front-page lead stories

were based on polls. In that election all the polls predicted a close result but in the event they were proved wrong as the Conservatives romped home with a 7 per cent margin over Labour. Intensive studies as to what went wrong suggested the organisations had not properly analysed the 'don't knows' and those who refused to be interviewed. It seemed a disproportionate number of Conservative voters were included in these categories, thus producing the wrong forecasts. Corrective measures went much of the way to restore the reputation of opinion polls by the time of the May 1997 election, when 59 national polls were conducted by the polling organisations for the media. In 2002 pollster Peter Kellner set up YouGov, a polling company which uses the Internet as its means of eliciting views. Some criticised this approach as being skewed to middle-class respondents.

The Market Research Association (the pollsters' trade organisation) claimed the polls had performed reasonably well in the 2001 general election, with most predicting Labour's share at 45 per cent when it was actually 42 per cent; predictions of the Conservative vote were on average 1.7 per cent out and only 0.6 per cent out in the case of the Liberal Democrats. The BBC/NOP exit polls were reasonably accurate, with errors of between 2 and 12 in terms of predicted seat numbers. However, the *Economist* (16 June 2001) disagreed. It pointed out that during the campaign predictions varied by double-digit figures (for example 28 per cent for MORI). Furthermore, there was bias: every one of the 29 polls put Labour's lead above the actual final figure of 9 per cent. The *Economist* went on to point out that this was the third election in a row when Labour's share of the vote had been overestimated. It concluded the polling organisations needed to 'conduct a thorough review of their methods'.

In the 2005 general election the polls did pretty well. They predicted, for Labour, the Conservatives and the Liberal Democrats respectively, the following party percentages of the vote (the actual result was 36–33–23): NOP, 36–33–23; MORI, 38–33–23; YouGov, 37–32–23; ICM, 38–32–22; Populus, 38–32–21. In 2010 the major polls again performed fairly well. The actual result was Conservatives 36 per cent, Labour 29 per cent, Liberal Democrats 23 per cent and others 12 per cent. In the predicted respective party percentages, Com Res overdid the Liberal Democrats at 37–28–28–7; Yougov also did so with 35–28–28–9; ICM was close on 36–28–26–10; Populus was another over-egging the Liberal Democrats, with 37–28–27–8; but Mori was close on 36–30–23–10 and Canadian pollsters Angus Reid probably closest on 36–29–24–11. The average of the pollsters was 35–28–27–10, which did not reflect the tendency of polls to overestimate Labour but did so in relation to the Liberal Democrats.

See also exit poll; focus group.

opposition

The second largest party in parliament. Given the provenance of British democracy from the institution of the crown, opposition carried a whiff of disloyalty to the monarch so, as government became more independent of the crown, the concept of 'Her Majesty's loyal opposition' became established, with a salaried leader plus an alternative team of government shadow ministers. However, the Conservative Party after 1997 failed to emerge as an effective opposition and the role was to a degree usurped by the media and elements within the governing party. In July 2004 the Liberal Democrats ran equal to the Conservatives in the polls. While Conservative leader Michael Howard was able to improve his party's morale in the Commons and to test Tony Blair occasionally in debate, he proved less persuasive at winning round the voters. After David Cameron's election in December 2005, the Conservatives soon emerged as a very effective opposition, with the old Etonian leader regularly flaying Gordon Brown in prime minister's questions and debate. As Labour's share of the diminished turnout

declined during the first decade of the new century, Labour MPs as a whole became less squeamish about providing their prime minister with some closer to home opposition.

> On Wednesday [4 July 2001] sharp criticism was directed at PM Blair by his own MPs. With only 59 per cent of voters voting the mandate of the new government was less impressive than in 1997 and restive elements in Labour were less constrained from expressing their dissatisfactions, especially over private–public partnerships (PPP). Parliament too is in a more assertive mood and unwilling to be treated as a doormat any longer. (Michael White in the *Guardian*, 5 July 2001)

opposition days

Days on which the subjects for debate in parliament are not decided by government. For 20 of the available days for debate the opposition leader has a choice of subject on 17 of them; the remaining three are decided by the leader of the third largest party (currently the Liberal Democrats).

Orange Order

www.grandorangelodge.co.uk
Established in 1795, the movement was a reaction to the threat of the United Irishmen and the Catholic secret societies associated with the Irish Rebellion (1795–98). Its organisation is via lodges and it has been heavily influenced by the freemasons. Today the order exists to defend and promote the interests of Protestants in Northern Ireland and on 12 July every year the Orangemen parade in celebration of William III's victory over James II at the Battle of the Boyne in 1690. Mid-July is thus the annual marching season, which provides a sparking point for trouble between the two communities. The parades in Drumcree, County Armagh, threatened the peace process in 1996 and 1997. The 1998 parade looked as if it might be accompanied by violence but the death of three young children in a fire bomb attack caused tempers to cool and the tension to pass. However, tension reappeared in subsequent years. In

2001 Drumcree was again the flashpoint, with its Orange Lodge insisting, as in previous years, that it had the right to ignore the government ban and march down the mainly nationalist Garvachy Road in adjoining Portadown. During the July 2009 marching season, there were outbreaks of petrol bombings on estates in Derry and Belfast but no major incidents.

order in council
A legislative order made by the Privy Council under the royal prerogative, much used during wartime to achieve rapid changes when the traditional legislative procedures would be too slow. The orders are issued in the name of the queen but in effect the lord president of the Council reads out a list of orders prepared by government and the queen says 'agreed' at regular intervals. The device is also used by the prime minister to protect measures from parliamentary criticism, such as Blair's order giving Alastair Campbell the authority to instruct civil servants.

Osmotherly rules, 1980
Series of rules governing civil servants, based on a memo by an assistant secretary in the Civil Service Department in 1980. These advise civil servants appearing before select committees not to allow themselves to become involved in anything politically controversial, for example advice to ministers, interdepartmental policy matters or information concerning foreign countries.

Ouseley report, 2001
Report on major riots in Bradford city centre, by former chairman of the Commission on Race Relations, Lord (Herman) Ouseley. His report attracted considerable attention. The thrust of the recommendations was to break down the separateness of the different communities and to make 'Bradford citizenship' the top consideration, ahead of ethnic identity. The report focused on 'community fragmentation' along social, cultural, ethnic and religious lines throughout the Bradford

district. Segregation in schools was seen as a symptom and a cause. Different communities tended to see others with suspicion and hostility. Political leadership had been weak, said the report.

> so-called community leaders maintain the status quo of control and segregation through fear and threats.

Outrage!
www.outraged.org.uk
Radical gay rights body co-founded in 1990 by the well known campaigner Peter Tatchell. It specialises in direct action and it is one of the most militant pressure groups in the country. A tactic of one of its factions was to 'out' well known people whom they accused of concealing their sexuality, for example Jason Donovan, but the phase passed and the tactic is no longer used. Outrage! campaigned strongly in favour of lowering the age of homosexual consent from 21 to 16 in 1994 – a measure which took place in 2000, by virtue of the Sexual Offences (Amendment) Act.

outsider group
A term invented by Wyn Grant of Warwick University as a category of pressure group. Outsider groups are the corollary of Grant's 'insider' groups and there are similarly three kinds: groups which seek closeness to the decision-making process; groups which lack the skills and resources to move closer; and ideological outsider groups, which deliberately place themselves beyond the values of Whitehall and the establishment. A good example of an outsider group is the Campaign for Nuclear Disarmament (CND), which, despite massive campaigning, failed to influence government policy whether Conservative or, more surprisingly, Labour.
See also insider group; pressure group.

overload
A critique of a democratic government popular in the 1970s, whereby it was deemed unable to meet the mounting demands of a complex society. One analysis located the source of the problem in the

civil service, where individual officers sought to advance their interests by expanding their departments as a means of enhancing their own careers, thus helping to cause excessive public expenditure, burgeoning numbers of civil servants and widespread inefficiency. Right-wing politicians prescribed privatisation and a new ethos for the public service which owed much to the private sector. Another attributed overload to the difficulty of coordinating the apparently infinite number of uncontrollable variables of which political problems are comprised.

Oxbridge

Name produced by elision of the names of the two elite British universities. As well as being the objective for the most able and ambitious, Oxbridge is important politically as so many of its products go on to dominate positions of power in Britain. On 1 November 1998 the *Observer* produced a list of the 300 most powerful people in the country and of them nearly one-third had attended either Oxford or Cambridge. As the paper commented:

> The Oxbridge system is a devastatingly efficient way of producing the nation's elites. The cosy Cambridge power club includes for example, the heir to the throne, the prime minister's press secretary, the permanent secretary to the Treasury, the Home Office and the Departments of Health and Social Security, cabinet secretary Richard Wilson, the head of MI5, the Governor of the Bank of England and the director of the CBI.

Oxford, if anything, is even closer to the reins of power: its graduates include Tony Blair, Rupert Murdoch, David Miliband, Jonathan Powell, Peter Mandelson and Ed Balls. Oxbridge still, it would seem, runs the country. In 2000 Gordon Brown seized upon the case of Laura Spence, a state secondary schoolgirl who was refused a place at Oxford despite excellent A-level results. Brown claimed she was the victim of discrimination and elitism but the facts tended to prove him wrong, as other students turned down had equally good results and the college concerned had a

good record for encouraging candidates from state schools.

Oxford Union

The debating society of Oxford University, which has helped train some of the country's greatest politicians in public speaking. Being elected president of the Union has long been seen as an indication of political promise and possible career. For example, William Hague was, and performances as Tory leader after 1997 against Tony Blair at prime minister's questions attracted praise for their wit and good comic timing. When he stood down as leader in June 2001 Blair acknowledged Hague as a 'worthy and formidable opponent'.

P

Palace of Westminster

Also known as houses of parliament, this embodies the Commons and the Lords, on the north bank of the Thames, in the heart of London. It was rebuilt in 1834 but retains its status as a royal palace for ceremonial purposes. Its origins go back to the first palace in the 11th century and was the primary residence of the monarch until 1512, when a fire destroyed the palace. It became the home of parliament until the second great fire of 1834. Architect Charles Barry won the competition to rebuild the palace, assisted by Augustus Pugin. 'Westminster' and its related 'village' have become synonyms for British political life, just like the world within the 'Washington Beltway' in the USA.

paramilitary

A technical term for a terrorist military unit or organisation which claims to represent the two religious groupings in Northern Ireland. The Ulster Defence Association

(UDA) is the best-known Protestant body and the IRA the best-known Catholic one. There had been occasional contacts between the British government and the Provisional IRA since 'the troubles' began but none came to anything until the peace process initiated by the Conservative government in the late 1980s. These culminated in a series of negotiations chaired by US senator George Mitchell which involved the paramilitaries. Many believe their inclusion was the reason for the success of the peace process.

See also Continuity IRA; dissident republican group; Irish Republican Army (IRA); Loyalist Volunteer Force; Provisional IRA; Real IRA; Ulster Defence Association; Ulster Volunteer Force.

parenting class
An initiative, around the middle of the first decade of the new century, to curb crime, based on the idea that parents of actual or potential offenders will benefit from some instruction in how to manage their children. Initial results were encouraging and so it was proposed to extend parenting classes to the parents of 3,000 young offenders held in secure facilities, to 'break the cycle of intergenerational criminality'. The white paper on the criminal justice system issued in July 2002 contained this along with many other ideas and policy proposals. The classes were made part of the 'respect agenda' and were made compulsory in some cases. John Reid as home secretary defended them as justifiable when a difficult child could have typically cost the state £70,000 by the age of 28 years.

parliament
www.parliament.uk
Usually considered to comprise the House of Commons, the House of Lords and the monarch. The British parliament, held to originate in 1265, is often regarded as the 'mother of parliaments', though the Icelandic Althing, from 930, is older. However, the British parliament is the usual model for large developed countries

and has been very influential, not least because of the far-flung nature of the British Empire.

The Norman kings used to convene a gathering of landowners called the curia regis, or great council, to which representatives of the shires were occasionally summoned. In 1265 Simon de Montfort (who had led a baronial revolt against Henry III but who then needed a counter to their influence) summoned representatives from the boroughs as well as the shires and these two groups began to meet separately from the barons, thus establishing the embryos of the Commons and the Lords.

Gradually parliament extracted from successive monarchs a number of rights in exchange for their support but they were still contested and it took the Civil War in the 1640s and the Glorious Revolution in 1688–89 to establish parliament's ultimate supremacy over the monarchy and the judiciary.

Two parliamentary groupings emerged in the 17th century, namely the Whigs and the Tories. The monarch began to invite their leaders to be ministers, depending on who commanded a majority in parliament. In 1707 the parliaments of England and Scotland were united and from 1801 to 1922 the Irish parliament was added too. Elections were fixed at every three years in 1694, every seven in 1716 and the current five in 1911. Parliament enjoyed a 'golden age' in the 19th century, when it was able to reject legislation and sack ministers on the floor of the House of Commons. However, the growth of disciplined parties made debates wholly predictable and 'majorities ruled'.

Critics argue that the massive majorities won by New Labour in 1997 and 2001, together with Tony Blair's apparent reluctance to consult the House of Commons, brought parliament to a low position of power and prestige. A group of leading MPs, including Tony Wright and Gwyneth Dunwoody, were keen to persuade the then leader of the house, Robin Cook, that the balance of power between legislature and executive needed to be changed in the former's favour. A series of reforms occurred in the autumn of 2002, including a 7.00 p.m. finish to evening sessions, but the crucial balance of power in favour of the executive did not change as a result.

In spring and summer 2009 a huge scandal erupted over MPs exploiting their generous expenses, which brought the reputation of politicians to a new low.

Parliament Act 1911

One of the landmarks in British constitutional history, in that it originated in the Lords' rejection of David Lloyd George's People's Budget in 1909. The upper chamber finally agreed to pass the 1911 measure only under threat that the king would create sufficient Liberal peers to ensure its passage. The act effectively made the Commons the more powerful chamber and the powers of the unrepresentative Lords were reduced to that of delay of one month for bills embodying financial proposals and two years for other bills (reduced to one year by the Parliament Act 1949). In addition, the 1911 act reduced the maximum time between general elections from seven years to five.

parliamentary candidate

See candidate for parliamentary election.

parliamentary commissioner for administration

See ombudsman.

parliamentary commissioner for standards

www.parliament.uk/about_commons/pcfs.cfm

Set up in 1995 following the recommendations of the Nolan committee. The commissioner reports to the Select Committee on Standards and Privileges, which also adjudicates on the commissioner's reports. The commissioner maintains the register of members' interests (but not the register of lords' interests, which is compiled by the Lords registrar under the authority of the clerk of the parliaments) and gives advice on the code

of conduct and the *Guide to the Rules Relating to the Conduct of Members.*

The first incumbent was Sir Gordon Downey and he was busily employed from the outset considering the case of Neil Hamilton MP, who was accused of accepting cash for questions from the owner of Harrods, Mohamed al-Fayed. His successor was Elizabeth Filkin, a former chair of the Citizens' Advice Bureau. She established a tenacious style of investigation and press reports in late June 2001 suggested she had succeeded in offending some senior politicians. She had pursued inquiries against John Major and William Hague regarding issues which some dismissed as trivial. The decision not to reappoint Filkin in January 2002 attracted considerable controversy. Her most famous investigation was into the loan of £300,000 made by Geoffrey Robinson MP to fellow Labour MP Peter Mandelson. She upheld two of the complaints against Mandelson, the outcome being his first resignation. She also investigated Robinson regarding undeclared financial interests from former business links with the disgraced Robert Maxwell. She experienced problems investigating accusations against Keith Vaz, regarding both the Hinduja brothers and his wife's business interests. Vaz, the member for Leicester East and minister for Europe, was cleared on several points but on others the commissioner indicated she had not received the cooperation she required. Vaz was re-elected in 2001 but lost his job in government.

Sir Philip Mawer was commissioner 2002–08 and investigated George Galloway and Derek Conway. John Lyon took over in 2008; he maintained a low profile, despite having to deal with the MPs' expenses scandal in 2009.

parliamentary counsel

Expert legal draughtsmen who put into words what legislators seek to do; they are in charge of the formal drawing up of bills, amendments to bills and statutory instruments placed before the legislature for approval. They are civil servants but

usually qualified solicitors or barristers. In
1996 contracting out this activity to private
practice was considered but not introduced.

parliamentary democracy
See parliamentary government.

parliamentary government
The mechanism producing both a government and democratic accountability. In
Britain a general election must take place
at least once every five years, at which
voters elect a new House of Commons.
The sovereign then invites the person who
can command a majority in the house
to become prime minister and form a
government. This person is usually the
leader of the largest party elected by the
public but in February 1974 Edward
Heath sought to form a government
supported by the Liberals, then led by
Jeremy Thorpe. The bid failed when all 14
Liberal MPs rejected Heath's proposed
coalition, and Harold Wilson went on to
become premier of a minority government.
Once an administration is formed it seeks
to implement its manifesto promises,
principally by means of legislation (public
bills). The prime minister and other senior
members of the government are responsible
to the House of Commons, and ultimately
to the electorate for their actions, policies
and overall management of the country.
Therefore, parliamentary government is
responsible and accountable for its actions,
two key features of the British political
system. However, in recent years changes
have taken place in these constitutional
principles. For example, some have
suggested that the development of executive
agencies has weakened the principle of
ministerial accountability; and Scottish and
Welsh devolution has diluted the idea of a
unified state run by a central government.

> The British, being brought up on team
> games, enter the House of Commons in the
> spirit of those who would rather be doing
> something else. If they cannot be playing
> golf or tennis, they can at least pretend that
> politics is a game with very similar rules.
> (C. Northcote Parkinson, 1962, British

political scientist, expressing 'Parkinson's
law' – work expands to fill the time available)

**Parliamentary Labour Party
(PLP)**
Members of parliament who accept the
Labour whip in the House of Commons.
Unlike the Conservative Party, Labour
elects a Parliamentary Committee, which
the leader uses as the basis of the shadow
cabinet. In this process each MP has as
many votes as there are candidates and,
since 1992, there must be at least four for
women candidates. Once in government
the leader is obliged to appoint the cabinet
from those who held shadow cabinet posts,
though later reshuffles can reflect the
leader's choices. Before Labour got into
government in 1997, the PLP contained
well defined factional groupings – the 'soft
left' Tribune Group and the harder-left
Campaign Group – but these groups faded
once it became clear Tony Blair rewarded
loyalty with government posts. However,
the passage of years in power led to
dissatisfaction with the leadership and the
groupings began to re-emerge, especially
after the Iraq war in 2003. Working-class
representation in the PLP declined from
about 75 per cent in the interwar period
to 13 per cent by 1997, while middle-class
MPs increased in proportion of the
whole, with two-thirds being graduates. In
1997, 101 women were elected but ethnic
representation was still relatively low.

parliamentary majority
A party's voting strength over and above
other parties in the House of Commons. It
is one of the cornerstones of the 'unwritten'
constitution, because the leader of the
largest party following a general election
will be invited by the sovereign to form a
government. Indeed, it is the voting strength
and whipping system of the governing party
which enables it to enact legislation and
implement its manifesto commitments. The
first past the post system of elections tends
to produce majority governments, which
can implement their legislation without
having to form coalitions with other parties

and make the inevitable compromises and 'deals' which proportional representation tends to foster. Critics of this system, for example the Liberal Democrats, point out that governments can be elected, and usually are, with much less than 50 per cent of the popular vote. They claim that this reduces the political legitimacy of an administration, a claim given greater force when governments are elected with very small overall parliamentary majorities (majority in parentheses): 1950, Labour (5); 1964, Labour (4); February 1974, Labour (33, short of an overall majority); and October 1974, Labour (3). Small overall majorities, or no majority at all, create difficulties for government, as demonstrated after February 1974, when Labour soon lost its majority and was forced to rely first on Liberal support (the Lib–Lab pact) and then on the support of the Scottish National Party. Margaret Thatcher was fortunate in having substantial majorities, John Major less so in 1992, when he gained only a 21-seat majority and had to deal with a dissenting group of Eurosceptics. Tony Blair's 1997 administration was elected with a massive majority of 179, the largest since 1945; in June 2001 he succeeded again with a majority of 167, although from a turnout of only 59.2 per cent. Some pointed out that almost as many people did not vote in this election as those who voted in the governing party. In 2005 Blair won a majority of 67 on the basis of 36.5 per cent of the vote.

Parliamentary Office of Science and Technology (POST)

www.parliament.uk/mps-lords-and-offices/offices/bicameral/post

Body that acts as an advisory and information service to both houses of parliament to help ensure parliamentarians can base their activities on the best possible scientific knowledge.

parliamentary party

After the Reform Acts of the 19th century, MPs were increasingly elected on party platforms and represented parties in addition to their constituents in the House of Commons. Today parties dominate the Commons, and to a lesser extent the Lords. The European parliament is dominated by groupings of national parties. Both Conservative and Labour have well organised internal parliamentary structures, namely the 1922 Committee and the Parliamentary Labour Party (PLP) respectively, with managing committees, and others which shadow the major policy areas. Elections to the committees serving the parties are often quite fiercely contested. Internal party committees provide training for MPs specialising in particular issues and policies, as well as a line of communication between backbenchers and the leadership. Parliamentary parties used to elect the party leaders but in 1981 Labour introduced an electoral college that represented constituency parties, unions and the PLP to perform the function instead. In 1998 the Conservatives changed their procedures to one whereby the parliamentary party would identify a short-list of two candidates but with the final vote delivered by the party members.

parliamentary private secretary (PPS)

The lowest rung on the ministerial ladder. The PPS is part of a department's ministerial team and sits in on policy discussions but is given little to do that is of importance. He or she often acts as a conduit between the minister and backbenchers and is often little more than a message carrier. However, the importance of promotion to the post should not be underestimated; it is effectively that of 'apprentice minister' and can be the prelude to either promotion or renewed political oblivion.

parliamentary privilege

The right of MPs to say whatever they like, within the bounds of parliamentary language, inside the confines of parliament, without fear of any court action being taken against them. It also includes the power of the house to prevent anyone impeding its work. 'Privilege' enables some MPs to make arguably slanderous statements in the House of Commons with impunity; saying them outside would lay them open to legal action. However, privilege goes beyond the individual MP to include the right of the house to regulate and control its own proceedings, as well as its power to punish MPs and others for breech of privilege. The Standards and Privileges Committee will examine misconduct and recommend punishment, ranging from suspension from the house to criminal prosecution. Even the testimony of witnesses to committees of the house is protected by privilege. Some MPs taken to court in 2010 over their expenses claims tried to invoke 'privilege' but did not succeed.

parliamentary reform
See House of Commons reform; House of Lords reform.

parliamentary session
Usually runs from November to November but can be altered. If an election is held in the spring, for example, then a long session can run through to the November of the following year (it has carried over in the past into December). Conversely, the calling of a general election can interrupt a session, producing a 'short' session. If the government's business programme is under pressure, the end of a session may be delayed. There are recesses at Christmas, Easter, Whitsun and summer. In 2004, both houses experimented with a two-week September sitting to facilitate a three-week recess for the conference season. The experiment proved very unpopular and was discontinued.

Bills, if not passed by both houses, fall at the end of the session, though there is now some provision for carrying over bills from one session to another. In the Commons, this can be accomplished by the passing of a motion. The House of Lords has agreed that the carry-over should normally apply only to bills that have been subject to pre-legislative scrutiny.

parliamentary sovereignty/ supremacy
It is important to note the distinction between sovereignty and supremacy. The former is used to describe the independence of the nation state from any outside authority and its special status in international law; the latter refers to the political authority which parliament exerts over the monarchy and courts. The legal entity of the United Kingdom comprises England, Wales, Scotland and Northern Ireland but it is a unitary state, not a federal one with defined powers for constituent elements. The explanation is historical, in that England absorbed the peripheral states and made them subject to its parliament: Wales in 1536; Scotland in 1707; and Ireland in 1801, although in 1922 only the northern part of Ireland was retained. European Community law appears to qualify British sovereignty in that it is held to be superior to British law but most constitutional lawyers would probably maintain that ultimately parliament could overturn European law and that sovereignty still resides with member legislatures until (if ever) the European Union becomes a genuine federation.

parliamentary terms of address
In the Commons members are required to address their remarks to or through the speaker. Other members are referred to as 'honourable members' and members of the same party as 'my honourable friend'. MPs who are members of the Privy Council are referred to as 'right honourable'. In the Lords members are 'noble lords'. There is some movement to reject the rather antique modes of address and language used in the chamber though some traditionalists love these aspects of parliament.

participation
See political participation.

partisan dealignment
Term associated with the work of the political scientist Ivor Crewe, among others, which describes how voters have

become detached from their class-based or 'natural' party (the Conservatives for the middle classes, Labour for the working classes). The proportion of voters identifying closely with 'their' party fell from 38 per cent in 1964 to under 20 per cent in 1997; by 2001 the figure was closer to 10 per cent. Voters became more 'instrumental', choosing the party which they believed would most benefit their interests. This tendency hit Labour particularly badly as working-class support fell sharply in the 1980s, and shifted over to the Conservatives, particularly in the C2 or skilled manual categories. This view, however, was questioned by Heath, Jowell and Curtice in the mid-1980s, who suggested that most of the electorate still voted according to class; however, to prove this they had to redefine the class categories. By 1997 the allegiance of working-class voters had moved back to Labour, along with support from the middle classes. In that general election social groups A and B swung from Conservative to Labour by an average of 10 per cent. Those in groups C1/C2, D and E swung by 21, 15 and 9 per cent, respectively. In 2001 A and B votes swung to Labour by 1.5 per cent and C1 votes by 2 per cent; however, working-class votes swung to the Conservatives: 2.5 per cent of C2 votes and 6.5 per cent of D and E votes.

The overall effect of partisan dealignment is to make elections less predictable, with huge waves of support likely to wash first one way then the other. Votes are much more 'up for grabs' than at any time in the history of British politics.

partition

The partition of Ireland in 1922 into Ulster and the Irish Free State. Partition can be seen from two perspectives. Nationalists see it as British imperialism, an attempt to maintain a foothold in Ireland having lost the war of independence. The religious and political differences, cited in justification for partition, are seen as a smoke screen for imperial interventions and impositions. The other view sees the partition as inevitable

and necessary given the militant determination of Protestants in the north to retain a separate identity and the link with Britain.

party election broadcast

Broadcast by a political party allowed during the course of an election campaign. Before 1998 broadcasts were allocated on the basis of: a party's voting performance in the previous election; or whether it was fielding at least 50 candidates. Since 2000, a party has to contest a sixth or more of the seats up for election to receive a party election broadcast. In the 2005 general election, for example, in England Labour and the Conservatives received five broadcasts each and the Liberal Democrats four. In Scotland, Northern Ireland and Wales, all four main parties received four broadcasts each.

See also party political broadcast.

party funding

A constant source of concern for all politicians. Running one of the main political parties costs upwards of £20 million a year and more in an election year. Both Labour and the Conservatives have tried hard to solve the problem but without total success.

Labour has traditionally derived its funding from trade unions but the political influence which unions exerted became a political liability and New Labour sought to reduce its dependence on them. The existence of direct funding, through the 'sponsoring' of members to support them financially, gave way after 1995 to 'constituency plan agreements', whereby unions contributed some money in exchange for representation on the constituency general management committee. New Labour did its best to increase individual donations and as the Conservative cause declined in the late 1990s Labour began to pick up wealthy supporters in business, the City and in the media. By 1994 unions donated only half of Labour's income. The party's national membership scheme also brought in substantial sums. The Ecclestone affair proved an embarrassment for Tony Blair and subsequent donations were accepted with more circumspection. David Sainsbury, publisher Paul Hamlyn and financier Chrisopher Ondaatje each donated £2 million in the autumn of 2000. Some said the gifts were squeezed in before the legal limits on donations were applied from February 2001.

The Conservative Party has traditionally been perceived as the 'rich' party and, indeed, business sources regularly provided the party with the wherewithal to fight expensive elections, often via 'front' organisations which fed funds through to the party indirectly for those who wished to keep their donations confidential. However, the Conservatives, with a declining membership, were forced to look further afield and ended up accepting money from some business sources abroad, for example the Greek shipping magnate John Latsis. These donations attracted adverse comment and were a gift to the Labour Party, which exploited the issue in the 1990s and linked it to 'sleaze'.

The Neill committee recommended that the amount of cash spent on elections should be capped and that regulations be introduced regarding donations to political parties and their identification. During the 2001 general election a cap of £20 million was placed on spending and neither party seemed to object; nor did the campaign seem especially 'cut price' from the voter's point of view.

In 1998 the Conservatives sought to escape their financial problems by appointing a Belize-based billionaire as their treasurer: Michael Ashcroft. He helped to erase Conservative debts but ran into criticism himself for his business dealings. More helpful perhaps were the rich donors who contributed millions of pounds over Christmas 2000. Stuart Wheeler, who made his money out of betting, donated £5 million and later Paul Sykes, a Eurosceptic businessman, donated several million pounds. However, the Electoral Commission released figures in April 2001 which revealed that Labour had received four times as much funding as the Conservatives in the February and

March preceding the general election. Most of Labour's money came from the unions, including the GMB, AEEU, TGWU, MSF and USDAW. In addition, it received donations of £10,000 each from several businessmen, including Lord Haskins. In 2002 several unions threatened to sever their traditional financial support for the Labour Party on the grounds that the party no longer served union interests.

In 2006–07 Sir Hayden Phillips chaired talks between the parties in an effort to agree an acceptable *modus vivendi*. Progress was stopped when a maximum of £50,000 per donation proved a problem. The Conservatives insisted union donations should be covered by such a rule as well as individual donations. Labour claimed union donations – which could be several hundred thousand pounds – were merely aggregates of many smaller donations from members. While Tories can command very many donors willing to give that maximum, Labour had relatively few, apart from the big unions. This problem proved insurmountable and the talks stalled in October 2007 without agreement being reached.

See also election campaign costs; Neill committee; Political Parties, Elections and Referendums Act 2000.

party identification
See partisan dealignment.

party leaders' televised debates
Televised debates by party leaders, introduced for the 2010 general election. Following the introduction of such debates in US presidential elections there were many suggestions that Britain should adopt the practice. However, the incumbent party usually refused, as it did not wish to give the opposition the publicity such debates would provide. In 1997, Tony Blair, as the front runner, refused prime minister John Major's request for debates. In October 2009, prime minister Gordon Brown, similarly behind in the polls, announced he was happy to debate with other party leaders. The rules were to be strict: an audience of 200 representative voters, no

applause or heckling allowed and strict time limits to be applied to speeches and reactions to audience questions. Three 90-minute debates were screened, on three consecutive Thursdays. The first, on 15 April, was watched by nearly 10 million people. Some viewers found it hard to decide who had 'won' but the polls showed Nick Clegg had proved most popular by far in the first debate and on the strength of that his party's poll ratings leapt from around 20 points to 30 or over. The debates had turned a two-party contest into a three-way one. Clegg sustained his performance in the second debate but had to concede the third and final one, and perhaps the series as a whole, to David Cameron, who seemed to adapt and improve after a shaky start. Brown, while competent and well informed, lacked the presentational charisma of the other two (radio listeners reckoned he won the third) and, perhaps unfairly, came last.

The party leaders' debates had been anticipated by a Channel 4 debate involving the chancellor and his two shadows; it was largely thought to have been an uneventful 'draw' but with Vince Cable, the Liberal Democrat, edging the best performance.

party list
See regional party list.

party membership
In the 1950s it was reckoned both big parties had over a million members but the affiliated union members distorted this for Labour, while the Conservatives had many non-active members. In 2007 the figures were: Conservatives 290,000, Labour 176,000 and Liberal Democrats 7,000. In 2002 the Greens claimed 5,000 – up from 3,500 in 1996 – and Plaid Cymru 11,000.

party political broadcast (PPB)
Broadcast created by and issued on behalf of a political party. Parties are allocated airtime in relation to their performance in previous elections and the number of candidates they are fielding in an election. Not surprisingly, the lion's share goes to the three main parties. The very first PPB appeared in 1951, given by Lord Samuel for the Liberals; it was faded out as it over-ran its time. Anthony Eden presented the Conservatives' first PPB in the same year. The politicians of the day were unskilled and tended to give awkward, stilted talks to the camera. Harold Macmillan was the first to show a flair for the medium of television, and was followed by the pipe-smoking Harold Wilson and folksy James Callaghan. Margaret Thatcher taught herself to be effective on television with help from her media guru Gordon Reece. In 1987 Labour produced a 'vox pop' broadcast that focused on Labour leader Neil Kinnock, directed by Hugh Hudson. This PPB pushed up Kinnock's personal ratings in the opinion polls and won praise from all sides; it stimulated a similar (though less praised) broadcast featuring John Major in the 1992 general election campaign. In 1997 John Major vetoed a PPB which represented Tony Blair as a Faust-like figure, prepared to sell his principles for electoral victory. PPBs now tend to attract small audiences.
See also party election broadcast.

party system
The relationships between the political parties operating in a state. Unlike the one-party systems of the former USSR and its eastern satellites, Britain, in common with other liberal democracies, offers voters a choice of party candidates in elections. Many European countries have multi-party systems (usually the result of a proportional system of representation), where more than two political parties either are competing for government or play a significant part in influencing government. Britain has been viewed as a two-party system, as either the Conservative or Labour party traditionally has control of the House of Commons. However, this was not always the case. Between 1929 and 1945 there were minority governments (1929–31) and coalitions (1931–45). It is only since 1945 that the 'two-party system' has been so clearly and well established but even then substantial

third-party voting has taken place. Thus, since the 1970s the rise of the Liberals, Ulster nationalists and Scottish and Welsh nationalists has come to challenge this two-party control, most especially in the mid to late 1970s. In the 1983 general election, the Alliance spectacularly pushed Labour into third place in a number of constituencies, and to many this signalled the beginning of the end of the two-party system. However, the breakthrough was short-lived and Labour recovered ground in the elections of 1987 and 1992, finally gaining office in 1997. The May 2010 coalition could lead to a realignment of parties on the centre left and centre right; a reformed voting system would cause even bigger changes. Indeed, the Celtic assemblies have seen coalitions between Labour and the Liberal Democrats and their party systems have proved more complex. In 2009 a Labour–Plaid Cymru coalition ruled in Wales and a minority Scottish National Party government Scotland.

paternalism

The tendency of the state to take responsibility for important aspects of individual and group behaviour. Liberalism originally was predicated on the idea of limited government, that the state should not usurp areas of life that were the proper responsibility of the individual citizen. However, certain theorists, notably T. H. Green, argued persuasively that citizens were not properly free until they had equal opportunities to become self-reliant. From this beginning grew the whole structure of the welfare state and fears in the Liberal Party as well as the Conservative Party that the state in the 20th century had become too protective and too intervention-ist, threatening private liberties and inhibiting private initiative. Labour shed some of its paternalism before its 1997 victory but could not escape accusations of paternalism by the Conservatives, usually expressed as attacks on the 'nanny state'; examples given included the proposed ban on fox hunting and advice given on diet by the Ministry of Health.

patient payments

The rule whereby patients paying for their expensive drugs were deemed to have opted out of the National Health Service (NHS) system and therefore were liable to pay for *all* their care was widely deemed to be unfair, especially to cancer sufferers. On 4 November 2008 a report by oncologist Mike Richards enabled Alan Johnson, the health minister, to overturn this rule. Moreover, some steps were taken to make expensive drugs more easily available. The National Institute for Health and Clinical Excellence (NICE) has a remit to get value for money and limit health care costs. Its approach is based upon assessing treatments and rejecting those which cost more than a certain amount for the achievement of one year extra of life. This is logical enough but experts point out that local health managers tend to price such a year at £12,000 while NICE allows £30,000. Yet NICE receives huge criticism when it turns down a treatment. Why? Because it works in public and not in the privacy in which most local NHS decisions are taken.

patriotism

See nationalism.

paymaster general

One of a number of non-departmental posts which the prime minister can use as he or she wishes, whether in the cabinet or outside. At the time of writing it was a position in the Treasury with specific responsibilities for customs and excise, European and various other tax issues. Geoffrey Robinson occupied the post after 1997 but resigned in December 1998 over the controversy surrounding his loan to Peter Mandelson. Dawn Primarolo held the post 1998–2007, when she was in charge of HM Revenue and Customs. Tessa Jowell then held it, with a cabinet seat, while also acting as minister for the 2012 Olympic Games. After the May 2010 election, Francis Maude assumed this role, as well as being minister for the Cabinet Office.

Peace and Progress Party

www.peaceandprogress.org
A political party 'for human rights', set up in 2004 by Vanessa Redgrave, and led by her brother Corin.

peace process

The complex of initiatives, accommodations and rhetoric which moved Northern Ireland towards its latest period of peace. It was initiated by revelations in the *Observer* in 1993 that the IRA would be prepared to end its armed struggle. From this beginning, talks between the IRA, the Irish government and the British government ensued and took off when the former US senator George Mitchell agreed to chair the peace negotiations. These culminated in the Good Friday agreement, which was signed by all sides in 1998. A power-sharing executive was eventually formed in 2007 between Sinn Fein and the Democratic Unionists, though some problems persisted.

See also Northern Ireland.

Peacock report, 1986

Report of a committee on the financing of the BBC. The Conservative Party in the 1970s and 1980s tended to view the BBC as excessively left wing. Consequently there was much support for the ending of the licence fee system of funding the BBC. Some Conservatives hoped such a recommendation would come from the Peacock committee, which reported in 1986, but it bitterly disappointed them by dismissing the idea that the BBC should accept advertising and by recommending that the licence fee be indexed to inflation.

peak organisation

An 'umbrella' body representing a collection of a certain type of pressure group. The Trades Union Congress, for example, covers trade unions, while the Confederation of British Industry represents the managements of the larger economic enterprises. Peak organisations are especially valued by the European Commission as they help to streamline the consultation processes in Brussels.

Peerage Act 1963

An act, called for by Anthony Wedgwood Benn, as he then styled himself, that enabled peers to surrender their titles. This allowed them to stand for the Commons. Benn was the first beneficiary but the second, ironically, was Lord Home, who became Alec Douglas-Home in 1964 in order to lead the Conservative Party and become prime minister.

penal policy

The approach to punishing offenders. In Britain this has, since the 20th century, tended to be liberal, with some element of rehabilitation. However, Conservative policies after 1979 tended to be less so. Margaret Thatcher called for tougher sentences and Michael Howard, home secretary 1993–97, claimed that 'prison works', despite the fact that several judges asserted the opposite. As always, the younger generation are singled out for special treatment, with Conservative politicians frequently calling for tougher action to be taken against young offenders. To this end William Whitelaw, home secretary 1979–83, introduced the 'short sharp shock' approach, based on a recycled borstal model. Preventive remedies, though, were not wholly neglected and several programmes were initiated which attempted to make contact with young offenders and persuade them to mend their ways before periods in youth detention and then adult prison turned them into hardened criminals.

Neighbourhood Watch schemes became more popular from the 1980s onwards; there was also the appearance from that time of vigilante movements, whereby residents organised their own patrols and, occasionally, punishments (for example of paedophiles).

Labour used to take a more liberal line on penal policy, based on the belief that the sources of crime were to be found in poverty and social injustice. However, Tony Blair, as shadow home secretary in the early 1990s, changed this balance with his more nuanced policy of attempting to

POLITICS

247

be 'tough on crime, tough on the causes of crime'. After Labour's 1997 election victory, Jack Straw as home secretary was not notably more liberal than his Conservative predecessors and his successor in 2001, David Blunkett, was rumoured to have no ambition to be more liberal than Straw. In July 2001 he announced a new approach which suggested he might be, as it emphasised the rehabilitation of prisoners. Studies had shown that the changes in penal policy had not deterred the 100,000 core offenders who committed half of all crimes. Blunkett marked a break with the 'prison works' approach when he stated that: 'The aims of sentencing should be prevention, punishment and reparation, reducing crime and rehabilitation'. In May 2003 Blunkett announced the establishment a new body, the Sentencing Guidelines Council (SGC), to set national guidelines for all offences. The SGC is advised by a sentencing advisory panel comprising judges, magistrates, academics and others.

See also crime; Prison Service; sentencing; vigilante movement.

pension
Payment from private or public source given to older people when they have stopped working. State pensions began under David Lloyd George at the beginning of the 20th century, as payments to the elderly, which were met out of general contributions to the exchequer. More recently employers began to pay occupational pensions, from an accumulated fund. The government sought to encourage this practice by making contributions to such funds tax deductible. By the early 1980s pension funds had become the largest holders, at 27 per cent, of financial assets in Britain. In 1997 Peter Lilley, the social security minister, proposed a new scheme, whereby individuals would contribute towards their own pensions as the state pension increasingly declined as a proportion of the average income. Labour condemned the plan but could offer only a row between senior policy makers when in office. Frank Field, the minister entrusted with 'thinking the unthinkable'

about welfare, suggested a second pension, of roughly the same value as the state one, funded by national insurance contributions and run by mutual societies. However, the chancellor, Gordon Brown, did not like it, as different-sized contributions, reflecting income, would be paid in for the same flat-rate pension. Higher payments for negligible extra benefits were judged unlikely to be acceptable and the scheme made no headway. Brown caused controversy in 1997 when he removed tax benefits paid to pension and insurance funds, thus taking for the Treasury an annual £5 billion out of pension funds, which a few years later were destined, in many cases, to run into deficit. Brown introduced 'stakeholder pensions' in 2001, a scheme targeted at lower income earners. Meanwhile, occupational pension schemes were quickly abandoning the 'final salary' pension on cost grounds, so that by 2009 only 10 per cent of them were still in place. Employees are now expected to accumulate their own pension pots. Resentment was also expressed by those in the private sector that public sector salaries still funded final-salary pensions.

The problem with pensions all over the developed world is that whereas they were originally intended to tide people over the last few years of their lives, they are now often claimed for two or three decades. Adair Turner's Pensions Commission report in 2004 identified the options for improving and reforming pensions: work beyond the standard retirement age (e.g. make it 70 instead of the current average, which is 63); encourage people to save more each month; fund better pensions through increased taxation; or accept a lower standard of living for pensioners. State pensions are the biggest slice of the welfare bill, at £63 billion a year. Increasing the qualifying age by a year might reduce that total by 3–6 per cent; two or three years more would do an even better job and it is not surprising all the major parties made such proposals in 2009–10. In 2009–10 the basic pension for a single person was £95.25 per week, and for a married couple £152.30. Aon Consulting reported in

November 2007 that the British pension is equivalent to just 17 per cent of average UK earnings. This is the lowest level of pensions in Europe, where the average stands at 57 per cent.

See also retirement age.

pensions credit
A benefit that comes in two types: a 'savings credit' to reward people with some savings but who are still not well off and a 'guarantee credit' available to people below a certain income threshold (£200 a week for a couple in 2010). People in receipt of such benefits are also eligible for housing benefit and full council tax benefit. It was introduced by chancellor Gordon Brown in 2003 to alleviate poverty among older people. It replaced the minimum income guarantee of 1997.

People's Panel
A group of 5,000 people set up in 1998 to help government keep in touch with public opinion. In practice it had few functions and was wound up early in 2002.

people's peer
Introduced in April 2001 in an attempt to make the Lords more representative of ordinary people. People's peers were appointed by the House of Lords Appointments Commission – comprising four Lords and two commoners – chaired at the time by Lord Stevenson. The list was immediately ridiculed for being exclusive – seven knights and three professors were included as well as Lady (Elspeth) Howe, wife of the former Conservative chancellor. John Edmonds, the union leader, commented that 'The club remains as exclusive as ever'.

See also House of Lords; House of Lords Appointments Commission; House of Lords reform.

permanent secretary
The senior official who runs each department of government in Whitehall. Permanent secretaries are often correctly characterised as being largely drawn from Oxbridge universities, though

some, exceptionally, have no university experience. They are the chief advisors to the ministerial heads of the departments and are responsible for the civil servants employed by them. Their pay in 2002 was a maximum of £179,000 but went up in 2007 to a maximum of around £269,000.

personal social services
Residential and visiting services provided to people in need. In 1970 integrated social services departments were set up within local authorities to provide these services. The departments have responsibility for a range of people who are unable to look after themselves, especially children, children at risk within families and the elderly.

petition
See early day motion; political participation.

Phillips report, 2000
Report into the outbreak of bovine spongiform encephalitis (BSE, or 'mad cow disease'). The report was critical of Stephen Dorrell and a number of other former Conservative ministers who had played down the risk of BSE-infected beef contaminating humans. John Major and some of his colleagues apologised, in the wake of the report, for their role in the BSE crisis.

Phillis report, 2004
Independent review of government communications. Bob Phillis, chief executive of the Guardian Media Group, chaired an inquiry into government communication following the case involving Jo Moore, the political advisor who advised colleagues to use the disaster in the USA on 11 September 2001 as a good day to 'bury bad news'. His report recommended that: the Government Information Service should be disbanded; a permanent secretary should head a new communication service; the prime minister's communications team – one civil service and one political appointee – should report to the permanent secretary; there should be televised lobby

briefings; the culture of secrecy should be reduced; the media should separate comment from news; there should be special training for political advisors; the manipulation of government statistics should be ended. The government proved sympathetic to most of these suggestions.

See also Moore's email, 2001.

photo-opportunity

Name given to the carefully prearranged circumstances when politicians are photographed in a way designed to be symbolic, for example trying to look tough while driving a tank, or appealing, like Margaret Thatcher when she once cuddled a cow in a field.

Pinochet case, 1999–2000

General Augusto Pinochet, the former military dictator of Chile, on a visit to Britain, was arrested by British police in early 1999 in response to a request from a Spanish judge who was seeking to try the Chilean leader for crimes committed against Spanish nationals. Amnesty International, the group campaigning on behalf of those suffering at the hands of governments worldwide, was delighted, as were those on the left in Britain who had supported the Allende regime deposed by Pinochet with the help of the CIA. But other political figures, notably Margaret Thatcher and Norman Lamont, condemned the decision by home secretary Jack Straw to imprison a 'friend of Britain'. After considerable delay the general was found to be too ill to stand trial and was returned to his home country, where, upon arrival, he triumphantly stood up from his wheelchair. He died in December 2006.

> The fact that Augusto Pinochet was arrested while travelling abroad – almost unthinkable just 16 months ago – has sent a powerful message: no one is above the law, even national laws protecting you from prosecution. (Amnesty International, 2 March 2000)

> Sometimes democracy must be bathed in blood. (Pinochet, when dictator of Chile, 1979)

Pirate Party

www.pirateparty.org.uk

Originally a Swedish political party set up to campaign for legal file-sharing on the web and abolition of the patent system. In August 2009 it was officially recognised as a party in the UK.

Plaid Cymru (Party of Wales)

www.plaidcymru.org

Party founded in 1925 by John Saunders Lewis. Its aim is independence for Wales within Europe and the United Nations. Its first MP was Gwynfor Evans, who won the Carmarthen by-election in 1966. By the end of the 1970s there were three Plaid Cymru MPs but the proposed assembly for Wales was heavily rejected in the referendum held in 1979. Throughout the 1980s the party's MPs, including its leader Dafydd Wigley, kept the flame alight and in 1997 the referendum vote for a Welsh assembly was passed, albeit by a whisker.

Welsh nationalism is more cultural and language-based than its Scottish equivalent. While the party was socialistic in the 1970s, it arguably moved to the centre and right during the 1980s and 1990s. Dafydd Wigley resigned as leader in the summer of 2000 to be replaced by Ieuan Wyn Jones.

planned economy

To some extent the brainchild of John Maynard Keynes, who argued the economy could be managed to produce certain desirable goals like full employment. During the 1930s these ideas were supported by those who believed the USSR's planned economy was a success, but it was ridiculed by most Conservatives, a notable exception being Harold Macmillan. The Second World War appeared to reinforce Keynes's ideas, in that thorough planning of the economy achieved both full employment and victory. After the war the nationalisation of 20 per cent of the British economy was initially thought to be a success but was soon judged to be inefficient and costly. Further government intervention in the 1970s was judged a failure and Margaret Thatcher came to power determined to 'roll back the state' in terms of economic planning. This aversion to planning characterised the 1980s and, while New Labour was not ideologically opposed to planning, it did not restore the machinery dismantled by its predecessor in government.

See also nationalisation; Keynes, John Maynard.

planning

Britain has a system of planning permissions, whereby any organisation or person seeking to build or otherwise change the environment has to apply for permission to a planning authority, usually the local authority. Minor proposals – such as home extensions – are dealt with routinely by officials reporting to a council's planning committee. The same committee will closely consider any major proposal – such as a new supermarket – from either individuals or developers. The aim of such a system is to ensure that new developments do not clash with existing conditions or unacceptably offend against historical or aesthetic values. Consideration of the idea is then given and it is often possible for objectors to raise their cases at public inquiries chaired by a planning inspector. However, the system has come in for criticism, mainly from business. The public inquiry concerning the building of Heathrow's terminal 5 took 524 days, spread over five years. Consequently, revision of the system, to speed it up, was mooted by ministers in 2002, whereby the government would decide on projects in principle and only the details would be worked out in public inquiries. The Commons Transport, Local Government and Regions Committee criticised this as 'unworkable' and 'deeply flawed' in July 2002. To date the new system has not provoked any major problems, although criticisms are still made.

Plant report, 1993

Labour Party report that recommended a change in the electoral system. It favoured a regional list system for the European elections and the 'supplementary vote' for Westminster elections, an amended form

of the alternative vote. In 1998 the Jenkins committee also reported on electoral reform.

See also alternative vote; electoral reform; Jenkins report; proportional representation; supplementary vote.

plebiscite
See referendum.

plum job

Expression derived from a 17th-century term for £1,000: a 'plum' (in rather the same way that a 'monkey' is a term for £500). In that century a government job usually carried a salary of £1,000 a year, often for not very much effort: hence, a 'plum job'.

pluralism

Term with both a descriptive and a normative or prescriptive meaning. As a description of a political system, the US political scientist Robert Dahl argued that in his country, where power is widely dispersed, major decisions are taken through a process of negotiation between competing groups, as no group holds a monopoly of power on all issues. The role of government is that of a neutral 'referee', who makes sure that all interest groups play by the 'rules of the game'. An alternative and contrasting view, however, is that government is best seen as a weather vane, turning in the direction which reflects the prevailing wind of group interests. In relation to the British system, journalist Paul Johnson in 1957 said that 'Cabinet ministers are little more than chairmen of arbitration committees'. The US expert on British politics Samuel Beer said much the same thing in his description of his 'new group politics'.

The normative or prescriptive element in the theory argues that group-based politics, despite its failings, is the guarantee of a free society, unencumbered by an oppressive or interfering government. However, critics have rounded on the theory, and have pointed out, for example, that some groups have more status, resources or contacts with decision makers than others. Government, it is argued, must accommodate the interests of powerful financial or business groups if it wishes to manage a capitalist economy efficiently and thus be re-elected. Moreover, many citizens do not belong to a pressure group, and thus may be shut out of the decision-making process; even those who do may not necessarily be effectively represented.

See also corporatism.

plurality
See first past the post.

pocket borough
Name given to a parliamentary constituency where the seat(s) were partly or wholly controlled by either an individual or a group, usually landowners. About 120 English borough seats were so influenced by private patrons in the 18th century and well over 300 by the beginning of the 19th century. The Great Reform Act 1832 helped to rid the electoral system of such features.

See also Great Reform Act 1832.

police
The modern police force can be dated to Robert Peel's Metropolitan Police Act 1829. This established an organised system of police 'constables' for London, whose job was to implement the law and prevent crime. They were to achieve this through regular street patrols. They wore a uniform but were armed only with a truncheon. The same system was introduced nationally in 1856 and by 1860 there were more than 200 borough or county forces in England and Wales, financed by public funds, though in Ireland the Royal Ulster Constabulary (renamed Northern Ireland Police Service after the Good Friday agreement) took on a different form, to take account of the special circumstances there. In the 20th century police foot patrols were seen as an important reassurance to the public and a deterrent to criminals, but in the 1960s motorised 'panda' car patrols were introduced, which led to the disappearance of the familiar 'bobby on the beat'. In the

early 1980s inner-city riots and industrial disorder encouraged more centralised coordination of the police nationwide, the use of community styles of policing and increased powers of stop and search.

The large increases in pay for the police and huge increases in the law and order budget led to criticism of the police in the 1980s as the crime rate continued to soar and public confidence continued to slump. Further concern was expressed about the attitudes of police officers; for example, the Macpherson report (of the inquiry into the death of Steven Lawrence) stated that the Metropolitan Police, along with other public service organisations, were institutionally racist. Moreover, individual officers, and some units, have been accused of corruption and sexism. In 1995 Lancashire Constabulary was the first force to appoint a woman, Pauline Clair, as its chief constable. There are some 56 forces in the country, under the general control of the Home Office. By 2009 police numbers had risen to a record 142,688.

Police Service of Northern Ireland
www.psni.police.uk
Police service originally set up as the Royal Ulster Constabulary (RUC) in 1922, when Ireland was partitioned. Few Catholics joined as they were mostly opposed to partition and the force became perceived as a Protestant stronghold: only 11 per cent of the force were Catholic in 1969; by the end of the century it was only 8 per cent. Consequently the RUC never enjoyed widespread support and its ability to control sectarian violence was therefore limited. In 1999 the Patten report urged a number of changes to the RUC, including a much-resisted change of name to Police Service of Northern Ireland as well as new symbols and flags. Sir Ronnie Flanagan, head of the RUC, described the name change as a 'great hurt'.

policy community
Political science term to describe the way in which democratic governments make policy. According to this view, in each

policy area there are actors who wish to have an input – ministers, professional lobbyists, group leaders and civil servants – who have a degree of mutual dependence. Such actors can move in and out of the community, depending on developments, but there will be some continuity. The community will sometimes unite against perceived threats.

See also policy network.

policy formulation

How policy is formulated and decisions taken in the British system. There several theories on this. The 'pluralist' model, for example, emphasises the negotiation which takes place between different pressure groups or centres of power in the country. 'Corporatism', sometimes referred to as neo-pluralism, emphasises the decisions taken by elite members of key power groups and then presented to the legislature as necessary. The conventional Westminster model sees ministers taking advice from civil servants, making a decision and civil servants carrying out their instructions, though few believe this actually happens. Many commentators argue that civil servants, far from being compliant imple-menters of policy, regularly play a major role in formulation, implementation and, often, when they disagree, policy neutralis-ation. The 'ruling class' model follows the Marxist analysis that those taking the decisions subscribe consciously or uncon-sciously to the values of the economically dominant class.

The Butler report in 2004 criticised the informal – and by implication sloppy – decision making of the Blair government, infamous for forming policy while chatting on Number 10's 'sofa'.

policy-influencing legislature

One of the three types of legislature delin-eated by Philip Norton: the policy-making one, as in the USA; the policy-influencing one, as in Britain, which can occasionally modify or reject proposals; and those with no policy effect, like those in the former communist regimes of eastern Europe.

policy network

An approach to the burgeoning area of policy studies, based on the idea of a policy community. The policy community comprises complex networks of people and groups who have input into policy. Actors win access through a willingness to accept the rules of the game. Professor Rod Rhodes from Newcastle University developed the idea of a looser 'network', with frequent changes of membership, as opposed to the more cohesive 'policy community'.

See also policy community.

Policy Network

www.policy-network.org
International think-tank set up in 2000 with the support of Tony Blair and Gerhard Schröder, among others. Peter Mandelson became its chair in September 2001 and described it as 'not like a conventional think-tank': it does not originate policy but rather 'enables policy-makers to meet and debate and exchange ideas so that policy is strengthened in practice'. He predicted he would use the new body to launch an attack on anti-globalisation protestors. In 2009 Mandelson was the body's president and its chair was Giles Radice.

Policy Unit (Downing Street)

Advisory body set up by Harold Wilson in 1974. It was first headed by Bernard, now Lord, Donoughue and was retained subsequently both by James Callaghan and by the Conservative administrations in the 1980s. John Hoskyns, a businessman turned Conservative supporter, headed it under Margaret Thatcher and tried to make it a forward-thinking strategic unit. However, its chief use has probably been as a source of non-departmental advice to the prime minister, which he or she can rely on as relatively disinterested. There were usually eight members in the unit, drawn from civil servants and the outside world, although in 2003 Tony Blair had 13 in his Policy Unit. After Hoskyns, Thatcher reduced the importance of the unit but John Major relied on it substantially and under

POLITICS

him its leader, Sarah Hogg, actually wrote the manifesto for the Conservative Party in 1992. Tony Blair invited journalists as well as think-tank experts to join his Policy Unit. It is now seen as a de facto element in an emergent prime minister's department. David Miliband headed the unit until 2001 and then became an MP. Following the 2001 general election the prime minister's Policy Unit was merged with his Private Office, with Jonathon Powell in overall command. In 2009 the head of the Gordon Brown's Policy Unit was Dan Quarry; it worked closely with the Strategy Unit in the Cabinet Office. Jeremy Heywood acts as permanent secretary within Number 10 Downing Street.

See also prime minister's department.

political advertising

The promotion of party, leader, policy or a combination of all three by use of commercially inspired advertising and marketing techniques. British electoral law does not allow paid broadcasting (unlike in the USA) but parties are given free airtime for party political broadcasts (PPBs) – issued between elections – and party election broadcasts (PEBs). Governments have often used the media surreptitiously to advance political messages. The Conservative 1989 white paper 'Working for Patients' was backed by a £1.25 million campaign and in the same year water privatisation was presaged by a £21 million campaign. Conservative government spending on advertising stood at over £200 million annually by the end of the 1980s. The Tories and Liberal Democrats complained about figures in 2001 showing that spending on advertising by Whitehall departments had been unusually high in the weeks leading up to May 2001, the month in which Tony Blair had originally planned to hold a general election. Spending was £16.2 million in January, £16.5 million in February and a surprising £30.2 million in March: twice as much for that month than was spent by either of the world's biggest advertisers, Unilever and Procter & Gamble.

political advisor

Someone, often classed as a temporary civil servant, employed by a minister to provide essentially political advice. Traditionally a US phenomenon, it is customary for an incoming administration to install its supporters in key posts. During the 1970s Labour ministers began to appoint special advisors; for example, Jack Straw was appointed by Barbara Castle and Bernard Donoughue became senior policy advisor to Harold Wilson and then James Callaghan. John Major was keener than Margaret Thatcher on non-elected advisors, appointing 32, but the Blair government quickly put more than 50 in place, especially in posts with special media liaison functions. Before the 2001 general election there were 78 special advisors, who cost the taxpayer nearly £4 million, with the average salary being £56,000; around 30 worked in the prime minister's office. Usually these jobs are not advertised but are the result of previous friendships and contacts. Anji Hunter – a close aide to Blair until she left for the private sector – had known Blair since school. When the 2001 general election was called the special advisors resigned. Some were reappointed or repositioned but others entered parliament, including David Milliband, James Purnell and Andy Burnham.

Some argue that importing a new 'tier' of government in the form of advisors makes for more effectiveness and greater clarity, as the idea of a neutral civil service has in recent years been thrown into question. Others suggest that such appointments undermine open government by encouraging the employment of unelected, and therefore unaccountable, individuals, and expose senior politicians to the charge of 'cronyism' and patronage. Lord Butler of Brockwell, the outgoing secretary to the cabinet in 1997, was critical of the role played by political advisors under New Labour. Following the Jo Moore email scandal, the Committee on Standards in Public Life chose to investigate the relationship between ministers, advisors and civil servants. On 10 May 2008 the *Guardian* reported that Gordon Brown's spending on advisors had increased by £500,000, to £6.3 million. Brown had 24 advisors, while Harriet Harman and Des Browne each had four, making a total of 54 special advisors employed by Brown's government. Some of these new appointments were used to beef up Brown's Internet output in terms of blogs and even Twitter. Francis Muad for the Conservatives criticised the 'staggering cost and extent of the Labour spin machine across Whitehall'.

See also campaign strategist; Moore's email; prime minister's department.

political agenda

Not all group or social concerns get into the arena of public or political debate and hence become candidates for some kind of political action. What defines something as political has been hotly debated by thinkers for many years; however, the political scientist Samuel Finer gives us a guide with his concept of the 'political predicament', as discussed in his *Comparative Government* (1970). This is where opinion is divided on a communal issue, or at least one which affects a substantial proportion of a community, and where an authoritative decision will have implications for all.

For example, a plan to build a bypass on agricultural land in order to relieve a congested village will provoke intense and irreconcilable opinions from the groups concerned, and thus becomes a matter for the political agenda of the local people, the county council and ultimately the Department for Environment, Food and Rural Affairs. Competing groups will attempt to control the political agenda by controlling the media agenda. In 1997 Labour was perceived as dominating the media agenda with welfare and social policy, while the Conservatives could not shift attention away from a poor economic record and damaging stories of sleaze.

See also agenda setting; politics; power.

political apathy

The Hansard Society conducts an annual audit of the nation regarding willingness to participate in politics. In March 2008 the results indicated the following: only 53 per cent of voters say they are certain to vote; only 4 per cent have ever made a political donation; 55 per cent say they know nothing much about politics and are indifferent about a bill of rights or a written constitution; and only 23 per cent of the 18–24 age group say they will vote, compared with 78 per cent of the over-65s. Worse, newspaper readership is falling, while television news and current affairs programmes struggle for audiences. People are good at grumbling about everything, yet they feel no inclination to lift a finger to change anything. The fact that young people are the most apathetic suggests the problem is not going to get better any time soon. If we continue down this road, where are we likely to end up? With political parties which are mere shells, lacking membership but customised to organising and winning the votes the constitution says are needed to win office. Concerned reformers detect a strong undercurrent of anger and disillusionment with politicians, especially since the MPs' expenses scandal of 2008–09. These are the perfect conditions for parties on the extreme to wade in with their seductively easy simplicities or, as de Tocqueville wrote, when the public 'assents to the clamour of the mountebank who knows the secret of stimulating its taste'.

political business cycle

Term used to describe the tendency of governments to arrange elections to coincide with upturns in the national economy and thus use a 'feel good' factor to electoral advantage. In 1986 chancellor Nigel Lawson expanded the economy for a projected election in 1987, one which the Conservatives easily won. However, a government can survive unpropitious economic cycles; for example, John Major fought and won the 1992 general election against the background of recession. Labour chancellor Gordon Brown claimed that he would avoid 'boom and bust' policies; however, some observers saw signs that he prepared the ground for the 2001 general election by increasing public spending and leaving the Monetary Policy Committee to take care of interest rates. His self-congratulatory claims to have broken the 'boom and bust' cycle looked more than tattered after 2007, when the economy careered into a major recession following the US banking crisis arising from the selling of sub-prime mortgages. Brown performed well under pressure to gather investment to save the British banking system but his reputation as a brilliant chancellor had faded away.

See also 'boom and bust'; Monetary Policy Committee.

political communications
The messages which link party or government to the voter through the central agencies of mass communication. Historically, the press was the first of the mass media, its origins being the tracts and pamphlets of the early 17th century. Indeed, in the 1750s political comment was often part and parcel of popular folk songs, which escaped the attention of the authorities and the serious criminal charge of sedition. During the 18th century, the political class was deeply suspicious of comment; indeed, reports of debates had to be smuggled out of parliament. Gradually the principle of the free press was established, a significant turning point being the abolition of the Stamp Act, and today the principle of a free press independent of government control is jealously guarded by newspapers, which retain the right to adopt political positions critical of government. Newspaper editors and many politicians insist that statutory controls to protect the privacy of prominent individuals would be a slippery slope to press censorship. This having been said, radical views which challenge the political order in Britain are seldom, if ever, supported in a national tabloid or quality newspaper. Although spin doctors and the prime minister's press secretary provide stories via lobby correspondents to the national dailies, broadcast media now dominate the communications of political parties and governments. Press

conferences, news releases and ministerial statements are timed to meet the deadlines of news organisations and are often presented against professionally designed exhibition backdrops. Other instances of this direct communication to the electorate is the practice, extensively developed since 1997, of ministerial announcements on policy initiatives being released to the media before parliament has been informed, concern about which was voiced in late summer 2000 by Betty Boothroyd, the retiring speaker of the House of Commons.

These changes have been reflected in the 'Political Communications' series of books (studies of British election campaigns published since 1979). They bring together senior politicians, campaign strategists, media professionals and academics, who provide specific insights into an election campaign, the most recent edition being *The General Election Campaign of 2005*, edited by Dominic Wring *et al.* (2007).

The development of the Internet and email has increased the opportunities for parties, governments and other campaigning organisations to communicate directly with voters and other interested parties, a trend that has led to a kind of 'virtual' democracy. However, as with all open polities, it can be exploited by those opposed to the very existence of democracy, like the neo-Nazi organisation Combat 18, and to a lesser extent far-right parties such as the British National Party. The political blogosphere in Britain has developed rapidly over the past decade, with more rightwing blogs such as Iain Dale's Diary and Guido Fawkes proving the most popular.

political correctness
See political language.

political culture
Popular attitudes towards politics in general and, in particular, political authority, the institutions of government and national leadership. Public opinion is what the majority of people think at any one point in time, whereas political culture refers to embedded attitudes. Gabriel Almond and

Sidney Verba's classic *Civic Culture* (1963) explored how some societies breed citizens who seem to trust their leaders and feel an identity with their governments, while others do not provide this basic requirement, with adverse consequences for their political stability. It is a fact that some societies seem to demonstrate continuity of characteristics. For example, Russia has always been led by a revered authoritarian and it was arguably the political culture which contributed to the emergence under the Soviet Union of Joseph Stalin, a leader with similar characteristics to the tsars of old. Similar things might be said of Chinese politics, where Mao resembled the old-fashioned emperors he outwardly damned.

political language
In *Politics and the English Language* (1947), George Orwell pointed to the use of language as an instrument of thought control, and in particular he warned against the use of terms which obscure meaning. In his 1949 novel *Nineteen Eighty-Four* he gave creative expression to this view in a nightmare vision of Britain, where the Ministry of Truth was responsible for propaganda, the Ministry of Love for internal control and the Thought Police were always on the look-out for deviant individuals who gave themselves away by using the wrong expressions. While Orwell mainly had Stalin's terror in mind, his ideas have currency in the world of modern British politics. 'Political correctness', which began on US campuses in the 1980s, is the concern not to use expressions or words which offend minority groups such as women, members of ethnic minorities or others disadvantaged by social circumstances. The practice was adopted in Britain and has now been absorbed into mainstream discourse, especially by many business and government organisations. While some have ridiculed the more absurd examples of the practice (see, for example, Henry Beard and Christopher Cerf's *The Official Politically Correct Dictionary and Handbook*, 1993), others have suggested that language carries powerful emotional

and psychological 'charges' which play their part in the transmission of ideological messages. During the 1980s and 1990s, 'new right' concepts such as 'market forces' and 'freedom of choice' quickly invaded everyday speech; school heads became 'managers' and spoke of 'buying teachers' for their institution. With the election of the New Labour government in 1997, a new language or discourse seemed to emerge. Norman Fairclough, Professor of Linguistics at Lancaster University, published a book entitled *New Labour, New Language?* (2000), which charted the way in which Labour politicians, Tony Blair in particular, made use of a distinctive type of language which furthered the 'third way' agenda.

political marketing
A many-faceted phenomenon clearly different to advertising. Advertising is concerned with the promotion of an existing product, whereas marketing is concerned with identifying the concerns of customers (or voters) and then supplying a product or service that satisfies them. As an approach to politics, it uses marketing concepts such as 'packaging', 'positioning' and 'targeting', and investigates the behaviour of political parties, which now compete for votes from an increasingly choosy, volatile electorate. Margaret Thatcher was probably the first modern-day leader to be 'packaged', in her instance by campaign consultant Gordon Reece, for the 1983 general election. Following its disastrous performance in that election, the Labour Party under Neil Kinnock invited marketing and advertising consultants to advise on how the party could recover lost voters. People often associate Peter Mandelson with this revolution in the party's thinking, but the process began before his arrival as communications director for the Labour Party in 1985. Major changes then took place within the party, including the development of New Labour, when Tony Blair, advised by political strategist Philip Gould, repositioned the party in the centre-ground of British politics. The party went on to use

focus groups extensively as tools by which to discover the motivational levers of voters. Although Labour won a landslide in the 1997 election, it is not at all clear whether this was wholly the result of changes in policy and presentation, or whether it was a by-product of voters' hostility to John Major's faction-ridden government, which was associated with sleaze and hypocrisy.

After 1997 marketing informed many aspects of the Labour government's programme of modernising Britain, including the citizens' panels, encouraging a consumer focus in public service provision, introducing the 'best value' initiative for local government and making central government departments, including the Cabinet Office and Number 10, more 'consumer-friendly' to voters. This concern for establishing a dialogue with voter citizens is shared by all major parties, which regularly conduct market research. It is for this reason that the communication arts of marketing and advertising have become a growth industry in British public life. Jennifer Lees-Marshment's book *Political Marketing and British Political Parties* (2001) asserts that parties now conceive their political strategies in marketing terms. It follows that ideology is less important, that politicians tend to follow rather than lead the voters or 'consumers' and that eliciting what the voter wants through focus groups, polling and so forth has become a key aspect of creating political programmes. Lees-Marshment argues that Labour in 1983 had a 'product-based' message which was not attuned to voter demands and consequently failed. By 1987 the party had moved to a 'sales-based' strategy but the product was too similar to that of 1983 and it failed again. The same thing happened again, though more narrowly, in 1992 but by 1997, under Blair, the product had been refashioned and remarketed, with the resultant landslide victory. However, Blair's determination to forge ahead with the hugely unpopular war on Iraq in March 2003 reveals that there are limits and exceptions to the extent to which New Labour based its approach on marketing.

Political Office

A section in 10 Downing Street. It deals with communication between the prime minister and the wider party machine, parliament and the country. The political secretary was a role which assumed great importance under Harold Wilson when Marcia Williams held it, though less so under Edward Heath, when Douglas Hurd held the post. The Political Office is funded from party sources and not the public purse. In June 2001 the office was changed as Sally Morgan moved to the Lords and Anji Hunter became head of the Office of Government Relations – however, she left for a post in industry in late 2001. With this departure Tony Blair, in November 2001, brought Sally Morgan, now in the House of Lords, back into Number 10 to replace Hunter with the title of director of political and government relations.

See also prime minister's department.

political participation

To work efficiently, democracies are predicated upon a degree of participation. In practice this is generally minimal, apart from the act of voting in elections, in which generally 60–80 per cent engage within Britain; at local elections, however, the level, often only 30–40 per cent, is so low there has been some concern at the apathy shown. Figures released at the end of January 2002 revealed that the three major parties between them had memberships totalling a mere two-thirds of a million and falling, or under 2 per cent of the population. Activist numbers are even lower.

There has been more activism in pressure groups over the past decades, with environmental ones witnessing sharp upturns in their memberships. Greenpeace, Friends of the Earth and the Royal Society for the Protection of Birds all increased their membership from 2000 to 2002.

Over 60 per cent of citizens have signed petitions on some issue; over 5 per cent have joined protest marches; and nearly 15 per cent have attended protest meetings of some kind. Studies show activism tends to increase both with age – 24 per cent of 35–54-year-olds described themselves as politically active, compared with only 3 per cent of 18–24-year-olds in a poll reported in the *Guardian* in January 1998 – and with social class – the lower down the occupational hierarchy voters are, the less likely they are to be politically active. In an article in the *Guardian* in September 2001 Paul Whiteley of Sheffield University reported his study which had shown that 16 per cent of voters were certainly willing to demonstrate on an issue about which they felt strongly and another 18 per cent said they might be. Protestors were more likely to be middle class, younger and more highly educated than non-protestors. Only 15 per cent of working-class respondents were likely protestors, compared with 19 per cent of middle-class ones.

Political Parties, Elections and Referendums Act 2000

Act limiting expenditure by parties on elections to £20 million per party. It banned donations from abroad and limited anonymous donations to political parties to £5,000. It also established the Electoral Commission, to monitor the expenditure and income of political parties engaging in elections and referendums.

political party

In democracies, organisations that seek to win sufficient public support to take control of the government. In the 19th century, when the electorate had been expanded, groups of politicians organised themselves to appeal to voters, so setting up party organisations and political programmes. By the end of that century political parties dominated the business of parliament. In the 20th century the struggle between the party of government and the main opposition party was made more formal and became the major daily feature of politics between elections. The Conservative Party was the first to organise and did so from its Tory provenance and base in parliament. The Liberal Party was somewhat similar. Labour, by contrast, originated outside

Westminster – in an alliance of unions and socialist societies – and was designed to establish a foothold in the legislature. Consequently, the organisations of the two main parties in Britain have tended to reflect the centralised, 'top down' history of the Conservatives and the grass roots, 'bottom up' democratic origins of Labour. The political scientist Robert McKenzie argued that despite Labour's apparent democratic organisation it was in reality led from the centre. Indeed, since the mid-1980s there has been increased centralisation in the Labour Party, which has come to embrace a corporate style of organisation and administration. The election of Tony Blair as a powerful individual leader and the need of the party to offer a united front to the voters accentuated these centralising tendencies.

The nationalist parties in Wales and Scotland and the parties in Northern Ireland appeal to different factions in the political culture. In 1997 there were 123 registered political parties. In the 1997 general election, 3,724 candidates stood, of whom 1,592 polled less than 5 per cent of the votes in their constituencies and therefore lost their deposits of £500.

political populism

A tendency to appeal to the opinions and preferences of ordinary people. The term takes its name from a US 19th-century movement when farmers expressed their disillusion that they had been let down by false political promises and left to drift into debt. More sophisticated politicians protest that such a populist political approach is irresponsible, as the mass of people are often ill-informed and likely to favour simple, short-term solutions to complex problems. British politicians often allow their policies or their rhetoric to become populist – the Thatcherite championing of capital punishment in the 1980s, for example – but they usually fall in line behind more responsible policies eventually, as in the case of home secretary Douglas Hurd's firm rejection of the death penalty during the key 1980s debates. Having said this, it is in the nature of politics – or at least British politics – to add some degree of populist gloss to most policies.

political satire

It has long been a part of British political culture that the 'ruled' enjoy a laugh at the expense of their rulers. This tendency has competed at times with a deference to the 'upper classes', most noticeable in the tendency of some working-class voters to support the Conservatives. The barrier of deference was broken in the late 1950s and early 1960s by the publication of the magazine *Private Eye* and *Beyond the Fringe*, the satirical revue featuring Dudley Moore, Peter Cook, Alan Bennett and Jonathan Miller. This revue-style approach was later used again in the hugely popular ground-breaking television show *That Was the Week That Was*, screened in 1962 and 1963, which introduced David Frost and many others to the airwaves. In the 1980s the rubberised puppet television show *Spitting Image* made a huge impact on audiences with a variety of satirical sketches of the great and good. Other satirical offerings have included Harry 'loadsamoney' Enfield, who, for many, epitomised the greed of the 1980s. With the coming of the Blair government in 1997, and the ineffectual Conservative opposition in the early years, some argued that satirists were the only true opposition to the new wunderkind, an example being Rory Bremner, with his brilliant, biting impressions. Since the departure of Blair, satire appears to have been reinforced by the brilliant *The Thick of It*, the ongoing *Have I Got News For You* and on Radio 4 the *News Quiz* and the *Now Show*.

political socialisation

The process by which individuals acquire attitudes towards politics and the political system. The principal agents in this process include:

1 family, especially mother and father, as significant adults who introduce the child to adult authority;

2 schooling, where the hidden curriculum of rules, teacher authority and the examination system represent a type of micro political system;
3 peer group pressure;
4 the disciplines of work;
5 the mass media.

The subtle mix of factors and the development of the personality are probably more important than any individual factor. Moreover, while parents and schooling may leave a powerful impression, young people, perhaps in their first years at university, may rebel against a conservative upbringing, become radicalised and enter student politics on either the left or right. In 1997, New Labour targeted first-time voters (18–29-year-olds), among other groups, with the result that they provided the party with one of its largest swings.

Political Studies Association (PSA)

www.psa.ac.uk
The national body for professional academics, graduates and others interested in the discipline. Membership is available to individuals and institutions (corporate membership). It holds an annual conference, where members participate in workshops and seminars. The PSA publishes: the *British Journal of Political and International Relations*; *Political Studies*; *Political Studies Review*; *Politics*; and its most recent magazine, *Political Insight*.

political violence

To some, a logically inconsistent term, in that politics is the peaceful resolution of conflict. British politics since the Civil War has been characterised by its generally peaceful nature. This may be because the country solved many of its major problems sequentially and was not overwhelmed by catastrophes as some other countries were. For example, the struggle between crown and church was over by the 16th century, that between crown and state by the end of the 17th and that between the aristocracy and bourgeoisie by the end of the 19th century. This is not to say British politics is always peaceful. Violence was

used by government as well as by protestors
during: the clashes between Mosleyites and
opponents in the East End of London in
the 1930s; the riots in the inner cities in the
early 1980s; the miners' strike in 1984–85;
and the riots over the poll tax in 1990.
Northern Ireland, of course, saw extreme
political violence from the late 1960s.

politics
Best understood as a multifaceted
phenomenon involving the shaping and
the sharing of power and the non-violent
resolution of conflict. As political scientist
Harold Lasswell put it: 'who gets what,
when and how'. For Bernard Crick, it is
a moral imperative: 'politics is not just a
necessary evil, it is a definite good. Political
activity is a type of moral activity; it is a
fine activity and it is inventive, flexible,
enjoyable and human.' The study of politics
dates back to Aristotle and Plato, and is
regarded as the oldest of the social sciences.
It is closely linked to history, law, sociology,
economics, psychology, systems theory and
behavioural science. It also has a number of
sub-branches: political philosophy, political
theory, political analysis, international
relations and psephology.

> Politics is like boxing – you try to knock out
> your opponent. (Idi Amin, 1976)

> I reject the cynical view that politics is
> inevitably, or even usually, dirty business.
> (Richard Nixon, 1973)

> Politics is the art of acquiring, holding and
> wielding power. (Indira Gandhi, 1975)

> I used to say that politics was the second
> oldest profession and have come to know it
> bears a gross similarity to the first. (Ronald
> Reagan, 1979)

> It is evident that the state is a creation of
> nature and that man is by nature a political
> animal. (Aristotle, *Politics*, 350 BC)

> Politics is a strife of interests masquerading
> as a contest of principles. (Ambrose Bierce,
> *The Devil's Dictionary*, 1906)

> Where some people are very wealthy and
> others have nothing, the result will either be
> extreme democracy or despotism will come
> from either of these excesses. (Aristotle,
> *Politics*, 350 BC)

Politics Association
www.politics-association.org.uk
Body set up by (Sir) Bernard Crick and
others in 1969 to campaign for political
literacy. It quickly became the professional
body of politics teachers in schools and
colleges and an active lobbyist for more
political education, as well as a provider
of a range of services to members. *Talking
Politics* was the organisation's high-quality
tri-annual journal. The Association was
(sadly) wound up in 2006.

poll tax
See community charge.

polyarchy
See pluralism.

Ponting affair, 1985
See Ponting, Clive.

Popular Front
Left-wing campaign in the mid-1930s
designed to augment the defence of
Republican Spain. It was an attempt to
harness the activism of communists with
the broader labour movement but the
involvement of communism set it beyond
the pale for the Labour Party leadership
and they expelled Stafford Cripps and
Aneurin Bevan for joining it. The left-wing
magazine *Tribune* was established as part of
the campaign.

populism
See political populism.

portfolio
Term used to describe the responsibilities
undertaken by a minister. A minister might
be said to have taken on the 'transport' or
'health' portfolio. Occasionally a prime
minister will appoint an all-purpose
non-departmental cabinet minister who is
known as 'minister without portfolio'.

positive discrimination
This is the practice of intervening to
improve the chances of a usually disadvantaged group in a particular area.

Examples include all-women short-lists for parliamentary candidates or preference for lower socio-economic groups for entry into higher education.

Post Office part privatisation

Margaret Thatcher shrank from privatising the Post Office but Peter Mandelson, business secretary in 2008, chose to enter this fraught area with a suggestion that part of its activities be sold off to a Dutch firm, TNT. The problem was that the volume of mail had shrunk as a result of email and text messaging, and was calculated to shrink further, by 8 per cent to April 2010, costing £560 million in revenue. Postcom, the regulator, reckoned the business was 40 per cent less efficient than its competitors. Royal Mail's pension fund was also heavily in deficit, by some £6 billion, but the government would have to shoulder that responsibility, as no private company would touch it. Labour MPs were very unhappy with the idea and a large revolt ensured in the summer of 2009 that the idea was dropped.

postal voting

The distribution and return of a ballot paper by post. In Britain anyone on the electoral register can opt for a postal vote, but they have to apply to their local electoral registration office. The ballot must be returned before the close of the poll (usually 10 p.m. on the day of the election).

Experiments in the wake of the poor voter turnout in the 2001 general election revealed that postal voting tends to increase turnout by several percentage points. Accordingly, wider experiments were tried in the local and European elections in 2004, when in some regions postal ballots were made compulsory and not optional. However, the original two areas designated were increased by the government to four, all of them in the north. The measures were criticised by the Electoral Commission and by the Conservatives, who saw it merely as an attempt by Labour to increase turnout in areas where it would be of party advantage. Problems were encountered, including a failure to distribute voting forms in good

time, as well as accusations of fraud and intimidation in certain areas, including Lancashire and Bradford. However, the experiment did succeed in raising turnout by an appreciable amount. In August 2004 the Electoral Commission concluded in a report that 'all-postal voting should no longer be pursued for use at UK elections'. The reasons given were that, despite the 5 percentage point increase in turnout it had produced, the experiment the previous June had been so beset with problems and alleged abuses that the public's faith in the new system had been badly damaged. Critics pointed out that postal voting addressed only a symptom, not the cause: loss of faith and interest in the political process.

postwar consensus

Term used to describe the bipartisan agreement between Labour and the Conservatives formed during the war, which continued into peace and for the two subsequent decades. It grew out of a number of common experiences and values: the shared wartime alliance against a common enemy; successful government economic intervention; the blunting of ideological conflict caused by cooperation in the coalition government; the Beveridge report on welfare services; and the acceptance of Keynesianism as a new orthodoxy in macro-economics. The main elements of the consensus were: a mixed economy with a large public sector but retaining a wealth-creating private one; a welfare state providing services to all citizens irrespective of status; close cooperation with the trade unions and employers' organisations; and an acceptance of compromise and consultation as the best means of governing. What economic failure had not destroyed of the consensus by the mid-1970s, Margaret Thatcher did much to complete when she came to power in 1979. Her alternative agenda of promoting the free market was arguably so successful that it had convinced Labour to adopt it by the middle of the 1990s and thus created a new consensus. By 2001 the Conservatives had moved from their policy of tight control on expenditure to one which was comparable to that of Labour, suggesting a leftward shift towards a new 'neo-Thatcher' consensus.

poverty
The lack of sufficient money to conduct a life of any comfort, either in absolute terms or in comparison with the rest of society. After the Second World War, many politicians assumed the welfare state had abolished poverty but during the 1960s academics like Peter Townsend and Colin Titmus revealed that widespread poverty still existed, especially in the inner cities. In the 1980s the concept was contested by Conservative ministers, who claimed that absolute poverty had been abolished; people classed as being in poverty then would not have been so classified earlier in the century. The Child Poverty Action Group has no such doubts, and stated in its 1996 study *Poverty: The Facts* that 'Poverty blights the lives of around a quarter of the UK's population and a third of its children'. Calculations by social statisticians revealed that during the Conservative administrations of Margaret Thatcher and John Major the poorest 10 per cent of the population suffered an absolute decrease in income in real terms, while the richest 10 per cent enjoyed over a 50 per cent increase. The United Nations *Human Development* annual report in September 1998 stated that deprivation, chronic unemployment and low literacy levels had turned Britain into one of the most poverty stricken of the developed countries. It found that 9 per cent of Britons would not reach the age of 60, over one-fifth of adults were functionally illiterate and 13.5 per cent were below the internationally recognised poverty line (50 per cent of median disposable income). To reinforce such worrying figures about British poverty a further report by the Child Poverty Action Group in June 2000 asserted that: 10 per cent of children go without school meals, as their families cannot afford them; differences in intellectual development between children in middle-class and poor families can be seen at 22 months; 2.5 million children live in households where

income support is the only finance available; 63 per cent of children in single-parent families live in poverty.

In July 2001 the Labour government reported that the income gap had not closed during its years in power. Roy Hattersley in the *Guardian* (16 July 2001) deplored the fact that the 'poorest 10 per cent of the population had fallen to 2.9 per cent of overall income. The richest 10 per cent still pocketed 27 per cent.' He was especially concerned that the government claimed it did not matter if the income gap grew. Alistair Darling, when minister for social security, argued that income growth in absolute terms was the most important factor for the poor. Between 1994–95 and 1998–99, income growth after household costs was 10 per cent for the bottom decile and 13 per cent for the top decile. Martin Barnes of the Child Poverty Action Group insisted:

> Concern about the growing gap between rich and poor should not be dismissed as just the politics of envy. Increasing the incomes of the poor will not, in itself, deliver social justice if inequalities in health, education, well-being and opportunity remain.

The economic crisis that began in 2007 removed any notion Gordon Brown might have entertained regarding eliminating child poverty in UK.

> Anyone who has struggled with poverty will know how extremely expensive it is to be poor. (James Baldwin, *Nobody Knows My Name*, 1961)

> Poverty makes you sad as well as wise. (Berthold Brecht, *Mother Courage and Her Children*, 1949)

> The child was diseased at birth – stricken with an hereditary illness that only the most vital of men can shake off. I mean poverty – the most deadly and prevalent of all diseases. (Eugene O'Neill, *All God's Chillun Got Wings*, 1924)

See also inequality; social exclusion.

power
A defining quality of politics and arguably the core of the subject, but also one of

the most hotly disputed concepts in social science. A baseline definition of power is given by the US political scientist Robert Dahl, whose intuitive idea of power 'is that A has power over B to the extent that he can get B to do something that B would otherwise not do'. Other interpretations demonstrate the complexity of the power relation. Bertrand Russell, the British mathematician and philosopher, stated that power is 'the production of intended effects'. Max Weber applied a sociological perspective: power is 'the probability that an actor in a social relationship will be in a position to carry out his own will despite resistance'. This points to the fact that power is the quality of a social relationship, not an absolute. As suggested by Hannah Arendt, a political scientist, power 'is not the property of an individual' but 'corresponds to the human ability not just to act but to act in concert'. Talcott Parson, one of the fathers of structural functionalism, elaborated the social roots of power by suggesting that it is 'a generalised facility or resource in the society, analogous to money, which enables the achievement of collective goods through the agreement of members of a society to legitimate leadership positions whose incumbents further the goals of the system'. Marxist writers like Nicos Poulantzas, however, prefer to focus upon class relationships; thus power is the 'capacity of a class to realise its specific objective interests'. Steven Lukes, a British political scientist, takes an altogether different approach: rather than focus on one definition he provides three 'faces' of power. The first 'face' is the ability of people, whether as individuals, groups or large institutions like government, to make decisions and get them implemented, an example of this being Jack Straw's proposals on law and order, which were successfully steered through the legislative process and became the Crime and Disorder Act 1998. The second 'face' of power is the control of the issues agenda or the list of issues which enter the policy arena, and more importantly those that do not. Pressure groups and political parties (the governing

one in particular) have a major role in placing issues on the agenda, for example New Labour's 1997 manifesto commitment to promote policies which would sustain the environment and develop an integrated transport policy. It is unlikely that Labour, or any other mainstream party, would allow a proposal to abolish private transport to get on to the political agenda. Here, then, is an example of power, exercised in the negative sense, of keeping items off the agenda, in other words a form of non-decision making. The third 'face' of power is what Lukes calls 'the shaping of desires', achieved through the prevailing ideas and values of a society. He claims that this is the most insidious and pervasive demonstration of power, where individuals are trapped within a system of thought and are thus 'brainwashed' by an ideology which prevents them from seeing their real, 'objective' interests. Former cabinet minister David Owen wrote a book on *The Hubris Syndrome* (2007) in which he suggested that politicians became ill through excessive periods in power to the extent that their judgement becomes seriously impeded.

> There are few minds to which tyranny is not delightful. (Samuel Johnson)

> So that in the first place I put for a general inclination of all mankind a perpetual and restless desire of power after power, that ceases only in death. (Thomas Hobbes, *Leviathan*, 1651)

> Tyrants seldom want pretexts. (Edmund Burke)

> What luck for the rulers that men do not think. (Adolf Hitler)

> The undesirable classes never liquidate themselves. (Joseph Stalin in reply to Lady Astor, who asked him when he was 'going to stop killing people')

> As long as men worship Caesars and Napoleons, Caesars and Napoleons will duly rise and make them miserable. (Aldous Huxley, 1937)

> I have no objection to politicians being interested in personal power. (Michael Foot, 1966)

Man is born to seek power, yet his actual condition makes him a slave to the power of others. (Hans J. Morganthau, US political scientist)

Power tends to corrupt and absolute power corrupts absolutely. (Lord Acton)

See also elite; hegemony; Marxism; pluralism; power elite.

power elite

Term associated with C. Wright Mills's radical elite theory of the 1950s. Mills argued that a 'military industrial complex' existed in the USA. This was a network of elites, dominant in government, the military and industry, who served their own interests. More loosely defined, Britain has its own power elites, known as the 'establishment'. In keeping with classical elite theory, these constantly recruit new members to perpetuate the rule of the few over the many. Thus the old elites associated with the Tory party, judiciary and civil service have been reinvigorated with new people. On 1 November 1998 the *Observer* published a list of the 300 most powerful people in Britain. In the run-up to the 2010 general election, there was much press coverage of the 'Notting Hill set', reputed to be David Cameron's clique of political friends and advisors.

power sharing

Used to describe an executive for Northern Ireland in which representatives of the nationalists and the loyalists share power. This was tried in January 1974 after the 1973 Sunningdale agreement but the loyalists opposed it, called a general strike, and the initiative foundered after only five months. A new initiative was established by the Good Friday agreement in 1998, with David Trimble as the first minister and Seamus Mallon as his deputy. However, the executive did not last long as it sundered on the issue of the IRA abandoning its weapons; in the autumn of 2002 it was suspended over a dispute arising from alleged spying but in 2007 the two largest parties in the assembly, Sinn Fein and the Democratic Unionists, agreed

to support a period of government. This led to the unlikely accession to power of Ian Paisley as first minister, succeeded by Peter Robinson a year later.

pre-legislative scrutiny

The consideration of a draft bill by a parliamentary committee before the bill is presented to parliament for its first reading. A number of bills are now subject to this process. Recently there has been a tendency for such 'draft bills' to be referred to ad hoc joint committees of both houses. Examples in the 2003–04 parliamentary session included the joint committee on the draft Civil Contingencies Bill and the joint committee on the draft Gambling Bill. In 1997 the Modernisation Committee of the House of Commons identified three purposes for this innovation: connecting with the public by involving outside bodies and individuals in the legislative process; changing a bill to produce better law; and achieving consensus so that a bill completes its passage more smoothly. While 10 bills were so scrutinised 2002–03 and 2003–04, only four received similar treatment during 2004–06.

prerogative powers

The legal powers and privileges of the sovereign. Many of them date back to medieval times, when the monarch had sweeping powers over all aspects of the nation's life. In the 16th century the scope of the prerogative was extended by Elizabeth I and included the appointment of ministers, the declaration of war, the signing of treaties and the summoning and dissolution of parliament. These powers became bones of contention under the Stuarts, who tried to exercise their powers while parliament sought to restrict them. This led to the English Civil War. The royal prerogative is now exercised only on the 'advice' of the minister responsible in virtually all cases; in other words, it has become the property no longer of the monarch but of the elected government. Gordon Brown expressed the desire to limit such prerogative power when he came to power in 2007 but little came of such good intentions.

'presidential' government

Many commentators argue that the prime minister in Britain has become such a dominant figure by virtue of the ability to appoint and dismiss ministers, to set priorities, to present the 'brand' of the party to the public and to establish the dominant policy drives of the government that the office has become more akin to the US president. This neglects the fact that the latter has to negotiate constantly with a reluctant Congress and has strict constitutional limits on powers, unlike the prime minister, who is more able to make of the job what he or she may.

press

Newspapers first appeared in the 18th century with the *Times* and the *Observer*; mass circulation arrived in the late 19th century with the *Daily Mail* and the *Daily Express*. New technology eventually enabled the tabloids to sell millions of copies every day and reach the majority of the working class. There are presently three 'popular' papers – the *Daily Mirror, Star* and *Sun*; two 'mid-market' papers – the *Daily Mail* and *Daily Express*; and five 'qualities' – the *Guardian, Times, Daily Telegraph, Independent* and *Financial Times*. In addition there are three popular Sunday papers, two mid-market Sunday papers and four qualities. After the Second World War, the Conservatives commanded support from the majority of newspapers and in the 1980s this imbalance became even more pronounced. In the 1990s, however, the press began to realign, most dramatically in the case of the *Sun*, which switched its allegiance to New Labour as soon as the 1997 general election campaign started.

The press has suffered substantial declines in circulation over the past decades but still performs valuable political functions in setting the political agenda and informing public debate. A spectacular example of the latter was in May–June 2009, when the *Daily Telegraph* published full details of MPs' expenses. For the last two to three decades, the British press, in common with the press virtually worldwide,

has been losing readers at the rate of some 2–3 per cent a year. Newspapers have tried to minimise the trend but the growth of free news outlets and the disinclination of young people to read newspapers seems to be irreversible. In 2009 Rupert Murdoch announced his intention to charge for online news content as a means of saving print journalism but most experts on the industry are doubtful he can make this work.

See also Murdoch, Rupert.

Press Complaints Commission (PCC)

www.pcc.org.uk

An independent body which deals with complaints from members of the public about the editorial content of newspapers and magazines. It was set up in 1991 to replace the Press Council (established in 1953). This industry body comprises editors and non-journalists as a result of the Calcutt committee's recommendations. The original concern related to low standards in tabloid journalism, as exemplified by press intrusions into privacy, inaccurate reporting and 'cheque-book' journalism. It was hoped the PCC would help put the industry in order through self-regulation by adherence to a 1991 code of conduct; few believe this has happened. Intrusions into privacy, for example, were thought to be a strong element in the road accident which killed Princess Diana in August 1997. The PCC has no real sanctions and newspapers can flout its rulings with impunity. However, complaints to the PCC rose from 1,500 in 1991 to 3,000 in 1997. In February 2002, the chair of the PCC, Lord Wakeham, resigned his post while he dealt with problems caused by his directorship of Enron, the massive energy conglomerate which crashed into near bankruptcy in January 2002. Sir Christopher Meyer was chair from 2002 and Baroness Buscombe took over in April 2009.

press conference

An event organised to attract journalists and other commentators to hear some sort of announcement from the government or someone else, with an opportunity for questions to be asked afterwards. The aim is to gain publicity.

pressure group

An organisation that seeks to influence government policy on a specific issue. Two kinds are usually discerned: sectional groups, which defend the interests of particular groups in society (for example trade unions, the Confederation of British Industry, the British Medical Association); and promotional groups, which advocate a certain cause (for example the Child Poverty Action Group, the Lord's Day Observance Society). Pressure groups seek to apply pressure on decision makers (political parties, politicians, ministers, civil servants) in connection with their causes, and use a variety of methods, including the press, broadcasting and marches. Wyn Grant of Warwick University distinguishes between 'insider' and 'outsider' groups, depending on the closeness of their relationships to decision makers. Insider groups (those close to government) tend to be drawn into the policy process and may well exert influence and make compromises out of the glare of the media. Insider and outsider groups will use a range of tactics to get their view on the policy agenda, including newspaper articles, pamphlets, speeches, media interviews, marches, demonstrations, threats, civil disobedience and strikes. Sometimes different groups will join together in pursuit of a single objective. For example, in the autumn of 2000 a loose coalition of farmers, small businesses and independent road hauliers protested against the high level of fuel excise duty levied by the government and their actions led to a national fuel crisis. International pressure groups are increasingly attacking the process of globalisation. At a G8 summit in Genoa in July 2001 there were protests by anarchists (some violent), non-violent communists like Ya Basta from Italy, radical reformists from the Genoa Social Forum and Globalise Resistance. Moderates like Bob Geldof and fellow rock star Bono maintained they were 'negotiating' with

world leaders to reduce third world debt but the more militant demonstrators claimed that their success in focusing attention upon such summits was the reason why the moderates were given an audience at all.

Prevention of Terrorism Act 1974

First brought in as a temporary measure following the 1974 Birmingham pub bombings by the IRA. It gave wide powers of detention to the police, who were enabled to hold suspects for five days without trial and to ban them from the British mainland.

prime minister

The head of the executive branch in the British system of government. The office emerged out of constitutional developments in the 18th century, when the new kings imported from Germany were unsure of the language and the politics of their adopted country. Robert Walpole was the first to exercise prime ministerial power via his strategic position as first lord of the Treasury (1721–42). He presided over the cabinet in the absence of the monarch and used his skills to become its dominant element. Pitt the Younger was the next to fill the role as head of the cabinet, itself embodying the shift of power from monarch to parliament which the Glorious Revolution had occasioned. In the 19th century it became the convention that the leader of the largest party in the Commons – hence able to command majorities – should be invited by the monarch to form a government, even though the latter could in theory invite anyone to do so. No member of the Lords has been prime minister since 1902, as they lack the necessary degree of political influence which membership of the Commons provides. During the 20th century the office grew in importance as successive premiers expanded its scope, especially David Lloyd George and Margaret Thatcher, not to mention Tony Blair. The focus of publicity upon prime ministers and the image they give to their party ensure the office remains of key importance. Some observers see an increasing 'presidentialisation' of the office, reflected in the innovation of televised party leaders' debates in 2010. Thatcher and Blair helped to develop the office in this way; it is too early, at the time of writing, to tell whether David Cameron, who acceded in May 2010, will continue the trend, though it seems likely.

See also first lord of the Treasury; Walpole, Robert.

prime minister as president

Many observers noticed how Tony Blair developed his office towards something more approaching that of a US president. In support they cite:

1. Blair's burgeoning private office, which became closer to a White House staff than that which preceded it;
2. the use of White House titles like 'chief of staff';
3. his close relationship with George W. Bush and subsequent worldwide travel to assist the coalition forming after the 11 September 2001 terrorist attacks;
4. his tendency to keep cabinet meetings short and infrequent;
5. his preference for small, ad hoc meetings with advisors and concerned individuals rather than consulting widely to seek consensus.

Against this it is obvious that the US president is given considerable powers via the constitution; in the British case prime ministers are not so empowered or so constrained and can virtually make of the office what they wish or are able.

prime minister's delivery unit

Unit in Cabinet Office set up in 2001, focusing on improving the way government implemented its key priorities in education, health, crime and transport. It was headed at first by Michael Barber, formerly a professor of education at London University. He was replaced in 2006 by Ian Whatmore and he, in 2007, by Ray Shostak. The unit worked in close cooperation with the Treasury and major departments to assess how delivery was progressing and to assist in improving this process.

prime minister's department

Some experts advocate a fully fledged prime minister's department with perhaps a permanent secretary and a bevy of junior ministers and high-flying civil servants to staff it. While this would bring it into line with other chief executives in the USA and Europe, some argue the cabinet and its office perform many of the functions of such a department and fear that such an innovation would act as a barrier between the prime minister and the rest of the government, especially leading members of the cabinet.

To some extent the Cabinet Office fulfils support functions for the prime minister but his personal office contains key aides and advisors. The evolution of the 24–7 media coverage of politics has naturally led to the growing importance of the prime minister's press secretary and press office. Sir Bernard Ingham, Margaret Thatcher's formidable press officer, probably reflected the arrival of this tendency and Alastair Campbell, Tony Blair's equivalent, reinforced it. Media briefings are given regularly by Number 10 and spokespersons have to be sure-footed.

The office was reorganised in 2001 into three directorates:

1. *Policy and government.* This subsumed the function of the private office and the Policy Unit (which provided independent advice to the prime minister). This section seeks to coordinate policy across Whitehall and assist with implementation.
2. *Communication and strategy.* This contains three units: the press office, responsible for relations with the media; the strategic communications unit, which tends to take an overview of government presentation; and the research and information unit, which provides factual information to Number 10.
3. *Government and political relations.* This seeks to supervise relations with the governing party and other public relations.

prime minister's questions (PMQs)

A practice that dates only from the time of Harold Macmillan (who confessed to being terrified by the questioning). From 1961 to 1997 the prime minister answered questions directly in the House of Commons during two 15-minute slots on Tuesdays and Thursdays. Tony Blair changed the rules: it now occurs once a week on Wednesdays at noon and takes 30 minutes. These occasions have become set-piece events that attract a full attendance on both sides of the house and the intense interest of the media, which love the party political and personal confrontation. Consequently, the house shows its less admirable side: the proceedings are characterised by much shouting and barracking; the exchanges are generally either insults or well crafted sound bites; most of the questions are deliberately open-ended; and many are 'planted' by the whips into the mouths of compliant backbenchers to show the government in a good light. The leader of the opposition is allowed to ask six questions and the leader of the third largest party two.

The occasion is seen by both sides as a piece of party political jousting in which it is important to be seen to be winning debating points. Some MPs, however, not to mention commentators, see the event as a meaningless charade and waste of time. Others argue that prime minister's questions are something to be proud of: no other chief executives in the world subject themselves to such a randomly searching weekly inquisition – certainly not the US president. David Cameron took to the robust form of debate with ease after 2005 and was seen as having more than the measure of Gordon Brown.

prison numbers
In April 2010 there were 80,757 male inmates in UK prisons, and 4,319 female inmates, making a total of 85,076. At 1.40 per 100,000 population, the UK has the highest rate of imprisonment in the European Union. Usable operational capacity in 2010 was 87,146, indicating how overcrowded British jails are. Over 2,417 additional prisoners are subject to Home Office detention supervision curfew. Bad, overcrowded conditions have triggered

a number of riots and hostage-taking incidents over the last two decades.

Jack Straw, when justice secretary, released a number of short-term prisoners early in order to relieve overcrowding. Critics of the Labour government pointed out how imprisonment levels had continued to soar since 1997, despite the number of crimes committed reducing by a claimed 40 per cent. In December 2007, the government announced plans to build three 'Titan' jails, each with a capacity of 2,500 and costing £350 million. However, in April 2009 Straw told the Commons that, instead, five 'modern, purpose-built' jails, with a capacity each of 1,500, would be built.

> The opportunity to sleep nine hours a night and really relax has been extremely good for me. I ask you to disabuse yourself of any idea that prison is harmful. (John Stonehouse, former Labour cabinet minister jailed for corruption in 1975)

Prison Service
www.hmprisons.gov.uk
An executive agency created following one of the recommendations in the Ibbs *Next Steps* report. The service is entrusted with the custody, discipline and rehabilitation of offenders. It came to public attention in the early 1990s when Derek Lewis, chief executive of the Prison Service, was sacked by home secretary Michael Howard for alleged incompetence following escapes from certain prisons. Howard insisted he was in charge of policy while Lewis was in charge of day-to-day running. The fine line between such distinctions in practice revealed some of the accountability problems of the new executive agencies.

See also executive agency; penal policy; prison numbers; private prison.

prisoners and voting
The ban on prisoners voting dates back to the reign of Edward III and the ancient Greek concept of 'civic death', whereby punishment for crimes often entailed the loss of human rights, including the right to vote. Section 3 of the Representation of the

People Act 1983 formally disenfranchised prisoners but in 2005 the European Court of Human Rights ruled such a practice to be illegal. In April 2009 Jack Straw, secretary of state for justice, announced he was considering giving the vote to prisoners serving sentences of less than four years (approximately 28,000 in number). In October of the same year, Straw said no changes would be possible until after the 2010 election, raising the possibility that some prisoners might sue the government for breach of their human rights.

private bill
A type of bill mainly introduced by companies and local authorities when they require legislative authority from parliament to undertake public works such as bridge or tunnel construction. Although their number declined in the 20th century, there was an increase around the turn of the century because of the greater involvement of the private sector in infrastructural projects. Such bills often begin life in the House of Lords, due to the high number of public bills passing through the Commons.

private education
Although only 7 per cent of children attend private school, they go on to dominate most of the positions of power in business, politics, public administration and journalism. The *Economist* (1 March 2008) considered the value for money of such investments in a child's education (up to the end of secondary school, parents might well pay out not far short of £200,000).

Writing in the *Guardian* (22 February 2008) David Kynaston, author of *Austerity Britain* (and privately educated himself), quoted the autumn 2007 Sutton report:

> This ranked the success of schools, over a five-year period, at getting their pupils into Oxbridge. Top was Westminster school with a staggering 49.9 per cent hit rate. In other words, if you pay your annual boarding fees of £25,956, you have a virtually evens chance of your child making it to Oxbridge – the pathway to the glittering prizes that will almost certainly lie ahead. Altogether, there

were 27 private schools in the top 30; 43 in the top 50 and 78 in the top 100. Put another way, the 70th brightest sixth-former at Westminster or Eton is as likely to get a place at Oxbridge as the very brightest sixth-formers at a large comprehensive.

He regretted that private education had ever been allowed to survive. But there is a strong consensus among the middle classes that state education is inferior and not good enough for their children. It is a fact that the staff–pupil ratio in private schools is about half that in state schools.

See also public school.

Private Eye
www.private-eye.co.uk
Satirical fortnightly magazine. It began life in the fee-paying Shrewsbury School in the 1950s, where Richard Ingrams, Willie Rushton, Paul Foot and Christopher Booker were involved in editing a school magazine. After national service Ingrams and Foot went to Oxford and met future collaborators, including Peter Usborne and John Wells. Usborne brought a knowledge of offset lithography to the magazine, which began to publish in the early 1960s. Early editions were filled with rather silly jokes, though it also reflected something of the ongoing rage for satire. It sold surprisingly well. Peter Cook and Nicolas Luard then provided more finance from the vantage point of the satire-based Establishment Club and the magazine was set fair. The first editor was Booker followed by Ingrams, to be followed by Ian Hislop. Paul Foot provided, until his much-mourned death in 2004, the investigative journalism for what has developed into a highly successful publication.

private finance initiative (PFI)
An approach inaugurated by the Conservative government in 1992 to finance public projects through private capital. Such projects included the Channel Tunnel rail link, the Skye bridge and Bridgend Prison. One consequence of the scheme was to focus government activity more narrowly and cost-effectively. For

instance, the Benefits Agency sold its offices in 1997 and then contracted out the office services it required. Labour, in keeping with its pragmatic approach to Tory policies, made increasing use of PFI after coming to power in 1997. By September 1998, projects worth £10.5 billion had been agreed. A Prison Service report revealed that Altcourse Prison, built under PFI, cost £54,000 per prisoner, compared with £20,000 under the old system, which suggests that PFI can be hugely more expensive than purely public sector ventures, rather than the cost-saving exercise the government claims it to be. PFI projects are useful to the Treasury as they reduce the amount of debt the government would otherwise have to incur.

In a *Guardian* article (17 August 2001) Mark Seddon noted the use made by Labour of PFI projects. Under the Conservatives there were only 50 such deals over a five-year period. After 1997 Labour had signed 300, worth £9.6 billion, and in the wake of its election victory in June 2001 promised a further 100 hospitals and 3,000 surgeries by 2010, financed through PFI. Critics – and there are many – claimed that PFI was nothing more than a long-term 'hire purchase' deal in which investors received excessive rewards for virtually no risk. Between 1992 and 2007 over 800 projects were initiated, totalling around £68 billion. The 2008–09 financial problems made PFI more difficult, but the government insisted the programme would continue. Unison, the union, according to the *Economist* (4 July 2009), estimated that PFI projects will garner private firms £227 billion in charges over the period 2009–33.

See also public–private partnership.

private members' legislation
One of the methods whereby back-bench MPs can initiate legislation in the Commons. The 20 MPs who come top in the annual ballot have the opportunity on 20 Fridays in a parliamentary session to debate bills they have themselves proposed. Despite the somewhat arbitrary nature of

the process, some important human rights legislation – including abolition of capital punishment and the liberalisation of the laws on homosexuality – have been passed in this way and it remains an important route for ordinary backbenchers to make their contribution. In recent years private members' bills have been 'talked out' by certain MPs, for example the (now late) Conservative MP Eric Forth.

See also 10-minute rule bill.

private notice question
See urgent question.

private office
Name given to the administrative unit which supports a minister, important official, or leader of the opposition. As part of their preparation for more senior office young members of the (fast-stream) administration grade in the civil service have traditionally served for a year or two as the personal private secretary of such a person. The prime minister's private office is especially sought after by ambitious officials and is staffed by the highest of the high-fliers of their generation. Robert Armstrong, who served as Edward Heath's private secretary, went on to be head of the civil service. Robin Butler had a similarly brilliant career.

private prison
The Conservative government of the early 1990s was attracted by the idea of private prisons, specially contracted from security companies to do the job previously performed by the Prison Service. In 1993 Michael Howard, home secretary, announced 12 contracts for private prisons, to much Labour criticism. Reports of their efficacy had been positive in the USA but were mixed in Britain. When in power, Labour embraced the idea it had once opposed. There were 12 private prisons in Britain in 2009, including Bronzefield, which is the only purpose-built women's prison in Britain and the largest of its kind in Europe.

See also Prison Service; private finance initiative.

private sector
Name given to the privately owned part
of the economy. Labour eroded this after
1945 by nationalising 20 per cent of the
economy but the Conservatives did their
best to strengthen the sector after 1979
through privatisation, which returned most
of the nationalised industries to the private
sector. In addition, they sought to change
the culture of these industries to one which
favoured enterprise and cost-consciousness,
in order to increase their efficiency and
profitability. After 1997 Tony Blair, in
keeping with 'third way' pragmatism,
showed no hostility to private-sector provision of services if it served the consumer
effectively. The result of these policies is
that the country still employs most of its
labour force in the private sector.

See also nationalisation; privatisation;
public–private partnerships; public sector.

privatisation
The sale of publicly owned enterprises
to the private sector. The thrust for this
policy emerged in the late 1970s when
the Conservatives, hostile to state control
of industry, decided to reduce the size of
the public sector, in line with 'new right'
thinking. The first major privatisation
was British Telecom in 1984. This had
originally been part of the General Post
Office and then converted into a public
corporation before being sold off to the
public via a Stock Exchange flotation. This
policy of establishing a separate corporation,
making it profitable and selling it off became
the norm and between 1982 and the early
1990s a raft of public sector industries
were sold off in this way, including coal,
gas, steel, forestry, electricity, water and the
railways. By the mid-1990s privatisation
had returned virtually all the nationalised
industries to the private sector and
generated huge revenues for the exchequer.
Dr Madsen Pirie of the Adam Smith
Institute listed the advantages of privatisation as 10-fold: government reduces its costs;
private companies are able to raise money
on the capital markets; the government
can concentrate on core domestic policies

and not on trading; private companies are
more responsive to consumers, have better
management, have higher capital spending
and better industrial relations; and privatisation results in wider share ownership, more
competition and choice, and lower prices.
Needless to say, others contested these
alleged benefits. Labour bitterly criticised
the privatisations, citing, for example,
the poor levels of service, and the pursuit
of profit above public service. Labour
promised to renationalise but when in power
after 1997 did not do so. Moreover, several
state-owned enterprises were earmarked by
Labour for possible privatisation, including
the Royal Mint. The National Air Traffic
Services was partially privatised in 2000.

See also compulsory competitive tendering; market testing.

Privy Council
www.privy-council.org.uk
Originally part of the King's Council, the
Privy Council became the chief mechanism
for governing the country until the 18th
century. All the great officers of state were
members and it met whenever the monarch
wished it. In the 18th century the cabinet,
a smaller body, came to take over the
functions of the Privy Council. The latter
now survives mainly as a ceremonial body,
membership of which is granted to cabinet
members, senior backbenchers, senior
opposition figures and senior judges. The
lord president of the (Privy) Council is a
cabinet member, though the post holder
often fulfils non-departmental duties, and
more commonly in modern times combines
the job with that of leader of the House of
Commons. The Privy Council Office looks
after bodies which hold a charter, such
as universities, the appointment of high
sheriffs and other appointments in the name
of the crown. Privy councillors take an oath
of secrecy, in the presence of the monarch.

The Judicial Committee of the Privy
Council acts as a final court of appeal
for some Commonwealth countries. This
function has survived many changes and
reforms and applies to New Zealand and
Canada, for example.

Procedure Select Committee
Committee that makes periodic reviews of legislative procedures and how they might be improved. For example, in 1978 its report recommended the new system of select committees, which have now become well established and shadow all the main departments of state, with wide terms of reference and powers to appoint specialist advisors. In 1979 Norman St John Stevas brought forward the recommendations in the form of parliamentary motions, which were then passed by 248 votes to 12.

procurator-fiscal
A local public prosecutor in Scotland who is a qualified advocate or solicitor. Procurators-fiscal initiate preliminary investigations into criminal cases within the area over which they have jurisdiction. They take statements from witnesses and conduct any resultant prosecution. The Crown Prosecution Service performs these services for the rest of the UK.

productivity
Normally taken as the value of goods or services divided by the number of hours of labour taken to produce them. High productivity is a long-term means of allowing unemployment to fall to low levels without risking inflation. Margaret Thatcher boasted in 1987 that Britain was back in the 'first division' in terms of economic productivity but studies in the late 1990s revealed the country was still trailing its major rivals. The productivity gap with the USA narrowed from the 1960s onwards and in certain industries it was exemplary. According to a measure called 'total factor productivity', which measures how efficiently both capital and labour are used, the USA and Germany are some 15 per cent in front of Britain and France 7 per cent ahead. No one is quite sure why British workers are less productive but when Japanese management is in control, as in Sunderland's Nissan plant, British workers can be the most productive in Europe. The management consultants McKinsey point to low investment and poor worker skills as the main reasons for relatively low productivity in Britain.

Profumo affair
One of the factors which marked the beginning of the end for the 1959 government of Harold Macmillan. War secretary John Profumo began an affair with Christine Keeler, a high-class call girl, who was also having a sexual relationship with a military attaché at the Russian embassy. When called to account in the Commons he denied the relationship. When the truth emerged he was forced to resign, bringing the Conservative Party into disrepute. Lord Denning conducted an investigation into the affair. Profumo's political career was over but he gained some dignity and respect by devoting his life to charity work. The film *Scandal*, made in 1988, was based on the affair.

programme order
A procedure for speeding up the legislative process. This originated in a report of the Modernisation Committee in October 2002. It was subsequently accepted by the House of Commons for a trial period. The idea was to find arrangements for 'programming' legislation that were more formal than the usual channels (i.e. the whips) but more flexible than the guillotine motion. Programme orders provide a more sophisticated tool to timetable the progress of a bill through the Commons. They are moved directly after a bill's second reading and set: the timetable for the further stages in the Commons: the committee option to be followed; the date by which the bill should emerge from the committee stage; and the time to be allowed on the report stage and third reading.

See also act of parliament; guillotine motion.

Progressive Unionist Party
www.pup-ni.org.uk
Protestant-based political party in Northern Ireland. Founded in 1979, it became known in the 1990s as the mouthpiece of the Ulster Volunteer Force. It took

POLITICS

273

part in the 1998 Good Friday agreement talks and supported it thereafter. In 1996 it won two seats in the Northern Ireland Forum; in 1998 it won two seats in the elections for the Northern Ireland assembly and in 2003 won one seat. In 2007 Dawn Purvis was elected as successor to the late David Ervine as leader.

project (the)
Tony Blair's plan to forge a permanent alliance between Labour and the Liberal Democrats and thus keep the Conservatives out of power. According to Paddy Ashdown's memoirs, Tony Blair thought that not including the Liberal Democrat leader in his first cabinet was his 'biggest mistake', as this move would have initiated the 'project'. However, Labour's huge majority and residual hostility to the Liberal Democrats in the Parliamentary Labour Party headed off this possibility. The personal chemistry which characterised relations between Ashdown and Blair was not replicated once Charles Kennedy assumed the top job for the Liberal Democrats.
See also third way.

propaganda
Political communication aimed at persuasion, typically with the presentation of overly selective or distorted facts and misinformation. During the Second World War, the British national government coined the phrase 'propaganda through truth' to describe the attempts of the Ministry of Information to counter the physical and psychological threat posed by Hitler's Germany. Today, commentators prefer to use the term 'news management', as practised during the Falklands war in 1982 and the American-led Gulf war of 1991.
See also political communications; political language.

proportional representation
Any of various voting systems which produce seats in an assembly or parliament in proportion to votes cast. The regional list system is the most widely used form of proportional representation in Europe, but

the form favoured by some in Britain is the additional member system, which is used in Germany and which has been adapted for elections to the devolved assemblies of Scotland and Wales and the Greater London Authority. The single transferable vote, used in Ireland and favoured by the Liberal Democrats, is not strictly proportional, although it is often thought to be, as is the definitely non-proportional alternative vote. Northern Ireland has had proportional representation for local elections for several years. Reformers argue it is necessary for general elections in Britain to be fair. Elections to the European parliament are now all via this system.
See also additional member system; alternative vote; alternative vote 'top-up'; Jenkins report; single transferable vote.

Provisional IRA
Break-away faction of the official Irish Republican Army (IRA). When violence broke out between extremists in the late 1960s in Northern Ireland, the official IRA was accused of cowardice for not protecting the Catholic community. A much quoted contemporary piece of graffiti read 'IRA = I Ran Away'. By 1970 a more radical group (the 'Provos') had broken away from the official movement but soon became synonymous with the IRA. Events like internment in 1971 and Bloody Sunday in 1972 hugely increased recruitment to the paramilitary grouping, which continued its campaign of terrorism in pursuit of political goals until the Good Friday agreement in 1998, when it seemed violence might be rejected as a vehicle for political change in favour of the ballot box. However, punishment beatings in the province continued and the initial refusal of the IRA to disarm prevented the newly formed Northern Ireland executive from functioning.

proxy voting
If voters are unable to vote personally, it is possible for them to ask someone to vote on their behalf. The appropriate form has to be completed and sent to the returning officer in the constituency concerned.

psephology

The study of elections. The first British psephologist is generally thought to be David Butler of Nuffield College, Oxford, who is the author or co-author of successive 'Nuffield' studies of general elections. Many others have subsequently joined him in this important subdivision of British political science.

pseudo-event

An event which exists solely to generate publicity, for example a press conference or a photo-opportunity.

Public Accounts Commission

See National Audit Office.

Public Accounts Committee (PAC)

Parliamentary select committee, founded in 1861. For a long time the PAC was one of only two select committees and it is arguably still the most important and powerful. It examines how public funds have been spent and checks whether such spending has been for the purposes intended. It is served by the staff of the comptroller and auditor general and has real influence in the government service. In January 1994 the PAC issued its broadside against sleaze, *The Proper Conduct of Public Business*, a report which discerned what its then chair, Robert Sheldon, described as a noticeable decline in levels of public probity and integrity, which threatened the traditional 'incorruptibility' of Britain's public services. The chair of the PAC after 1997, by convention an opposition MP, was David Davis, who established a formidable reputation for getting things done. One study calculated that 95 per cent of the committee's recommendations were implemented under Davis's chairmanship. Edward Leigh MP (Conservative) took over in 2001 as chair.

> the queen of the select committees ... [which] by its very existence exert[s] a cleansing effect in all government departments. (Professor Peter Hennessy)

See also National Audit Office.

Public Appointments Commission

See Office of the Commissioner for Public Appointments.

public bill

Any bill concerned with the interests of the public as a whole. There are two types of public bill: those promoted by the government and those promoted by private members. The former are government measures that are designed to implement manifesto promises – they take up 80 per cent of the parliamentary timetable. They are announced by the sovereign in the queen's speech at the opening of a new parliamentary session. Private members' bills have to compete for limited time and follow a separate procedure.

public corporation

The legal entity for a nationalised industry. Public corporations usually have a charter that lays down their constitutions and the powers of the governing boards. The most important difference with public companies is that there are no shareholder rights. They are in theory independent of the state and responsible to the governing board, the members of which are appointed by the government. Two of the first, established in the 1920s, were the Central Electricity Board and the BBC. Corporations have a sponsoring department in Whitehall which will oversee their activities and be accountable for them in parliament.

public expenditure

The money spent by the government on public services. During the Second World War, public expenditure in relation to gross domestic product was over 60 per cent, and while it dropped to 35–40 per cent in 1945–50 it then rose to a peak of nearly 50 per cent in the mid-1970s. It hovered in the mid-40s during the 1980s, fell to under 40 per cent at the end of the decade and levelled off in the low 40s in the 1990s. During the early years of the present century it climbed up beyond 45 per cent as Labour boosted public spending and then took an additional leap as the 2007–09 economic crisis arrived, requiring large amounts of borrowing to save the banking system and to inject a 'fiscal stimulus' into the economy. The four biggest categories of public expenditure, which totalled £618 billion in 2008–09 were: social security £169 billion; education £82 billion; health £111 billion; and defence £33 billion.

public expenditure survey

The annual process known as 'the survey' whereby the government reviews, confirms, allocates or reallocates funding between the spending departments. It involves all chief departmental officers as well as senior Treasury officials. The process starts in May with departmental submissions on desired expenditure. In June the cabinet sets the limits for the survey and nominates a subcommittee (named PX and chaired by the chancellor) to oversee the process. The chief secretary to the Treasury considers the submissions and responds with papers to the PX, which meets throughout the autumn. Recipients of funding are consulted beforehand and are informed of the outcome, though usually without any explanation. PX then submits its report to full cabinet, usually in November. Allocations are then ready to be announced in the spring budget.

public inquiry

These occur after major disasters, failures or embarrassments. They are designed to find the causes and advise on remedial action if at all possible; they are often chaired by senior judicial figures. Examples have included Lord Justice Taylor's inquiry into safety at sports grounds, Lord Bingham's into the collapse of the BCCI bank and Lord Nolan's into standards in public life. Most public inquiries are set up at the behest of the prime minister or another government minister, who sets their terms of reference and their time frames. The best-known inquiry in recent years was the one producing the Hutton report (January 2004) into the death of the Ministry of Defence scientist Dr David Kelly. The Butler inquiry (reported July

2004) into intelligence regarding the Iraq war was also controversial. The Saville inquiry into 'Bloody Sunday' was set up in 1998 and reported in 2010 at a cost estimated at £400 million.

public interest immunity (PII) certificate

Issued by government to prevent the release of secret documents where disclosure could threaten the national interest. These 'gagging orders' were little heard of before the 'arms to Iraq' scandal in 1992, when a number of PIIs were overturned by the judge in the Matrix Churchill trial.

public opinion

Since the dawn of the democratic age the views of the public have been considered important, not least because they are likely to influence the way votes will be cast at election times. In the past, popular opinion was thought to be so ill-informed it was frequently ignored, but the modern practice is to respect even ill-informed opinion and to measure it assiduously in public and private opinion polls. Public opinion on an issue seldom arises spontaneously – it is often the result of opinion formers, who operate in interest groups, the media and political parties. In an age of mass media, governments and political parties are highly sensitive to this phenomenon and try to monitor and predict the twists and turns of opinion through focus groups and other forms of opinion research. New Labour's People's Panel, among other devices, was a sophisticated attempt to monitor popular concerns; however, it was disbanded after a relatively short time.

public opinion poll
See opinion poll.

public–private partnership (PPP)

Collaboration between the government and the private sector, in theory to their mutual advantage and that of the public as well. PPPs became especially controversial when, after the June 2001 general election, Tony Blair announced his goal of 'world class' public services, which he felt could be achieved through the involvement of the private sector. In January 2000 Arthur Andersen Accounting released a report, commissioned by the Treasury, on 17 private finance initiatives (PFIs). It concluded that the 'average percentage estimated saving against the public sector comparator [i.e. traditional costings] for our sample of projects was 17 per cent'. This finding was used by ministers to justify more projects but was furiously disputed by the unions and other critics, who pointed out that Arthur Andersen had made millions from the advice it had tendered.

The promise on public services had helped Labour win a second landslide in 2001 but worries continued that the £180 billion pledged to be spent on education, health and transport would not be enough. It was hoped the private sector would be able to help carry some of the financial and management burden. Much of the uproar focused on a report (*Building Better Partnerships*, 24 June 2001) by the Institute of Public Policy Research (IPPR) which envisaged substantial cooperation with the private sector. The IPPR report argued that the view that public services 'should always and everywhere be provided by the public sector' was wrong. However, it also maintained that private involvement should be limited to those occasions when public finance was not available or when current services were poor. Its main message was that ideological approaches were less attractive than pragmatic solutions. It urged the government to look beyond the PFI for a suitable model, as it had proved expensive in some cases. As the *Economist* noted (30 June 2001), almost 20 per cent of public capital spending in 2001 was via the PFI route. PFI projects are attractive mainly because 'they allow spending departments to escape the Treasury's purse strings'. Trade unionists had visited the prime minister three weeks after the June 2001 general election victory to protest at plans to increase the role of private business in the public sector but had been roundly rebuffed.

On 11 July 2001 a MORI poll revealed that only one in nine of the general population believed the extension of private sector involvement would improve public services. Two-thirds said that better pay and conditions would be more likely to improve services. In February 2002 Tony Blair came under sustained pressure at the party's spring conference from trade unions objecting to plans to involve the private sector in public sector activities.

public–private split: European comparisons

During the 2001 general election campaign Tony Blair emphasised how public services would face reform and greater involvement of private companies. Critics accused the prime minister of the Thatcherite mind-set of 'Public bad, private good'. However, European experience suggests there are ways of involving the private sector to the benefit of the public sector. The *Economist* (14 July 2001) reported that health services in the European Union spent about the same percentages of state funding as in Britain – about 5–7 per cent – but added up to 2 per cent from the private sector. Some experts claim Britain could achieve similar levels of health service to Germany, France and the Netherlands if the public were allowed to pay for private 'top-up' care. In France, for example, patients pay for their own care and then claim up to 85 per cent back from the state; however, doing this for simple visits to a general practitioner would not be easy to introduce in Britain.

Public Record Office
See National Archives.

Public Records Act 1958
Act that stipulates a 30-year delay in the release to the public of some 40 categories of government information. The reasons may vary from state security to the embarrassment which might be caused to living people. Some cabinet and other papers are permanently secret. In 2009 there were some indications that the government would relax the 30-year rule.

public school

Term used paradoxically for private schools in England and Wales. Originally the ancient schools, such as Eton, Harrow, Rugby and Winchester, were intended to provide education for the sons of poor families but the quality of what they came to provide led to their clients becoming the rich and influential. Middle-class people with money sought the cachet of a prestigious education for their children and the number of such schools expanded in the 19th and 20th centuries. Roedean and Benenden are examples of girls' public schools. Some predicted the demise of public schools after the Education Act 1944 reformed the state secondary education system. The resultant state-run grammar schools – access to which was via an examination taken at the age of 11 – certainly competed scholastically with private education but postwar Labour governments, in their desire to remove selection in education, sought to phase them out. Partly as a result, public schools survived and then prospered as the quality of state education was seen to be substandard compared with private education. This has produced a two-tier system of education, with some 7 per cent of children, mostly from well-off backgrounds, receiving an education which enables them to win a disproportionate share of places at the older prestigious universities and to dominate the elite levels of government, the professions, the civil service and most other centres of power in Britain. A report in May 2002 from the Organisation for Economic Cooperation and Development revealed that British public schools produce the best academic results of any in the world. In 2009 public schools faced a dual threat to their continuing success: an initiative by the Charities Commission to look into whether private schools did enough for the general community to merit the advantages of their charitable status; and the reduction of new enrolments following the 2007–09 recession.

See also private education.

public sector

Economic functions controlled or funded by government. After 1945 nationalisation moved over 20 per cent of the economy into the public sector but Margaret Thatcher ensured privatisation 'rolled back the frontiers of the state' and enlarged the private sector, which she admired, at the expense of the public, which she disliked. This tended to encourage a culture in which public was seen as 'bad' and 'private' as 'good' (i.e. more efficient and better managed). The absence in the public sector of the constraining disciplines of profit making and competition were particularly emphasised by the right, while the left argued that wastefulness was not the exclusive preserve of the public sector and that profits were irrelevant in the delivery of services like health. The size of the public sector varies according to region, being biggest in Northern Ireland (31 per cent) and the north-east of England.

See also nationalisation; private sector; privatisation; public–private partnership.

public sector borrowing requirement (PSBR)

The difference between what the government spends and brings in via revenue and therefore needs to borrow from the market. Borrowing is done by selling certain kinds of government stock, for example gilt-edged stocks, national savings and local authority stocks and bonds. In the early 1990s the Conservatives had to raise taxation to cover a £50 billion PSBR which had built up during the recession at the end of the 1980s. After 1997 the Labour government made much of its financial virtue in paying off government debt during its first term but sceptics doubted the spending plans could be fully implemented throughout Labour's second term without recourse to some expansion of government borrowing. By July 2009 government borrowing was calculated to be 57 per cent of GDP.

public service agreement (PSA)

Agreement with government departments made by the Treasury regarding the way funding will be spent. PSAs appeared after the 1998 comprehensive spending review and set out what departments aim to achieve in terms of priorities and direction over a specific period. Similar agreements are made with local authorities; in 2004, 60 of them had agreed 'local PSAs', which link national targets with local priorities. To provide incentives for improved performance, extra funding is made available if targets are met. Some commentators have seen in PSAs a device by the Treasury for controlling the work of departments.

public service guarantee
Government guarantee that originated with a 2002 report from the Cabinet Office's Performance and Innovation Unit, *Privacy and Data-Sharing*. This recommended that public bodies should have a 'public service guarantee on data handling' to inform people of their rights when they supply personal information to the public sector. Such guarantees ensure people know why information is required by a government agency and that it will not be made available to anyone else.

Q

qualified majority voting (QMV)
A system of voting used in the European Union's Council of Ministers. Euro-enthusiasts seek extensions of QMV, while Eurosceptics are less keen on surrendering the veto. It is a system of weighted voting which replaced the previous unanimity requirement (which gave each member a veto) and which is based on population sizes of member countries. Before expansion of the European Union in May 2004, Britain, along with the other large countries, had 10 votes. There were 87 votes in the Council distributed among members and a qualified majority required 62 votes to pass

a proposal, instead of the mathematical majority of 44. The Nice treaty of 2000 adjusted the weightings to take account of new members: 345 votes in total on the Council, with the larger countries having 29 each, reducing down to 4 for Latvia and 3 for Malta. A qualified majority requires both a majority of the member states and 255 votes (74 per cent of the whole). These arrangements are due to be modified by the Lisbon treaty of 2009, but not until 2014–17. Only a few subjects now carry the veto (i.e. require unanimity) apart from foreign and defence policy and justice and home affairs, and these will be even fewer in number under Lisbon.

quantitative easing
A government device for increasing the amount of money circulating in an economy, used by the Labour government in 2008–09. Quantitative easing was also used by Japan to alleviate its own economic recession in 2000. Essentially, the government increases the amount of money available simply by adding figures to its credit balance (not so very different to 'printing money'). In the UK some £200 billion was created in this way over 2009–10 to help stimulate the depressed economy. This money is then used to buy bonds from insurance companies, banks and pension funds. The recipients are able to use such funds for lending purposes or for purchasing other products. The danger of the policy is that it can increase the money supply by too much and cause hyperinflation.

quasi-autonomous non-governmental organisation (quango)
A body that is not attached to a government department and usually has no formal close contact with a minister but still performs a government function of sorts. Quangos are part of the 'shadow world' of government. According to the Whitehall manual *Non-Departmental Public Bodies*, there are three subdivisions:
1 Executive bodies, like the Medical Research Council, the Equality and

Human Rights Commission and the Atomic Energy Authority. They are set up by statute and are headed by boards appointed by government. There are well over 300 such bodies, spending in total £12 billion per annum.

2 Advisory bodies, like the Bovine Spongiform Encephalopathy Committee, the Industrial Injuries Advisory Council and the royal commissions. There are over 800 advisory bodies, most of which comprise part-time experts.

3 Tribunals and other quasi-judicial bodies, like the Central Arbitration Committee, the Social Security Appeal Tribunals and the Value Added Tax Tribunal. These have delegated jurisdiction in a specialised area. There are around 70 such bodies plus another 130 or more which exist for monitoring the conditions of prisons and prisoners.

The Conservative government of 1979 denounced quangos but invented a number, which took over functions previously performed by central or local government. Labour furiously criticised them as undemocratic refuges for Conservative placement but did not dismantle them en masse once in power.

The Office of the Commissioner for Public Appointments, set up by Labour to ensure fairness in ministerial appointments to quangos, criticised a number of National Health Service trusts for packing their boards with Labour activists – in parallel to the accusation made by Labour against the Conservatives when they were in government. In July 2009, David Cameron alleged there were millions to be saved by culling the existing 790 quangos (the number is disputed), citing the broadcasting regulator Ofcom as a candidate, which annually spends over £100 million. He claimed that 68 of them were led by executives earning more than the prime minister. He vowed to retain only those that give technical advice (like the Bank of England's Monetary Policy Committee), that make impartial decisions (like the research councils) or that aid transparency (like the Office for National Statistics).

Labour retorted that the Conservatives planned to create 17 new quangos if elected; the biggest of these would be an independent board to run the National Health Service.

> A body which has a role in the processes of national government, but is not a government department or part of one, and which accordingly operates to a greater or lesser extent at arm's length from Ministers. (Government definition of a quango, 1997)

quasi-government
Those government institutions which are government funded but not staffed by civil servants. As the scope of government has expanded so rapidly since 1945, new bodies have sprung up to administer the enlarged public sector, including nationalised corporations and quangos. For example, independent specialised agencies include bodies like the Urban Regeneration Agency (renamed New English Partnerships after a merger with the New Towns Commission in 1999), which helps reclaim derelict urban areas. Critics accuse such 'government at arm's length' of not being properly accountable to parliament and subject to public control.

queen's counsel (QC)
The elite of courtroom advocates. QCs originated in the 16th century under Elizabeth I, who wanted the best lawyers to advise her. Eventually the title became merely a form of promotion: QCs were able to earn more than ordinary barristers. However, in 2001 the Office of Fair Trading condemned them as 'uncompetitive' and the Bar Council, the body representing barristers, criticised the secretive way in which the lord chancellor collected information about candidates before awarding 'silks'. In 2004 the queen's counsel selection panel was established to consider applications for selection as a QC. References are taken and interviews carried out in a process which is transparent and based on merit. Writing in the *Guardian* (28 January 2008), Marcel Berlins regretted

the failure of the new panel to select more women and ethnic minorities: 'the white male continues to rule'.

See also judge.

queen's counsel selection panel

See queen's counsel.

queen's (or king's) speech

Speech delivered by the monarch on the occasion of the state opening of parliament. It is not written by the queen but by government ministers, who are advised by civil servants. It lays down the legislative measures which the government intends to pass during the forthcoming parliamentary session. The speech is delivered by the queen in the House of Lords and the members of the House of Commons come through to listen, traditionally in silence. There then follows a six-day debate on the programme and the opposition tables critical amendments. Defeat on any resultant divisions (votes) causes the resignation of the government, as in 1924, when Stanley Baldwin's minority government was defeated by Labour and the Liberals on the king's speech and Ramsay MacDonald was invited to take over. In February 1974 Wilson issued his queen's speech for his minority administration, daring the Conservatives to defeat it and precipitate another election, which might have improved Labour's position.

question time (Commons)

An hour-long opportunity for MPs to question ministers. It occurs Monday to Thursday at 2.30 p.m. and finishes at 3.30 p.m. MPs are restricted to eight questions in every 10 sitting days and never more than two on any one day. Questions must be precisely worded on areas which are appropriate for the minister concerned to answer; some areas, like arms sales and budgetary contracts, are ruled out of bounds. Most ministers appear on a rota to answer every four weeks. Usually about 20 questions are answered in each question time.

See also prime minister's questions.

question time (Lords)

A period of no more than 30 minutes (Monday to Friday, at the beginning of the day's business) when peers can pose questions to the government as a whole (not to individual departments, as in the Commons). There are two types of questions in the Lords: starred and unstarred. The former are oral and non-debatable while the latter are written and can be the subject of short debates lasting no more than 20 minutes.

R

racism

A belief in the superiority of certain races over others, used as a justification for discrimination. The existence of the National Front, British National Party and other groups generally taking their inspiration from Oswald Mosley indicates that racism is a theme in British politics. The country's imperialist history makes it likely that feelings of superiority should be felt in the 'home' of the Empire towards its member races, especially when so many small wars and military operations were made against them. Most commentators would suggest that racism is not a very powerful theme in Britain as a whole, but there is evidence to suggest there is considerable embedded racism in the culture of large institutions. This is especially so in the case of the police, and was referred to as institutionalised racism by the Macpherson report on the bungled investigation into the murder of Steven Lawrence in 1998.

In a study by Warwick University in September 1998, 16 per cent of white respondents interviewed felt race relations were improving, 38 per cent thought that they were getting worse and 39 per cent felt that the situation was about the same. For black respondents the figures were 7, 79 and

14 per cent respectively, while for Asians they were 9, 50 and 33 per cent. Despite the fact that six black and Asian MPs were elected in 1997, rising to 12 in 2001, only 55 per cent of those eligible to vote from these communities were actually registered to do so. It is significant also that black people are twice as likely as whites to be unemployed, and they are much more likely to be stopped and searched by the police, to receive longer prison sentences and to die in custody.

On 30 June 2001 a report to the United Nations from 11 British organisations led by Liberty claimed that 'politicians and the media alike have been encouraging racist hostility in their public attitudes towards asylum seekers…. In our view the recent race riots in Oldham and Bradford are to an extent directly linked to [this].' Lord Tebbit did not agree and accused the 'race relations industry' of being the 'main recruiting ground for the British National Party'.

See also British National Party; immigration; National Front.

radical
Term associated with the reformist movements of the 19th century, often the vigorously reformist wing of the Liberal Party. Radical movements had sprung up in England in the late 18th century and proposed fundamental reform of the British political and social order, similar to that which had taken place in revolutionary France and the American colonies. An even earlier form of radicalism was that of John Lilburne and his Leveller supporters, who were active in Cromwell's New Model Army in the middle of the 17th century. Historically in Britain, radicalism has been 'managed' or defused by gradual accommodation to pressure, as occurred during the 19th century when electoral reform took place from 1832. In the late 1970s and 1980s Margaret Thatcher was happy to use the term to describe her own political beliefs.

radio
Radio broadcasts were first introduced in the 1920s by the BBC, founded upon a mission to 'inform, educate and entertain'.

It was used by Stanley Baldwin for political purposes with his folksy 'fireside chats'. Winston Churchill and the Ministry of Information were more interested in using radio to rouse the nation in the Second World War and his broadcasts inspired the country to survive the difficult years and win through against the might of Nazi Germany. After the war television increasingly came to dominate political attention, but radio still carries party political broadcasts and its current affairs coverage is widely listened to and admired. The *Today* programme on Radio 4 has been used by politicians to communicate directly with the 1 million or so people who listen to it every morning. Included in this number are members of Britain's political, media and economic elite, and of course teachers and students of politics.

Ragged Trousered Philanthropists
Novel written in the early 1900s by Robert Noonan, under the pen-name Robert Tressell, set in Hastings and in a sub-Dickensian style, about the painting and decorating trade at the turn of the century. It dealt with: the poor standards of workmanship which private enterprise encouraged; the problems of poverty wages; and the plight of young unmarried women who become pregnant. It also contained arguments for an early kind of utopian socialism, which succeeded in convincing thousands of people, including the future union leader Jack Jones, that they should convert to socialism and join the Labour Party.

rail travel
See Network Rail.

Ramblers' Association
www.ramblers.org.uk
Founded in 1935, a pressure group currently with some 130,000 members. It has campaigned for years for a 'right to roam' – freedom for walkers to traverse the 12 per cent of Britain classed as mountain, moorland, heath and common land.
See also right to roam.

Rasmussen

www.rasmussenreports.com

US polling organisation which participated briefly in British politics in 2001, with some success. It worked for the *Independent* and introduced the novel idea of computerised interviewing by telephone (i.e. a disembodied voice seeking responses).

rate support grant

A block grant given from 1967 to 1980 by central government to local authorities to spend according to their needs. It comprised a 'resources' element for small authorities, a 'needs' element based on population and a 'domestic' element to reimburse local government for rate reductions. The addition of a complex formula in the 1970s undermined its utility and led to calls for reform. During the 1980s and early 1990s it was used by the Conservative government as a weapon to curb local government spending.

See also local government finance; rates.

rates

Local taxes based on the notional rental value of property (effectively, home occupiers had to pay in proportion to the size of their property). This was thought to be unfair by some, as large families often paid no more than small ones or single people. Conservative governments after 1979 reduced the amount given to local authorities through the rate support grant and also 'capped' the amount local authorities could levy via the rates. In 1986, the green paper 'Paying for Local Government' suggested the idea of a community charge (poll tax) which would, it was argued, more fairly reflect the link between voting and paying for local services. The charge was introduced in April 1990, and so the rates ended, only to be replaced three years later by the council tax.

See also community charge; council tax; rate support grant.

Real IRA

Hard-line group which emerged in the wake of the Good Friday agreement of 1998, committed to continuing the armed struggle against the British government. It was behind the Omagh bombing in 1998, which killed 29 people; it also exploded bombs in London, notably outside the BBC early in 2001. A *Sunday Times* article in July 2001 reported that MI5 operations against the group had weakened it significantly and reduced its capacity to obtain weapons from eastern Europe. On 7 March 2009 two young soldiers were murdered by the Real IRA in the Massereene army barracks when they stepped outside to collect a pizza.

realignment

The process by which movements in voter support for parties create changes in the party system. Four phases of realignment can be identified in British politics:

1 In 1918, support for the Liberal Party declined, marking the beginning of the rise of the Labour Party. The reason for this can be found in the split between Herbert Asquith and David Lloyd George and the massive increase in the size of the electorate, when, for the first time, all adult males (over the age of 21) could vote, as could women over the age of 30.
2 The Liberal vote revived in the early 1970s, marked by the Rochdale by-election, when the party took the seat from Labour. In the October 1974 general election, Liberal support had increased to 18 per cent, and the Scottish and Welsh nationalists received 2.6 per cent of the total vote. Since then third-party support in general elections has fallen below 20 per cent only once, in 1979.
3 In the 1983 general election, third-party support reached 31 per cent, the Alliance and others achieving 44 seats in the House of Commons. Indeed, up to the 1987 general election many commentators spoke of a significant realignment taking place in the party system, which would involve the Alliance displacing Labour as the second major party.
4 Labour's decline was halted at the 1987 general election and the party went on to win a landslide victory in

1997. However, third-party voting did not collapse, as the Liberal Democrats achieved 17 per cent and other parties 7.2 per cent in 1997, giving them a total of 75 seats in the House of Commons, the highest number since 1945. In 2001 the Liberal Democrats did even better in the general election, polling 18.8 per cent of the vote and garnering 52 seats.

The extraordinary 2010 general election produced one of those rare hung parliaments, with the Conservatives needing another 20 seats to rule but Labour needing much more. After three days of negotiations, David Cameron's Conservatives agreed a coalition deal with the Liberal Democrats, with Nick Clegg as his deputy prime minister and four other Liberal Democrat cabinet members. This realignment, if successful, might prove permanent, entailing the absorption of the smaller party into the bigger grouping, thus cementing a centre-left–right realignment instead of the left-centre–left, most sought (and anticipated) hitherto.

See also partisan dealignment; tactical voting.

rebate
See European rebate to Britain.

recall (of MPs)
Reform proposal to make MPs more accountable to voters. This device resembles procedures in the USA whereby a group of constituents can recall their representative from the legislature and, if necessary, subject them to re-election. The number of voters required to trigger such a process varies but 10 per cent has been mentioned as a possible figure.

> Recall means allowing local people trigger a by-election to sack an MP who fails to deliver. Or who makes promises, but doesn't keep them. Or who is indolent, lazy, or fiddles their expenses. (Blog of Douglas Carswell, Conservative MP, 7 April 2010)

recession
A period when the economy has begun to contract, officially for more than two

quarters in succession. Recessions are times of hardship, with bankruptcies and high unemployment and problems for the government in raising revenue from taxation. There have been regular recessions in recent British history, in 1979–81, 1990–92 and most dramatically 2007–09.

Reclaim the Streets
http://rts.gn.apc.org
A group that virtually took over the City of London in an anti-capitalist demonstration in June 1999. Many of the participants were prepared to use violence. One quoted in the *Observer* (31 October 1999) said:

> We tried tree hugging at the Newbury bypass. It did get some great publicity but the road still got built. We lost. There are a lot of us who now recognise we can't pick individual battles; we have to take on the whole system.

Activists arrived for the demonstration from all over the world – the Internet was used for their coordination. Similar demonstrations were expected on 1 May 2003 but in the event police outnumbered the demonstrators.

'Red Flag'
The anthem of the Labour Party for virtually the whole of its history. It was written in 1889 by Jim Connell. In 1997 it was downgraded at the party conference to a set-piece performance by a school choir after a rendition of the theme song for the 1997 campaign, 'Things Can Only Get Better'. When new converts joined the party, for example Peter Hain, news editors used to have fun focusing cameras on them during the finale singing of the 'Red Flag' to check whether they knew the words. They usually did not. The chorus is as follows:

> Then raise the scarlet standard high!
> Beneath its shade we'll live and die
> Though cowards flinch and traitors sneer
> We'll keep the red flag flying here!

red lines
Policy areas on which Britain said it would not surrender sovereignty in the negotiations over the proposed new European

Union (EU) constitution in 2004. In the face of sharp Eurosceptic criticism, the Labour government indicated that, while it supported the draft constitution in principle, it would not compromise domestic control over: tax and social security, labour laws, foreign and defence policy, crime and immigration, or voting systems within the EU. Britain's EU partners were concerned that if too many countries laid down similar 'red lines', agreement would prove impossible. Conservative opponents of the draft constitution dismissed the red lines as irrelevant.

See also Lisbon treaty.

'red Toryism'
See ResPublica.

Redcliffe-Maud report, 1969
Report of the Royal Commission on Local Government Reform. The Commission was set up in 1966 to consider the structure of local government in England outside Greater London. As local government had become, over time, a baffling patchwork, the report was not before its time. The Commission accepted the need for local government and believed it should be efficient, adaptable and supported by the electorate. There were clearly too many fragmented units for efficiency but the Commission could not agree on the best structure of reform. The majority report favoured 58 unitary authorities for the country outside London, but a minority report urged the two-tier structure which was eventually introduced by the Conservatives in the Local Government Act 1972.

Redistribution of Seats Act 1944
This established the boundary commissions and guaranteed minimum numbers of seats for Scotland and Wales, which were proportionally higher than for the rest of the country. This benefited Labour: in 1987 it won 24 of the 40 Welsh seats and 50 of the 72 Scottish ones. In 1997 the Conservatives held no seats in either Scotland or Wales for the first time ever,

although one was recovered in 2001. In 2010 the Conservatives won just one Scottish seat out of the 59 now available. They did better in Wales, winning eight out of the 40 contested.

redress of grievance
Although Britain does not have an entrenched or 'written' constitution to protect citizens' rights, there are a number of channels available for the redress of grievance against government and other statutory authorities. The main ones are: the MP; the parliamentary ombudsman; judicial review; the European Court of Human Rights; and tribunals. Under the various citizens' charters or public service guarantees, users of public services such as the National Health Service can make a complaint about the quality of service.

referendum
A special poll of the electorate, usually on a specific issue of public policy. Referendums have traditionally been alien to the British tradition of parliamentary democracy. At the time of writing there has been only one national referendum, in 1975 on whether Britain should remain in the European Community; it was passed with a two to one majority. Regional referendums were held on devolution to Scotland and Wales in 1979. The former registered a majority in favour but not sufficiently large to meet the 40 per cent of the electorate required (quite a difficult criterion given the variability in turnout). The Wales vote registered a four to one majority against the proposal. In September 1997, however, the results were different: a heavy victory for devolution in Scotland and a very narrow one in Wales. Future referendums are promised on British entry into a single currency and any new constitution of the European Union, and on proposals to reform the electoral system. Although not a feature of constitutional practice in the past, it would seem a referendum is now standard practice before a major constitutional reform goes forward.

See also regional assembly.

Referendum Party

Party founded by Sir James Goldsmith in 1996 to campaign for a referendum on British membership of the European single currency. Goldsmith allegedly spent £20 million on the campaign but received precious little in return, as the party failed to register more than 800,000 votes. The most that could be said for the party is that it made life difficult for those Conservatives who refused to support the referendum, as Labour did, and consequently lost votes to the Referendum candidates – and in some cases consequently lost their seats.

Reform Act

Any of a series of acts from 1832 to 1928 affecting the franchise. The British political system has escaped the type of revolutionary movements which transformed the political order in France (1789) and Russia (1917). In the 19th and 20th centuries a series of Reform Acts enlarged the franchise. The Great Reform Act of 1832 increased the size of the electorate by nearly a half and abolished many of the archaic features of the system, like 'rotten boroughs'. The Reform Act 1867 further enlarged the electorate by nearly 90 per cent, and in 1884 it was enlarged still further to include working-class voters. In the 20th century most women aged over 30 were enfranchised in 1918 by the act that extended the franchise to nearly all men aged 21 or more; the age discrepancy for women was removed in 1928. The most recent reform was in 1969, when 18-year-olds were given the vote.

Refugee Council

www.refugeecouncil.org.uk
Body working to assist refugees in Britain. Its provenance lay in the 1981 merging of two independent organisations dating back to 1951: the British Council for Aid to Refugees (BCAR) and the Standing Conference on Refugees (SCOR).
The Council's main role is to provide a source of information and advice for the benefit of asylum seekers and refugees but it also assists new refugees in resettling in different parts of the country and receives government funding as well as charitable donations to this end. It also runs regular campaigns to advance and improve the conditions under which both groups live within Britain. Since 2007 the chief executive has been Donna Covey.

regional aid

Labour governments in the 1960s believed in channelling government aid into regions with high unemployment but Conservative governments reduced this drastically, as it did not conform with their market-based philosophy. The European Union (EU), however, is keen to encourage development in particular regions and Britain has been a net beneficiary of such assistance: in the mid-1990s British citizens made up 20 million of the 50 million people living in some of the most economically deprived areas of Europe. In 1989 Britain had a standard of living 100.7 per cent of the EU average but this concealed a large variation, from 121 per cent for the south-east of England to 74 per cent for Northern Ireland. The north-east and Merseyside were other major recipients of EU funds, together with the Scottish Highlands and Islands Enterprise Area. EU grants mainly come from the European Regional Development Fund, the European Social Fund and the European Agricultural Guidance and Guarantee Fund. In addition, there are business loans and business support. Following the entry of 10 new members into the EU in 2004 regional aid to Britain has decreased.

regional assembly

Appointed assemblies set up in all eight English regions after the Regional Development Agencies Act 1998, which also set up the regional development agencies (RDAs). Over half of those appointed to these assemblies are elected councillors.

As a logical development of Scottish and Welsh devolution, the supporters of regional government suggest that the next step might be the creation of elected regional assemblies for all of the English regions.

In May 2002 deputy prime minister John Prescott launched a white paper 'Your Region, Your Choice', which proposed more resources and flexibility for the RDAs and more powers to the unelected regional assemblies. It also set out how regions could have elected assemblies if this was endorsed in a regional referendum. The initial three regional referendums on regional assemblies scheduled for autumn 2004 had, by the summer of that year, been reduced to one, in the north-east, scheduled for November. When it took place the result was a crushing defeat for the advocates of regionalism: 78 per cent no to 22 per cent yes. Some optimists have suggested that the defeat might not be final and noted that Welsh devolution eventually happened despite defeat in the 1970s referendum.

regional development agency (RDA)
Set up in 1999 in eight English regions. The ninth followed in London in July 2000. The RDAs aim: to provide coordinated regional economic development and regeneration; to reduce economic imbalances between regions; and to improve competitiveness. In 2001 chancellor Gordon Brown announced an increase of funding for the RDAs from £1.2 billion to £1.7 billion.

regional government
See regional assembly.

regional party list (voting system)
Introduced by the Labour government in 1998 for the election to the European parliament in 1999, this is a variant of the national party list system and as such is a significant move to proportional representation. Britain is divided into a number of multi-member constituencies to return the 72 MEPs. Each party pre-selects a 'slate' or list of candidates in order of preference; voters then choose parties, not candidates. In other words the party has a major say in which of its candidates are 'elected', and for this reason many have criticised the system as placing too much power in the hands of political parties. Northern Ireland was not included in the change, the province having used the single transferable vote (STV) system of election since 1979.

register of members' interests
A register which records the financial interests of MPs, including fees paid for directorships and consultancies. In the 19th century it was accepted that MPs would have economic interests outside parliament; indeed, it was seen as beneficial to democracy, mainly because government's links with the economy were not as many-layered as now. However, MPs paid by organisations to speak for them in parliament were gradually perceived as injurious to democratic government, as their contributions were tainted by personal financial gain. Consequently, a register of interests was introduced in 1975 on the basis of a parliamentary resolution, although MPs were not obliged by law to make such declarations. They are asked to provide information under a variety of headings: paid directorships, paid employment, trades and professions, clients, financial sponsorship or gifts, overseas visits, payment from abroad, land and property and shareholding. Some MPs refused to make declarations, like Edward Heath and Enoch Powell, while others made incomplete ones, by excluding, for example, the size of fees received for consultancy work. The blizzard of revelations about MPs working for outside concerns in 1994 prompted John Major to set up an extra-parliamentary committee under judge Lord Nolan to investigate standards in public life. A new system was introduced as a result of Nolan's recommendations which obliged MPs to disclose earnings according to income bands, forbade them from tabling questions and amendments on behalf of outside interests, limited what they could say in the chamber on behalf of such interests and obliged them to register all details of contracts with a powerful parliamentary commissioner. In the wake of the MPs' expenses scandal in June 2009, declarations on the register became even more important and David Cameron

suggested the tendency of some of his MPs to take outside jobs on top of being MPs should be brought to an end, a proposal which was not especially well received.

See also Nolan committee; parliamentary commissioner for standards.

regulation
See Council of Ministers; delegated legislation.

regulator
An office invented as a result of privatisation to ensure that the privatised industry concerned does not operate inefficiently or against the public interest. All the major utilities have a regulator, such as Ofgem for gas and electricity and Ofcom for the communications industries. In Britain regulators: control prices; specify operating requirements; set rules of behaviour; and encourage competition.

religion and politics
Following the Norman conquest, the English church was integrated into the Roman Catholic establishment. However, in the 16th century Henry VIII broke with Rome when the Pope refused to annul his marriage to Catherine of Aragon. Henry therefore set up an English church. Religious persecution occurred during the 17th century but after that the role of the church declined as an intense political issue, except in Ireland. Religion is now generally not a powerful cleavage in British society; other divisions such as class have greater effect. This is reflected in the fact that, with the exception of Northern Ireland (where national identity blends with religious affiliation), British politics is largely free of religion. Nonetheless, most mainstream politicians are careful to claim a belief in God and membership of a church. Margaret Thatcher occasionally made speeches which seemed to be related to the church but more often she was responding to criticisms from a church which soon became disenchanted with her individualistic philosophy. Tony Blair was a high-profile

member of the Church of England but also attended mass at Catholic churches (Cherie, his wife, is Roman Catholic) before converting to Catholicism in June 2007. When he was a student Blair allegedly considered becoming a priest. Some politicians have successfully combined a political career with a commitment to the church; for example, former MP and minister John Gummer was a lay member of the General Synod of the Church of England. Others attract publicity when they change churches (for example Ann Widdecombe, who converted to the Catholic Church).

> Politicians should not be preachers. (Enoch Powell)

Renewal
www.renewal.org.uk
Blairite journal founded in 1993, subtitled *A Journal of Social Democracy*. Set up as a discussion forum for the Blairite modernisers, it boasts an appropriate board, currently including David Miliband, Ed Miliband, Geoff Mulgan, Jon Cruddas and Tony Wright. For most of its life the journal performed its role loyally but in August 2004 published a swingeing attack on the direction in which Tony Blair had taken the party.

> Tragically Blair still appears to believe that if he can only explain it one more time, we will get it. But Tony, we get the message – we just don't accept it.

report stage
See act of parliament; legislative process.

Representation of the People Act
See Reform Act.

representative
Someone who, in political terms, is held to stand for or speak for a group of people from which he or she is drawn. This person may be appointed but more often, and desirably from the democratic point of view, is elected by some recognised process.
See also delegate.

representative democracy

The system used in most advanced western economies, including Britain. As distinct from direct democracy, it involves electors choosing representatives to make law and form governments. Jeremy Bentham, James Mill and his son John Stuart Mill were the chief philosophical advocates of this form of government, which they believed was the best safeguard against bad rulers and 'sinister interests'. All three believed individuals were the best judge of their own interests and so it followed each must have a vote, although James Mill sought to restrict it to men over 40. In contrast his son urged universal suffrage in principle for all adult men and women, though only if they passed a literacy test, in a system which would give more votes to the educated classes. He believed participation in government through voting would contribute to the moral education of society: 'Democracy creates a morally better person because it forces people to develop their potentialities'.

See also direct democracy; political participation; Bentham, Jeremy; Mill, James; Mill, John Stuart.

republicanism

A strand of political thinking usually associated with Irish nationalists although the embryo of republicanism has long existed in mainland Britain, mostly in the Labour Party and sections of the press. Because of the monarchy's perceived popularity, republicanism has never been embraced by Labour's leadership. James Callaghan and Neil Kinnock were careful to bow in the direction of the crown and Tony Blair declared himself an 'ardent monarchist' in 2000 when Mo Mowlam suggested the royal family should move out of Buckingham Palace. However, in January 2002 the *Guardian* reported that a group of former Labour frontbenchers led by Roy Hattersley had formed the new All Party Parliamentary Republican Group. They met in secret to prevent Labour whips from intervening. Twenty Labour MPs were said to support it, plus Norman Baker from the Liberal Democrats.

Research Department (Conservative)

Founded in the 1920s and revived by R. A. Butler after the Second World War. Three of its early members – Enoch Powell, Ian Macleod and Reginald Maudling – went on to serve in the cabinet. Its function is to undertake long-term research and help formulate policy. It also provides secretaries for the parliamentary committees of the party. From 1945 to 1975 it was a useful source of ideas and personnel but Margaret Thatcher tended to see it as a centre of consensual 'wet' influence and the more monetarist Centre for Policy Studies stole much of its role in the party. Future cabinet members who worked in the Research Department in the late 1970s included Chris Patten, William Waldegrave, David Willets and David Howell. Chancellor Nigel Lawson, who once turned down the offer of directing the department, used to include its head in weekly policy discussions at the Treasury in the 1980s. It produces the invaluable campaign guides before general elections for Conservative candidates.

reselection (of MPs)

The process whereby a constituency party confirms or revokes its support for a sitting parliamentary candidate. This practice is associated with all the main parties, but Labour is particularly noteworthy in this respect. In the late 1980s it subjected its sitting MPs to mandatory reselection before a general election, which, on occasion, resulted in deselection. The thinking behind Labour's system was to 'test' whether the MP had reflected constituency party interests; in practice during the early 1980s it reflected the agenda of left-wing party activists, who wanted to secure greater control over an MP's behaviour in the Commons, in line with the delegate theory of representation. However, under the leadership of Neil Kinnock the left was marginalised and sitting MPs enjoyed more independence. Under Tony Blair, the reduction of the block vote by trade unions at conference was applied also to the selection of candidates in 1995, where union influence could previously have been decisive. After 1995 and a close conference decision, one member one vote (OMOV) was adopted for the selection of candidates. However, Labour's central party machine often intervenes in the selection of parliamentary candidates by local parties: Shaun Woodward, for example, who joined Labour from the Tories, was all but parachuted into his safe constituency of St Helens.

The Conservatives tend to reselect automatically but in the case of Neil Hamilton, Central Office would probably have liked to intervene and force the Tatton MP to stand down. Under reforms introduced by William Hague after 1997 this kind of intervention is easier, though local autonomy is a strongly held principle in the Conservative Party.

A popular reform proposal in the wake of the 2009 MPs' expenses scandal was that an MP can be 'recalled' and a new contest held if a sufficient number of constituents (e.g. 10 per cent) support this.

See also candidate for parliamentary election; deselection; recall (of MPs).

Respect (party)
www.therespectparty.net
Party established in 2004, when it was focused on opposition to the Iraq war. One of the main founding influences was George Galloway, the maverick former Labour MP. Respect campaigned in the local and European elections in June 2004 and, while it did not win any seats in the latter contest, it polled a quarter of a million votes overall and did relatively well in Birmingham and in certain London boroughs, for example gaining 20 per cent of the vote in Tower Hamlets. In 2005 Galloway caused a sensation by defeating Oona King in Bethnal Green and Bow but he failed to win in Poplar and Limehouse in May 2010.

'respect' agenda
Labour government attempt to curb anti-social behaviour by young people. Polls and focus groups report widespread public dissatisfaction with anti-social behaviour

and the Labour government under Tony Blair and Gordon Brown believed it was the result of poor parenting, poverty, poor schooling, unemployment and low-level crime. Its response was to introduce measures like 'asbos' (anti-social behaviour orders) and parenting classes. By May 2010 few believed such measures had even begun to solve the problem and many more believed David Cameron's analysis that Britain was a 'broken society'.

ResPublica
www.respublica.org.uk
Right-of-centre think-tank created 2009 by theologian Phillip Blond. He is the originator of so-called 'red Toryism'. This approach, based to a degree on his hostility to what Thatcherism did to his home town of Liverpool, has allegedly appealed to David Cameron and his circle, as it aims to use the state to assist poorer people but from a distinctive, rather more traditional moral basis. Blond argues for the reinvention of communities and objective values.

restorative justice
Confronting criminals with their victims. This approach was pioneered in New Zealand, where it registered some success. The aim is to heal the wounds of the victim, offender and community through various forms of mediation between the victim and the offender, as well as delivering some reparation of the hurt caused. In spring 2003 home secretary David Blunkett announced that this theme would receive a new emphasis in coming years. The Restorative Justice Consortium (www.restorativejustice.org.uk) claims this approach works:

> Restorative Justice also helps offenders and UK trials have proven that Restorative Justice reduces the number of crimes offenders commit (results indicate that an average of 27 per cent fewer crimes are committed by offenders who took part in a restorative justice conference). Restorative Justice saves the criminal justice system up to £8 for every £1 spent delivering the Restorative Justice service.

retirement age

The age at which the state pension can be drawn. The state pension age for British men and women will increase to 66 in 2024, to 67 in 2034 and 68 in 2044. Each rise will be phased in over two years. PricewaterhouseCoopers produced a report on 25 February 2010 that suggested the retirement age would have to increase to 70 to enable public finances to afford to pay pensions. The Tories suggested an even faster schedule for increases (possibly 66 by 2016 and 65 for women by 2020).

Along with many other countries, the UK's population is ageing. In 1950 only one in 10 was over 65; in 2010 it was one in six and by 2035 it will be one in four. In 2007 there were 11.8 million over state pension age: for the first time ever a number exceeding those aged 16 and under.

returning officer

The officer appointed by local authorities to be responsible for and to supervise the count on election night. The sight of returning officers announcing results in front of the television cameras has become an essential aspect of British election nights.

revenue support grant

A local government finance term, meaning, according to Exeter county council: 'A grant paid by government to meet a proportion of the local authority expenditure necessary to provide a standard level of service throughout the country'.

revisionism

The name given to the ideas of those in the Labour Party who disagreed with members who wished to extend the programme of Clement Attlee's 1945 Labour government into the 1950s and beyond. Those who conducted the rethink were intellectuals for the most part and included Hugh Gaitskell, Anthony Crosland, Denis Healey and Roy Jenkins. Harold Wilson pursued basically revisionist policies during the 1960s and 1970s but the left-wing backlash in the early 1980s so alienated voters it took a decade or so of a more full-blooded

revisionism by Neil Kinnock and John Smith, but most of all by modernisers such as Tony Blair and Peter Mandelson, to reposition Labour in the electoral 'market' to make victory possible again.

See also clause 4.

right honourable

See parliamentary terms of address.

right to buy

The right of a council tenant to buy the house being rented. Margaret Thatcher's unerring sense of popular concerns was evident soon after 1979, when she identified the wish of many council house tenants to own their own homes. Accordingly the 'right to buy' policy was introduced, whereby tenants were allowed to buy their own houses at substantial discounts. It was criticised for reducing the housing stock and contributing to homelessness, but it was very popular with tenants and 1.7 million council houses were sold. However, the funds raised were returned to the Treasury, and local authorities were barred from using the receipts as a subsidy for general expenditure or to build additional houses.

See also council housing.

right to roam

Slogan of the Ramblers' Association, expressing its objective of achieving freedom for walkers to use the 12 per cent of Britain classed as mountain, moorland, heath and common land. Such a right was in Labour's manifesto in 1997 but lobbying by the landed gentry caused the government to think again, especially after the Countryside Alliance's march in 1997 included opposition to it. Instead, the government decided on a consultation exercise; in this, 80 per cent of the over 2,000 responses favoured the 'right to roam'. Opposition continued in 1998 from the Country Land and Business Association, a 50,000-strong organisation that threatened to sue the government for the losses such a right would cause. Nonetheless, the measure was passed and celebrated by walkers in September 2004.

riot
Term originally derived from Old French *riote*, meaning 'to have a good time'. Apart from the riots in the 1930s centred around Oswald Mosley, modern British political culture has not generally featured violence. Many commentators predicted riots in the streets when unemployment approached 3 million in the early 1980s. However, the streets remained surprisingly quiet until disturbances broke out in Toxteth, Liverpool, in 1981. Similar riots occurred in many British cities, including Manchester and London. Michael Heseltine produced a paper for the cabinet entitled 'It Took a Riot' and advocated substantial expenditure to remove the social causes of the violence. His advice was rejected but Margaret Thatcher was at least momentarily worried by the apparent breakdown in law and order. Eventually peace returned but several areas of the country remained uneasily balanced on the edge of disorder for many years and, indeed, many still are. One of the most serious cases of rioting took place in Trafalgar Square as part of the anti-poll tax demonstrations in 1990; stewards lost control of the protest and the police, according to many protestors, actively provoked public disorder by their methods. In June 2001 riots broke out in Oldham, Burnley and Bradford; these had a racial component exacerbated by the activities of far-right parties like the British National Party.
See also anarchism.

RMT
See National Union of Rail, Maritime and Transport Workers.

Rockall
A small uninhabited column of rock, 83 feet long, 100 feet wide and 70 feet high, jutting out of the sea to the west of St Kilda. It was annexed to Britain in 1972 but because it cannot sustain habitation there cannot be any exclusive economic zone or continental shelf, according to the 1997 UN Convention on the Law

of the Sea, though the island falls within the British zone, which extends for a distance of 12 miles around it. Rights to the surrounding continental shelf and any underlying natural resources are disputed by Britain, Iceland, Ireland and Denmark.

rotten borough
Borough constituencies that sent MPs to parliament and that were so decayed they deserved Pitt the Elder's remark that borough representation was the 'rotten part of the constitution'. Examples include Old Sarum, which was a green mound populated by sheep, and Dunwich, which had been submerged for hundreds of years under the North Sea and whose patrons secured election through straightforward bribery or simple nomination.

Royal Air Force
See armed forces.

royal assent
Final stage of the legislative process after a bill has passed through both houses of parliament, when it thereby becomes an act. Queen Anne was the last monarch to deny the royal assent, in 1707 over the Scottish Militia Bill. The queen no longer gives the royal assent personally; since the passing of the Royal Assent Act 1967, commissioners in the Assent Office communicate the fact of assent to both houses of parliament.
See also legislative process.

royal commission
Appointed by the sovereign, on the request of the prime minister, to investigate a matter of public concern. Royal commissions are usually chaired by a member of the 'great and the good' and therefore unlikely to produce anything too radical. They make recommendations for future action and can mark watersheds in the aspects of public life into which they inquire. Margaret Thatcher did not establish any such bodies during her period in office, as she tended to believe she did not need research into what was wrong: she already knew this and merely wanted action to remedy it.

Royal Commission on Criminal Justice

Set up by John Major in 1992, it produced 352 recommendations, including a suggestion for a new independent body to refer cases of miscarriages of justice to the Appeal Court.

Royal Commission on Environmental Pollution, Transport and the Environment

Raised concerns in its 1994 report about the health implications of transport policy and recommended the halving of road building over the next decade plus the doubling of the real price of petrol. The Conservative government was unreceptive to the proposals but Labour deputy prime minister John Prescott was more sympathetic, though whether action will follow along such lines is still unclear. In September 2000 road hauliers and farmers led direct action against petrol taxation by blockading refineries. The public, it seemed, was not prepared to accept that high fuel prices were justified environmentally (or indeed in any other way).

See also fuel protest.

Royal Commission on Local Government in England

See Redcliffe-Maud report.

Royal Mail

www.royalmailgroup.com

The Post Office decided to change its name to Consignia in January 2001 on the grounds that its existing name no longer adequately described what it did. The change coincided with the transition of the Post Office to a government-owned public limited company in March 2001. Union critics complained that 350 years of history and the brand name 'Royal Mail' were being carelessly abandoned and that such a move threatened a move to privatisation. Consignia reported financial problems early in 2002 – it allegedly lost over £1 million per day and was forced to consider the abandonment of second deliveries. Consignia announced restructuring plans which would entail 17,000 redundancies; some reports suggested the true figure was closer to 40,000. The name Royal Mail was subsequently reclaimed. In June 2004 a consumer watchdog claimed over 14 million letters were wrongly delivered every week. When losses increased, many post offices were closed in both urban and rural areas, causing much anger and dissent by MPs. Some years later it was suggested that the Royal Mail be partly privatised, provoking a rebellion on Labour back benches. On 2 July 2009 Lord Mandelson announced the partial sell-off would not go ahead on account of 'business conditions'. Cynics concluded that Gordon Brown lacked the political capital to progress the proposal. The Conservative–Liberal Democrat coalition in May 2010 revived plans to push through a partial privatisation of the Mail; the size of its pension fund deficit was anticipated to be a major problem in such a transition.

Royal Navy

See armed forces.

royal prerogative

See prerogative powers.

Royal Ulster Constabulary

See Police Service of Northern Ireland.

royal wealth

Being a hereditary monarch in a democracy is something of an anomaly and the scale of royal wealth attracts criticism: why should the queen receive money via the civil list when she is already fabulously wealthy? Some estimates of her wealth include her palaces and art collection, which is inappropriate in that such items belong to the nation and are not convertible into any other form of wealth by the queen. An estimate of her wealth appeared in the *Guardian* in October 2001 and reckoned it to be £1.15 billion. This included: property valued at £61 million; racehorses worth £3.6 million (the queen owns 30 racehorses, which cost £500,000 a year to keep); jewels worth £72 million

POLITICS

(including the Cullinan diamonds, valued
at £29 million); cars valued at £7.1 million
(the queen owns over a dozen cars); stamps
and medals worth £102 million (the queen
has the biggest collection of stamps in the
world, kept in 300 albums and 200 boxes).

rule of law
The great constitutional lawyer
A. V. Dicey defined this as one of the
twin pillars of the British constitution and
a principal element of a free and civilised
society. Included in its provisions is the
normative rule that governments must act
within the law with respect to their own
actions, as well as the treatment of individuals and groups. In particular, it posits an
impartial judiciary, which must also be
independent in order to provide fair trials
and freedom from arbitrary imprisonment.
However, jurists and political scientists
have criticised the doctrine on a number
of counts. For example, parliamentary
sovereignty could in theory override any
prior law. Moreover, ministers of the crown
enjoy certain quasi-judicial and legislative
powers which may undermine a citizen's
protection under due process of law.

ruling class
Karl Marx argued that in stratified
societies a ruling class owns the means of
production and exploits and oppresses a
subject class. Westergard and Resler, two
sociologists, suggested in the 1970s that
the ruling class amounted to 5–10 per cent
of the population, and included owners of
the means of production, chief executives of
major companies, higher professionals and
administrators, a large number of whom
were major shareholders. Many of these
people have similar social and educational
backgrounds, usually having attended
public school and Oxbridge, and go on to
marry people with a similar background,
thus perpetuating the class. Many have
challenged this view as a simplistic explanation of the complex nature of economic and
political decision making.
    See also elite; meritocracy; pluralism;
upper class.

S

safe seat
See marginal seat.

Saint Kilda
Small group of islands in the Outer
Hebrides notable politically only for the
St Kilda parliament, which sat in the 19th
century and comprised all the adult males
on the island and conducted its proceedings
purely in Gaelic. The island was evacuated
in 1930, thus ending settlement. The
island now belongs to the National Trust of
Scotland.

salariat
Term used – prefixed by 'higher' and
'lower' – by Oxford sociologist John
Goldthorpe as an alternative to 'middle-
class professional' in his analysis of social
groupings. Both categories collectively
were roughly equivalent to the groupings
A, B and C1 according to the more widely
accepted British Market Research Society's
analysis. Others in Goldthorpe's scheme
were 'routine clerical', 'petty bourgeois',
'foremen and technicians', 'skilled manual'
and 'unskilled manual'.
    See also class.

Salisbury doctrine
A rule that the Lords will not oppose a
measure that has wide public support. It is
named after the fifth Marquess of Salisbury,
the Conservative leader of the Lords
from 1945 to 1950 who formulated it. In
practice, after the Second World War, this
meant the Lords would oppose only Labour
legislation that had not been mentioned in
its manifesto. Margaret Thatcher invoked
the doctrine in 1988 when she refused to
accept the Lords' opposition to the poll tax
on the grounds that it had been mentioned
in the Conservative 1987 manifesto; the
Lords responded that mere mention of
'reform of local government finance' was not
the same as the 'poll tax' and that therefore

the government did not have a mandate – but they passed it nevertheless.

Salisbury Group

Right-wing intellectual grouping, founded 1976, linked to but not part of the Conservative Party exerting influence through its journal, founded in 1982 by philosopher Roger Scruton, the *Salisbury Review*.

Saville inquiry

www.bloody-sunday-inquiry.org
Set up in 2000 to investigate the deaths of 14 civil rights marchers on 'Bloody Sunday' in 1972. It reconsidered the ground supposedly covered by the 1972 Widgery report, the anodyne conclusions of which did nothing to assuage the sense of outrage felt by the families of those killed. That report had favoured the army and had been conducted in an adversarial manner. By contrast, the Saville inquiry avoided those mistakes and summoned more than 900 witnesses, including senior politicians (for example Edward Heath), army officers and the soldiers who fired on and killed the marchers. After three years of exhaustive hearings – the opening statement alone took 176 hours – the inquiry heard its last oral testimony in February 2004. So time consuming and expensive – with estimates as high as £400 million by its conclusion – was the process that it probably ruled out anything similar for some time. In February 2008 Shaun Woodward, secretary of state for Northern Ireland, revealed the inquiry was still costing £500,000 per month and a total of over £180 million, more than half of the costs in the form of legal bills. Time alone will tell whether the conclusions of the report will render the mammoth undertaking worthwhile; Lord Saville was expected to publish his report in early 2010 although such dates have been progressively pushed into the future since 2004.

See also Bloody Sunday.

Scarman report, 1981

Following the riots in Brixton, Lord Scarman was appointed to investigate its causes. He focused on the absence of a police complaints procedure as a major reason for the breakdown in police–community relations. He came down in favour of measures to reduce racial discrimination, including positive discrimination.

Schengen agreement, 1985

An EU agreement that removed border controls. It includes most members of the EU but Britain implemented only some of the border controls, fearing the dangers of crime and terrorism.

Scotland

A northern region of the British Isles of 79,000 km^2 (30,400 square miles) and a population of some 5 million. There were successive wars between England and Scotland but in 1603, when Elizabeth I died, the two separate kingdoms were united under a single monarch, as James IV of Scotland became James I of England. Scotland became part of the United Kingdom with the Act of Union in 1707. This was far from an 'annexation', as the agreement was to some extent negotiated and the Scots were allowed to retain some independence. Scotland retained its distinctive educational and legal systems as well as bank notes. This sense of identity fuelled the Scottish National Party (SNP), which began to attract support during the 1960s. There was substantial support for increased autonomy from Westminster in the 1970s but not enough to bring about devolution in that decade. However, national feeling continued to grow under the Thatcher governments in the 1980s and beyond until New Labour came to power in 1997. This was evidenced by the large 'yes' in the referendum for a Scottish assembly in September 1997; the summer of 1998 saw increasing support for the SNP. In 1999, the queen opened the Scottish parliament in Edinburgh, signalling an era of (renewed) Scottish devolution. In the 1999 elections to the Scottish parliament Labour was the biggest party but had to govern in coalition with the Liberal Democrats. Despite losses in 2003 the same coalition remained in power. As a consequence of

devolution the Boundary Commission reduced the number of Scottish Westminster
seats from 72 to 59 in 2005. After the May
2007 election the SNP was the largest
party in the Scottish parliament, by just one
seat (47 seats to Labour's 46), and Alex
Salmond became first minister in a minority
administration. Despite this insecure political position, Salmond governed shrewdly
and maintained high levels of popularity for
his party. In the May 2010 parliamentary
elections there was a 0.8 percentage point
swing to Labour, which won back two
seats the party had lost in by-elections
since 2005, giving it 41 out of the 59 seats
contested. The Conservatives managed to
win only one seat, the Liberal Democrats
11 and the SNP 6.

See also devolution.

Scotland Act 1998
See Scottish parliament.

Scott report, 1996
The *Report of the Inquiry into the Export
of Defence Equipment and Dual-Use
Goods to Iraq and Related Prosecutions.*
Sir Richard Scott was asked to inquire into
the circumstances of the 1992 collapse of
the Matrix Churchill trial of three British
businessmen accused of selling arms
to Iraq in contravention of government
guidelines. The trial ended when a junior
defence minister, Alan Clarke, admitted
the businessmen had received an informal
indication that their proposed sale could
go ahead. The report uncovered a disturbing mixture of maladministration and
departmental self-interest taking precedence
over policy objectives. Several ministers,
including William Waldegrave, and officials
were criticised, though Michael Heseletine,
president of the Board of Trade at the
time, emerged unscathed. Robin Cook was
notable for the excoriating attacks he made
on the government over this issue.

See also Matrix Churchill case.

Scottish Grand Committee
Set up in 1981 to deal with Scottish legislative matters. Second and third readings

of bills relating to Scotland were read in
the committee, which often met in Scotland
itself. Initially it comprised all Scottish
MPs. During the Conservative years of
government in the 1980s and early 1990s,
therefore, it had a Labour majority. This
led the Scottish secretary to point out to
Labour members that Westminster had the
'absolute veto' and that the committee was
not a 'Scottish parliament'. The committee
survived devolution and in 2003 comprised
72 members, though bills relating exclusively
to Scotland have been a rarity since the
establishment of the Scottish parliament.

Scottish Labour Party (SLP)
Set up in 1976 by Scottish members of the
Labour Party who felt the then government's devolution proposals did not go far
enough. James Sillars and John Robertson
became members but continued to take the
Labour whip until late in 1976. The party
suffered entryism from the International
Marxist Group and a very early bout of
factionalism. Sillars saved his deposit in the
1979 election but the other two candidates
did not. Sillars joined the Scottish National
Party once the SLP was wound up.

Scottish National Liberation Army (SNLA)
Militant faction seeking the end of English
immigration into Scotland and the
establishment of a Scottish republic. It was
thought to be behind the sending of parcels
containing toxic substances to a number of
political figures in March 2002, including
Cherie Blair. The chief suspect was Adam
Busby, the founder of the SNLA, who
lives in Ireland and has evaded attempts
to extradite him. The organisation was
involved in earlier hoax threats to poison
water supplies in England and in sending
hoax anthrax letters to Prince William.

Scottish National Party (SNP)
www.snp.org
Founded in 1934 by John McCormick,
who believed his country received a poor
deal from the union with England effected
in 1707. The party asserts that Scotland

could pay its own way through domestic taxes and pursues a policy of independence within the European Union. The party's fortunes improved after the discovery of North Sea oil in the 1970s, when the proposition that this oil belonged to Scotland attracted support in a country beset with unemployment as traditional industries declined. In February 1974 it returned seven MPs and in October 1974 11 MPs – whose vote against Labour in 1979 precipitated the vote of confidence which then led to an election at which the party returned only two MPs. There were only three SNP MPs elected in 1992. In 1997 the SNP supported the 'yes' vote on the referendum for a Scottish parliament and it may be that Labour's policy of assuaging nationalist feeling with devolution paradoxically merely whetted the Scots' appetite for more autonomy. The SNP's standing in the polls was equal to Labour's in the autumn of 1998, which augured badly for Labour in the elections to the Scottish parliament scheduled for 1999. In the event the SNP emerged as the second largest party after Labour, with 35 MSPs. In 2000 Alex Salmond stood down as leader of the SNP and John Swinney took over. In the June 2001 Westminster election the SNP won 20 per cent of the Scottish vote (two points down on 1997) and five seats (one down on 1997). The election was something of a setback for the SNP, leaving it 8 percentage points down on the 1999 Scottish parliament elections. In the May 2003 elections to the Scottish parliament the SNP lost eight seats; Swinney resigned in 2004 and Alex Salmond was re-elected as leader that September. In May 2007 the SNP won 47 seats, one more than Labour, and Salmond became first minister in a minority administration, which proved able to rule with some popular success.

Scottish Office

The department of state concerned with governing Scotland. It was established in 1885 and disappeared once the Scottish parliament came into being in 1999.

In June 2003 the secretary of state for Scotland was downgraded to a part-time job, when it was tacked on to that of the transport secretary but with political authority given to the new Department of Constitutional Affairs.

Scottish parliament

www.scottish.parliament.uk

As promised in Labour's 1997 manifesto, a referendum was held on two proposals: a Scottish parliament and a parliament with tax-varying powers. The voters approved the first proposal by 74 to 26 per cent, the second by 64 to 36 per cent. Turnout was 60 per cent. The Scotland Act establishing the parliament received its royal assent in May 1998. Just over a year later, on 6 May 1999, elections took place for the 129 members of the Scottish parliament (called MSPs) by the amended additional member system (AMS): 73 from constituencies plus 56 members by party list. Labour emerged the largest party but needed Liberal Democrat support, which came at a price: seats in the cabinet and an inquiry into student tuition fees, which eventually led to their abolition in Scotland.

The parliament has legislative and executive powers, except in the following areas: UK constitutional issues, foreign affairs, defence and national security, macro-economic policy, employment, social security, and transport safety and regulation. Income tax could be varied by plus or minus 3 pence in the pound. Those powers not defined are devolved and become the responsibility of the Scottish executive, led by a first minister. The late Donald Dewar became the first holder of this office (he died in the autumn of 2000) and Jim Wallace (Liberal Democrats) his deputy. David Steel became presiding officer of the parliament. Jack McConnell took over as first minister and survived the second elections to the parliament on 1 May 2003. Labour lost six seats but the SNP fared even worse, losing eight. The Greens gained seven seats and the Scottish Socialists a surprising six seats. After four years of the parliament, voters did not seem to be especially pleased

POLITICS

with the performance of the coalition. In May 2007 Alex Salmond became first minister as leader of the SNP, having won 47 seats to Labour's 46.

See also devolution; Sewel convention.

second chamber
See House of Lords.

Second World War
A war with a profound effect on the development of Britain. Among the consequences were the fact that Britain, though triumphant, was now economically bankrupt, which ensured its days as a world power were numbered. Despite this, the experience of war unified the country and established a powerful myth of togetherness, sharing and equality, which was exploited by the Labour Party in the 1945 general election. Moreover, wartime social policy carried over into the peace with the founding of the National Health Service, social security and other elements of the welfare state during the 1945–51 Attlee administrations. Centralised planning of the economy, in particular of labour, fuel and manufacturing, which helped win the war, made Labour's programme of nationalisation more acceptable, as did a recognition that trade unions were effectively part of the state and had a right to be consulted. Full employment during the war nourished a desire for it in peacetime and the demand management theories of John Maynard Keynes were to underpin much of the economic thinking for the next 30 years or so. The public and the armed forces had been radicalised by a war fought against a barbaric system, Nazism, and many wanted a new start, which meant that the Conservative Party, despite the triumph of Winston Churchill, was discredited as the party of appeasement and unemployment. Finally, the carve-up of Germany and Europe at Potsdam and Yalta was eventually to lead, along with Marshall aid and the Berlin blockade, to Britain's membership of NATO in 1949, a military alliance led by the USA – an indication that the Cold War was already well under way.

secondary legislation
See delegated legislation.

secondary modern school
Established by the 1944 'Butler' Education Act, which introduced three types of secondary school – grammar, technical and secondary modern. Grammar and some technical schools were well resourced and catered for mostly middle-class children who had passed the 11-plus, an examination also introduced by the act. The majority of children, who failed, were condemned to a poorly funded education in the secondary modern sector, where the teaching and the results were often dire. In the 1960s Labour decided to scrap the 11 plus and introduce comprehensive education as a substitute for grammar schools, secondary modern schools and technical schools; however, some areas retained these types of school.

secondary picketing
Picketing (industrial action) by trade unionists of a place of work not directly involved in an industrial dispute. It was used extensively during the miners' strikes in 1972 and 1974 and during the public sector disputes in late 1978, now known as the 'winter of discontent'. To curtail union power, the Employment Act 1980 outlawed the practice, a measure which was retained by New Labour when it came to power in 1997.

secrecy
Sir John Hoskyns, former head of Margaret Thatcher's Policy Unit, wrote that the culture of secrecy, sustained by the Official Secrets Act and the 30-year rule, was convenient for government by 'hiding peacetime fiascos as if they were military secrets or issues of national security, thus protecting ministers and officials from embarrassment'. Despite hopes of reform under New Labour, many were disappointed by the relatively modest changes of Jack Straw's Freedom of Information Act 2000.

See also Freedom of Information Act 2000; Official Secrets Act; open government.

secret ballot
See ballot.

Secret Intelligence Service (MI6)
See security services.

section 28
A clause of the Local Government Act
1988, accepted as an amendment, which
made it illegal for local authorities to
engage in the 'deliberate promotion' of
homosexuality. This vague wording was
used by some local authorities, claimed
activists, to justify homophobic policies.
Many teachers saw the clause as a veto on
open discussion of the issue in class and
a barrier to their tackling of homophobic
bullying. After 1997 Labour promised
to repeal the section, but support for
its retention proved surprisingly robust,
especially in Scotland, according to a
privately funded poll. It was finally repealed
in November 2003. In the summer of 2009
gay cabinet minister Ben Bradshaw warned
gay voters that the Conservatives were not
genuinely sympathetic to them. This caused
a row, with David Cameron denying this
but having to accept that he had voted for
section 28 in the Commons.

sectional interest group
See pressure group.

Security Commission
Cabinet Office body tasked with investigating breaches of national security. It was
established in 1964 to 'investigate and
report upon the circumstances in which a
breach of security is known to have occurred
in the public service'. The Right Honorable
Lady Justice Sloss was chair in 2004, supported by six other members. The members
form a panel from which three or four,
including the chair, are normally selected
on each occasion when the Commission is
invited by the prime minister to investigate a
suspected breach of security.

Security Service Act 1989
Placed MI5 on a statutory basis with a
specified range of functions. In 1997 the

latter were increased to include the prevention of crime and its detection. The act also
set up a security services commissioner to
monitor phone tapping and interference
with property by the security services, and
to deliver an annual report to the prime
minister.

security services
www.mi5.gov.uk; www.mi6.gov.uk
Britain's security services comprise
MI5, the Security Service (the counter-
intelligence agency for domestic matters),
and MI6, the Secret Intelligence Service
(the overseas intelligence service). The
police have an internal agency called
Special Branch and radio surveillance
is carried out by SIGINT, Signals
Intelligence. MI5 reports to the Home
Office; MI6 collects intelligence on matters
relevant to the security of the state and
reports to the Foreign Office. MI5 used to
worry about the Communist Party but since
that party's demise has focused on extremist
political movements. Despite these different
lines of accountability, important matters
can be taken direct to the prime minister
when necessary. There are cabinet committees that overlook the security services:
one, MIS, is chaired by the prime minister,
and three, PSIS plus two others, by the
cabinet secretary. Under the provisions
of the Intelligence Services Act 1994 the
Intelligence and Security Committee was
set up to oversee the security services. In the
mid-1980s there were about 10,000 people
employed by the security services. Security
chiefs are also represented at COBRA,
the name given to the Civil Contingencies
Committee dealing with emergencies.

select committee
An investigative committee of the House
of Commons. Select committees have
been used since Tudor times but more so
recently. For much of the 20th century
there were only two such committees, the
Public Accounts Committee (PAC) and
the Estimates Committee. These were
supplemented by the Statutory Instruments
Committee in the 1940s and in the

POLITICS

1950s by a committee dealing with the nationalised industries. Richard Crossman strove to expand their role in the 1960s but with limited success. It was not until the 1980s, when Norman St John Stevas was leader of the House of Commons, that real progress was made and a raft of departmental select committees were set up. The committees have powers to call for persons, papers and records; they may also hold hearings in public.

See also departmental select committee; non-departmental select committee; Public Accounts Committee.

Select Committee on Science and Technology (Commons)

www.parliament.uk/business/committees/committees-archive/science-technology
The Select Committee on Innovation, Universities, Science and Skills, set up on 6 November 2007, was the occasion of the abolition of the old Science and Technology Select Committee. A year and a half later, however, the latter was re-established after the Department of Innovation, Universities and Skills was merged with the Department of Business, Enterprise and Regulatory Reform in June 2009. The Committee's remit is to examine the work of the Government Office for Science.

Select Committee on Science and Technology (Lords)

www.parliament.uk/business/committees/committees-archive/lords-s-t-select
The remit of the Lords Committee, set up in 1979, is as wide as possible: to 'consider science and technology'. It investigates via subcommittees set up afresh for each inquiry. It directs its attention to such matters as: public policy areas which ought to be informed by scientific research, such as the health effects of air travel and the legal status of cannabis; technological challenges and opportunities, like resistance to antibiotics and the management of nuclear waste; and public policy towards science itself, for example as it affects the research councils, schools and universities.

Selsdon Group

www.selsdongroup.co.uk
Formed in 1973 to champion free market policies in the Conservative Party. It took its name from the Selsdon Park Hotel at which the Conservative Party formulated its manifesto in 1970. Many of Edward Heath's critics felt he had departed from these principles and the group was designed to direct him back to the chosen path after his famous U-turns. It advocated privatisation, the scrapping of quangos, private initiatives in the welfare state and strict control of both the money supply and public expenditure. It was an important fringe group at party conferences in the 1980s.

sentencing

A controversial aspect of penal policy, as few people can agree what punishment fits which crime. Parliament makes laws and the Home Office may issue guidelines on the maximum sentences for certain offences. Courts are allowed wide discretion based on the particular circumstances of each crime. Consequently there is not always consistency in the sentences handed down in different parts of the country. The Conservatives, influenced by the party rank and file, tend to favour tougher sentences, such as the return of the death penalty – though after much debate during the 1980s it was not readopted and is not party policy. Sentences for rape, robbery and the use of firearms did increase markedly during the middle of the decade. Tory home secretary Michael Howard was famous for adducing the simplistic claim that 'prison works' but criminologists and High Court judges tended to disagree strongly and in September 1998 the Home Affairs Select Committee reported that the increase in the prison population of Britain – then over 66,000 – was 'unsustainable' and that 20,000 inmates should be released and dealt with via community punishments. Its chair, Chris Mullin MP, said 'Prison is only an ineffective and very expensive means of containment'. In January 2003 the lord chancellor, Lord Irvine, and the lord chief justice, Lord Justice Woolf, caused controversy by suggesting that burglars should not necessarily be imprisoned for their first or second offences. To provide guidance on sentencing the Sentencing Guidelines Council was set up in 2003 by the Criminal Justice Act 2003. It gives authoritative guidance on sentencing to the courts of England and Wales.

See also death penalty; penal policy; Prison Service.

Sentencing Advisory Panel and Sentencing Guidelines Council
www.sentencing-guidelines.gov.uk
Two closely related independent bodies that work together to encourage consistency in sentencing. The Sentencing Advisory Panel advises the Sentencing Guidelines Council on the appropriate sentences for certain offences or categories of offence. Its remit is to carry out wide consultation and research if called upon. The Council uses the advice to formulate sentencing guidelines to be used by sentencers, after further consultation.

separation of powers
Montesquieu, the 18th-century French political theorist, developed a doctrine, first evinced in medieval Europe, that political power was too potent a force to be vested in one body or authority. So fearful was he that a despot or tyrant would come to overwhelm a kingdom that he examined the British parliamentary system and believed, wrongly, that he could discern three functions in government: a legislature which made the law; a judiciary which interpreted and judged the laws; and an executive which implemented the laws and performed other governmental functions. He believed the three elements should be kept separate and his ideas were taken up by the framers of the US constitution, who built into their fledgling political system clear separation between the Congress (the legislature), the Supreme Court (the judiciary) and the president (the executive), and an elaborate checking procedure between them, an arrangement which survives to this day.

At the time he was writing, the political system in Britain (under George III) was rather different from his ideals, and this remains so today in a number of significant respects. First, the executive or government is mostly drawn from the legislature (the House of Commons) in that the government is usually formed by the largest party returned to the legislature in elections. Nearly all members of the cabinet are MPs. Furthermore, cabinet ministers have quasi-judicial and legislative powers, which enable them to make executive decisions without necessarily having to seek prior approval of parliament.

The lord chancellor used to be head of the judiciary, to appoint judges as well as QCs, to serve as a cabinet member and to preside over the House of Lords. This concentration of roles 'fused' the supposedly separate functions of government and attracted much criticism from reformers. In spring 2003 the government sought to resolve some of these anomalies by establishing: a secretary of state for constitutional affairs to take charge of the courts system instead of the lord chancellor; and new procedures for appointing judges and QCs. In addition, the establishment of the Supreme Court in 2008 ended the arrangement whereby senior members of the judiciary sat as law lords in the House of Lords as the highest court of appeal in Britain.

The separation of functions is therefore not sharp and is to some extent 'fused' but, despite this, advocates of the system maintain that there are extensive mechanisms of accountability and for the redress of grievance.

See also elective dictatorship.

Septennial Act 1716
Act, passed by the Whigs, that extended the maximum period between elections from three to seven years. It contributed to the greater stability of parliament and the authority of the House of Commons. The Parliament Act 1911 reduced the period to the present five years.

Serious Fraud Office (SFO)
www.sfo.gov.uk
An independent government department,
formed in 1988, that investigates and
prosecutes serious or complex fraud. The
Office is headed by its director (Richard
Alderman from April 2008), who is appointed by and accountable to the attorney
general. The SFO has been criticised for
some of its investigations including: when
the BAE illegal payments inquiry was
stopped by ministers, who claimed it was
jeopardising national security; drug sales
to the National Health Service; and a
£16 million inquiry into the Phoenix Four
businessmen, who made millions out of
buying MG Rover in 2005.

Serious Organised Crime Agency (SOCA)
www.soca.gov.uk
Executive non-departmental public
body sponsored by, but operationally
independent from, the Home Office, with
law enforcement powers. The Agency was
announced in the white paper 'One Step
Ahead' in 2004, and was presented in the
media as a kind of British equivalent of
the US Federal Bureau of Investigation.
Its aim is to find the big figures who
run multimillion pound drug, vice and
money-laundering rackets. Organised crime
is believed to cost Britain £40 billion per
year. SOCA combines the National Crime
Squad, the National Criminal Intelligence
Customs and fraud investigations. The
intelligence agencies support the work of
the new agency, which has around 4,000
staff, including experts in finance and high
technology. SOCA has been criticised
for inefficiency and poor results since its
inception.

service (or tertiary) sector of the economy
The part of the economy which provides
services to consumers, including tourism,
leisure, financial services and information
technology. As the manufacturing sector
has declined, the service sector has
expanded, so that it provided jobs for 70
per cent of the workforce in 2004. The
service sector is more labour intensive and
cannot cut costs as easily as manufacturing,
where advances in production technology
can reduce labour costs. Moreover, the
service sector boomed in the 1990s while
manufacturing declined, creating the
'two-speed' economy.

settlement
See Act of Settlement 1701

7/7 bombings (London, 2005)
Coordinated suicide bombings on London
transport, 7 July 2005. The bombers were
four Muslim men opposed to the invasion
of Iraq. Three of the bombs exploded, the
first at 8.50 a.m., on Underground trains,
while the fourth detonated on a bus, an
hour later, in Tavistock Square. The four
bombers were: Mohammad Sidique Khan
(aged 30, from Dewsbury) (Edgware
Road Tube); Shehzad Tanweer (22, from
Leeds) (Aldgate Tube); Germaine Lindsay
(19, from Aylesbury, Buckinghamshire)
(Russell Square); and Hasib Hussain (18,
from Leeds) (bus at Tavistock Square).
Including these four, 56 people were killed
and 700 wounded. The attacks caused
outrage, especially as all four bombers were
British nationals, three of whom were born
and raised in Britain.

Sewel convention
The convention, not law, that Westminster
can legislate in respect of Scotland only
with the full consent of its parliament.

Sex Discrimination (Election Candidates) Act 2001
Act that enabled political parties to use
affirmative action to increase the selection
of female representatives. The legislation
is permissive and removes the possibility of
prosecution under British law, though not
European law. In 1996 all-women short-
lists enabled more women to be adopted as
candidates in the Labour Party – which
contributed to a record number being
elected in 1997 – but an employment
tribunal in 1996 found this to be illegal.

The act made such short-lists legal but it is up to individual parties to adopt the procedures they think appropriate.

Sexual Offences Act 1967
Decriminalised homosexual acts conducted in private between consenting adults aged over 21 in England and Wales. The provisions of the act were extended to Scotland and Northern Ireland in 1982. The Sexual Offences Amendment Act 2000 lowered the age of consent for all gay, lesbian and heterosexual acts to 16, though it introduced the new offence of 'having sexual intercourse or engaging in any other sexual activity with a person under 18 if in a position of trust in relation to that person'.

shadow cabinet
The team of opposition politicians, drawn largely from the House of Commons, chosen to specialise in the various departmental portfolios of government ministers – in effect a 'government in waiting'. An election within the Parliamentary Labour Party in theory determines the composition of its shadow cabinet and the actual cabinet once the party is elected to office. However, in May 1997 Tony Blair left out two members of his former shadow cabinet on the grounds that there were not enough cabinet posts available. In the more hierarchical Conservative Party, the leader has the power to appoint cabinets and shadow cabinets. Appointment is eagerly sought by MPs, who recognise that a creditable effort in opposing their minister will reinforce their claims to office and possible promotion. Blair served in several shadow jobs – employment, Home Office and energy – before winning the leadership in 1994. The practice of creating an alternative 'government in waiting' from the biggest opposition party is not emulated in other systems. For example, it would be difficult to do this in a multi-party system or in the USA, where the executive is elected in the person of the president and the losing candidate is not even a member of any legislative chamber and has no status once the election is over.

share ownership
Individual share ownership increased in the 1980s as millions of people bought shares in privatised industries. The Conservative government celebrated this as part of a change in national culture, a move to a 'people's capitalism'. However, shortly after buying them most people sold their shares to take a profit. The proportion of shares owned by individuals fell from over 30 per cent in the mid-1980s to just over 20 per cent in the early 1990s; the majority of shares are held by large financial institutions, especially pension funds and insurance companies.

Sheehy report, 1993
Report into the management of the police force. Sir Patrick Sheehy, a prominent businessman, was asked by home secretary Michael Howard to undertake the inquiry. The report criticised the top-heavy management structure of the police, overlapping responsibilities and promotion based on length of service, not merit or individual performance. It recommended: the abolition of three senior ranks; fixed-term, possibly 10-year contracts; performance-related pay; and less generous terms of sick pay. The Police Federation, the force's professional association, was incensed and attacked the report bitterly; even the former Labour prime minister James Callaghan, once a representative of the Federation, was called in to rubbish its 'dogmatic conclusions based on inaccurate analysis'. In the light of this robust response Howard agreed to ignore some of the more contentious proposals.

Shelter
www.shelter.org.uk
National campaign for the homeless founded in 1966 by the former social campaigner Des Wilson. It campaigns for housing projects and undertakes studies of homelessness. Shelter has 300 voluntary groups throughout the country which give advice on housing and tenancy issues.

Sierra Leone operation, 2000
On 10 September 2000 six hostages held by a militia group, the West Side Boys,

POLITICS

were recaptured by a group of 150 SAS soldiers supported by five helicopters. The action was hazardous but executed with great efficiency; 25 militia were killed to one SAS soldier.

silly season
Period in the summer when parliament is in recess, many politicians are on holiday and there seems to be very little hard news. This is traditionally when newspapers run apocryphal stories like 'man bites dog', or in August 2004 a story about two Greek athletes' failure to take a drugs test at the Olympic Games, which filled the headlines for several days.

single currency
See euro.

Single European Act (SEA), 1986
European act revising the treaty of Rome. As soon as he became president of the European Commission in 1985, Jacques Delors became a catalyst for integration. He pushed for rapid movement towards the single internal market in Europe, defined by freedom of goods, people, capital and services. A single market was proposed for 1992 after the December 1985 European Council meeting in Luxembourg. During the following year it was ratified by the national parliaments. Geoffrey Howe as foreign secretary steered it through the British parliament with little fuss. The necessary British legislation was passed in July 1987, and the single market came into being in January 1993. It was a massive leap towards an integrated Europe since it strengthened the European parliament and established qualified majority voting in the Council of Ministers. However, it seems Margaret Thatcher, that great enemy of integration, allowed the act to pass because she was unaware of its importance for the future and its supranational implications.

single transferable vote (STV)
The voting system used in the Irish Republic and favoured by the Liberal Democrats as a model for Britain. The

country is divided into multi-member constituencies, in which voters register their preferences from 1 to whatever the number of candidates there might be. To take a four-member constituency as an example, a quota is set at one-fifth of the votes cast, plus one. Only four candidates can possibly reach this quota figure. Any candidates reaching it after the first count are elected but if four do not do so, the next stage sees the elimination of the lowest-ranking candidate and a redistribution of the second preferences to all the others so that their votes are thereby increased. This continues until quotas are reached and then, if necessary, the other preferences are redistributed if quotas remain to be filled. Many consider the STV system to be inappropriate for Britain, as it would weaken the link between MPs and their constituents. However, it is used in Northern Ireland elections and in Scottish local elections.

sink estate
A council estate in which social problems such as unemployment, delinquency and vandalism are concentrated. It is calculated there are 2,000 such estates in Britain. This was exacerbated by the 'right to buy' policy, which led to 1.7 million council houses – the best of them – being sold while 3.4 million remained, many of them of poor quality. Low pay and unemployment create a culture of despair and social exclusion in which groups of youngsters roam the estate, cause a nuisance to neighbours and get into trouble with the police. Initially the physical state of the housing was good but it then suffered years of neglect. The overall result is an estate on which no one wants to live, wrecked by crime and drugs: a 'sink estate' where 'problem families' are forced to live and bring up children, which establishes a set of vicious circles.
See also social exclusion; underclass.

Sinn Fein
Gaelic for 'we ourselves'. The movement was founded in 1907 by Arthur Griffith as an Irish nationalist party. Over time it became identified as the 'political wing'

of the Irish Republican Army. It more or
less maintained this relationship, though
its leaders found it convenient from time to
time to distance themselves from the IRA's
excesses. It steadfastly supported the armed
struggle throughout the 1970s and 1980s,
refusing to condemn terrorist atrocities, but
eventually, in the early 1990s, its president,
Gerry Adams, elected in 1978, decided the
armed part of the struggle was not worth
continuing. The result of this change of
heart was the peace negotiations chaired
by Senator Mitchell, which culminated
in the Good Friday agreement. In June
1998 elections were held for the resultant
Northern Ireland assembly, which met on
14 September, Adams declaring he wished
to 'make friends' with Ian Paisley. In the
November 2003 elections to the assembly,
the need for closer relations between the
nationalists and hard-line Protestants was
heightened by the squeezing of the centre,
which saw Sinn Fein gain six seats, the
Democratic Unionist Party 10 and the
Social Democratic and Labour Party
lose six. In May 2007 Sinn Fein formed
a new Northern Ireland executive in
collaboration with its one-time arch enemy,
the Democratic Unionist Party. Martin
McGuinness of Sinn Fein became deputy
first minister.

See also Northern Ireland; Northern
Ireland assembly; Adams, Gerry.

sleaze
Term that originated in the final years
of the Major government of 1992–97. In
November 1993 Major circulated a memo
inviting ministers to come up with ideas
around the theme of 'back to basics', which
was the focus of his Conservative Party
conference speech. Interpreted by some
right-wingers and journalists as a campaign
for a return to family values and traditional
sexual morality, it backfired badly. Between
October 1993 and February 1994 eight
MPs, some of them ministers, were
exposed by the tabloids as currently having
or having had illicit sexual affairs. The
scandals of 'cash for questions' followed
shortly after, together with a number of

other revelations. A poll on 12 February
1994 revealed that more than half the
respondents believed the Conservatives
gave an impression of 'sleaze'. It was a
label which stuck to them right up until
the general election in May 1997, and
certainly made Labour's landslide easier to
achieve. The defeat of MP Neil Hamilton
by Martin Bell in the previously safe Tory
seat of Tatton exemplified the problem the
party faced.

After 1997 Labour had its own
problems, with donations to the party from
rich businessmen, in exchange, it is alleged,
for special favours. One full of drama and
intrigue concerned the Hinduja brothers,
one of whom gained a British passport
in an unusually short time following their
sponsorship of the Faith Zone in the
ill-fated Millennium Dome; the affair
ensnared Peter Mandelson, the Northern
Ireland secretary, who was forced to resign,
for a second time, from the government
in January 2001. Labour's penchant for
cosying up to business brought more grief
in February 2002, when a letter from Tony
Blair to the Romanian prime minister
on behalf of an Indian businessman who
had contributed to Labour Party funds
was exploited by the Conservative Party.
A poll published in the *Sunday Times*
on 17 February 2002 suggested that
60 per cent of the public regarded Labour
as 'sleazy and disreputable', compared
with only 41 per cent who felt the same
about the Conservatives. Further Labour
'sleaze' stories included the alleged 'cash
for coronets' allegations in which Blair
was implicated and questioned by police.
Both Labour and Conservative MPs were
heavily involved with the MPs' expenses
Scandal of June 2009.

Smith Square
Westminster headquarters of the
Conservative Party for many years. In
the summer of 2002 Iain Duncan Smith
moved his office to the House of Commons;
William Hague had followed other
Conservative leaders and worked from
an office in Smith Square but Duncan

Smith decided a closer relationship with the parliamentary party was necessary. In addition the party faced financial problems and such a move saved thousands of pounds in rent and rates. Following the accession to the leadership of Michael Howard in November 2003 it was announced that the Smith Square building was to be sold. In July 2004 Conservative Party headquarters moved to Victoria Street and in March 2007 to Millbank Tower.

Snowdrop Campaign
Campaign to ban the use of handguns following the Dunblane massacre of school children by a deranged resident in March 1986. It gained some 750,000 signatures in six weeks and ultimately led to the passing of the Firearms (Amendment) Act 1997, a measure criticised by some as too draconian and unfair to genuine sports enthusiast.

Social Affairs Unit
www.socialaffairsunit.org.uk
Think-tank founded in 1980 by Digby Anderson, a right-wing journalist. According to the *Economist* (6 May 1989), 'it is concerned less with advocating free market economics than with promoting social morality and preserving the social fabric'. It has not been especially influential since the fall of Margaret Thatcher.

Social and Liberal Democratic Party
See Liberal Democrats.

Social Chapter
Part of the treaty on European Union (TEU) signed at Maastricht in 1992. It concerned employment policy and dealt with such matters as workers' health and safety, works councils, a minimum wage and working conditions. These had not been received sympathetically by the Conservative government as they were thought to relate to the sort of trade union demands which, it was alleged, had caused British goods to be overpriced and of poor quality. The Conservatives under John Major negotiated an 'opt-out': the Social Chapter was added as a protocol to the TEU, to which 11

members subscribed but not Britain. For a number of years Britain was excluded from most social policy measures, though some were binding, including children's working time, equality for pensioners and women's rights. In 1997 Labour accepted the Social Chapter in its entirety as one of its first acts in government.

social class
See class.

Social Contract
Agreement in 1975 between the Labour government and the trade unions. It was in response to a crisis that June which had seen wages and inflation soaring. It focused narrowly on wages, which unions agreed to hold down to a set level, in exchange for which their members would receive benefits such as controls over prices and rents. This fragile agreement succeeded in bringing down inflation; it continued until the autumn of 1978, when the Trades Union Congress refused to accept the government's wage guidelines and the disastrous 'winter of discontent' resulted.

social democracy
See Social Democratic Party (SDP).

Social Democratic and Labour Party (SDLP)
www.sdlp.ie
Northern Ireland political party formed in 1970. It is moderately left wing and favours eventual Irish unification, though by peaceful means. Its leader up to 2001, John Hume, consistently condemned the terrorist tactics of the nationalists and helped to encourage the peace process in the late 1980s and early 1990s. Seamus Mallon, as deputy leader of the party, was made deputy to the first minister in the first Northern Ireland executive, produced by the elections in June 1998. In the November 2003 elections the SDLP suffered a disaster, losing six seats as the centre was squeezed by the extremes of the Democratic Unionist Party and Sinn Fein.
See also Northern Ireland assembly.

Social Democratic Federation

Britain's first Marxist party, formed in 1881 by H. M. Hyndman. For a while it recruited well, especially among middle-class intellectuals. It organised meetings in the 1880s and 1890s and was present at the foundation of the Labour Party in 1900. But its factionalism and dogmatism stunted its growth and its appeal waned; former members seemed to find a more agreeable home in the Communist Party of Great Britain, formed in 1920.

Social Democratic Party

Political party in existence from 1981 to 1990. Social democracy is a blend of free market economics (economic liberalism) combined with a strong commitment to social welfare and the responsibilities of the state in this regard (social reformism or reformist liberalism). This type of thinking had existed uneasily alongside democratic socialist doctrines (for example nationalisation) in the Labour Party until the early 1980s. Matters came to a head on 1 August 1980, when Shirley Williams, David Owen and William Rodgers published an open letter to the Labour Party expressing their discontent at its leftward drift. When this drift accelerated and Roy Jenkins came on board to make up the 'gang of four', the formation of a new party was only a matter of time. In January 1981 the Social Democratic Party (SDP) was formed. Media interest was intense and many disillusioned Labour members were attracted by the new banner. Labour supporters complained of betrayal. Opinion polls registered astonishing levels of support for the SDP: it attracted 70,000 members and won two sensational by-elections, at Crosby and Hillhead. It fought the 1983 general election in the Alliance with the Liberal Party, when it mustered an impressive 25.4 per cent of the vote, although only 23 seats. However, many of the defectors from the Parliamentary Labour Party lost their seats and some of the forward momentum had been stalled. After the 1983 election Owen replaced Jenkins as leader of the SDP. In 1987 the Alliance needed nearly 40 per cent of the vote to win a majority and 30–34 per cent to hold the balance of power; it won 22.6 per cent and 22 seats, a major disappointment. Liberal leader David Steel called for merger negotiations but the SDP split into 'mergerite' and 'Owenite' factions. Owen resigned and at the 1987 conference the SDP voted to merge with the Liberal Party that year. Owen defiantly led a small rump SDP but it was hopeless and it was wound up in 1990. From euphoric beginnings the SDP ended up as a party of protest with limited appeal outside the middle classes. However, the experience had a salutary effect upon Labour and helped to nudge it back towards an electable position in the late 1980s and early 1990s.

See also Alliance; Liberal Democrats.

social engineering

Changing the basic nature of human beings. Political philosophers have debated the intrinsic nature of humankind for centuries and some have suggested that it can be improved by changing social arrangements, a view propounded by Karl Marx, who stated that as 'environment creates consciousness', it follows that a change to the environment will change consciousness. This approach became known as social engineering. For the socialist utopians in the Labour Party this was seen as a mission to change the British people from selfish, competitive members of a capitalist society into cooperative, sharing members of a socialist one. Traditional Conservatives condemn 'social engineering' as an artificial intervention in the natural order which can only damage society, but Margaret Thatcher seemed to be doing something very similar with her efforts to create an 'enterprise society'. Despite the experience of failure, politicians seem irrevocably wedded to the idea that the acceptance of their political ideas will transform, invigorate and renew the nation, a visionary aim which underpinned the project of Tony Blair and others no doubt in the future.

social exclusion

The inability of a poor section or 'underclass' of society to participate fully in the life of a community. The term, within the context of New Labour, neatly combines a sociological description with an ideological imperative: that those excluded have suffered an injustice which should be righted, and that those shut out should be included, possibly irrespective of their own wishes. The term was associated with Labour's approach to reforming welfare in Britain. When Tony Blair came to power in 1997 he formed the Social Exclusion Unit in the Cabinet Office. It produced a report in September 1998 on 2,000 rundown council estates, which called for more tenant-owned estates, an end to new estates which tend to break up communities and cheaper supermarket food to be made available to poor estates. Nearly £1 billion was allocated to the programme. In Whitehall 18 task forces were established to coordinate policy to tackle crime, education and youth disaffection.

See also poverty; sink estate.

social justice

A fair and proper distribution within society of benefits and burdens. The idea that there should be social justice underlies much of the welfare state. It originates in the gulf between the rich and the poor, the powerful and the weak, and suggests the political 'playing field' ought to be level. Accordingly, advocates of social justice in Britain, usually in the Liberal and Labour parties, have called for redistributive taxation to fund free education, health and pensions. The Conservatives have argued that such ideas are false in that they substitute passive state dependence and moral decline for energetic self-reliance. After Tony Blair became leader of the Labour Party in 1994, 'third way' thinking recast the party's traditional commitment to welfare into a modern, critics would say pragmatic, safety net approach to the welfare state and social justice, possibly involving the private sector, where this was advantageous.

Social Market Foundation

www.smf.co.uk

Think-tank founded in 1989 by the Social Democratic Party luminary Robert Skidelsky, which survived the demise of its social democratic creators and became independent. The Foundation has produced some influential work identifying where markets can be usefully applied to the public sector and where they cannot. The group has some links with Conservative thinkers like David Willets.

social mobility

The extent to which an individual's social status can change during their lifetime. In May 2002 the Institute for Social and Economic Research at Essex University reported a study showing that social mobility had slowed in Britain in recent years. It seems that the sons and daughters of people who joined the middle classes in the 1960s are tending to block the ascent of children from working-class backgrounds by occupying the available middle-class jobs. Another causal factor is that people tend to marry within their own class and thereby close off another access route to potential new members of the stratum. According to the *Guardian*:

> Based on a 5000 strong sample of families which have been tracked and questioned repeatedly since the late 1950s the study finds that people with parents in better earning jobs are more likely to be in higher earning positions themselves and are more likely to marry someone with parents in higher earning occupations.

A report by former Labour cabinet minister Alan Milburn into social mobility in July 2009 concluded that Britain had become one of the least socially mobile countries in Europe. He pointed out how the 7 per cent of privately educated children went on as adults to dominate all the major professions, including the law, business, the military and the civil service. Only 29 per cent of university students came from lower socio-economic backgrounds, despite comprising 50 per cent of young people. He perceived the middle-class hold on important jobs to be increasing, causing division in society and a sense of hopelessness among those with the ambition to better themselves. He suggested a £5,000 personal training grant be given to all young people, to be spent as they think fit, whether on university or professional or vocational training. He was critical of government initiatives like Connexions, the careers advice and teenage support body, as well as Aim Higher and the Gifted and Talented programme. He also urged the creation of a social mobility commission to give an annual progress report.

Social Mobility Foundation
www.socialmobility.org.uk
A charitable body dedicated to better social mobility by enabling bright year-12 students from disadvantaged backgrounds to receive mentoring, internships and assistance with university applications.

social security
The provision of support for people in need as a result of age, poverty, unemployment, illness and so forth. Britain's annual public expenditure by the Department for Work and Pensions was £135 billion in 2009.

social structure
See class.

socialism
Originated out of the indignation created by the inequalities and suffering caused by early capitalism in the west. This critique, expressed most powerfully in Robert Tressell's novel *The Ragged Trousered Philanthropists* (1914), focused on: the exploitation of workers, who create wealth for the 'bosses'; the inequalities between workers who have to bring up large families on a weekly sum their employer might spend on a single meal; the lack of responsibility bosses have for workers, who become a mere commodity; and the climate of brutal competition which infects and corrupts all concerned. Early socialists in Britain, such as the Social Democratic Federation and the Independent Labour Party,

offered an alternative vision. This was of a commonly owned economy and workers who cooperated willingly in the creation of a better society, using free time to develop their individual talents and skills, and enjoy the full fruits of life. The foundation of the Labour Party and its successes after the First World War brought this ideal closer and it was refined into a set of policies based on nationalisation of the main economic enterprises plus improved social services. This programme was enacted by Clement Attlee's huge postwar majority but thereafter socialism was split between those who wished to continue nationalisation and create a command economy, and those revisionists who believed management of the economy through Keynesian techniques could bring the fruits of socialism without the fractures of destroying capitalism. This struggle reached its climax in the early 1980s with a full-blooded capitalist Conservative government. Left-wing activists made significant inroads into the Labour Party but the wider public was not impressed and its version of socialism received a blast of dismissive contempt by voters in 1983. From then on Labour inched away from socialism under Neil Kinnock; under Tony Blair socialism was a word very rarely used, even in Labour Party manifestos, in public and leadership speeches or by party activists in public. Margaret Thatcher swore one of her missions was to destroy socialism; while the Labour Party lived on to win famously in 1997 it is a moot point whether or not she succeeded.

Socialist Alliance (SA)
www.socialistalliance.org.uk
Umbrella organisation for left-wing parties which fought the 2001 general election. It was chaired by former Militant MP Dave Nellist. Its manifesto was a scathing critique of New Labour as no better than Thatcherism, but it did also put forward an 'alternative to the global unregulated free market'. Despite the effort expended in healing factional differences, the SA's six candidates garnered no more than 2 per cent of the vote in any contest.

Socialist Campaign Group
See Campaign Group.

Socialist Labour Party
www.socialist-labour-party.org.uk
A left-wing socialist party launched by
miners' leader Arthur Scargill in 1996.
He was disgusted with what he saw as the
anodyne revisionism of New Labour and
wished to inject some 'real' socialism into
the body politic. The party subscribes to
a fundamentalist programme of measures,
including full employment, better benefits
and salaries, a planned economy, plus
the ending of outsourcing of labour and
cheap migrant labour. It has attracted
some publicity but few votes in local and
national elections. Scargill stood against
Peter Mandelson, the sitting Labour MP
for Hartlepool, in the 2001 general election
but mustered fewer than 1,000 votes.

Socialist League (SL)
Originally the International Marxist Group,
the SL was founded in 1964 out of splits
between feuding Trotskyites. Ken Coates
was a leading figure, as was Tariq Ali.
Prominent during student political action
in the 1960s, the SL was more influenced
by new left thinking, which stressed the
importance of 'transforming consciousness'
and the ending of 'alienation'.

Socialist Party of Great Britain
www.worldsocialism.org/spgb
An unreconstructed Marxist party
dedicated to world revolution and the
destruction of capitalism, founded in
1904. It is against war but in favour of
parliamentary democracy. Its attempts to
get candidates elected have proved wholly
unsuccessful.

Socialist Workers Party
www.swp.org.uk
Trotskyite party founded by Duncan
Hallas in 1950 as the International
Socialists. It changed its name in 1977. It
existed as an non-entryist party that sought
to influence the Labour Party. It was active
in the Anti-Nazi League in the 1970s and
the Right to Work Movement. Until his
much-mourned death in July 2004, journalist Paul Foot was probably the best-known
member of the party.

Society for the Protection of Unborn Children (SPUC)
www.spuc.org.uk
Classic 'cause' pressure group established
to campaign against abortion, founded in
1966 to oppose the bill that became the
Abortion Act 1967. Gynaecologist Aleck
Bourne was a prime mover in this. Its aim
is to 'uphold the principle of respect for
the life of the unborn child'. It concentrates
much of its work on parliamentary
campaigns against euthanasia and embryo
research, for example. The SPUC is
funded by voluntary contributions and
raises over £1 million annually.

solicitor general
www.lslo.gov.uk
Since the 16th century, one of the two
senior government legal officers, the other
being the attorney general, both of whom
lead for the government in major court
cases as well as advise the government on
legal matters.

sound bite
Short pithy statement of the type news
editors like to use in bulletins. Having
realised this, politicians now serve them
up in a never-ending stream. In the late
1960s the average uninterrupted broadcast
statement by a US presidential candidate
was over 40 seconds. By 1996 it had
shrunk to just 8 seconds. During election
campaigns sound bites are even more
important, as they can sum up the message
for the day. Spin doctors try hard to dream
up high-quality ones and then beg or bully
news editors to include them on their television bulletins, watched in Britain by up to
20 million people each evening. Tony Blair
was particularly good at inserting televisual
sound bites into his performances at prime
minister's questions, as such high-profile
jousting often wins news coverage. Some
commentators voice concern that important

political messages are being compressed into such short time spaces and possibly distorted in the process.

See also political marketing; political language; spin; spin doctors.

sovereignty

The absolute power which states exercise over matters of government within their own borders. More a legal term than a behavioural reality, it has, however, become an emotive symbol for many patriots. Eurosceptics and opponents of the European Union (EU) are hotly opposed to what they see as a dilution of the essence of Britain's nationhood through membership of the EU. The supremacy of European law over domestic law rankles especially and led opponents in the 1970s, not to mention the present day, to argue for withdrawal. Constitutional experts assert that the ability of the nation to withdraw ultimately is the final guarantee of national sovereignty. Others argue that the erosion of sovereignty by membership of international organisations like the United Nations and NATO, not to mention the international economy and other aspects of globalisation, make discussion of such matters redundant: in other words, why talk about complete control of the nation's destiny when it has not been within Britain's power for several decades?

See also parliamentary sovereignty.

speaker

www.parliament.uk/about/how/principal/speaker.cfm

Chief officer of the House of Commons. In the 14th century the speaker conveyed the wishes of the house to the king. For this service nine of the early speakers were executed, thus explaining the ritual show of reluctance by speakers to sit in their chair upon inauguration. Over the centuries the speaker ceased to play a political role and became an 'umpire' of proceedings, above the partisan fray. Elected by MPs, usually on a non-partisan basis, the speaker has an authority which is jealously guarded, as Margaret Thatcher discovered in 1983

when she favoured Humphrey Atkins to succeed the legendary George Thomas, while the Commons insisted on a back-bencher, eventually the modestly effective Bernard Weatherill. Similarly, John Major wanted his colleague Peter Brooke in 1992 but the Conservative-dominated Commons chose Labour's Betty Boothroyd.

The speaker presides at sittings of the Commons, calls on members to speak and keeps their contributions within the rules of parliament and good order. He or she also decides on requests for emergency debates under standing order number 10 and private notice questions. MPs who offend against the rules can be reprimanded, suspended or even excluded. In the event of a tied vote in a division the speaker by tradition gives the casting vote against any amendment. The speaker's procession starts each day's proceedings after lunch. The speaker also heads the Commons Commission, which runs the house. At election times the speaker is traditionally returned unopposed, though this has attracted criticism from those who say constituents are thereby denied a choice and arguably effective representation. The colourful Betty Boothroyd stood down in 2000, after eight years in the job, and was replaced by Labour's Michael Martin, a former shop steward who attracted some criticism, centred on the fact that he was a Labour MP following a Labour MP, spoke with a broad Glaswegian accent and tended to make somewhat eccentric interventions. These allegations were angrily rejected by the speaker's supporters, who included chancellor Gordon Brown and a number of other Scottish members. By 2003 the criticisms had virtually ceased but they returned redoubled in May 2009 during the MPs' expenses scandal, when Martin was believed to have possibly transgressed himself while doing his best to frustrate attempts to bring transparency to MPs' expenses. Eventually he lost the confidence of the house and even Brown, according to some reports, had indicated Martin should stand down. This he eventually did, with as much dignity as he could muster.

In the ensuing election for a new speaker on 22 June 2009 the Conservative John Bercow was elected, largely through the votes of Labour MPs keen to elect someone unpopular in his own party.

See also deputy speaker.

speaker's conference

Occasionally matters relating to arrangements affecting elections are considered in a conference chaired by the speaker, with representation from all parties. Examples include consideration of changing the voting system in 1917 and the lowering of the voting age in 1969.

special advisor

See political advisor.

special relationship

Term often used to describe the relationship between Britain and the USA. Despite the War of Independence which the USA fought in the 18th century to separate from the 'home' country, the two nations have a history of alliances against shared foes, including Germany in two world wars and the USSR during the Cold War. In addition, Britain supported the USA in a number of Cold War conflicts and the link was so close it helped explain why French leader Charles de Gaulle – suspicious of 'Anglo-Saxon' ganging up – vetoed British applications to join the Common Market in 1963 and 1967.

The relationship has not always been smooth: the USA opposed Britain's Middle Eastern war in defence of the Suez Canal in 1956–57 and ignored Harold Wilson's advice over Vietnam. Margaret Thatcher was very close to US President Ronald Reagan, however, in his 'cold warrior' attitude to the USSR and Britain allied to the USA during the Gulf war in 1991. Tony Blair had a close relationship with Bill Clinton and was quick to establish good relations with George W. Bush. He displayed assiduous loyalty over most issues and his degree of support after the terrorist attacks on the USA on 11 September 2001 and the subsequent war against the Taliban

in Afghanistan served to cement the alliance still further. However, many European countries were less enthusiastic and in 2003 Blair faced tension at home and abroad regarding his slavish support for the US-led invasion of Iraq. Gordon Brown sought to establish a certain distance from Bush but tried hard to establish good relations with the newly elected Barack Obama in 2008.

special standing committee

In 1980 the House of Commons sanctioned the creation of special standing committees, to which a number of bills were referred. These committees were allowed to hold up to four meetings before the normal standing committee stage, with three of them being public sessions in which witnesses could be questioned. The general conclusion was that this experiment was worthwhile but there was little further use of the approach.

Spectator

www.spectator.co.uk

Weekly journal of comment and analysis. Founded in 1828, it has established a reputation for good writing which has helped see it through occasional hard times. Its editors have tended to come from the right in postwar years and have included Ian Gilmour, Ian Macleod, Nigel Lawson, Charles Moore, Dominic Lawson and Boris Johnson. Predictably its policy line has tended to be right-wing independent but it can rock the boat a little, as when Lawson junior published in July 1990 a transcript of cabinet minister Nick Ridley's unflattering comments about Germany; Ridley was subsequently forced to resign. Lawson senior, in his memoirs (*The View From No. 11*, 1993), commented that Ridley made the remarks only because he had heard Margaret Thatcher saying similar things in private.

speech from the throne

See queen's (or king's) speech.

spin

The process by which messages are changed or otherwise massaged by politicians, especially by specialist spin doctors, to improve their acceptability to the public. The word is most closely associated with the refashioned New Labour Party, which revolutionised its media presentation during the mid-1980s under the influence of Peter Mandelson. However, most commentators agree the use of 'spin' in opposition was maintained in government, when it became counterproductive. In May 2002 both Mandelson and Tony Blair's press secretary, Alastair Campbell, admitted their party had relied too much on spin and called for a more open approach, in which senior politicians would be more accountable to the voters. On 16 July 2002 Blair met the chairs of the select committees in a ground-breaking session. He agreed his government had been too obsessed with spin and attributed this to the 18 years of opposition, during which the 'announcement was the reality'. The session was judged a success by most – though not all – commentators and an effective way of being held accountable, thereby negating accusations of spin, and it has been repeated.

See also spin doctor.

spin doctor
Media advisor to a politician who devises and manipulates messages to opinion formers in the media and hence voters. The phrase originates in the USA, where the science of managing the media began. One of the first spin doctors in Britain was (later Sir) Gordon Reece, who trained Margaret Thatcher in media presentation and, by accentuating her strengths and minimising her weaknesses, turned her into a formidable performer on the television. Bernard Ingham, her press secretary, became another highly respected though, on the left, much disliked figure – perhaps the inevitable fate of spin doctors. On the Labour side Peter Mandelson emerged in the 1980s as the master of the same black arts; he was able to understand the chemistry of the interaction between the media and the public and to make it work for Labour. Tony Blair's press secretary,

Alastair Campbell, was another spinner in chief and his background in the tabloids gave him a special advantage. His coining of the phrase 'the people's Princess' for Blair to use in his supposedly impromptu speech after Diana's death was a perfect example of this skill in action.

During the run-up to the 2001 election there was some adverse comment about Labour's reliance on 'spin' and the feeling was widely expressed that the government relied too much on presentation and neglected delivery of promises. In a Radio 4 programme *Why Do People Hate Spin-Doctors?* (25 June 2001), Charlie Whelan, former controversial 'spinner' for chancellor Gordon Brown, finished his presentation by unashamedly celebrating spin doctors and the role they had played in delivering a second huge majority to Labour, which would 'enable the enactment of the most radical programme of government for 50 years'. The Conservatives' communications director during the 2001 general election, Amanda Platell, was generally thought to have performed poorly and the effectiveness of Conservative media management over the previous decade was probably inferior to Labour's. Campbell was called more than once to give evidence on his role before a select committee and on each occasion did so with combative panache. As the decade wore on Campbell retired as Blair's spin-meister and Brown did not appoint anyone quite so high profile. However, Damien McBride, one of his close media advisors, became involved in a messy scandal in spring 2009 when he suggested in emails to a colleague (later made public) that scandalous untruths be disseminated about Conservative politicians.

See also Moore's email; political communication; spin.

Spirit Level, The
Book by Richard Wilkinson and Kate Pickett, two respected epidemiologists, published in 2009, on the repercussions of social inequality upon western societies. It is subtitled *Why More Equal Societies Almost Always Do Better* and is arguably the

POLITICS

most important book for the Labour Party since Anthony Crosland's *The Future of Socialism* (1956). It relates socio-economic inequality to social dysfunction and finds a wealth of evidence. For example, on low levels of trust the book shows how countries with low relative inequality (such as Japan, Scandinavia, northern Europe) have high levels of response to the question 'most people can be trusted' – about 60 per cent – while those with high inequality (such as the USA, Britain, Portugal, Singapore) register low levels – in one case 10 per cent. Near identical graph profiles result from asking the question in states of the USA: high values in low-inequality states like New Hampshire; very low in the likes of Mississippi and New York.

The book also reports that about a quarter of all people in Britain and the USA suffer mental health problems, compared with only 10 per cent in Japan, Sweden and Germany. The chapters continue relentlessly to illustrate, via scatter graphs, such astonishingly high correlations. We see it with drug abuse, physical health and life expectancy, educational performance, teenage births, violent offences, incarceration, social mobility, even obesity. And, mark this, even the rich have more mental illness and lower life expectancy in high-inequality countries. The USA in the 1960s had relatively high levels of equality but salaries for senior executives took off along with the 'rediscovery' of market forces in the 1970s and rocketed to the end of the century, ultimately feeding causally into the banking collapse and recessions of 2007–09.

> Early socialists and others believed that material inequality was an obstacle to wider human harmony…. The data we present in this chapter [on community life and social relations] suggest that this intuition was sound: inequality is divisive, and even small differences seem to make an important difference. (*The Spirit Level*, p. 52)

sport
Harold Wilson used to suggest that he lost the 1970 election because voters blamed him for England's defeat by Germany in

the World Cup soccer tournament in that year. John Major recognised how important sport can be to the morale of the nation and did his best to support a number of sports, especially cricket. Minister of sport is a post in the Department for Culture, Media and Sport, and former cabinet minister Chris Smith argued in July 2001 that more big sporting occasions should be made available on terrestrial television and not limited to those who pay for cable television.

Sporting metaphors pervade the political culture – for example, Wilson likened his role as prime minister to a 'half-back providing the ball to the forwards to score' and Whitehall civil servants talk about 'close of play' and 'batting first' at meetings. Margaret Thatcher used to say she was 'batting for Britain' but the metaphor came back to haunt her in Geoffrey Howe's devastating resignation speech which effectively ended her tenure in power.

See also Department for Culture, Media and Sport; Wembley stadium.

Spycatcher affair
Case involving the attempted banning in 1987 of the memoirs of a former intelligence officer, Peter Wright, entitled *Spycatcher*, and elements of which breached the Official Secrets Act. In particular, he alleged that MI5 bugged and burgled its way around London, attempted to bug Number 10 Downing Street, and most sensationally of all tried to subvert the government of Harold Wilson in the mid-1960s. Legal injunctions launched by the government had the effect of banning the book and its newspaper serialisation in Britain, despite the fact that the book could be purchased in Moscow. Further action was taken against Wright in Australia and Sir Robert Armstrong, the cabinet secretary, was sent out to put the government's case. He proved to be no match for Wright's clever lawyer, Malcolm Turnbull, who forced him to admit on one occasion he had lied or, in his own words, had been 'economical with the truth', a phrase that has entered the language as a serviceable synonym for lying.

See also Official Secrets Act.

stagflation
The combination of high inflation with
high unemployment. It was once thought
by economists that inflation stimulated
economic growth, so that it would not be
likely to cause unemployment. However,
the British economy in the 1970s exhibited
both record high inflation and soaring
unemployment, which proved this assumption to be false.

stakeholder society
Idea most closely associated with former
Observer editor Will Hutton, whose book
The State We're In (1995) became a best
seller. The essence of the approach is the
acceptance of a 'mutual reciprocity', that
capitalism needs to be broadened from
its neo-liberal individualism to encompass
long-term social objectives for everyone,
with rights given to citizens regarding
education and training, job security and
basic welfare. Germany was held up as
a stakeholder society in operation. The
corollary of these rights are the obligations
citizens would shoulder regarding the need
to create an internationally competitive
economy and to save in order to minimise
the welfare burden. The stakeholder
society, along with communitarian ideas,
was briefly hailed in the mid-1990s as
Labour's 'big idea' but enthusiasm waned
somewhat in the run-up to the general
election in 1997, possibly because it lacked
sharp definition and a clear plan for
implementation.

Stamp Act, 1765
Act which attempted to raise sufficient tax
from the American colonies to pay for their
defence. The idea was to levy a charge
('stamp') on every publication and legal
document issued in these colonies. The act
was widely disobeyed and was repealed the
following year but the upset caused helped
precipitate the American Revolution.

standard spending assessment (SSA)
A means of limiting local government
spending through the setting of local
authority grants via centrally defined
calculations, introduced in 1990. This
meant in effect central government was
establishing the levels at which local government should spend; any spending beyond
these levels constituted overspending and
penalties could be applied. 'It amounts',
wrote David Wilson and Chris Game in
2001, 'to governments setting a ceiling for
every council in the country, leaving locally
elected politicians in the position of having
the framework of their budgets, if not the
detailed content, determined for them'. The
Independent Audit Commission in 1993
studied the SSA and gave it only 2 marks
out of 12: it was judged to be unaccountable
and hard to understand.

Standards and Privileges Committee
www.parliament.uk/parliamentary_
committees/standards_and_privileges.cfm
Commons committee set up in 1995,
in the wake of the 'cash for questions'
scandal, though the original function of
the Members' Interests Committee was
subsumed into it. It set out the code of
conduct for MPs, which was designed to
assist them in discharging their duties.
Complaints regarding breaches of the code
are referred to the parliamentary commissioner for standards and also reported
to the committee. In 2004 it was chaired by
Sir George Young. In 2009 he remained
in the chair of the committee, which also
included Nicholas Soames, Kevin Barron
and Chris Mullin.
   See also Committee on Standards in
Public Life; parliamentary commissioner
for standards; select committee.

standards in public life
See Committee on Standards in Public
Life; Neill committee; Nolan committee.

standing committee
Committee established to consider a bill
in detail as part of the legislative process
following the second reading. Standing
committees are set up afresh for each new
bill and so are not really 'standing' or
in any way permanent. Each comprises

POLITICS

around 18 members and is constituted to reflect party strengths in the Commons. A bill is considered clause by clause and amendments are moved and debated, though none is allowed that is contrary to the underlying theme of the bill. If debate drags on in a partisan fashion, as it often does, the government can introduce a timetable or 'guillotine' motion, which often means the later clauses receive little or no close attention.

Star Chamber
Originally used by medieval kings to administer their own brand of justice. In modern times the name has been attached to a cabinet committee which resolves disputes between the Treasury and spending departments (or indeed to any committee of dubious legitimacy sitting in judgement). The meetings were chaired by the chief secretary to the Treasury. The Star Chamber was abolished by Tony Blair in 1997 but then reinvented to adjudicate over the expenditure cuts due to be implemented by the new coalition government after May 2010.

state
See nation state.

Statistics Authority
See UK Statistics Authority.

statute law
Term used for acts of parliament and subordinate or delegated legislation made under the authority of a 'parent' act. A distinction is made between public acts, which comprise those passed by the government of the day, as well as those initiated and piloted through by private members who have won a high place in the annual ballot, and private acts, which are prepared often by private interests, such as local authorities or private companies. Statutes may consolidate existing laws or amend them. Ultimately parliament can pass whatever law it wishes but cannot bind its potential future actions, although this has been severely curtailed by European

Community law (which is superior to domestic statute law) and the European Court of Justice, as well as by devolution.

See also act of parliament; money bill; private bill; public bill.

Statute of Westminster, 1931
Enacted the decision of the 1926 Imperial Conference which gave full independence and equal status with the UK to the Dominions, namely Canada, Newfoundland, Australia, the Irish Free State, New Zealand and South Africa.

statutory instrument
See delegated legislation.

stealth tax
See indirect taxation.

Stephen Lawrence inquiry
See Macpherson report, 1999.

Stevens inquiry, 1999–2003
Inquiry into allegations that collusion had occurred between the army and the police in Northern Ireland and Protestant terrorist groups to murder prominent Catholics. Foremost among the latter was Pat Finucane in 1989, a solicitor who defended many nationalists against charges of terrorism. It had long been alleged that he had been murdered on army instructions, as he was too effective in his job. It emerged that the army Force Research Unit placed an agent, Brian Nelson, with the Ulster Defence Association, who, the report alleged, was responsible for at least 30 murders: in other words, these were state-sanctioned murders. Stevens condemned the practices he had unearthed and recommended a full review of procedures for investigating terrorist activities.

Stonewall
www.stonewall.org.uk
Gay rights campaigning body formed in 1989, named after the 1969 Stonewall riots in New York. Sir Ian McKellen and Michael Cashman were founder members. The body claims some credit for the repeal

of section 28 and for the Civil Partnership Act 2004.

Stormont

After partition in 1922 the Northern Ireland parliament sat in Stormont Castle outside Belfast. After direct rule was introduced in 1972 it ceased to be used but came back into use in 1998 when the new Northern Ireland assembly was elected.

sub-prime mortgage crisis, 2006–08

A crisis caused by fluctuations in the US housing market and by the issuing of loans to people who could not afford to sustain the repayments. The causes of this crisis were many and complex. Most mortgages in the USA were on an adjustable rate, and when the rates went up as house prices declined there were many foreclosures and repossessions. This was exacerbated by the practice of some banks and mortgage companies of lending to people who had no jobs, no income and no assets, so that they folded as soon as rates increased. An additional problem was the practice of financial investment banks of wrapping up these 'toxic' mortgages with other debts and selling them as securities on international markets – the so-called 'collateralised debt obligations' (CDOs), which were widely distributed and purchased abroad but were worthless. So great was the reach of such toxic loans that as soon as its extent became known in 2007–08 there were huge repercussions on the international markets. In Britain, the Northern Rock Bank effectively went bust and had to be taken over by the government. Iceland's banks, also heavily into the bad loans, went bust and big US investment banks began to slide into bankruptcy, most sensationally Lehman Brothers, in September 2008. This triggered other failures and shock waves which threatened the world's banking system. The major industrialised countries fed billions of dollars into ailing banks and still more into economies which were sliding into recession all over the world. By the summer of 2009 there were some signs that the economic crisis caused by bad debt was

beginning to abate, but there was still some way to go before recovery could be said to have happened.

subsidiarity

Principle set out in article 3b of the Maastricht treaty (the treaty on European Union, 1992). This was seen as providing a check on the centralising tendencies in the European Union (EU), as it stipulated that all actions that could be taken at the national level should be so taken, although the interpretation of the principle was not identical for each nation. To John Major this was a way of counteracting the fears of British Eurosceptics that a European super-state was emerging that would seriously undermine national sovereignty. In the technical language of the EU, article 3b stated that the EU would take action 'in accordance with the subsidiarity principle, only if and in so far as the objectives of the proposed action cannot be sufficiently achieved by the Member States and can therefore, by reason of the scale or effects of the proposed action, be the better achieved by the Community'.

See also Maastricht treaty.

succession (to the throne)

Under the Act of Succession Prince Charles will automatically become king upon his mother's death. He will not be allowed to renounce his right to succeed unless a special act of parliament is passed, as in 1936. Some opinion polls have indicated a preference from a section of the population for Prince William to be king and for the succession to jump a generation. However, many have suggested that this would be unwise, as the young prince has already been burdened by the premature death of his mother and is known to be already less than enchanted with the life of being a high-profile member of the royal family.

Suez crisis, 1956–57

A landmark in Britain's retreat as a world power. It began when Egyptian leader and pan-Arabist Colonel Nasser nationalised the Suez Canal on 26 July 1956. The

317

POLITICS

canal had been owned by the Suez Canal Company, controlled by British and French interests. After abortive negotiations Britain and France secretly conspired to support an armed attack by Israel, the plan being for the two European powers to intervene ostensibly as peacemakers to occupy the canal and keep it open. Israel invaded in October, followed by 8,000 Anglo-French troops in November. However, the action provoked intense dissent in Britain and even more abroad. The USA refused to support the initiative and threatened to withdraw financial support for sterling on the foreign exchanges. The military action stopped on 6 November, western troops were withdrawn and the United Nations sent in a peacekeeping force. The whole episode was a disaster for prime minister Anthony Eden: it ruined his reputation, his political career and his health. It also demonstrated spectacularly how Britain's world position had declined from the status of a first-class world power to one almost wholly dependent on US political and military support.

> We are not at war with Egypt. We are in armed conflict. (Anthony Eden, 1956)

suffrage
See franchise; Reform Act.

suffragette
Campaigner for votes for women in the early 20th century. Emmeline Pankhurst and her daughter Christabel inspired and led the Women's Social and Political Union, established in 1903. It took the First World War and the new role which it brought women to help win them the vote in 1918, though this was restricted to those over 30 years of age and who met a property criterion. In 1928 all discrepancies between men and women regarding the vote were removed and there was equality.

Sun
www.thesun.co.uk
Tabloid newspaper which emerged from the ashes of the Labour-supporting *Daily Herald* in 1964. It was purchased by

Rupert Murdoch, the Australian media tycoon, who appointed Larry Lamb as its first editor. Under the brooding tutelage of its proprietor, Lamb established the publication's profile as light on news and heavy on trivia and titillation. The next editor was the now legendary (for his brash irreverence) Kelvin MacKenzie, who transformed the tabloid into the leading British title, with a circulation of over 5 million per day. The political stance of the paper was pro-Conservative in the 1970s and 1980s, though this was probably more a reflection of its proprietor's views. During the Falklands war it was rabidly jingoistic, and produced the notorious headline on 4 May 1982 'Gotcha', when the Argentinean battle cruiser the *General Belgrano* was sunk by the British submarine HMS *Conqueror*. It also developed an expertise in soft porn, with its daily topless page 3 girl, and MacKenzie was unafraid of intruding into the privacy of many well known people, especially Princess Diana. In 1992 the *Sun* was sneeringly dismissive of Neil Kinnock and did its best to destroy his reputation, by using what the media analyist Colin Seymore-Ure calls 'infofantasy', a mixture of comic book fantasy and hard-hitting political comment. Other media experts reckoned the *Sun* delivered hundreds of thousands of votes to the Conservatives in the election of that year, though others contest the extent of its own assessment that 'It's the Sun Wot Won It', delivered soon after the Conservative win. With John Major as prime minister in his second term, however, the editorial line became critical and almost as hostile as it had been to Kinnock. Murdoch and Tony Blair became friendly after 1995 and it was not too much of a surprise when, on 18 March 1997, the *Sun* came out strongly in support for Blair. Blair was said to lay great store by the good opinion of the tabloids and his press secretary Alastair Campbell was recruited from their ranks. The honeymoon continued until 24 June 1998, when the paper ran a front-page headline 'Is this the most dangerous man in Britain?' over a picture of the prime minister, in relation to his stance on the European Union. When circulation began to dip a new editor, David Yelland, took over, with the alleged aim of taking the tabloid 'up market', to serve a supposedly increasingly sophisticated readership. During the 2001 general election the *Sun* sustained its support of New Labour but under Rebekah Wade (soon to become Brooks), appointed editor in February 2003, the paper was more critical of the government. In the autumn of 2009 the *Sun* came out in support of the Conservatives, and Dominic Mohan was made editor in September of the same year.

Sunningdale agreement, 1973
A power-sharing initiative in Northern Ireland involving Catholics and Protestants but the latter bitterly opposed the part of the agreement which provided for the Council of Ireland and destroyed it by calling a general strike in the province. There were several other attempts to achieve a settlement: 1975 Constitutional Convention; 1980 Constitutional Conference; 1982 Northern Ireland assembly; 1984 New Ireland Forum; and 1985 Anglo-Irish agreement. The Good Friday agreement in 1998 was the most successful power-sharing initiative, though it took until 2007 for anything like a stable Northern Ireland executive to be formed.

super class
Term invented by Andrew Adonis and Stephen Pollard in their book *A Class Act* (1997) to describe the new elite of top professionals and managers which is increasingly divorced from the rest of society: almost a complementary class to the 'underclass' at the bottom of society. Examples include Cedric Brown, the chief executive of British Gas, who received a much publicised 75 per cent increase in his salary for running a private monopoly utility. Nick Leeson, the high-flying Barings Bank trader, bankrupted his bank by reckless dealing, so that it was eventually sold for a mere £1. Nevertheless, his supervisors still received their bonuses. The authors trace the super class culture to the

USA and argue it was imported during the 1980s, when it raised expectations and attracted the cream of Oxbridge graduates to go for jobs in law, accountancy or the City, rather than public service jobs like teaching or the civil service. Further grist to this mill was provided by Polly Toynbee and David Walker in their book *Unjust Rewards: Exposing Greed and Inequality in Britain Today* (2008).

supplementary vote (SV)
Electoral system similar to the alternative vote, in that the voter can record a first and second choice of candidate for a single-member constituency. If a candidate gets over half the first-preference votes then he or she is elected. If not, all but the top two are eliminated. Any second-preference votes for either of the top two candidates on the ballot papers for eliminated candidates are then duly allocated, and the person with the biggest share of the resultant vote is deemed to be elected. The system is used to elect the mayor of London.
See also alternative vote.

supply-side economics
See monetarism.

supra-nationalism
When a policy or event affects other countries beyond national boundaries.

Supreme Court of the United Kingdom
www.supremecourt.gov.uk
The final court of appeal for civil cases; it also hears appeals in criminal cases from England, Wales and Northern Ireland, as well as cases of public or constitutional importance. Such matters were previously the preserve of the law lords in the House of Lords. Appeals must relate to a general point of law and are heard by a committee drawn from the 12 members of the Court. Critics of the British system had long argued that the judiciary should be independent of the legislature, yet the law lords, as part of the legislature, precluded this. In June 2003 critics had

POLITICS

their way when the government declared its intention of setting up such a court, but on 5 November 2003 six of the law lords declared themselves opposed to the plan as 'unnecessary and harmful' and because 'the present system works well'. Only four of their lordships argued in favour of the proposal. However, the government thought otherwise and pressed ahead with its plans. The UK Supreme Court was set up by the Constitutional Reform Act 2005 and started work on 1 October 2009. It performs all the judicial functions of the House of Lords exercised by the law lords (lords of appeal in ordinary). It also took over some functions of the Judicial Committee of the Privy Council. The Court is located in the Middlesex Guildhall, Parliament Square.

Sure Start
Programme introduced by Labour, in 1998, aiming to provide a holistic addi-tion – child care, nursery education, health and family support – to the upbringing of disadvantaged children. It owes something to policies in Scandinavian countries and Australia, as well as Head Start in USA, which has returned a valuable dividend in terms of education and family life. The basic idea is that children brought up in poor areas tend to suffer from emotional, educational and family neglect and that government intervention can minimise the damage which would otherwise be incurred by such children, thus giving them a much better start in life. Areas were chosen for their degree of disadvantage and were given a wide degree of autonomy to proceed as they thought fit. In the most disadvantaged areas, for example, provision was to include: integrated early learning and child care (early-years provision) for a minimum of 10 hours a day, five days a week, 48 weeks a year; and support for child-minder provision. The results of assessment have been modest to date but supporters passionately believe this is the best way to remove the scars which poverty inflicts upon modern societies. They also fear that, in an atmosphere of financial cuts,

the coalition government that took office in May 2010 might choose to reduce Sure Start provision.

Sustainable Development Commission
www.sd-commission.org.uk
The government's independent advisor on sustainable development. It reports direct to the prime minister and the first ministers of the devolved executives, seeking to put sustainable development at the heart of government policy. From its establishment in 2000 its chair was Jonathon Porritt, the doyen of green campaigners. Porritt left the job in July 2009, feeling that many of his arguments with government, non-governmental organisations and business had been substantially won. On 1 February 2009, the Sustainable Development Commission became an executive non-departmental body.

> I am unapologetic about asking people to connect up their own responsibility for their total environmental footprint and how they decide to procreate and how many children they think are appropriate. (Jonathan Porritt)

swing
Measure used by psephologists to indicate movements in voting behaviour. It is calculated by adding the percentage of votes gained by one party to that lost by another and then dividing by two. For example, if the Conservatives lose 8 per cent at an election and Labour gains 6 per cent, the average swing is half of 14 per cent, which is 7 per cent.

swingometer
A relatively crude piece of machinery used by veteran political scientist Bob McKenzie in the 1950s and 1960s when commenting in BBC studios on general elections. It comprised a large arrow which swung to show how many seats would change hands between the parties, depending on the percentage swing from one to another. For example, a 1 per cent swing from Labour to Conservative usually indicated that 18 seats

would change hands. In those early days it was easier to make such predictions, as percentage swings would largely be reflected across the country. During the 1970s and 1980s swings became less uniform. Moreover, television techniques advanced so that computer graphics replaced the swingometer in election coverage, which often featured the irrepressible Peter Snow using a lifelike House of Commons that would fill up with the requisite numbers of blue or red MPs, depending on swings or computer predictions.

T

tabloid press

These comprise the 'red tops', the *Sun*, *Daily Mirror* and *Daily Star*, catering for lower-income, less well educated groups. The *Daily Mail* and the *Daily Express* are also tabloid size but are aimed at the so-called 'mid-market', comprising people in social class C1. Some 'quality' papers have also come to adopt the tabloid size but are not included in the 'tabloid' category. The Sunday tabloids are also important, with the *News of the World*, *Sunday Mirror* and *People* shadowing the three daily papers. The three daily tabloids sell predominantly to C2, D and E groups, that is, working-class readers. In 2002 the tabloids had over 7 million of the 13 million daily newspaper sales. The *Star* and *Sun* supported the Conservatives in 1992 and many experts believed their support, especially that of the *Sun*, swung hundreds of thousands of votes to the governing party – though such views are hotly contested by other experts. However, in the 1997 campaign a huge shift in press loyalty occurred and Rupert Murdoch's *Sun* swung behind New Labour, as did the *Star*. This meant that the previously close relationship with the tabloids no longer

benefited the Conservative leadership as it had in previous elections, when the tabloids ran stories closely correlated with those of Central Office. Tony Blair's press secretary Alastair Campbell believed he was chosen for his job by Blair because 'We both acknowledge the significance to the political debate of the tabloids'.

tactical voting

When voters do not vote for the candidate of their preferred party but choose one who will most likely defeat their most disliked candidate. For example, in a seat held by a Conservative, Labour voters might choose to support the second-placed Liberal Democrat candidate as a way of defeating the Conservative. For tactical voting to take place electors usually need to have opinion poll information on which to base their calculations as to who is most likely to defeat the least wanted candidate. The practice is sometimes referred to as 'negative' voting, in the sense that electors are not really making a positive democratic decision – they are in effect blocking or vetoing the choices of others. However, tactical voting can have important consequences. In the 1997 general election anti-Conservative tactical voting helped the Labour Party to gain more MPs (419) than it had expected, resulting in a parliamentary majority of 179. Part of this effect was the result of information published in the *Observer* before polling day.

After the June 2001 general election, Peter Kellner wrote in the *Observer* that tactical voting was still significant and still hurt the Tories. In one seat Labour gained in that election, Dorset South, Ian Bruce, the sitting Conservative MP, actually increased his share of the vote but Labour's increased by much more and the Liberal Democrats' vote dropped from 20 per cent to 14 per cent. In nearby Totnes and Teignbridge it was Labour voters who switched and helped elect a Liberal Democrat. Guilford and Ludlow were also gained by the Liberal Democrats through tactical voting and many of that party's majorities were boosted by the same effect.

In the 2010 election Labour marginals stood up better than expected, indicating tactical voting by Liberal Democrat supporters and the same could be said for some Liberal Democrat marginals, where the Labour vote shrunk by much more than the national swing would have suggested.

Taff Vale decision, 1901

Legal decision that badly affected the power of trade unions by making them liable for damages if sued in relation to actions by their officers. The Taff Vale Railway Company sued the railway workers' union after a strike and was awarded £23,000. This superseded the previous understanding that a union was not a legal corporation and could not be sued for the actions of its members. This decision, in the light of the Liberal Party's less than fulsome opposition, was one of the major reasons why the unions proceeded to seek independent Labour representation and to form the Labour Party.

'take note' motion

A motion on which the House of Lords debates reports from select committees or discusses topics on which the government would like to hear a view from the upper chamber.

Tamworth manifesto, 1835

Election address by Robert Peel which is usually seen as the first manifesto. It is also taken to mark the emergence of the new Conservative Party from the more nebulous Tory group in parliament. Peel declared that he accepted the Reform Act of 1832 and favoured moderate reform which balanced the interests of aristocracy and commerce.

task force

Body appointed by government to look into a particular matter, usually with a membership of civil servants and experts. New Labour came into office in 1997 with a flurry of task force creation in response to a myriad of different topics. Within two years 238 such bodies had been set up and these

employed a total of 1,500 people. Not all of them reported on time and their proliferation attracted much dubious comment and a feeling that they were an excuse for failing to deal with the issues in question. There was a task force on Near Earth Asteroids and Comets which reported in 2001 and a Northern Ireland Organised Crime Task Force was set up in 2000.

taxation

The means whereby the government raises money in order for it to be able to provide services (public goods) such as the armed forces, education and the National Health Service. Income tax is a direct form of taxation which was first introduced in 1799. During the Second World War the standard rate of income tax rose to 50 per cent but the Conservatives brought it down gradually when in power to 23 pence in the pound by 1997. In 1998 it brought in £84.3 billion, or around a quarter of the £330.2 billion total expenditure. Corporation tax is a direct tax on company profits and brings in around £30 billion each year.

Indirect taxation, mainly value added tax (VAT), is preferred by the Conservatives, as taxpayers tend not to notice it as much as money deducted from wage packets. It is paid on the value added to a product at every stage of the production or distribution process. Other forms of indirect taxation include the duties on goods like alcohol and tobacco.

In the 1992 general election the Conservatives were able to alarm voters into thinking Labour would put up taxation by large amounts, as they had done in the past to fund high government spending. When Labour lost that election the party decided to pursue a policy of low direct taxation and in 1997 promised not to increase spending above the Conservative level for at least two years into the next government.

Taxation is also one of the tools of macro-economic management and fiscal policy, although since the 1980s its role in this respect has largely been replaced by interest rates. Traditionally Labour

POLITICS

governments have attempted to redistribute wealth by taxing higher earners and using the receipts to finance social security or other benefits, although New Labour claimed to have abandoned a policy of 'tax and spend'. Instead, the party sought to extract more revenue via indirect taxes, such as the excise duty on petrol, which was bitterly criticised when the price of oil rose sharply in 2000 and again in 2004 (as some 75 per cent of the cost of petrol went to the exchequer). The Conservatives made much of these 'stealth' taxes in the run-up to elections. Many critics of New Labour felt the party should have braved the consequences of supporting higher taxation during the 2001 election campaign.

In 2010–11, taxpayers received a tax-free allowance of £6,475 and paid the standard rate of income tax at 20p in the pound. For taxpayers earning above £37,400 the higher rate of 40p applied.

In 2008–09 total receipts from taxation were £575 billion; national insurance garnered £105 billion; income tax £160 billion; corporation tax £52 billion; and VAT £84 billion.

See also income tax; indirect taxation; value added tax.

televised debate
See party leaders' televised debates.

televising of parliament
First proposed in 1966 but then heavily defeated. While radio coverage was introduced into both houses in 1978 and television into the Lords in 1985, the Commons refused on the grounds that such a presence would destroy the unique, intimate atmosphere of the place. But opinion changed. If Margaret Thatcher had not been opposed, it would have become a reality before 2 November 1989, when the cameras, subject to various restrictions, were coyly allowed onto the floor of the 'mother of parliaments'. In January 1990 many of the restrictions were relaxed; in July of that year the Commons voted 131 to 32 to make the arrangement permanent.

television
John Logie Baird's 1920s invention came into production in the 1930s. Television broadcasts ceased during the Second World War and television was still secondary to radio after it. The 1953 coronation was the catalyst for television in Britain and politicians realised its potential at about the same time. Winston Churchill had already appeared on US television, aboard the *Queen Mary* in 1951; later he agreed that cameras should televise his 80th birthday celebrations in Westminster Hall. In 1954 he took part in a secret television screen test at Number 10; the results were not positive, as he did not suit the medium. Harold Macmillan was arguably the first cleverly to exploit television, soon followed by Harold Wilson. After 1959 all election campaigns concentrated much expense and energy on transmitting political messages via the television sets most families owned. The BBC's monopoly was broken in the 1950s with the arrival of independent television. Interviewers like Robin Day began to structure the coverage the medium gave to politics. Broadcasts became controversial; for example, Wilson objected bitterly to the BBC programme *Yesterday's Men*, on the Labour Party, produced in 1971. In the 1970s politicians began to take television even more seriously and Margaret Thatcher benefited from the services of a 'spin doctor', Gordon Reece, in adjusting her presentation to the cameras.

During election campaigns politicians try their best to make an impression in news bulletins with well turned sound bites. The evolution of every election into a 'television election' helps to explain the sensitivity of the medium regarding funding and operating frameworks. Being good on television is now so important that it influenced some of those keen to remove Gordon Brown as leader in autumn 2008 and the summer of 2009. The Conservatives, meanwhile have, in the person of David Cameron, someone who is a good all-round communicator and very good on television.

POLITICS

10 Downing Street
www.number-10.gov.uk
Official London home of British prime
ministers since the time of Robert Walpole.
It is located in a row of 17th-century houses
in Westminster. Number 11 is the home
of the chancellor of the exchequer. The
street is named after Sir George Downing
(1623–84), who was an early secretary to
the Treasury. In 1997 Tony Blair swapped
sleeping accommodation with his chancellor
neighbour Gordon Brown, as Number 10
had insufficient room for his three (later
four) children. Portraits of all former prime
ministers adorn the walls of Number 10.
    See also Downing, George.

10-minute rule bill
One of the methods whereby back-bench
MPs can initiate legislation in the
Commons. Revived in 1950, this device
enables members to introduce a bill
after question time on Tuesdays and
Wednesdays, with a speech not exceeding
10 minutes. A speech of equal length is
allowed in opposition and then the bill
is put; if it is unopposed or passed it can
progress further. The procedure is available
to those MPs who are first in a queue at the
Public Bill Office; it is valued in that the
house is usually well attended for question
time. The bill to abolish the death penalty
and that which legalised homosexual acts
were both introduced in this way.

10 pence tax rate
In his final budget as chancellor Gordon
Brown raised a huge cheer from his MPs
when he announced the standard rate of
tax was to be reduced from 22p to 20p. He
paid for this reduction by abolishing the
lower tax band of 10p in the pound paid by
those earning above the personal allowance
level of just over £5,000 and below the level
at which the standard rate was required.
Several newspapers pointed out that the
poorest people in the country would suffer
as a result of this measure and Frank
Field MP made personal approaches to
Brown to plead for reconsideration. Brown,
however, proved immovable and denied

there would be any 'losers'. It was only
later, when it came into force in April 2008
(and Brown had become prime minister)
that it became clear that 5.3 million of the
nation's poorest, to whose cause Brown
had always claimed support, would lose
out by a relatively large percentage of their
small earnings. A revolt by Labour MPs
produced a compensatory package but this
did not prevent the issue becoming a potent
loser of votes in the Crewe and Nantwich
by-election, which Labour lost disastrously
on 22 May of that year.

terrorism
A pejorative term used by state authorities
and mainstream media to describe those
'extremist' and violent groups that they
oppose and accuse of not subscribing to
the liberal democratic consensus. However,
these groups or their representatives may
cross the line and sign up to democratic
principles, and thus be rehabilitated by
state authorities as recognised politicians,
an example of this being Britain's recognition of former 'terrorists' as legitimate
representatives of the people in Ireland,
Cyprus, Palestine and, more recently,
Northern Ireland. Political conflict in
Britain is for the most part channelled
through the system of parliamentary
democracy and the operation of pressure
groups in the policy-making process.
However, the 'troubles' in Northern Ireland
were a sharp reminder that this is not
always the case and that some demands
cannot be accommodated within the British
political system.
    The 7/7 bombings in London in 2005,
involving four coordinated bombings on
public transport which killed 56 people,
presented a wholly new perspective on
terrorism. The worrying aspect of these
attacks was that the perpetrators emerged
from within Britain's own Muslim community: young men who had been educated
and employed in this country, something
which had not happened, for example,
in the USA. The law was tightened up
again in 2005 and 2006 to make virtually
any association with terrorism a criminal

offence. In 2006 another scare emerged when suspects were arrested accused of planning to blow up airplanes mid-Atlantic using liquid explosives. Government sources have reported the foiling of several plots by the security agencies and the risk remained 'substantial' according to official classifications in 2009.

See also Afghanistan; 9/11 2001; Northern Ireland; 7/7 bombings.

Terrorism Act 2000

Came into force in February 2001 and replaced a range of temporary legislation relating to Britain and Northern Ireland. It gave, among other things:

1 a new definition of terrorism;
2 new powers to seize suspects at borders;
3 a new offence of inciting terrorism abroad from within Britain;
4 new extensions of rights to detain suspected terrorists;
5 a new offence of training terrorists.

Terrorism Act 2001

Piece of legislation that complemented the Terrorism Act 2000. It was passed in December 2001 in the wake of the attacks on the USA on 11 September 2001. Its main provision was for the indefinite detention of suspected terrorists but it also contained clauses on the incitement of religious hatred, hoax threats of terrorist action, aiding the development of chemical, nuclear, biological or radiological weapons, the withholding of information regarding a terrorist attack, refusing police requests to remove hand and face coverings in public-order situations, and the financial support of terrorist activities. The new act was much criticised for its alleged breach of civil rights and encountered difficulties during its passage through the House of Lords.

Thatcherism

Margaret Thatcher is one of the few prime ministers to have an 'ism' attached to her name. Her ideas were so clear and consistent everyone in government and probably most voters understood them and either loved or loathed them, as they did their

author. In essence Thatcherism reasserted classical liberalism with traditional political authority, delivered in a populist and assertive style of leadership. A set of policy orientations, which later became known as Thatcherism, were developed around this ideological framework, and included:

1 tight control of the money supply to control inflation;
2 the notion that individual freedom is inseparable from the free enterprise economy;
3 the idea that market forces work automatically for the benefit of all;
4 the belief that capitalism works, and that state intervention destroys freedom and efficiency;
5 the belief that trade union power endangers competitiveness and the government's ability to run the country in the interests of all;
6 the idea that state welfare is excessive, inefficient and saps the self-reliance of those who depend upon it.

Perhaps its greatest achievement was to reshape the political terrain of Britain and with it the Labour Party. Thatcher continued to exert influence over the rank and file of the Conservative Party even after her departure from office; her presence at the 1999 party conference, for example, helped to reinforce the rightward shift made by William Hague towards the 'commonsense revolution'. She also appeared prominently during the 2001 general election campaign. Experts considered the rightward shift of the Conservatives to be a bad mistake and that it ensured another beating at the polls, and the presence of the former prime minister during the campaign as another mistake as she tended to speak 'off message' and to remind voters of unhappy aspects of her period in office. Others believed Tony Blair's second general election victory enabled him to move out from under the shadow of Thatcherism, many of whose tenets he had espoused in government. He made no secret of his admiration for the formidable former Conservative leader. The election as leader of David Cameron in 2005, marked a shift towards the centre and a more liberal version of Conservatism regarding public spending, social policy and cultural questions like attitudes towards homosexuality.

See also classical liberalism.

think-tank

A research and development organisation which brings together academics, technocrats and politicians who wish to advance a specific policy or ideological agenda. Think-tanks are often associated with the USA, where there are more than 1,000 non-profit political research institutes, with 100 based around Washington, DC. Britain, though, has had think-tanks for over a century. Two of the first were the Fabian Society (1884) and the more academic Royal Institute of International Affairs (1920). In the 1930s two more, both academically orientated, emerged: the Policy Studies Institute (PSI) and the National Institute for Economic and Social Research (NIESR). In the 1950s the first right-wing organisation, the Institute of Economic Affairs (IEA), was founded, followed in the 1970s by the Centre for Policy Studies, the Adam Smith Institute and the Policy Studies Institute. In the 1980s the left contributed with the Institute for Public Policy Research (IPPR). In the 1980s and 1990s some more left-wing think-tanks were founded, including Demos, the think-tank perhaps currently closest to the Labour Party. In September 1996 the Centre for European Reform was set up by David Miliband, a member of the Downing Street Policy Unit (and minister after 2001). In the autumn of 1997 the Smith Institute was set up with chancellor Gordon Brown's support in honour of the former Labour Party leader John Smith. Robin Cook at the Foreign Office also got in on the act with the Foreign Policy Centre. All these recent think-tanks were set up by New Labour but Catalyst is more in the Old Labour camp, with Lord Hattersley as the head of its editorial board. Unlike the Conservatives, who used them to prepare for their period in power, the Labour Party seemed in 1997 to have got into power

first and then looked to the think-tanks for ideas. During the early part of Labour's second term the think-tank closest to the Labour government was the IPPR and its report on public–private partnerships caused controversy in June 2001.

third-party voting

Voting for any party other than the two main ones in Britain's first past the post electoral system. Just after the Second World War the Liberal Party attracted a small fraction of the popular vote and the two big parties commanded 95 per cent. By the 1980s third-party voting had increased to over 20 per cent and in 1983 the Alliance polled 26 per cent for a mere 3.5 per cent (23) of the seats, strengthening the argument for electoral reform. Since then the nationalist parties have continued to prosper, though the voting system does not so severely penalise small parties where their vote is geographically concentrated. On 19 July 2009 Andrew Rawnsley wrote an article in the *Observer* suggesting the flight of voters away from the two big parties had caused a crisis in British politics, whereby neither could safely assume it could govern on its own in the future. Peter Kellner in the *Sunday Times* on 9 May 2010 argued that the rise of third-party voting made big majorities a thing of the past: 'As well as the 57 contingent of Liberal Democrats, 28 represented eight smaller parties. To secure an overall majority of just two, the Tories would have needed 86 more MPs than Labour.'

See also tactical voting.

third reading

See act of parliament; legislative process.

third way

Term associated with Tony Blair's approach to politics, sometimes referred to as 'Blairism'. In September 1998 Blair published a Fabian pamphlet called *The Third Way*; it was an attempt to characterise his approach as neither old socialist nor Conservative, but a distinctively radical third direction. The pamphlet was received with doubt in most political circles. Critics claim that the third way was merely a clever piece of political pragmatism, in that it targeted disillusioned middle-class voters with a repackaged version of somewhat moderated Conservative economic policies. Supporters of third way politics suggest that Blair had a core of beliefs which qualify him as a progenitor of a new political movement. Moreover, these beliefs have found echoes in the work of social and political commentators such as Amitai Etzioni and Anthony Giddens, as well as the New Democrat thinking of Bill Clinton and the ideas of German chancellor Gerhard Schroeder.

The third way is best understood as a set of themes or propositions:

1 It recognises that globalisation and new technology have created a world of rapid change, which requires new thinking and the application of treasured values in new ways.

2 It synthesises the best of old left and new right ideologies to meet the challenges of today. In particular, it combines the efficiencies of dynamic markets with social justice and inclusion.

3 It employs pragmatic and technological managerialism – third way thinking emphasises 'delivery' and it therefore follows that what matters is not public or private sector provision, but the quality of the provision, however sourced. (New Labour in office indeed used the public, private and voluntary sectors, and various mixtures of all three at once, in the delivery of public services.)

4 It does not take a mechanistic view of the state as too big (new right) or too small (old left), but rather asks whether it is doing enough in terms of regulation or policy initiatives, for example in the area of pensions or encouraging parental responsibility. It became well known in Whitehall that Blair believed essentially in the 'non-ideological' notion of 'what works'.

5 It asserts that both the state and the market should serve the public interest. Citizens should expect high-quality

services from both public and private sectors, which should serve the community fairly, efficiently and effectively. Thus, if market providers treat their workers unfairly or engage in uncompetitive practices, then reform should take place. Equally, if public services are inefficient, or do not respond to the needs of those they are there to serve, then government should bring about change.

6 It emphasises social inclusion. The third way rejects the idea that individuals have only themselves to blame for lack of success in life; it therefore insists that all have access to the full range of life resources, including health, income, work, education and public order. However, it also rejects the idea of equality of outcomes, where individual effort or merit is not recognised by additional income, social status or other rewards.

7 It offers a new contract between citizen and state. The third way emphasises the interdependence of individuals, groups and the state, each type of actor having rights but also obligations or responsibilities. Thus the state has a duty to provide work, or pathways into work or training, but equally the citizen is expected to take advantage of these opportunities, not only for individual improvement but also as a responsible citizen who has a duty to contribute towards society and the economy.

8 It also offers a new vision of politics. Third way thinking seeks to influence the political landscape, as did the Conservatives did in the early 1980s. It seeks to reshape the political agenda and establish a new consensus between all major political parties, and in so doing contribute to the governance of modern British society. In this sense Blair's third way had a powerful ideological agenda.

On 26 March 2002 'Bagehot' (David Lipsey) in the *Economist* wrote a valedictory piece in which he saw Blair's achievement through slightly different eyes:

By turning Labour into New Labour, abandoning socialism, befriending business and promising not to squeeze the rich,

POLITICS

Mr Blair has done more than build an election winning party. He has broken the tribal pattern of British politics in just the way the Social Democrats who broke from Labour in the 1980s hoped but failed to.... By finally breaking the old relationship between Labour and the interests it was created to represent, Mr Blair has twisted the whole of British politics into a new shape. It is the system he broke rather than the machine he built that makes his premiership so interesting.

The third way has been tested in the cauldron; those principles are still valid. However, some of the softer edges have been shown to be flaky. (Stephen Byers, *Guardian*, 14 January 2002)

See also political language.

38 degrees
http://38degrees.org.uk
Radical change movement, set up in May 2009, that seeks to exploit the Internet and other means to achieve change. Its executive director is David Babbs, formerly with Friends of the Earth. The body is based upon US campaigning groups like Aavaz and Moveon. Issues chosen include climate change, sustainable environment and change for greater democracy.

three-day week, 1974
A rationing of energy to industry announced by Edward Heath in January 1974. Energy supplies were being threatened by: the oil crisis caused by the price hikes determined by the Organization of Petroleum Exporting Countries (OPEC); the industrial action of the miners' union; and the winter weather. The measure caused an atmosphere of crisis in the country but industrial production did not decrease initially – an indication of the degree of overstaffing which characterised British industry at that time. In February Heath called an election on the theme of 'Who Governs Britain?', which he lost, thus ending his time in Downing Street and setting the scene for the emergence of Margaret Thatcher.

See also miners' strikes, 1972 and 1974.

three-line whip
Written instruction issued to MPs by the whips' office with three underlinings to indicate that voting for the party line on a debate is mandatory.

Times, the
www.timesonline.co.uk
Daily newspaper nicknamed the 'Thunderer'. It was founded in 1785 as the *Daily Universal Register* and became the *Times* in 1788. It was owned by Lord Northcliffe from 1908 and then by J. Astor after 1922. The Thomson Organisation bought it in 1966 and then Rupert Murdoch's News International in 1981. The *Times* has always been the mouthpiece of the establishment and has pursued an independent Conservative line on most major issues. Murdoch lowered the price of the newspaper in the 1990s in an attempt to put the *Independent* out of business and to hurt the *Daily Telegraph*. The *Times* backed Labour for the first time in a general election in 2001. In 2010 both the *Times* and *Sunday Times* endorsed the Conservative Party.

Today programme
www.bbc.co.uk/radio4/today
Early-morning Radio 4 programme introduced during the 1970s that has become something of a national institution. It commands an audience of over a million, who include many of the nation's political elite. Its presenters – the most well known of whom include John Humphrys, James Naughtie, Evan Davies and Caroline Quinn – are famous for the tenacity of their interrogations and are regularly criticised for being rude or for interrupting excessively. In April 2002 the general secretary of the Labour Party, David Triesman, criticised the programme for treating politicians as if they were 'consummate liars trying to line their own pockets' (ironic in view of the 2009 MPs' expenses scandal). He went on to blame this tendency for encouraging disengagement from politics and apathy. Rod Liddle, the then editor of the programme, denied such

a tendency and insisted 'Today listeners expect to hear politicians challenged'. Margaret Thatcher, when prime minister, once famously rang up the programme to comment live on something which she had just heard. On 29 May 2003, Today reporter Andrew Gilligan in a live interview accused Downing Street of embellishing the dossier on Iraqi weapons published by the government in September 2002, saying that the threat posed by Iraqi weapons of mass destruction (WMD) was exaggerated in order to justify the government's backing of the US policy of invading Iraq. This triggered the biggest crisis ever in relations between the BBC and the government and led to the resignations of the BBC chair of governors as well as Greg Dyke, its director general.

toleration

John Locke was the liberal philosopher in an age of religious conflict who advocated the advantages of toleration and compromise over dogmatism and conflict. British political culture has allegedly been characterised by a strong element of toleration ever since, though examples of racist bigotry and closed minds over a whole range of issues are not difficult to find and are revealed regularly in opinion surveys.

top-up fee

Variable charge on students for their further education. This proposal caused much dissension within the Labour Party in the autumn of 2003 and was opposed, for example, by Estelle Morris when she was in charge of education. The proposal was to allow universities to increase the fees charged to students from just over £1,000 to £3,000. The condition was that they were to make special efforts to encourage students from disadvantaged homes. The key difference was that the funds raised were to go direct to the parent institution and not via the Treasury. Opponents argued that such a dispensation would allow elite universities to charge more and would open the way for variable salaries for academics instead of universal rates.

Tory

The word was probably derived from the Irish term *toraidhe*, meaning a brigand, cattle thief or outlaw. It was applied to supporters of the Duke of York (James II) in the 'exclusion crisis' of 1679–81, when great political energies were directed towards the exclusion of the Catholic son of Charles II from the succession. The Whigs supported exclusion whereas their opponents became associated with support for the Church and the king, and included many squires and large landowners. They were excluded from power by George I and George II for most of the 18th century, but George III decided to favour them. The French Revolution strengthened Tory principles and therefore their political profile in Britain. The term was still used abusively by Whigs to describe their opponents but gradually it came to be accepted as a non-pejorative term, especially after the Tory Benjamin Disraeli used it. Robert Peel preferred the term Conservative when he reorganised the party after the Great Reform Act of 1832 and the two terms are now used interchangeably, with the former being favoured by the right wing for its historical connotations.

Tory Action

Right-wing grouping, active in the 1970s and 1980s, led by a former head of MI6, George Young. It held views on immigration close to those of the Monday Club and claimed to have several hundred members, who included about a dozen Tory MPs. The group was still active in 1990 but is now thought not to be.

See also Monday Club.

Tory Reform Group

www.trg.org.uk
Set up in 1975 to defend the 'one nation' tradition within the Conservative Party, which was under fire from the new right. In the early 1990s it had around two dozen MP members. Several MPs defected to other parties, for example Emma Nicholson to the Liberal Democrats, and Shaun Woodward and Alan Howarth to Labour.

Ken Clarke is president of the group, which also includes Lord Hurd and John Bercow, now the speaker of the House of Commons.

'tough on crime, tough on the causes of crime'

Tony Blair sound bite produced when he was shadow home secretary in 1994. It cleverly combined the essence of 'Old' Labour's approach – that crime reflected an unjust social system – with the more populist and voter-sensitive New Labour – that criminals should be caught and punished, possibly severely. By straddling both points of view it also provided maximum policy options. In power Labour proved as tough on crime as its predecessor in government, with the prison population soaring despite falling crime statistics.

Toynbee Hall

www.toynbeehall.org.uk
Founded 1884 by Samuel and Henrietta Barnet in Whitechapel as the original 'university settlement' where university graduates could experience something of the nature of poverty. The centre still operates a series of programmes to assist poorer families at the younger, adult and old age levels, to advance their potential and overcome the disadvantages of poverty. Residents have included R. H. Tawney, Clement Attlee and, perhaps most notably, John Profumo, the minister who was at the centre of the Christine Keeler scandal in the early 1960s.

Trade Union and Labour Party Liaison Organisation (TULO)

www2.labour.org.uk/tulo
Organisation established in 1994 that links nationally affiliated unions (currently 15) with the party. On 6 August 2004 TULO negotiated a series of commitments to the public services from Labour in exchange for continuing union support for the party. They included extending workforce protection in local government across all public services, an agreement to tackle unequal pay in local government and a commitment not to extend selection by ability in schools.

trade unionism

Emerged in the 18th century with the appearance of mutual self-help organisations mostly for skilled workers. With the industrial revolution workers became more easily organised, especially in the 19th century, but employers were hostile and the Combination Acts (1799–1825) made trade union membership a serious criminal offence. The 'new model unions', which developed in the late 19th century, were reluctant to strike and sought rational settlement of disputes through negotiation rather than direct action. Membership grew in times of prosperity and slumped in depressions. In the 1920s the Transport and General Workers' Union (TGWU) had a third of a million members; by the mid-1970s this had grown to 2 million though it had slumped back to under 1 million by 2001. During the 1970s unions were instrumental in the fall of Ted Heath's government (1974) and it was said quite seriously that Hugh Scanlon of the Amalgamated Union of Engineering Workers and Jack Jones of the TGWU were the two most powerful men in Britain. Margaret Thatcher came to power determined to reduce their power for political and economic reasons. The sharp rise in unemployment in the early 1980s weakened the hands of unions, in that workers prove to be less willing to strike when their jobs are at risk. Legislation designed to make industrial action more difficult also contributed to their decline, but the single most effective blow was the failure of the protracted miners' strike of 1984–85. Union membership slumped in the 1980s from 12 million to just over 7 million and the national political role they had played under Labour administrations had long since vanished. Under Tony Blair the unions were promised 'fairness not favours' and were lectured at the annual conference of the Trades Union Congress (TUC) on the need for modernisation by him in 1997 and by Peter Mandelson in 1998.

Several new union leaders surfaced during the early part of 2002 who threatened to be the 'awkward squad'. Tony Blair had himself blamed 'wreckers' for preventing his attempted reforms of the public sector at a conference in January 2002. It was clear to most observers that his later claim that he had meant the Conservatives was disingenuous – he had also meant those union leaders who disagreed with him. On 18 February 2002 the *Guardian* identified six members of this 'awkward squad': Dave Prentis of Unison, Britain's biggest union; Billy Hayes of the Communication Workers' Union (CWU); Mark Serwotka of the civil service union (PCS); Mick Rix of the Associated Society of Locomotive Engineers and Firemen (ASLEF); Bob Crowe of the National Union of Rail, Maritime and Transport Workers (RMT); and Andy Gilchrist of the Fire Brigades Union (FBU).

Unions are especially strong in the public sector; 60 per cent of this workforce are unionised compared with 19 per cent in the private sector. More surprising is that middle-class workers are more unionised than blue-collar workers. Younger workers seem apathetic regarding joining unions as well as political parties: only 18 per cent of the 18–29 age group are members of unions. By 2009 industrial relations were still fairly good under the Labour government, apart from a few isolated strikes, mostly in the public sector. Labour was keen to keep the unions onside so that the party's parlous finances could be replenished for the general election campaign that was due in 2010.

See also awkward squad; industrial relations; Trade Union and Labour Party Liaison Organisation; Trades Union Congress; unemployment.

Trades Disputes Acts 1906 and 1927
The 1906 act removed the legal liability of unions for the actions of their members, thus reversing the legal significance of the Taff Vale decision of 1901. A further act passed in 1927, after the General Strike, banned general strikes and civil servants joining unions affiliated to the Trades Union Congress. It also required a positive decision on the part of members to 'contract

in' to make financial contributions the Labour Party via union dues, rather than the automatic deduction which applied before the act. The result deprived the party of about one-third of its financial support until 1945, when the measure was reversed. Norman Tebbit's Employment Act 1983 required ballots to be held by trade unions to decide whether their members wished a political levy to be passed on to the Labour Party. In the event most union memberships confirmed the political contribution.

See also Taff Vale decision.

Trades Union Congress (TUC)
www.tuc.org.uk
Founded in Manchester in 1868 to organise union activity more effectively and to hold annual conferences. Initially it involved only skilled workers but it grew in the later part of the 19th century as union activity increased. By 1900 it represented over 250,000 workers and by 1914 this figure had risen sharply, to 2.5 million. Militant activity during the First World War helped to increase membership to 6 million by 1920. The TUC was damaged by the failure of the General Strike in 1926, which discouraged it from politically related activity separate from its Labour links. During the Second World War union influence grew as leaders cooperated with government; Ernest Bevin, for example, who had been general secretary of the Transport and General Workers' Union before the war, became minister of labour in the wartime coalition government and a household name. Membership rose to over 8 million. Thereafter the TUC became for a time one of the 'estates of the realm' and was consulted and listened to as a matter of course. In the 1970s, however, union power was generally believed to be excessive and against the public interest. The 'winter of discontent' of 1978–79 was the culmination of this disaffection and Margaret Thatcher found a country not unreceptive to her measures to curb the trade unions during the 1980s. By the 1990s the TUC seemed to have accepted the legal framework

created by the Conservatives (together with ballots for strikes and political donations) as normal. Its general secretary, John Monks, set about reforming the TUC's structure in the 1990s.

The TUC has a General Council and a body of officers who help coordinate union activity and resolve disputes. An annual conference is organised for each September. Following Labour's 2001 general election victory, trade union representatives visited Tony Blair in Downing Street in late June and frankly stated their hostility to attempts to introduce more private sector involvement in the public sector. He listened sympathetically but refused to move from his reform agenda. He did the same at Labour's spring conference, held in February 2002. On 3 July 2001, the *Guardian* reported that Blair would be seeing the unions 'five or six times a year' in order to defuse the growing conflict between the government and Labour's main donors. In 2005 the TUC had 58 unions affiliated and nearly 7 million members.

See also Trade Union and Labour Party Liaison Organisation (TULO); trade unionism.

transparency
Procedures which make decisions (notably on the part of government) open and clear to everyone.

Transco
Privatised monopoly which owned the gas distribution network. It came in for much criticism for poor maintenance and in June 2001 the Health and Safety Executive insisted Transco replace its mains equipment in Batley after an explosion killed a whole family. Clare Spottiswoode, the former gas regulator, accused the company of playing the game of demanding investment, not spending it and then giving it to shareholders in dividends.

Transport and General Workers' Union (TGWU)
Formed from a merger of unions in 1922. It represents workers mostly in manual

occupations in transport, construction, the public sector and agriculture. It has a famous history as the union once led by Ernest Bevin and has played an important role in Labour Party history, sometimes as a bastion of the right, for example under Bevin, and at other times of the left, for instance when Jack Jones was leader in the 1970s. In 2001 the leader was Bill Morris, who was generally supportive of New Labour but who was also outspoken in his criticisms. He retired in 2003 and his place taken by Tony Woodley. The TGWU was the second largest union after the public sector union Unison, but its membership was declining. It merged with Amicus in May 2007 to form Unite.

See also Unite.

transport policy
The Department for Transport is responsible for the country's 2,700 km of motorways and 7,800 km of trunk roads. Strategic planning is undertaken by the core but maintenance and construction are undertaken by the Highways Agency. In 1997 transport was included in deputy prime minister John Prescott's Department of Environment, Transport and the Regions. During his stewardship policy seemed to move against the car and in favour of public transport but this shift was not sustained in practice and environmentalists criticised Labour for not fulfilling promises. In September 1999 a poll revealed that 65 per cent of respondents felt the government had not improved public transport. In a poll published on 18 July 2001, two-thirds of respondents were in favour of paying more in tax in exchange for better public transport. Two-fifths ranked transport as their 'major' local issue, higher even than crime. Fifty-four per cent backed congestion charging, provided the money raised was ploughed back into transport improvements.

In 1997 the government promised a renaissance in public transport but by 2001 figures for the previous year indicated an increase in the miles travelled by motorists compared with the previous year. Given the number of vehicles on the road even a small increase in journeys brings about incalculable jams and related traffic problems. Experts argued that problems would continue to increase as long as motoring costs continued to fall and public transport costs to increase. Green groups accused the government of reneging on its promises, citing in evidence the new motorway projects initiated in 2001. Lord (Andrew) Adonis was made transport secretary in June 2009 and expressed an interest in: high-speed trains; a disinclination to continue subsidising railway companies; and the possibility of 'pay as you go' road travel.

> Britain spends half as much on public transport as Germany, France and Italy. We have also some of the highest bus and train fares. Ageing rolling stock, vandalised buses and a Tube system where summer temperatures exceed the legal limit for transporting live animals make public transport the last resort for more and more commuters. (*Observer*, 31 March 2002)

> I will have failed if in five years there are not many more people using public transport and far fewer car journeys. It is a tall order but I want you to hold me to it. (John Prescott, 1997)

> If the railways don't improve, I take the blame – fine. At the next election I'm going to be judged by the quality of our travelling experience. (Stephen Byers, 14 January 2002; he was sacked later in the year)

See also Department for Transport; Network Rail.

Treason and Felony Act 1848

Passed at a time when European capitals were being rocked by revolution and London by a surge in Irish nationalism. The act sought to make criticism of the monarchy in print an offence punishable by life imprisonment. Several prosecutions were made in the 19th century – especially against editors in Dublin – but none has been made since 1883, though historians judge it had a 'chilling effect' on the British press during Victoria's reign and inhibited open statements of republicanism into the 20th century. In June 2001 the editor of the

Guardian attempted to challenge the law and to claim it violated the Human Rights Act. Two senior law lords replied that the application for judicial review could not be allowed, though the reasoning was largely technical.

Treasury

www.hm-treasury.gov.uk

The government department with responsibility for the economy. The Treasury has its origins in medieval times; since the 18th century the chancellor of the exchequer has been its senior member. By the 20th century it had become the most important department in the government and its head second in the hierarchy of importance. Its aims are: to provide the monetary and fiscal conditions necessary for continued economic growth; to run a stable financial system; to balance spending with taxation revenue; to advance Britain's overseas financial interests; and to manage the pay, conditions of service and industrial relations of the civil service. The Treasury has interests in all departments and especially big-spending ones like defence and health. It constantly seeks to control public expenditure and consequently has few friends in the Whitehall spending departments. The Treasury also monitors 'delivery' of service – the mantra of Tony Blair's second term. It agrees performance targets with all the other government departments and does its best to ensure they keep to their side of these agreements. The Treasury also negotiates 'public service agreements' with departments, which are a collection of agreed targets for departments, agencies and local councils.

treaty of accession, 1972

The treaty signed by prime minister Edward Heath in 1972 whereby the UK became a member of the European Community as of 1 January 1973.

treaty of Rome, 1957

The treaty which founded the European Economic Community. It was explicitly aimed at establishing institutions which would encourage the integration of

POLITICS

Europe, in accordance with the wishes of its founding fathers: Jean Monnet, Robert Schuman, Paul Spaak and others. The treaty was signed on 25 March 1957 and it established the Common Market. There was also another treaty of Rome of the same year which set up the European Atomic Energy Community (Euratom). Once ratified by member parliaments the treaties came into force on 1 January 1958.

treaty on European Union, 1992
See Maastricht treaty.

triangulation
Name given to the US Democrats' strategy under Bill Clinton of 'neutralising' controversial policy areas by adopting positions which were midway between traditional Democratic ones and the Republican equivalent. It has been suggested that New Labour adopted a similar approach. Nick Cohen in his book *Pretty Straight Guys* (2004) suggested an example was New Labour policy on asylum seekers, which emerged as an issue on which the Conservatives were strong in the run-up to the 2001 general election, as Labour decided to be 'as nasty or nastier still' than the Conservatives. He concluded the result of triangulation of policies for the Labour Party was to move the political spectrum consistently rightwards.

tribunal
An important quasi-judicial means of redressing a grievance. According to the *Times Guide to the New British State* (1995), they decide on the 'rights and obligations of individuals to each other and to the state' and are part of the 'peripheral state', as non-departmental public bodies (NDPBs). They all have 'quasi-judicial powers in a specialised field of law'. There were 68 at the time, served by over 22,000 appointees and included the Social Security Appeal Tribunal, the Disability Appeals Tribunal and the Value Added Tax Tribunal. Probably the best known, however, are the employment tribunals. Applications to these – on issues such as unfair dismissal,

discrimination and pay – have been increasing in recent years and the Confederation of British Industry was keen to reduce their role, as the average cost of defending a case for an employer was £2,000 plus 27 hours of management time. In November 2007, the Council on Tribunals was abolished and replaced by the Administrative Justice and Tribunals Council. At the same time, 107 tribunals were transferred to the supervision of the Council.

Tribune
www.tribunemagazine.co.uk
Socialist weekly magazine founded in 1936 by wealthy Labour MP George Strauss and the socialist barrister and future chancellor Stafford Cripps, to advance the arguments for a popular front against fascism. Before the war it fell under the control of 'fellow travellers', who were communists in all but name, but was then edited by Aneurin Bevan and later by Michael Foot. The circulation of the journal was not great but it appealed to working-class socialists and received contributions from the likes of George Orwell, Barbara Castle and Ian Mikardo, as well as Cripps himself.

After the war it gave its name to a group of left-wing MPs associated with Michael Foot, Tony Benn and then Neil Kinnock. It ceased to be a critical group but became more supportive of the party leadership once Kinnock became leader.

The group of MPs is no longer important but the publication *Tribune* still continues to play a role and might even be said to have offered a critical yet supportive voice to Tony Blair. In 2009 the magazine was taken over by Kevin McGrath, who wanted to keep it as a left-of-centre publication.

Trident
US nuclear missile made available to Britain to install in its nuclear submarine deterrent force. These missiles have enabled the British deterrent to operate with credibility for several decades but the perceived need to update the technology has created

the DSW Life Extension Programme, which will extend the life of Trident missiles until 2040. Both Tony Blair and Gordon Brown, not to mention the Tories, affirmed their intention to update the system, but the likely £60 billion price tag has made it a candidate for the public expenditure cuts which both parties deem necessary in view of the damage to the economy caused by the 2007–09 economic crisis.

tripartism
Term used to describe the close cooperation between government, employers' organisations and trade unions from the 1950s to the 1980s. In 1961 the Conservative government created the National Economic Development Council (NEDC, or Neddy), a forum which included representatives of employers, trade unions and government. It met regularly to consider ways of improving economic growth. In the 1970s with the Social Contract some commentators predicted Britain was moving in the same direction as Germany: a corporate state or 'tripartism'. However, the Social Contract ended in the 'winter of discontent'. Critics saw tripartism as a form of undemocratic corporatism which excluded parliament and other interests, and Margaret Thatcher would have no truck with Neddies of any kind, although it was left to John Major to abolish it in April 1993.
See also corporatism.

'triple lock'
Mechanism devised by Liberal Democrats, at their 1998 conference in Southport, to ensure their leadership cannot take the party in a direction it does not wish to go. It entails backing from three-quarters of all Liberal Democrat MPs, plus three-quarters of the party's federal executive. Failing those two safeguards, a two-thirds majority of a special party conference is required.

Trotskyism
The ideas associated with the Russian revolutionary Leon Trotsky. He urged a state of 'permanent revolution' as a means

of achieving the fall of capitalism worldwide. Stalin had him assassinated in 1940. Followers of Trotsky sought to influence the Labour Party in the 1960s. Ted Grant had been a member of the Revolutionary Communist Party, which eventually transformed into the Revolutionary Socialist League. He joined up with Peter Taafe in Liverpool in 1964 and together they set up a newspaper called *Militant* and devised the tactic of entryism. This entailed members of their group joining a constituency Labour party and then attempting to take it over for the faction, to pursue left-wing policies. The ultimate hope was to lead the imminent revolution and direct it towards a Trotskyist vision of society. The activities of the Militant Tendency were effectively countered during the 1980s and whatever Trotskyist activity continues in Britain is not very politically visible.
See also Militant Tendency.

'troubles', the (Northern Ireland)
Name given to the political upheavals and sectarian murders in Northern Ireland from around 1969 to the Good Friday agreement in 1998. Some commentators close to the province believe civil strife has been only suppressed, not eliminated, and could break out in the future.

trust
Clearly, voters' trust in the government is a key factor in determining electoral success as well as, more generally, electoral turnout. Trust became a key issue under Tony Blair in the wake of the Iraq war, when he appeared to many to be not telling the truth. The *Observer* (15 February 2004) published a review of trust and the Blair government which revealed that, in the wake of the Hutton report on the death of Iraqi weapons expert Dr David Kelly, 54 per cent thought Blair had 'lied to the nation' over the threat posed by Iraq. In September 2003, 35 per cent of those polled thought Blair was trustworthy, while 58 per cent thought him untrustworthy. However, as pollster Bob Worcester pointed out, the matching figures for September 2000 were

37 and 56 per cent, respectively – and yet he still went on to win a landslide in the 2001 general election. Only 18 per cent of people in February 2004 thought politicians could be trusted.

> Trust you lose precipitately and regain glacially. You regain it by evidence, you cannot do it by rhetoric. (Bob Worcester, *Observer*, 15 February 2004)

turnout

The percentage of registered voters who exercise their right and cast a vote (or spoil their ballot paper) in an election. Political scientists use turnout as one of the indicators of citizens' political participation in a nation's political system. It is also evidence of the degree of legitimacy that a system of government enjoys from the population. The performance of Britain in these respects is mixed. Turnout in British general elections is generally high, averaging around 70 per cent until the 1990s, although the figure has, on a trend, been falling since 1945. However, figures for local government contests and elections to the European parliament are far lower: in the 1999 European elections under 25 per cent of those registered to vote actually did so, though in 2004, with the assistance of postal voting, turnout was up to 39 per cent. Despite this, voting still remains, at least in Britain, one of the most significant ways by which citizens participate in the political life of their country. In the 2001 general election the turnout was the lowest since the birth of liberal democracy, at 59.2 per cent. (Although turnout was lower in 1918, those figures were distorted by the majority of voters who were voting for the first time.) In 2005 turnout was slightly higher, at 61 per cent, and in 2010 up again at 65 per cent. Other elections, though, registered even lower figures: 49 per cent for the Scottish parliament in 2003, 38 per cent for the Welsh assembly in 2003, and 38 per cent for the Euro-elections in 2004, falling to 35 per cent in 2009.

two-party system

See party system.

U

UK Border Agency

www.bia.homeoffice.gov.uk
Government agency formed from a merger in 2008 of the Border and Immigration Agency, the UK Visa Services and the border customs work of HM Revenue and Customs. It comprises three sections:
1 external controls (including visa issue in overseas posts);
2 borders (passport and customs controls);
3 internal immigration controls (including asylum, management of applications for further stay and enforcement).

UK Independence Party (UKIP)

www.ukip.org
Party founded in 1993 by university lecturer Alan Sked, who later left the party and disowned its leadership. It stands unambiguously on a platform of British withdrawal from the European Union. UKIP was overshadowed in the 1997 general election by the well funded Referendum Party, led by James Goldsmith, but in the 1999 Euro-elections the party picked up 7 per cent of the vote to win three seats. By 2004 it had won about 30 local council seats and in June of that year it captured a rising tide of Euroscepticism, strengthened possibly by anti-immigrant sentiment, to claim 16 per cent of the vote and 12 seats in the European parliament election. Studies showed that 45 per cent of UKIP's vote came from disaffected Conservatives and 20 per cent from former Labour voters. In the 2009 European elections, UKIP beat the governing Labour Party into second place; it increased its share of the vote to 16.5 per cent, giving it 13 MEPs. It won no seats in the 2010 general election.

UK Statistics Authority

www.statisticsauthority.gov.uk
Body that came into being on 1 April 2008, set up by the Statistics and

Registration Service Act 2007. Independent of government and reporting directly to parliament, it has a brief to oversee all official statistics. The Office for National Statistics (www.ons.gov.uk) is the executive office of the Authority.

Polls show that a large majority of the public believe official statistics are subject to political interference and that the government uses such figures dishonestly. Unlike the Statistics Commission which it replaced, the new authority has the power to enforce remedial action. In relation to figures from departments dealing, for instance, with crime, examination results and health statistics like waiting lists, there was concern that policy staff – who usually had a week's notice of new statistics – could massage the figures or 'spin' the best possible interpretation of them. Under the new regime they will have only a day for such creativity – still more than best international practice, where such a period is three hours or less. On 17 March 2009 Lord (David) Lipsey set up a 'Campaign for Real Statistics' to complement the work of the new authority.

Ulster
See Northern Ireland.

Ulster Defence Association (UDA)
Launched in 1971 (effectively as an umbrella organisation for such groups as the Ulster Freedom Fighters) in Belfast to protect Protestants from IRA violence. Based in the Shankhill area, the group has links with the Ulster Democratic Party. The leading figure is Johnny ('Mad Dog') Adair, who was imprisoned for inciting sectarian attacks in the early 1990s, and who left the Maze Prison in 2000 under the terms of the Good Friday agreement, only to return in August of the same year for breaching the terms of his release. He was forced to leave Northern Ireland in 2003 by other loyalists. The UDA is suspected of involvement in drug racketeering and extortion, and has approximately 600 members. It officially ended its campaign of violence in November 2007,

when it ordered its militant wing, the Ulster Freedom Fighters (UFF), to stand down.

Ulster Freedom Fighters
See Ulster Defence Association (UDA).

Ulster Unionist Party
www.uup.org
Unionist political party in Northern Ireland. It formed in 1905 and effectively ruled the province between 1921 and 1972. It is right wing on most issues and insists the province should be treated on a par with the rest of the United Kingdom. It hotly opposes any union with the Republic of Ireland. It was represented in Westminster after the 2001 general election by five MPs (down from 10 after the 1997 election) and eight peers. While opposing any drift towards eventual union with the south, the party proved willing to negotiate with all parties in the conflict, including the hated IRA and Sinn Fein. David Trimble, the party leader, became the first minister of the province after elections to the assembly in June 1998, and in September of that year met up with Gerry Adams, although he studiously avoided any symbolic handshakes. In June 2001 Trimble's position in the party came under fire when the party lost ground in the local and general elections to the more militant Democratic Unionist Party. Trimble threatened to resign as first minister in July if the IRA refused to disarm. He fulfilled his threat but resumed his role when the IRA seemed to move on decommissioning. In October 2002 the executive was suspended following the discovery of a Sinn Fein spying conspiracy in the Northern Ireland Office in Belfast. In November 2003, the UUP was eclipsed in the assembly elections by Paisley's hard-line Democratic Unionist Party. Currently led by Sir Reg Empey, the party forged an electoral alliance with the Conservative Party for the 2010 election, under the banner 'Ulster Conservatives – New Force'. In 2010 it had no MPs at Westminster, 18 members of the Northern Ireland assembly and 115 local councillors.

Ulster Volunteer Force (UVF)

Paramilitary organisation established in 1966, with the same name as Carson's 1912 army, which was formed to fight Irish independence. It linked to the Progressive Unionist Party led by David Ervine. Gusty Spence was a hero figure who helped broker the loyalist cease-fire. Billy Hutchinson was another leading member. It has long been a proscribed terrorist organisation and reckoned to be involved in drug dealing of various kinds. In 2007 it claimed to be 'decommissioning' its weapons but conclusive evidence that it has done so has not been forthcoming.

ultra vires

Being beyond one's legal powers or authority. In practice it means the actions of an individual or body have been beyond the legal authority granted by statute law. The term is specifically associated with the rulings from tribunals and judicial review, and is frequently applied to the actions of local authorities and ministers of the crown which are adjudged to be illegal. Examples include *Conway* v. *Rimmer* (1968) and *Laker Airways* v. *Department of Trade* (1977). One of the most significant cases was *R.* v. *The Greater London Council ex parte Bromley* (1981), where the House of Lords upheld the decision of the Appeal Court that the Greater London Council (GLC) was acting beyond its powers in introducing a supplementary rate to subsidise fares on London Transport. This is historically important because judges became involved in party political squabbles between a Labour-controlled GLC and a Conservative council adhering to government policy.

underclass

Name given by US writer Charles Murray to the poorest sector of society, often on minimum wage and/or welfare benefit, who subscribe to a set of values at odds with conventional society. He believes the sources of such a class can be found in unemployment, the lack of hope and expectation, and illegitimacy with its associated lack of male role models to influence growing children in a fashion supportive to society. After diagnosing such problems in the USA, Murray came to Britain and did the same; he wrote a number of influential articles in the *Sunday Times* in the 1980s. His term has subsequently entered the language of social debate. However, some sociologists dispute the term, arguing that many poorer people spend only periods in the so-called 'underclass' and cannot be described as lifetime members of it. Moreover, they suggest that it is a value-loaded, pejorative term, heavily influenced by the ideas of the new right.

See also meritocracy; social exclusion.

unemployment

In the 1930s unemployment soared to over 3 million and great hardship was suffered by families all over Britain, but especially in the north of England. During the Second World War full employment arrived of necessity and politicians, supported by Keynesian thinking, resolved that full employment would continue into peacetime. For 30 years this more or less happened; in the mid-1970s unemployment was under 1 million, about the number of people likely to be unemployable anyway through disability or sickness, or for other non-economic reasons. However, full employment tended, by way of the law of supply and demand, to push up wages, which fuelled inflation. The Conservative government under Margaret Thatcher resolved to allow inefficient and non-competitive enterprises to fail and her policy of high interest rates to keep down inflation forced bankruptcies through the prohibitive cost of credit and the high exchange rate which it encouraged. During the 1980s unemployment rose to over 3 million and probably much more as the government resorted to a number of statistical sleights of hand to reduce the figures. Some commentators had predicted that a rate of 3 million unemployed would lead to riots and widespread social dislocation. This did not happen but there were riots in the inner cities in the early

1980s and the crime rate soared; this was almost certainly linked to unemployment, according to Home Office studies. Critics of the Conservatives maintain the valuable revenues from North Sea oil in the 1980s were lost paying unemployment benefit to those millions made unemployed by in-effective government policies. Levels edged down as the 1980s came to an end and during the 1990s were consistently below 2 million. Some economists claim this is the minimum level required by the market to keep inflation in check, though this is disputed by other experts. After 1997 the figure continued to fall until it was just under 1 million by the time of the 2001 general election (6.5 per cent of the work-ing population). Studies submitted to the annual meeting of the British Association in September 2001 suggested the low unemployment rate in Britain masked a relatively large group of people who were classified as 'long-term sick' and claiming benefit. Seven per cent of the workforce was seen as economically inactive, com-pared with 2.1 per cent in Germany and 0.3 per cent in France. It seems that large groups of unemployed people may have deliberately moved on to sickness benefit, as it is more generous than unemployment benefit. If the 1.5 million claiming sickness benefit were included in the statistics the unemployment figure would have been worryingly high. Subsequently a tougher regime regarding sickness or incapacity benefit was introduced. The 2007–09 economic crisis caused unemployment to soar in the summer of 2009 to the point when 3 million was expected to be soon reached.

unilateralism
The giving up of nuclear weapons outside the framework of international (multilateral) agreements. In the 1980s, 'unilateralist' was used to describe a variety of different groups, prominent Labour politicians and others in Britain who were hostile to nuclear weapons. Although all unilateralists oppose the concept of nuclear force on moral or strategic grounds, the term is used to refer to a range of positions on the issue. For example, one strand of unilateralism opposes Britain's membership of NATO as a military alliance, which, ultimately, has recourse to weapons of mass destruction. For pragmatists in the Labour Party, unilateralism was perceived by many, including Neil Kinnock, as an obstacle to winning a general election. For the 1992 general election the Labour manifesto removed all traces of its previous unilateralist stance, a position enhanced by the relaxation in tension between NATO and eastern Europe after the disintegration of the Soviet Union. The pragmatism of New Labour saw no reversal of the party's multilateralist position.

union bashing
Colloquial term which entered the language in the 1980s and was associated with Margaret Thatcher's drive to reduce the powers and rights of the trade unions. Thatcher sought to do so as a means of allowing market forces to operate freely and to further the political objectives of the new right. The term, much used by trade unionists and Labour politicians in the 1980s, obscures the fact that Thatcher, a barrister by training, mainly used a raft of new industrial relations laws as a mechanism of reform. However, most commentators agree that one of her most significant acts was the facing down of the most powerful trade union, the National Union of Minerworkers, in its strike of 1984–85. Left-wing Labour members were angered by Tony Blair's and Gordon Brown's coolness towards the unions and probably felt their injunctions to restrain wage demands and toe the party line amounted to something akin to 'union bashing'.
See also trade unionism.

Union of Shop, Distributive and Allied Workers (USDAW)
www.usdaw.org.uk
Founded in 1947 to represent workers in shops, stores and transport, this union has over 300,000 members.

POLITICS

Unison
www.unison.org.uk
The second largest union in Britain, Unison was formed out of a merger of unions for health service, public service and local government workers in 1993. Half of its 1.4 million members are in the local government sector. Unison's leader, Dave Prentis, was greatly upset by the failure of the government to end 'two-tier' workforces, whereby private sector employees are brought in to perform former public sector jobs on lower rates of pay. Unison also campaigns on a number of issues, recently against the private finance initiative (PFI) and identity cards.

unitary authority
A level of local government to replace county and district councils, first proposed by the Redcliffe-Maud report in 1966. It recommended the creation of 58 unitary authorities, in charge of all functions within their boundaries. The incoming 1970 Conservative government opted for two-tier authorities, which the public found confusing. After 1979 the Conservative government initiated a rethink and in 1992, under John Major, John Banham was appointed to the Local Government Commission in England with a brief to create new unitary authorities. The Welsh Office's internal review had already led to the replacement of 8 county councils and 37 district ones by 21 new unitary authorities. Scottish Office proposals also replaced 68 regional and district councils with 28 unitary ones. Banham's progress was uneasy and he was eventually sacked by John Gummer, secretary of state for the environment, in 1995. His successor, Sir David Cuckney, managed to increase the number of authorities recommended for unitary status but controversy remained and no wider reorganisation resulted from his tenure in the post.
See also Redcliffe-Maud report.

unitary state
Where the central government controls all the major decisions within a given territory,

irrespective of sub-national authorities. Most countries are unitary and Britain used to be one of the most centralised. However, since devolution Scotland and Wales have delegated powers. Others argue that, as Westminster could rescind such powers, the UK is still unitary.

Unite
www.unitetheunion.com
The UK's biggest trade union formed by the merger of Amicus with the Transport and General Workers' Union in May 2007. The respective secretaries of the two merged unions – Derek Simpson and Tony Woodley – became the joint secretaries of the new organisation.
Amicus itself had resulted from the merger between the Amalgamated Electrical Engineering Union (AEEU) and the Manufacturing, Science and Finance Union in 2001. During the 1970s the Amalgamated Engineering Union (AEU) under Hugh Scanlon had been one of the most powerful unions in the country. The AEU merged with the Electrical, Electronic, Telecommunications and Plumbing Union (EETPU) to become the AEEU.
Following the falling off of rich donors to the Labour Party, Unite became the single biggest donor and this closeness was exploited by the Conservatives in the run-up to the 2010 general election.

United Irishmen (Society of)
Formed in 1791 as a revolutionary reform society. Initially it included Catholics and Protestants but it soon became strongly republican and in 1795 was driven underground. During the Irish rebellion of 1795–98 the society tried to link up with revolutionary French forces and organise disaffected activists in England but it collapsed once the rebellion failed. In 1796 Wolfe Tone accompanied a French fleet containing 15,000 troops to invade Ireland but bad weather foiled the attempt. Many of the group then emigrated to the USA. Tone tried to invade Ireland, at Donegal in 1798 with 3,000 French troops, but a

Royal Navy squadron intervened and Tone was captured. He cheated the hangman by committing suicide in jail.

United Kingdom
The United Kingdom of Great Britain and Northern Ireland. It is not synonymous with 'Britain' in that Northern Ireland is not part of Britain but is part of the UK. The UK was established by the Acts of Union of 1536 (Wales), 1707 (Scotland) and 1800 (Ireland). England, united since 900, has 90 per cent of the population. The union with the whole of Ireland was broken in 1920 by the Government of Ireland Act, which partitioned the country, leaving the six northern counties as part of the UK and causing a civil war in consequence.

United Kingdom crown dependencies
See Channel Islands; Isle of Man.

university education (quality questioned)
In 1961, as the *Economist* noted (20 September 2008), Kingsley Amis, the novelist, wrote of university expansion 'more means worse'. Since then the polytechnics became universities in the 1990s and several other 'new' universities have been established. The proportion of young people going to university has risen from 5–10 per cent in the 1960s to some 40 per cent now. In 2008, a record 430,000 youngsters began their university careers. Professor Paul Buckland at Bournemouth University was overruled when he failed 10 of his students, so he resigned and won his case for 'constructive dismissal' against his former employers. Other critics argue universities award absurd numbers of firsts to push their way up league tables, as this will attract yet more students. Plagiarism is also a common problem, as is the enlisting of students from abroad whose English language skills are poor. University top-up fees from parents currently stand at £3,000 maximum, but it is likely that this cap will increase to allow more differentiation. A survey by Sodexo (11 September 2008)

showed that most students attend university to enhance their career prospects; only 9 per cent did so because of interest in the subject. In 2006 an estimate of how much a degree enhances salary suggested it was as high as £160,000 over a lifetime but this varies enormously according to subject, with arts degrees offering virtually no enhancement but rather a negative effect instead. One study by Kent University discovered in 2006 that a third of graduates ended up doing jobs which did not require a degree.

Unjust Rewards
Book published in 2008 by *Guardian* journalists Polly Toynbee and David Walker on the income gap in Britain. Toynbee and Walker present their case basically in the first 35 pages of their book. 'Parental income pretty accurately predicts whether a child will win or lose in life: the more unequal income is, the tighter the link becomes.' And income is distributed more unequally in Britain than anywhere apart from the USA. The top 10 per cent of income earners get 27.3 per cent of the cake; the bottom 10 per cent get 2.6 per cent. In 1988 'the average chief executive of a FTSE company earned 17 times the average employee's pay. By 2008 the typical FTSE boss earned 75 times the average'. An ICM poll in February 2008 showed 75 per cent of respondents thought the gap between rich and poor was too wide. Worryingly, social mobility seems to have ground to a halt, in that the middle classes have ensured the lion's share of the good jobs are occupied by them and their children. Everyone is now aware of the large US-style salaries earned by top executives, some getting more money than they could spend in a lifetime. Toynbee and Walker point out that the super-rich can employ super-accountants to minimise their tax liabilities. Out of the 54 billionaires living in Britain, 32 paid no income tax at all and the whole group paid only a tiny fraction of their earnings. Thereby, calculate Toynbee and Walker, the Treasury (that is, the taxpayer) is denied some £12 billion a year.

The authors report on two focus group meetings with a clutch of lawyers and bankers on the subject of wealth and poverty. They displayed an astonishing ignorance of salary levels, claiming they were way down the top 10 per cent of earners when they were easily in the top 1 per cent. They also had no idea that 90 per cent of people earned less than £39,825, the higher tax limit. They seemed locked in a denial that they were rich at all. When questioned on the morality of their high incomes they justified them by citing their extraordinarily hard work and desire to get ahead. They also seemed to accept unquestioningly the 'trickle down' theory, while even the Conservatives admit that it is wrong to 'pretend a rising tide raises all boats'.

Unlock Democracy

www.unlockdemocracy.org.uk
Group that campaigns for democracy, rights and freedoms, including electoral and constitutional reform, and popular participation in politics. It resulted from a merger of Charter 88 (created after an article in the *New Statesman* in 1988) and the New Politics Network, which had emerged in 1999 from the Democratic Left, the successor to the Communist Party of Great Britain.

upper class

Term used to describe the aristocracy and upper stratum of British society. In the 19th century few would have quarrelled with this term but as the number of aristocrats reduced relative to the numbers of rich middle-class people and their influence receded, the term was avoided by social scientists as misleading. They prefer other categorisations and tend to refer only to the working and middle classes.

urban development corporation (UDC)

Type of body set up in the 1980s by the Thatcher government to bypass local authorities, which were perceived as too respectful of planning regulations,

obstructive of the wealth-creating process and insufficiently entrepreneurial. Consequently, development responsibilities were given not to local government but to UDCs, for example in Liverpool and the London Docklands. Local authorities therefore lost power to these well resourced quangos, which had considerable discretionary powers. Relations between UDCs and local authorities varied but in some cities, for example Manchester, they were generally conducive to change and improvement.

urgent question

A question which the speaker of the House of Commons considers to be urgent and worthy of immediate discussion. 'Urgent questions' were previously (before 2003) called 'private notice questions'. They have, for example, concerned the wreck of an oil tanker, a strike affecting essential services and threats to the liberty of the citizen. They are taken at the end of question time if the speaker agrees to the request in advance; the minister concerned always knows such questions are going to be put.

'usual channels'

Term used to describe the close working relationship between the whips' offices of all the parliamentary parties, though in practice it usually refers to those of the government and opposition. The latter party is concerned to oppose the government, naturally, but its minority of parliamentary votes means it has to make arrangements with government on such matters as when key debates are going to occur and what type of debate is appropriate to the topic and occasion. Critics sometimes claim the relationship between the whips is too close and cosy and works to curtail inner party dissent.

utilitarianism

A philosophy first espoused by Jeremy Bentham and James Mill, and further elaborated by the latter's son, John Stuart Mill. The thesis stated that whatever was conducive to producing happiness was 'good' and what tended to produce pain was 'bad'. Translated into political action it posited that 'The action is best which procures the greatest happiness of the greatest number'. Bentham argued it should be possible to calculate quite precisely the good and bad effects of an act: the 'felicific calculus'. Policy making could almost be an automatic process. Though crude and philosophically flawed, this approach strongly influenced policy, especially welfare policy relating to prisons, the new Poor Law and sanitary reform. Charles Dickens mocked the ideas of utilitarianism in *Hard Times* (1854), with his memorable character of Thomas Gradgrind: 'Now, what I want is, Facts…. Facts alone are wanted in life.'

V

Valuation and Lands Agency

Set up in 1993 by the Home Office, this provides a valuation list for the purpose of levying rates plus estate management and information on property in Northern Ireland. It has now become the Land and Property Services.

Valuation Office Agency

www.voa.gov.uk

Executive agency of the Inland Revenue in England, Wales and Scotland. The VOA has 85 offices and employs 4,000 people. Its functions are: to compile and maintain business rating and council tax valuations lists for England and Wales; and to advise ministers on property valuation matters.

value added tax (VAT)

A tax of European provenance that was introduced in 1973 at a rate of 10 per cent. It is applied at each stage of the production process to reflect the resultant added value. Producers can reclaim it if their turnover falls under the VAT threshold. It was

introduced to replace purchase tax and to make British taxation compatible with the European system. It is collected by HM Revenue and Customs. A proportion of the tax collected – according to a complex formula – goes to finance the European Union (EU). In meetings of EU finance ministers in 1987 and 1992 it was agreed to levy a standard rate of 15 per cent and a maximum of 25 per cent throughout the EU. In December 2008 chancellor Alistair Darling controversially reduced VAT for one year from 17.5 per cent to 15 per cent in order to release a 'fiscal stimulus' to stimulate the economy.

veto

A unilateral right to reject proposals. Although the veto is used by a number of states (for example the US president can exercise a veto) and international organisations (for example permanent members of the UN Security Council), the device is not recognised in the British system of government. The monarch's legal right to veto bills has not been used since 1707. However, the veto is important in Britain's relations with the European Union (EU); twice, in 1962 and 1967, French leader Charles de Gaulle blocked Britain's application to join the organisation. The veto was also used by Britain when John Major vetoed the candidate Jean-Luc Dehaene for the presidency of the Commission in succession to Jacques Delors at the Corfu summit in 1994. While the veto is not used much, the threat of its use can exert quite an ongoing influence.

See also qualified majority voting.

vigilante movement

Name given to the attempts by residents to police their own property as crime rates soared in the 1980s and 1990s. Usually these amounted to no more than regular patrols to dissuade offenders, but occasionally they took the law into their own hands and delivered illegal punishments to suspects. The employment of security companies to undertake patrols is now a regular aspect of life on some estates. The dangers of vigilantism were vividly demonstrated in August 2000 when, following a 'name and shame' campaign on convicted paedophiles by the *News of the World*, residents on a number of estates attacked the homes of suspected child abusers, some of whom were innocent, including that of a consultant paediatrician, whom they mistakenly believed was a paedophile by virtue of her professional title.

violent crime
The murder of two French students in London on 29 June 2008, according to the *Economist*, directed attention to the fact that Britain is a relatively violent society. Injuries from guns had trebled since 2000. Media sensationalism can make it appear that people are being stabbed constantly in British streets, which is clearly not the case, but a comparison for the year 2004 of 'attacks or threats per 100 of the population' revealed Italy at the bottom (with just 1 attack per 100), Germany, Norway, Poland and Canada (3) in the middle, the USA (4) and the Netherlands (4) second and third, but sitting on top of the table: England and Wales (6). However, on 'homicides per 100,000 population', England and Wales, with 1.6 (around average for Europe), were well behind the USA on 5.6.

virtual politics
Term used to describe the virtual democracy which has developed with interactive media such as television and the Internet. Radio 'phone-ins', telephone opinion polls and email comments solicited by political parties and other organisations are now part of the 'wired' society. Only time will tell whether this interactive technology will expand or restrict democratic choices and the voice of the people.
    See also e-voting.

virtual representation
Idea associated with Edmund Burke, the conservative thinker who stated that it is possible for a group of people to represent others without them having been formally

elected by ballot. Burke argued that there is a communion of interests between a section of people and those whose concerns they express in an assembly. This view was rejected by those who supported electoral reform in the debates which took place in the 19th century. After the Great Reform Act of 1832, and subsequent electoral reforms, the principle was firmly established that the people must give their approval for a candidate or government by means of secret and free ballots.

volcanic ash
In mid-April 2010 the Icelandic volcano Eyjafjallajoekull erupted and spewed ash into the stratosphere. High winds caused the cloud to spread over northern Europe; in consequence air flights had to be cancelled and thousands were left stranded. The government was in the middle of the 2010 election campaign but efforts were made to assist those in need, some involving use of naval vessels.

voluntary sector
Comprises all those organisations that organise volunteers to work for specific social groups. Britain is unusual in having many such organisations, so much so that working for charities and small voluntary groups can be said to be part of the British way of life. In the 19th century these groups were the precursors to government action and the voluntary sector still works closely with government agencies. Most charities are funded by contributions but since its inception the National Lottery has channelled millions of pounds into the voluntary sector. In early 2001 chancellor Gordon Brown announced a programme of support for the sector.

voting behaviour
After the Second World War voting behaviour appeared to be essentially about class divisions, with working-class people generally voting Labour and middle-class voters supporting the Conservatives. There was nonetheless a significant minority of working-class Conservative voters and

certain sections of the middle class who were Labour supporters. However, most psephologists argued that this pattern started to change for a number of reasons:

1 Party loyalty began to decline, with the proportion of voters identifying strongly with either of the two main parties falling from 38 per cent in 1964 to 20 per cent and below this by 1997. This partisan dealignment made the outcomes of elections less predictable and meant voters were more amenable to persuasion.

2 Regional variations have long been discernible, with the north inclined to support Labour and the south the Conservatives. However, this pattern was altered in 1979–83, when both parts of the country swung to the Conservatives, and in 1997, when the swing was to Labour.

3 Third-party voting increased during the 1970s and the proportion supporting both main parties fell from 90 per cent in 1950 to only 70 per cent in 1983.

4 Mass media and television in particular assumed greater importance from the 1960s onwards.

5 In 1997, Labour turned the tide by attracting back not only former Labour voters but also formerly Conservative 'middle England'. Some on the left, such as Tony Benn, have argued that Labour would still have won with a socialist agenda – which would have presented the electorate with a real choice. However, it is unlikely for socio-economic and political reasons to see a return to the traditional two-class, two-party voting which characterised the postwar years.

See also partisan dealignment; third-party voting.

voting system

The mechanism used to convert electors' choices of party or candidate into seats in assemblies, legislative and otherwise. Voting systems can broadly be divided into majoritarian, proportional and hybrid systems. All have advantages and disadvantages for majority and minority parties, and reflect different national and political traditions. Britain has the first past the post system, which has the advantage of producing strong executives but which suffers from discriminating against smaller parties and under-representing certain elements of the population.

See also additional member system; first past the post; regional party list; single transferable vote; third-party voting.

W

Wakeham report, 2000

Report of a royal commission established in 1999 to look at further reform of the House of Lords. Lord Wakeham's plan for the second chamber was essentially that it should not challenge the legitimacy of the Commons. Accordingly he proposed a 550-strong chamber with only a small proportion elected. The options outlined were: 65 regional members elected on election day; 87 regional peers; or 195 elected peers. One-third were to be elected at successive elections via closed party lists. The majority, however, would be appointed by an independent appointments commission, with the largest group of members still being nominated by political parties. The award of a peerage would no longer entitle the holder to membership of the upper chamber. Life peers would retain membership. The law lords would continue to sit in the upper chamber and the functions would remain the same. The report influenced the debate but did not provide an accepted structure for any reform.

See also House of Lords reform.

Wales

Originally occupied by Celts from central Europe. What is now Wales became part of the Roman empire about 50 AD and was a Celtic stronghold against the Saxons during the 'Dark Ages'. There was

345

conflict with neighbours over the border for many centuries. Wales was formally joined to England in 1536 by an Act of Union after its 13th-century conquest by Edward I. It now has 2.9 million people, 19 per cent of whom speak Welsh. The coal and iron industries developed in the south and a militant tradition of unionism was inaugurated. The main nationalist party, Plaid Cymru, is more cultural and language based than its Scottish equivalent.

The region returns 40 MPs to Westminster. Plaid Cymru seeks independence for the country but the Welsh people supported the devolved assembly by only a thin margin in the referendum vote in September 1997. The secretary of state for Wales was downgraded in June 2003 to a part-time role performed by the leader of the House of Commons, Peter Hain. Hain returned to this role in June 2009. In 2007 Labour agreed to rule in coalition with Plaid Cymru.

See also Plaid Cymru; Welsh assembly and government.

Wapping

Part of London's borough of Tower Hamlets. Its political significance is in the move to Wapping by News International from Fleet Street in 1986, when its owner, Rupert Murdoch, decided to outflank the print unions and use labour-saving technology to cut production costs. Other parts of the press benefited from Murdoch's decisive action. The result was the weakening of the print unions' power and a renaissance in the press, with the launch of new titles.

war cabinet

During wartime, political control has been vested in a smaller body than the usual full cabinet. This happened in the two world wars as well as the Falklands war in 1982. David Lloyd George's war cabinet – the first modern one to be formed – included Labour's Arthur Henderson. Winston Churchill's first war cabinet numbered five and included Labour members Clement Attlee and Arthur Greenwood; later Ernest Bevin was brought in as well as

Stafford Cripps. Margaret Thatcher's war cabinet included Cecil Parkinson, John Nott, William Whitelaw and Francis Pym, as well as Lord Lewin, the chief of the defence staff. Tony Blair's Iraq war cabinet contained John Prescott, Gordon Brown and Jack Straw, as well as Sir Michael Boyce, chief of the defence staff, the security chiefs of MI5 and MI6 and the occasional attendance of Alastair Campbell and chief of staff Jonathan Powell. Blair was criticised by the 2004 Butler report for holding meetings on Iraq which were over-casual and not minuted.

See also cabinet.

war on terror

Tony Blair's determination to express political solidarity with the USA led him to go to war alongside George Bush in Afghanistan in 2001 and, to much greater domestic dissent, Iraq in 2003. After the Afghan war a number of British citizens were detained in the US Cuban base of Gauntanamo. In February 2004, it was announced that five were to be returned to Britain. However, the dozen suspects detained in Belmarsh Prison stayed in jail, with no clear explanation being given for the continued detention. In the same month David Blunkett announced more stringent measures for the handling of suspected terrorists as well as more financial and personnel resources for the secret services. The term 'war on terror' has now been abandoned on both sides of the Atlantic.

wash-up

The short period (two to four days) between the time an election is announced and the end of that parliament. It is used to try to push through bills which have not completed their stages. Professor Philip Norton calculates that in the five parliaments 1983–2005 a total of 82 bills became law in this way, along with 29 private members' bills.

water privatisation

The sale of the 10 public water authorities in 1989. Opinion polls registered a 5 to 1

majority against the idea of privatisation
when it was mooted but the public still
turned out to grab the quick profit when
shares were floated on the Stock Exchange.
The National Rivers Authority (NRA)
was created to take over pollution control,
fisheries and protection of the environment.
In 1996 the NRA was subsumed within
the Environment Agency. In 1991 Ian
Byatt, the head of the Office of Regulation
for Water (Ofwat), was criticised for
allowing rises of over 100 per cent in
the domestic charges for water supply.
Also criticised were huge self-awarded
pay increases for the directors of these
private monopolies. In September 1998
John Prescott, the deputy prime minister,
imposed tough new restrictions on the
water companies, including a 10 per cent
reduction in water prices, an end to excess
profits for shareholders and an insistence
that more money be spent on environmental
clean-ups.

ways and means
See Committee of Ways and Means.

wealth
Wealth is very concentrated in all
developed capitalist economies and Britain
is no exception (though to a lesser extent
than the USA). In 1992 the richest 1 per
cent of the British population owned 18 per
cent of all marketable wealth, or 29 per cent
if the value of dwellings is subtracted (that
is, property values for ordinary families
served to reduce the wealth gap). For the
richest 10 per cent the figures were 49 per
cent and 65 per cent, respectively. This
distribution has remained similar for over
half a century though some redistribution
has occurred from the very rich to the
merely rich, partly as a tactic to avoid death
duties.
See also underclass.

**weapons of mass destruction
(WMD)**
Nuclear, biological or chemical weapons.
Weapons of mass destruction were claimed
to be in the possession of Saddam Hussein

in the autumn of 2002, when Tony Blair
was trying hard to find reasons for supporting US president George W. Bush's policy
of 'regime change' in Iraq through military
invasion. Invading merely to remove a vile
dictator was arguably justifiable morally
but not in terms of international law.
Self-defence, however, was a legitimate
casus belli – hence Blair's eagerness to
prove British forces faced a danger from a
possible Iraqi attack. His office produced
a dossier in September 2002 based on
intelligence reports which argued Iraq could
launch an attack on Britain within 45 minutes: a clearly absurd claim but one which
helped deliver a majority in the House of
Commons for the eventual joint attack.
However, the removal of Saddam did not
lead to the exposure of such weapons and
critics loudly accused Blair of fabricating
reasons to go to war. BBC reporters were
prominent in this process, citing 'senior
intelligence' sources; in retaliation Blair's
press secretary, Alastair Campbell, denied
the charges and demanded an apology.
Eventually an advisor to the Ministry
of Defence, Dr David Kelly, a scientist
and former Iraq weapons inspector, was
named as the source of the story. He gave
evidence to the Foreign Affairs Select
Committee but denied being the source of
the embarrassing parts of the BBC reports;
shortly afterwards, at the centre of much
media pressure, he committed suicide. In
July Lord Hutton was appointed to make a
full inquiry amid the most intense crisis of
public trust in New Labour since 1997. A
new inquiry into the war was announced by
Gordon Brown in July 2009.
See also Chilcott inquiry; Hutton
inquiry.

welfare state
Term given to the battery of services
supplied by the state since the early 20th
century to improve the living conditions of
the population. The National Insurance
Act 1911, passed by David Lloyd George,
introduced pensions for older people. The
Beveridge report of 1942 committed the
government to construct a welfare state after

the war, with a whole set of new benefits and services. To unemployment benefit was added sickness benefit, family allowances and family income supplement. As well as benefits disbursed by the Department for Work and Pensions there is free health care, compulsory state education for children aged 5 to 16, and personal social services. Welfare spending takes up the largest share of public expenditure – nearly 30 per cent – and a long-running debate has been conducted in both main parties about the best means of welfare reform. Conservative politicians have long argued that the welfare state erodes self-reliance and the desire to fend for oneself, because it provides overgenerous benefits. Certainly, benefit fraud is widespread and both parties have sought to squeeze it out of the system. The right wishes to reduce welfare spending – social security spending, at £170 billion in 2008–09, is the biggest single item of government expenditure – by encouraging people at best to buy into private education and health or at worst pay a significant proportion of such costs personally. Labour came into power in 1997 talking of welfare reform but a clash emerged between Frank Field (minister for welfare reform in the Department of Social Security, 1997–98), who favoured cash transfers and no means tests, and others who favoured targeting benefits via means tests and adopting what were basically right-wing solutions. By 2000, despite some isolated changes to traditional Labour policy, such as the New Deal, no all-embracing or radical changes had been introduced.

Welsh assembly and government
http://wales.gov.uk
Bodies for the devolved government of Wales. For historical and economic reasons, Welsh nationalism has developed as a cultural rather than as a political phenomenon – that is, mainly as a concern to preserve the Welsh language, sport, the arts and its nonconformist religion. It was therefore no surprise that the referendum on devolution held in September 1997 should

have produced the narrowest of results: 50.3 per cent to 49.7 per cent in favour of the proposition. The assembly is composed of 60 members: 40 elected from existing parliamentary constituencies (using the first past the post system) and 20 using the party list system. In 1999 Labour won 28 seats; Plaid Cymru raided Welsh Labour heartlands to pick up 17; the Conservatives won 9; and the Liberal Democrats 6.

The assembly and executive (drawn from the majority party or coalition) has a number of devolved powers, including economic development, agriculture, forestry, fisheries and food, social services, education, the Welsh language and the arts. However, despite its nominal control of a £15 billion budget in 2009–10, unlike the Scottish parliament it cannot pass its own legislation or vary levels of taxation (other than council tax). In key areas final responsibility stays with Westminster: foreign affairs (including the European Union), defence, taxation, economic and finance policy, social security and broadcasting control.

Welsh politics faced a series of crises during the first session of the assembly, which included the resignation of the leader of the Welsh Labour Party, Ron Davies, following a scandal involving an apparent 'cruising' incident on Clapham Common. Tony Blair was unhappy to endorse the popular but allegedly 'off message' Rhodri Morgan as his successor and an unseemly process of manipulation resulted in the Blairite Alun Michael being appointed first minister instead. In February 2000 Michael lost a no-confidence motion centring on matching funds from London for European Union regional aid. Michael resigned and was replaced by Morgan; Blair then let it be known he had misjudged the popular Welshman. After governing in a minority for a while Labour formed a coalition with the Liberal Democrats but after the 2003 elections Labour's 30 seats (including heartland retrievals) enabled the party to rule unencumbered by a coalition partner. In 2007 Labour won 26 seats, Plaid Cymru 15, Conservatives 11 and

Liberal democrats 6. The outcome was a Labour–Plaid Cymru coalition, with Rhodri Morgan remaining as first minister.

Welsh Grand Committee

Established in 1960 but weaker than its Scottish equivalent. This is partly because there is little legislation which relates specifically to Wales. New standing order regulations in 1996 made it possible for Welsh questions plus second reading debates and other debates to be held in the Committee. However, this occurred only twice in the 1996–97 session (it did, however, enjoy a revival under Labour after 1997, but debates are still rare).

Welsh nationalism

See Plaid Cymru.

Welsh Office

This was the department of state concerned with governing Wales 1964–99. It disappeared once the devolved Welsh government came into being. However, a new Wales Office was established in 1999 to look after residual matters after devolution.

Welsh Republican Movement (WRM)

Small faction set up in 1949 in response to what some perceived as the passivity of Plaid Cymru. In 1949 some 50 of the latter's senior members walked out to set up their own party dedicated to a more muscular approach to Welsh independence. The modern incarnation of the movement is Cymru Annibynnol (Independence for Wales), established in 1999, which seeks a 'new free Wales'.

Wembley Stadium

The project to build a new national football stadium encountered funding problems as the Football Association, despite the millions made by the game, was unable to provide sufficient funding to make the idea viable. City banks were also wary of advancing cash as they doubted the financial viability of the new complex. The government was nervous of funding something which the public might think the sport itself should pay for; it was also afraid of another 'Millennium Dome' instance of spiralling costs and warring factions. The sports minister Kate Hooey was widely believed to have been sacked in June 2001 because she was unable to solve the problems surrounding the project.

West Lothian question

A term associated with the Labour MP representing West Lothian, Tam Dalyell. In 1977 he questioned an aspect of the proposed devolution process (later abandoned) whereby over 100 MPs from Scotland, Wales and Northern Ireland could influence legislation for England but English MPs would not be able to do the same in relation to the proposed new devolved assemblies. At the time of writing no solution has been found. The Conservatives did at one point suggest a separate parliament for England, though this attracted little support. Some point out that a similar position existed in relation to Stormont for 50 years (1922–72) and few complaints were made regarding that particular anomaly. Optimists speculated that criticism might abate after the number of Scottish Westminster seats had been reduced, by the Boundary Commission, from 72 to 59 in 2006; in practice it did not.

Westland affair, 1985–86

A dispute over the future of the Westland helicopter company. It gave a fascinating insight into the workings of cabinet government under Margaret Thatcher. The affair began when Michael Heseltine, the defence secretary, wanted the ailing enterprise to be taken over by a European consortium, while Thatcher and others favoured the US Sikorski company. Heseltine was convinced the matter was being kept off the cabinet agenda, to block discussion of the issue. Behind the scenes the argument continued but on 6 January 1986 a crucial action occurred: the deliberate leaking by an official at the Department of Trade and Industry (DTI) of a letter from the solicitor general, Sir Patrick Mayhew, to Heseltine pointing out 'material inaccuracies' in an earlier letter by Heseltine to Lloyds Merchant Bank. This leak was designed to damage the defence secretary's credibility over the issue but to leak a law officer's communication is illegal and that is when the real row started: who authorised the leak? At the time Leon Brittan at the DTI accepted the blame and resigned but he subsequently admitted he received direction from the prime minister's office to release the information. In the cabinet on 9 January the issue was discussed and Thatcher tried to defeat Heseltine using all the advantages of her office. When it was obvious he had been isolated he claimed collective responsibility had been violated, gathered his papers and walked out. Thatcher was probably happy to see the troublesome minister go but she could have called him back had he not seen journalists outside the door of Number 10 and, still angry, told them he had resigned. The crisis could have escalated to the point where the future of the government was threatened but an indifferent Commons speech by Neil Kinnock, as leader of the opposition, let the prime minister off the hook and the repercussions of the crisis were played down for the most part in a select committee where key participants in the drama were questioned, before the affair fizzled out. However, Heseltine used his freedom to campaign up and down the country for the time when he could stand as leader of the Conservative Party. When he finally did, in 1990, he was instrumental in removing Thatcher but failed to win the crown; this passed to the unassuming John Major.

Westminster City Council

See 'homes for votes' scandal.

Westminster Hall Chamber

A room, called the Grand Committee Room (adjoining Westminster Hall in the Palace of Westminster), has been used for some parliamentary debates since December 1999. The idea was experimental to begin with, to give MPs an additional forum in which to raise issues. The conduct of its business features the use of desks and microphones and is presided over usually by a deputy speaker. Topics chosen are usually non-contentious and votes are not taken. The practice has not won the media's attention and debates are as poorly attended as they are in the main chamber, but it has been made permanent as it enables MPs to place items of business before the government, as a junior minister replies to each debate. The initiative has increased the time available to MPs by 25 per cent.

Westminster model

The much copied British form of liberal democracy, which gives executive power to the largest party after a first past the post election. This model has been much criticised for giving the government excessive powers between elections but is defended by those who prefer a strong executive rather than a coalition, which can cause immobility and lack of action. Defenders insist it is accountable to the voters, who can easily vote out the government if it proves inefficient or unpopular. The model has also been criticised for its lack of democratic credentials without proportional representation and its poor representation in parliament of women and ethnic minorities.

wet

Contemptuous description given by Margaret Thatcher to those who supported the 'one nation' consensual approach to politics often associated with Benjamin Disraeli. Her brand of uncompromising free market monetarism was consequently described as 'dry', though this was less popular than the 'wet' designation, which some came to wear as a badge of pride rather than the shame intended. Prominent wets included Jim Prior, Peter Walker and Ian Gilmour. Others more on the right, like Chris Patten and Douglas Hurd, were perceived as somewhat 'damp' if not wholly wet.

Whig

Term derived from 'whiggamore' and applied to those who opposed the king in the 'exclusion crisis' of 1679–81, when Charles II tried to ensure the succession for his Catholic brother James, Duke of York. The Whigs became a grouping in parliament devoted to promoting civil and political liberties and mild, controlled political reform. Between 1715 and 1760 there was said to be a 'Whig oligarchy' dominating all aspects of the political system; they supported the Great Reform Act of 1832. Eventually the Whigs were subsumed into the new Liberal Party during the middle of the 19th century.

whip
An officer of a parliamentary party who ensures members know on which side to vote in divisions and who also acts as a channel of information between the leadership and the back benches. Whips are also used as a mechanism for reporting on MPs who fail to 'toe the party line' in Commons votes. Though often the lowliest form of appointment for government parties, the whips' office can also be an escalator to high office, as in the case of Edward Heath and Francis Pym.
See also chief whip.

white paper
Statement of proposed policy by government. White papers are carefully constructed and often follow comments made by government inquiries, royal commissions or green papers circulated earlier. Pressure groups strive to influence white papers as they often, but not always, determine the eventual shape of legislation.

Whitehall
The wide street, in Westminster, leading up to the houses of parliament, containing a range of government departments. Because it contains so many government buildings 'Whitehall' is often used as short-hand for government as a whole, but especially the civil service part. The name derives from the Palace of Whitehall, which was destroyed by fire in 1698; the Banqueting Hall (where Charles I was beheaded in 1649) is the only surviving element.

Whitty report, 1985
Report, drawn up by Labour Party general secretary Larry Whitty, on how the Militant Tendency had infiltrated the Liverpool branch of the party and seized control of the local authority. It urged specific expulsions and presaged the coordinated assault which ended the Tendency's period of excessive influence.
See also entryism; Hayward report; Militant Tendency.

'winter of discontent'
The winter of 1978–79, when low-paid workers in the public and private sectors revolted against the government-proposed pay norm of 5 per cent and went on strike. The term was coined in the newspaper coverage of the time and is a reference to the opening line of Shakespeare's King Richard III ('Now is the winter of our discontent'). Especially harmful to the nation's life was the strike by transport workers. The Labour government was weak at this time. James Callaghan returned from a conference in the West Indies, relaxed and calm, and was reported to have stated: 'Crisis, what crisis?' (In fact he did not use those precise words.) The impression that the trade unions were more powerful than the government proved damaging to Labour and strengthened the arguments of Margaret Thatcher that they needed reform. When the government lost a vote of confidence following its defeat over a devolution vote in March 1979, even Callaghan discerned a sea change in opinion which swept the Conservatives into office.

Witangemot
Meeting of nobility with Anglo-Saxon kings when the monarch sought counsel. The Witangemot was the precursor to parliament, which placed a check upon unlimited royal power. Because this ancient council represented the nobility, the subsequent shape of the councils which advised the monarch – the Lords and the Commons – reflected similar representation and provided the basis for representative democratic government.

POLITICS

Wolfenden report, 1957
Report of a royal commission on homosexuality and prostitution, chaired by John Wolfenden. It recommended the legalisation of homosexual acts between consenting adults (aged over 21) if they were performed in private. However, the law was changed only in 1967 and reflected, in part, the changing moral climate of the 1960s.

Women's Coalition
Women's party in Northern Ireland. The coalition was formed in 1996 as an attempt to contribute a distinctive women's voice to the negotiations concerning the future of the province. It was cross-community and involved Catholics and Protestants, nationalists and unionists as well as others. It was the only party in the world founded by women to have elected representatives – in its case in the Northern Ireland assembly. The Coalition, though, failed to win or retain seats in the 2003 elections to the assembly and it was officially wound up in May 2006.

women's movement
Although Mary Wollstonecraft advocated women's political rights in 1789, it took the direct action of the suffragettes, and in particular Emmeline Pankhurst, to win for most women over 30 the right to vote in 1918, and then for all women over 21 in 1928. Reformist feminists argue the Equal Pay Act 1970 and the Sexual Discrimination Act 1975 achieved much of what women were after and that the political battle was being won when over 100 Labour women MPs were elected in 1997, as there had also been a fundamental change in attitudes towards women. Radical and Marxist feminists say the battle against an inferior position of women at work, in education and in politics is only just the beginning of a more thorough-going reformation of the social order. The cutting edge of the women's movement has been blunted a little by the retirement from the political fray of leading campaigners and the gradual opening up of political

and corporate elites to ambitious women. Nonetheless, women are still faced with major economic, cultural and psychological obstacles from a male-dominated society. Margaret Thatcher remains the only woman to have achieved the highest political office of prime minister; she is the exception which proves the rule. In 2001 women constituted 18.5 per cent of MPs in the UK – better than the 11 per cent equivalent in France and 13 per cent in the USA but worse than 31 per cent in Germany and 43 per cent in Sweden. Percentages in the Scottish and Welsh assemblies were also better at 37 per cent and 42 per cent, respectively. Many parties in European Union countries use positive discrimination in the form of quotas for women candidates. In 2005 the number of women MPs in Britain was 128, 20 per cent of the whole.

See also feminism; inequality (gender).

woolsack
A large red cushion upon which the lord chancellor sat when presiding over debates and other business in the House of Lords. The accepted version of its provenance is that it was placed in the house in the 14th century during the reign of Edward III as a symbol of how the country benefited from the wool trade. It has no arms or backrest and is thought to be uncomfortable to sit on for long periods. It is still used by the lord speaker of the House of Lords and is still, presumably, as uncomfortable.

Workers' Educational Association (WEA)
www.wea.org.uk
Body founded by Albert Mansbridge in 1903. The Association sought to educate working men and women to give them a chance in an otherwise elitist educational system. In practice it provided day and night classes for thousands of working people over the years but perhaps its political significance was greatest for the many Labour politicians who worked as tutors at some time, including Richard Crossman, Neil Kinnock and R. H. Tawney.

Workers' Revolutionary Party (WRP)

www.wrp.org.uk

Trotskyist party dating back to the Revolutionary Communist Party of the early 1940s. Gerry Healy was originally a member of the Revolutionary Communist Party but left to stimulate similar ideas in the Labour Party, and was expelled for his pains in 1959. He then concentrated on building up his own party, which became the WRP. It seeks government control of the economy as well as withdrawal from the European Union and NATO. It expanded in the 1970s, especially after the high-profile Vanessa and Corin Redgrave joined. As with all such parties, the WRP offers a disciplined cadre of activists to seize control once the final crisis of capitalism arrives. Training is undertaken in a Derbyshire mansion and in centres throughout the country. Gerry Healy was expelled in 1985 for sexual offences. The party is said to have assets worth £1.5 million. In the 2001 general election it fielded six candidates and polled 607 votes in total.

working class

It is a truism that all adult British citizens who are in employment are working people, including Tony Blair, the governor of the Bank of England and counter hands in a McDonald's fast-food outlet. However, when sociologists and others use the term 'working class' they are describing a section of the population who differ from others in terms of a number of socio-economic characteristics, including education, occupational status, housing tenure, lifestyle and life chances. Karl Marx and Max Weber were divided over the true nature of this group, the former claiming that they were those who had nothing to sell except their labour (the proletariat), the latter examining the characteristics of occupational status groups. Taking this Weberian form of analysis, the British working class have traditionally been those people employed for wages in return for their labour, in manual occupations where they work under the close supervision of others, and have

little autonomy in the planning and control of their work.

In Britain at the turn of the 20th century, 80 per cent of the population were working class, while in 1998 the total of the C2, D, E groups – generally perceived collectively as the 'working class' – was 46 per cent of the population.

The social structure has been changing radically since the Second World War, as the occupational pattern has been transformed by changes in production technology and the labour market. Working-class jobs have disappeared, with traditional heavy industries such as mining, shipbuilding and iron and steel production being replaced by jobs in the burgeoning service sector of employment. Automation has replaced many routine assembly-line tasks in manufacturing, for example in the car industry. The information revolution that has swept across many sectors of the economy and the labour market now demands workers who are competent in a range of transferable skills, including communications and information technology. The net effect of this, according to some sociologists, is the shrinkage of the traditional working class and the enlargement of the middle class. Some also detect a new grouping lying beneath the old working class and to some extent antipathetic to the values of mainstream society. US sociologist Charles Murray sees a new 'underclass', comprising older people, single-parent families and the long-term unemployed, who live on state benefits. Moreover, some of the individuals in these groups, in particular young unemployed males, make a life for themselves in the so-called black economy of petty crime and social security fraud.

See also class; underclass.

working families tax credit (WFTC)

Introduced by chancellor Gordon Brown in Labour's first term to help families in work but on low incomes. In the budget of March 2001 poorer families in work could claim under the new system a minimum of £214 per week, raised to £225 by October 2001.

POLITICS

POLITICS

World War II
See Second World War.

World Wide Web
See Internet.

writ
Originally a command of the sovereign but more commonly understood as an order of the court summoning someone to attend a hearing.

writ of acceleration
A relatively antique writ of summons to the House of Lords that makes it possible for the eldest son and heir apparent of a peer with multiple peerage titles to attend the British House of Lords using one of his father's lesser titles. Most examples date back to medieval times but a relatively recent one was the son of the Marquess of Salisbury, who, thanks to such a writ, has sat as Viscount Cranborne in the Lords since 1992.

xenophobia
From the Greek, literally meaning fear of foreigners or strangers but in political usage more usually applied to a hatred or hostility towards people who are perceived or labelled as different and do not belong to the national or cultural group. As such, xenophobia is closely related to racism and extreme nationalism. It is thus a central feature of far-right belief systems. Some writers have suggested that it is associated with rapid social change in communities where traditional beliefs and practices are challenged by new forces. Ethnic minority groups are particularly vulnerable to xenophobic attitudes because they may have distinctive characteristics of language, dress, religious observance or physical

appearance. While Britain is generally devoid of xenophobic politics, there are occasions when the fear of foreigners or strangers is used, for example when Margaret Thatcher claimed that people had a fear of being 'swamped' by immigrants, or when Conservative politicians accused the Labour government of being soft on alleged bogus asylum seekers in the summer of 2000.

See also British National Party; fascism; National Front; nationalism; racism.

YouGov
www.yougov.com
Polling organisation specialising in Internet interactions. This body was set up by Stefan Shakespeare in 2002 and involves journalist Peter Kellner, broadcaster John Humphrys and former campaigner Des Wilson. It seeks to stimulate e-democracy and polls sample groups of 2,500–3,500 to seek opinion measures on a wide range of social and political issues. The *Daily Telegraph* regularly feature polls by YouGov (in preference to the once-favoured Gallup), employing Professor Anthony King as its analyst.

Young Conservatives
See Conservative Future.

Young Labour
www.labour.org.uk/younglabour
Youth body of the Labour Party. In the 1980s Labour's Young Socialists acquired a reputation for unruly behaviour and left-wing if not Militant political sympathies. In 1994 a new structure was introduced. It has an upper age limit of 27 and claims a membership of 30,000. Young Labour has no structure and no elected officers. Youth conferences occur every two years.

yuppie (or yuppy)
A colloquial term derived as an acronym
for 'young urban professional'. The term,
which came into use during the 1980s,
refers to young, upwardly mobile professional people – implicitly those working
and living in London. After the deregulation of the financial services in the City
of London in the mid-1980s, yuppy-dom
became a lifestyle term to denote a 'class'
of big-earning, fast-living and aggressively
acquisitive young people who cared only for
themselves.
   See also City (the); new right;
Thatcherism.

Z

Zimbabwe
Originally Southern Rhodesia, one of
the three parts of the Central African
Federation established in 1953. The
federation was dissolved in 1963 but
Rhodesia refused to accept democratic rule
and declared independence unilaterally
under prime minister Ian Smith. In 1979
Margaret Thatcher negotiated majority
rule and Smith finally resigned. However,
Zimbabwe's president Robert Mugabe

allowed many white-owned farms to
be taken over by black 'war veterans' in
1999–2000, and further claimed that
Britain still owed responsibility to black
farmers dispossessed by the whites. Faced
with a powerful opposition led by Morgan
Tsvangirai, Mugabe still tries to blame his
country's problems on 'British colonialism'.

Zinoviev letter, 1924
Forged letter purportedly from Grigory
Zinoviev, leader of the Communist
International, calling for British workers
to start a revolution. It was published in
the British press shortly before the general
election in 1924, called by Ramsay
MacDonald's fragile Labour government.
Labour had recognised the Bolshevik
government in Russia and attracted the
accusation from the right of being overly
sympathetic to the revolutionary state. The
use of the 'red menace' ploy contributed to
Labour losing the election and the forgery
was not revealed for many years.

***Zircon Affair*, 1987**
A BBC film made by *Guardian* journalist
Duncan Campbell about the Zircon
spy satellite. Special Branch raided the
Scottish offices of the BBC and confiscated
the film. The Conservative government
claimed the film compromised the country's
security, while sceptics concluded they
merely wished to conceal how far behind its
timetable the project had fallen.

POLITICS

People

Note by author
Inevitably there were problems in deciding
whom to include and whom to leave out of
this section. The aim has been to include
the 'giants' of British political history
from before the Second World War, such
as Gladstone and Disraeli, and those
who have since made or are making an
important contribution to British politics.
In addition, some leading British political
scientists have been included. The use
of the present tense has generally been
avoided, because of the fast-changing
nature of political careers.

Abbott, Diane (1953–)
First black female MP (Labour). She was
educated at Harrow County Grammar
School and then at Newnham College,
Oxford. She worked as a career civil servant
but was active as a councillor in Westminster
1982–86 and was then elected MP for
Hackney North and Stoke Newington in
1987; she was re-elected in 2010 with a
majority of 14,461. She has tended to be
seen as a left-wing rebel in the Labour
Party who has diverted some of her energies
into becoming a media performer. To some
surprise, she announced she would stand for
the Labour leadership in May 2010.

Adams, 'Gerry' (Gerald) (1948–)
Irish nationalist leader born in Belfast. He
joined Sinn Fein and was interned and
later imprisoned in the Maze for his IRA

connections during the 1970s. He was first
elected to Westminster in 1983 (for Belfast
West) but refused to take his seat because
he felt he could not make the oath of allegiance. However, in a conciliatory gesture,
he was allowed to use office facilities and
take up Westminster allowances in January
2002. As Sinn Fein's president from 1983,
he took part in the negotiations surrounding
the 1994–96 IRA cease-fire and the
subsequent peace process that culminated
in the Good Friday agreement in 1998. He
was elected to the new Northern Ireland
assembly in July 1998. He was re-elected to
Westminster in May 2010 for Belfast West
with a majority of 17,578.

Adonis, Andrew (1963–), Lord
Political advisor and Labour cabinet
minister. Son of an immigrant waiter, he
had a tough upbringing which involved
several years in care until he was 11. He
was educated (via a local authority grant)
at Kingham School and then Keble
College, Oxford, where he took a first in
modern history. He completed a DPhil
before becoming a fellow of Nuffield
College. He served as an Oxford City
Liberal Democrat councillor 1987–94; in
1995 he joined the Labour Party. He went
on to work for the *Financial Times* and
the *Observer* before he became an advisor
to Tony Blair. He was seen as influential
on Labour's education policy, though he
had a wider brief in practice, especially
after being made head of the Policy Unit.
His book *A Class Act* (1997) was an
acute analysis of Britain's class system. He
was a member of the Number 10 Policy
Unit from 1998. In 2003 he was officially
given a 'cross-cutting policy role' as the
prime minister's senior policy advisor on
education, public services and constitutional

reform. In May 2005 he was raised to the peerage and became a junior education minister. In October 2008 he was made a minister of state at the Department of Transport and in June 2009 he was promoted to the cabinet as transport secretary. His energy and ideas attracted favourable comments. He was also chosen by Gordon Brown to provide political advice and was a member of the Labour Party's negotiating delegation after the hung parliament election of May 2010.

Ainsworth, Bob (1952–)

Labour MP and secretary for defence from 2009. He was educated at Foxford Comprehensive. As a trade unionist at Jaguars he rose within the Manufacturing, Science and Finance Union (MSF). In 1984 he became a Labour councillor in Coventry and then deputy leader of the group. He was elected for the safe seat of Coventry North East in 1992; he served as a whip 1995–2001 and then became a junior minister in the Department for Environment, Transport and the Regions. After the 2001 election he was moved to the Home Office and then became deputy chief whip. In June 2007 he became a minister of state in defence, moving up to full cabinet status in June 2009. Few saw him as anything but a basically very competent minister who was perhaps fortunate to be promoted in Gordon Brown's somewhat desperate reshuffle in early June 2009. He re-elected in May 2010 with a majority of 11,775.

Aitken, Jonathan (1942–)

Conservative MP and minister. He was educated at Eton and Christ Church, Oxford, where he studied law. He was personal secretary to Selwyn Lloyd 1964–66 and *Evening Standard* foreign correspondent 1966–71. He worked for Slater Walker in the Middle East 1973–75. He was Conservative MP for Thanet South 1974–83 and then Thanet East 1983–97. He was a member of the Select Committee for Employment 1979–82 and a director of TV AM 1981–88. He served as minister

of defence procurement 1992–94 and chief secretary to the Treasury 1994–95. A *Guardian* article accused him of staying in the Paris Ritz hotel at the expense of a Middle Eastern arms dealer. He denied this and sued, with much talk about the 'sword of truth'. He came unstuck when his claim that his wife had paid his bill was proved wrong, as airline tickets showed she was in Switzerland at the time. A brilliant career – and Aitken is able – was cut short, it would seem, through an apparent belief that he could lie and bluster his way out of trouble. He was sentenced in June 1999 to a term of imprisonment for perjury in the case he brought against the *Guardian*. On release he decided to study theology, having acquired an enthusiasm for it while in prison. An attempted political comeback was crushed by Michael Howard in 2004. He has since published, with his subject's cooperation, an admiring biography of the president of Kazakhstan, Nursultan Nazarbayev (*Nazarbayev and the Making of Kazakhstan*, 2009). So far, it is yet to receive an admiring review.

Alexander, Danny (1972–)

Liberal Democrat MP, chief secretary to the Treasury and briefly before that secretary of state for Scotland. He was educated in Lochaber High School in Fort William and St Anne's College, Oxford, where he studied philosophy, politics and economics (PPE). After working for the Liberal Democrats in communications, he was elected for Inverness, Nairn, Badenoch and Strathspey in 2005. He fulfilled various shadow posts for his party before playing a role in the negotiation of the coalition in May 2010 and emerged with secretary of state for Scotland but took over the Treasury post when David Laws resigned on 28 May 2010.

Alexander, Douglas (1967–)

Labour MP and minister, and key election planner. He was educated at Park Mains High School, Lester Pearson College, Vancouver, Edinburgh University and Pennsylvania University. He worked as a researcher for Gordon Brown and as a solicitor before he became MP for Paisley South in 1997. He was Labour's election campaign coordinator from 1999 and orchestrator of Labour's 2001 general election campaign. He was minister of state for the Cabinet Office and chancellor of the Duchy of Lancaster from June 2003. In June 2007 he was appointed international development secretary. He was rumoured to be Gordon Brown's aide most in favour of a 'snap election' in the autumn of 2007, when Brown briefly rode high in the polls. The unravelling of this plan is thought to have reduced the status of Alexander's advice to the prime minister. However, he was general election coordinator from June 2007 and during the May 2010 election.

Amos, Valerie Ann (1954–), Baroness

Labour politician and the first black woman to sit in cabinet. She was born in Guyana and educated at the Universities of Warwick and East Anglia. After working in local government in London she became chief executive of the Equal Opportunities Commission 1989–94. She was given a life peerage in 1997 and became spokesperson on international development in the House of Lords as well as Tony Blair's 'envoy to Africa'. She stepped up to become secretary of state for international development when Clare Short resigned in May 2003, so becoming the first black woman to serve in the cabinet. She was then appointed leader of the House of Lords (where she had earlier served as chief whip) and president of the Privy Council in October 2003. When Gordon Brown became prime minister she left the cabinet. In October 2009 she was appointed British high commissioner to Australia.

Ancram, Michael (1945–)

Conservative MP and minister. He was educated at Ampleforth, and then Oxford and Edinburgh Universities. He practised at the Scottish bar before he entered the House of Commons for Berwick and East Lothian in February 1974 (until October 1974), for Edinburgh South 1979–87 and for Devizes since 1992. He served in the Scottish Office as well as the Northern Ireland Office 1993–97, where he was judged to have been unusually effective. He was one of the few aristocrats left in the Commons, as he stood, on the death of his father, to become the 13th Marquis of Lothian (at the time he held the courtesy title Earl of Ancram). He was chair of the Conservative Party 1998–2001 under William Hague. After the electoral disaster of June 2001 he stood for the leadership, allegedly in response to many colleagues who had asked him to. He espoused the 'one nation' brand of Conservatism and was widely seen as a moderate as well as a highly clubbable colleague. Some said his participation in the contest was an extension of the 'Stop Portillo' tendency and the support offered to him by Ann Widdecombe appeared to support this view. However, his bid failed when he polled only 17 votes in the second ballot and was eliminated. He was made shadow foreign secretary by Iain Duncan Smith in 2001 and he was the only person to retain his portfolio when Michael Howard took over as leader in November 2003. Following the House of Lords Act 1999, Ancram was entitled to continue serving in the House of Commons even after inheriting his father's title, an opportunity of which he availed himself, although he stood down at the 2010 election, for health reasons. He is known by his friends as 'Crumb', following a party in the 1960s at which he introduced himself as 'Lord Ancram' but was announced as 'Norman Crumb'.

Archer, Jeffrey (1940–), Lord

One of the most colourful and controversial figures of his day. He was Conservative MP for Louth 1969–74 before financial disaster led to near bankruptcy (which disbars a person from the House of Commons). To pay his debts he started writing novels and became hugely successful after *Not a Penny More, Not a Penny Less* (1975) became a best-seller. He was deputy chairman of the Conservative Party 1985–86 but resigned after being accused of giving money to a prostitute, Monica Coghlan. In 1987 he successfully sued the *Daily Star* over the allegation. Scandal also followed him in 1994, when it was alleged he used inside information via his wife's directorship of Anglia Television to make a large profit on the Stock Exchange. His biographer, Michael Crick, raised a number of questions relating to the veracity of his version of his education at Wellington and Oxford, where he was a noted athlete. He remained a stalwart supporter of his party and a close friend of both Margaret Thatcher and John Major. He was made a life peer in 1992; Thatcher had tried and failed to convince the Honours Scrutiny Committee that Archer should be made a peer in 1990 but his cricketing chum, John Major, succeeded in 1992. Attempts to make Archer a junior minister for sport failed when David Mellor refused to accept him. Archer put himself forward in 1998 as a candidate for the mayor of London but he withdrew from the party's selection procedure in late 1999 amid allegations that he had asked a friend to provide a 'cover' story in the 1987 libel case. His reputation in tatters, he seemed finished as a politician and as an influential member of the party. More unseemly publicity surrounded the perjury trial in the summer of 2001 when sordid details of Lord Archer's personal life were revealed to the world. His former secretary exposed him as a liar and a womaniser. The jury found him guilty of perjury and he was sentenced to four years' imprisonment, the judge observing that it was the most serious case of perjury he had 'been able to find in the books'. In the wake of the verdict, the *Star* announced it would be seeking £2.2 million in damages for the libel action Archer's lies had caused it to lose. Archer eventually repaid most of the sums he had received. In 2004 it was rumoured he might have been one of the people financing the abortive coup on Equatorial New Guinea in which Mark Thatcher was heavily implicated. He has continued to

write novels but his public rehabilitation is yet to take place.

> It is most unlikely that he has been involved in any wrongdoing. Nothing would give me more pleasure than to know of his innocence. (Michael Portillo, July 1994)

> This candidate is a candidate of probity and integrity. I am going to back him to the full. (William Hague, October 1999)

> Lord Archer is my friend, has been my friend and will remain my friend. (John Major, April 2000)

> He is not a Robert Maxwell figure, he is not someone who eats babies for breakfast. But there was something about Jeffrey, his ambition, and his inability to separate fact from fiction, that meant he was a ticking time bomb throughout his time in the Tory party. (David Mellor, July 2001)

Armstrong, Hilary (1945–)

Labour MP and minister. She was educated at Monkwearmouth Comprehensive, West Ham College of Technology and Birmingham University. She was MP for North West Durham from 1987. She was opposition spokesperson on Treasury matters 1994–95; parliamentary private secretary to John Smith 1992–94; education spokesperson 1988–92, minister for local government in the Department for Environment, Transport and the Regions from 1997. From 2001 she was parliamentary secretary to the Treasury and chief whip. She encountered trouble in July 2001 when she was involved in the attempted sacking of Gwyneth Dunwoody and Donald Anderson as chairs (respectively) of the Transport and Foreign Affairs Select Committees. Backbenchers of all hues, including Labour, rebelled, and they were reinstated in the same month. She also received criticism in 2005 for some key votes which the government lost. In 2006 she was appointed chancellor of the Duchy of Lancaster and minister for social exclusion. She left government when Brown became prime minister in June 2007 and in July 2009 announced she would stand down at the next general election. She was made a life peer in May 2010.

Armstrong, Robert (1927–)

Cabinet secretary 1979–87 and head of the civil service 1983–87. He was educated at Dragon School, Oxford, Eton and Christ Church, Oxford. He joined the Treasury in 1950 and was principal private secretary to Roy Jenkins 1967–68; permanent private secretary to the prime minister under Heath and Wilson; and deputy under-secretary at the Home Office 1975–77. Then, the perfect establishment bureaucrat, he served Margaret Thatcher – though he was not politically sympathetic to her – through a series of crises, including the Ponting, Westland and *Spycatcher* affairs. He sits as a crossbencher in the Lords and is probably now best known for coining the wonderful euphemism for lying in the sentence quoted below, spoken in legal proceedings in Australia during the *Spycatcher* affair.

> It contains a misleading impression, not a lie. It was being economical with the truth. (Armstrong referring to a letter in the *Spycatcher* trial, 1986, New South Wales)

Armstrong, William (1915–80)

Head of the civil service 1968–74. He was joint permanent secretary at the Treasury in 1962 before being given the top job in 1968. He became very close to Edward Heath and was closely involved with his anti-inflation strategy, many say too closely involved for a supposedly neutral civil servant. He was even dubbed the deputy prime minister by some critics. He suffered a nervous breakdown in the mid-1970s and retired soon after.

Ashcroft, Michael (1946–), Lord

Conservative Party treasurer 1998–2001. Ashcroft became rich through financial dealings, principally in Belize (where he had spent much of his life), which he represented at the United Nations from 1998 to 2000. Controversy surrounded his appointment regarding the propriety of his finances and a court case for libel involving the *Times* was narrowly averted in 1998. His candidature for a peerage was initially rejected but approved once he made his home back in Britain. In

June 2001 it emerged that he had served writs on two cabinet ministers, the foreign secretary and the international development secretary, Clare Short, under the European Convention on Human Rights. He argued that the government had breached his human rights by failing to prevent government documents from being leaked which formed the basis for hostile press stories. Ashcroft felt the leaks were part of a campaign to undermine his good name. He became one of the major donors to the Conservative Party, funnelling in some £6 million over the years. He was noted in Labour circles for funding candidates in marginal constituencies. While there are limits on such funding during election campaigns, there is none between elections. Both Ashcroft and senior Conservatives were reticent for several years over whether he was registered as domiciled for tax purposes. However, in March 2010 he admitted that he did not pay any tax on his own earnings.

Ashdown, 'Paddy' Jeremy John Durham (1941–), Lord

Liberal Democrat leader 1988–99. He was born in India and spent his childhood there and in Ulster before he joined the Royal Marines, when he served in the Special Boat Squadron and Northern Ireland. He gained a first-class honours degree in Mandarin at Hong Kong University and entered the diplomatic service but decided to stand as a Liberal for the Yeovil constituency, where he overthrew a Conservative majority in 1983. An astute and aggressive political operator he made his mark with his ability to speak directly and powerfully. He was made leader of the new Social and Liberal Democratic Party in 1988 (which in 1989 shortened its name to the Liberal Democrats). He eschewed 'equi-distance' between the two main parties in favour of 'constructive opposition' to Tony Blair's government and was rewarded with a seat on a cabinet committee and a prospect of his party's principal objective: electoral reform. However, Blair was always famously 'unpersuaded' on proportional representation and in September 1998 at the Labour Party conference made comments suggesting that the much spoken of referendum on the voting system might be delayed for some time. Ashdown stood down as Liberal Democrat leader and was replaced by Charles Kennedy in August 1999. He was made a peer in 2001. In May 2002 he took on the task of international high representative in Bosnia, a role he performed until 2006. In his 2009 autobiography he revealed that he had worked from time to time as a spy for the British government. Ashdown was a little sceptical about the Liberal Democrat–Tory coalition in 2010 but was generally supportive of it.

Ashley, Jackie (1964–)
Guardian journalist and broadcaster. Born the daughter of Jack Ashley, the Labour MP and campaigner for the disabled, she attended the Roseberry Grammar School, Epsom and Oxford, where she studied philosophy, politics and economics (PPE). She was once political editor of the *New Statesman* but now writes a weekly column for the *Guardian* as well as presenting radio and television programmes on current affairs. She is married to journalist and presenter Andrew Marr.

Asquith, Herbert (1852–1928)
Liberal prime minister 1908–16. He was educated at City of London School and Oxford. He practised as a barrister before becoming MP for East Fife 1886–1918 and MP for Paisley 1920–24. He was home secretary 1892–95; chancellor 1905–08; leader of the Liberal Party 1908–26; and secretary for war 1914. He was prime minister from 1908 but resigned in 1916 and became leader of the opposition. He was outmanoeuvred by David Lloyd George, who, for all his brilliance, succeeded in splitting his party between his own supporters and those of Asquith.

Astor, Nancy (1879–1964)
US-born politician who in 1919 succeeded her husband as Conservative MP for

Plymouth. She made history by becoming the first woman to win a seat in the House of Commons. Her interests lay in social problems, temperance and women's rights. She was a member of the pro-appeasement 'Cliveden set'.

Attlee, Clement Richard (1883–1967)
Labour prime minister 1945–51. He was born in Putney and educated at Haileybury and University College, Oxford. He was called to the bar in 1905. His work in Stepney slums converted him to socialism. He lectured at the London School of Economics 1913–23 except for when he undertook war service, when he attained the rank of major. He was elected mayor of Stepney 1919 and then elected into parliament in 1922. He was parliamentary private secretary to Ramsay MacDonald 1922–24; junior minister for war 1924; member of the Simon Commission on India 1927–30; and postmaster general 1931. He then became deputy leader of the opposition 1931–35 and leader of the opposition in 1935. During the war he was deputy prime minister to Winston Churchill. Labour won a landslide in the general election of 1945 and Attlee thereafter presided over six years of Labour majority rule, during which the party nationalised the utilities, introduced the welfare state, gave independence to India and Burma (1947) and signed the NATO treaty, which joined Britain's defence to that of the USA. He served as leader of the opposition 1951–55 before he resigned and entered the Lords as the 1st Earl Attlee. One of his great passions was cricket and he took a keen interest in the game's statistics.

I must remind the Right Honourable Gentleman that a monologue is not a decision. (Attlee to Churchill, 1945)

He is a sheep in sheep's clothing. (Churchill on Attlee)

He seems determined to make a trumpet sound like a tin whistle.... He brings to the fierce struggle of politics the tepid enthusiasm of a lazy summer afternoon at a cricket match. (Aneurin Bevan on Attlee)

I am a diffident man. I find it hard to carry on a conversation. But if any of you wish to come and see me, I will welcome you. (Attlee to his junior ministers, 1945)

I have none of the qualities which create publicity. (1949)

Democracy means government by discussion, but it is only effective if you can stop people talking. (1962)

Avon, Lord
See Eden, Anthony

B

Bagehot, Walter (1826–77)
Author and editor, born in Somerset, studied mathematics at University College London. He was called to the bar in 1852 and succeeded his father-in-law in 1860 as editor of the *Economist*. His *English Constitution* still remains one of the most perceptive analyses of British politics and has been reissued many times, most notably in an edition introduced by Richard Crossman. He advocated many constitutional reforms in his writings, including the introduction of life peerages. The *Economist*, in deference to its former editor, still carries a column on British politics by 'Bagehot'.

Baker, Kenneth (1934–), Lord
Conservative politician and cabinet minister. He was educated at Magdalen College, Oxford, then did national service 1953–55 as a lieutenant in the Gunners. He was a member of Twickenham borough council, was elected MP for Acton in 1968 and later for Mole Valley. He was a junior minister in the Civil Service Department 1972–74 and parliamentary private secretary to the leader of the opposition (Edward Heath) 1974–75. He was minister for information technology

1981–84 and local government 1985–86; education secretary 1986–89; chancellor of the Duchy of Lancaster 1989–90; chair of the Conservative Party 1989–90; and home secretary 1990–92. Baker was one of the most articulate and persuasive of Margaret Thatcher's ministers; he served her faithfully despite being a committed Heath-ite when younger. When chairman of his party his greatest coup as a 'spinner' of news was in the 1990 local government elections, when his insistence that the poll tax worked was apparently vindicated when Wandsworth and Westminster, 'flagship' councils with exemplary low charges, increased their majorities. The (admittedly pro-Tory) press accepted this version of events and neglected to emphasise the huge losses made by the party countrywide. He has a special retirement interest in political cartoons.

Baldwin, Stanley (1867–1947)
Three times Conservative prime minister (1923–24, 1924–29, 1935–37). He was born into a wealthy family with interests in iron and steel manufacturing, and educated at Harrow and Trinity College, Cambridge. He entered the House of Commons in 1908, was president of the Board of Trade 1921–22 and chancellor 1922–23. He was unexpectedly selected as prime minister when Andrew Bonar Law retired through ill-health. He managed to be the dominant personality in his party for over a decade through cultivating a relaxed, pipe-smoking and reliable image: 'the man you can trust'. He was, however, a tough politician: he led the revolt against David Lloyd George in October 1922, overcame the threat of the Trades Union Congress during the General Strike in 1926 and forced King Edward VIII to give way over the abdication crisis in 1936. He was the first senior British politician to become familiar with the media and he mastered perfectly the art of the 'confidential' talk to the nation via radio. He goes down as an under-rated prime minister of resilience and generally sound judgement, though his insistence on returning to the gold standard was unwise and his complacent attitude

towards the rise of fascism myopic. In 1937 he became Earl Baldwin of Bewdley.

> I hate elections, but you have to have them – they are medicine. (1931)

Balfour, Arthur (1848–1930)

Conservative prime minister 1902–05 and foreign secretary 1916–19, when he issued the Balfour declaration. He was born in Scotland and educated at Eton and Cambridge; he initially combined politics with scholarship and wrote *A Defence of Philosophic Doubt* (1879). He was elected to the House of Commons at the age of 26 and was soon made personal secretary to his uncle, then foreign secretary, the Marquess of Salisbury. Balfour was made president of the Local Government Board 1885 and soon after secretary for Scotland and then chief secretary for Ireland 1887–91, where he strongly opposed home rule. His elevation, through the patronage of his uncle, led to the common phrase 'Bob's your uncle'. He became first lord of the Treasury in 1891 (before that title became synonymous with the office of prime minister) and led his party in the Commons while his uncle was prime minister in the Lords. When Salisbury resigned in 1902 Balfour became prime minister. A destructive battle followed in the Conservative Party, with Joseph Chamberlain (colonial secretary in Salisbury's government) pressing imperial preference and being opposed by the advocates of free trade, and Balfour resigned as prime minister (though not as party leader) in December 1905. The Conservatives mustered only 156 seats in the 1906 general election. Balfour lost his seat but was soon in again as the member for the City of London. As leader of the opposition his patrician style was not well received; he encountered a 'Balfour Must Go' movement and in 1911 he resigned the leadership. However, David Lloyd George brought him into the wartime government eventually as foreign secretary, as which he issued the Balfour declaration in 1917 and played a role in the Versailles peace treaty in 1919. He managed to serve again in Stanley Baldwin's government as lord president of the Council 1925–29. He left office in 1929, having served 27 years in the cabinet, and died soon afterwards. Possibly one of the most elegant and cerebral prime ministers ever to serve in Downing Street, but by no means one of the most distinguished.

> I would rather take advice from my valet than from the [Conservative] party conference.

> Nothing matters very much, and few things matter at all.

Balls, Ed (1967–)

Labour MP, minister, and advisor to Gordon Brown when chancellor. He was educated at the private Nottingham High School, then Oxford and Harvard Universities. He worked as a leader writer at the *Financial Times* 1994–97 before becoming advisor to Brown. According to the *Observer* (25 February 2001) he was 'one of the handful of people the chancellor will listen to, he is a prime mover behind the Americanisation of economic policy'. Regarded as the 'deputy chancellor', he saw every key Treasury paper and was an advocate of welfare to work and promoting individual opportunity. A 'closet Keynesian', said the *Observer*, who 'believes in income redistribution'. On 1 July 2004 he was made Labour candidate for the safe seat of Normanton and was elected in 2005. In 2007 he was appointed to the cabinet as secretary of state for children, schools and families. He is reckoned to be a wily politician, given to 'briefing wars', and was a close colleague of Damian McBride, the Brown aide disgraced for planning to issue damaging smears about leading Conservatives. In June 2009 he was allegedly intended to take over from Alistair Darling as chancellor but James Purnell's resignation as secretary of state for work and pensions meant a weakened Gordon Brown was unable to shift his resident chancellor, who defiantly stayed put. Balls later ridiculed Purnell's resignation as a sign of a 'mid-life crisis'. His wife, Yvette Cooper, was work and pensions secretary and also in the cabinet. In May 2010 he declared himself a candidate for the Labour leadership.

Barber, Anthony (1920–), Lord
Conservative chancellor under Edward Heath. Born to a Danish mother, he was educated at Retford Grammar School, Oxford, and was a barrister before being elected for Doncaster 1951–64 and then Altrincham and Sale 1965–74. He began his ministerial career as a whip, moved on to the Treasury, and then became the minister of health and chairman of the Conservative Party 1967–70. He was chancellor of the Duchy of Lancaster in 1970 and chancellor of the exchequer 1970–74. He was generally reckoned to have precipitated the inflationary spiral of the 1970s as a result of high borrowing. He was made a life peer in 1974.

Barber, Brendan (1951–)
General secretary of the Trades Union Congress (TUC) from 2003. He was educated at St Mary's College grammar school, Crosby, then spent a year on Voluntary Service Overseas (VSO) before going to City University, where he was president of the Student Union. He worked for a while as a university researcher before he joined the TUC in 1974. He became a head of section one year later and head of press in 1979 and deputy general secretary in 1993.

Barber, Michael (1951–), Sir
Former head of Tony Blair's Delivery Unit. He was educated at Oxford and became a professor of education at London University. From 1997 to 2001 he was chief advisor to the education secretary on school standards, when he helped to implement Labour's school reforms. From 2001 to 2005 he was head of the Delivery Unit, tasked with discovering ways of ensuring that government policies were successfully delivered. His book on this latter period, *Instruction to Deliver: Tony Blair, the Public Services and the Challenge*

of Achieving Targets (2007), has been widely praised.

Barnett, Joel (1923–), Lord
Labour politician who devised the Barnett formula. He was educated at Manchester High School. He became an accountant and businessman in Greater Manchester after serving in the Royal Army Service Corps and the British military government in Germany. He was MP for Heywood and Royton 1964–83 and entered the House of Lords in 1983. He was a member of the Public Accounts Committee 1961–71 and its chair 1979–83. He served as shadow Treasury spokesman 1970–74 and chief secretary to the Treasury 1974–79, with the last two years as a cabinet member. He devised the 'Barnett formula': the basis on which public expenditure was to be divided between the constituent countries of the UK. He was known for his canny, folksy style, his right-of-centre opinions, his tough negotiating with departments on behalf of the Treasury and subsequently for his revealing memoirs, which were said to be a favourite of Margaret Thatcher.

Barry, Brian (1936–2009)
Distinguished British political scientist who was Lieber Professor of Political Philosophy, Columbia University, New York, from 1998. He was educated at Taunton School, Southampton University and Queen's College, Oxford, and was Rockefeller Fellow, Harvard, 1961–62. He worked at the Universities of Keele, Southampton, Oxford, Essex (1969–72), Chicago (1972–83), the California Institute of Technology (1982–86), European University, Florence (1986–91) and the London School Economics (1987–98). He won the Johan Skytte Prize in Political Science 2001 and the W. J. M. Mackenzie Prize (of the Political Studies Association) for the best book published in the previous year for *Theories of Justice* (1989), *Justice as Impartiality* (1995), and *Culture and Equality* (2000). In 2005 his *Social Justice Matters*, a critique of new Labour, was highly praised.

Beaverbrook, Max (1879–1964), Lord

Newspaper magnate, historian and Conservative politician. He was born in Ontario, Canada (as William Maxwell Aitken), moved to Britain in 1910 and in same year entered the Commons for Ashton-under-Lyne; soon afterwards he became parliamentary private secretary to his friend Andrew Bonar Law. Under David Lloyd George he was made minister of information in 1918. In 1916 he took over control of the struggling *Daily Express* and made it the newspaper with the largest circulation of his generation. He founded the *Sunday Express* in 1921 and bought the *Evening Standard* in 1929. During the Second World War he was made minister of aircraft production and displayed unusual energy and effectiveness. He held the post of minister of supply 1941–42 but his political career fizzled out after the war. His newspapers stoutly supported the British Empire and tended to be opposed to an integrated Europe. Beaverbrook was one of the great original 'press barons', who probably did not fulfil his own dreams of power and effectiveness. The fact that he had close friends among left-wing journalists and politicians – including the likes of Michael Foot and Aneurin Bevan – attests to his charm and ability to rise above his own prejudices.

> I learnt one thing from my father – and that was to hate, to hate! (1935)

> He is a magnet for all young men and I warn you if you talk to him no good will become of it. Beware of flattery. (Clement Attlee warning junior ministers against Beaverbrook, 1945)

Beckett, Margaret (1943–)

Labour MP and cabinet minister. She was educated at Notre Dame High School, Norwich, and studied metallurgy at Manchester College of Science and Technology before she became a research assistant to the Labour Party 1970–74. She was elected MP for Lincoln in 1974, lost her seat in 1979 but re-entered parliament in 1983 as MP for Derby South. She went through a period of closeness to the hard left in the early 1980s (which is still remembered with some bitterness by older Labour MPs). She soon forgot her leftist past though and held a number of posts with evident competence before becoming deputy leader of the Labour Party from 1992 to 1994 and briefly (acting) leader in 1994 when John Smith died. She shadowed social security, the Treasury and trade and industry, and was made president of the Board of Trade in 1997. She was moved to leader of the house in July 1998, played an active part in the 2001 general election campaign and was made the new secretary for environment, food and rural affairs in the reshuffle following the election. She was surprisingly appointed foreign secretary in 2006, though her tenure was not widely viewed as a success. After Tony Blair left office in June 2007 she was out of government until 2008, when Gordon Brown appointed her as minister of state for housing and planning. She resigned from that post in June 2009. In that same month she stood in the contest for a new speaker of the Commons, withdrawing after the second round of voting, though she polled respectably. She retained her Derby South seat in 2010 with a majority of 6,122.

Beith, Alan (1943–)

Liberal Democrat MP. He was educated at Macclesfield School and Balliol College, Oxford, and was a lecturer in politics at Newcastle University. He won Berwick upon Tweed at a by-election in 1973. He was deputy leader of the Liberals from 1985 and deputy leader of the Liberal Democrats from 1992 (having lost to Paddy Ashdown in the 1988 leadership contest). He was chief whip for the Liberals 1976–85; served as Treasury and home affairs spokesman and served on the Treasury and Civil Service Select Committee. He was appointed chair of the select committee set up to scrutinise the Lord Chancellor's Department in January 2003. He was briefly spoken of as a compromise candidate for the leadership in 2007 but he disowned the idea. He was awarded a knighthood in 2008. He retained his seat in 2010 with a majority of 2,670.

Bell, Martin (1938–)

BBC news correspondent and independent MP, 1997–2001. He was educated at Cambridge and joined the BBC in 1962. He became an award-winning foreign correspondent in Washington, Berlin and Vienna, as well as a war correspondent, notably in Bosnia, where he was celebrated for his bravery and his trademark white suit. In 1997 he decided to fight Tatton as an 'anti-sleaze' candidate. Complete with white suit, he campaigned against former Conservative trade minister Neil Hamilton, the MP at the centre of the 'cash for questions' scandal. He won by a majority of 11,000 and served as an effective constituency MP in a job he came to enjoy. However, he was forced, in line with his stated 1997 intention, not to stand in 2001. Instead, he fought Brentwood and Ongar in 2001 and, while his campaign against the alleged infiltration of local Conservatives by a religious faction was effective, his opponent, Eric Pickles, won by a majority of 2,800 – down from over 10,000 in 1997. Since then Bell has made several television programmes and has tried to encourage independents to stand for parliament with his Independent Network.

> Does the Prime Minister agree that the perception of wrong-doing can be as damaging to public confidence as the wrong-doing itself? Have we slain one dragon only to have another take its place, with a red rose in its mouth? (Question to Tony Blair in 1997, to Conservative cheers)

Benn, Hilary (1953–)

Labour MP and minister. He was educated at Holland Park Comprehensive School and the University of Sussex, where he studied Russian and East European Studies. He worked for trade unions in the 1980s and became active in local politics. He stood for Ealing North in 1983 and 1987. He was head of policy

and communications at the Manufacturing, Science and Finance union (MSF) and in 1997 became special advisor to education secretary David Blunkett. He was elected to the Commons in 1999 for Leeds Central and became a junior minister in the Department for International Development in June 2001; he became minister of state in May 2002 after a sojourn in the Home Office, May 2002–03. His accession to the cabinet meant three generations of his family had served in this way: his father Tony and his grandfather before that. He stood for the deputy leadership of the Labour Party in 2007. When Gordon Brown became prime minister was appointed secretary for environment, food and rural affairs in 2007. He was re-elected in 2010 with a majority of 10,645.

Benn, Tony (1925–)

Labour MP, cabinet minister, diarist and left-wing ideologue. He was originally known as Anthony Wedgwood Benn, son of Viscount Stansgate. He was educated at Westminster and New College, Oxford. He was Labour MP 1950–60 but was then barred from the Commons when he inherited his father's title. He fought this and succeeded in changing the law so that he could re-enter the Commons in 1963. In Harold Wilson's first governments he was postmaster general 1964–66 and minister of technology 1966–70. In opposition 1970–74 he shadowed trade and industry and briefly held this ministry after Labour's 1974 election victory, until Wilson moved him to the less sensitive position of secretary of state for energy 1976–79, because of concern at the left-wing stance his ambitious protégé had uncompromisingly adopted. In opposition after 1979 he led the left wing of the Labour Party and was responsible, according to some critics, for much of the internecine fighting which characterised Labour in the early 1980s and helped keep the party out of power. His attempt to become deputy leader in 1981 narrowly failed and he lost his seat in 1983 but came back for Chesterfield in 1984. He challenged Neil Kinnock for the leadership in 1988 but failed by a wide margin. He remains true to his left-wing ideals but is now seen with affection, even by his opponents, as a great radical dissenter, a wonderful speaker and (important to the Tories) scrupulously polite, whose time for leadership passed decisively in the mid-1980s. His prolific diaries (eight volumes), culled from the tape recordings he assiduously made on every aspect of his varied life, provide a unique insight into British political history. He stood down as MP for Chesterfield in June 2001 to 'devote more time to politics'. He remains an active campaigner on many issues and, though he would hate the phrase, has become something of a 'national institution'. Benn insists there are five questions that should be asked of any powerful person: 'What power have you got? Where did you get it from? In whose interests do you use it? To whom are you accountable? How do we get rid of you?'

Bentham, Jeremy (1748–1832)

Political thinker and author of 'utilitarianism'. He was a child prodigy who entered Queen's College, Oxford, aged 12 and entered Lincoln's Inn three years later. His fame, however, was established not at the bar but as the creator of the philosophy of utilitarianism, which is based on the premise that the aim of all legislation should be the achievement of 'the greatest happiness for the greatest number'. He invented a model prison named the Panopticon and a special school, the Chrestomathia. He travelled widely in Europe and wrote on economics, politics and penal reform. He founded University College London, where his clothed skeleton was preserved and remains on public view.

Bercow, John (1963–)

Conservative MP and speaker of House of Commons. Born the son of a Jewish taxi driver, Bercow attended Finchley Manorhill comprehensive school in north London. He was a talented tennis player until glandular fever ended his career. He took a first in politics at Essex University,

before becoming an activist on the right of the Conservative Party. He was chairman of the National Federation of Conservative Students 1986–87. Bercow worked in the City and as a lobbyist for a while before being elected for Buckingham in 1997. He filled several shadow positions on the front bench but resigned over a vote on gay rights in November 2002. Michael Howard appointed him shadow for international development but he fell out with his leader and was sacked. In June 2007 there were rumours he might defect to Labour (his wife is a known Labour sympathiser). Bercow had long harboured ambitions to become speaker and stood in June 2009. Conservatives generally dislike him so Labour MPs were pleased to foist him onto them by voting heavily for the Tory MP. Being relatively young, Bercow is likely to remain in office for many years. In the 2010 general election he saw off a challenge from the UK Independence Party's Nigel Farage, who broke the convention that the speaker is returned unopposed. His majority was over 12,000.

Bevan, Aneurin ('Nye') (1897–1960)

Labour minister of health after the Second World War, whose energy and speaking talent made him a rival to Hugh Gaitskell for the party leadership. He was born in Tredegar as one of a miner's 13 children; he himself entered the pits aged 13. He became active in the miners' union and led the Welsh miners during the 1926 General Strike. He was elected Independent Labour Party member for Ebbw Vale in 1929 and joined the Labour Party in 1931. In the Commons he soon established a reputation as a brilliant orator, whose wit excoriated the Conservatives and anyone else he disagreed with, including some in his own party, which expelled him for a while for supporting the Popular Front campaign. As part of that campaign he had been a co-founder of the left-wing magazine *Tribune*. During the war he criticised Winston Churchill for 'conducting wars like a debate and debates like a war'. In 1945 he was made minister of health and was instrumental in establishing the National Health Service in 1948. As minister of labour in 1951 he resigned over the imposition of prescription charges and led a left-wing faction of 50 or so MPs against the leadership of Clement Attlee and then the 'desiccated calculating machine' Hugh Gaitskell (who easily defeated him in the 1955 Labour leadership contest). He was passionately opposed to nuclear weapons but abandoned his stand in the 1957 conference when, as shadow foreign secretary, he claimed Britain could not go 'naked into the conference chamber' (to negotiate arms reductions with the Soviet Union).

> No attempt at ethical or social education can eradicate from my heart a deep burning hatred for the Tory Party.... So far as I am concerned, they are lower than vermin. (4 July 1948)

> The language of priorities is the religion of socialism. (Labour Party conference, 8 June 1949)

> Like an old man approaching a young bride – fascinated, sluggish, apprehensive. (On the Allies' advance into Italy, 1943)

> He was like a fire in a room on a cold day. (Constance Cummings on Bevan)

Beveridge, William Henry (1879–1963)

Liberal academic and thinker credited with framing the modern welfare state. He was born in India of Scottish descent and educated at Charterhouse and Balliol College, Oxford. Initially a journalist he became an authority on unemployment insurance and compiled his report *Unemployment* in 1909. At the Board of Trade he became director of labour exchanges 1909–16 and then director of the London School of Economics 1919–37 and master of University College, Oxford, 1937–45. He served on many official committees and chaired the one which produced the famous report associated with his name in 1942, *Social Insurance and Allied Services*. This was a comprehensive blueprint for social insurance for the whole

of the national community aiming to eliminate the five 'giants' of 'Want, Disease, Ignorance, Squalor and Idleness'. It was endorsed by the wartime government and provided the basis for the postwar welfare state. Beveridge was elected as a Liberal MP in 1944 but lost his seat in 1945; he was made a peer in 1946.

> Ignorance is an evil weed which dictators may cultivate among their dupes, but which no democracy can afford among its citizens. (*Social Insurance and Allied Services*, 1942)

Bevin, Ernest (1881–1951)

Trade union leader and Labour foreign secretary 1945–51. He was born to poor parents in Somerset, who abandoned him at an early age. He first worked as a van driver in Bristol and soon entered the world of the trade union movement, which he did so much to form into its modern shape. He became a paid official of the Dockers' Union at the age of 30. His brilliant conduct of a case in front of a wage tribunal earned him the title of 'the dockers' KC'. He amalgamated over 30 unions to form the massive Transport and General Workers' Union (destined to become the largest union in Europe) and became its general secretary 1921–40. He was active in the 1930s on the Macmillan Committee on Finance and Industry, where he absorbed early Keynesian ideas. In 1940 he became minister of labour, when he achieved near complete mobilisation of the workforce, and served in the war cabinet. He was foreign secretary in Clement Attlee's postwar government, when he was scrupulously loyal to his premier and the architect of the formation and Britain's membership of NATO. Unlike many in his own party, and by no means a left-winger, he soon perceived the USSR as a potential threat to the peace achieved in 1945. Bevin was not without idealism, as many of his speeches attest, but he was essentially a realist, used to tough negotiations, who would not allow Soviet claims to obscure the USSR's advance into eastern Europe. The original John Bull of British trade unionism, he died in office in

1951, mourned by Labour politicians and Foreign Office officials alike.

> The most conservative man in the world is the British trades unionist when you want to change him. (1927)

> I do not know whether Marx really educated anybody. What he did was to confuse me. (House of Commons, July 1948)

> The familiar saying is that Bevin always treated the Soviet Union as if it were a breakaway faction of the Transport and General Workers' Union. (Kingsley Martin, when editor of *New Statesman*)

> A speech from Ernest Bevin on a major occasion had all the horrid fascination of a public execution. If the mind were left immune, eyes and ears and emotions were riveted. (Michael Foot)

Biffen, John (1930–2007), Lord

Conservative MP and cabinet minister. He was born the son of a Somerset tenant farmer and was educated at his local grammar school, followed by Jesus College, Cambridge. He worked in industry and for the Economist Intelligence Unit before winning the seat for Oswestry in 1961. A 'one nation' Tory, he became a supporter of Enoch Powell's economic ideas, a convinced Eurosceptic and a close advisor and confidant of Margaret Thatcher. She made him chief secretary to the Treasury, trade and industry secretary and then leader of the House of Commons. In 1986 he began to question the direction of her leadership – he preferred a team approach and was sacked in 1987 after the Conservatives' general election victory of that year. Bernard Ingham, Thatcher's press secretary, responded famously to his dissent by describing him as a 'semi-detached' member of the cabinet. Biffen responded by calling Ingham 'the sewer and not the sewage', though they had cordial personal relations in retirement. He was made a life peer in 1997.

Bingham, Tom (1934–), Lord

Law lord, educated at Sedbergh School and Balliol College, Oxford. As lord chief justice 1996–2000 he tended to reinforce

the rights of the accused: he opposed cuts in legal aid on the grounds that it would disadvantage the poor; he opposed the plan to remove the right of men on rape charges to cross-examine their accusers; and he argued that sections of the Prevention of Terrorism Act 1989 violated the presumption of innocence in a 'blatant and obvious way'. He was also opposed to the 2003 invasion of Iraq, calling it 'a serious violation of international law'.

Birt, John (1944–), Lord

Director general of the BBC 1992–2000. He was born in Liverpool and educated at St Mary's College, Oxford. Initially he worked for London Weekend Television, where he developed the philosophy that current affairs coverage should provide the background to politics and also where he met and became friends with Peter Mandelson. When he moved to the BBC there was much criticism – some of it virulent – that he used management jargon to disguise swingeing cuts and a deprofessionalisation of the Corporation, referred to by critics as 'Birtism'. However, he defended his policy vigorously and won the trust of government, both Conservative and Labour. He was raised to the peerage in 2000 and performed an advisory role on crime for a while, though evidence of any influence remained slight. In the summer of 2001 Birt was given a role in helping to reform Whitehall, which was widely perceived as failing to 'deliver' the results government wanted. Tony Blair then asked him to assist in the field of transport, where he was commissioned to think 'blue sky' thoughts on how related thorny problems could be resolved. His suggestion that toll-paying motorways be built alongside existing ones was not well received and subsequently his profile rarely rose above that of a 'Tony's crony'.

Black, Conrad (1944–)

Press magnate. He was educated at Carleton, Laval and McGill Universities. He was the third most powerful press magnate in the world, with interests in Canada and the USA, and owner of Telegraph newspapers and the *Spectator*. He failed to win control of the *Independent* in 1994. He was close politically to Margaret Thatcher and became a peer in 2001, though his home government in Canada objected to the elevation. In 2004 Black was forced to give up control of the *Telegraph* and it was sold to the financiers and newspaper owners the Barclay bothers. He was tried in a US court for illegal financial practices – designed to fund what appeared to be a grossly extravagant lifestyle. He was found guilty and is currently residing in the Coleman Federal Correctional Complex in Florida.

Blair, Cherie (1954–)

Recorder since 1998 though probably best (perhaps unfairly) known as Tony Blair's wife. Her father, actor Tony Booth, also had a high profile, which created problems during her schooldays. She was educated at Seafield Grammar School and the London School of Economics. She was called to the bar in 1976 and specialised in public and employment law and human rights after joining Matrix chambers. She was thought to earn in the region of £200,000 a year. Cherie was reckoned to have been a better lawyer than her husband and she too had political ambitions at one time, though these soon took second place to Tony's. In the autumn of 2002 she was involved in 'Cheriegate' when the *Daily Mail* and other tabloids revealed she had bought two flats in Bristol (one for her student son, Euan) partially on the advice of convicted conman Peter Foster, boyfriend of her style advisor Carole Caplin. The story ran for longer perhaps than it merited. She was often pilloried in the right-wing tabloid press for being over acquisitive – a possible reaction to her less than comfortably off childhood – and rather naively loyal to politically inappropriate friends. However, no one criticised her passionate loyalty to her husband and her children.

Blair, Tony (1953–)

Labour leader from 1994 and prime minister from 1997. He was born in Scotland and educated at Fettes College and St John's College, Oxford, where he studied law. He was always a rebellious pupil but showed more interest in Christianity (and perhaps drama) than politics until he left university. He was called to the bar in 1976. He sought a parliamentary seat and fought a by-election in Beaconsfield before he won the safe seat of Sedgefield in 1983. He shadowed the Treasury, trade and industry and energy before 1988, employment in 1989 and home affairs in 1992. After the death of Labour leader John Smith in 1994 he was elected leader and did much to 'modernise' the party; this included abolishing clause 4 of Labour's constitution and steering the party into the electable centre-ground on economic and social policy. He was helped by colleagues such as Gordon Brown and key advisors such as Peter Mandelson. His stunning general election victory in 1997 gave him unparalleled power in his party; Blair was highly telegenic and his performances on television helped to win the landslide victory. As prime minister his high poll ratings lasted for many months into his premiership but critical voices began to be raised regarding his bevy of advisors, including his press secretary, Alastair Campbell, upon whom, it was alleged, he placed a disproportionate reliance for advice, at the expense of cabinet and parliament. On 9 September 1998 a *Guardian* ICM poll revealed what the newspaper announced was the true end of the 'honeymoon', with a 'disaffected electorate beginning to view him as just another politician'. His personal ratings then appeared to plummet for trust and effectiveness as prime minister. He won the 2001 general election by another landslide but on a worryingly low turnout. As 2002 progressed he came in for criticism for excessive use of 'spin' and for offering such uncritical support for US president George W. Bush. By the spring of 2003 Blair had faced near fatal opposition from his side of the house to his plans for foundation hospitals and university top-up fees but these were small beer compared with party as well as wider opposition to the US plan to invade Iraq. The 2003 Iraq war and its barbaric aftermath became a running sore in Blair's standing, damaged as it already was by the repercussions of the David Kelly affair and the Hutton and Butler reports. By the autumn of 2004 there was open talk of Blair being replaced as leader, possibly by Gordon Brown. To quell the discontent, Blair announced that he would not contest the election after the next one. He went on to win the May 2005 election with a majority of 67 but the victory did not feel especially like one and continuing criticism over the Iraq war caused more rumblings against his leadership. After a series of bad news stories in the spring of 2006, rebel MPs conspired to bring him down in the autumn, forcing him to stand down before his stated intention to leave at the end of the parliamentary session. Brown was suspected of orchestrating the plot but after some tense days before the Manchester party annual conference peace broke out once again, with Blair agreeing to go in a year's time. All this meant that he became something of a 'lame duck' prime minister, whose time to establish the 'legacy' achievements about which he cared so much was fast running out. He finally handed over to Brown in June 2007 and took on a role as a peace envoy in the Middle East for the 'quartet' players of Russia, the USA, the European Union and the United Nations. He was criticised for taking large fees for lecturing tours in the USA and elsewhere. It was rumoured that if the Lisbon treaty measures were implemented, he would be a candidate for the president of Europe but his closeness to the USA made him unacceptable and this did not happen (it was allegedly vetoed by German chancellor Angela Merkel). He made a brief return to British politics when he campaigned for Brown during the 2010 election campaign.

> Labour is the party of law and order in Britain today. Tough on crime and tough on the causes of crime. (Labour Party conference, 1993)

> Ask me my three main priorities for government, and I tell you: education, education, education. (Labour Party conference, 1996)

> We are not the masters. The people are the masters. We are the servants of the people … what the electorate gives, the electorate can take away. (1997)

> I now have more respect for judgement than intellect. (Attributed to Blair by John Prescott and cited as a sign of his increasing wisdom, BBC2 programme, 4 May 2003)

> I don't really believe what Tony says, not after the Iraq war. But I would still prefer him to Gordon Brown for prime minister because he's a class act. (Voter Khalid Hussein, after being canvassed by Blair in April 2010)

Blears, Hazel (1956–)
Diminutive Labour MP and former cabinet member. She attended Wardley Grammar School and then Trent Polytechnic, where she studied law. She worked as a solicitor in local government, was elected to Salford council 1984–92 and in 1997 was elected for her native Salford as MP. She served as a junior minister in health, then as minister of state at the Home Office. In May 2006 she became party chair. However, when she stood for the post of deputy leader of the party in 2007 she came last. Gordon Brown named her as his communities and local government secretary. She survived a reshuffle in 2008 but was fatally embroiled in the MPs' expenses scandal. It transpired she had 'flipped' houses three times to benefit from an allowances system which provided substantial assistance for designated 'second homes'. She had also claimed for expensive furniture and hotel stays. By designating her London home as her 'main' one for tax purposes, she was able to avoid capital gains tax even though it was her 'second home' for parliamentary expenses purposes. She publicly repaid over £13,000 to cover this omission but Brown upset her by describing her behaviour as 'totally unacceptable'. Her resignation on the eve of the local elections – with some added venom aimed at the beleaguered Brown – was held to be spiteful and disloyal. In June 2009 the

police said they would not pursue any matters in connection with expenses claims and payments. Despite her expenses ignominy she was re-elected in 2010 by a majority of 5,725 (reduced from 13,784 in 2005).

Blunkett, David (1947–)

Labour MP and cabinet minister, remarkable for the fact that he is blind. He was educated at Sheffield University and later lectured in industrial relations at Barnsley College of Technology. He was leader of Sheffield city council in the 1980s before he became a Labour MP in 1987. He was opposition spokesman on health, education and employment and chairman of the party 1993–94. He was made secretary of state for education in 1997 and judged to have angered teaching unions by his support for chief inspector of Ofsted, Chris Woodhead. Blunkett was home secretary from June 2001, a post in which he was controversial in pursuing relatively hard-line authoritarian policies on crime and antisocial behaviour. However, his hard-line stance was not unpopular with voters and the reasons for his resignation in December 2004 were unusual to say the least. It transpired that he had been having a passionate affair with the rich American married publisher of the right-wing *Spectator* magazine, Kimberly Quinn. While the tabloid press were delighted with the story – it seemed Mrs Quinn had already given birth to a son by the home secretary and was again pregnant – it was evidence that he had used his position to fast-track an application for residence submitted by Mrs Quinn's nanny which brought him down. However, he did not have long to wait for another stint in the cabinet, this time as work and pensions secretary, after the 2005 election victory. But this was short-lived: he was again forced to resign once it transpired he had not properly followed required procedures regarding shares he owned in a company called DNA Bioscience. His brief emergence into the limelight in the autumn of 2006 when his diaries were published

was interpreted by some as evidence that he did not necessarily believe his political career to be over under a possible Gordon Brown prime ministership. However, the call never came. In office, he had pioneered the idea of identity cards for British people but in April 2009 he called for the scheme to be scrapped. He was returned in 2010 by 13,632 votes.

> Mr Blunkett grew up blind in dreadful poverty, the son of a factory foreman who died in an accident and whose family did not have enough money to give the grave a headstone. (*Economist*, 12 January 2002)

Bogdanor, Vernon (1943–)

A professor at Oxford from 1996 and an expert on the British constitution. He was educated at Bishopshalt School and Queen's College, Oxford. He was a fellow of Brasenose College, Oxford, from 1966. He was special advisor to the Select Committee on European Communities and to foreign governments, including those of the Czech Republic and Israel. In 2009 he wrote a book *The New British Constitution* in which he argued that, in practice, as a result of all the changes which had happened since 1972 – joining the European Union, devolution, the Human Rights Act 1998 and so forth – Britain effectively had a 'new' constitution.

Bonar Law, Andrew (1858–1923)

Conservative prime minister 1922–23. He made money through being an iron merchant in Glasgow and became a Conservative MP in 1900. He was colonial secretary in Herbert Asquith's wartime coalition and chancellor in David Lloyd George's 1916–19 cabinet and later became lord privy seal. In March 1921 he retired through ill-health but came out of retirement to help defeat Lloyd George's coalition government in 1922. He then resumed the position of party leader and became prime minister in October 1922 but the following May was again forced to resign because of ill-health. One of the least known or lauded prime ministers of the 20th century, he also deserves to be known as the politician who helped end the ministerial career of the greatest politician of his time – Lloyd George.

> I must follow them, I am their leader.

> I am afraid I shall have to show myself very vicious, Mr Asquith, this session. I hope you will understand. (When leader of the house, 1912)

> If I am a great man, then a good many of the great men of history are frauds. (During the Ulster crisis)

Booth, Cherie
See Blair, Cherie.

Boothroyd, Betty (1929–), Baroness
Speaker of the House of Commons 1992–2000. She was educated at Dewsbury College of Commerce and Art. She entered the house for West Bromwich West in 1974, served variously in the whips' office and on select committees before becoming deputy chair of the Ways and Means Committee 1979–87, the second in line to the speaker. Boothroyd was a colourful character whose used to dance as a Tiller Girl in the war. She developed an effective blend of humour and firmness to keep the house on the civilised side of the unruliness it frequently threatens. Her command of the house was much admired also in the USA, where video clips of the proceedings stimulated considerable interest. In 2000, to general acclaim, she retired from the speakership and went into the Lords.

Bourn, John (1934–)
Comptroller and auditor general 1988–2008. He was educated at Southgate Grammar School and the London School of Economics. He worked as a civil servant in the Air Ministry, Treasury and Civil Service College but his main career was in the Northern Ireland Department, where he was deputy secretary 1982–84, and the Ministry of Defence, where he rose to deputy under-secretary (defence procurement) 1985–88. He was not afraid to make critical reports on government activity,

whether Conservative or Labour. He was a visiting professor at the London School of Economics from 1983. *Private Eye* ran a campaign highlighting his extravagant use of restaurants, expensive hotels and overseas trips, often accompanied by his wife. It also accused him of neglecting aspects of government expenditure. The mainstream press eventually took up the story and he resigned in October 2008.

Boyce, Michael (1943–)
Admiral and chief of defence staff (CDS). He was educated at Hurstpierpoint School and Britannia Royal Naval College, Dartmouth. He joined the Royal Navy in 1961 and had a distinguished career as a submariner and then staff officer. He was first sea lord before he became CDS in 2001. He was thought to be sceptical on US missile policy. He resigned in 2003.

Bradshaw, Ben (1960–)
Labour politician, one of the first openly gay MPs and a cabinet member. He was educated at Thorpe St Andrews Grammar School, Norwich, and the Universities of Sussex and Frieburg. After some time spent teaching and in journalism, he joined the BBC, working in local radio and then on Radio 4's *World at One*. His election campaign in 1997 for the seat of Exeter was bitter, as his openly gay candidacy was opposed by someone from the religious right. He was parliamentary private secretary to John Denham at the Department of Health but became a junior minister in the Foreign Office after 2001. He was deputy leader of the house in 2002 and a junior minister at the Department for the Environment, Food and Rural Affairs 2003–06. In June 2007 he was became as minister of state for health and in June 2009 joined the cabinet as secretary for culture, media and sport. He retained his seat in 2010 by 2,721 votes.

Brandreth, Gyles (1948–)
Conservative MP and diarist. He was educated at Bedales and New College, Oxford, where he was president of the

Oxford Union debating society. He built a career in television, the theatre and writing, especially novels and children's books. Many would have thought him an unlikely politician but he entered the house as MP for Chester in 1992 and became a government whip 1995–97, but was defeated in the 1997 general election. He earns a small footnote in political history through his witty and perceptive diaries published as *Breaking the Code* (1999), which were widely praised.

Branson, Richard (1950–), Sir
Entrepreneur whose gift for publicity led politicians to seek his support. He was educated at Stowe School. He first made money through founding Virgin Records but moved swiftly into air travel, radio, pensions and other enterprises, not all of which proved successful. Political parties wooed him and he gave low-level support to Tony Blair in 1997. There was some talk later that he might stand for London mayor but nothing came of it. In August 2000 his People's Lottery initially defeated Camelot as the agency to run the National Lottery for the next seven years but later he saw this victory overturned in the Court of Appeal. He was knighted in 1999; he has been courted by both main parties but remains unaligned. He is thought to be worth over £3 billion.

Bremner, Rory (1961–)
Britain's premier political satirist. He was educated at Wellington College and King's College, London. He was lauded with awards from BAFTA, RTS and elsewhere and was the nation's favourite impressionist and satirist of politicians. Along with fellow satirists John Bird and John Fortune, his Channel 4 programme became a 'must see' event for anyone interested in British politics and who also had a sense of humour; this, fortunately, seemed to include most of the politicians pilloried on the shows. The arrival of David Cameron and Nick Clegg in power in 2010 posed problems as both are so difficult to impersonate.

Bright, John (1811–89)
One of the leading Radical Liberals of the mid-19th century, who spoke out for trade, peace and reform. He was born in Rochdale and became a leading member of the Anti-Corn Law League after 1839, when he gained a reputation as a brilliantly fiery speaker. After 1843 he was MP for Durham. Later he represented Birmingham and campaigned for what became the second Reform Act (1867). He was briefly president of Board of Trade in 1868 but retired through ill-health in 1870. He returned to office in 1881 as chancellor of the Duchy of Lancaster.

Brittan, Leon (1939–), Lord
Conservative politician who became a cabinet minister and then a European commissioner. He was educated at Cambridge and Harvard, and qualified as a barrister. He became a Conservative MP in 1974 and from 1979 held office under Margaret Thatcher: chief secretary to the Treasury 1981–83 and home secretary 1983–86. He resigned in 1986 over the Westland affair, though most insiders believed him to have taken the blame for the actions of others. He became a European commissioner in 1989, with responsibility for competition policy, and was vice president of the Commission 1995–99. Brittan was not afraid to criticise his Eurosceptic party (though with no discernible effect). His brother is the well known economic journalist Sam Brittan.

Brooks, Rebekah (née Wade) (1968–)
Journalist, former editor of the *Sun* and subsequently chief executive of News International. She was educated at Appleton Hall County Grammar School, Warrington. Her first job was on a French architecture magazine in Paris but she returned to work in Eddie Shah's Messenger group. She joined the *News of the World* in 1989 as a secretary and rose through the ranks to become a feature writer for its Sunday magazine before becoming deputy editor. In 1998 she moved

to become deputy editor of the *Sun* but returned as editor to *News of the World* in 2000. Here she initiated the 'name and shame' campaign against paedophiles. She took over at the *Sun* in 2003. In September 2009 she became chief executive of the paper's parent body News International. In 1996 she married soap actor Ross Kemp and in 2002 was arrested for an alleged assault on her husband but no charges were made. In June 2009 she married Charlie Brooks, a former racehorse trainer and author.

Brown, George (1914–85), Lord

Unpredictable, quick-tempered foreign secretary under Harold Wilson 1966–68. He left school at 15 to become a van driver. He became an official of the Transport and General Workers' Union and established himself as a robust critic of the left. He entered the House of Commons in 1945 and gained junior office. He was minister of works in 1951. His talents, perhaps, suited opposition. He defended the leadership against 'Bevanism' and was elected deputy leader in 1960. He lost to Harold Wilson in the Labour Party leadership election following Hugh Gaitskell's death in 1963. He became secretary of state for economic affairs in 1964. His National Plan for the economy, however, was never really practical or acceptable to the cabinet. He was moved to the Foreign Office, where he pursued his enthusiasm for Europe and hostility to US involvement in Vietnam. He resigned in 1968 over his exclusion from a key economic decision. He went to the Lords after his defeat in 1970 as Lord George Brown but was not offered office again and he became a critic of the government. He joined the Social Democrats in 1982.

Brown, Gordon (1951–)

Labour chancellor and prime minister. He was educated at Edinburgh University, where he gained a first-class history degree and then a doctorate. He entered the house in 1983 for Dunfermline East. At the age of 38 and already a party 'heavyweight', his destructive debating and media-friendly

style placed him top of the party's shadow cabinet poll. In 1994, it was rumoured, he agreed to stand down as the successor to Labour Party leader John Smith, in favour of his friend and colleague the even more telegenic Tony Blair, with whom he had been assiduously 'modernising' the Labour Party. Once in office in 1997 he immediately gave the Bank of England the right to set interest rates, advised by a Monetary Policy Committee. He soon established a reputation as the 'iron chancellor', partly because he insisted on restraining public expenditure for two years. However, in July 1998 he delighted 'Old' Labour by announcing substantial increases in planned social spending over the forthcoming three years. His press advisor Charlie Whelan was criticised for exceeding his authority and misrepresenting Brown's policies as well as urging Brown's advancement to the detriment of other colleagues. Labour's general election victory of June 2001 was widely attributed to Brown's sound record on the economy. He retained his position as chancellor, though talk of rivalry with Blair continued. Brown's dream of becoming prime minister seemed to be no closer in 2004, when the two colleagues are said to have had a huge row. Possibly to assuage Brown, Blair promised to stand down before the next election, allowing time for his successor to bed himself in before the next general election. Brown was reluctant to throw himself into the 2005 election campaign initially but did so in the end to help Blair win a majority of 67. Brown's supporters, however, were still not satisfied with their champion's lack of elevation to the top job and, after a dismal run of political reverses in 2006, a 'coup' was attempted in the autumn, allegedly by 'Brownites'. The Manchester party annual conference succeeded in smoothing over the divisions and Blair eventually agreed to go within a year, most expecting him to go by the summer of 2007. At the end of 2006, Brown could confidently look forward to 2007 as the year in which he would become prime minister, as no credible candidate seemed to be coming forward to challenge him at that time. Eventually Blair departed and Brown was 'crowned' the new king with no contest. Initially he saw his poll ratings rise and there was talk of a 'snap election' to exploit them. However, Brown could not decide and when the Tories' inheritance tax proposal boosted their ratings, Brown decided against an election, though he claimed, feebly, it was not connected with poll ratings. Things seldom improved from then on, with Brown exhibiting no gift for communicating with voters – rather, he failed to inspire or impress. The 2007–09 banking and economic crisis was a severe blow to a government which had relied upon continuing economic growth but Brown's idea of 'fiscal stimulus' via huge influxes of money into banks and the economy probably saved the banks and helped the economy stabilise. In 2008 and 2009 attempts were made to remove Brown but he was able to resist them, latterly with the help of former arch Blairite and mortal enemy now turned ally Peter Mandelson. After Brown became prime minister in 2007 Labour went on to lose four by-elections, lost control of all county councils, lost the London mayoral election and came third, behind the UK Independence Party, in the June 2009 Euro-elections. In May 2010 he was judged third in all three televised leaders' debates and Labour came second in the election, losing over 90 seats. He resigned on 10 May with dignity and left Number 10 with his wife and two sons.

> Many people could outperform Mr Brown on YouTube; very few can claim to have served country and planet with his level of dedication. (*Observer*, 18 May 2010)

Brown, Nick (1950–)
Labour politician and chief whip from 1997. He was educated at Tunbridge Wells Technical School and Manchester University. He was a legal advisor to the GMB union before he entered the House of Commons in 1983 for a Newcastle constituency. He served as Treasury opposition spokesman under Labour leader John Smith. Brown was seen as a loyal

supporter of Gordon Brown. In office after 1997 he had a difficult time at the Ministry of Agriculture, Fisheries and Food (MAFF), both through the tail-end of the crisis over bovine spongiform encephalitis ('mad cow disease') and the epidemic of foot-and-mouth disease in 2001, which he was perceived to have handled ineptly. In June 2001 he lost his job at MAFF, which was subsumed into a new ministry, but was appointed to the ministry of work and pensions as minister for work. Brown reappointed him for a second spell as chief whip in June 2009.

Brown, Simon (1938–), Lord Justice
Intelligence services commissioner from 2000. He was a judge of the High Court Queen's Bench Division 1984–92 and lord justice of appeal from 1992. He was appointed commissioner for security services under the Security Act 1994 and then for intelligence services under the Regulation of Investigatory Powers Act 2000.

Browne, Des (1952–)
Labour MP and defence secretary. He was educated in the Catholic St Michael's Academy, Kilwinning, and then Glasgow University, where he studied law. After practising as a solicitor he won Argyll and Bute in 1997. He served as a junior minister in the Northern Ireland Department and the Department for Work and Pensions, and was chief secretary to the Treasury before becoming defence secretary in May 2006. He was given additional responsibility as secretary of state for Scotland when Gordon Brown became prime minister but stood down in October 2008. He did not stand for re-election and was made a life peer in May 2010.

Budd, Alan (1937–), Sir
Head of the Office of Budget Responsibility from May 2010. He was educated in Oundle School, then the London School of Economics and Cambridge. He taught at Southampton University and universities in the USA and Australia. He was senior economic advisor to the Treasury 1970–74

and director of the Centre for Economic
Forecasting at the London Business School
during the 1980s. He sat on a number of
government committees, the most important
of which was the Monetary Policy
Committee, set up by Gordon Brown to
advise on interests rates in 1997.

Burke, Edmund (1729–97)

Great Conservative thinker. He was born
in Dublin and educated at Trinity College.
He became secretary for Ireland but is
better known as the major philosophical
founder of modern Conservatism. He was
horrified by the French Revolution and
asserted that humans are not able to change
their basic nature; thus change has to be
slow and gradual, and continuity between
past, present and future is essential for
stability. He also supported the right of
the American colonists to oppose taxation
without representation and insisted the
duty of an MP is not to reflect the views of
constituents but to use judgement on their
behalf in the government of the country.

> All government – indeed every human bene-
> fit and enjoyment and every prudent act – is
> founded on compromise and barter. (1775)

> The only thing necessary for the triumph of
> evil is that good men do nothing.

Burnham, Andrew (1970–)

Labour MP for Leigh and cabinet member.
He was secretary for culture and sport
from January 2008 and secretary for health
from June 2009. He was born in Liverpool
and grew up in Warrington, where he
attended St Aelred's Roman Catholic High
School. He went on to Fitzwilliam College,
Cambridge. Joining the Labour Party at 14
he did a number of researcher jobs before
becoming special advisor to Chris Smith
at the Department for Culture, Media and
Sport in 1998. He was elected for Leigh in
2001. After stints as parliamentary private
secretary to David Blunkett and Ruth Kelly,
he was made a junior minister at the Home
Office. In May 2006 he became a minister
of state at the Department of Health.
Gordon Brown appointed him to the cabinet

as chief secretary to the Treasury in June
2007. His expenses claims for his London
flat were criticised as excessive in June 2009.
He retained his seat in 2010 with a majority
of 12,011. In May 2010 he declared himself
a candidate for the Labour leadership.

Butler, David (1924–)

Political scientist. He was educated at
St Paul's and New College, Oxford.
He became a fellow at Nuffield College,
Oxford, where he established himself as the
'father' of modern psephology, the study of
voting behaviour. He has appeared regularly
on television and has written, with a variety
of collaborators, the series of Nuffield
studies on British general elections.

Butler, Richard Austen ('Rab') (1902–82)

Conservative politician, cabinet minister,
thinker and candidate for leadership who
never quite made it. He was educated
at Marlborough and Cambridge, where
he became a fellow before he entered the
Commons for Saffron Walden in 1929. He
served as a junior minister before becoming
minister of education 1941–45. His name
is still associated with the Education Act
1944, which reorganised secondary education and introduced the much criticised
11-plus examination. He was chancellor
1951–55 before he went on to become a
liberal home secretary 1957–62. Harold
Macmillan believed him to be unsuited
to leadership at the very top and did his
(successful) best to frustrate Butler's efforts
to achieve the premiership. Consequently
Butler failed to win the succession to
Anthony Eden in 1957, losing out to
Macmillan, who also prevented him gaining
the prize when he retired through ill-health
in 1963. Butler served briefly as foreign
secretary under Alec Douglas-Home. In
1964 he became master of Trinity College,
Cambridge, and a peer. He was one of
the most able and thoughtful Conservative
politicians of his generation, very much
of the consensual school but ultimately
perhaps lacking the steel, and the luck, to
become prime minister.

Butler, (Frederick Edward) Robin (1938–), Lord

Able British 'mandarin' who rose to be head of the civil service. He was educated at Harrow and University College, Oxford, where he was a rugby blue and later played first-class rugby for Harlequins. He joined the Treasury in 1961, was principal private secretary to Edward Heath 1972–74 and Harold Wilson 1974–75; then principal private secretary to the prime minister 1982–85, permanent secretary at the Treasury 1985–87, secretary to the cabinet and head of the civil service 1988–97. He served five prime ministers in all, including Tony Blair for a short time before retiring and being raised to a life peerage. In February 2004 was called back from retirement to chair an inquiry into the intelligence upon which the decision to go to war against Iraq had been based. He was the archetypal smooth mandarin, with the traditional upper-middle-class background, who, in the classic mode, seemed to achieve his success effortlessly.

> The deal is that you give people very considerable power for five years and then they can be thrown out. And, in the meantime, if things get bad enough, there are ways of getting rid of them. That is the deal of our constitution. (1998)

> What can a few special advisers do against thousands of civil servants? We'll swat them like flies. (Butler quoted in the *Times*, 3 February 2004)

Byers, Stephen (1953–)

Labour politician and cabinet minister. He was educated at Chester City Grammar School and Liverpool Polytechnic. He became a lecturer at Newcastle Polytechnic before becoming MP for Wallsend in 1992. He was education spokesman in opposition. After the 1997 general election he became a junior minister at the Department of Education and Employment, then in July 1997 he moved to the Treasury as chief secretary. Byers was an earnest Blairite high-flier and was even mentioned as a potential future leader, though critics complained that he had little charisma. In June

2001 he moved to secretary for transport and local government, where he inherited problems from deputy prime minister John Prescott, who had had responsibility in this area. Byers ran into heavy criticism from the right and from the world of finance for declaring Railtrack bankrupt and appointing a receiver. He also attracted criticism for supporting the private–public partnership favoured by chancellor Gordon Brown for the London Underground. His cup of woe overflowed in February 2002 when he faced a scandal involving his political advisor Jo Moore and his press secretary Martin Sixsmith. To make matters even worse he was blamed for a financial crisis involving the National Air Traffic Services (NATS). Byers survived one crisis of confidence in the autumn of 2001 through the support he commanded from the Labour back benches over his Railtrack moves, which forced the privatised company into a kind of renationalisation. However, such support could not stop the gaffes and alleged misleading statements to the House of Commons taking their toll and in May 2002 he resigned and returned to the back benches. After Gordon Brown became prime minister Byers criticised aspects of his government. He was also caught up in accusations of over-claiming on his expenses after revelations in the *Daily Telegraph*. In March 2010 Byers, along with Geoff Hoon and Patricia Hewitt, was caught by undercover journalists, agreeing to sell his services as a lobbyist for several thousand pounds per day.

C

Cable, Vince (1943–)

Liberal Democrat MP for Twickenham since 1997 and deputy leader of the party since 2006. Educated at Nunthorpe Grammar School and Cambridge

University, where he was president of the Union, 1965. He was awarded a PhD in economics at Glasgow University. He lectured at Glasgow University and at the London School of Economics. He worked in Kenya for a while, was chief advisor to John Smith when he was industry secretary and chief economist at Shell, 1995. Initially a Labour councillor, he joined the Social Democratic Party in 1981, finally winning Twickenham a decade and a half later. In 2005 he was instrumental in persuading Charles Kennedy to quit as leader and in 2006 passed up the chance of standing in a leadership contest he might well have won, in order to back Ming Campbell. He became even more respected during the 2007–09 financial crisis and popular with voters, something which his expertise as a ballroom dancer served to enhance. (Cable danced on television with *Strictly Come Dancing* winner Alesah Dixon.) In May 2010 he became business secretary as a member of the Liberal Democrat–Tory coalition.

Callaghan, James (1912–2005), Lord
Labour prime minister 1976–79. He was born in Portsmouth. He joined the civil service in 1929, became involved in trade union matters, and served in the Royal Navy during the war as a midshipman. He was elected MP for South Cardiff in 1945 but rose to prominence in the 1960s when he was chancellor 1964–67 and home secretary 1967–70. In Harold Wilson's second administration he was foreign secretary 1974–76 and after Wilson's surprise resignation became prime minister 1976–79. As premier he operated with relaxed aplomb and survived some awesome financial crises as well as the two-year period when he had to operate with the support of the Liberals (the Lib–Lab pact of 1977–79). His decision to peg wage increases to 5 per cent in 1978 proved unacceptable to the Trades Union Congress and the so-called 'winter of discontent' of industrial unrest resulted. This destroyed the authority of the government and the notion that it could

keep the unions in check. Callaghan lost the 1979 general election but remained as leader of the opposition until 1980, when he resigned. He took up a seat in the Lords in 1987. He was the only prime minister to have served beforehand in all three of the great offices of state and he proved remarkably effective as the incumbent of Number 10. As his luck ran out towards the end of the 1970s, when events began to engulf him, his political judgement as to when to go to the country deserted him also.

> Crisis? What crisis? (*Sun* headline, 11 January 1979, which wrongly quoted the prime minister at a press conference in which he had actually said 'I don't think that other people in the world would share the view that there is mounting chaos')

> You can never reach the promised land. You can march towards it. (1978)

Cameron, David (1966–)
Leader of the Conservative Party from 2005 and prime minister from May 2010. Born to a stockbroker with family links to King William IV and married to the daughter of a baronet, Cameron certainly has a privileged social background. An education at Eton and then Oxford continued this pattern. While joining in the usual dissipations of student life, he was sufficiently assiduous to gain a first in philosophy, politics and economics (PPE) and was described by Professor Vernon Bogdanor as one of his 'ablest students', who had 'sensible Conservative views'. He worked in the Conservative Research Department 1988–92, also assisting Number 10 at the same time. He then worked as an advisor to chancellor Norman Lamont and later to Michael Howard at the Home Office. From 1994 to 2005 he was director corporate affairs at Carlton Communications. He was elected as MP for Witney 2001 and soon made his mark as a promising backbencher. It was no surprise when he put himself forward as a candidate in the election to replace Michael Howard after the Conservatives' defeat in the 2005 election. At the 2005 party conference he made an immense

impression with a speech in the leadership contest, arguing for a rethink of the party's policies and branding. In December he was elected by the membership as leader and then set about moving the party from the right into the centre on such matters as taxation (no immediate cuts), the National Health Service (more market reforms), education (more power to headmasters), social issues (pro-gay marriages), and law and order (more understanding for young law-breakers). While more traditional Conservatives like Lord Tebbit and the *Daily Telegraph* were slightly appalled by these changes, they succeeded in altering public perceptions of the party, which, by the autumn of 2006, was winning leads over Labour in the polls. Cameron was at the time criticised for being too much like Tony Blair and for featuring his disabled son, Ivan, too much in photo-shoots (Ivan died in 2009). During the MPs' expenses crisis in 2009 he took a very tough line, assuming this was in tune with the mood of voters. However, some of his own MPs complained that while he was being very tough with some of the better-established backbenchers, he was less tough with his own close aides and members of his shadow cabinet. By autumn 2009 his party had enjoyed a year of unopposed electoral success at the local level and in by-elections, and few believed Labour would be able to prevent a Conservative victory in 2010. In the event, he did not win an overall majority. The Conservatives, though, formed a coalition with Nick Clegg's Liberal Democrats and Cameron became prime minister in May 2010.

Campbell, Alastair (1950–)

Famously tough press secretary to Tony Blair from 1994. After Oxford Campbell entered journalism, specialising in the tabloids: he was political editor for the *Daily Mirror* and *Today*, where he was a colourful Fleet Street figure known for a taste for alcohol and with a quick temper. In 1994 he became Blair's press secretary – technically a civil servant though his role was intensely political. He quickly gained

a reputation for aggression towards the Conservative press and fierce loyalty to his boss, which virtually equalled that of Bernard Ingham, Margaret Thatcher's formidable equivalent during the Tory 1980s. Some commentators described him as the second most powerful man in the government – the 'deputy prime minister', even though in June 1998 he assured the Public Administration Committee he was no more than a humble 'mouthpiece'. In 2000 he was given a new title – director of communications and strategy – and a less conspicuous role, as the chore of daily press briefings was given to his deputy, Godric Smith. In the summer of 2002 New Labour was engaged in a bitter war with the media and some, including Roy Hattersley, a former deputy leader of the party, blamed part of the trouble on a press secretary who had outlived his usefulness and should go. By the summer of 2003 Campbell had been hit by the aftermath of the war on Iraq, when attention focused on how the case for war had been presented. Campbell himself was accused by the BBC of having 'sexed up' an intelligence-based dossier issued in September 2002 to justify the attack on Iraq. Campbell demanded an apology but the exposure of the BBC's source, Dr David Kelly, an advisor to the Ministry of Defence, was quickly followed by his tragic suicide. This prompted the Hutton inquiry, out of which Campbell emerged officially exonerated but hardly spotless. However, he had already resigned in September, apparently of his own volition, though the criticism occasioned by Hutton made his going opportune. He denied his diaries – quotations from which had an explosive effect at the Hutton investigations – were intended for publication, but few believed him. His decision to take to the 'road' with a stage show in January 2004 was initially successful, though attendances dropped off. Campbell had officially stood down from Blair's side by the time of the 2005 election but he returned to offer advice. He also kept a voluminous diary, parts of which were published in *The Blair Years* (2007).

When Gordon Brown became prime minister in 2007 Campbell still continued to advise from time to time and was a major advisor on the 2010 election campaign.

> G[eoff] H[oon] and I agreed it would fuck Gilligan if that was his source. (Campbell's diary, read in evidence to the Hutton inquiry, 22 September 2003, in which he and the defence secretary agreed the exposure of David Kelly's name would help his side of his row with the BBC)

> This is diary writing – it doesn't actually express what is going on. It's me, at the end of the day, scribbling whatever comes into my head. (Evidence to Hutton, 22 September 2003)

Campbell, Menzies ('Ming') (1941–)

Leader of the Liberal Democrats, March 2006–October 2007. 'Ming' Campbell was educated at Hillhead High School and Glasgow University, where he studied law. In 1964 he represented Britain in the Tokyo Olympics and held the British record for the 100 metres 1967–74. He became a barrister in 1968 and a QC in 1982. He entered the Commons for North East Fife in 1987 and soon specialised in foreign affairs, becoming his party's spokesman in 1992 and shadow foreign secretary in 1997. In 2002 he recovered from lymphatic cancer. From 2003 he acted as deputy leader and strongly opposed the decision to invade Iraq. He attacked Tony Blair's policy of 'undue deference' to the USA. This position, apparently justified by the failure of the invasion, gave him a high profile in the party, which in turn helped make him the front runner when Charles Kennedy stood down as leader early in 2006 as a result of his drinking problems. In the resultant leadership contest, Campbell beat Chris Huhne by 30,000 votes to 22,000 in the second ballot. Initially he faced criticism for being ineffective at prime minister's questions but by the time of the party conference in September 2006 he had established himself as a respected leader of his party. However, criticism of his performance as leader continued. In October he finally

stood down and Nick Clegg took over. He expressed support for the Liberal Democrat–Tory coalition in 2010.

Campbell-Bannerman, Henry (1836–1908)

Liberal prime minister 1905–08. He was educated at Glasgow High School and Cambridge. He was Liberal MP for Stirling Burghs 1868–1908 and held junior office in the War Office and Admiralty before becoming secretary for war 1892–95. He became leader of the Liberal Party when Herbert Asquith was seen as too young for the job and managed to hold a divided party together during the Boer war, which he and David Lloyd George opposed. When the Conservative prime minister Arthur Balfour resigned in December 1905, thinking the Liberals would be even more divided than the Conservatives, Campbell-Bannerman took office. He proved an astute and effective manager of his party and led it to the historic 1906 landslide election victory. The unassuming typical Liberal, 'CB' ended up leading a great reforming administration and succeeded in harnessing the talents of the likes of Asquith and Lloyd George. He resigned in 1908 through ill-health and died shortly afterwards; having stayed on in Downing Street after his resignation, he is the only (former) prime minister to have died there.

Carey, George (1935–)

Archbishop of Canterbury. Born in London's East End he failed his 11-plus and was educated at Bifron Secondary Modern School, Barking. As an adult, he studied at King's College, London, and gained a doctorate. He was appointed archbishop in 1991, as someone with an evangelical tinge to his Christianity. He took a conservative line on homosexuality in the 1998 Lambeth Conference votes. He was succeeded in 2002 by Rowan Williams.

Carrington, Peter (1919–), Lord

Conservative politician in office in the late 20th century. He trained in Sandhurst and won the Military Cross in the Second World War. He held junior posts in government in the early 1950s before becoming high commissioner to Australia 1956–59, first lord of the Admiralty 1959–63 and leader of the House of Lords 1963–64. He was defence secretary under Edward Heath 1970–74 and briefly energy secretary in 1974, while also chairman of the Conservative Party 1972–74. He was foreign secretary 1979–82 but resigned over the Falklands crisis. He was secretary general of NATO 1984–88. Carrington was one of those competent, loyal, aristocratic (and in his case very clubbable) Conservatives who devoted their lives to public service and occupied Tory cabinets out of a sense of *noblesse oblige*. It was in character that he should tender his resignation over the Falklands when, arguably, others were more responsible.

Carter, Stephen (1964–), Lord

Labour peer and minister for communications. He was educated at Curie High School and Aberdeen University, where he studied law. He later studied at the London and Harvard Business Schools. He became managing director of J. Walter Thompson's in 1995 and chief executive in 1997. He then moved to NTL, where he managed the company's bankruptcy. In 2003 he became chief executive of media watchdog Ofcom. In January 2008 he became Gordon Brown's chief of strategy and principal advisor – though it would be hard to accept such advice had especially helped him politically. In October 2008, Carter was made parliamentary under-secretary of state for communications, technology and broadcasting. In June 2009, following the publication of his report *Digital Britain*, he announced he was resigning from government after 18 months in post.

> What I tell them is nine-tenths bullshit and one-tenth selected facts. (Carter's alleged comment about NTL shareholders)

Cash, Bill (1940–)

Conservative MP and noted Eurosceptic. He was educated at Stonyhurst College

and Oxford, and went on to practise as a solicitor. He was known as a monomaniac Europhobe who was central to the rebellions over this subject during John Major's troubled years as prime minister (1992–97). Colleagues complained he bored them relentlessly on his pet subject and many were surprised, especially on the moderate wing of the party, when in September 2001 the new Conservative leader, Iain Duncan Smith, appointed him to a senior shadow job, claiming it would require a much wider knowledge than merely things European. Under Michael Howard, however, he did not receive similar or indeed any preference. He successfully defended his constituency of Stone in 2010.

Castle, Barbara (1911–2000), Baroness

Labour cabinet minister during the 1960s and 1970s. She was educated at Bradford Girls' Grammar School and St Hugh's College, Oxford. She worked as a journalist before the Second World War and entered the House of Commons in 1945 for Blackburn. She was a supporter of Aneurin Bevan and a chair of the Labour Party in the 1950s. She served as minister of overseas development 1964–65, transport 1965–68 (where she introduced the breathalyser and the 70 mph limit) and employment and productivity 1968–70. She was minister of health and social security 1974–76 but was not a favourite of James Callaghan and returned to the back benches when he came to power in 1976. She acted as vice chair of the socialist group in the European parliament 1979–84 and campaigned for better pensions during the 1990s. As a much-respected Labour veteran, the New Labour hierarchy allowed her to have her say but chose to disregard her advice. She was ennobled in 1990.

Chamberlain, Austen (1863–1937)

Conservative chancellor 1903–05 and 1919–21, leader of the party 1921–22, and foreign secretary 1924–29. He was the eldest son of Joseph Chamberlain and was educated at Rugby and Trinity College, Cambridge. He was returned as MP for East Worcester in 1892 and soon began to climb the ladder into the cabinet. In the wartime coalition government he was secretary for India 1915–17. Following Andrew Bonar Law's resignation he was elected leader of the Conservative Party 1921–22. He was opposed to back-bench pressure to end the coalition government with the Liberals, but in 1922 the famous meeting in the Carlton Club voted to take Law and Baldwin's advice to end it. While foreign secretary 1924–29 he negotiated the 1925 Locarno pact, which many thought was a guarantee against a renewed outbreak of war, and for which he was awarded the Nobel Peace Prize in 1925. He was a sensitive man who somewhat misjudged the political climate of his times and consequently arguably missed being made prime minister.

A man who played the game and always lost. (Winston Churchill's acid comment on Austen Chamberlain)

All governments are pretty much alike, with the tendency, on the part of the last, to be the worst. (1911)

Chamberlain, Joseph (1836–1914)

Liberal politician and secretary of state for the colonies 1895–1903, who split his party over Irish home rule. He was educated at University College School, which he left aged 16, and then went to work for Nettlefolds screw factory, from which he retired in 1874 a wealthy man, aged 38. He began his political career as a Radical councillor and then mayor of Birmingham 1873–76, where he made a reputation as something of a 'machine politician', even in those days. He entered the House of Commons for Birmingham via a by-election in 1876 and by 1880 was president of the Board of Trade and then president of the Local Government Board in 1886, but was seen in cabinet as an extremist by some. He resigned over William Gladstone's home rule plans for Ireland and went on to lead a faction called the Liberal Unionists, who were destined to merge

with the Conservatives. In the Conservative government of 1895 he was colonial secretary but, unlike the Radical Liberals, supported the Boer war. He resigned in 1903 to advocate tariff reform to protect British industries from foreign competition. In 1906 he suffered a stroke, which drove him out of public life, though he lived on for several more years. He was one of the great talents of 19th-century politics but never quite fulfilled his potential.

The day of small nations has passed away. The day of Empires has come. (1904)

The manners of a cad and the tongue of a bargee. (H. H. Asquith on Chamberlain, 1900)

Chamberlain, Neville (1869–1940)

Conservative chancellor 1923–24 and 1931–37, and prime minister 1937–40. He was the son of Joseph Chamberlain by second marriage. He was educated at Rugby and Mason College, Birmingham, and became a successful businessman in his own right before serving as lord mayor of Birmingham 1915–16. Then he entered national politics as Conservative MP for Birmingham Ladywood. He was a minister in his early 20s and then chancellor until 1924, followed by a period as minister of health. In 1931 he was appointed chancellor again and remained in the post until 1937, when he became prime minister. He was out of his depth in foreign affairs and was unable to gauge the danger of Hitler – he believed a policy of appeasement was morally and politically justified. In 1938 he returned from Munich with an agreement which he thought offered 'peace in our time' but it soon fell apart and he was forced to declare war: the direct opposite of his policy objective. As the war went against Britain in the early months the Conservative Party turned against him and in a crucial vote of confidence he could muster a majority of only 80 instead of the party's 200. He therefore resigned as prime minister (though not as party leader) before ill-health forced him to allow Winston Churchill to take over, with historic consequences. He died, of cancer, a broken man, six months later.

Some defend his appeasement policy for allowing Britain to gather strength in time to cope with the war when it came.

> How horrible, fantastic, incredible it is that we should be digging trenches and trying on gas-masks here because of a quarrel between people in a faraway country of whom we know nothing. (Reference to Czechoslovakia in a radio broadcast, 27 September 1938)

> This is the second time in our history that there has come back from Germany to Downing Street, peace with honour. I believe it is peace for our time. (From a window in Number 10 Downing Street, on returning from Munich, 30 September 1938)

Charles, Prince of Wales (1948–)

Heir to the throne. He was educated at Gordonstoun School and Cambridge University. He also studied Welsh at Aberystwyth University for a while in 1969. Faced with the problem of a high public profile and the longevity of his mother, Charles busied himself with the Prince's Trust, which seeks to put young people into worthwhile work. He also advocated traditional opinions on architecture and conservationist ones on the environment. His disastrous marriage to Diana left him appearing more the sinner than the sinned against, though after her death the press presented him more favourably as a father trying desperately hard to bring up his two sons in a loving fashion. His affair with Camilla Parker Bowles was not popular with the public and he tried to usher her into the public limelight discreetly, preparing the way for the more permanent connection which occurred in April 2005 when they married. He continued with his campaigns and enthusiasms – still uneasy with his position but, to his credit, still trying to perform a useful role in public life.

Churchill, Winston (1874–1965)

Heroic, world-famous, long-serving states-man whose career spanned two centuries and included most of the senior political offices. He was the son of Lord Randolph Churchill and was educated at Harrow and Sandhurst. His life was quite astonishing in its longevity, variety, excitement and historic achievement. He joined the 4th Hussars in 1895 and fought at Omdurman. He reported the Boer war as a journalist. He became Conservative MP for Oldham in 1900 but joined the Liberals in 1904 and served in junior office before becoming president of the Board of Trade 1908–10 and home secretary 1910–11, first lord of the Admiralty 1911 and munitions minister in David Lloyd George's wartime government 1917, war minister 1919–21 and, from 1924 when he rejoined the Conservatives, chancellor until 1929. During the 1930s he inveighed against the spinelessness of the national government in the face of the threat of fascism and as a result of his furious assaults on appeasement was regarded by his party as a dangerous maverick. In 1939 he returned to the Admiralty in Neville Chamberlain's wartime coalition government and when Chamberlain fell in 1940 Churchill took over as prime minister. This was the greatest period of his career, perhaps of any British political career, when he promised the country nothing except 'blood, toil, tears and sweat'. After working closely with the Allies and under his inspiring leadership, in which his gift of oratory ranked as a major weapon in the war, Britain eventually emerged triumphant. However, a country transformed by war denied him re-election and he led the opposition – not with conspicuous distinction – until 1951, when he became prime minister again. He finally retired in 1955. During this final phase he was sick and for a while, after he suffered a stroke, the government was run discreetly in his name. As well as a great orator he was also an accomplished writer and journalist. He wrote enthralling histories of the English-speaking peoples and the Second World War; he was awarded the Nobel Prize for Literature in 1950.

> I have nothing to offer but blood, toil, tears and sweat. (4 June 1940)

> We shall fight them on the beaches, we shall fight them on the landing grounds, we shall fight them in the fields and streets. (4 June 1940)

If the British Empire and Commonwealth last for a thousand years, men will say, 'This was their finest hour'. (Anticipating the Battle of Britain, September 1940)

From Stettin in the Baltic to Trieste in the Adriatic, an iron curtain has descended across the Continent. (Fulton, Missouri, 5 March 1946)

Victory at all costs, victory in spite of all terror, victory however long and hard the road may be, for without victory there is no survival. (1940)

Give us the tools and we will finish the job. (1941)

Clark, Alan (1928–99)

Conservative politician, historian and diarist. He was educated at Eton and Christ Church, Oxford, and became a member of the Household Cavalry and a barrister. He was MP for Plymouth Sutton 1974–92, then retired from politics, but he decided to return in 1997, for Kensington and Chelsea. An ardent Thatcher supporter, he was a junior minister for employment and defence, where, as a minister of state, he admitted the defendants in the Matrix Churchill affair had been 'tipped the wink' by the government regarding how to sell arms to the Middle East which ended up in Iraq. He is best known for his witty and scandalous diaries, published in 1993 and later televised. His abilities – and ambitions for cabinet office – were not taken as seriously by the higher echelons of the party as he took them himself.

Clarke, Charles (1950–)

Labour MP and cabinet minister. He was educated at Highgate School and King's College, London, as well as Cambridge. He was president of National Union of Students in the 1970s. He was elected to the House of Commons for Norwich South in 1997, after working as chief of staff to Neil Kinnock. In 1999 he became a Home Office minister and he was soon tipped as a 'coming man' and even possible future leader. He was promoted to cabinet in 2001 as party chair. This resembled Conservative practice – Clarke

was paid a cabinet minister's salary but by the Labour Party and not the taxpayer. He saw his role as assisting the delivery of the election promises by reconnecting the government with the party membership (which was falling). Critics pointed out that the party already had a chairperson elected by the party's National Executive Committee. He was appointed secretary of state for education when Estelle Morris resigned unexpectedly in autumn 2002. He was home secretary 2004–06 but was forced to resign some months after the April 2006 'foreign prisoners' scandal rocked the government. This involved over 1,000 prisoners – some in prison for the most serious of crimes – who should have been deported upon release. He survived a few weeks until May but was then axed in a reshuffle. From the back benches he was outspoken in criticising colleagues, especially John Reid, his successor as home secretary, and Gordon Brown. He also tried to suggest new policy themes for the Labour Party. He lost his Norwich South seat narrowly in May 2010.

Clarke, Kenneth (1940–)

Conservative politician and versatile cabinet minister. He was educated at Nottingham High School and Cambridge University. He practised as a barrister before being elected MP for Nottingham Rushcliffe in 1970. He became a member of the 'one nation' Bow Group and served as junior minister under Edward Heath 1970–74 but won senior office under Margaret Thatcher. He became health secretary in 1988. Under John Major he was home secretary 1992 and chancellor of the exchequer 1993–97. He stood for the leadership of his party in 1997, in the wake of its general election defeat, but was beaten by William Hague, even though he made a surprising alliance with fellow candidate John Redwood. In the wake of the 2001 general election defeat Clarke was initially absent on a business trip to Vietnam in pursuance of his (not uncriticised) role as deputy chairman of the British American Tobacco Company. However, he returned to declare his candidature in late June, though refused to compromise on his robustly pro-Europe views. In the first ballot he polled a disappointing 36 and came third. In the second round he increased his votes to 39 but few expected his winning 59 in the third ballot on 17 July. Some predicted more 'civil war' over Europe with a right-wing Iain Duncan Smith pitted against him for the party members' ballot. However, the ballot by party members, used for the first time by the Conservatives to elect a leader, found heavily for the Eurosceptic, more right-wing Duncan Smith in September 2001. He chose not to contest the leadership in 2003 but did so in 2005, when he was eliminated in the first round. David Cameron made him chair of his 'democracy task force' and in January 2009 brought him back into the shadow cabinet to take the business portfolio, shadowing Peter Mandelson. Clarke is unusual in frontline politics for having a full 'outside' life, involving jazz – he presented an authoritative Radio 4 programme on it – as well as bird-watching, political history and supporting Nottingham Forest. He is also unusual for being scrupulous in speaking the truth as he sees it, even when – as on the European Union and his opposition to the Iraq war – his views embarrass his party. This might explain why he has consistently been the most popular Conservative politician without ever being elected leader. He easily retained his seat in 2010, whereupon he was made secretary of state for justice and lord chancellor (some were hoping he would be made chancellor of the exchequer).

Clegg, Nick (1967–)
Leader of Liberal Democrats from 2007 and deputy prime minister from May 2010. He was educated Westminster School and Cambridge University. He spent time, when younger, campaigning, writing a thesis on 'deep green' ideas, working for Christopher Hitchens at *The Nation*, more generally as a journalist and then in Brussels working for the Commission. He served as an MEP 1999–2004 and was

then elected MP for Sheffield Hallam in 2005. His leadership period has been generally thought a qualified success; his party's poll ratings overtook Labour in May 2009. His performance in the televised leaders' debates catapulted his party into a three-way contest for the 2010 election. His final tally of seats – 57 – was disappointing but his coalition with the Tories elevated him to deputy prime minister.

Cobden, Richard (1804–65)
Early Radical Liberal. He was born in Sussex but educated in Yorkshire, and settled in Manchester as a calico merchant in 1831. He became an advocate of free trade. He contested the Stockport seat in 1837 on a free trade ticket but lost. He became the most prominent member of the Anti-Corn Law League and was returned for Stockport in 1841. He spoke regularly against the Corn Laws, which were repealed in 1846 once Peel, leader of the Conservatives, was won over. With John Bright he opposed the Crimean war and Henry Palmerston's foreign policy in China. He supported the North during the US Civil War. He was one of the great radical politicians of the 19th century and was dubbed 'the apostle of free trade'.

Cockerell, Michael (1940–)
Distinguished British broadcaster and journalist, specialising in documentary profiles of senior politicians. He was educated at Corpus Christi College, Oxford, then joined the BBC, where he reported for the current affairs programme *Panorama*, before moving into documentaries, especially biographical profiles of the likes of Roy Jenkins, Edward Heath, Margaret Thatcher and Barbara Castle. He presented a series called *The Great Offices of State* (BBC 4, 2010), on the Home Office, the Foreign Office and the Treasury.

Cohen, Nick (1960–)
Journalist on the *Observer* and author/broadcaster. He was educated in Manchester and later Hertford College,

Oxford, where he read philosophy, politics and economics (PPE). He was a constant critic of Tony Blair's foreign policy and of him personally for mendacity and other crimes. His books include: *Cruel Britannia: Reports on the Sinister and the Preposterous* (1999); *Pretty Straight Guys* (2003), a highly critical account of the New Labour project; *What's Left?* (2007), which he describes as the story of how the liberal left of the 20th century came to support the far right of the 21st; and *Waiting for the Etonians: Reports from the Sickbed of Liberal England* (2009).

Coke, Edward (1552–1634)
Leading Elizabethan jurist who provided the definitive writings on the common law. The product of Norfolk gentry, he settled in London and soon became a leading lawyer under Elizabeth I, becoming her solicitor general and then attorney general. In this role he prosecuted Sir Walter Raleigh and the Gunpowder Plot conspirators. In 1613 he became lord chief justice. He demonstrated great respect for the common law – something resented by monarchs, who had statute law to set against it. He insisted the royal will had to submit to the common law, thus providing grounds for the Levellers and American revolutionaries.

Conway, Derek (1953–)
Conservative MP caught up in the early stages of the MPs' expenses scandal. He was educated at Beacon Hill Comprehensive and at Newcastle Polytechnic. He was elected to Gateshead council aged 21 and became Conservative leader in 1974. He was elected to the Commons in 1983 for Shrewsbury and Atcham. He held the seat until defeated in 1997. He served as parliamentary private secretary to Wyn Roberts in the Welsh Office 1988 and Michael Forsyth in the Scottish Office 1992. In 1993 he became a government whip and remained so until he lost his seat in 1997. He returned to the Commons in 2001 for Bexley and Old Sidcup. Conway became embroiled in scandal when it was revealed his son

Freddie, a full-time student at Newcastle University, was employed as a researcher. Over three years his pay amounted to over £40,000. The Standards and Privileges Committee criticised this arrangement in January 2008 and David Cameron withdrew the Conservative whip from him, effectively expelling him from the parliamentary party. His second son, Henry, was also said to be employed on a similar basis. Conway's travails merely anticipated those of so many MPs when the full row over expenses broke in May–June 2009. In his book *The Political Animal* (2002), Jeremy Paxman recounts Conway's reflections on losing his seat in 1997: "'Had it not been for James Goldsmith's intervention I'd have won. He died of pancreatic cancer," he [Conway] says, and then adds in the most chilling tone, "I hear it's the most painful of deaths. I'm so pleased.'"

Cook, Robin (1946–2005)
Labour MP and foreign secretary. He studied at Edinburgh University and trained as a teacher before becoming MP in 1974 for Edinburgh Central; after 1983 he represented Livingston. He served in the shadow Treasury team 1980–83, before taking on health and social security 1987–92. After Labour leader John Smith died in 1994 he became spokesman on trade and industry and then, under Tony Blair, foreign affairs 1994–97. After Labour's election victory he served as foreign secretary 1997–2001. Generally seen as the cleverest member of Labour's front bench, he lacked television appeal and his divorce and remarriage (1997/98) earned him unflattering publicity. The general opinion of commentators – though the view was contested – was that this fearsomely intellectually able man under-performed in office and was prone to misjudgements. He introduced an awkwardly 'ethical dimension' into foreign policy, although many diplomats doubted whether the national self-interest could be reconciled with consistently high moral principles. His negotiation of the end of the Kosovan war was widely regarded as a success. In June

2001 his demotion to leader of the house and Jack Straw's appointment to Cook's old job was the surprise of the post-election reshuffle. There were some early signs that in his new role he might seek to strengthen parliament against the executive. His reforms in autumn 2002 were welcomed by reformers but few felt the balance of power had been altered. In March 2003 he resigned over the imminent war in Iraq and made an impressive, principled speech in support of his decision. He thereupon became a measured critic of the government's foreign policy from the back benches. Cook was a well known aficionado of horse-racing and something of a *bon viveur*. His marriage broke down shortly after the 1997 election and he married his former secretary, Gaynor, in 1998. He worked hard and successfully to heal the major rift he had with Gordon Brown and there was speculation in 2005 that he would return to government when his former enemy stepped up to take over. However, this was not to be: in August 2005, aged 59, he died of a heart attack when walking in the Scottish hills. At a time when Labour was striving to find a new rationale and mission, his absence was keenly felt.

> Bin Laden was, though, a product of a monumental miscalculation by western security agencies. Throughout the 80s he was armed by the CIA and funded by the Saudis to wage jihad against the Russian occupation of Afghanistan. Al-Qaida, literally 'the database', was originally the computer file of the thousands of mujahideen who were recruited and trained with help from the CIA to defeat the Russians. (*Guardian*, 25 July 2005)

> Our foreign policy must have an ethical dimension. (1997)

Coulson, Andy (1968–)
Journalist and director communications for the Conservative Party under David Cameron. He attended Beauchamps Comprehensive School, 1979–86. He began work on a local paper but soon moved to the *Sun* to work with Piers Morgan on the show-biz page. After

working briefly on the *Daily Mail* he returned to the *Sun* and then moved to the *News of the World* as editor in 2003, replacing Rebekah Wade. He resigned in January 2007 when involved in journalists tapping royal mobile phones. He later claimed – though this was received with widespread scepticism by journalists who know editors are bound to know of such major operations – to the Commons Culture Committee that he knew nothing of his journalists' activities. In 2007 he took up his post with the Conservative Party and was generally judged to have improved its media operation. In the wake of the Conservatives' failure to achieve an overall majority in May 2010, however, there was criticism of Coulson and Cameron's small 'clique'.

Cranbourne, Robert (1946–), Viscount
Conservative leader in the Lords. He was educated at Eton and Christ Church, Oxford. He entered the House of Commons in 1979 for Dorset South. He spent some time in Afghanistan resisting the Soviet occupation. He served as a junior minister in the 1980s and then returned to the back benches until John Major elevated him to the Lords via a 'writ of acceleration', necessary as his father, the Marquess of Salisbury, was still a sitting member. He became Conservative leader in the Lords with a place in the cabinet in 1994. He made several speeches opposing Labour plans to end the role of hereditary peers when the Conservatives were in government. In a *volte face* in December 1998 he conducted a series of secret meetings with Number 10 Downing Street and reached a compromise agreement whereby he accepted a two-stage abolition of peers; during the interim stage 92 hereditary peers would continue to sit and vote. When his party leader, William Hague, heard of these unauthorised meetings and agreements – the events were exposed very publicly at prime minister's questions on 3 December 1998 – he was both embarrassed and angry. Cranbourne was sacked immediately, though still retained

the support of some Tory peers. He left the House of Lords in November 2001.

Crewe, Ivor (1945–), Sir

Political scientist and master of University College, Oxford. He was educated at Manchester Grammar School, Exeter College, Oxford, and the London School of Economics. He became professor of government at Essex University in 1982 and its vice chancellor in 1995. He has been a leading British psephologist who has appeared regularly on television, especially during election campaigns. His book with Anthony King on the history of the Social Democratic Party was received with critical acclaim (*SDP: The Birth, Life, and Death of the Social Democratic Party*, 1995). He received the Political Studies Association's Isaiah Berlin Prize 2004. He was knighted in 2004. He succeeded Lord Butler of Brockwell as master of University College in July 2008.

Crick, Bernard (1929–2008), Sir

Political scientist. He was educated at Whitgift School, University College, London, and Harvard, McGill and Berkeley Universities. He lectured at the London School of Economics and became professor at Sheffield and Birkbeck. He was joint editor of *Political Quarterly*. On David Blunkett's invitation, he chaired Labour's working party on citizenship, which established citizenship as a taught subject in schools. He was also a joint founder, with Derek Heater, of the Politics Association in 1969. His books include *In Defence of Politics* (1962) and a praised biography of George Orwell (1980). He was knighted in 2002. He died of prostate cancer in 2008.

Crick, Michael (1958–)

Author, investigative BBC2 *Newsnight* reporter and its political editor. He was educated at Manchester Grammar School and Oxford University, where he was awarded a first in philosophy, politics and economics (PPE) and was president of the Union. He started work for Independent Television News in Washington before moving to the BBC's *Panorama* and then *Newsnight* programmes. He has written praised biographies of Arthur Scargill (1985), Michael Heseltine (1997) and, most famously, Jeffrey Archer (1995), in which he exposed much of the fantasy on which the Conservative peer's life had been based. He entered the news in October 2003 by submitting a dossier accusing Iain Duncan Smith of employing his wife Betsy on tax payers' money as a secretary when there was no substantive job performed.

Cripps, Stafford (1889–1952)

Labour MP and minister. He was educated at Winchester and New College, Oxford, where he showed brilliant promise as a chemist but chose the law. He then became the youngest barrister in Britain and went on to make his fortune out of patent and compensation cases. He became solicitor general in 1930 but refused to join Ramsay MacDonald's coalition, preferring to support a succession of left-wing causes, culminating in the Popular Front campaign to rally a broad swathe of support against Nazism. For this he was expelled from the Labour Party and he sat through the war as an independent. He served as ambassador to Moscow 1940–42 and then returned to hold a number of posts, including minister of aircraft production. He became president of the Board of Trade in 1945 and chancellor in 1947, when Hugh Dalton was forced to resign for leaking budget secrets. He presided over a period of austerity, which he seemed to relish. He lost political credibility when he devalued the pound in 1949. He became ill from overwork in 1950 and retired – dying shortly afterwards.

> There, but for the grace of God, goes God. (Winston Churchill on Cripps)

> He has all the virtues I dislike and none of the vices I admire. (Churchill on Cripps again)

Cromwell, Oliver (1599–1658)

Revolutionary English politician and general. He was born into lesser gentry from Huntingdon. He became an MP in

1629 and his conversion to Puritanism followed in the 1630s. He led the parliamentary resistance to Charles I. In the Civil War he was responsible for the cavalry forces – called Ironsides – which contributed towards a decisive victory at Edgehill in 1642 and Marston Moor in 1644. Along with Fairfax he was the creator of the New Model Army, which won the decisive victory at Naseby in 1645. Following the execution of Charles he declared a republic in 1649. He became lord protector in 1653, when he dismissed parliamentary government for a number of years. He was a harsh ruler in some respects, executing the radical Levellers and crushing the Irish rebellion of 1649–50, not to mention the Scots at Dunbar in 1650 and Worcester in 1651. He brooked no parliamentary interference and was essentially a dictator during the period of his 'protectorship'. He was successful militarily against the Dutch and the Spanish. He refused those who pressed him to become king, though he was one in all but name. He introduced a high degree of religious toleration and was responsible for the readmission of the Jews into the country in 1655. When the crown was restored in the person of Charles II, Cromwell's body was dug up from Westminster Abbey and 'ceremonially executed'. It seems incredible in retrospect that an ordinary member of parliament should have risen to lead a revolt against an over-mighty executive, and that he should turn out to be such a gifted military leader. He is a contradictory figure in British history: devout and unambitious; yet ruthless and dictatorial.

Necessity hath no law. (1654)

I need pity. I know what I feel. Great place and business in the world is not worth looking for. (1650)

The people would be just as noisy if they were going to see me hanged. (In response to a friend who pointed to the cheering crowds)

Crosland, Anthony (1918–77)
Labour politician and writer on socialism. He was educated at Oxford, where he

also taught after war service. He became an MP in 1950. His seminal revisionist text *The Future of Socialism* (1956) argued that Keynesian economics made socialist revolution unnecessary, as the fruits of revolution could be won without one. His passion was equality and he believed it could be won largely through reforming the education system. As education secretary 1965–67 he tried but his vision of comprehensive schools eventually failed to deliver his dreams. He also served in the cabinet at the Board of Trade 1967–69, local government and planning 1969–70 and environment 1974–76, and as foreign secretary 1976–77. His premature death denied Labour his great talents at a time when arguably they were sorely needed.

If it's the last thing I do I'm going to destroy every fucking grammar school in England and Wales and Northern Ireland. (Quoted by his wife, Susan, 1982)

Crossman, Richard (1907–74)
Labour politician, journalist and writer. He was educated at Winchester and New College, Oxford, where he taught for a while for the Workers' Educational Association, before leading the Labour group on the city council 1934–40. He joined *New Statesman* in 1938 as a journalist and worked in psychological warfare during the war before being elected Labour MP for Coventry East in 1945. His brilliance in debate, criticising Labour's foreign policy, earned the anger of Ernest Bevin and Clement Attlee. In the 1950s, ever the rebel, he became a leading supporter of Aneurin Bevan. Harold Wilson made him a minister of local government 1964–66 and leader of the house 1966–68, where he initiated some reform of the select committee system, and social services and health 1968–70. He edited *New Statesman* 1970–72 and wrote a classic introduction to Walter Bagehot's *British Constitution* in 1963. His *Diaries of a Cabinet Minister* (published in three volumes, 1975–77) proved a goldmine for historians and

lovers of Labour political gossip in equal measure.

> I view this able and energetic man with some detachment. He is loyal to his own career but only incidentally to anything or anyone else. (Hugh Dalton on Crossman, 1941)

Cruddas, Jon (1962–)

Labour MP. He was educated at a comprehensive school near Portsmouth and then Warwick University, where he gained an MA and doctorate. He also studied at the University Wisconsin 1987–88. He worked as an assistant to the general secretary of the Labour Party and stepped up to work in Number 10 for Tony Blair in 1997 as deputy political secretary in charge of linking with the unions. He became MP for Dagenham in 2001 and was a candidate for deputy leadership of the Labour Party in 2007; he did well in the contest but was narrowly beaten by Harriet Harman. He was regularly seen as a potential challenger for the leadership of the party; however, in May 2010 he declined to be a candidate following Gordon Brown's resignation.

Cubbon, Sir Brian (1928–)

Permanent secretary at the Northern Ireland Office (1976–79) and the Home Office (1979–1988). He was educated at Bury Grammar School and Trinity College, Cambridge, before entering the Home Civil Service. He was in the car in July 1976 which was blown up by the IRA, killing the British ambassador to Ireland, Christopher Ewart-Biggs; Margaret Thatcher mentioned in the House of Commons at the time that he had once served as her private secretary. He served as a member of the Press Complaints Commission 1995–2002.

Currie, Edwina (1946–)

Colourful junior health minister under Margaret Thatcher. She was educated at Liverpool Institute for Girls, St Anne's College, Oxford, and then at the London School of Economics. She was a lecturer 1972–81 before becoming active as a Birmingham city councillor, where she specialised in social services and housing. She was MP for Derbyshire South 1983–97. She became a junior minister at education and health 1986–88 but lost the latter job after unwisely describing the British chicken stock as being infected with salmonella, thus damaging the egg industry. Despite her expectations she failed to win office again but won attention through her broadcasting and her novels (the best-known being A *Parliamentary Affair*, 1994). In 2002 she caused a sensation when her published diaries revealed she had conducted a four-year affair with John Major, before he became prime minister. She was a clever and interesting politician whose reach perhaps exceeded her grasp.

> Edwina was once a virtually permanent fixture on the nation's TV screen saying something outrageous about just about anything – a habit which finally and inevitably killed off her political career – and flirting with her hosts. (Nick Assinder, BBC, 28 September 2002)

D

Dacre, Paul (1948–)

Editor in chief at Associated Newspapers and editor of the *Daily Mail*. He was educated at University College School, Leeds, and Leeds University. He succeeded to the editorship on the death of David English in 1998 and sustained the tabloid's position as the second (to the *Sun*) best-selling daily newspaper, with over 2 million daily sales. His newspaper was reportedly regularly read and respected by Tony Blair and he was said to be close to Gordon Brown too. Dacre was credited with being able to 'feel the pulse of middle England' and was known for campaigns like that over the death of Stephen Lawrence.

Dale, Iain (1962–)

Britain's most popular blogger (http://iaindale.blogspot.com), author, Conservative politician and commentator. He was educated at Saffron Walden County High School and the University of East Anglia, where he studied languages and linguistics. In 1985 he worked in Germany teaching English as a foreign language. He worked variously as a financial journalist, a businessman and a researcher for an MP. In 1997 he founded the Politico's Bookshop, specialising in political writing. In 2003 he sold the business to Methuen. He set up his blog, Iain Dale's Diary, and developed it into, at 130,000 visits a month, the nation's most popular political blog. He stood for Norfolk North in 2005 but was heavily beaten by Norman Lamb, the Liberal Democrat. He also writes for the *Spectator, Daily Telegraph, Guardian* and *Independent*. He also appears on television from time to time and is quite open about being gay.

Dalton, Hugh (1887–1962)

Labour politician and cabinet minister. He was the son of the chaplain to Queen Victoria. He was educated at Eton, King's College, Cambridge, and the London School of Economics before serving in the First World War. He was a Labour MP from 1924 to 1931 and then again from 1935. He was minister for economic warfare 1940 and president of the Board of Trade 1942. In 1945 he became chancellor of the exchequer but disclosed the contents of the 1947 budget to a journalist before his speech to parliament and, in the honourable custom of the time, resigned. He was made a life peer in 1960. One of the founding fathers of modern Labour, he was influential in economic and foreign policy. An extrovert with a high self-regard, he attracted enemies as easily as friends but had a record of encouraging younger colleagues to advance themselves, including Hugh Gaitskell. His diaries (lodged at the London School of Economics, and on which he based his 1957 *Memoirs*) have been a rich source for historians; his biography by Ben Pimlott (1985) has been highly praised.

Dalyell, Tam (1932–)

Formidable old Etonian Labour backbencher with reputation for persevering with his campaigns. He was educated at Eton and King's College, Cambridge – where he was chair of the Conservative Association – and then trained and practised as a teacher before joining the Labour Party in 1956, entering parliament for West Lothian 1962–83 and Linlithgow from 1983. The 'backbencher's backbencher', Dalyell had no experience of office and little of shadow office either. Rather, he channelled his formidable talents of research and perseverance into particular campaigns like the one on the circumstances surrounding the sinking of the *General Belgrano* in the Falklands war and the discovery of the authors of the Lockerbie disaster. He took over from Sir Edward Heath in 2001 as the father of the house. He stood down as an MP in 2005.

> Since Mr Blair is going ahead with his support for a US attack without unambiguous UN authorisation, he should be branded as a war criminal and sent to The Hague. (2003)

D'Ancona, Matthew (1968–)

Deputy editor of the *Sunday Telegraph* and editor of the *Spectator* from 2006. Born to a Maltese father who played football for Newcastle, he was educated at St Dunstan's College and then Magdalen College, Oxford, where he was awarded top first of his year in modern history; he was elected a fellow of All Souls the same year. He joined the *Times* as a trainee and was assistant editor by the age of 26. He joined the *Sunday Telegraph* in 1996, for which he continued to write a weekly column. He also writes for *Prospect* and has written two history books as well as two novels.

Dannatt, General Sir Richard (1950–)

Chief of general staff 2006–09. Educated Felsted School, St Lawrence College, Ramsgate, and Durham University. He was commissioned in the Royal Green

Howards and won the Military Cross in Northern Ireland before serving in Germany. He commanded the Armoured Brigade in Bosnia and commanded British forces in Kosovo 1999. He went on to command NATO's Allied Rapid Reaction Corps and was then commander in chief of Land Command. In 2009 he publicly criticised the Labour government for failing to provide sufficient funding to equip British forces in Afghanistan and then controversially agreed to advise and possibly serve as a minister in a future Conservative government.

Darling, Alistair (1953–)

Labour MP and chancellor. He was born into a Conservative family and was educated at Lorretto School and Aberdeen University. He served on Lothian Regional Council 1982–87. After being elected Labour MP for Edinburgh South West in 1987 he was opposition Treasury spokes-man. In government after 1997 he was an impressive chief secretary to the Treasury before he moved to become secretary of state for social security after the reshuffle in July 1998. He was made secretary for work and pensions in June 2001. In June 2002 he took over from the sacked Stephen Byers at the Department of Transport, to attempt to sort out Labour's possibly most intractable policy area. He was given the 'part-time' job of spokesman for Scotland in June 2003 when the residual functions of the secretaries of state for Scotland and Wales were subsumed into the new Department of Constitutional Affairs. He was always seen as a clever, competent minister but only average with media skills and a bit boring to listen to. However, he was rewarded for loyalty to his fellow Scot when Gordon Brown appointed him chancellor in 2007. Many assumed he would be little more than 'his master's voice' but during the 2007–09 banking and related economic crisis he restrained Brown's urge to borrow more and in June 2009 stoutly resisted Brown's attempt to replace him in a reshuffle with his favourite: Ed Balls. On balance, he was a 'success'

during the Brown years, something which few of his fellow cabinet colleagues could claim. In 2010 he held Edinburgh South West with a majority of 8,447. Along with Brown and Jack Straw, he served in the cabinet continuously from 1997 to 2010.

Davies, Clement (1884–1962)

Liberal politician and leader. He was born in Llanfyllin, Montgomeryshire, and educated at Cambridge. He was elected for his home county in 1929 and served until his death. He was leader of the Liberal Party 1945–56 and in 1951 refused Winston Churchill's offer of a post as education secretary, to avoid his party being subsumed, as had the National Liberals, into the Conservative Party.

Davies, Gavyn (1952–)

Chairman of the BBC 2000–04. He was educated at both Cambridge and Oxford. He had a hugely lucrative career as an investment banker for Philips and Drew, Simon and Coates, and then Goldman Sachs, where sale of shares made him a very rich man. He was attached to the Policy Unit of Number 10 Downing Street 1974–79 and subsequently was a regular advisor to governments of both main parties. The Conservatives complained bitterly when in 2001 he was appointed as chairman of the BBC, as his wife, Sue Nye, worked for chancellor Gordon Brown and Davies was known to be a generous donor to the Labour Party, as was the BBC's then director general, Greg Dyke. Davies defended himself by saying he had worked for governments of both left and right and was able to suspend personal bias in a professional capacity. His role in the BBC was anticipated when he chaired a committee into the future funding of the BBC in 1999. The previous chairman, Sir Christopher Bland, had been a well known Conservative supporter. Davies was forced to resign when the Hutton report criticised the BBC in the wake of the row caused by Andrew Gilligan's controversial broadcast on 29 May 2003 regarding the government's presentation of the case for war with Iraq. Since his resignation he has returned to business and has, if anything, been critical of the Labour government.

Davies, Ron (1946–)

Former Labour secretary of state for Wales whose flourishing career was sadly ended by scandal. He was educated at Barasleg Grammar School, Portsmouth Polytechnic and Cardiff University. He was a teacher and tutor for the Workers' Educational Association 1968–74 before he became a councillor and then MP for Caerphilly. He served in the whips' office and as shadow spokesman on Wales. He became secretary of state 1997–98 and was instrumental in setting up the Welsh assembly. After serving as a member of the Welsh assembly from 1999 he decided to resign from politics after a bizarre scandal involving a late-night walk on Clapham Common in an area frequented by gays.

Davis, David (1948–)

Conservative MP and leadership hopeful in 2001. He went from humble beginnings in a council house to study at grammar school, then had substantial success at Warwick and Harvard Universities. A member of the Territorial Army's SAS Regiment, he became a successful businessman at Tate and Lyle. He entered the House of Commons in 1987 for Boothferry but changed to Haltemprice and Howde in 1997. He was made a whip in 1990 and became Foreign Office minister of state for Europe under John Major 1994–97, who hoped Davis's Eurosceptic views would help him sell the idea of the European Union to fellow MPs. After the Conservative defeat in the 1997 general election he became a highly regarded chair of the Public Accounts Committee, 95 per cent of whose recommendations were accepted by government during his time in the chair. After the 2001 election defeat of his party he stood as a candidate in the leadership contest, when he was widely seen as a 'dark horse', but he came joint last with Michael Ancram. He decided to drop out shortly afterwards. Iain Duncan Smith made

him party chair but in July 2002 he was sacked amid some damaging circumstances involving accusations of a dilatory attitude and residual designs on the leadership. He was re-established as deputy leader but was seen by many as a less than loyal member of the shadow cabinet as the chorus of complaint against Duncan Smith grew in 2003. When the latter was defeated in the vote of confidence in October 2003, Davis, after some hesitation, decided not to stand for the leadership and stood aside to allow the 'coronation' of Michael Howard. He stood for the leadership of his party in 2005 and, despite building a big early lead, lost out to David Cameron's charismatic speech-making. He served as shadow home secretary 2003–08 but in June 2008 resigned to fight a by-election on the subject of civil liberties: he duly won the following month. However, in the process, he lost his shadow position and went to the back benches. He held his seat with a majority of 11,602 in May 2010 but received no office in the coalition government.

Davis, Evan (1962–)

BBC economics editor and radio/television presenter. He was educated at the Ashcombe School, Dorking, and then read philosophy, politics and economics (PPE) at St John's College, Oxford. He began work as an economist at the Institute for Fiscal Studies and moved to the London Business School before joining the BBC in 1993. He became economics editor in 2001 and joined Radio 4's *Today* programme in 2007, where he fitted in smoothly.

Day, Robin (1923–2000)

Leading television interviewer of his day. He served in the artillery during the Second World War and then studied law at Oxford and was called to the bar in 1952. He worked as a broadcaster for Independent Television News 1955–59 and then joined BBC's *Panorama* 1967–72 and played a leading role as an interviewer and political commentator, especially during election campaigns. He fronted the BBC's *Question Time* for many years. He was arguably the first interviewer to shake off the deferential attitude towards senior politicians and brought to interviews a freshness and irreverence, not to mention abrasiveness, which others have assiduously copied and developed.

> But why should the public, on this issue, as regards the future of the Royal Navy, believe you, a transient, here-today and, if I may say so, gone-tomorrow politician, rather than a senior officer of many years? (October 1982, during an interview with the Conservative secretary of state for defence John Nott, while pursuing a line of questioning regarding cuts in defence expenditure – Nott then walked out of the interview)

de Chastelain, John (1938–), General

Head of the Independent International Commission on Decommissioning in Northern Ireland. Son of an American mother and Scottish father, he was educated in Fettes School, Edinburgh, moved to Canada when aged 18, and entered the Canadian military. He soon rose through the ranks and distinguished himself before becoming his country's ambassador to the United Nations in 1993. In 1995 he was invited by Senator George Mitchell to head up the new Commission.

Delors, Jacques (1925–)

French politician of the left who became president of the European Commission 1985, reappointed 1988 (a term extended to 1995). Given his length of time in office he is rightly seen as one of the major influences on the evolution of European political and economic integration. Accordingly he was disliked by Conservative Eurosceptics, including Margaret Thatcher, and the *Sun* newspaper, which once led with the headline 'Up Yours Delors'.

Denham, John (1953–)

Labour MP and cabinet minister. He was educated at Woodroffe Comprehensive, Devon, and Southampton University, where he studied chemistry and was

president of the Union. He worked for a number of charities including Oxfam, Friends of the Earth and War on Want before becoming a councillor in Southampton 1981–93. He was elected for Southampton Itchen in 1992. He was spokesperson on social security 1995 and after 1997 became a minister of state within that ministry by 1998. In 1999 he was moved to the Department of Health and then the Home Office after 2001 but did not agree with the Iraq invasion and made a highly effective speech against it when he resigned in 2003. As chair of the Home Affairs Committee he was a regular critic of Tony Blair. Gordon Brown made him secretary for universities and skills in 2007; in June 2009 he replaced Hazel Blears as secretary for communities and local government. In July 2009 he disappointed some Labour supporters by judging social and economic equality was no longer a viable goal for the Labour Party.

> The left needs to stop holding up egalitarianism as the ideal. If we continue to believe that the egalitarian approach is really the right one, and we, somehow, have to find more cunning ways of getting there, we will fail.

Denning, Tom (1899–1999), Lord

One of the most distinguished judges in postwar British public life. He was educated at Oxford and called to the bar in 1923. He became a High Court justice in 1944 and was made a lord of appeal in ordinary in 1957. He led an inquiry into the Profumo affair in 1963. He was master of the rolls 1962–82 and the author of many controversial judgements. He believed judges should make the right decisions on behalf of individuals now and 'not leave it to Parliament years afterwards'. Consequently he was more than once over-ruled by the Lords.

> We shouldn't have all these campaigns to get the Birmingham Six released. If they'd been hanged they'd have been forgotten and the whole community would have been satisfied. (1990)

Dewar, Donald (1937–2000)
Labour MP and minister. He was
educated at Glasgow Academy and
Glasgow University. He was a silkily clever
and ambitious Scottish politician who
became his country's first minister after the
votes for the parliament in 1999. Labour
scandals in Scotland in the early years
of the parliament did not help his cause
and the Scottish National Party posed a
constant threat to his dreams. Following a
period of ill-health, he died in the autumn
of 2000.

Dicey, Albert Venn (1835–1922)
Author of the definitive work on the constitution *Lectures Introductory to the Study
of the Law of the Constitution* (1885). He
was Vinerian professor of jurisprudence
at Oxford. His work emphasised the rule
of law and the supremacy of parliament
and was instrumental in creating the much
imitated Westminster model of liberal
democratic government. He was fervently
opposed to Irish home rule.

Disraeli, Benjamin (1804–81)
Conservative prime minister 1868 and
1874–80. He was privately educated but
trained as a solicitor. Of Jewish origin but
baptised in boyhood, he was a best-selling
novelist as well as a leading politician
(*Coningsby*, 1844, and *Sybil*, 1845, being
his best-known works). He became leader
of the Young England movement, was
critical of industrialism and advocated an
alliance between the aristocracy and the
working class. He became well known
for his acidic criticism of Robert Peel's
repealing of the Corn Laws. He led the
Conservative Party after Peelites left and
was made chancellor in 1867, piloting the
second Reform Act through parliament.
As prime minister he helped secure
ownership of the Suez Canal for Britain
and pleased Queen Victoria by making
her empress of India. He was judged to
have achieved a diplomatic triumph at the
Congress of Berlin in 1878, which settled
disputes between the Russians and the
Turks in the Balkans. For many Tories his

name remains synonymous with 'one nation'
Toryism. He is the most exotic and unusual
man to achieve high office in Britain, let
alone become prime minister as leader of
the Conservative Party.

> Though I sit down now, the time will come
> when you will hear me. (Following the
> derisive reaction to his maiden speech in the
> Commons, 1837)

> I will not go down to posterity talking bad
> grammar. (Correcting *Hansard* proofs on his
> deathbed)

> At the top of the greasy pole. (Describing
> his position as prime minister, 1868)

> A Conservative government is an organised
> hypocrisy. (1845)

> England does not love coalitions. (1852)

> He is a self-made man and worships his
> creator. (John Bright on Disraeli)

Dobson, Frank (1940–)
Labour MP and minister. He was
educated at Archbishop Holgate Grammar
School, York, and the London School of
Economics. He worked for the Central
Electricity Generating Board 1962–70
before becoming a local councillor in
Camden 1971–76, where he was council
leader 1973–75. He was the MP for
Holborn and St Pancras after 1979 and
had various shadow portfolios before he
became health secretary 1997–99. He left
office to stand as Labour mayoral candidate; however, the leadership's hope that he
would stop Ken Livingstone winning the
election as an ex-Labour independent was
dashed. As a backbencher he opposed the
Iraq war, was the leader of the campaign
against foundation hospitals and became
a critic of Tony Blair's government and
something of a serial rebel on the Labour
back benches. He retained his seat in 2010
with a majority of 9,942.

**Donaldson, John Francis (1920–
2005), Lord**
Cambridge-educated British judge
specialising, when a barrister, in commercial law. He was made a judge in 1966,

justice of appeal 1979–82 and master of the rolls 1982, in succession to Lord Denning. He achieved a high profile in 1971 when he became president of the National Industrial Relations Court, which was regarded by unions and Labour alike as a Conservative anti-union instrument. He sat on the cross-benches in the House of Lords.

Donoughue, Bernard (1934–), Lord

An early political advisor, author, working peer and businessman. He was educated in Northampton Grammar School after a spell in a secondary modern. He went on to Lincoln College, Oxford, followed by Nuffield College, where he completed a doctorate in 1963. He lectured at the London School of Economics and worked at the *Economist* for a while – and even edited the *Times* briefly until Rupert Murdoch dismissed him – before, famously, he became a political advisor to Harold Wilson. He was raised to the peerage in 1985 and was active on Labour's behalf as a spokesman on Treasury matters. From 1997 to 1999 he was a junior minister at the Department of Agriculture, Fisheries and Food.

Douglas-Home, Alec (1903–95), Earl of Home

Conservative prime minister. He was educated at Eton and Oxford, where he was elected head of the prestigious 'Pop'. He entered parliament in 1931 and served as secretary to Neville Chamberlain during the appeasement years. In the 1950s as the Earl of Home (after 1951) he had junior office and was then promoted to foreign secretary 1960–63, as which he was successful and popular. He astonished the political world when he emerged out of the then undemocratic 'magic circle' system of appointing Conservative leaders and became the compromise candidate between rivals R. A. Butler and Reginald Maudling. He went on, with the support of Harold Macmillan – who wished to stop Butler – to become prime minister in November 1963, when he renounced his

peerage and won Kinross at a by-election. As premier he was popular with his party but perceived as ineffectual and out of touch with ordinary people, a deficiency exploited effectively by Harold Wilson in the 1964 general election campaign. He served as leader of the opposition until 1965 and then as foreign secretary under Edward Heath 1970–74. He became a life peer in 1974. He was the only senior politician of his day to have played (first class) county cricket.

> The doctor unfortunately said I was fit. (On taking office as prime minister, 1964)

> There are two problems in my life. The political ones are insoluble and the economic ones are incomprehensible. (1964)

> After half a century of democratic advance, the whole process ground to a halt with a fourteenth earl. (Harold Wilson on the new Conservative prime minister, Sir Alec Douglas-Home, 1963)

Downing, George (1623–84), Sir

Anglo-Irish politician after whom the street containing the home of the British prime minister is named. He was born in Dublin but lived for some time in America, being a member of the first graduating class from Harvard and later was hired as that college's first tutor. After a stint as an instructor to seamen and a preacher he opted for a military career back in England when he became chaplain to Colonel John Okey, whose support proved valuable for his advancement. He was initially a strong supporter of Oliver Cromwell and received an income from him, in part, according to one account, for providing intelligence on Cromwell's enemies. He became a diplomat in the Hague but later began to adapt to a changing atmosphere. After the fall of Richard Cromwell, he was able to convince the restored Charles II that he now 'saw the error' of his previous ways. He was consequently knighted and given the patch of land on which he eventually built Downing Street. It was his information which led to the arrest of the regicides, John Barkstead, Miles Corbet and his former commander and sponsor John Okey. All were hanged, drawn and quartered. Samuel Pepys was not impressed by such behaviour, describing him as a 'perfidious rogue' and remarking that 'all the world took notice of him for a most ungrateful villain for his pains'. He was created a baronet in 1663, went on to accumulate yet more status and material wealth and died in 1684, one of the largest landowners in Cambridgeshire.

Drummond, Stuart (1973–)

Mayor of Hartlepool from 2002 (twice re-elected). He was educated at Salford University but became known locally as H'Angus the Monkey, the mascot of Hartlepool Football Club. Initially his candidacy was a publicity stunt but, despite his total lack of participation in his own campaign, voters were engaged by the idea and gave him a narrow majority over the Labour candidate. The reaction to a 'monkey' winning generated international hilarity but in post Drummond has clearly been more than a feeble joke, as he was re-elected in 2005 and 2009 – which begs the question of how many other apparently non-political people could be encouraged to stand for public office and make a success of the responsibility.

Dugdale, Thomas (1897–1977)

Conservative minister of agriculture. He is usually quoted as the minister who resigned in recognition of his ultimate responsibility for mistakes made by his officials, in his case in 1954, over the reselling of land, Crichel Down, requisitioned during the war. In more recent times few ministers have emulated his behaviour despite dire mistakes in their departments.

Duncan, Alan (1957–)

Conservative MP and minister. He was educated at Merchant Taylors School, where he was head boy, and St John's College, Oxford, where he coxed the college first eight. He was president of the Union 1979. He won a Kennedy scholarship to Harvard 1981–82. He

then worked in the oil industry for various companies before becoming a consultant to foreign governments. He won Rutland and Meldon in 1992 and served two ministers as their parliamentary private secretary. He was close to William Hague when the latter won the leadership in 1997 but held no major shadow office until David Cameron became leader in 2005. He became shadow business secretary 2007 and shadow leader of the house 2009. He was the first Tory MP to come out as openly gay. He was made minister of state at the Department of International Development in 2010.

> Our Achilles heel, though, has been our social attitude. Censorious judgmentalism from the moralising wing, which treats half our own countrymen as enemies, must be rooted out. (*Guardian*, July 2005)

Duncan Smith, Iain ('IDS') (1954–)

Conservative MP and party leader. He was educated at Sandhurst and became an MP for Chingford. He was shadow defence spokesman under William Hague and he decided to stand in the elections for Conservative leadership after Hague stepped down in June 2001. His advantages included support from the right, including Margaret Thatcher and Norman Tebbit, but disadvantages included lack of name recognition and, in the television age, his baldness. He believed the party had to broaden its appeal while remaining true to its traditions. He did well in the first ballot, winning 39 votes, coming second behind Michael Portillo. In the second ballot he edged up to 42, and in the final ballot on 17 July he failed to beat Ken Clarke but came second to him with 54 votes (to the ex-chancellor's 59). The stage was then set for the choice of 330,000 party members, who now, under rules introduced by Hague, had the opportunity to vote on the two candidates produced by the parliamentary party: Duncan Smith was resolutely right-wing – opposing gays in the military, in favour of education vouchers, a supporter of caning in schools and a Eurosceptic – while Clarke was defiantly pro-Europe, pro-euro and more liberal on most social issues. Duncan Smith won easily. As leader he initially steered a right-wing course but then signalled a shift to the centre on social policy in 2002. He seemed to be leading his party into the centre ground but in February 2003 became embroiled in a crisis when he sacked a former Portillo supporter as executive head of the party organisation. This caused a major crisis of confidence and contributed to polls which suggested most voters did not know what the party stood for. After talk of a leadership challenge in autumn 2002 it was assumed a good Tory performance in the 2003 local elections would be crucial for his continued leadership. In the event the party won well over 500 seats and Duncan Smith hailed a great victory – but the rumblings against him did not altogether cease. At the 2003 party conference in Blackpool there was much talk of a leadership challenge but his speech, more aggressive and rehearsed, won support in the hall and some improvement in the polls: 'the Quiet Man is turning up the volume' he claimed. In the longer term, however, the speech was seen as over-coached and risible. Support continued to ebb away and on 28 October 2003 Sir Michael Spicer, chair of the 1922 Committee, announced that the requisite 25 letters had been received asking for a vote of confidence in the leader. Duncan Smith made an inspired speech to the party's MPs the next day but he lost the vote of confidence 60 to 90. The problem with the Hague leadership rules was that Duncan Smith won the leadership battle in 2001 with the support of only a third of the parliamentary party and it took his failure as leader to reveal that it is support in the legislature which still really counts. He declared that he was considering a new career as a writer but must have been desolate when the *Telegraph*'s reviewer judged his first novel as 'terrible, terrible, terrible'. Michael Howard took over from Duncan Smith unopposed. In March 2004 the commissioner for standards in public life exonerated him of any wrongdoing regarding the employment

of his wife as a secretary. 'Betsygate', as the row was dubbed, centred on whether his wife actually put in enough work to justify the £15,000 a year of public money she was given. In 2010 he was made secretary of state for work and pensions, with a known interest in relieving poverty.

Dunleavy, Patrick (1952–)
Professor of politics at the London School of Economics from 1989. He was educated at St Mary's Grammar School, Sidcup, and Corpus Christie College, Oxford, followed by Nuffield College, where he became a research fellow 1976–85. He is the author of many influential works on British politics and was an advisor to the Jenkins commission on the reform of the electoral system.

Dyke, Greg (1947–)
Director general of the BBC 2000–04. He was educated at Hayes Grammar School and York University. His early career encompassed TV AM 1965–83, London Weekend Television 1987–91, GMTV 1993–94 and Pearson Ltd 1995–99. His appointment at the BBC was controversial in that he was a known Labour supporter and donor. In the summer of 2000 he made a widely publicised speech criticising the legacy of his predecessor, John Birt. He was ranked by the *Guardian* as the second most important person in the media for taking the BBC 'by the scruff of the neck to raise morale, rejuvenate the ratings and seize control of digital terrestrial television following ITV Digital's collapse'. He was forced to resign by BBC governors in February 2004 when the Hutton report criticised the reporting and editing of news stories in the wake of Andrew Gilligan's accusatory broadcast on 29 May 2003. In his memoirs, published August 2004, Dyke bitterly attacked New Labour and accused Blair of either incompetence if he did not understand the 45-minute claim or lying if he did, when he 'duped' the country into the Iraq war; Alastair Campbell he called a 'deranged, vindictive bastard'.

E

Eagle, Angela (1962–)

Labour MP and minister. She is openly gay and is unusual in that her twin sister, Maria, is also an MP. She was educated at Formby High School and St John's College, Oxford, where she read philosophy, politics and economics (PPE). She worked briefly for the Confederation of British Industry (CBI) before working for the Confederation for Health Service Employees (COHSE). She was elected for Wallasey in 1992 and in 1996 became a whip before becoming a junior minister at the Department for the Environment, Transport and the Regions after 1997 followed by Social Security and the Home Office in 2001. She was sacked by Tony Blair in 2002 but returned to government under Gordon Brown in 2007 in a new post: exchequer secretary to the Treasury. She served as minister of state for ageing and pensions 2009–10, and held her seat in the 2010 election with a majority of 8,507.

Eden, Anthony (1897–1977)

Conservative foreign secretary and prime minister. He was born to an upper-class landed family, and educated at Eton and Christ Church, Oxford. He was awarded the Military Cross during his war service in 1917. He stood for parliament in 1923 and represented Warwick and Leamington for 30 years. He was a junior minister in the Foreign Office 1931 and foreign secretary 1935 but resigned over the policy of appeasement towards Fascist Italy and Nazi Germany. After Winston Churchill replaced Neville Chamberlain as prime minister he again served as foreign secretary, from December 1940, when he helped to negotiate all the major wartime and immediate postwar agreements. He was deputy leader of the opposition from 1945 and then went back to the Foreign Office in 1951. In 1955 he succeeded Churchill, at long last, as prime minister. However,

his premiership was not as celebrated as his service in the Foreign Office. Secretly in league with Israel, in November 1956 he ordered British and French forces to occupy the Suez Canal Zone in the wake of an invading Israeli army, which provoked a furious political protest at home and in the United Nations as well as Washington. Eventually the USA's threat to withdraw support for the pound, combined with his ill-health, forced Eden to climb down humiliatingly over Suez and to withdraw. He resigned in January 1957 and became a peer in the early 1960s.

> He is forever poised between a cliché and an indiscretion. (Aneurin Bevan on Eden)

> Beneath the sophistication of his appearance and manner, he has all the unplumbable stupidities and unawareness of his class and type. (Bevan again on Eden)

Elizabeth II (1926–)

Monarch, head of state. She was educated privately at home. She succeeded to the throne when her father died in 1952; her coronation was the first major public event to be televised. She has been revered as a slave to duty and has escaped many of the scandals which surrounded the royal family during the 1980s. However, the death of Diana in 1997 revealed the family in an unflattering light and the queen as a possibly unfeeling and vindictive woman. The queen looked to reform the royal family so that it could become once again the centre of the nation's affections. Her depiction by Helen Mirren in the film *The Queen* (2006) suggested she was reliant on Tony Blair during the crisis over the death of Diana but most reviewers felt the film showed the monarch in a sympathetic light.

> The British constitution has always been puzzling and always will be. (Elizabeth II, 1995)

> Please don't be effusive. (To prime minister Tony Blair on the speech he was about to make to celebrate her golden wedding, 18 November 1997)

> I for one believe there are lessons to be drawn from her life and from the

extraordinary and moving reaction to her death. (Broadcast from the Palace on the evening before the funeral of Diana, Princess of Wales, 5 September 1997)

Erskine May, Thomas (1815–86)

Famous clerk of the House of Commons who wrote *Parliamentary Practice*, the bible of anyone wishing to discover the complexities of parliamentary procedure. It is regularly updated and currently exceeds 1,200 pages.

F

Falconer, Charles (1953–), Lord

Labour peer and minister. He was educated at Fettes with Tony Blair and became a successful barrister. He was made a life peer early in the Blair administration and took a pay cut when appointed solicitor general. The appointment was criticised, as Falconer's only apparent political qualification for office was having shared a flat with Blair when they were both young barristers. In July 1998 he moved to the Cabinet Office and was chair of many cabinet committees, where his ability and judgement were allegedly greatly valued by the prime minister. He sailed into a gale of criticism when placed in charge of the Millennium Dome. The financial and other problems of that fiasco were frequently blamed on him as the minister responsible but he resolutely refused to resign. In June 2003 he was made the new secretary of state for constitutional affairs, a combination of the old lord chancellor's department and the residual functions of the secretaries of state for Wales and Scotland. Again the 'Tony's cronies' jibe was frequently deployed but Falconer chose to ignore them, claiming his record in office was good. His easy charm certainly helped him to deflect criticism in a way denied to his predecessor, Lord Irvine.

He left office once Gordon Brown acceded to Number 10 and took up various jobs in business. He spoke against the proposed 'rainbow coalition' with the Liberal Democrats and others in May 2010.

> We need to have an arrangement whereby the regions, and Scotland and Wales and Northern Ireland, are better represented in the House of Lords. (On the subject of an English parliament)

Falkender, Lady

See Williams, Marcia.

Farage, Nigel (1964–)

Former leader of the UK Independence Party (UKIP) and an MEP for South-East England. Educated at the private Dulwich College, he went on to work in the City as a commodities broker. He supported the Conservative Party until John Major signed the Maastricht treaty in 1992, whereupon he became a founding member of UKIP in 1993. He was elected to the European parliament in 1999 and was re-elected in 2004 and 2009. He became leader of UKIP in 2006 and stood for Westminster five times before being elected an MEP. In 2009 he stood down as leader to contest the seat of the speaker, John Bercow, in Buckingham. The day before polling, 5 May 2010, he was a passenger in a light plane trailing a UKIP banner. When the banner got caught in the propeller the plane crashed and he was exceedingly fortunate to escape death. He was forced to watch the count from his hospital bed, where he managed to come only third, with 8,401 votes. Farage is an unusual politician – very astute and quick on his intellectual feet, and who seems always to be spoiling for a fight; maybe someone one either loves or hates.

> We've got three social democratic parties in Britain – Labour, Lib Dem and Conservative are virtually indistinguishable from each other on nearly all the main issues … you can't put a cigarette paper between them and that is why there are nine million people who don't vote now in general elections that did back in 1992.

I found most things easy. (p. 14 of his 2010 autobiography *Fighting Bull*)

You have all the charisma of a damp rag and the appearance of a low-grade bank clerk. (When insulting Herman van Rompuy, president of the European Union, in an open session of the European parliament, 24 February 2010)

Field, Frank (1942–)

Pressure group leader turned Labour MP and a prolific author on poverty and welfare issues. He was educated at St Clement's Dane Grammar School and Hull University. He was director Child Poverty Action 1969–79, the Low Pay Unit 1974–80 and MP for Birkenhead from 1979. He was chair of the Social Services Committee for many years, in which role he won widespread admiration. He was made minister for welfare reform in the Department of Social Security 1997–98 but his brief to 'think the unthinkable' proved short-lived as his proposals were too costly for the Treasury to support and he departed, not without a degree of bitterness, to the back benches. From there he became an outspoken critic of the government over foundation hospitals, the abolition of the 10p tax band (on which he led an effective revolt) and, in June 2009, Gordon Brown's leadership. He toyed briefly with contesting the speakership in June 2009. Field is a maverick, much admired by Conservatives, who describes Margaret Thatcher as a 'hero'. On 5 June 2010 it was announced that Field – a Labour MP always highly respected by the Conservatives – would become the 'poverty czar' and head a review into poverty in Britain. More particularly, the review would scrutinise: the validity of the definition of poverty as 60 per cent of the median income; and how to encourage nurturing of children by parents and local services.

We welcome the expertise he will bring to the table. In order to effectively address deep-seated poverty and its associated problems, we will need cross-party support. (Iain Duncan Smith, 5 June 2010)

Filkin, Elizabeth (1940–)

Former parliamentary commissioner for standards. She was educated at Clifton High School and the University of Birmingham. She worked for London local authorities, Liverpool University, the Citizens' Advice Bureau, London Docklands Development Corporation and the Inland Revenue before becoming parliament's watchdog in 1999. Her job was to report to the House of Commons Committee on Standards in Public Life. She soon established a reputation as a tough investigator who was no respecter of political rank: she investigated, among others, John Reid, Peter Mandelson, Geoffrey Robinson and Keith Vaz. However, she began to attract criticism for being allegedly 'politically naive' and a process began whereby she was marginalised and then effectively sacked in 2001 when she was told to reapply for her job. She resigned in protest amid accusations that parliament had sought to rid itself of a watchdog whose bite was too fierce for its liking. Her successor was Philip Mawer, appointed in February 2002. On 16 February 2001 she told the *Guardian* she would be 'going down the Job Centre on Monday' as she had no job to go to.

Flint, Caroline (1961–)

Labour MP for Don Valley and former minister. She was educated Twickenham Girls School and Richmond Tertiary College before attending the University East Anglia, where she took film studies and American literature and history. She worked for the Inner London Education Authority 1984–85; the National Union of Students 1988–89; Lambeth council 1989–93; and the GMB union 1994–97. After her election in 1997, she served as parliamentary private secretary to Peter Hain and John Reid before becoming a junior minister at the Home Office in 2003, moving to the Department of Health in 2005, where she became minister of state, May 2006. In June 2007 she moved to the Department for Work and Pensions as minister for employment and welfare reform. In

January 2008 she became secretary of state for housing and planning, and attended cabinet by invitation. In October 2008 she was moved to the Foreign Office as minister for Europe. From there on things began to go slightly wrong for the fast-rising politician. In March 2009 she attracted ridicule by admitting she had not read the Lisbon treaty, despite being in charge of introducing it. She resigned in June 2009, not without some rancour, claiming Gordon Brown used women as 'window dressing' rather than give them proper responsibility. She also complained of 'constant pressure, negative bullying'. Apart from being obviously bright and able, Flint appeared to be a little over-fond of her own image, and featured in a glamour photo-shoot for a newspaper. She also seemed to feel she had a right to be promoted to the cabinet and had resigned in something of a huff when she failed to be. Such sentiments seldom produce political advancement. She retained her seat in 2010 by 3,395 votes.

Foot, Michael (1913–2010)

Labour politician, scholar and journalist. Son of Liberal MP Isaac Foot, Michael was educated at Leighton Park School, Reading, and Wadham College, Oxford. During the war he worked as a journalist on left-wing publications and for the right-wing, Beaverbrook-owned *Daily Express*. He was elected for Devonport in 1945 and defeated in 1955 but returned for Ebbw Vale (the constituency of his idol, Aneurin Bevan) in 1960. He was thereafter a perennial rebel over expenditure, industrial relations and Vietnam in the 1960s. He stepped up to real power in 1974 as employment secretary. Under James Callaghan he became lord president of the Council and leader of the house, as well as a key conduit between the left and right in the party, then dangerously wide apart. Aged 67 he was elected as leader of the Labour Party in 1980 and there began three tortured years when Margaret Thatcher was supreme and Foot synonymous with a discredited and largely ungovernable left-wing Labour Party. He

lost the 1983 election heavily and gave way to Neil Kinnock but continued campaigning, writing and espousing his many causes. Possibly the most brilliant public speaker and parliamentarian of his day as well as one of the most cultured and civilised politicians of the century, he was widely popular in many sections of the party, but suffered from a poor media image.

> The members of our Secret Service have spent so much time looking under the bed for Communists, that they haven't had time to look in the bed. (On the Profumo affair, 1963)

> It is not necessary that every time he rises he should give the impression of being a semi-house trained polecat. (On Norman Tebbit, 1978)

Forsyth, Michael (1954–), Lord

Conservative MP and cabinet minister. He was educated at Arbroath High School and St Andrew's University (where he was president of the Union). He was MP for Stirling 1983–97 and junior minister in the Scottish Office before becoming secretary of state for Scotland in 1995. He was known to be a staunch Thatcherite and was created a life peer in 1997 (as Lord Drumlean).

Fox, Charles James (1749–1806)

Whig politician with a reputation as a radical. He was son of Baron Holland, entered parliament in 1769 as a supporter of the monarchy but crossed to the Whigs in 1774. He led the opposition to Pitt the Younger's war of intervention against the French Revolution, which he supported. He was made foreign secretary in 1782 (so becoming the first office holder) and again in 1806. He succeeded in abolishing the slave trade.

> How much the greatest event it is that has ever happened in the world! and how much the best! (On the fall of the Bastille, 1789)

> I will not close my politics in that foolish way. (On being offered a peerage)

Fox, Liam (1961–)

Conservative MP. He was educated at St Bride's High School and Glasgow

University, where he qualified in medicine. He was elected MP for Woodspring in 1992 and soon made a mark as a lively right-winger. He shadowed health under Conservative leader Iain Duncan Smith but helped Michael Howard with his leadership campaign in November 2003. He was joint Conservative Party chair from November 2003. He then became shadow defence secretary and remained so after 2005, when David Cameron defeated him in the contest for leadership of the party. He became secretary of state for defence in May 2010.

France, Elizabeth (1950–)

Commissioner for information from 2002. She was educated at Beauchamp's School, Leicester, and University College Wales, Aberystwyth. She entered the elite grade of the civil service and by 1986 had risen to be in charge of the Criminal Justice and Constitutional Department. She was data protection registrar 1994–2002.

Freedland, Jonathan, (1967–)

Journalist on the *Guardian* and *Jewish Chronicle* and broadcaster. He was educated at University College School and Wadham College, Oxford. Apart from his twice-weekly columns in the *Guardian*, he is an author of fiction and non-fiction as well as a broadcaster on television and Radio 4.

Friedman, Milton (1912–2006)

US monetarist economist who argued in *Free to Choose* (1980) that in order to control inflation governments should control the supply of cash and credit in the economy through the manipulation of interest rates. Many governments and right-of-centre politicians were influenced by him, not least Margaret Thatcher, Keith Joseph and Nigel Lawson, who applied a brand of monetarism closely related to Friedman's ideas. He won the Nobel Prize for Economics in 1976 and advised the governments of Chile and Israel.

> There's no such thing as a free lunch.

> A society that puts equality – in the sense of equality of outcome – ahead of freedom will end up with neither equality or freedom.

Frost, David (1939–)

Broadcaster and interviewer. He was educated at Oxford and began his career by presenting *That Was the Week That Was* in the 1960s. He went on to *The Frost Report* and *Breakfast with Frost*. He assisted the trend towards irreverent, sharp questioning which began with Robin Day in the late 1950s. His interviews with Richard Nixon in the 1970s were much praised and were the subject of a play by Peter Morgan, *Frost/Nixon* (2006), in 2008 made into a film directed by Ron Howard.

G

Gaitskell, Hugh (1906–63)

Labour MP, minister and party leader. He was born to a middle-class family and educated at Winchester and Oxford. He became a socialist in the 1920s and an adult education tutor before teaching economics at the University of London. He worked as a civil servant with Hugh Dalton during the war and was elected for Leeds South in 1945. After junior posts he replaced Stafford Cripps as chancellor in 1950. His 1951 budget proposed massive rearmament in response to the Korean war, which provoked Aneurin Bevan and Harold Wilson to resign their ministries. Bevan led a faction in the party but lost the battle to succeed Clement Attlee in 1955, when Gaitskell won, with the support of the unions. Gaitskell lost the 1959 general election and was rebuffed over unilateralism at the 1961 Labour Party conference. However, he reacted passionately and overthrew the decision at the following year's conference. Gaitskell was brilliant intellectually though he lacked the charisma and common touch of his rival, Bevan. He died suddenly and tragically in 1963 but left his disciples in the form of Anthony Crosland and Roy Jenkins. He was very much a moderate socialist, was in favour of scrapping clause 4 of the party's constitution, and led the way to the revisionist approach which dominated the 1960s and 1970s Labour governments and established the context within which it was possible for New Labour to emerge.

> There are some of us Mr Chairman who will fight, fight and fight again to defend the party we love. (Labour Party conference, 1960)

Galloway, George (1954–)

Labour MP expelled in 2003 for persistent rebellious behaviour. He was educated at Harris Academy, Dundee, but left school aged 16 and worked for a tyre factory before becoming active in politics. He became Labour chair in Scotland when 26, and later became chair of the charity War on Want. He raised its profile but there were some doubts about its finances. In 1987 he defeated Roy Jenkins to become MP for Glasgow Hillhead (later Kelvin). He espoused several causes in the Middle East, including that of the Palestinians and sanctions against Iraq under Saddam Hussein. He met the Iraqi dictator several times and was accused, somewhat unfairly, of being his apologist. On 23 October 2003 Labour expelled him for allegedly urging soldiers to disobey orders during the 2003 war against Iraq. He set up the anti-Iraq war Respect party, which contested the European and local elections in June 2004. In 2005 he sensationally won Bethnal Green and Bow from sitting Labour MP Oona King; in refuting various accusations made against him he was generally judged to have come off the better. In May 2005 he testified in the US Senate before Senator Norm Coleman. In 2006 he had an embarrassing stint on *Celebrity Big Brother*. He failed to win Poplar and Limehouse in 2010. He was, though, one of the most brilliant natural orators in the House of Commons and, given a different career trajectory, might easily have fulfilled his ambition of becoming a foreign office minister.

> Sir, I salute your courage, your strength and your indefatigability and I want you to know

that we are with you. (In a televised meeting with Saddam Hussein, 1994)

> I have no expectation of justice from a group of Christian fundamentalist and Zionist activists under the chairmanship of a neo-con George Bush. (Upon arriving in the USA to testify in front of the Senate, 2005)

Gamble, Andrew (1947–), Professor

Leading political scientist, at Cambridge University. He was educated at Brighton College and then Cambridge. He acquired his MA at Durham and returned to Cambridge for his doctorate. He lectured for several years at Sheffield University, becoming a professor in 1986. He moved to Cambridge in 2007. His works include *Politics and Fate* (2000), *Between Europe and America* (2003) and *The Spectre at the Feast* (2009).

Garton-Ash, Timothy (1965–)

Academic, author and journalist. He studied modern history at Oxford University then lived for some years in Germany, where he wrote widely on the break-up of communist eastern Europe. He moved into academic posts and has written nine books on political topics. He writes a weekly column in the *Guardian* and for the *New York Review of Books*. He is professor of European studies at Oxford, Isaiah Berlin fellow at St Anthony's College, Oxford, and senior fellow at the Hoover Institution, Stanford University.

George, Eddie (1938–2009), Sir

Governor of the Bank of England 1993–2003. He was educated at Dulwich College and Cambridge University. A lifetime employee of the Bank he developed a reputation for cool judgement and reliability. After 1997 he and members of the Monetary Policy Committee were given responsibility for fixing interest rates. In an interview he once admitted to be hopeless with his private finances and estimated the cost of a pint of milk at £1. He was nicknamed 'Steady Eddie' but could make gaffes, as when he said unemployment in the north was a price worth paying for low inflation.

Gibson, Ian (1938–)
Former Labour MP for Norwich North.
He was educated at Dumphries Academy
and Edinburgh University. He also
studied at the Universities of Indiana
and Washington before working at the
University of East Anglia as a lecturer in
biology. Initially in the Socialist Workers
Party, he joined Labour in 1983, finally
entering the Commons in 1997. As an MP
he was a regular rebel over various aspects
of government policy but came unstuck
when it transpired he had bought a London
flat with the help of the MPs' second
homes allowance and then sold it to his
daughter – who had lived in it rent free – at
half the market price. He was forced to
appear before a Labour Party panel, who
insisted he stand down at the next election.
Instead he resigned and a by-election was
held in July 2009, which was won easily by
the Conservative candidate.

Giddens, Anthony (1938–)
Director of the London School of
Economics and professor of sociology at
Cambridge. He is said to have influenced
New Labour thinking in the 1980s
and 1990s. He was educated at Hull,
the London School of Economics and
Cambridge. He became a fellow of King's
College, Cambridge, in 1969. He is
the author of many books on sociology,
which have been influential worldwide. In
particular, his book *The Third Way* (1998)
was said both to express and to influence
New Labour's approach to politics. His
influence soon declined as New Labour
moved into its second term.

Gieve, John (1950–), Sir
Permanent secretary at the Home Office
2001–05 and subsequently deputy
governor of the Bank of England. He was
educated Charterhouse School and New
College, Oxford, where he got a first in
philosophy, politics and economics (PPE),
and he added an MPhil in philosophy
to his bachelor's degree. He joined the
civil service in 1974 and served in the
Treasury, where he was private secretary

to Nigel Lawson, John Major and Norman
Lamont. He moved to the Home Office
and helped develop defences against
terrorism and measures against anti-
social behaviour. He served three home
secretaries while he was the most senior
official: Jack Straw, David Blunkett and
Charles Clarke. A report by the National
Audit Office in January 2006 criticised
his financial stewardship of his department
but, nevertheless, he was appointed deputy
governor of the Bank of England.

Gillan, Cheryl (1952–)
Conservative MP and secretary of state for
Wales. She was educated at Cheltenham
Ladies College before entering the business
world. She became a senior marketing
consultant with Ernst and Young in 1986.
She chaired the Bow Group 1987–88.
She tried unsuccessfully for an MEP seat
in 1989 and was elected for Chesham and
Amersham in 1992. She served as a junior
minister in Education and Employment
from 1995 and then held several opposition
posts after 1997 in trade and industry, and
foreign affairs. She made it to the shadow
cabinet for her present post in 2005 and in
2010 was appointed to it.

Gilligan, Andrew (1968–)
BBC defence and diplomatic correspondent
1999–2004. Gilligan was educated at a
comprehensive school in south-west London
before going on to Cambridge University.
He worked for the *Sunday Telegraph* for
five years as its defence correspondent
and joined the BBC in 1999. He was
unusual in that his BBC reports sometimes
involved seeking news exclusives rather
than merely reporting news. This practice
proved problematic on 29 May 2003 when
he was interviewed on Radio 4's *Today*
programme and claimed an intelligence
source had told him the government had
deliberately embellished the intelligence
dossier produced in September 2002
on Iraq's weapons of mass destruction, a
document used to justify the war on Iraq
launched in 2003. Soon the name of the
informant, Dr David Kelly, came out and

his subsequent suicide led Tony Blair to set up the Hutton inquiry into the circumstances leading to Kelly's death. Hutton's report, in January 2004, heavily criticised the BBC's news editing procedures and led to the resignations of the corporation's chairman, director general and, on 30 January 2004, Gilligan.

Gilmour, Ian (1926–2007), Lord
Conservative cabinet minister who was too 'wet' for Margaret Thatcher. He was educated Eton and Balliol College, Oxford. He served in the Grenadier Guards before being called to the bar in 1952. He edited the *Spectator* 1954–59. He was MP for Norfolk Central 1962–74, Chesham and Amersham 1974–92. He was a junior defence minister in Edward Heath's government and lord privy seal under Thatcher 1979–81. He wrote several books on British party politics and was made a life peer in 1992. He was popular in his party as an erudite and witty companion.

Gladstone, William Ewart (1809–98)
Liberal prime minister. He started his political life as a reactionary high Tory and served in government at the Board of Trade under Robert Peel, whose high-mindedness made a great impression on him. His sympathy with Italian nationalism influenced his views on foreign policy. His first ministry (1868–74) initiated landmark reforms in the army, civil service and local government as well as taxation and education. He came out of retirement to fight, successfully, the Conservative seat of Midlothian in an attack on Benjamin Disraeli's foreign policy in the Middle East. His inspiring speeches revealed how politicians can win power through appeals to the mass electorate. He returned to be prime minister in 1880–85, 1886 and 1892–94 but the Irish home rule question was a constant distraction to the 'Grand Old Man' in his later years. One of the greatest politicians of his age in terms of both his administrative and his speaking abilities, he was notable for injecting his

own high-minded morality into the lifeblood of the nation's politics.

> My mission is to pacify Ireland. (On hearing he was to become prime minister, 1868)

> He has not a single redeeming defect. (Disraeli on Gladstone)

> He speaks to me as if I were a public meeting. (Queen Victoria on Gladstone)

Goldsmith, James (1933–97)
Wealthy businessman who established the Referendum Party. He was born in Paris though educated in Britain. He developed a network of publishing and food companies but became rich through being a financier, cleverly selling stocks before the mid-1980s crash and buying when prices were low. He was calculated to be worth over £1 billion and owned a huge estate in Mexico. He was elected as a member of the European parliament 1995–97 and intervened in the 1997 British general election with his lavishly funded Referendum Party, which argued against closer European integration. The party ran candidates all over the country but was perceived by voters as a fringe oddity for the most part and it had little overall impact on the outcome. Shortly afterwards the charismatic and highly controversial Sir James died of cancer. He was also well known for his aggressive libel action against the satirical magazine *Private Eye* in the 1970s. He was knighted in 1976.

Goldsmith, Peter (1950–), Lord
Labour peer. He was educated in Liverpool Queen's School and Cambridge University as well as University College, London. He was called to the bar in 1972 and became queen's counsel in 1997. He sat as a recorder from 1987 and a deputy High Court judge after 1994. He was created a life peer in 1999 and made a privy counsellor in 2002. He served as chairman of the bar in England and Wales and was chairman of the International Bar Association. In 1996 he was the prime minister's personal representative at the Convention for Fundamental Rights. He

was attorney general from June 2001, and became embroiled in controversy when his advice that the war on Iraq was legal was subsequently challenged. When he resigned in June 2007, he was the longest serving Labour attorney general.

Goodwin, Sir Fred (1958–)

Former head of the Royal Bank of Scotland (RBS). Born the son of an electrician, he attended Paisley Grammar School and then Glasgow University, where he studied law. He qualified as an accountant in 1983, becoming a partner in Touche Roche in 1988. He rapidly rose to the top of the National Australia Bank by 1996. He joined RBS in 1998 and was chief executive 2001–08. He acquired a reputation as 'Fred the Shred', a ruthless cost cutter, although he rapidly expanded the bank to make it one of the largest in the world. However, his acquisition of Dutch bank ABN Amro proved a disaster and led his bank to the brink of ruin in 2008. It was also one of the world's top three underwriters of sub-prime mortgage securities, which exposed it critically to the 'credit crunch' which arrived in 2007–08. Goodwin resigned in 2008 but insisted his annual pension of £700,000 should be paid, despite his former bank being bailed out by taxpayers and furious objections from both public and government. This outcry was redoubled when it was revealed RBS had made a loss of £28 billion during the last year of Sir Fred's leadership. He eventually agreed to repay about a quarter of his pension. Along with fellow leading bankers Sir Fred appeared before the Treasury Select Committee in 2009 and all said 'sorry' for anything they might have done to precipitate the banking meltdown.

Gordon Walker, Patrick (1907–80), Lord

Academic and Labour foreign secretary in the 1960s. He was educated at Wellington and Oxford. He worked as a university lecturer before he became MP for Smethwick 1945–64 and Leyton 1966–74. He held junior office under Clement Attlee, then

was foreign secretary 1964–65 and minister for education and science 1967–68. He was defeated in Smethwick in the 1964 general election by an opponent who played the 'race card' but was appointed foreign secretary nevertheless when Reg Sorensen accepted a peerage from Harold Wilson so that Gordon Walker could (eventually) be re-elected to the Commons.

Gould, Philip (1950–)

Tony Blair's aide and pollster. He was educated at Knaphill Secondary Modern, East College, London, the University of Sussex, the London School of Economics and the London Business School. He worked as a marketing consultant in the 1970s and 1980s before he assisted the Labour Party. He founded Philip Gould Associates in 1985 and was a partner of Gould, Greenberg, Carville Ltd from 1997. He married Gail Rebuck, head of Random House publishers. Memos to and from Blair in 2000 were leaked and provoked bad publicity, as they suggested Blair was anxiously obsessed with short-term popularity. Gould is generally seen as the champion of focus groups in Labour campaign strategy, and in his book *The Unfinished Revolution* (1998) he defended them as aides to democratic government. He was made a Labour peer in 2004.

> The New Labour brand has been badly contaminated. It is the object of constant criticism and, even worse, ridicule. (Memo to Tony Blair, May 2000, leaked to press)

Gove, Michael (1967–)

Conservative MP and minister. He was born in Edinburgh and educated at both state and private schools, having won a scholarship to Robert Gordon's College. From there he went to Oxford, where he studied English and was president of the Union. He was originally a Labour supporter and considered entering the church. He tried to join the Conservative Research Department but was told he was 'insufficiently political'. He chose instead to become a journalist, starting on the *Press and Journal* in Aberdeen and then moving on to the *Times* in 1996 as a leader writer. He has written widely for other publications, including the *Spectator*, as well as becoming a regular broadcaster on BBC radio and television. His book on Northern Ireland, *The Price of Peace* (2000), won the Charles Douglas Home prize. He chaired the right-leaning think-tank Policy Exchange in 2002 and was elected for Surrey Heath in 2005. He was seen as close to David Cameron's 'modernising' social circle and shadowed education before being appointed secretary of state for education in May 2010.

Grade, Michael (1943–)

Chairman of the BBC, 2004–06. He was educated St Dunstan's College, London. Undoubtedly highly imaginative and talented in his field, Grade has been a somewhat maverick figure in the British media. He began his career as a journalist with the *Daily Mirror* and then moved to London Weekend Television in 1973; he became director of programmes in 1977. Next he was BBC1's controller 1986–88 and director of programmes 1987. He moved to become Channel 4's chief executive 1988–97. When he failed to obtain the key jobs he wanted – mostly at the BBC – during the 1990s he switched careers to become chief executive of Camelot in 1997 and then chairman 2000–04. His appointment by Tessa Jowell as the BBC's chairman in 2004, following the upheavals of the Huttton report, was controversial – the *Daily Mail* attacked him as 'pornographer in chief' at Channel 4 – but the appointment was welcomed in the media and on the left. He moved to ITV in 2006 and stood down in 2009.

Grayling, Chris (1962–)

Conservative MP and minister. He was educated at Royal Grammar School, High Wycombe, and Sidney Sussex College, Cambridge. He worked as a producer for the BBC, worked for Channel 4 and then became a management consultant before being elected for Epsom and Ewell in 2001. In 2002 he became whip and then

shadowed health. Michael Howard made him a spokesman on education in 2003 as well as shadowing the leader of the house until 2005. Under David Cameron he shadowed transport, work and pensions and then the Home Office, January 2009. He failed to be made home secretary in 2010 but did become minister of state at the Department of Work and Pensions.

Green, Damien (1956–)

Conservative MP and minister. He was educated at Reading school and Balliol College, Oxford, where he studied philosophy, politics and economics (PPE) and was president of the Union. He worked in journalism and television before becoming a member of John Major's Policy Unit in 1992 and then running his own public affairs consultancy. He was elected for Ashford in 1997. He shadowed at various junior levels before becoming shadow education secretary 2001 and then transport 2003. He left the front bench of his own accord in 2004 but rejoined under David Cameron, speaking on home affairs. He was arrested in November 2008 in connection with 'aiding and abetting misconduct in public office' and 'conspiring to commit misconduct in a public office'. This related to a leak made by a Home Office official keen to work for the Conservatives. Green claimed he was merely doing his job when making public information in the public interest – most of the media agreed he had done no wrong but Green was held for several hours and his home searched as well as his office in the Commons. Vernon Bogdanor claimed it was a 'storm in a tea-cup' but it caused huge perturbations in the media and political life for several days. He was made minister of state for immigration at the Home Office in May 2010.

Green, T. H. (1836–82)

Philosopher and social theorist. He was educated at Rugby and Oxford. He was influenced by the German idealists Kant and Hegel. Not a prolific writer, his influence was disseminated more through his lectures and teaching. He did not go the way of

Hegel in idealising the state but insisted on individual responsibility and rights. He put forward the view that to be free one had to have the opportunity to fulfil one's potential – a crucial element in thinking, a century later, on the welfare state.

Greer, Germaine (1939–)

Leading Australian feminist academic, author and broadcaster. She was educated at Universities in Melbourne and Cambridge, and lectured at Warwick University. Her *Female Eunuch* (1970) portrayed marriage as a legalised form of slavery and she attacked the way in which women's sexuality was misrepresented and denied by males. Later in her career her early radicalism was modified a little.

Grieve, Dominic (1956–)

Conservative MP and attorney general. He was educated at the Lycée Français and Westminster School before Magdalen College, Oxford, where he was president of the university Conservative Association. He studied law at the University of Westminster and was called to the bar in 1980; he became queen's counsel in 2008. He won Beaconsfield in 1997 and became spokesman on Scotland 1999, criminal justice 2001 and shadow attorney general 2003. He gave the impression of quiet competence, albeit from a position of almost cloned establishment credentials, and in January 2009 became shadow justice secretary. After the May 2010 election he became attorney general and rocked the boat a little by praising the Human Rights Act, which his party wished to appeal.

Griffin, Nick (1959–)

Leader of British National Party (BNP). He was born in Barnett but educated at Woodbridge School in Suffolk. From there he won a sixth-form scholarship to the independent Saint Felix School in Southwold: one of only two boys in the all-girls school. His father was a former Conservative councillor but the son was clearly more interested in a more robust form of political belief. He read *Mein*

Kampf when he was 14 and joined the National Front (NF). He went on to study history and then law at Downing College, Cambridge. He gained a lower second degree but won a 'blue' for boxing for his university. He went on to work for the NF at national level and contested Croydon Northwest in 1981 and 1983 but lost his deposit both times. He left the NF in 1989 and, when he lost an eye in an accident, he gave up politics for a while. He joined the BNP in 1995, having been persuaded by John Tyndall. He was convicted in 1998 of distributing material likely to incite racial hatred but other court cases were less successful for the prosecution. Griffin worked hard to draw the BNP away from its extremist image and to seek mainstream success. This began with successes at the local level in towns like Burnley in the north and Barking in the south, and in June 2009 Griffin was able to win one of two seats in the Euro-elections for the BNP in the north-west. In October 2009 he appeared on BBC1's *Question Time* discussion programme but did not impress many. During the 2010 election he stood for Barking against Margaret Hodge but was defeated easily, together with all his councillors at the local level in the same town. Partly as a result of discontent at his leadership during the 2010 elections, Griffin announced he would step down as leader in 2113.

> The electors of Millwall did not back a post-modernist rightist party, but what they perceived to be a strong, disciplined organisation with the ability to back up its slogan 'Defend Rights for Whites' with well-directed boots and fists. (Griffin upon the BNP winning a council by-election in 1993)

Grimond, Joseph (Jo) (1913–93)

Liberal MP and party leader in the 1950s and 1960s. He was educated at Eton and Balliol College, Oxford. He married Herbert Asquith's grand-daughter. He practised as barrister and fought in the Second World War. He was elected MP for Orkney and Shetland from 1950 and was leader of the Liberal Party 1956–67. During this time the number of Liberal MPs doubled: he thereby ended the decline in Liberal fortunes which began when David Lloyd George split the party in 1916. He was made a life peer in 1983.

> I look forward to the day when there is a strike not because a firm has introduced automation, but because it has not. (1956)

Gummer, John Selwyn (1943–)
Conservative MP and cabinet minister. He was educated at King's School, Rochester, and Selwyn College, Cambridge, where he was chair of the Cambridge University Conservative Party and Federation of Conservative Students. He was MP for Suffolk (Eye) 1979–83 and Suffolk Coastal 1983. He served as a junior minister at the Departments of Agriculture and Employment before he became secretary of state for the environment 1993–97. He was also chairman of the Conservative Party 1983–85. He was one of the faithful Thatcherite ministers who served during the 1980s; he reinforced her enthusiasm for the environment and won plaudits even from the green lobby. He famously once fed a beefburger to his daughter in front of the press during the crisis over bovine spongiform encephalitis ('mad cow disease'), to demonstrate the safety of British beef. He was also well known as a member of the General Synod of the Church of England, 1979–92. He stood down as an MP and became a life peer in May 2010.

H

Hague, William Jefferson (1961–)
Conservative MP, party leader 1997–2001, and cabinet minister. He was educated at Wath Comprehensive School, near Rotherham. He received a standing ovation when aged only 16 after an address to the

Conservative Party annual conference. He moved on to Oxford, where he was president of the Union and attained a first-class honours degree. He became a McKinsey management consultant and then an MP in 1989. He served as parliamentary private secretary to Norman Lamont 1990–93, became a junior minister and then secretary of state for social security and secretary of state for Wales 1995–97, when he met his wife, Ffion. Initially he was approached by Michael Howard to run with him as deputy leader in the 1997 leadership fight but he decided to stand in his own right after Kenneth Clarke and John Redwood tried to form a united front. He came through to win the contest decisively on the third ballot, by 92 votes to Clarke's 70. He became thereby the youngest party leader since William Pitt the Younger. Many commentators thought little of Hague's performance as leader during his first year but he reorganised party structures and developed a sharp style at prime minister's questions, which frequently rattled the normally serene Tony Blair. After an initial attempt to introduce a species of 'compassionate Conservatism', Hague swung to the right and presided over a Thatcherite 'commonsense revolution' in 1999, which sealed the fate of his party at the 2001 general election. His anti-Europe stance may have led to Tory gains in the 1999 European elections but this was on a low poll. During the 2001 general election campaign Hague decided to stress issues like (bogus) asylum seekers, taxation and the perils of Europe, especially joining the single currency. Almost certainly as a result, Conservative support barely rose above 30 per cent throughout the campaign: about the level of the party's core vote. On 7 June 2001 the Conservatives' representation rose by only one seat, to 166, while Labour had won 412 and had a majority of 167. Immediately in the wake of the defeat – despite widespread tributes to his resilience and courage – Hague resigned his position, leaving the field open for rivals to contest the leadership. Hague was the first Conservative leader since Austen Chamberlain in 1922 not to become prime minister. Not unusually for failed leaders he became more highly thought of subsequently, partly through his wit and acuity and also through his brilliant biographies of the Younger Pitt (2004) and William Wilberforce (2007). His career as an after-dinner speaker enabled him to earn up to £1 million a year. In 2005 David Cameron made him shadow foreign secretary. He retained his Yorkshire Richmond seat with a majority of over 20,000 in the May 2010 election and became foreign secretary.

> People work and save hard to own a car. They do not want to be told they cannot drive it by the deputy prime minister whose idea of a park and ride scheme is to park one Jaguar and ride away in another. (1999)

Hailsham, Lord (Douglas Quintin Hogg) (1907–2002)

Leading postwar Conservative lawyer, thinker and cabinet minister. He was educated at Eton and Christ Church, Oxford, where he was president of the Union. He was a fellow of All Souls 1932, and from 1938 to 1950 served as MP for Oxford City. He succeeded as the 2nd Viscount of Marylebone in 1950 and served as first lord of the Admiralty 1956–57, education minister 1957, lord president of the Council 1957–59 and 1960–64, minister for science and technology 1959–64 and chairman of the Conservative Party 1957–59. He then renounced his peerage in order to become eligible for the leadership of the Tory party after Harold Macmillan resigned and was re-elected to the Commons in a by-election for Marylebone. He was made a life peer in 1970 and became lord chancellor 1970–74 and 1979–87. He was thus one of the longest-serving Conservative grandees, with a fine legal mind and a combative political style slightly out of step with his party, though he served both Edward Heath and Margaret Thatcher loyally. He was also a distinguished writer on politics and the constitution. In the mid-1970s he claimed the ability of Labour to introduce radical reforms on the basis of well under half of

the electorate's vote indicated Britain had become an 'elective dictatorship', where the majority in parliament delivered too much power to the government. However, his enthusiasm for reform disappeared once he was back in government.

> A great party has been brought down because of a squalid affair between a woman of easy virtue and a proven liar. (In a television interview with Robert McKenzie about the Profumo affair, 13 June 1963)

> Mercy is not what every criminal is entitled to. What he is entitled to is justice. (1975)

> The best way to win an argument is to start by being in the right. (1960)

Hain, Peter (1950–)

Labour MP and minister. He was born in South Africa but his family were forced to leave in 1966. He was educated at Pretoria Boys High School, the University of London and Sussex University. He later took part in anti-apartheid activities, especially against rugby links with his home country. He was chairman of the Young Liberals 1971–73 and was active with the Anti-Nazi League (as its press officer). In the 1970s he worked for a number of unions. He contested Putney for Labour in the 1980s but was elected for Neath in South Wales in a by-election in 1991. He served in the whips' office and was spokesman on employment matters as well as Welsh affairs. Once Labour gained power in 1997 he served in the Welsh Office and the Department of Trade and Industry and was minister for Europe in the Foreign Office, before becoming secretary of state for Wales. In 2003 he was given the job of speaking for Wales in cabinet and the Commons, as well as being leader of the house. He was seen as a street-wise, loyal, thoughtful but ambitious minister marked for further promotion in the cabinet. He stood for deputy leader of the Labour Party in 2007 but did not do well. Afterwards he was caught up in a scandal about his funding of his campaign for the deputy leadership election and he resigned in January 2008. Gordon Brown reappointed him as Welsh secretary in 2009. He held Neath in 2010 by 9,775 votes.

Hamilton, Neil (1949–)

Conservative junior minister who was embroiled in the 'cash for questions' scandal in the mid-1990s and sensationally defeated by Martin Bell in the 1997 general election. He was educated at Amman Valley Grammar School and University College Wales, Aberystwyth, then studied law at Cambridge. He worked as a barrister until he was elected for Tatton in 1979. He served as a junior minister in the Department of Trade and Industry. The *Guardian* claimed he had regularly accepted favours and cash from the owner of Harrods, Mohamed al Fayed, in exchange for asking parliamentary questions on his behalf and other lobbying activities. Hamilton declared he would sue (he had sued the BBC for libel in the mid-1980s and won, over an accusation that he had fascist tendencies). However, in October 1996 Hamilton pulled out of the action through lack of money and the *Guardian* responded by calling him a 'Liar and a Cheat' on its front page. In the 1997 general election the BBC war correspondent Martin Bell stood against Hamilton – who was supported by his formidable wife, Christine – in this rock-solid Conservative seat and won it by a majority of 11,000; Bell served only one term as an MP and the constituency returned to the Tories in the 2001 general election. In August 2001 a bizarre follow-up to the Hamiltons' notoriety occurred when a single mother in Essex claimed both Hamiltons had been involved in an incident in which she was raped. Both Neil and Christine hotly denied the story and, after huge media interest, the police decided there was no case to answer and dropped their inquiries. After the scandal they both sought, with some bravery, to develop careers in the media, though with varying degrees of success.

> I've found it's much better making political jokes than being one. (Neil Hamilton after the scandal)

Hardie, Keir (1856–1915)

One of the founders of the Labour Party. He worked in the mines from childhood and became an organiser of the men and a journalist. He was defeated as a parliamentary candidate in Mid Lanark in 1888 but sat for West Ham South 1892–95 and then Merthyr Tydfil 1900–15. He founded and edited *Labour Leader* and handed it to the Independent Labour Party in 1903, which he chaired 1893–1900 and 1913–14. He supported the formation of a separate Labour Party. He was a dedicated pacifist and opposed the Boer war and the First World War.

Harmsworth, Alfred (Lord Northcliffe) (1865–1922)

Newspaper magnate. He was born in Ireland and rapidly rose to prominence in the emerging newspaper business at the end of the 19th century. He founded the *Daily Mail* in 1896, when it was priced a halfpenny. This success prompted the launch of the *Daily Mirror* in 1903. He then acquired the *Observer* and in 1908 the *Times*. He was openly political and attacked the government of the day, especially Herbert Asquith and Horatio Kitchener in the First World War. During the war he held office as director of propaganda. He had a nervous breakdown before his death in 1922.

Harmsworth, Harold (Lord Rothermere) (1868–1940)

Younger brother of Alfred Harmsworth and owner of the *Daily Mirror* after 1914. He controlled Associated Newspapers for 10 years from 1922 and was one of the 'press barons' who featured so strongly in politics at the start of the 20th century. He used his newspapers to support appeasement of Nazi Germany. In 1934 he wrote a *Daily Mail* editorial entitled 'Hurrah for the Black Shirts'.

Haskins, Christopher (1937–), Lord

Special advisor on rural policy and chairman of Northern Foods. He was educated at Trinity College, Dublin, then worked for Fords in Dagenham before moving to Northern Foods. He was a member of several government task forces set up after 1997 and had a controversial role as a government advisor on agriculture, as he was himself a farmer. In 2005 he contributed money to a Scottish Liberal Democrat campaign and was expelled from the Labour Party as a result.

Hastings, Sir Max (1945–)

Leading journalist and historian. He was educated at Charterhouse and Oxford, then pursued a distinguished career in journalism. He reported on dozens of wars for British television, especially the Falklands conflict in 1983. He edited the *Daily Telegraph* and the *Evening Standard* and currently writes columns in the *Daily Mail* and the *Guardian*. He is also a recognised as a military historian of distinction.

Hattersley, Roy (1932–), Lord

Former Labour cabinet minister and journalist. He was educated at Hull University and was a journalist and local politician before entering the Commons in 1964. Always pro-Europe, he served as a minister in the Foreign Office 1974–76 and then as cabinet minister for prices and consumer protection 1976–79. He was opposition spokesman on the environment and home affairs in the 1980s and was elected on the so-called 'dream ticket' to be deputy party leader 1983–92 to Neil Kinnock. He was made a life peer in 1993. His age was probably why he was not appointed to office on Labour's return to power in 1997. However, witty, perceptive and fluent he continued his prolific journalistic and broadcasting career, often appearing as a left-wing critic of New Labour, which is an irony as throughout his political career the left regarded him as hopelessly revisionist and right wing. On 24 June 2001 he wrote an article in the *Observer* highly critical of Tony Blair. He called for a 'counter-coup' against New Labour to restore the party's principles. He attacked Blair for being contemptuous

of ideology and described the pursuance of 'social justice' a 'vacuous platitude'.

> One by one the policies which define our philosophy have been rejected by the Prime Minister. (*Observer*, 24 June 2001)

> Opposition is four or five years' humiliation in which there is no escape from the indignity of no longer controlling events. (1995)

Hatton, Derek (1948–)

Deputy leader of Liverpool council 1983–87. He was educated at Liverpool Institute and Goldsmith's College, London University. He briefly followed his father to become a fireman before finding a profession closer to his political instincts: a community social worker. Study in London introduced him to the world of local politics and he carried this experience back to Liverpool, where he met Peter Taafe, who led him to support the Trotskyist Militant Tendency, a group which, while outwardly democratic, strove to take over the Labour Party from within. He became deputy leader of Liverpool council in 1983 (though most saw him as the effective leader himself), leading a left-wing programme for jobs and housing. He led the fight for the council against the Thatcher government's attempts to starve left-wing councils of funding. Hatton, who had become a bogey figure for the right-wing press, clashed bitterly with the Labour leadership and was denounced at the 1985 conference by Neil Kinnock in a famous speech. By 1987 the fight was lost and Hatton departed politics; he used his loquacious talents to become, variously, a public relations consultant, after-dinner speaker and local radio broadcaster.

> People have often accused me of being a show-off, a showman, someone who loves hogging the limelight. I suppose there's a degree of truth in it too. (1988)

Hayek, Friedrich von (1899–1992)

Austrian-born British economist. After being director of the Austrian Institute for Economic Research 1927–31 he moved to become Tooke Professor at London University 1931–50. He was appointed professor at the University of Chicago 1950, then worked in Frieburg 1962–69. His work was a reaction to Keynesianism, especially his *The Road to Serfdom* (1944) and *The Constitution of Liberty* (1960). His work demonstrates a passionate opposition to controls on the economy from the government. He saw Britain as a bulwark of freedom, which took the regulatory 'road to serfdom' in the late 19th century. He jointly won the Nobel Prize for Economics in 1974. He influenced Conservative leaders Keith Joseph, Nigel Lawson and Margaret Thatcher, along with his colleague Milton Friedman, and was partly responsible for the monetarist stance of the party during the 1980s. Thus he was one of the rare but important people who changed the way politicians think about economics.

Healey, Denis (1917–), Lord

Labour MP and cabinet minister. He was educated at Bradford Grammar School and Balliol College, Oxford. He served in the army during the war, rising to the rank of major, and won distinction as a beach master at Anzio. In 1945 he became secretary to the International Department of the Labour Party, where he made myriad contacts all over Europe and influenced the evolution of Ernest Bevin's anti-Soviet stance, which ultimately led to Britain joining NATO in 1949. He entered the house via a by-election in 1952 in Leeds South East (later Leeds East, which he held until his retirement in 1992). He helped refashion the 'revisionist' version of Labour's socialism during the 1950s and was a supporter of Hugh Gaitskell. Harold Wilson made him minister of defence, in which post he initiated cuts, restructurings and the crucial 'east of Suez' withdrawal. He was then shadow foreign secretary 1970–74 and on Labour's return to power chancellor 1974–79, when he weathered horrendous political storms as inflation roared uncontrolled and the dissenting left wing of the Labour Party almost

undermined the government. He stood for the party leadership in 1981 but was beaten by Michael Foot, by 139 votes to 129 (he subsequently served Foot loyally in opposition). He must have been sympathetic to the aims of the breakaway Social Democratic Party in 1981 but resisted any temptation to join and continued as shadow foreign secretary until 1987, when he retired to the back benches; he left the Commons in 1992 and was made a life peer. Healey was a natural politician who revelled in extroverted performances in front of the media. Brilliant intellectually – and with intense interests in music, literature, philosophy and languages – he suffered fools not at all and made enemies as a result, which may explain why this most able of politicians did not achieve his just reward of being party leader. It is often said he was the 'best prime minister we never had'.

> That part of his speech was rather like being savaged by a dead sheep. (Replying to a Commons attack by Sir Geoffrey Howe, 14 June 1978)

Heath, Edward (1916–2005)

Conservative prime minister 1970–74. He was the son of a carpenter and domestic servant. He was educated at Chatham School, Ramsgate, and Balliol College, Oxford, where he was president of the Union. He had a distinguished war record and returned to enter parliament in 1950 for Bexley (Old Bexley and Sidcup after 1974). His maiden speech was a call for European unity and this ideal informed the whole of his career. He moved up through the whips' office and served as chief whip 1955–59. In 1960 he was appointed lord privy seal, in charge of negotiations for Britain's entry into the European Community. Under Alec Douglas-Home he was at the Board of Trade, where he abolished resale price maintenance, which won him credit in his party; this, along with his humble origins and similar age to Harold Wilson, helps to explain his victory in the first democratic election (within the parliamentary party) for a Conservative leader: 150 votes to Reginald Maudling's

133. He developed a right-wing alternative to Labour and had the opportunity to put it into practice after he surprisingly won the 1970 election. However, his initial attempts to impose his 'Selsdon' programme ran into trouble and he resorted to full-blooded Keynesianism investment. This came unstuck when the unions refused to accept his reforms, as well as his prices and incomes policy, and oil prices rose sharply. The record number of days lost in strikes and 'the troubles' in Northern Ireland, not to mention the stand-off with the miners, were not overshadowed by Heath's success-ful negotiation of entry into the European Community in 1972. He called a 'Who Governs Britain?' election in February 1974 and lost narrowly to Wilson. His govern-ment was regarded by many Conservatives as unsuccessful and after his second general election defeat, in October 1974, he was challenged by Margaret Thatcher as leader and lost in the 1975 leadership election. He never forgave Margaret Thatcher for standing against him and remained a dissenting presence on the back benches throughout her period in opposition and then in government. His somewhat curmudgeonly style and tense appearances on television prevented this talented and capable politician from fulfilling his true potential. Despite his well publicised love of music and yachting, the electorate never warmed to him. He went on to become the father of the house in 1997, but retired in 2001. He died in July 2005.

It is the unpleasant, unacceptable face of capitalism. (On the Lonrho affair in the Commons, 15 May 1973)

From 31 December, they [most industrial and commercial premises] will be limited [in the use of electricity] to three specified days each week. (Commons, 13 December 1973)

I am not a product of privilege, I am a product of opportunity. (1974)

If politicians lived on praise and thanks, they'd be forced into some other line of business. (1973)

Power ... has the ability to mellow some of those who achieve it ... in Heath's case

changed his personality overnight. When prime minister he became authoritarian and intolerant. (Journalist James Margach, 1978)

Heffer, Simon (1960–)

British Conservative-supporting journalist. He was educated at King Edward VI Grammar School, Chelmsford, and Corpus Christi College, Cambridge. Heffer wrote for the *Daily Mail* from 1995 but rejoined the *Daily Telegraph* in 2005, a more suitable home, perhaps, for his well thought through and trenchantly expressed views. He has also written biographies, the best known of which is on Enoch Powell (*Like the Roman*, 1998).

If the Government wishes to prime the economy, it should bulldoze the Norris Green estate in Liverpool, where the murderer and his gang live, and split up the gang by redistributing them around the country, preferably to remote islands. Until we stop paying people to be an underclass, we'll have an underclass. (*Daily Telegraph*, about the case of the murder of Rhys Jones, February 2009)

Henderson, Arthur (1863–1935)

Labour cabinet member and party leader in early years of the 20th century. He left school aged 12 to work in an iron foundry and became active in the Ironfounders' Union. He was Labour MP for Barnard Castle 1903–18, Widnes 1919–22, Newcastle East 1923, Burnley 1924–31 and Clay Cross 1931–35. He served as Labour leader in the Commons 1908–10 and 1914–17, chief whip 1914, education minister 1915–16, as a member of the war cabinet 1916–17 (resigned 1917), chief whip again 1920–24 and 1925–27, home secretary 1924, foreign secretary 1929–31 and leader of the opposition 1931–32. He was perceived as a wise and committed socialist who tried manfully as foreign secretary to achieve disarmament.

Hennessy, Peter (1947–)

Political scientist and leading historian of government. He was educated at Marling and St John's College, Cambridge, the

London School of Economics and Harvard University. He worked as a journalist on the *Times, Times Higher Education Supplement, Financial Times, Economist, New Statesman* and *Independent*. He founded the Institute of Contemporary British History and became a well known broadcaster. He has been professor of modern history at Queen Mary and Westfield College, London University, since 1992. His books include: *Cabinet* (1986), *Whitehall* (1989), *Never Again: Britain, 1945–51* (1993), *The Hidden Wiring: Unearthing the British Constitution* (1995), *The Prime Minister: The Job and Its Holders Since 1945* (2001), *The Secret State* (2002), *Having It So Good* (2003), *Cabinets and the Bomb* (2007) and *The Secret State: Preparing for the Worst 1945–2010* (2010). He is an innovative academic who developed his journalistic skills into an extravagant gift for narrative history writing.

Heseltine, Michael (1933–), Lord
Conservative MP and cabinet minister. The son of a wealthy businessman, he was educated at Shrewsbury School and Oxford, where he was president of the Union. He served as MP for Tavistock 1966–74 and for Henley from 1974. He became rich from property and publishing (Haymarket Press) – he was a millionaire by the time he was 30. He held junior office under Edward Heath and served in Margaret Thatcher's cabinet as secretary of state for environment from 1979; he maintained his close concern for Liverpool and its surrounds following his support for government action after the 1981 riots. In 1983 he moved to defence and fought an effective battle against the Campaign for Nuclear Disarmament and the protestors outside Greenham Common. In 1986 he clashed with his prime minister over the fate of the Westlands helicopter company and her refusal to accept his European consortium solution. In December 1985 the clash became public when he walked out of the cabinet and accused Thatcher of unfairly and unconstitutionally keeping the item off the cabinet agenda. Thatcher – always suspicious of Heseltine's

ambition to be prime minister – survived the crisis but Heseltine did not languish on the back benches. Instead he began an unofficial campaign for the leadership, travelling the country to speak at party meetings. He was not shy about pointing out that his green paper on local government finance when he was at the Department of the Environment had ruled out a poll tax as unfair, before the government unwisely pressed through its introduction as the community charge. When in October 1990 Geoffrey Howe resigned as foreign secretary and accused Thatcher of poor leadership, Heseltine decided the situation was such that his earlier pledge not to stand against her could safely be ignored. He mustered 152 votes on the first ballot to her 204; she was four short of the majority required by party rules. His ambition to be prime minister was thwarted, however, when John Major came through to win the resultant contest with Heseltine and Douglas Hurd. He served as secretary of state for environment under Major, when he abolished the hated poll tax, and then as president of the Board of Trade. He lost some credibility when he accepted the Coal Board's recommendation to close 30 pits and was forced under pressure to rescind the decision. He recovered well from a mild heart attack in 1993 and was regarded as the most likely successor to Major. However, he decided to support Major when he resigned his leadership of the party in July 1995 and dared opponents to stand against him. In the event Major won but Heseltine 'won' the post of deputy prime minister and much power over policy formulation. He fought a vigorous election campaign in 1997 but his heart condition prevented him from standing in the leadership contest which followed his party's defeat. Famously ambitious, this colourful and able politician had accepted that deputy prime minister was the highest position he would attain when he retired from the Commons in 2001. He was subsequently made a life peer.

> I knew that 'He who wields the knife never wears the crown'. (On his failure to win the leadership contest he initiated against Thatcher in November 1990)

The market has no morality. (1988)

Polluted rivers, filthy streets, bodies bedded down in doorways are no advertisement for a prosperous and caring society. (Speech to Conservative Party conference, 1989)

Hewitt, Patricia (1948–)

Labour MP and cabinet minister. An Australian by birth, she was educated at Canberra High School, the Australian National University and Newham College, Cambridge. She worked for a number of pressure groups, including Age Concern and the National Council for Civil Liberties, as well as Andersen Consulting, before being elected MP for Leicester West 1997. She was soon appointed a junior Treasury minister and then moved to the Department of Trade and Industry before she entered the cabinet for the same department in 2001 as secretary of state and minister for women. She was caught by undercover journalists in March 2010 offering her services as a lobbyist. She stood down as an MP in 2010.

Heywood, Jeremy (1962–)

Civil servant. He was educated at Bootham School, York, Oxford, the London School of Economics and Harvard University. He then became a Treasury civil servant who worked in Washington for the International Monetary Fund 1988–90. He worked closely with Norman Lamont when he was chancellor as his personal private secretary 1991–94. He was in charge of securities and markets policy in 1997 when he transferred to Number 10 as liaison with his department on economic and domestic briefs. Thereafter he became principal private secretary to Tony Blair and then to Gordon Brown. David Cameron retained him in this role after May 2010.

One of the most important chefs in Blair's kitchen cabinet. (*Sunday Times*, 26 September 1999)

Hill, David (1947–)

Tony Blair's director of communications from 2003. He was educated at King Edward VI School, Birmingham, and Brasenose College, Oxford. He was assistant to Roy Hattersley 1972–74, policy advisor in the Department of Prices and Consumer Protection 1976–79; head of staff for the deputy leader of the Labour Party (Hattersley again) 1979–83, and director of campaigns and communications for the Labour Party 1991–93. He was generally regarded – especially by Hattersley – as a 'safe pair of hands', who was also popular with the press.

Hilton, Steve (1969–)

Director of strategy to the Conservative Party. Born the son of Hungarian refugees, his name was anglicised. He was educated Christ's Hospital School in Sussex before doing philosophy, politics and economics (PPE) at Oxford. Soon after graduating Hilton joined the Conservative Party, where he met his future wife, Rachel Whetstone, who worked for Google. In 1997 he was responsible for the 'demon eyes' poster campaign aimed at Tony Blair, which, though it won an award, was much criticised. David Cameron seems to depend on Hilton's judgement to quite a degree, according to insider reports, but failure to achieve an overall majority in 2010 was blamed by some Tories on Hilton's 'Big Society' idea.

Hislop, Ian (1960–)

Editor of *Private Eye*, writer and broadcaster. He was educated at Ardingley College, and Magdalen College, Oxford. He became a 'disciple' of Peter Cook and Richard Ingrams (former editor of *Private Eye*) and served as deputy editor 1985–86 before becoming editor in 1986. Initially he intended to do the job only for two years but he decided to stay longer. He survived a number of expensive libel cases to make the magazine financially stable. Together with Paul Merton, Hislop is the star of the BBC's satirical television show *Have I Got News For You*.

I have more influence as an editor of the *Eye* than I would have as a back-bench MP. (At a book signing in Manchester, 1998)

Hoare, Samuel (Viscount Templewood) (1880–1959)

Conservative cabinet minister in the 1930s. He was educated at Harrow and Oxford. He was elected MP for Chelsea 1910–44 and served in the Air Ministry 1922–29 and India Office 1931–35, before becoming foreign secretary 1935, first lord of the Admiralty 1936–37 and home secretary 1937–39; he was lord privy seal 1939–40 and ambassador to Spain 1940–44. His part in the Hoare–Laval plan in 1935 to concede much of Abyssinia to Italy was believed to have neutered the League of Nations' attempts to act collectively. He was a committed supporter of appeasement and continued to defend it even after the war had ended. Also, perhaps surprisingly for a Conservative at this time, he was a vigorous opponent of capital punishment.

Hobbes, Thomas (1588–1679)

One of the greatest British political philosophers. Educated at Oxford, he kept himself by tutoring the sons of the rich, including Charles II during his exile in Paris in 1642. Hobbes can be understood only within the context of the civil strife of his time. His great work *The Leviathan* (1651) was posited on the social contract idea, that in a state of nature life would be 'solitary, nasty, brutish, and short'. To achieve some sort of decent life it was necessary for people to create civil government and Hobbes believed a powerful king – and his power had to be absolute – should be supported by the populace, provided the king could deliver effective law and order. The significance of these ideas was that, in a climate where support for the divine right of kings was in decline (Charles I had been beheaded in 1649), his formulation provided a basis for authority without a religious underpinning. Hobbes lived a vigorous and prolific life, dying at the age of 91.

> During the time men live without a common power to keep them all in awe … the life of man [is] solitary, poor, nasty, brutish, and short. (*Leviathan*, 1651)

> I put for a general inclination of all mankind, a perpetual and restless desire after power, that ceaseth only in death. (*Leviathan*, 1651)

Hobhouse, L. T. (1864–1929)

Social and political theorist. He was educated at Oxford University and became a fellow at Merton College. He wrote for the *Manchester Guardian* for a while and became a social philosopher of the left. His writings marked the completion of the shift of left-wing thought from economic liberalism to paternalism, in which he saw the state as an 'overparent' providing the 'basis of the rights of a child, of his protection against neglect, of the equality of opportunity which he may claim as a "future citizen"'. Hobhouse prepared the intellectual ground for what later became the welfare state.

Hobson, J. A. (1858–1940)

Liberal economist. He was educated at Oxford. He believed that capitalism was fatally flawed – because it produced a rich minority who accumulated unspent profits, which led to under-consumption. This tended to create slumps and booms and the phenomenon whereby surplus wealth was invested abroad, thus creating overseas economic interests, colonies and then imperialism. He suggested the solution was the redirection of resources from the rich to the poor via progressive taxation. His thinking anticipated that of John Maynard Keynes and was especially attractive to socialist politicians.

Hogg, Douglas Quintin

See Hailsham, Lord.

Hoggart, Simon (1946–)

Journalist and broadcaster. He was educated Hymer's College, Hull, Wyggeston Grammar School, Leicester, and King's College, Cambridge. He joined the *Guardian* in 1968 and undertook most roles there – reporter, columnist, political editor – until he became parliamentary correspondent and daily sketch writer. Whether he is as accomplished in his present role as his predecessor, Michael White, is a topic of *Guardian* reader debate. From 1996 to 2006 he chaired, with some aplomb, the highly rated *News Quiz* on Radio 4. He has published collections of his sketches as well as several books based on readers' contributions, including 'round robin' Christmas circulars.

Hoon, Geoff (1953–)

Labour MP and cabinet minister. He was educated at Nottingham High School and Jesus College, Cambridge. He was a barrister before he became an MP for Ashfield 1992. He also served as a member of the European parliament 1984–94. He shadowed the solicitor general and information technology, then, after Labour came to power in 1997, served as minister of state in the Lord Chancellor's Department 1997–99 and secretary of state for defence from 1999. He was viewed as a competent Blairite but, in the perception of critics, another colourless New Labour operative. He had, by general consent, a 'good war' against Iraq. In October 2008 he was made secretary for transport but in June 2009 he resigned his job before a reshuffle. He was seen by many as a guilty party in the MPs' expenses scandal and in 2010 he was caught with others by undercover television journalists in a *Dispatches* sting, trying to sell his services as a lobbyist. He did not stand for election in 2010.

Howard, Michael (1941–)

Conservative MP and minister and leader of the Conservative Party from November 2003. Son of a Romanian-born ethnic Jew, he attended Llanelli grammar school and then went to Cambridge University, where he was president of the Union. He was called to bar 1964 and elected MP 1983. He held several junior posts before entering cabinet in charge of employment 1990–92 and environment 1992–93. He was a somewhat controversial home secretary, 1993–97, when he was known as a 'prison works' advocate and a high-profile politician who was found to have exceeded his legal powers as a minister some eight times.

In 1994 he introduced his Criminal Justice and Public Order Bill, which, among other things: modified a suspect's right to remain silent; introduced new measures against terrorists; gave tougher penalties for young offenders; gave new powers for the police to evict squatters and stop trespassers; and reduced the amount of paperwork required of police officers. He also initiated the building of six new prisons. His dismissal of the director of prisons, Derek Lewis, brought him up against his shadow, Jack Straw, a debating contest between two barristers which he easily won. However, when he stood for the leadership of his party in the wake of the Tories' 1997 defeat, his former junior minister, Ann Widdicombe, ruined his chances with a series of criticisms in which she alleged there was 'something of the night' about him. He performed badly in the contest and the person whom he had invited to stand with him as deputy leader, William Hague, eventually won it on his own. Some were surprised when Iain Duncan Smith ('IDS') gave him the brief of shadow chancellor after 2001, but he performed well against Gordon Brown – so well that many believed he would make a better leader than the much criticised IDS. When dissatisfaction with the latter reached its height in the autumn of 2003, Howard was seen as the competent, experienced heavyweight, who could rescue the Conservatives electorally. When IDS lost a vote of confidence on 29 October 2003, Howard was widely seen as his most credible replacement. Possible candidates stood down so that he was the only person available for the competition, which consequently became a 'coronation' on 6 November 2003. His first few weeks as leader were deemed a success by most commentators. He proved effective at prime minister's questions; he appointed a credible and smaller team of shadow ministers, when he managed to involve most of the previously alienated 'heavyweights'; he struck a more conciliatory note on social issues; and pledged, perhaps optimistically, in February 2004 to maintain or increase spending on public services, if elected, but to effect eventual tax savings through cutting down on wasted expenditure. As summer closed in 2004, Howard was forced to contemplate polls which in some cases showed his party level with the Liberal Democrats. Despite this he led his party into the 2005 general election on a right-wing manifesto which invoked fears about immigration ('Are you thinking what we're thinking?') but even this could not prevent a third Labour victory. In 2006 he announced he would stand down as an MP at the next election. In May 2010 he was made a life peer.

> Prison works…. I know what causes crime: criminals. (When home secretary in John Major's government)

> There is tidal wave of crime in this country. I am not going to ignore it. I am going to take action. Tough action. (As home secretary to Conservative Party conference, 1993)

> I am proud of Britain's history as a safe haven for refugees over the centuries. People have always wanted to come to Britain, as my own family did.

> I'm probably a bit more mellow than I was. (6 November 2003)

> There is something of the night about him. (Ann Widdecombe placing the kiss of death on her former boss's then leadership ambitions, 2001)

Howe, Geoffrey (1926–), Lord

Conservative chancellor, then foreign secretary, to Margaret Thatcher, who finally turned on his patron. He was educated at Winchester and Cambridge. He was a Conservative MP from 1964, was knighted in 1970, and served as solicitor general 1970–72, at trade and consumer affairs 1972–74, as chancellor 1979–83, foreign secretary 1983–89 and deputy prime minister 1989 (effectively a demotion). He resigned in 1990 and precipitated the fall of Thatcher. Always diffident – Healey famously said debating with him was like being 'savaged by a dead sheep' – and loyal, Howe also was highly ambitious and his years of accepting

his prime minister's dismissive scorn were revenged in his brilliant resignation speech, when he ridiculed Thatcher's management of the cabinet and the issue of Britain's relations with Europe. As chancellor he pursued a rigidly deflationary policy which produced a deep recession. He was created Baron Howe of Aberavon upon his retirement from the Commons.

> It is rather like sending your opening batsmen to the crease only for them to find that the moment the first balls are bowled, their bats have been broken before the game by the team captain. (Resignation speech, 13 November 1990)

Huhne, Chris (1954–)

Liberal Democrat MP for Eastleigh, since 2005. He was educated at Westminster School, the Sorbonne, Paris, and Oxford University, where he took a first in philosophy, politics and economics (PPE). He was an economics/business journalist at the *Guardian* and *Independent* and a City economist, heading his own team. He served as an MEP 1999–2005, then moved to Westminster as an MP. He shadowed the Treasury and established a green version of economic policies. He stood against Ming Campbell for the leadership, receiving 21,600 to Campbell's 29,700 votes. In the October 2007 contest he came a close second to his colleague Nick Clegg. In May 2010 he was made secretary of state for energy and climate change.

Hume, John (1937–)

Leader of Northern Ireland's Social and Democratic Labour Party and Westminster MP. He was educated at St Columb's College, Derry, and St Patrick's College, Maynooth. He was a strong advocate of peace in Northern Ireland via democratic consent; he took a risk in joining in talks with Sinn Fein leader Gerry Adams in 1988. This dialogue helped create the Good Friday agreement in 1998. He won the Nobel Peace Prize in 1998, shared with David Trimble.

> Over the years, the barriers of the past – the distrust and prejudices of the past – will be

eroded, and a new society will evolve, a new Ireland based on agreement and respect for difference.

I thought that I had a duty to help those that weren't as lucky as me.

Humphrey (the Downing Street Cat) (c. 1988–2006)

This was a 'mouser' black and white cat who lived at Number 10 Downing Street. He originally arrived as a stray but lived with Margaret Thatcher, John Major and then the Blair family. It was rumoured Cherie Blair did not like cats and within six months of the Labour victory he was rehomed with an elderly couple in the suburbs. However, his disappearance led to press rumours that he had been shot. In March 2006 it was announced he had sadly died.

Humphrys, John (1943–)

Presenter of the *Today* programme on Radio 4, BBC1's *On the Record* and a newsreader. He was educated at Cardiff High School. After the death of Brian Redhead in 1994, Humphrys became, along with James Naughtie, the voice of this daily wake-up programme for the nation's chattering classes. His tenacious questioning style made him unpopular with certain politicians. Others see him as an adornment to the nation's life. In his Mactaggart memorial lecture in August 2004 Humphrys savaged the 'seedy and cynical' television which was 'coarsening society'. He reserved some of his sharpest criticism for reality television shows like *Big Brother* and concluded by questioning whether Mary Whitehouse, the long-time 'clean-up TV' evangelist much mocked by liberals, had not been right all along. He is the author of several books including *Devil's Advocate* (2000).

> The bad television of today (compared to 'the old days') is worse. It is not only bad – it is damaging, meretricious, seedy and cynical.

Hunter, Anji (1955–)

Special assistant for presentation and planning to Tony Blair and a key member of his kitchen cabinet. She was educated at Oxford, where she sustained her childhood friendship with the future prime minister; she ran his office from 1986 to 2001, when she left government service to work in industry. She was seen as guarding the door to Blair's office.

> She is no fawning Blair babe, but one of Britain's most powerful women. (*Sunday Times*, 26 September 1999)

Hurd, Douglas (1930–), Lord

Conservative MP and cabinet minister. He was born into lesser landed gentry and educated at Eton and Cambridge. He joined the diplomatic corps in 1952; he learnt Chinese when posted in China. He joined the Conservative Party Research Department in 1966 and served as an office manager to Edward Heath and then as his political secretary after Heath became prime minister 1968–74, after which Hurd entered the House of Commons. Under Margaret Thatcher he was Northern Ireland secretary 1984, home secretary 1985 and foreign secretary 1989–95. He stood as a candidate in the leadership election in 1990 but mustered only 56 votes on the second ballot. He became a peer in 1997. Unusual in a world of driven politicians, he also writes occasional novels, usually political thrillers.

Hutton, Brian Edward (1931–), Lord

Lord of appeal in ordinary from 1997. He was educated at Shrewsbury School, Oxford University and Queen's University, Belfast. He was called to the Northern Ireland bar in 1954 and the English bar in 1972. He served as lord chief justice in Northern Ireland 1988–97. He chaired the inquiry in 2003 into the death of Dr David Kelly, the scientific weapons advisor to the Ministry of Defence who committed suicide in July 2003. He reported on 28 January 2004, when he cleared ministers and civil servants of any wrongdoing regarding the circumstances leading to Kelly's death and allocated most of the blame to the BBC, which thereupon suffered the resignations of its chairman and director general. The press generally greeted the report with scepticism and criticised his excessively narrow interpretation of the inquiry's remit; the press also made the accusation of a 'whitewash' of the establishment by a classic establishment figure.

Hutton, John (1955–)

Labour politician and cabinet minister. He was educated at Westcliff High School for Boys and Magdalen College, Oxford. He taught law at Newcastle Polytechnic 1981–92 before being elected for Barrow and Furness in 1992. After 1997 he served in the Department of Health and then as chancellor of the Duchy of Lancaster and minister for the Cabinet Office. In November 2005 he replaced David Blunkett at the Department for Work and Pensions. As a 'Blairite' minister he was expected to be dropped in 2007 when Gordon Brown took over but he was kept on as secretary of state for business, enterprise and regulatory reform. This was the more surprising as he had been reported as saying in 2006 that Brown 'would make a f****** awful prime minister'. He subsequently admitted he did make the comment. He was moved to defence in October 2008 and resigned in June 2009 when he also announced he would not contest the next election. He was made a peer in the 2010 dissolution honours.

Hutton, Will (1950–)

Economist, journalist and social commentator. He was educated at Chislehurst and Sidcup Grammar School and Bristol University. He entered the BBC and worked as a radio producer at Radio 4 before moving to television to feature on *The Money Programme* and *Newsnight*. He was named political journalist of the year in 1993. He became editor of the *Observer* in 1996. He is best known for his mammoth critique of British institutions, *The State We're In* (1995), in which he developed the thesis of a partnership between employees, employers and others in modern capitalism (the stakeholder economy). He writes a

regular column in the *Observer*. In May 2010 he agreed to head a public pay sector review for the new coalition government.

I

Ibbs, Robin (1926–)

Author of the *Next Steps* report (1988). He was educated at Toronto University and Trinity College, Cambridge. He served as a lieutenant in the Royal Navy 1947–49 then practised at the bar 1949–52. He joined ICI in 1952 and became a director 1976–80 and 1982–88. He was head of the Central Policy Review Staff (CPRS) 1980–82, of the Efficiency Unit 1983–88 and author of the *Next Steps* report, which established executive agencies. He was also associated with many banking and business concerns, as well as several public bodies, like the Top Salaries Review Body 1983–89.

Ingham, Bernard (1932–), Sir

Redoubtable press secretary to Margaret Thatcher during the 1980s. He was born in Yorkshire and educated at Hebden Bridge Grammar School. He worked as a journalist on local papers before he moved to the *Guardian* 1962–67 and then into government service as a press advisor in the 1970s, when he rose to under-secretary at the Department of Energy under Tony Benn 1978–79. In 1979 he became chief press secretary to Thatcher and became nationally known for his gruff yet highly competent performances at press conferences and in the media. He also managed to become one of Thatcher's closest and most trusted advisors. He was knighted in 1990.

Irvine, Alexander Andrew Mackay (1940–), Lord

Labour peer and minister. He was made lord chancellor after Labour's victory in

1997. He was educated at Hutcheson's Grammar School, and Glasgow and Cambridge Universities. He lectured at the London School of Economics 1965–69, was called to the bar 1967, became queen's counsel 1978 and a deputy judge in the High Court 1987. He was Tony Blair's head of chambers when Blair (as well as Cherie Booth, his future wife) practised as a barrister. He was made a life peer in 1987 and served as shadow lord chancellor 1992–97 and then lord chancellor after Labour's 1997 election victory. He proved a controversial member of Blair's cabinet, though it was rumoured that Blair depended upon him for advice. He chaired several cabinet committees and his undoubted influence encouraged him to compare himself in a public talk to Cardinal Wolsey. His aloof manner won him few friends and his expensive refurbishing of the lord chancellor's rooms in the House of Lords, especially the heavy wallpaper, attracted much criticism and satirical comment. He remained unrepentant and predicted the nation would be 'grateful' for his foresight. In January 2000 he was at the centre of the 'wigs for cash' scandal when he invited senior lawyers – whose future advancement he could determine – to a fund-raising dinner for the Labour Party. On a more positive assessment, he did drive through the devolution legislation in 1997/98 which led to the first Scottish parliament in three centuries. In addition he introduced the revolutionary Human Rights Act 1998. In June 2003 Blair removed his former boss as part of his restructuring of the judiciary. The 1,400-year-old office – much criticised for involving the law-making function with the law-implementing judiciary – was effectively replaced by the Constitutional Affairs Department, although the vestigial title lives on. Irvine was known to oppose the measures and this possibly helps explain why it was pushed through with indecent haste. In the 1990s Donald Dewar's wife left him for Irvine. The two remained unreconciled despite being in the same government.

J

Jackson, Ken (1937–)
General secretary of Amicus 1995–2002. He was educated at St Joseph's School, Wigan. In 1956 he joined the Royal Air Force as a technician and later was an electrician in the engineering industry. He became an official of the electrical union (EEPTU) in 1966 and rose through the ranks to be president in 1992. He was general secretary of the Amalgamated Engineering and Electrical Union before heading up the new union, Amicus, in 1995. He was defeated by Derek Simpson in 2002 for the office of general secretary. He was known as Tony Blair's 'favourite trade unionist' for his loyal support of the prime minister. In retirement he chaired Nirex, a company which disposes of nuclear waste.

Jay, Margaret (1940–), Baroness
Labour peer. She was educated at Blackheath High School and Somerville College, Oxford. She was the daughter of James Callaghan and at one time was married to Peter Jay, the journalist and broadcaster. She was a *Panorama* reporter and a director of the National Aids Trust. She gained a peerage in 1992 and served as a whip in opposition. A highly sociable socialist, she described herself as a 'moderniser'. She was made leader of House of Lords in July 1998 and was put in charge of reform of that chamber. She oversaw the abolition of hereditary peers in 1999 but decided to give up her cabinet post in June 2001.

Jenkins, Roy (1920–2002), Lord
Apparently ageless Labour politician with a passion for Europe who joined the Social Democratic Party (SDP) and then the Liberal Democrats. He was born in Wales to a mining family, though his father was a Labour MP. He was educated at a local grammar school and Balliol

College, Oxford, where he took a first in modern greats. He was the youngest MP when elected for Central Southwark in 1948 and sat for the Stechford Division, Birmingham, 1950–76. He served as minister for aviation 1964–65 before gaining the Home Office. He then swapped offices with James Callaghan in 1967 to become chancellor. He became deputy leader in opposition, when he rebelled against his party's opposition to Europe. He was home secretary again 1974–76. He then left Westminster politics in 1977 to become president of the European Commission, until 1981. He was a founder member of the Social Democratic Party (SDP) and part of its joint leadership 1981–82 before he stood down in favour of David Owen. He won Glasgow Hillhead for the SDP in 1982, lost it in 1987 and then was made a peer. He was elected chancellor of Oxford University 1987. A noted journalist and biographer, Jenkins was one of the 1930s-educated polymaths, like Denis Healey, who led the Labour Party after the war. He was very able intellectually and as a minister but his aloof manner belied his humble origins. His passionate advocacy of most things European discouraged the support he might otherwise have commanded. He was a powerful figure in British and European politics for a generation. In 1997 he was asked to chair Labour's commission into the voting system and he produced a controversial report recommending the alternative vote 'top-up' system. In his final years he became an intimate advisor to Tony Blair. Arguably one of Labour's greatest ever politicians.

Johnson, Alan (1950–)

Labour MP and home secretary. He was orphaned at 12 when his mother died and then cared for by his older sister in a council flat. He attended Sloane Grammar School in Chelsea before leaving school at the age of 15 to stack shelves at Tesco. Aged 18 he became postman and was active in the Union of Communication Workers; he soon was appointed a branch official and, despite being far to the left of

it, joined the Labour Party in 1971. He was a full-time union official after 1987 and became general secretary of the newly formed Communication Workers' Union (CWU) in 1993. He was elected for Hull West and Hessle in 1997, entering government first as parliamentary private secretary to Dawn Primarolo and then as a junior minister at the Department of Trade and Industry in 1999. In 2003, despite his lack of university experience, he was put in charge of higher education. He became work and pensions secretary in 2005 and moved to the Department of Education and Skills in 2006. Under Gordon Brown in 2007 he became health secretary and then home secretary in June 2009. After the departure of Tony Blair and the demise of David Miliband's challenge, he became the commentator's favourite candidate to take over from the unpopular Brown. However, when the moment arrived in June 2009 he chose to praise Brown as the best man for the job and to accept promotion to home secretary as a possible reward for his loyalty. After Labour's 2010 defeat he expressed no interest in the leadership, opting to support David Miliband.

Johnson, Boris (1964–)

Editor of the *Spectator*, Conservative MP known for his sense of humour, and London mayor. He was educated at Eton and Balliol College, Oxford. He became a journalist at the *Times* and the *Daily Telegraph* before assuming the editorship of the right-leaning *Spectator* in 1995, where he helped to increase circulation. He became MP for Henley on Thames 2001, though still appeared on the comedy news programme *Have I Got News for You* from time to time. In 2004 he was sacked from his shadow post for denying to his party leader that he was having an affair with Petronella Wyatt. Prone to gaffes, there was much doubt over his candidacy for the mayor of London but he easily won the 2008 contest against Ken Livingstone and has generally been perceived as a popular and successful mayor; and surprisingly gaffe free into the bargain. Some claim his long-term aim is to head the Conservative Party.

Jones, Digby (1955–)

Director general of the Confederation British Industry (CBI), 2000–06. He was educated at Bromsgrove School and University College, London, where he studied law. He became a solicitor in 1980 and more recently worked for business consultants KPMG. He was made a junior minister for trade in 2007 by Gordon Brown as part of his 'government of all talents' but he did not last long: he resigned in April 2008, not without criticism of the government.

Jones, Jack (1913–2009)

Leader of the Transport and General Workers' Union (TGWU) in the 1970s. He was born in Liverpool and left school at 14 to work on the docks and in engineering before moving into union activism; after reading Robert Tressell's *Ragged Trousered Philanthropists* at this time he was converted to socialism. He fought in the Spanish Civil War and was wounded in 1938. He became district organiser in Coventry before moving up in the organisation and becoming general secretary of the TGWU 1969–78 at the same time as Hugh Scanlon was leading the engineering union. Between them they dominated the union scene in the 1970s and were often described as the two most powerful men in the country, responsible for making the unions too influential and provoking the backlash by Margaret Thatcher's administration. Jones served on the General Council of the Trades Union Congress 1968–78 and, much respected throughout the world of politics, dedicated his retirement to campaigning for a better deal for old-age pensioners.

Joseph, Keith (1918–94)

Leading postwar new right ideologue and Conservative cabinet minister. He was educated at Oxford University and practised as a barrister before becoming a Conservative MP 1956. He was secretary of state for social security 1970–74 under Edward Heath and he might have become leader but for an ill-advised speech which appeared to advocate eugenics. However, his elaboration of a 'common ground' in the mid-1970s, which he claimed was to the right of the postwar consensus and on to which he urged his party to move, was justified by future events. He became one of Margaret Thatcher's most closely trusted policy advisors in opposition and in government served as secretary of state for education 1981–86. He founded the Centre for Policy Studies with Thatcher in 1975.

> It needs to be said that the poor are poor because they don't have enough money. (1970)

Jowell, Tessa (1947–)

Labour MP and minister. She was educated at Aberdeen, Edinburgh and London Universities. She was MP for Dulwich from 1992 and served as junior minister at the Departments of Health 1997–98 and Education 1998–2001. In 2001 she was made secretary of state for culture, media and sport. In 2006 her husband was accused of wrongdoings in Italy where he had acted as a lawyer for Silvio Berlusconi, the Italian prime minister. Tony Blair cleared her of any clash of interest but she separated from her husband and this quietened down the controversy. Under Gordon Brown she took on four simultaneous jobs: minister for the Olympics, minister for the Cabinet Office, minister for London (until 2008) and paymaster general. However, she attended cabinet only by invitation, not as a full member. In 2010 she retained her Dulwich and West Norwood seat, with a majority of 9,365. London mayor Boris Johnson was keen to retain her services regarding the London 2012 Olympic Games.

K

studies of the prime minister and cabinet and a series of Nuffield election studies co-authored with David Butler.

Kaufman, Gerald (1930–)

Leading postwar Labour politician whose long years in opposition denied him the chance of senior office. He was educated at Leeds Grammar School and Queen's College, Oxford. He then worked for the Fabian Society and various newspapers before becoming press officer to the Labour Party, when he worked for a while in Downing Street after 1966. He was elected MP for Ardwick in 1970 and then Gorton from 1983. He served as a junior minister for environment and industry before becoming minister of state for industry 1975–79. He was shadow home and foreign secretary in the 1980s. He was an able politician with a wicked wit and good ministerial record but was too young to achieve high office in the 1960s and too old to return to office after 1997. He was the author of the much quoted *How To Be a Minister* (1980). In 1992 he became chairman of the Culture and Heritage Select Committee and, despite his well known hostility to such committees, proceeded to chair it with great panache and effectiveness. He was involved in the 2009 expenses affair by virtue of his desire to charge a large television to parliamentary expenses. He retained his seat in 2010 by 4,703 votes.

> The longest suicide note in history. (Kaufman's much quoted comment on Labour's 1983 manifesto)

Kavanagh, Dennis (1941–)

Emeritus professor of politics at the University of Liverpool 1996–2008. He was educated at St Anslem's College, Birkenhead, and Manchester University. He then taught at the Universities of Hull and Manchester before becoming professor at Nottingham 1982–95 and then Liverpool. His writings include *Political Culture* (1972), *Thatcherism* (1986),

Kavanagh, Trevor (1943–)

Political editor of the *Sun* 1983–2005. He was educated at Reigate Grammar School, then emigrated to Australia. He joined News International in 1974 and returned to Britain in 1978. He took over as political editor of the *Sun* in 1983 and became one of the country's most influential journalists. He was known to be a supporter of Margaret Thatcher and her policies and to have opposed Rupert Murdoch's switching of support to Tony Blair in 1997.

Keeler, Christine (1942–)

Model who conducted a dual affair with the minister of war, John Profumo, and a Soviet naval attaché, Eugene Ivanov, in 1963, which raised questions of state security. Profumo denied the affair in the house and when his deceit was revealed he resigned. The scandal damaged the final months of Harold Macmillan's government.

Kelly, David (1944–2003)

Government advisor whose suicide on 18 July 2003 precipitated an acute crisis in the BBC's relations with government and public trust in Tony Blair's New Labour regime. He was the son of an officer in the Royal Air Force. He was born in the Rhondda but moved to Tunbridge Wells. He studied agricultural science at Oxford, moved into microbiology and subsequently worked at the Ministry of Defence's Porton Down 1984–92, engaged in biological warfare research. In the 1980s he worked for the government as a weapons inspector in Russia and then for the United Nations 1994–99 as a weapons inspector in Iraq. Some experts claimed he was pre-eminent in his field, not just nationally but worldwide. However, he had doubts in 2002 about the government's determination to use the supposed threat of Iraqi weapons of mass destruction to justify going to war with that country. When such weapons failed to appear at the end of the war his conversations with BBC journalists fed into reports that a 'senior intelligence' source had claimed the government had 'sexed up' intelligence reports to help justify the war on Iraq. He was soon identified and subsequently gave evidence, clearly under strain, to the Foreign Affairs Select Committee but in July 2003, as the media frenzy grew, committed suicide. Lord Hutton was appointed to head the judicial inquiry into the affair, which eventually exonerated the government but pointed the finger at the BBC.

Kelly, Ruth (1968–)

Labour MP and cabinet member. Having lived part of her life in Ireland (her father fought for Irish independence and she is a devout Catholic), she was educated at Sutton High School and then won a scholarship to Westminster School, where she sat her A levels. She went on study philosophy, politics and economics (PPE) at Queen's College, Oxford, and then completed a masters at the London School of Economics. She was a journalist on the *Guardian* from 1990 and then worked for the Bank of England from 1994. She was elected for Bolton West in 1997 and was soon parliamentary private secretary to Nick Brown when agriculture minister. After 2001 she became economic secretary to the Treasury but was soon promoted to financial secretary. In September 2004 she became minister for the Cabinet Office and shortly afterwards education secretary. In May 2006 she was moved to be secretary for communities and local government and then transport once Gordon Brown was in post. She stood down in October 2008 and announced she would stand down as an MP at the next election. In May 2010 she took up work with the HSBC bank.

Kemp, Peter (1934–2008), Sir

Senior civil servant who master-minded the 'Next Steps' reform of the civil service. He was educated at Millfield and Royal Naval College, Dartmouth. He entered the civil service in 1967, serving in the Department of Transport before moving to the Treasury

and then the Cabinet Office. He rose to second permanent secretary at the Treasury and was engaged on the Next Steps reform as project manager within the Cabinet Office during the late 1980s. He left the service in 1992.

Kennedy, Charles (1959–)

Liberal Democrat MP and leader of the party. He was educated at Lochaber High School, Fort William, and the University of Glasgow, where he was the president of the Union. He was a Fulbright scholar and lecturer at Indiana University. He was elected MP for Ross, Skye and Inverness for the Social Democratic Party in 1983 and was president of the Liberal Democrats 1990–94. He won the contest to replace Paddy Ashdown as leader in August 1999 but was initially thought by some to be too diffident and a bit too lazy to be an effective leader. However, his laid-back style went down well in the 2001 general election campaign and he led his party to a good result. His opposition to the Iraq war in 2003 was well judged and his party benefited politically, for example winning the Leicester South by-election in July 2004, when many Muslims deserted Labour to vote in a Liberal Democrat. Kennedy presided over a very good general election result in 2005, in which the Liberal Democrats garnered 62 seats, but, maybe through raised expectations, Kennedy was not thought to be actively driving the party forward. Consequently, a whispering campaign began against him, focusing on allegations of a drink problem which had dogged him for a number of years. By December 2005, several senior MPs in his party had openly criticised him. Finally he was forced to admit the problem and, when this confession failed to still the discontent, to resign, on 7 January 2006. Ming Campbell was elected as successor in March that year. A year later he too had resigned and Nick Clegg took over.

Kennedy, Helena (1950–), Baroness

Labour life peer and queen's counsel. She was educated at Holyrood Secondary

Grammar and Glasgow University. One of the country's leading female lawyers, she has headed government inquiries, sits on important bodies and, perhaps crucially, is a close personal friend of the Blairs.

Kennedy, Ian (1941–), Sir

Chair of the Independent Parliamentary Standards Authority. He was educated King Edward School, Stourbridge, and University College London. He went on to be a Fulbright scholar and studied at Berkeley, University of California. He is a specialist on the law and ethics of medicine and is emeritus professor of health law, ethics and policy at University College London. He chaired the Healthcare Commission 2003–09 and served on several government committees. He has been a member of the General Medical Council for a number of years and is a former president of the Centre of Medical Laws and Ethics, which he founded in 1978. His salary of £100,000 a year was criticised by some MPs as excessive.

Kerr, John (1942–), Baron

Civil servant. He was educated at Glasgow Academy and Oxford. As a diplomat he served in Moscow and Rawalapindi as well as being permanent representative to the European Union 1990–95. He was ambassador to the USA 1995–97. He was permanent under-secretary to the Foreign Office and head of the Diplomatic Service after 1997. He became a close advisor to Tony Blair in the aftermath of the terror attacks on the USA on 11 September 2001 but retired at the end of that year and was raised to the peerage.

Keynes, John Maynard (1883–1946)

Economist. He was born into an academic Cambridge family and studied at Eton and King's College, Cambridge, where he became one of the so-called Bloomsbury group of intellectuals. He lectured at Cambridge in economics then served as a member of the Royal Commission on India. He advised the Treasury during the First World War and was opposed to the peace

terms, which he criticised in his *Economic Consequences of the Peace* (1919). He attacked Winston Churchill's restoration of the gold standard in 1925. He was influenced by J. A. Hobson's under-consumption theories and developed them in response to the unemployment in the 1930s, most famously in his *General Theory of Employment, Interest and Money* (1936). His view that recessions could be combated through investment to stimulate growth was revolutionary and was not initially widely accepted. His idea that the economy could be planned influenced US president Roosevelt's New Deal and many thinking politicians in both British main political parties, such as Harold Macmillan and Hugh Dalton, began to study his ideas and adapt them. During the Second World War his views gradually became orthodoxies and the 1945 white paper on employment embodied his views on the achievability of full employment. He was one of the architects of the international economic order agreed at Bretton Woods (1944–46), which established the International Monetary Fund. He also helped form the Vic-Wells ballet and the Cambridge Arts Theatre. One of the truly great intellects of his time, or any time, he achieved more in one lifetime in the field of economic thought, public affairs and the arts than a team of gifted people might reasonably hope to achieve. His contributions to economics revolutionised government not only in Britain but all over the world. The problems of inflation in the 1970s initiated a reaction against Keynesianism and for a while monetarism eclipsed it, but the fundamental analyses and ideas were not jettisoned and live on as tools of analysis if not articles of faith. Indeed, his ideas were still notably influential during the 2007–09 banking and economic crisis, when Gordon Brown and others urged massive fiscal stimuli to kick start a recovery (at the time of writing, however, it is unclear if the remedy has worked).

> They [Conservative MPs] are a lot of hard faced men who look as if they have done well out of the war. (Quoting a Conservative

politician, often thought to be Stanley
Baldwin, in *Economic Consequences of the
Peace*, 1919)

I work for a government I despise for ends
which I think criminal. (1917)

Kiley, Robert (Bob) (1935–)

Commissioner for transport for London,
2001. A US citizen, he was born in
Minneapolis and educated at Notre
Dame University, Indiana, and Harvard
University. He began his career in 1963
as a CIA agent and remained with the
Agency until 1970. He was deputy mayor
of Boston, 1972–75, chief executive
of Massachusetts Bay Transportation
Authority, Boston, 1979–83, chairman of
the Metropolitan Transportation Authority,
New York, 1983–90, and president of New
York Chamber of Commerce, 1995–2000.
He then came to Britain and served as
chairman of London Transport January–
July 2001, appointed by Ken Livingstone,
but his opposition to the Treasury's plan
for the London Underground led to his
dismissal after only 10 weeks in post,
though he remained commissioner for
transport for London. He stood down from
his post in 2006.

Kilroy-Silk, Robert (1942–)

Labour MP, chat-show presenter and
MEP. He was educated at Saltley
Grammar School, despite failing the
11-plus, and then the London School of
Economics. After a period lecturing in
political philosophy, he was elected Labour
MP for Knowsley in 1970 and surprised
some of his colleagues by predicting he
would soon lead the party and become
prime minister. In 1985 he was deselected
by his Militant-dominated constituency
party. He then turned to the media and
became the presenter of *Kilroy*, a successful
and long-running morning chat-show
with an emphasis on shocking viewers.
In January 2004 he was dismissed by the
BBC for making anti-Arab remarks in a
newspaper column but, again undeterred,
in June 2004 he successfully stood as a
candidate in the European elections for the

UK Independence Party (UKIP); his new
party garnered 17 per cent of the national
vote. Some predicted he would soon go
on to challenge former Conservative MP
Roger Knapman as leader of the party.
This he failed to do, so he set up his own
party, Veritas, which was short-lived,
and he soon resigned from that too. His
membership of the European parliament
ended in July 2009. In a quiz held during
I'm a Celebrity … Get me Out of Here!
(from which he was rapidly expelled), in
2008, he was unable to name the chancellor of the exchequer.

> Robert has never really lost his love of
> politics. He wants to influence things, to
> shake up opinion formers. (Liz Barron,
> former editor of *Kilroy*)

King, Anthony (1934–)

Professor of government at Essex
University from 1969 and a member of
the Committee on Standards in Public
Life after 1994. He was educated at
Queen's University, Kingston, Ontario,
and Magdalen College, Oxford (he was
a Rhodes scholar). As one of the leading
political scientists in Britain, King analyses
polls regularly in the press and provides
shrewd commentary on television on
election nights. He wrote *The Birth, Life
and Death of the Social Democratic Party*
(1997) with his Essex colleague Ivor Crewe
and in 2008 *The British Constitution*.

Kinnock, Neil (1942–), Lord

Labour leader who lost the general elections
of 1987 and 1992 before becoming a
European commissioner. He was the son of
a coalminer and was educated at University
College, Cardiff, before becoming a tutor
with the Workers' Educational Association,
and then Labour MP for Bedwellty in
1970 and then, from 1983, Islwyn. He immediately became a champion of left-wing
policies and made a name as a powerful
speaker. He was elected to Labour's
National Executive Committee in 1978
and the shadow cabinet in 1980. Michael
Foot's election to the leadership reflected
the leftward swing of the party, which went

down to a disastrous defeat in the 1983 general election. In its wake Kinnock, the popular left-wing rebel, was favoured in the elections for a new leader. His was the first election under the rules introduced in 1980 which gave 70 per cent of the decision to extra-parliamentary constituency parties and trade unionists. He was successful and was initially welcomed as a dynamic force. However, his movement towards the centre ground in response to the new right-wing Thatcherite agenda annoyed some of his erstwhile left-wing supporters and his performances in parliament were not judged impressive; Margaret Thatcher, in particular, seemed to treat him with contempt at prime minister's questions. His assiduous efforts to gain control over the party's machinery paid some dividends and in 1986 he appointed Peter Mandelson as its communications director. Both men moved the party even further towards the centre and poll ratings began to improve. However, the 1987 general election proved a bitter disappointment. He persevered with even more centrist policy reviews and further moves to neutralise the electorally embarrassing left-wing groups, especially Militant, which he had excoriated triumphantly at the 1985 Labour Party conference. By 1992, with John Major as premier and the economy deep in recession, it seemed his time had come. But it was not to be and Labour – despite appearing to be marginally ahead in the polls – lost yet again. Kinnock resigned and John Smith took over. When making his election victory speech in 1997, Tony Blair was careful to acknowledge the debt he owed to Kinnock as the man who had prepared the way. Kinnock went on to become the European commissioner for transport in 1994 and eventually became a vice president of the Commission (up to November 2004). He was raised to the peerage in 2005. He was a gifted party politician who used his hugely likeable personality to build a power base in the unions and constituencies. However, he was let down by a tendency to be prolix in media interviews and muddled when making crucial speeches in the

house. Maybe his renunciation of so many left-wing opinions strained the electorate's credulity. He is historically significant as the man who presided over the introduction of political marketing and managerialism into the modern Labour Party.

> If Margaret Thatcher wins on Thursday, I warn you now not to be ordinary, I warn you not to be young, I warn you not to fall ill, I warn you not to grow old. (To supporters in Bridgend as the general election campaign closed, 8 June 1983)

> The grotesque chaos of a Labour council – a Labour council – hiring taxis to scuttle round the city handing out redundancy notices to its own workers. (Attacking Militant councillors in Liverpool, in his party conference speech at Bournemouth, 1985)

> I have a lot of sympathy with him. I too was once a young, bald Leader of the Opposition. (On William Hague, 3 October 1999)

L

Lamb, Norman (1957–)

Liberal Democrat MP for Norfolk North. He was educated at state boarding school, Wymondham College, then studied law at the University of Leicester, before studying for the NNEB childcare qualification at the City of London Polytechnic. He worked as a solicitor until 2001 when he entered the Commons. He shadowed international development, trade and then health. He is known as a vigorous, adhesive campaigner with a good eye for media coverage.

Lamont, Norman (1942–), Lord

Conservative chancellor under John Major who took the country out of the European Exchange Rate Mechanism (ERM). He was educated at Cambridge, after which he worked for the Conservative Research Department and in the City as a merchant banker and journalist. He was elected

Conservative MP for Kingston on Thames 1972. He served as financial secretary to the Treasury under Margaret Thatcher 1986 and was promoted to the cabinet 1989. Following Thatcher's departure in 1990 he managed Major's election campaign and was rewarded with the chancellorship. His credibility in this office was shattered by Black Wednesday, in September 1992, when Britain was forced to leave the ERM. However, membership of the ERM was the prime minister's policy, too, and perhaps because of this Lamont kept his job, in the face of clamorous criticism, until the following year, when he was replaced by Ken Clarke. His 2003 resignation speech was bitter – he accused Major of giving the impression of being 'in office but not in power'. On the back benches he became ever more Eurosceptic; he also supported General Pinochet throughout the former Chilean dictator's period of arrest in Britain.

Lansbury, George (1859–1940)

Leader of the Labour Party during the 1930s. He was an activist for reform and against poverty before he entered politics. He was elected MP for Bow and Bromley in 1910 but he resigned in 1912 and was not elected again until 1922. He founded the *Daily Herald* and edited it for a while. He became the Labour leader after the debacle of the 1931 election robbed the party of so many leading figures (Labour gained only 52 seats after Ramsay MacDonald had formed the national government coalition with the Conservatives). He was a successful leader for much of the time but his pacifism was inappropriate as Hitler's power was on the increase. At the 1935 party conference he suffered a devastating personal assault over his pacifism from the trade unionist Ernest Bevin and resigned shortly afterwards.

> It is placing the Executive and the Movement in an absolutely wrong position to be *hawking* your conscience round from body to body asking to be told what to do with it. (Bevin on Lansbury at the 1935 Labour conference)

Lansley, Andrew (1956–)

Conservative MP and secretary of state for health. He was educated at Brentwood School and Exeter University, where he studied politics. As a civil servant he worked as a private secretary for Norman Tebbit at the Department of Trade and Industry in 1984. He became head of the Conservative Research Department in 1990 and ran the successful 1992 campaign. He suffered a minor stroke in 1992 but made a full recovery. He was elected as MP for South Cambridgeshire in 1997. In 2001 he became a vice chairman of the party but was not given a shadow job until 2005, when Michael Howard gave him the health portfolio. This he held until 2010, when he took over the job for real.

> people who see more fat people around them may themselves be more likely to gain weight. Young people who think many of their friends binge-drink are likely to do so themselves.

Laws, David (1964–)

Prominent Liberal Democrat MP who was briefly chief secretary to the Treasury (for three weeks) following the formation of the Tory–Liberal Democrat coalition in May 2010. He was educated at the independent school for Catholic day pupils in Weybridge, Surrey, and then at King's College, Cambridge, where he gained a double first in economics. He joined J. P. Morgan bank and became a vice president by the age of 22 and at 25 managing director of Barclays de Zoette Wedd. In 1994 he became an advisor to the Liberal Democrats. He was elected for Yeovil in 2001, Paddy Ashdown's old seat, and in 2004 he co-authored the *Orange Book*, a series of essays by Liberal Democrats emphasising the primacy of market forces. In May 2010 his Treasury post was crucial, in that he would be the face of the coalition's policy of deep cuts in public expenditure. But on 28 May it transpired he had been paying rent to his male partner for accommodation, something which a 2006 rule change had excluded. He reluctantly resigned; both David Cameron and Nick Clegg hoped he would soon be able to return to office in their government.

Lawson, Dominic (1956–)
Journalist educated at Westminster School
and Christ Church, Oxford. He started
his career with the BBC, moved to the
Financial Times and then edited the
Spectator 1990–95, a job his father, Nigel,
had once filled. He edited the *Sunday
Telegraph* 1995–2005. He now writes for
the *Mail on Sunday*, the *Independent* and
the *Sunday Times*. Like his father he does
not believe arguments that human action
has caused global warming.

Lawson, Nigel (1932–), Lord
Conservative chancellor whose resignation
from the government in 1989 anticipated
and helped hasten Margaret Thatcher's
own fall a year later. He was educated at
Westminster school, and Christ Church,
Oxford. He worked as a speech writer
to Alec Douglas-Home 1963–64 and
edited the *Spectator* 1966–70. He was
elected Conservative MP for Blaby in
1974. By 1977 he was an opposition
Treasury spokesman. He served as
financial secretary to the Treasury 1979
and energy secretary (in cabinet) 1981. In
1983 he was made chancellor and served
for six years. He reformed the tax system
but was best known for lowering the top
rate of income tax to 40 per cent. He
was opposed to the poll tax. He argued
strongly for membership of the European
Exchange Rate Mechanism as the best
guarantee against inflation and for growth.
Thatcher was advised differently by Sir
Alan Walters and a clash ensued in 1989.
When Thatcher refused to dismiss her
advisor Lawson resigned sensationally and
the first stage of Thatcher's downfall was
completed. He laid the foundations for the
Conservative election victory of 1987 with
his 1986 budget. However, his reputation
was damaged by his reduction of interest
rates in the late 1980s, which fuelled
inflation; the resultant high rates produced
the recession which damaged John Major's
government in the early 1990s. He also
had a reputation for arrogance and for
alienating colleagues. He worked for a
bank after his retirement and took his seat

in the Lords in 1992. His memoirs, *The
View from Number 11* (1992), provided
a fascinating insight into economic policy
making during his years as chancellor.

Letwin, Oliver (1956–)
Conservative MP and minister. He was
educated at Eton and Trinity College,
Cambridge. He was elected MP for Dorset
West 1997. This cerebral Conservative
politician (who has written books on
philosophy) made an embarrassing gaffe
during the 2001 election campaign when
he made an incautious remark about his
party's tax-cutting plans as shadow chief
secretary to the Treasury; he was nonetheless promoted under Iain Duncan Smith to
shadow home secretary. He was tipped as
a possible replacement leader at the time
of Duncan Smith's removal in November
2003 but bowed out of the contest in favour
of the popular choice, Michael Howard,
who then made him shadow chancellor in
2003. He was appointed shadow environment secretary May 2005. During the age
of David Cameron he became chair of the
Conservative Research Department and
the party's policy review. He was influential
in the May 2010 election campaign and
subsequently became minister of state in the
Cabinet Office.

Liddell, Helen (1950–)
Labour MP and secretary of state for
Scotland 2001–03. She became MP for
Airdrie and Shotts in 1997. She served as
junior minister for transport, energy and
competitiveness, and at the Treasury and
Scottish Office before stepping up to the
cabinet. She was a famously tough operator
but after devolution was not left with much
of a departmental remit and left the cabinet
in June 2003. She was made a life peer in
May 2010.

Lilley, Peter (1943–)
Conservative cabinet minister in the 1990s
and deputy leader of the party 1998–99.
He was educated at Dulwich College and
Clare College, Cambridge. He worked in
finance during the 1960s and became an

MP in 1983. He served as parliamentary private secretary to chancellor Nigel Lawson 1985–87 and was then economic secretary 1987–89, financial and economic secretary 1989–90, secretary of state for trade and industry 1990–92 and social security 1992–97. He was a quiet, even uncharismatic politician but formidably clever, with a talent for policy initiatives. He was not unambitious, as he demonstrated by standing for the leadership in 1997, though he withdrew after the first ballot. He shadowed the Treasury under William Hague, then moved in 1998 to become deputy leader but was sacked after two years and returned to the back benches. Apart from opposing Labour's identity cards and undertaking some policy research tasks for David Cameron, his political life became uneventful for several years. He won the redrawn seat of Hitchin and Harpenden in May 2010, but was not given any ministerial office in the coalition government.

Livingstone, Kenneth (Ken) (1945–)

Mayor of London 2000–08 and Labour MP for Brent East 1987–2000. He was educated at Tulse Hill Comprehensive and Philippa Fawcett Teacher Training College. He was a Lambeth councillor 1971–78, vice-chair of housing 1971–73 and 1978–82, and chair of Camden council 1978–80. A lifelong, though idiosyncratic, left-winger, he was leader of the Greater London Council (GLC) 1981–86, when he stoutly resisted the Conservative government's decision to abolish it. He considered standing as a candidate for the Labour leadership in 1992 but had no deep support in the party. He was a frequent critic of Labour's leaders, especially Tony Blair and Gordon Brown. His decision to stand as the mayor of London was in defiance of the Labour Party, whose official candidate he had failed to become; he stood as an independent and was expelled from the party. After a noisy campaign he defeated Frank Dobson (Labour's candidate) by a comfortable margin on 4 May 2000. His achievements in his first years as mayor were slight and were constrained by his

battle with the Treasury on the future of the London Underground. He attracted some bad, though short-lived, publicity in June 2002 when it was alleged he had been involved in a skirmish with a journalist at a London party. The apparent success of his brave London traffic congestion charges in February 2003 strengthened his reputation. He was re-elected in June 2004. His second election as mayor was won on a 55–45 per cent majority over the Conservative, Steven Norris, after second preferences had been redistributed. In 2008, though, the maverick Boris Johnson proved a good campaigner and Livingstone lost by 53.2 per cent to 46.8 per cent after first and second preferences had been distributed.

> I'd like to pay tribute to the very considerable achievements of the last mayor of London who has been a very considerable public servant. You shaped the office of mayor. You gave it national prominence and when London was attacked on 7 July 2005 you spoke for London. (Boris Johnson, after the count, 2008)

> He was never a leftwinger. What passed for his philosophy was the devout belief that a day without a mention on the front page of a national newspaper was a day wasted.... He is not fit to be mayor of London. (Roy Hattersley, *Guardian*, 8 July 2002)

Lloyd George, David (1863–1945)

British chancellor and then wartime prime minister (nicknamed the 'Welsh wizard'). He was born in Manchester, the son of a schoolteacher who died when David was young, and brought up in rural North Wales by his uncle Lloyd. He became a solicitor but won the seat of Carnaervon Boroughs for the Liberals in 1890 at a by-election and then held the seat for 55 years. In 1905 he was made president of the Board of Trade, then took over from Herbert Asquith as chancellor and in 1909 submitted his famous tax-raising budget which precipitated the reform of the Lords with the Parliament Act 1911. He passed more social legislation, including the National Insurance Act 1911. During the First World War his administrative skills were needed to improve the supply of munitions. He was secretary for war 1916. When Asquith refused to accept a small war cabinet he resigned and out of the resultant crisis Lloyd George emerged as prime minister. The Liberal Party never really recovered from the split this occasioned between Lloyd George and Asquith. He was energetic in modernising the government machine – he set up a five-man war cabinet (the first ever formed) and invented the Cabinet Office. He clashed with field marshall Douglas Haig but could not get rid of him. In 1918 he led the coalition government to a landslide but it was largely a victory for the Conservatives rather than the Liberals. Lloyd George had a presidential-style role and treated his ministers badly, particularly George Curzon, his foreign secretary. In 1922 he fixed a temporary peace in Ireland at the price of the Black and Tans' excesses in the postwar period. In October 1922 Conservative MPs' loss of faith in the 'Welsh wizard' was such that they voted to end the coalition. Lloyd George was meanwhile selling political honours and building a political war chest but he never returned to high office, even though he lived throughout the interwar years. The main reason for this failure was the lack of trust he inspired and his tendency to create divisions. He espoused Keynesianism before most of his contemporaries and was at all times perceived as a powerful figure. He refused an offer of a post by Winston Churchill in his wartime government. He is one of the two or three greatest political figures of the 20th century and few have equalled his mastery of the political arts.

You mean Mr Balfour's poodle! It fetches and carries for him. It bites anybody that he sets it on to. (To H. Chaplin MP, who claimed the House of Lords was the watchdog of the constitution, 26 July 1907)

What is our task? To make Britain a fit country for heroes to live in. (24 November 1918)

How these dukes harass us. They're as expensive to keep as a dreadnought and not half as useful. (1909)

I do not believe you could point to any case where men work better for the state than they work for syndicates. (1919)

I hate fences. I always feel like knocking down every fence I come across. (1915)

He could not see a belt without hitting below it. (Margot Asquith on Lloyd George)

He did not care in which direction the car was travelling, so long as he remained in the driver's seat. (Lord Beaverbrook on Lloyd George, 1963)

He spent the whole of his life in plastering together the true and the false and therefore manufacturing the plausible. (Stanley Baldwin quoting Carlyle to attack Lloyd George)

Locke, John (1632–1704)

One of greatest figures in British political philosophy, who helped provide some of its essential character. He was educated at Westminster School and Christ Church, Oxford, where he studied philosophy. At first he was interested in science and actually qualified with a medical degree. Descartes' thought, however, stimulated his thinking, which continued to develop while he worked for his patron, the Earl of Shaftesbury, who became lord chancellor in 1672. When the Earl died Locke fell from favour; he retired to Holland, where his writing prospered. His *Two Treatises of Government* appeared in 1690 and drew on most of the advanced thinking of the time. He was keen to refute the idea that the monarch had any God-given right to rule: on the contrary, the monarch had a duty to provide good, if strictly limited, government and, if he did not, might be legitimately removed. However, Locke was no democrat and while he believed people to be basically rational and cooperative he did not trust democratic assemblies. He was in favour of a separation of powers and favoured a tolerant approach towards Dissenters. He is often seen as the father of the liberal enlightenment and a huge influence on the formation of liberal democracy in Britain and elsewhere, especially the USA, where his views influenced the colonists to seek independence.

M

MacDonald, Gus (1941–)

Labour peer and minister. He left school aged 14 to work as an apprentice machine fitter in a Glasgow shipyard and evolved into a left-wing activist who became a journalist for *Tribune*. He worked as circulation manager before he moved to the *Scotsman* and then Granada Television, where he worked as a presenter and senior executive before becoming director of programmes with Border Television in 1985. In July 1998 Donald Dewar invited him to become a minister in the Scottish Office. There was an immediate outcry – echoed by disappointed Scottish Labour MPs – that New Labour was again appointing its 'cronies' to top jobs. However, MacDonald was deemed to be an energetic, tough and effective minister – he was, after all, used to running large organisations. He served as chancellor of the Duchy of Lancaster 2001–03 within the Cabinet Office, charged with the 'enforcer' role in relation to government policy. Thereafter he did not serve in government.

MacDonald, Ramsay (1866–1937)

First Labour prime minister. He sprang from the most humble of origins as the illegitimate son of a Scottish farm labourer and received only a rudimentary education. He moved to England when 18 and flirted with the idea of becoming a Liberal MP but in 1894 joined the Independent Labour Party. He was secretary to the Labour Representation Committee, formed in 1900 and, thanks to the pact with the Liberals which he negotiated, became MP for Leicester in 1906 along with 28 other early Labour MPs, a group which he came to lead by 1914. Ideologically MacDonald was no revolutionary; he was more an evolutionary socialist and a vague one at that. However, his resignation as leader and his opposition to the war gave him an undeserved reputation for radicalism,

something which helped his subsequent career. He was elected MP for Aberavon in 1922 and elected chairman of the Labour Party. He became prime minister in a minority government in January 1924. This short period in power achieved little but did, as MacDonald hoped, reassure doubters that Labour was not made up of revolutionary Bolsheviks. He became premier again in 1929 but had to face the mounting financial crisis of the day. A committee recommended to the cabinet a package of deep cuts in pubic spending, including unemployment benefit. The cabinet was unable to agree. MacDonald saw the king but returned having been persuaded to lead an all-party government to deal with the crisis. MacDonald went ahead but the majority of his party, who did not follow his lead, regarded him as a traitor. These feelings were compounded when the resultant general election returned MacDonald's coalition but almost wiped out Labour. MacDonald was the prisoner of the Conservative majority in parliament and cabinet and achieved little of note, degenerating into a pathetic figure. He was defeated in his Seaham seat in 1935 but returned for the Scottish Universities 1936–37. MacDonald's life story is one of the most unusual in British political history. From the most crippling of starts in life he became the architect of the Labour Party and then three times prime minister. However, he lacked the intellectual weight to deal with the fearsome economic problems which beset his times and was weakened by an overweening vanity. He is seen in retrospect by his party as a renegade and a disgrace – a poor reward, perhaps, for his remarkable contributions to the genesis of the Labour Party. Some draw parallels with Tony Blair, as a charismatic leader who was drawn by the glamour of social high life, just as Blair seemed to be by the mega-rich. Moreover, claim critics, both betrayed their party's traditional principles, in pursuit of power.

> Sit down man, you're a bloody tragedy!'
> (James Maxton to MacDonald, 1933, as he was making one of his last speeches to the Commons)

If God were to ask me and say 'Ramsay, would you rather be a country gentleman than Prime Minister?' I should reply, 'Please God, a country gentleman'. (1930)

Macleod, Ian (1913–70)

Leading Conservative politician who died before fulfilling his potential. He was educated at Fettes, Gonville and Caius Colleges, Cambridge. He was injured in the Second World War and suffered from rheumatoid arthritis. He worked in the Conservative Research Department 1948–50. He became MP for Enfield West 1950 and was appointed minister of health following a brilliant attack on Anuerin Bevan in the house, and minister of labour 1959. The Marquess of Salisbury, a Tory grandee of the old school, described him in May 1961 as 'too clever by half' – a serious 'crime' in the party at the time. Along with Enoch Powell he refused to serve under Alec Douglas-Home (Macleod had supported R. A. Butler). He was editor of the *Spectator* for a while in the 1960s as well as shadow chancellor and was briefly chancellor before his death (from a heart attack) in 1970. Macleod was one of the most brilliant minds in postwar British politics, blessed with exceptional debating skills. He was a founder member of the 'one nation' group of Conservative MPs. His death was a huge loss to the Conservative Party in the 1970s; he was held up as a model by Conservatives of the centre left, like John Major.

Equality is a futile pursuit, equality of opportunity is a noble cause. (1969)

Macmillan, Harold (1894–1986)

One of the most successful British prime ministers, 1957–63. He was educated at Eton and Balliol College, Oxford. He served in the Grenadier Guards and was injured three times in the First World War, bearing his serious third injury with typical sangfroid, by reading classical Greek in no-man's land. His experience in the war and his service as Conservative MP for Stockton 1924–29 and 1931–45 during the Depression deeply affected his political

philosophy: he became a paternalist Keynesian, advocating a 'middle way' – the title of his 1930s book – of government regulation and intervention in a free enterprise economy. He served as a junior minister in 1940 and then was attached to Allied forces in the Mediterranean, where he met future US president Dwight Eisenhower. He lost his Stockton seat in 1945 but won a by-election in Bromley and went on to become a leading opposition spokesman. In 1951 he became a cabinet minister for housing and managed to achieve his own ambitious target – 300,000 – for house construction. He was rewarded with defence in 1954 and became Anthony Eden's foreign secretary in 1955 and chancellor in December of the same year. However, the Suez debacle ruined Eden, and Macmillan, who had been an enthusiast for going in quickly, became equally keen to pull out when US support was not forthcoming. Despite his lack of consistency, he was preferred in the ensuing Conservative Party leadership process to his rival, R. A. Butler, and became prime minister. His gift in the highest office was to exude calmness and confidence, sentiments belied by his intense inner nervousness and an unhappy personal life. His laid-back campaigning included shrewd use of modern media and he won handsomely in the 1959 general election. His reputation as 'Supermac', however, did not last long and he ran into economic difficulties as well as failing to achieve, as a result of De Gaulle's veto, his goal of joining the Common Market. In 1962 he tried to reverse growing unpopularity by sacking one-third of his cabinet in the so-called Night of the Long Knives. Now 'events', as he ruefully observed, took over and the Profumo affair took its toll. In October 1963 he entered hospital with prostatitis and prematurely resigned (he had over 20 years left to live). From his hospital bed he choreographed the fight for the succession, when he ignored Butler. He first favoured Lord Hailsham and then, when he proved excessively histrionic at the party conference, Alec Douglas-Home.

And so that unlikely, mild-mannered aristocrat – and Macmillan admired the aristocracy intensely – briefly became prime minister with Macmillan's blessing. Macmillan lived out an active retirement, writing memoirs and acting as chancellor of Oxford University. He accepted a hereditary peerage in 1984 and caused a stir when he criticised Margaret Thatcher's privatisation policies as 'selling the family silver'. He clearly did not enjoy seeing his consensual 'middle way' being overturned by one of his successors as party leader.

> Let us be frank about it, most people have never had it so good. (Party rally, 21 July 1957)

> I thought the best thing was to settle up these little local difficulties, and then turn to the wider vision of the Commonwealth. (Referring to the resignations of Treasury ministers before flying off for a Commonwealth tour, 7 January 1958)

> The wind of change is blowing through this continent [Africa], and whether we like it or not, this growth of national consciousness is a political fact. (Cape Town, 3 February 1960)

> Events dear boy, events. (In reply to a young journalist who asked what kept him awake at night when prime minister)

Major, John (1941–), Sir

Successor to Margaret Thatcher as Conservative prime minister, 1990–97. He was born the son of a trapeze artist and, unlike either Edward Heath or Margaret Thatcher, did not go to university. He did attend grammar school but left at 16. He joined the Standard Bank and worked in Nigeria before a serious accident encouraged him to come home. He was elected Conservative councillor for Lambeth, was adopted for the safe Tory seat of Huntingdon and entered the Commons in 1979. After junior office as a whip, then as a junior minister in social security, he became one of Thatcher's favourites; he was made chief secretary to the Treasury in 1987 under Nigel Lawson. In July 1989 he took over from Geoffrey Howe at the

Foreign Office and then from Lawson as chancellor that October. When Thatcher fell he stood in the resultant leadership contest and, as one of her proposers in the contest she lost, inherited some of her mantle in the perceptions of Conservative MPs. He won the contest in the second ballot by 185 votes to Michael Heseltine's 131 and Douglas Hurd's 56. He soon belied his apparent strong Thatcherism by revealing a moderate Conservatism, not hostile to the public sector, but the main thrust of his programme in terms of privatisation and welfare reform was still essentially Thatcherite. After an extended 'honeymoon' he soon attracted criticism for being weak and vacillating but the economic recession did more to damage him. In 1992 he called an election which most expected him to lose but his defiant electioneering and clarity compared with Neil Kinnock's more passionate but opaque style for Labour proved decisive and, in spite of the polls, which (wrongly) showed Labour slightly in front throughout, he won by a 7 per cent margin, though with a majority of less than 30 in the Commons. His first disaster in his new government was Black Wednesday, in September 1992, when Britain withdrew from the European Exchange Rate Mechanism, which destroyed his party's reputation for economic competence. Divisions over Europe exacerbated the Tories' poor image. However, he won respect and credit for persevering with Northern Ireland, where he combined with Irish premier Albert Reynolds to initiate a process which ultimately led to the Good Friday agreement in 1998. To answer critics within his own parliamentary party he resigned as leader in July 1995 and stood again for his own job, when he won by a margin that did not still criticism. His government staggered on until 1997, riven by splits and discredited by evidence of corruption, sexual peccadilloes and incompetence. Few were surprised when he lost by a landslide but the scale of his defeat reflected the deep pit into which the Conservatives had slipped. He resigned as leader after the election, to be replaced by William Hague. He stood down from parliament in 2001. He was a decent, competent politician who became prime minister at a time when the Conservatives' long tenure in power had reduced their majority and splits over Europe were, arguably, making the party unleadable.

> So right, OK. We lost. (On election night, 1 May 1997)

> Margaret has been at her happiest confronting political dragons: I choose consensus. (1999)

> Fifty years from now Britain will still be the country of long shadows on county grounds, warm beer, invincible green suburbs, dog lovers, and – as George Orwell said – old maids bicycling to Holy Communion through the morning mist. (1993)

> In the next 10 years, we will make changes that will make the whole of this country a genuinely classless society. (1990, soon after becoming prime minister)

> A decent and honourable man. (Paddy Ashdown)

Malloch-Brown, Mark (1953–), Lord

UN administrator and minister of state. He was educated at Marlborough and Oxford University, where he took a first in history; he also gained a degree in politics from the University of Michigan. He worked for the UN with refugees. He briefly contemplated running for the Social Democratic Party (SDP) in 1983. In 1986 he became a political consultant advising the likes of Aquino in Philippines and the anti-Pinochet opposition in Chile. In 1994 he joined the World Bank but went back to the UN in 1999, where he worked closely with Kofi Annan. He was briefly deputy to the UN general secretary (March–April 2006). He was outspoken in criticising George W. Bush on occasions. He also worked closely with the financier George Soros at certain times. He was appointed in 2007 as one of Gordon Brown's 'government of all talents' (goats) to the Foreign Office, where he was a minister of state with responsibility for Africa, Asia and the United Nations (UN). He stood down in October 2009.

Mallon, Seamus (1936–)

Deputy leader of the Social Democratic and Labour Party (SDLP) 1979–2002 and MP. He was educated at Brothers Abbey Grammar School, Newry, and St Joseph's College of Education. He was elected for Newry and Armagh in 1986, though he had become deputy leader of the SDLP in 1979. He was deputy first minister of the Northern Ireland executive 1999–2001. He retired in 2005.

Mandelson, Peter (1954–), Lord

Labour MP and minister. His grandfather was Labour MP Herbert Morrison. He was educated at Hendon County Grammar School and St Catherine's College, Oxford. As a student he was a member of the Young Communist League and notoriously earned an MI5 file as a result. He worked for the Trades Union Congress and for London Weekend Television as a producer. He was made Labour's director of communications in 1985 and was a close ally of Neil Kinnock in moving the party into the centre. He played an important role in the 1987 general election and a bigger one in 1992, when he himself was elected MP for Hartlepool. He advised Tony Blair on his leadership campaign in 1994 following John Smith's death, though secretly. In 1997 he became minister without portfolio in charge of monitoring policy delivery and the ill-fated Millennium Dome. In 1998 he was made secretary of state for trade and industry but was forced to resign that autumn when it became known he was the secret recipient of a large house loan from fellow (Treasury) minister Geoffrey Robinson. In 1999 he came back into the cabinet as secretary of state for Northern Ireland. He prospered until it was alleged he had intervened on behalf of a Dome contributor, one of the Hinduja brothers, to advance his application for citizenship. The story attracted much criticism and eventually he was forced to resign by Blair. He never accepted any guilt and remained bitter, despite his continued contacts with Blair. In July 2004 Blair announced that his old friend was to be sent to Brussels as

Britain's European commissioner. Some criticised another example of cronyism, while others reflected that the 'Prince of Darkness' was at least three hours' travel away from Downing Street. After Blair stood down in June 2007, most commentators thought his time in the spotlight was over. However, Gordon Brown, known as Mandelson's sworn enemy, amazed everyone by calling him back into the cabinet in October 2008 as business secretary, via a seat in the Lords. Soon he was omnipresent as a spokesperson for the government, but his value was most observed in June 2009 when he stage-managed the reshuffle which enabled a weakened Brown to stay in office. In the process he managed to acquire substantial extra responsibilities in a 'super department' and the virtual role of 'deputy prime minister'; thereafter he sat on no less than 35 cabinet committees. He played a major role in Labour's 2010 election campaign and was in favour of a coalition with the Liberal Democrats.

> New Labour is extremely relaxed about people becoming filthy rich. (1998)

> I'm a fighter and not a quitter. (Speech after being re-elected at Hartlepool, June 2001)

Manning, David (1949–), Sir

Civil servant and foreign policy advisor to the prime minister. He was educated at Ardingly Hall, Oxford University, John Hopkins University and in Bologna. He had appointments in eastern Europe, India, Moscow, Israel (as ambassador), the Cabinet Office 1985–90 and was British representative to the Contact Group on Bosnia. He came to public attention following the terrorist attacks in the USA in September 2001 as someone advising Tony Blair on foreign policy at the highest level. He was knighted in 2008 and had an advisory role regarding Princes William and Harry.

Marquand, David (1934–)

Political scientist and author. He was educated at Emanuel School and Magdalen College, Oxford. He worked at the University of California 1955–59, was a leader writer for the *Guardian* 1956–62 and then worked at the University of Sussex 1964–66. He was MP for Ashfield 1966–77 and parliamentary private secretary to the minister for overseas development 1967–69. He contested a seat for the Social Democratic Party in 1983 but rejoined Labour when Tony Blair became leader. He was a professor at Salford University 1978–91 and Sheffield University 1991–96, and then became master of Mansfield College, Oxford, 1996–2002. His books include *Ramsay MacDonald* (1977), *Social Theory and Radical Change* (1982), *Thatcherism* (1987) and *The Unprincipled Society* (1988). He won the Sir Isaiah Berlin Prize for Lifetime Contribution to Political Studies in 2001.

Marr, Andrew (1959–)

Leading journalist and television presenter of current affairs programmes. He was educated at the High School of Dundee, Craigflower School and at Loretto, an independent private boarding school in East Lothian. He went on to study English at Cambridge (Trinity Hall). He began his career at the *Scotsman* but his mentor Tony Bevins led him into the *Independent*'s orbit. After a spell as the *Economist*'s lead columnist on British politics ('Bagehot') and political editor, he returned to the *Independent* as political editor in 1992, becoming full editor in 1996. His period was notable for its boldness but being asked to work with Rosie Boycott and then Simon Kelner led him to leave in 1998. In 2000 he became the BBC's political editor and a national figure until he stood down in 2005. His *Andrew Marr Show* on BBC1 on Sunday mornings is an influential programme; he also hosts *Start the Week* on Monday mornings on Radio 4. He has written several books on British politics and a much praised book *History of Modern Britain* (2007).

Martin, Michael (1945–), Lord

Speaker of the House of Commons 2000–09 (the first Roman Catholic to have held the office) and Labour MP for

Glasgow Springburn from 1979. He was educated at St Patrick's School, Glasgow, and was later a councillor, a trade union officer and a sheet-metal worker. He served on a variety of house committees and was deputy speaker 1998–2000. He was parliamentary private secretary to Denis Healey. His strong Glaswegian accent and general conduct in post were criticised by some in his own party. His friends and defenders included Gordon Brown and Tam Dalyell, who tended to dismiss such criticism as 'southern snobbery'. In the summer of 2009 he was deeply involved in the MPs' expenses scandal, partly in his own right and partly for appearing to be opposed to the transparency regarding MPs' expenses which the public seemed to be demanding. Eventually he was openly challenged in the house and, when Brown removed his support, resigned, being replaced by John Bercow in the 22 June 2009 speaker's election. He was made a life peer in August 2009.

Marx, Karl (1818–83)

Revolutionary intellectual, author of international communism, who spent much of his life studying and writing in England. Of Jewish extraction, he was educated at Bonn and Berlin Universities, where he became one of the 'Young Hegelians'. He emigrated to Paris in 1843 (after being warned that his militant journalism might lead to his arrest), where he became a revolutionary and friend of Friedrich Engels – with whom he wrote *The Communist Manifesto* (1848). He believed that the social group, or class, which controls the means of production effectively controls society. He argued that this was true of all stages in history and that each dominant class provokes opposition from a subordinate class, making all history the story of class conflict. In the 19th century he argued a small group of property-owning capitalists (the 'bourgeoisie') were dominant at the expense of a huge working class (the 'proletariat'). He predicted that the latter would (inevitably) eventually rise up and overthrow the former, thus creating

a classless society. He also ordained that it was the duty of enlightened people to assist in the revolution, which would end exploitation and usher in a new era of dignity and happiness for those who suffered from the workings of capitalism. He moved via Brussels to London and began his research in the Reading Room of the British Museum, which led in 1867 to the first volume of *Das Kapital*. Engels helped support the impoverished Marx and his family during these years. He is buried in Highgate Cemetery. Despite basing much of his work on British experience, Marx never exerted much influence on British politics, apart from the tiny Communist Party of Great Britain and the more peripheral fringes of Labour's left wing.

Maude, Francis (1953–)

Minister for the Cabinet Office and paymaster general. Son of former Tory minister Angus Maude, he attended Abingdon School and Corpus Christi College, Cambridge, before becoming a criminal lawyer. He was a City of Westminster councillor 1978–84 but was elected to the Commons for North Warwickshire in 1983. After junior office at the Department of Employment and the Foreign Office he became financial secretary to the Treasury under John Major in 1990. He lost his seat in 1992 and took up a variety of business roles, including banking and working for the Asda Group. He was returned to the Commons for Horsham in 1997 and took up a variety of opposition portfolios, including shadow chancellor and shadow foreign secretary. He managed Michael Portillo's bid for the leadership in 2001 and was seen as a keen 'moderniser'. In 2005 he was made chairman of the Conservative Party and after 2007 shadow chancellor of the Duchy of Lancaster and Cabinet Office minister. He assumed his new office in May 2010.

> David [Cameron] has asked me to lead an implementation team that will ensure that we are as well-prepared as any incoming government has ever been. Our priorities rigorously sorted. Our teams armed with the

knowledge and capabilities that will enable new ministers to start making a difference from day one. (Statement to the party conference, 2007)

Maudling, Reginald (1917–79)

Leading Conservative politician who served as chancellor and was a leadership candidate. He was educated at Merchant Taylor's School and Merton College, Oxford. He practised at the bar and was elected to the Commons in 1950 as MP for Barnett. He held a succession of junior and senior posts in the 1950s, principally at the Department of Trade. In 1962 he became chancellor after Harold Macmillan's 'Night of the Long Knives' and retained this post under Alec Douglas-Home. He was widely expected to win the party leadership election when the latter stepped down (the first election for Conservative leader) but was beaten by Edward Heath, by 150 votes to 133. He was home secretary under Heath in 1970 but resigned when his business partner, John Poulson, was investigated for corruption. He briefly held shadow office under Margaret Thatcher until she sacked him in 1976. He escaped expulsion from the House of Commons – a reflection of his popularity – following censure in respect of his dealings with Poulson.

> We're a Conservative country that votes Labour from time to time.

Mawer, Philip (1947–), Sir

Parliamentary commissioner for standards 2002–08. He was educated at Hull Grammar School and Edinburgh University. He joined the civil service where he was principal private secretary to Douglas Hurd and worked on the Scarman report. In 1990 he became general secretary of the Church of England. As commissioner he conducted a four-year investigation into George Galloway. In January 2009 he became advisor to Gordon Brown on breaches of the ministerial code of conduct. In May 2009 he cleared Shahid Malik, when justice minister, of an alleged expenses violation.

Maxwell, Robert (1923–91)

Media tycoon and Labour politician who proved to be a fraud as well as a bully. Originally Ludwig Hoch, Maxwell was a Czech who served in the Second World War and then settled in Britain. A born survivor, fluent in several languages, he worked for intelligence, possibly for the east as well as the west. He set up Pergamon Press, which established his reputation as a brilliant businessman. He was elected Labour MP for Buckingham 1964–70 but retained extensive business interests in the media. In 1984 he became chair of the Mirror Group and did his best to influence editorial policy. A man never to do things in half measure, he left this world in dramatic style: his body was found floating alongside his luxury yacht in 1991 near the Canary Islands; the conclusion of suicide seemed to follow from the parlous state of his business finances, but many have disputed this and conspiracy theories abound. After his death it was discovered he had emptied the pension fund belonging to *Daily Mirror* employees in a vain attempt to save his business empire. After his death he was initially praised as a generous and brilliant businessman, known and respected by the world's most powerful leaders, but as revelations emerged he was condemned as a fraudster, bully and hypocrite.

May, Theresa (1956–)

Conservative MP, former party chair, and home secretary. She represented Maidenhead after 1997. She shadowed education before 2001, when she was generally judged to have been ineffective. As transport spokesperson, her opposition to Stephen Byers won her some commendations and she was made the first ever woman Conservative Party chair, in succession to David Davis, in July 2002. She quickly became identified as a leader of the 'moderniser' faction in the party, controversially urging it to lose the label of 'the nasty party'. She was the only woman selected in Michael Howard's shadow leadership team in 2003, becoming shadow secretary of state for the family. After

2005 she became shadow secretary for culture, media and sport but then moved to shadowing work and pensions, while retaining responsibility for women. In May 2010 she was made home secretary instead of the expected Chris Grayling.

Mayhew, Patrick (1929–), Lord
Conservative cabinet minister under Margaret Thatcher, who proved a tenacious Northern Ireland secretary. He was educated at Tonbridge and Balliol, Oxford, where he was president of the Union in 1952; he was a barrister before becoming MP for Tunbridge Wells 1983–97. He was a junior minister in the Home Office and for employment before becoming successively solicitor general, attorney general and then secretary of state for Northern Ireland from 1992. He was a key player in the events leading to the Downing Street declaration, itself the precursor to the Good Friday agreement in 1998.

McBride, Damian (1974–)
Civil servant, and then political aide working for Gordon Brown, caught out in a scandal involving proposed smears on a Labour blog. He was educated at Peterhouse College, Cambridge, and began his career in the Inland Revenue, before becoming head of communications at the Treasury, a position he held until 2008. In 2009 he sent emails suggesting to fellow Labour supporter Derek Draper that they disseminate scandalous fabrications about the private lives of senior Conservatives. These emails came into the hands of blogger Paul Staines, the plot was exposed and McBride resigned. Many wondered how commonplace such political skulduggery was within Brown's court, given his reputation for briefing against Tony Blair during the time he was seeking to replace him as prime minister.

McCartney, Ian (1951–), Sir
Labour MP and minister. He was state educated and then worked variously as a seaman and a manual worker for local government. He served as a local councillor

in Wigan 1982–87 and was elected MP for Makerfield 1987. After a number of shadow jobs at the Departments of Health, Employment, Education and Social Services he became minister of state at the Department of Trade and Industry 1997–99, the Cabinet Office 1999–2001 and Work and Pensions 2001–03. From 2003 he was a minister without portfolio and Labour Party chair. Short of stature but with dynamic energy, this Scotsman provided a vital link between the government and the unions and was a credible loyal connection between 'New' and 'Old' Labour. In May 2009 he announced he would not contest the next election. He was knighted in May 2010.

McFadden, Pat (1965–)
Labour MP and minister. He was educated at Holyrood Roman Catholic School in Crosshill, Glasgow, and then Edinburgh University. He was active as a student and became a political aide to John Smith the Labour leader; he was Tony Blair's political secretary from 2002. He was elected for Wolverhampton South East 2005 and was appointed junior minister in the Cabinet Office 2006. In 2007 he took on minister of state for business, innovation and skills, attending cabinet by invitation, and became deputy to Peter (Lord) Mandelson in 2008 in order to speak on departmental matters in the Commons. He was re-elected in May 2010 by 6,503 votes.

McGuinness, Martin (1950–)
Sinn Fein leader who joined Gerry Adams in supporting the peace process that culminated in the Good Friday agreement in 1998. Catholic born in Derry's Bogside, he joined the IRA in the 1960s and became a senior officer in Derry. In 1972 he joined Gerry Adams in talks with Northern Ireland secretary Willie Whitelaw. His close relationship with Adams was a crucial element in the process towards peace and the Good Friday agreement, with McGuinness seen as the 'hard' negotiator, with credibility with the IRA, as opposed to Adams' more

subtle and political approach. In September 1998 it was announced he would be 'liaison officer' between Sinn Fein and the body set up to oversee decommissioning of paramilitary weapons. He was made minister of education in the new Northern Ireland executive after 1998, though his period in office was soon interrupted when the executive was suspended. In 2007 he became deputy first minister to Ian Paisley in the newly formed executive.

McLoughlin, Patrick (1957–)

Conservative MP and chief whip from 2010. He was educated at the Cardinal Griffin Roman Catholic School in Cannock and the Staffordshire College of Agriculture. He is one of the few working-class Conservative MPs, being the son of a miner and having himself worked down the mines and as a farm labourer. He began his political career as a councillor for Staffordshire county council and was elected MP for West Derbyshire in 1984 by a wafer-thin majority; the constituency was renamed the Derbyshire Dales in 2010. He served as a junior minister in Trade and Industry and Transport and then, under John Major, Employment. He became a whip in 1995 and deputy chief whip in opposition after 1997. He had a majority of 13,866 in the 2010 election and was appointed government chief whip in the House of Commons by David Cameron.

McShane, Denis (1948–)

Labour MP and minister for Europe. Born of an Irish mother and a Polish father who fought in the war and took British nationality in 1950, he was educated at St Benedict's School, Ealing, and then at Merton College, Oxford. He went on to complete a PhD at the London School of Economics in international relations. He worked in the BBC 1969–77 before becoming active in the National Union of Journalists and other unions. He was married for a while to the newsreader Carol Barnes. He was elected for Rotheram in a 1994 by-election and went on to serve as parliamentary private secretary to a number

of ministers. In 2002 he became minister of state for Europe, where his six languages proved an asset. His occasional frank statements of opinion probably explained why he did not serve after 2005, especially as he was critical of Brown's 'five tests' for entry into the euro. He was re-elected in May 2010 by 10,462 votes.

Meacher, Michael (1939–)

Labour MP and minister, and allegedly the most 'green' member of New Labour. He was educated at Berkhamstead and New College, Oxford. He was elected MP for Oldham West and Royton in 1970 and served in junior capacity at the Departments of Trade and Industry and Health and Social Security 1974–79. He was seen as a left-wing ally of Tony Benn in the early 1980s but moved back into the centre under Neil Kinnock. In opposition he shadowed employment, transport, social security and then environmental affairs. He was minister of the environment 1997–2001 but then returned to the back benches. In August 2002 he was left out of the official delegation to the world environment conference in Johannesburg but was reinstated when green groups said they would pay his fare themselves. Once out of government he became a regular critic of it. In the spring of 2007, he claimed he would stand for the leadership of the party but there was tension with John McDonnell, also keen to stand, as the two candidates would split the left-wing vote. In the end Meacher stood down, among disputed estimates of how many pledged MP supporters he had. He retained his seat in 2010 with a majority of 9,352.

Mellor, David (1949–)

Former Conservative cabinet member turned broadcaster and journalist. He was educated at Swanage Grammar School and Cambridge. He became a barrister and was made queen's counsel 1978. He served as MP for Putney 1979–97, a junior minister in the Home Office and Foreign Office under Margaret Thatcher and chief secretary to the Treasury 1990–92 before becoming secretary of state for national heritage under John Major. He was forced to resign in 1992 after a scandal involving an actress with whom he had an affair. After he lost his seat in 1997 he became a member of the football task force 1997–99. He continues a career in the media as a journalist and broadcaster.

Meyer, Anthony (1920–2002)

Conservative backbencher who earns a footnote in history for standing against Margaret Thatcher in the 1989 party leadership election. He was educated at Eton and New College, Oxford. He fought in the Second World War in the Scots Guards, then worked in the Treasury and Foreign Service (Paris, Moscow). He became MP for Eton and Slough 1964–66, West Flint 1966–83, and Clywd North West 1983–92. He was a pro-European backbencher with an unexceptional career but was notable for standing against Thatcher in 1989 in the annual leadership contest. He mustered only 30 votes but, with an equal number abstaining, he helped show that his party was unhappy with its leader; she was deposed a year later.

> I question the right of that great Moloch, national sovereignty, to burn its children, to save its pride. (In a speech against the Falklands war, 1982)

Michael, Alun (1943–)

Labour MP and minister, and former first minister in Wales. He was educated at Colwyn Bay Grammar School and Keele University. He worked as a journalist before becoming MP for Penarth from 1987 and Cardiff South from 1997. He was spokesman for Wales in opposition, then, after 1997, served initially as Home Office junior minister before taking over from Ron Davies as secretary of state. When Davies was no longer leader of the Welsh Labour Party he was controversially 'installed' by the party machine (according to most commentators) as Davies's successor and thereafter as first minister of Wales. Following problems over government

funding for Wales he resigned and was replaced by the more popular Rhodri Morgan. He was made minister of state in the Department of Environment and Rural Affairs in June 2001. In 2005 he was moved to the Department of Trade and Industry and in May 2006 was reshuffled out of office and back to the back benches. He held his seat in 2010 by 4,710 votes.

Milburn, Alan (1958–)

Labour MP and minister. He was educated at John Marley and Stokesley Schools (Newcastle and Cleveland, respectively), and Lancaster and Newcastle Universities. He was elected MP for Darlington in 1992 and was opposition spokesman on health and Treasury matters 1995–97. He was chief secretary to the Treasury 1998–99 and secretary of state for health 1999–2003. Former left-wing firebrand turned Blairite, he was widely seen as competent and tough but perhaps lacking in personality. He surprised the world of politics in June 2003 by suddenly declaring he was giving up front-line politics to bring up his young family. Nonetheless, he was appointed to the cabinet again in September 2004, as chancellor of the Duchy of Lancaster, in which role he was to develop policy for the next general election. During the 2005 election there was tension with Gordon Brown when Tony Blair tried to make Milburn his campaign coordinator, a role Brown had usually performed. In the summer of 2009 Milburn presented a report on social mobility. He stood down at the 2010 election.

Miliband, David (1965–)

Labour advisor, MP and foreign secretary. The son of Ralph Miliband, a Marxist academic, he was educated at Oxford University and the Massachusetts Institute of Technology. He was made head of the Downing Street Policy Unit in 1998. He left Number 10 in June 2001 to become a Labour MP for South Shields and, tipped as a high-flier, was made a junior education minister (for schools) in 2002. He helped to set up the Centre for European Reform.

He went on to be environment secretary, in which role he emphasised the importance of climate change. In 2007 he became the youngest foreign secretary for 30 years. In 2009 he declined to join James Purnell's example in resigning when Gordon Brown's leadership came under very critical scrutiny. Peter Mandelson was believed to have played an important role in persuading the young foreign secretary to stay in post and thus save Brown's premiership. In May 2010 he declared he would stand for the leadership of his party.

Miliband, Ed (1969–)

Labour MP, secretary for energy and climate change and brother of David. He was educated at Haverstock Comprehensive School and Corpus Christi College, Oxford, and later the London School of Economics, where he studied for a masters. He worked for a while as a television journalist before becoming a political advisor to Harriet Harman in 1993 and then Gordon Brown. In 2004 he became chair of the Treasury's Economic Advisors' Council before being elected MP for Doncaster North 2005. He began his ministerial career as a junior cabinet minister in 2005, stepping up to cabinet in 2007 under Brown. In October 2008 he was put in charge of the new Department for Energy and Climate Change. He declared the government's objective was to cut carbon dioxide emissions by 80 per cent by 2050. While brother David is the person most often cited as a future leader, some argue Ed is the better communicator and more likely eventual leader. In May 2010 he declared himself a candidate for the leadership, as did his brother. Neil Kinnock supported him.

Mill, James (1773–1836)

British liberal political philosopher. He was ordained in 1798 and moved from Scotland to London, where he worked as a journalist and became an admirer of Jeremy Bentham and part of his 'utilitarian' school of thought. Mill helped form University College London in 1825. He worked for

the British India Company while writing books, which included *Elements of Political Economy* (1821).

Mill, John Stuart (1806–73)

One of the most famous political thinkers and a founder of liberal thought as well as the concept of representative democracy. Son of James Mill, this remarkable child prodigy, taught by his father, was similarly a follower of Jeremy Bentham. He joined his father at the India Office and retired prematurely in 1858 to write. After a nervous crisis relating to his cloistered childhood he rediscovered equanimity and wrote *On Liberty* (1859), followed by *Considerations on Representative Government* (1861) and *Utilitarianism* (1863). He defined freedom as the right to do anything which did not impinge on another's freedom and argued for the protection of liberties against both the power of government and popular democracy. He developed the case for: electoral reform – he favoured a form of proportional representation; improved living conditions for the working class; and representative government – he argued that participation in the political process was the best education in citizenship. Mill was the intellectual father of Britain's liberal democracy. He was elected to the Commons in 1865 and campaigned for the enfranchisement of women. He is probably the best-known British liberal thinker worldwide.

> The Conservatives ... being by their law of existence the stupidest party. (1861)

> The only freedom worth the name is that of pursuing our own good in our own way. (1859)

> The liberty of the individual must be thus far limited; he must not make himself a nuisance to other people. (1859)

Mitchell, Andrew (1956–)

Conservative MP and minister. He was educated Rugby School and Cambridge University, where he was chairman of the university's Conservatives and president of the Union. He represented Gedling in

Nottinghamshire 1987–97, when he also served as junior minister. In 2001 he was elected for Sutton Coldfield and came to shadow the secretary of state for international development, the post to which he was appointed in May 2010.

Mitchell, George (1933–)

US politician who played a crucial role in achieving the 1998 Good Friday agreement in Northern Ireland. He was educated at Bowdoin College in Maine and Georgetown University, Washington, DC. He served in the US army in counter-intelligence, then worked as a lawyer in the US Department of Justice 1960–62 and in public office in Maine. He became a US senator 1982 and was re-elected 1988. He was made majority leader 1988 but surprisingly retired 1994. He accepted an invitation to chair the peace commission in Northern Ireland and performed a delicate job with great sensitivity up to the Good Friday agreement. He won praise from all sides.

> I never said it would be easy– and that was an understatement. (1998)

> Peace, political stability and reconciliation are not too much to ask for. They are the minimum that a decent society provides. (1998)

Monks, John (1945–)

General secretary of the Trades Union Congress (TUC). He was educated at Dulcie Technical High School, Manchester, and Nottingham University. He joined the TUC after university and worked his way up through the ranks, serving as deputy general secretary 1987–93 before becoming general secretary after 1993. He was seen as a moderate 'moderniser' and a skilled diplomatic operator who was less than happy with New Labour's plans to introduce more private sector involvement in the public sector. He was elected general secretary of the European Trade Union Confederation in 2007. In May 2010 he was made a life peer.

Moore, Charles (1956–)

Leading right-wing columnist and editor of the *Daily Telegraph*. He was educated at Eton and Trinity College, Cambridge. He worked for *Daily Express*, the *Sunday Telegraph* and *Daily Telegraph* and as editor of the *Spectator* and then of the *Telegraph* 1995–2003. He continues to write regular columns for both the publications he used to edit.

Morgan, Piers (1965–)

Editor of the *Daily Mirror*. He worked for the *Sun* before he moved to the *Mirror*, where he did not prevent the *Daily Mail* from overtaking its ailing circulation of 2.3 million daily; the *Mirror* is still the third best-selling daily newspaper. He suffered some bad publicity when he was associated with some suspect share reporting by two of his financial journalists. He was sacked in May 2004 for publishing pictures of British servicemen abusing Iraqi prisoners which turned out to be fakes. He has written a well received set of name-dropping memoirs (*The Insider: The Private Diaries of a Scandalous Decade*, 2005) and has made a career for himself as a television celebrity.

Morgan, Rhodri (1939–)

Labour first minister of Wales 2000–09. He was educated Whitchurch Grammar School and St John's College, Oxford, where he studied philosophy, politics and economics (PPE). He later gained an MA from Harvard. He was elected MP for Cardiff West in 1987 and went on to serve as a shadow environment spokesman and chair of the Public Administration Committee. In 1999 he came runner-up to Ron Davies as leader of the Labour group in the Welsh assembly. Alun Michael – widely seen as Blair's placeman – then briefly served as first minister but was replaced by Morgan in February 2001. He stood down from the Commons at the 2001 election. In May 2003 Morgan was able to lead a Labour-only administration. The third Welsh assembly election, in 2007, left Labour the biggest party but Morgan had to lead a minority government before allying with Plaid Cymru. He retired, aged 70, in December 2009.

Morgan, Sally (1959–), Baroness
Labour peer and Downing Street aide. She was educated at Belvedere Girls' School, Liverpool, and Durham and London Universities. She was a teacher 1981–85, student organiser in the Labour Party 1985–87, director of campaigns and elections in the Labour Party 1993–95, head of party liaison for the leader of opposition 1995–97 and political secretary to the prime minister 1997–2001. She was briefly a minister of state in the Cabinet Office before she became director of political and government relations based in Downing Street in 2001. She left Downing Street in 2005.

Morris, Bill (1938–), Sir
General secretary of the Transport and General Workers' Union (TGWU). He was educated at Mizpah School, Manchester, Jamaica. In 1954 he moved to Handsworth, Birmingham, and joined the TGWU in 1954. He was deputy general secretary 1986 and was elected general secretary 1991 and re-elected 1995. He retired in 2003. He is still active in public life as a board member of numerous public organisations.

Morris, Estelle (1952–)
Labour MP and minister. She was educated at Whalley Range High School, Manchester, and Coventry College of Education, then worked as a teacher. She was active in local government before entering the House of Commons and was leader of Warwick district council 1979–81. She was elected MP for Birmingham Yardley 1992, became a junior education minister after 1997 and then secretary of state 2001. However, after just over a year in the post she resigned, claiming the demands of the job were beyond her. She was later made minister for the arts but declared in September 2004 that she would not contest the next election.

Morrison, Herbert (1888–1965)
Leading Labour politician who helped develop the policy of nationalisation. Self-educated, he helped to found the London Labour Party and became leader of London County Council from 1934. He did much to establish transport in the capital and to protect 'green belt' land from development. He was elected an MP in 1923 and helped formulate Labour's policies on nationalisation. He served in Winston Churchill's war cabinet as home secretary. After Labour's 1945 election victory he was deputy prime minister 1945–51 and leader of the house. He succeeded Ernest Bevin as foreign secretary for a few months after the latter's resignation but was not a success in the post. He was defeated by Hugh Gaitskell in the party leadership contest in 1955. He was made a life peer in 1959. His grandson is Peter Mandelson.

Mosley, Oswald (1896–1980)
Gifted British politician who became leader of the 1930s fascist movement and failed to achieve any power. He was born into a landed family and educated at Winchester and Sandhurst. He was elected Conservative MP in 1918, retained his seat as an independent in 1922 and 1924 and then joined the Labour Party, when he made a name for himself as a left-wing rebel. He served as chancellor of the Duchy of Lancaster in the 1929 Labour government, when he was in charge of tackling unemployment, the major problem of the day. His Mosley Memorandum was a proposal to spend money on public works and anticipated much Keynesian thinking. His ideas were rejected and he resigned. He formed the socialist New Party in 1930, lost his seat in 1931 and then looked to other routes to power. He was clearly influenced by the fascist movement on the Continent and set up the British Union of Fascists in 1932. His Blackshirts took part in violent rallies, which contained strong anti-Semitic overtones. Their excessive violence in demonstrations in 1934 and 1936 led to the passing of the Public Order Act 1936. Mosley's demeanour as a

political leader seemed to ape that of Adolf
Hitler in appearance, style and manner
of political meeting. However, the British
political culture was not receptive to such
messages and he never prospered. During
the war he was interned, though he was
released on health grounds in 1943. He
attempted to be active in politics after the
war and in the late 1950s stood unsuccessfully for the Commons. A vigorous
and imaginative politician, he could have
achieved much but his desperate wish to
acquire power by whatever means ultimately
destroyed his career.

> Jewish international finance, the nameless,
> homeless and all powerful force which
> stretches its greedy fingers from the shelter of
> England to throttle the trade and menace the
> peace of the world.

> I am not, and have never been, a man of the
> right. My position was on the left and is now
> in the centre of politics. (1968)

Mottram, Richard (1946–)
Civil servant. He was educated at Edward
VI Camp Hill School, Birmingham,
and Keele University. He worked in the
Ministry of Defence, the Cabinet Office
and Office of Public Service and Science
before moving to be permanent secretary
in the Department of Transport, Local
Government and the Regions in 1998.
He was involved in public controversy in
February 2002, when his minister, Stephen
Byers, demanded the resignation of his
head of communications, Martin Sixsmith.
The latter claimed he had not offered his
resignation and an unseemly public dispute
ensued, with Sir Richard insisting he had
told Sixsmith his 'position was untenable'
and that the ex-BBC man had agreed to
resign as long as Jo Moore (with whom
he had difficulties) did the same and that
his resignation did not appear to blame
him for any wrongdoing. Sir Richard's
highly unusual statement was published in
the press on 26 February 2002. Shortly
afterwards he was moved to become the
top mandarin at the Department of Work
and Pensions.

> We're all fucked. I'm fucked. You're fucked.
> The whole department is fucked. It's the
> biggest cock-up ever. We're all completely
> fucked. (Attributed to Mottram by Sixsmith
> in the wake of the Jo Moore affair)

**Mowlam, Mo (Marjorie) (1949–
2005)**
Labour MP and cabinet minister with
the popular touch. She was educated at
Conodon Comprehensive, and Durham and
Iowa Universities. She lectured at Florida
University before becoming MP for Redcar
1987. She was shadow Northern Ireland
spokeswoman then, after 1997, secretary of
state for Northern Ireland. She is credited
with playing a big part in obtaining the
Good Friday agreement in 1998 but was
replaced by Peter Mandelson and took over
the Cabinet Office job once performed by
Jack Cunningham. She left the house in
2001 to do different things; this included
being critical of the government on a number
of issues, especially Iraq. She had suffered
from a brain tumour for several years and in
August 2005 she died after a fall.

> You can't switch on peace like a light. (1999)

Mulgan, Geoff (1961–)
Head of policy at 10 Downing Street for
several years and now director of the Young
Foundation. He was educated at Oxford
University and the Polytechnic of Central
London. After working for Gordon Brown
as an advisor 1990–92, he founded the
independent think-tank Demos in 1993.
He became a member of the Cabinet Office
Performance and Innovation Unit before
joining the Downing Street Policy Unit,
where he was responsible for the social
exclusion issue. In June 2001 he became
head of policy, charged with undertaking
'blue skies policy thinking for the prime
minister' and 'strategy projects at request'.
In 2004 he became director of the Young
Foundation.

Mullin, Chris (1947–)
Labour MP for Sunderland South from
1987. He read law at Hull University and
became a journalist. He worked for ITV's

World in Action and was editor of *Tribune* 1982–84. He led campaigns for the release of the Birmingham Six and other wrongful IRA imprisonments. A political activist from an early age, and supporter of Tony Benn, he soon achieved prominence as chair of the Home Affairs Committee 1997–99 and again 2001–03. He served three times as junior minister: at the Departments of Environment, Transport and the Regions 1999–2001, International Development 2001, and the Foreign Office 2003–05. He stood down as an MP at the 2010 election. His novel *A Very British Coup* (1982) was televised and won a BAFTA and his witty, insightful volume of diaries (1999–2005), *A View From the Foothills* (2009), is warmly recommended.

Murdoch, Rupert (1931–)
Media tycoon with a big stake in the British media, who decided to support Tony Blair in 1997. He was educated at Geelong Grammar School and Oxford University. He then worked for a while on the *Daily Express* before returning to his homeland, Australia, to run the paper he inherited, the *News* in Adelaide. Using this as a base he bought newspapers in Hong Kong and the USA, as well as others in his home country. In Britain his News International owns the *Times, Sunday Times, News of the World* and the biggest-selling British tabloid, the *Sun*. He also moved into satellite television with Sky TV in Europe, Fox in the USA and Star TV in Asia. He owns Random House and other publishing interests. He was known for astute though legal tax avoidance, for his ruthless use of the law to advance his business interests (as occurred when he broke the power of British trade unions by moving to Wapping and employing new technology in defiance of the print unions), for his wooing of politicians, and for his editorial intervention to influence the content of the newspapers he owns. Murdoch is one of the world's most influential media moguls. He is clever at maximising his influence,

for example inviting Tony Blair to address his company's executives in 1995. The *Sun* supported Blair in 1997 and thereafter commentators discerned a desire by Blair to retain Murdoch's support – Blair allegedly assisted him in 1998 by contacting the Italian prime minister on a business matter on Murdoch's behalf. More traditional Labour supporters were deeply troubled by the Blair–Murdoch connection. The *Sun* supported Blair in the 2001 general election and Murdoch was an early visitor to Number 10 after the victory. For several years, while Blair was prime minister he was sometimes designated a 'silent member of the cabinet' as his known views, especially on the European Union, acted as a veto on certain policy options. In recent years he has drawn back from the front line of his business and left his children – for example Elizabeth and James – to take over day to day running. In 2009 he announced he would charge for online news content in an attempt to recoup some of the advantage lost to the Internet. Some greeted this as a bold decision but others doubted the success of a move in a world where online news is expected to be free.

Murphy, Paul (1948–)
Labour MP and former minister. He was educated at St Francis School, Abersychan, and Oriel College, Oxford. He worked as a technical college lecturer. He became MP for Torfaen in 1987. He served as minister of state at the Northern Ireland Office 1997–99, where his ability was noticed. He was opposition spokesperson on Wales 1988–94, Northern Ireland 1994–95 and defence 1995–97. He was secretary of state for Wales from 1999 but devolution had not left his department much to do. He was moved to take charge of the Northern Ireland Office in October 2002. He was replaced as secretary of state for Wales, to which Gordon Brown had reappointed him, by Peter Hain in June 2009. He retained his seat in 2010 by 9,306 votes.

PEOPLE

N

Naughtie, James (1951–)

Known, along with John Humphrys, as the voice of Radio 4's *Today* programme. He was educated at Keith Grammar School, Aberdeen University and Syracuse University, New York. He worked for a variety of newspapers but principally the *Guardian* before he joined the BBC to present *The World at One* and from 1994 *Today*. He wrote a study of Gordon Brown and Tony Blair entitled *The Rivals* (2000).

Neville-Jones, Pauline (1939–), Baroness

Chair of the Joint Intelligence Committee 1993–94 and Conservative peer and minister. She was educated at Leeds High School and Oxford University (Harkness fellow 1961–63). She was a career member of the Diplomatic Service 1963–96. She was seconded to the European Commission, where she acted as chef de cabinet to the budget and financial institutions commissioner Christopher Tugendhat. She became political director of the Foreign Office 1994–96 and led the British delegation to the Dayton negotiations on peace in Bosnia. She was made a governor of the BBC in 1998. Anticipating the Butler report, in 2004 she said that responsibility for any intelligence failure rested ultimately with the prime minister. In July 2007 she was made shadow security minister by David Cameron and in October 2007 entered the House of Lords. In May 2010 she became minister of state for security at the Home Office.

Normington, David (1951–), Sir

Permanent secretary at the Home Office from 2006. He was educated at Bradford Grammar School and Corpus Christi College, Oxford, where he obtained a first in modern history. He began his career in the Department of Employment, where he was private secretary to Tom King when

secretary of state 1983–84. In 1995 he was central to the merging of the Departments of Employment and Education. He was director general for schools, responsible for raising standards, 1998–2001, and then permanent secretary at the Department of Education 2001–06 before moving on to the Home Office. He was dubbed by some 'the smiling assassin' in consequence of his urbanity and charming manner, which were alleged to disguise a ruthless streak. However, despite his opposition to home secretary John Reid's proposals, he had to accept the hiving off of the Ministry of Justice from the Home Office in 2006–07. He was a candidate for cabinet secretary but was beaten to it by Gus O'Donnell.

Norton, Philip (1951–), Lord

The leading academic authority on parliament. He was educated at King Edward's Grammar School, Louth, Sheffield University and the University of Pennsylvania. He has written over 20 books, including *The Conservative Party* (1996) and *Legislatures* (1990). He served as president of the Politics Association for many years and in 1998 was elevated to the House of Lords as a Conservative peer – one of the few political scientists in the upper chamber.

Nott, John (1932–), Sir

Conservative MP and minister. He was educated at Kings Mead, Seaford, and Trinity College, Cambridge, where he was president of the Union. He was called to the bar in 1959 and worked as a merchant banker 1959–66. He was MP for St Ives 1972–83, and served as a junior minister in the Treasury under Edward Heath, and under Margaret Thatcher as secretary of state for trade 1979–81 and defence secretary 1981–83, during the Falklands war. After leaving politics he filled a number of jobs in the City.

Nye, Sue (1955–)

Former close personal aide to Gordon Brown. She was educated at Westcliff High School for Girls. She married

Gavyn Davies, merchant banker and later chairman of the BBC. She became diary secretary to Brown but was much more important than this role suggests, being the chancellor's and then prime minister's effective 'minder'. Her friendship with Anji Hunter, close aide to Tony Blair, enabled her to play an important mediating role between the two feuding politicians. She was made a life peer in May 2010.

Oakeshott, Michael (1901–99)
English philosopher who influenced the Conservatives. He was educated at Cambridge, where he also taught, 1929–49. He moved to the London School of Economics in 1950 as professor of political science. His *Experience and Its Modes* appeared in 1933 and *Rationalism in British Politics* in 1962. He was sceptical of ideological approaches and trusted a pragmatic approach to politics.

Oborne, Peter (1957–)
Widely respected journalist, author and broadcaster. He was educated at Sherborne School and Cambridge. He has written books on cricket, a biography of Alastair Campbell (1999), *The Rise of Political Lying* (2005) and *The Triumph of the Political Class* (2007). He has written for the *Evening Standard*, for most of the quality dailies and Sundays and been political editor of the *Spectator*.

O'Donnell, Gus (1952–), Sir
Civil servant. He was educated at Salesian College, Warwick University and Oxford University. He became a career civil servant who was moving smoothly upwards when he was made press secretary to John Major. He resigned in 1993 and returned to the Treasury to head the monetary group and became a member of Gordon Brown's inner circle on the economy as chief economist at the Treasury. In 2005 he became secretary to the cabinet, the highest-ranking civil servant in the government service, the prime minister's most senior advisor and effectively head of the civil service.

Omand, David (1947–), Sir
Civil servant. He was educated at Glasgow Academy and Cambridge University. He started his civil service career in the Ministry of Defence and moved to head Government Communications Headquarters at Cheltenham and then became permanent secretary at the Home Office. He was mentioned as a candidate to take over from Sir Richard Wilson as cabinet secretary in April 2002 but was eventually – after a period of ill-health – given the job of security coordinator as well as day-to-day manager of the Cabinet Office. He was centrally involved with the David Kelly affair and gave evidence to the Hutton inquiry in 2003. He retired from the Cabinet Office in 2006. In 2010 he gave evidence to the Iraq inquiry.

Orwell, George (pen name for Eric Blair) (1903–50)
English political writer. He was born in India and educated at Eton. He spent the early 1930s empathising with and writing about people living in oppressed circumstances before he fought in Spain on the Republican side (as depicted in *Homage to Catalonia*, 1938). He was associated with left-wing socialist ideas and groupings but was a firm opponent of communism and the USSR. Apart from his influential and prolific journalism he wrote two world-famous books inspired by the Soviet Union: *Animal Farm* (1945), a satirical parody; and *Nineteen Eighty-Four* (1949), a dystopian view of the future. His was a genuinely honest and perceptive voice with lasting relevance.

> Most revolutionaries are potential Tories, because they imagine that everything can be put right by altering the shape of society. Once that change is effected – as

it sometimes is – they see no need for any other. (*Inside the Whale*, 1940)

War is peace. Freedom is slavery. Ignorance is strength. (Example of 'doublespeak', *Nineteen Eighty-Four*, 1949).

Osborne, George (1971–)

Conservative MP and chancellor from May 2010. He was educated at the exclusive St Paul's and went on to study history at Oxford. He is married to the daughter of former Conservative cabinet minister David Howell. He joined the Conservative Research Department in 1994, from where he went on to advise the Ministry of Agriculture and Number 10, 1995–97. He served as political secretary to William Hague, 1997–2001. In 2001 he became the youngest MP, being elected for Tatton, replacing the independent Martin Bell. He became shadow chief secretary to the Treasury in September 2004 and then shadow chancellor in May 2005. He remained in post after managing David Cameron's successful leadership campaign. He was closely identified with Cameron's cautious policy of not promising tax cuts unless the economy was sufficiently stable to absorb them and with the general movement of the party into the electoral centre ground. Some voices in the party favoured Kenneth Clarke as chancellor but his old friend, Cameron, placed him in his expected post in May 2010.

Owen, David (1938–), Lord

One time Labour minister and leader of the Social Democratic Party (SDP). At Cambridge University he studied medicine. He became Labour MP for Plymouth Sutton in 1966 and held the seat until 1974; thereafter he held Plymouth Devonport until 1992, when he stood down. He had junior posts in health and defence, then became second in command at the Foreign Office until Anthony Crosland died and he took over, aged 39, 1977–79. At this time many spoke of him as a future leader but he became disaffected with Labour's drift to the left, especially in the wake of the 1979 general election,

and he formed the so-called 'gang of four' (with William Rodgers, Shirley Williams and Roy Jenkins) to form the SDP, which was initially led by Roy Jenkins, and which in the autumn of 1981 joined up with the Liberals to form the Alliance (for electoral purposes). Owen led the party after 1983 and insisted on leading it even after a majority of members voted to merge with the Liberals in 1987. In 1991 he offered John Major support in exchange for the Tories not fielding candidates in the constituencies of the two remaining MPs loyal to his banner. Even when this could not be done Owen declared his support for the Conservatives. He resigned from the House of Commons in 1992 and was given a role in the former Yugoslavia, promoting peace, though little came of his efforts. Owen was one of the most able of politicians of his generation but his self-confidence, bordering on arrogance, alienated many potential allies and a life of the highest achievement passed him by.

The price of championing human rights is a little inconsistency at times. (1977)

We are fed up with fudging and mudging, with mush and slush. We need courage, conviction, and hard work. (Labour Party conference, 1980)

P

Paine, Thomas (1737–1809)

Revolutionary writer. Born in Norfolk, he was first a corset-maker, then a sailor and later a schoolmaster. In 1774 he arrived in Philadelphia and almost at once argued for American independence, and even served for a while in the US army. He returned to Britain in 1887, where he wrote *The Rights of Man* (1791/92), which supported the French Revolution. He fled to Paris, where he became a deputy to the National Convention. His views were unacceptable, however, even to his French hosts and he was imprisoned until 1796, when he wrote *The Age of Reason* (1794). He returned to the USA in 1802.

> Government, even in its best state, is a necessary evil; in its worst state, an intolerable one. Government, like dress, is the badge of lost innocence; the palaces of kings are built upon the ruins of the bowers of paradise. (1776)

> Of more worth is one honest man to society, and in the sight of God, than all the crowned ruffians that ever lived. (1791)

Paisley, Ian (1926–), Reverend

Uninhibited Protestant leader in Northern Ireland famous on the 'mainland' for his intractability but respected by his own community. He was born in Armagh, Northern Ireland, and educated at Ballymena Technical High School and Belfast Reformed Presbyterian Theological College. He was ordained in 1946 and set up his own Free Presbyterian Church of Ulster in 1951. He gained a doctorate from an American university which did not entail a thesis and was not widely recognised in Britain. In the 1960s he became involved in the politics of the province as an outspoken activist on the Protestant side. He was imprisoned for a while in 1966 following his behaviour during a riot. He founded the Democratic Unionist Party (DUP) in 1972 and represented North Antrim in its name. In 1979 he was elected to the European parliament. Paisley always provoked strong reactions. He was strongly opposed to any move which hinted at an eventual unification of Ireland and maintained a powerful suspicion of Catholics and the Dublin government. For many Protestants he was the authentic voice of unionism; for others he epitomised the bigotry and inflexibility which made Northern Ireland a political tragedy. Those who hoped hard-line Protestantism might fade as a result of the peace process were disappointed in November 2003 when the DUP won an extra 10 assembly seats, placing Paisley at the head of loyalist representation and making compromise with

Sinn Fein even less likely – Paisley declared the elections spelt the end of the Good Friday agreement. So it was to widespread amazement in May 2007 that, as the leader of the largest party in the assembly, he was elected first minister, with Martin McGuinness of Sinn Fein his deputy. In June 2008 he stood down and was replaced by Peter Robinson of the DUP. He was made a life peer in May 2010.

> The Mother of all Treachery. (On the Good Friday agreement, April 1998)

> Trusting in the God of our fathers and confident that our cause is just, we will never surrender our heritage. (1968)

Palme Dutt, Rajani (1896–1974)

Leading intellectual in the Communist Party of Great Britain (CPGB). He was the son of an Indian doctor and a Swedish mother. He was suspended from Oxford University for opposing the First World War. He joined the CPGB in 1920 and established the *Labour Monthly*, which he edited until his death. He served on the executive committee of the party 1923–65 and was responsible in part for the party's slavish obedience to the Moscow line. He was also active in the communist international body, the Comintern, as well as the Communist Party of India. He willingly stood in to take the place of the dissenting Harry Pollitt in the chaos caused in 1939 when Stalin decreed the war against Hitler was an 'imperialist' war which communists should resist. Palme Dutt never lost his allegiance to the USSR and remained loyal to it, throughout the convulsions caused by the invasion of Czeckoslovakia and the growth of Eurocommunism in the 1970s.

Pankhurst, Emmeline (1857–1928)

Founder of the suffragette movement. She was born in Manchester. She founded the Women's Franchise League in 1889 and the Women's Social and Political Union in 1903, along with her daughter Christabel Harriette (1880–1958). She embraced violent methods for her struggle and went on hunger strike in prison several times.

Parkinson, Cecil (1931–), Lord

Thatcherite loyalist cabinet minister whose career was badly damaged by an affair with his secretary. From humble beginnings, he was an early Labour supporter. He was educated at Royal Lancaster Grammar School and Emmanuel College, Cambridge. He was in management at Metal Box Company then a chartered accountant, founding Parkinson Hart Securities in 1967. He was elected at a by-election in 1970 as MP for Enfield West and served as parliamentary private secretary to Michael Heseltine 1972–74 and then became a whip. He was opposition spokesman on trade and then in 1979 a junior minister in the Department of Trade and Industry (DTI). He was made chairman of the party by Margaret Thatcher in 1981 and paymaster general. Popular in the party, he successfully led the election campaign in 1983 and sat in the cabinet for the DTI but was overwhelmed by the scandal involving his lover, Sarah Keays, who bore his child. After much vacillating he decided to stay with his wife and lost much credibility within his party and the country. Margaret Thatcher brought him back to serve as energy minister 1987–89 and transport minister 1989–90. He resigned the day Thatcher resigned and returned to business but, despite leaving the Commons in 1992, was still involved in politics. Most commentators were surprised when William Hague made him party chairman again in 1997. He stood down a year later.

Parris, Matthew (1949–)

Well known Conservative MP who reinvented himself as a successful journalist, author and broadcaster. He was educated at Waterford School, Swaziland, and Clare College, Cambridge, as well as Yale University. He worked in the Foreign Office and then the Conservative Research Department and the office of Margaret Thatcher. He was MP for West Derbyshire 1979–86, then left the Commons to become the presenter of *Weekend World* and a columnist on the *Times* and other newspapers. In November 1998 he caused uproar by saying 'Peter Mandelson is certainly gay'. Parris maintained this was an unexceptional thing to say as the *News of the World* had 'outed' him in 1987 but he lost his column in the *Sun* as a result and attracted criticism from those who pointed out that, as long as he served as an MP, he had not divulged that he, too, was gay. He continues a successful career in the media.

Paterson, Owen (1956–)

Conservative MP and secretary of state for Northern Ireland. He was educated at Radley Hall School and Corpus Christi College, Cambridge. He was managing director of the British Leather Company 1993–99. He won North Shropshire in 1997 and has retained his seat since then. He was made shadow Northern Ireland secretary in 2007, the post to which he was appointed in May 2010.

Patten, Chris (1944–), Lord

Conservative cabinet minister and governor of Hong Kong. He was educated at Balliol College, Oxford. He joined the Conservative Research Department (CRD), then worked in the Home Office and Cabinet Office. He directed the CRD 1974–79 and entered the house as MP for Bath in 1979, after which he served as junior minister in a number of departments before becoming minister for overseas development 1986 and environment 1989. He lost his seat in 1992 and became the last governor of Hong Kong before returning to Britain to speculation as to his ambitions in Conservative politics. In the end he became a European commissioner in charge of external affairs, courtesy of Tony Blair. He criticised the 2001 Conservative campaign and joined Leon Brittan as a pro-European critic of his former party. In 2005 he was raised to the peerage. He is the chancellor of Newcastle and Oxford Universities.

Paxman, Jeremy (1950–)

Formidable interviewer and BBC presenter of current affairs television programmes. He was educated at Malvern College and St Catherine's College, Cambridge. He worked variously for the BBC, mostly on current affairs programmes, as well as Breakfast Television, but is most closely associated with *Newsnight*, which he began to present in 1989. Feared by many politicians for his deliberately lofty intellectual style and tenacious questioning, he once won an award for his persistence in repeating the same question to home secretary Michael Howard 14 times in a vain attempt to elicit a clear answer. Paxman is also a highly accomplished author, with a number of volumes to his name.

Pepys, Samuel (1633–1703)

English diarist. Pepys was administrator of the Royal Navy. His diary 1660–69 provides a unique insight into the atmosphere of the day, with many entries covering corruption, scandals and court gossip. He thereby set a tradition which ever since other politicians and public people have sought to extend.

> I went to Charing Cross, to see Major General Harrison hanged, drawn, and quartered; which was done there, he looking as cheerful as any man could do in that condition.

> I see it is impossible for the King to have things done as cheap as other men.

Peston, Robert (1962–)

Journalist and BBC business editor. He is the son of former Labour peer Lord Peston. He was educated at Highgate Wood High School and then Balliol College, Oxford, and the Université Libre de Bruxelles. He worked for a number of newspapers including the *Independent*, the *Sunday Correspondent* and then the *Financial Times* 1991–2000. As political editor he used to clash with Alastair Campbell, who once responded to a press conference inquiry with: 'Another question from the Peston school of smart-arse journalism'. He went on to write for the *Spectator*, *Daily Telegraph* and *Sunday Times*, before joining the BBC in 2005. His slightly idiosyncratic broadcasting style, which mangles words, has become his

trademark and did not prevent his becoming a national figure during the banking crisis 2007–09, when his explanations were highly regarded and even influential.

Philby, Kim (1912–88)

British intelligence officer and Soviet spy. He became a communist while at Cambridge in the 1930s and a Soviet agent in 1940. His real use to the USSR, however, came later when he was liaison officer in Washington, 1949–51. He was unmasked as a double agent and asked to resign but fled to the USSR in 1963 when it became public knowledge that he had warned the spies Guy Burgess and Donald MacLean in the early 1950s that they were about to be exposed. He became a Soviet citizen and a general in the KGB.

> To betray, you first have to belong. (1967)

Pickles, Eric (1952–)

Conservative MP, former party chairman and cabinet minister. He was educated at Greenhead Grammar School and Leeds Polytechnic. He was born into a Labour-supporting family but joined the Tories in 1968. He made his name as a leading Young Conservative and campaigner against racism. He was leader of Bradford council 1988–90. He won Brentwood and Ongar in 1992. In 2001 Martin Bell stood against him and reduced his majority to a little over 2,000 but he regained his usual majority in 2005. He served as party chairman 2009–10. In May 2010 he was made secretary of state for communities and local government.

Pimlott, Ben (1945–2004)

Leading political biographer and professor of politics and modern history, Birkbeck College, London University. His biographies *Harold Wilson* (1992), *Hugh Dalton: A Life* (1995, Whitbread Biography Prize) and *The Queen: Biography of Elizabeth II* (1996) were acclaimed as superlative examples of this elusive art. He died, much mourned, of leukaemia in 2004.

> The best political biographer now writing. (Andrew Marr)

Plant, Raymond (1945–)
Professor of jurisprudence at King's
College, London University, and Labour
peer. He was educated at Grimsby
Havelock School, King's College, London,
and Hull University. He was a senior
lecturer in philosophy at Manchester
University and then professor of politics at
Southampton University. He was made a
life peer in 1989 (Lord Plant of Highfield)
and subsequently Neil Kinnock asked him
to study alternative electoral systems for
Britain. He is the author of several books
on political philosophy.

Pollitt, Harry (1890–1960)
Former general secretary of the Communist
Party of Great Britain (CPGB). He
was born in Droylsden, Lancashire, and
educated in local schools; he left school
aged 13 to work in a Benson's mill but later
became a boiler maker. Despite working
53 hours a week, Pollitt attended evening
classes and became active in union affairs
and socialist campaigning. He joined the
fledgling CPGB in 1920 and in 1929
became its respected general secretary.
Under him membership rose from 3,000 at
the start of the 1930s to 18,000 by the end
of that decade. In 1939 he refused to obey
the Moscow line that the war against Hitler
was to be opposed and in consequence
stood down from his post, when he was
replaced by Rajani Palme Dutt. However,
after the USSR joined the war in 1941 he
was reinstated. He stood down as general
secretary in 1956. In 1971 the Soviet
Union named a ship after him.

Ponting, Clive (1946–)
Civil servant in the Ministry of Defence
who, in 1985, passed secret information to
Labour MP Tam Dalyell about the sinking
of the *General Belgrano* in the Falklands
war. He was prosecuted under the Official
Secrets Acts; Ponting defended himself on
the basis of being responsible not primarily
to his minister but to parliament. He was
found not guilty by the jury, who had been
specifically directed to convict by the judge.
The case highlighted the ambiguity of a

civil servant's duty – whether to his/her
minister or to parliament and the public –
when something in the national interest is
involved. To clarify the matter, the head of
the civil service, Sir Robert Armstrong,
issued a statement which asserted that the
'duty of the individual civil servant is first
and foremost to the minister of the crown
who is in charge of the department'. After
leaving the civil service Ponting settled in
Wales, and became a writer and academic.

Portillo, Michael (1953–)
Conservative MP and minister. He was
educated at Harrow and Peterhouse,
Cambridge. He worked for the Conservative
Research Department 1976–79 and was
a policy advisor on energy 1979–81. He
then worked for an oil company 1981–83.
He was elected MP for Enfield Southgate
in 1984 and served as a junior minister
at the Department of Health and Social
Security and at Local Government and
Transport before becoming chief secretary
to the Treasury 1992–94 and then
secretary of state for employment 1994. In
the small hours of election night, 2 May
1997, he was defeated by Steven Twigg,
his young Labour opponent, giving birth
to the humorous question among Labour
supporters 'Were you up for Portillo?'
He was therefore unable to stand in the
ensuing leadership contest after John Major
resigned, which most commentators think
he would otherwise have won. Portillo
attempted at the Conservative Party conference later that year to refashion his brand
of Conservatism, offering a much more 'one
nation' version than the right-wing attitudes
he supported when a minister. In the
autumn of 1998 he presented a television
programme called *Portillo's Progress*, in
which the new, non-arrogant, voter-friendly
ex-minister talked to a range of people about
why the Conservatives lost the election. In
1999 he was elected for Kensington and
Chelsea and almost immediately became
shadow chancellor. In the aftermath of
the Conservatives' defeat in 2001 he
did stand for the leadership of his party,
advocating a gentler, more inclusive form of

Conservatism. However, his admission in 2000 that he had indulged in homosexual experiences when at Cambridge lost him the support of certain sections of the party. In the first round of the contest he polled 49 seats, in the second ballot 50 and by the time the third and final ballot came it was clear his candidature was in trouble, but his third place on 53 votes was a shock to everyone and in its wake he announced he was standing down from 'front line' politics, though continuing his role as a back-bench MP. In June 2002 the Conservative grouping Conservative Change was formed to advance his political cause. Portillo announced in November 2003 that he would not be contesting the next election. He continues a successful media career.

> You cannot ditch policies that succeeded so convincingly that they were adopted by our opponents. (1999)

Powell, Charles (1941–), Lord

Diplomat and key foreign policy advisor to Margaret Thatcher during her years in power. He was educated at King's School, Canterbury, and then read modern history at New College, Oxford. He joined the diplomatic corps in 1963 and filled posts all over the world. He was private secretary to Thatcher 1983–90 and then to John Major 1990–91. He helped broker the huge Yamamah arms deal with Saudi Arabia. Suave, witty and hugely well connected, he also picked up a wide range of consultancies and directorships as a result of his service in government. His brother Jonathan played something of a similar role for Tony Blair as a key advisor and aide.

Powell, Enoch (1912–98)

MP, cabinet minister and writer. He was educated at King Edward School, Birmingham, and Trinity College, Cambridge. A brilliant scholar, he became a professor at Sydney University aged 25. He joined the Conservative Party Research Department in 1945 and was elected for Wolverhampton South West in 1950. He served a year as a junior Treasury minister before resigning over levels of public expenditure. He became minister of health 1960–63 but refused to serve under Alec Douglas-Home, as he had supported R. A. Butler for the leadership. He himself stood for the party leadership in 1965 but mustered only 15 votes, coming third. However, he became best known for his unorthodox but well argued ideas: an early form of monetarism at odds with the postwar consensus; withdrawal from east of Suez; opposition to Britain's joining the Common Market; against capital punishment; and opposition to continued immigration. His views on race – most vividly expressed on 20 April 1968, when he said he foresaw 'rivers of blood' in British city streets – were unacceptable to Edward Heath and he lost his chance of office in the 1970–74 administration. In 1974 he believed he helped Labour win its narrow victory by urging voters to support Labour as the party most likely to withdraw from Europe. In October 1974 he was elected for South Down as an Ulster Unionist, a seat he held until 1987.

> As I look ahead, I am filled with foreboding. Like the Roman, I seem to see the Tiber foaming with much blood. (Speech to Conservative Political Centre meeting in Birmingham, 20 April 1968, when he dramatically put race on the political agenda and indicated his future maverick tendencies)

> An almost unlimited faith in the ability of people to get what they want through price, capital, profit and a competitive market. (On his economic beliefs, 1968)

> If we had a presidential system, on polls I would no doubt be a candidate. (1974)

> For a politician to complain about the press is like a ship's captain complaining about the sea. (1984)

> All political lives, unless they are cut off in mid stream at a happy juncture, end in failure, because that is the nature of politics and human affairs. (1977)

> I was born a Tory. I am a Tory and shall die a Tory.

Powell, Jonathan (1956–)

Chief of staff to the prime minister. He was educated at Oxford and Pennsylvania

Universities. He originally pursued a diplomatic career, like his brother Charles, who for several years advised Margaret Thatcher, but was persuaded to join Tony Blair in 1995 and acted as his fixer, making crucial contacts with civil servants. After the departure of Alastair Campbell (Blair's press secretary) in 2003 he was made the prime minister's chief of staff and was rated as the person with the most intimate influence within the Blair government. He was made head of Number 10's combined private office and Policy Unit, when he was officially responsible for 'leading and coordinating operations across Number 10, reporting to the prime minister'. In 2007 he joined the Morgan Stanley Bank as a full-time senior managing director in its investment banking division.

Prescott, John (1938–)

Labour MP and deputy prime minister 1997–2007. He was first secretary of state after 1997. He was born in Prestatyn, North Wales, and, after failing his 11-plus, educated at Ruskin College, Oxford, and Hull University. He served in the merchant navy 1955–63, when he was a steward and also an officer in the National Union of Seamen. He was elected as a Labour MP in 1970. He was also elected to the European parliament in 1975 and, though then opposed to the concept of Europe, became Labour group leader 1976–79. In the shadow cabinet he served as spokesman for energy, employment and transport. He became deputy leader in 1994 and deputy prime minister with the job of secretary of state for environment and transport. His 1998 transport white paper, which suggested cars should be used less, caused controversy and was, according to some reports, opposed by the prime minister. He retained his post after the June 2001 general election, surviving the celebrated incident when he punched a Welsh demonstrator who threw an egg at him. Prescott, given his working-class provenance and no-nonsense style, was seen as something of the left-wing conscience of the party, as well as not especially bright. The latter

judgement was probably unfair, though it is true his communication abilities were not brilliant. In April 2006 he admitted to a two-year affair with his diary secretary, Tracey Temple; the tabloids really enjoyed that, though so did most of the rest of the country. Somehow his marriage survived. He stood down with Blair in June 2007 and thereafter played the role of Labour loyalist, supporting Gordon Brown and insisting Labour could win the next election. In August 2007 he announced he would not contest the next election and in May 2010 he was made a life peer.

> People like me were branded, pigeon holed, a ceiling put on their ambitions. (On failing his 11-plus)

> We did it! Let's wallow in our victory! (Speech to the Labour Party conference, September 1997)

> John Prescott is the best deputy leader Labour has ever had. (Roy Hattersley, *Guardian*, 9 August 2004)

> Our Willie Whitelaw. (Peter Mandelson on Prescott, 2004)

Primarolo, Dawn (1954–)

Labour MP and former minister. She was educated at Thomas Bennet Comprehensive School, Crawley, Bristol Polytechnic and Bristol University. She was elected for Bristol South in 1997. Over her years in parliament she moved from hard left to uncritical New Labour loyalist, from supporting the Campaign for Nuclear Disarmament to advocating renewal of Trident. She was financial secretary to the Treasury 1997 and paymaster general 1999–2007, when she was credited with introducing the tax credit system. In June 2007 Brown moved her to the Department of Health and then to minister of state for children, young people and families in June 2009. She retained her seat in May 2010 with a majority of 4,734.

Prior, James (1927–), Lord

Conservative MP and minister. He was educated at Charterhouse and Pembroke College, Cambridge, where he took a first in estate management. He was MP for Lowestoft 1959–83 and Waveney 1983–87 and served as parliamentary private secretary to several cabinet ministers during the 1960s. He rose quickly under Edward Heath and served Margaret Thatcher as employment secretary 1979–81 and Northern Ireland secretary 1981–84 but was always seen as too 'wet' for the Iron Lady. He chaired the General Electric Company 1984–98. He was made a life peer in 1987.

Profumo, John (1915–2001)
Conservative defence secretary at the heart of a scandal which helped bring down Harold Macmillan in 1963. He initially denied his involvement with Christine Keeler, a glamorous young woman who also shared her favours with a Soviet naval attaché. When exposed he was forced to resign and the scandalous aftermath damaged Macmillan's government. He devoted the rest of his life to charity, becoming administrator of the social and educational settlement Toynbee Hall in 1982. When he died, Profumo was the last remaining MP who had voted against Chamberlain in the 1940 debate which presaged Winston Churchill becoming prime minister.

Purnell, James (1970–)
Labour MP and cabinet member who resigned on 4 June 2009 in an attempt to bring down Gordon Brown's premiership. He was educated mostly in France before attending the Royal Grammar School, Guildford, and going on to Oxford, where he took a first in philosophy, politics and economics (PPE). He worked during holidays as a researcher for Tony Blair, then as a fellow at the Institute for Public Policy Research before becoming head of corporate planning at the BBC. He won the seat of Stalybridge and Hyde in 2001. He was parliamentary private secretary to Ruth Kelly, then, after 2005, a junior minister in the Department of Culture, Media and Sport. In 2006 he was promoted to minister of state at the Department for Work and Pensions. In 2007 he entered cabinet as

secretary of state for culture, media and sport, before moving again to Work and Pensions in January 2008. His resignation was designed to produce more resignations and the downfall of Brown as prime minister. But colleagues like David Miliband, whose resignation might have sealed Brown's fate, merely agreed to disagree about Brown as prime minister – possibly under pressure from Peter Mandelson – and Brown survived. Purnell moved to the back benches but was still spoken of as a future leadership prospect. Unfortunately for his supporters he stood down as an MP in 2010, and went to work for Open Left, part of the think-tank Demos.

Pym, Francis (1922–2008), Lord
Conservative MP and cabinet minister. He was educated at Eton and Cambridge. He served in the Second World War. He became a Cambridgeshire MP in 1961 and served as chief whip 1970–73, secretary of state for defence 1979–81 and foreign secretary 1982–83. He was associated with the liberal wing of the Conservative Party and clashed with Margaret Thatcher over a number of issues before bowing out of mainstream politics, perhaps before his full contribution had been made. He was made a life peer in 1987.

R

Rawnsley, Andrew (1962–)
Associate editor and chief columnist of the *Observer*. He was educated at Lawrence Sherif Grammar School and Cambridge University. He then worked for the BBC and the *Guardian* before the *Observer*. He presented and produced several television programmes and wrote *Servants of the People* (2000), the widely accepted though highly controversial account of New Labour in power, in which he detailed

Tony Blair's obsession with presentation and the rivalry between him and his chancellor, Gordon Brown. He has made a number of well received documentaries for Channel 4: *Bye Bye Blues*, on John Major's government (1997); *Blair's Year* (1998); *The Rise and Fall of Tony Blair* (2007); and *Gordon Brown: Where Did It All Go Wrong?* (2008). His *The End of the Party* (2010) made damaging allegations regarding Brown's character and suitability as prime minister.

Raynor, Derek (1926–), Lord
Long-time advisor to Margaret Thatcher on efficiency in government. He was educated at City College, Norwich, and Selwyn College, Cambridge. He joined Marks and Spencer in 1953 and rose to be its managing director 1973–91. He started to advise the prime minister on efficiency in government in 1979 and for a number of years headed the Efficiency Unit in the Cabinet Office. The Whitehall expert Peter Hennessy wrote of 'Raynerism' in his book *Whitehall* (1989), so profound was his impact upon the civil service culture.

Redwood, John (1951–)
Conservative MP and cabinet minister. He was educated at Oxford University, then worked for a merchant bank before his intellectual brilliance led to him heading Margaret Thatcher's Policy Unit in 1983. He was Conservative MP for Wokingham from 1987 and served as a junior minister for trade until he was made secretary of state for Wales 1993–95. He resigned from cabinet in 1995 and stood against John Major when he recontested the party leadership. His support was sufficient to encourage him to stand again in the contest following his party's election defeat in 1997. In 1998 he shadowed trade and industry under William Hague. He has campaigned and written on Eurosceptic and pro-US capitalism themes. He chaired his party's policy group on competitiveness, to which he was appointed in 2005. He won a 13,492 majority in May 2010 but was not given office in the coalition government.

Reece, Gordon (1929–), Sir
Influential public relations consultant and political advisor. He was educated at Ratcliffe College and Downing College, Cambridge. He was a television producer 1960–70 and an advisor to Margaret Thatcher 1975–79, during which time he transformed her image to one that was more acceptable on television. He was director of publicity at Conservative Central Office 1978–80.

Reid, John (1947–)
Labour MP and seven times a cabinet minister. He left school at 16 but later completed a BA and PhD at Stirling University. He became the MP for Hamilton North in 1987 (previously named Motherwell North and Beshill). He served as minister of transport 1997–99, minister of state defence 1997–98 and secretary of state for Northern Ireland 2000. He was a tough Scottish political operator, an effective Labour government advocate and apologist on the media. He was brought in to cover after the forced resignation of Peter Mandelson and was leader of the house after the resignation of Robin Cook and then health minister after Alan Milburn resigned in June 2003. In 2006 he replaced Charles Clarke as home secretary and accused his department of being not 'fit for purpose'. He left government in 2007 along with Tony Blair, later announcing he would stand down at the next election. He was made a life peer in May 2010. In the aftermath of the 2010 election, his excoriation of a proposed coalition of Labour with the Liberal Democrats as a 'coalition of losers' helped to condemn the idea.

Reith, John (1889–1971), Lord
First director general of the BBC (1927–38). Born in Scotland, he was educated at Glasgow Academy and Gresham School, Holt. He began life humbly as an engineering apprentice but found his *métier* in radio communication. In 1922 he became the first general manager of the BBC and managed its transition to a public corporation in 1927. He resisted the

attempts by politicians and business people to exert influence and pursued a high-minded mission for the BBC to 'educate, enlighten and entertain'. His influence helped make the BBC an international template for public service broadcasting. He served as minister of information in 1940 and then minister of works 1940–42, before falling out with Winston Churchill, who once described the imposing but dour Scot as 'that wuthering height'.

Richards, Steve (1960–)

Chief political columnist for the *Independent* and a radio and television broadcaster. He was educated at Christ's College school, north London, and then at York University. In 1996 he became political editor of the *New Statesman*. He presents programmes on Radio 4 and on various television channels as well as producing columns for the *Independent* and *Independent on Sunday*.

Riddell, Peter (1948–)

Leading columnist and commentator on British government. He was educated at Oxford. He worked on the *Financial Times* and the *Times*, of which he was the assistant editor. He is a highly respected authority on British government and politics and the author of several much-praised books, including *Honest Opportunism* (1993), *Parliament Under Pressure* (1998) and *The Unfulfilled Prime Minister: Tony Blair's Quest for a Legacy* (2006).

Ridley, Nicolas (1929–93)

Thatcherite Conservative cabinet member. He was educated at Oxford and became a Conservative MP in 1959. He held junior posts until Margaret Thatcher made him secretary of state for transport 1983–86. He moved to the Department of the Environment 1986–89, where he had responsibility for the hated poll tax, and then to Trade and Industry 1989–90. He resigned after making unflattering remarks about Germany, for example that the European Exchange Rate Mechanism was a 'German racket to take over Europe' and that Britain might just as well have given in

to Hitler. Ridley was very close ideologically to Thatcher and some felt that he said what she could not say in public.

Rimington, Stella (1935–), Dame

Former director general of MI5 and the world's first female head of national security. She was educated at Nottingham High School for Girls and Edinburgh University. She joined MI5 in 1969 and rose to be its director in 1992; she retired in 1996. She favoured a more public face for the secret service but was herself criticised for publishing her memoirs, *Open Secret* (2001). She responded to this exclusion from her previous 'insider' status by calling for a reform of the Official Secrets Act.

Robertson, George (1946–), Lord

Labour MP and secretary of state for defence in 1997 then secretary general of NATO 1999–2003. He was educated at Dunoon Grammar School and Dundee University. He then worked as a trade union official before being elected MP for Hamilton in 1978 (Hamilton South from 1997). He served as shadow spokesman for Scotland, foreign affairs and defence before entering government. He was perceived to have been calm and effective during the Kosovo crisis and became secretary general of NATO shortly after its conclusion. He was made a life peer in 1999.

Robinson, Geoffrey (1938–)

Labour MP and paymaster general sacked by Tony Blair in the wake of the first ministerial resignation of Peter Mandelson. He was educated at Emmanuel College, Cambridge, and Yale. He was a Labour Party researcher in the 1960s, worked for British Leyland in the 1970s and became chief executive of Jaguar 1973–75, as well as an unpaid director of the Meriden motor cycle cooperative 1978–80. He has been MP for Coventry North West since 1976. He made a considerable fortune in the 1980s through his engineering company, TransTec. He was made a minister by his friend Tony Blair but was criticised by the Conservatives for his alleged failure to register all his financial interests. A connection with the disgraced tycoon Robert Maxwell also figured in the criticisms made in the press and by the opposition. Blair, however, seemed to believe he was perfectly acceptable as 1998 drew to a close. Robertson made a loan to Mandelson of £330,000 to assist a house purchase but was embroiled in the crisis which arose when it transpired Mandelson had not told his permanent secretary at the Department of Trade and Industry of the loan, even though his department was investigating Robinson's finances. From 1996 to 2008 he was owner of the *New Statesman* magazine. He retained his seat in May 2010 by 6,288 votes.

Robinson, Nick (1963–)

Political editor at the BBC. He was born in Macclesfield and attended Cheadle Hulme School and University College, Oxford, where he read philosophy, politics and economics (PPE). He was president of the Oxford University Conservative Association and then national chairman of the Young Conservatives. He joined the BBC as a production trainee and produced a variety of radio and television programmes, including *Panorama*, on which he spent three years as deputy editor. In 1996 he became a political correspondent and covered the 1997 election for BBC radio. From 2002 to 2005 he was political editor at ITN but he returned in 2005 to take the place of Andrew Marr in his current position. During the 2010 election he seemed to be ubiquitously present on television screens, spending exceptionally long days on reporting, interviewing and blog writing. Shortly after the election there were rumours he might move jobs again.

Rodgers, William (1928–), Lord

Labour MP who became one of the 'gang of four'. He was educated at Oxford, served as general secretary of the Fabian Society 1953–60, then was elected MP for Stockton on Tees in 1962. He held a series of junior posts in the 1960s and 1970s, including transport minister 1976–79.

He was a strong pro-European and was unimpressed with the left. He joined the gang of four in 1981 and helped found the Social Democratic Party (SDP). He lost his seat in 1983 but served as vice president of the SDP 1982–87 and was influential in the Alliance. He withdrew from politics in 1987 to become director general at the Royal Institute of British Architects. He stood down as leader of the Liberal Democrats in the House of Lords in 2001.

Rose, Richard (1933–)

American-born leading political scientist and director of public policy at the University of Aberdeen. He was educated at Clayton High School, Missouri, USA, Johns Hopkins University, the London School of Economics 1953–54 and Oxford University 1957–60. He worked as a journalist in the USA 1955–57 then as a lecturer at Manchester University 1961–66 before moving to Strathclyde 1966–82. Rose has been possibly the most prolific author on his subject since the war and has displayed an extraordinary and distinguished eclecticism, writing highly original studies of psephology, urban problems, public policy and the territorial dimension, as well as books on the presidency in the USA, Russia and Europe. One of his books (*Do Parties Make a Difference?*, 1998) daringly suggested parties had little effect upon politics; now every textbook on British politics includes a rebuttal of this well argued but flawed thesis.

Rothermere, Viscount (1968–)

Succeeded his father, Vere, in 1998 as owner and chairman of the *Daily Mail* and General Trust as well as being hugely rich through property. He has been a big player in the media though was still unsure about investing in broadcasting after losses with Channel One TV. He is a 'non-dom' in the UK, registered as a resident of France, allowing him to pay tax in that country.

Rushdie, Salman (1947–)

Celebrated novelist. He was educated at Catholic School, Bombay, Rugby and

King's College, Cambridge. He won
the Booker Prize (1981 for *Midnight's
Children*) but his fourth novel, *Satanic
Verses* (1988), was condemned in February
1989 by the Iranian religious leader
Ayatollah Khomeini, who pronounced a
fatwa against the author. He then lived for
nine years in secret, making virtually no
public appearances, until February 1993,
when he announced he was coming out of
hiding. According to Rushdie over 20 hit
squads during this period sought to fulfil
the *fatwa*. On 26 September 1998 Iran
announced it had withdrawn its support for
the *fatwa* but danger still persisted for the
author from extremist enemies. Among his
honours was a knighthood in 2007.

Russell, Bertrand (1872–1970)

Philosopher and mathematician of
Welsh extraction, who became known
as a tireless campaigner for peace and
disarmament. He was the second son
of Viscount Amberley, the third son of
prime minister Lord John Russell. He was
educated privately and at Trinity College,
Cambridge, where he was awarded a first
in mathematics and philosophy. He worked
briefly as a diplomat and an academic
before writing the first of many books. His
joint work with Alfred North Whitehead,
the three-volume *Principia Mathematica*
(1910, 1912, 1913), became a landmark
and his pupil Ludwig Wittgenstein went
on to achieve similar ground-breaking
works in philosophy and logic. He was
imprisoned for his pacifism in 1918 but
renounced it in 1939, on the eve of the
fight against fascism. He won the Nobel
Prize for Literature in 1950. In the
1950s he became obsessed with nuclear
weapons and assumed a leading role in the
Campaign for Nuclear Disarmament. He
retired to live the last years of his long and
highly productive life in North Wales.

Envy is the basis of democracy. (1930)

Few people can be happy unless they hate
some other person, nation or creed.

The trouble with the world is that the stupid
are cocksure and the intelligent full of doubt.

S

Saatchi, Charles (1943–); Saatchi, Maurice (1946–)

Brothers who owned the Saatchi and
Saatchi advertising agency. Political parties
had used advertising agencies since the
1950s but the involvement of Charles and
Maurice Saatchi's agency, already well
known in their field in the late 1970s, as the
advisors of the Conservative Party, marked
a new departure in British politics in terms
of the scale and intensity of their involvement. It was Gordon Reece, Margaret
Thatcher's media advisor, made director
of publicity in 1981, who employed the
firm, and gave it full responsibility for all
aspects – from press and poster advertising
to television. Managing director Tim Bell
got on well with Thatcher and the 1979
election saw the famous poster of a long
dole queue (in reality dragooned Young
Conservatives) under the caption 'Labour
isn't working'. The firm worked for the
party again in the 1983 and 1987 general
elections but in 1992 there was disagreement and after the 1997 general election
debacle for the Tories the party parted
company with the agency, which had by
now lost some of its previous international
lustre and had split due to disagreements
between the two Saatchi brothers.
Maurice was elected joint chairman of the
Conservative Party in 2003. He was made
a peer in 1996 for his services to politics
via the Conservative Party. He became a
Treasury spokesman in the upper house
in 1999 and on the Cabinet Office after
2001. Maurice stepped down from active
politics after assisting the 2005 campaign.
Charles became renowned for his collection
of modern art and was less active politically.
He married celebrity cook Nigella Lawson
in 2003.

Sainsbury, David (1940–), Lord

Labour peer, minister and patron of centre-
left politics. He was educated at Eton,

PEOPLE

Cambridge and Colombia. He was hugely rich from his family's supermarket business, was elevated to the Lords by Tony Blair and made a trade minister. He had previously funded the Social Democratic Party as long as David Owen was involved but shifted allegiance to New Labour in the 1990s. He donated £2 million in late 2000 to the party. He resigned ministerial office in 2004 but continued as a generous donor to Labour.

Salmond, Alex (1954–)

Scottish National Party (SNP) MP and leader. He was educated at Linlithgoe Academy and St Andrews University. He worked as an economist before entering politics, as MP for Banff and Buchan in 1987. He became SNP leader in 1990. He fought for the devolved assembly in Scotland 1997–99, as he believed it was a halfway house to full independence. He proved an effective speaker and media performer. He resigned as leader of the party in the autumn of 2000. He was elected to the Scottish parliament in 1999 but left in 2001 to lead the SNP at Westminster. After the resignation of John Swinney as party leader, in September 2004 Salmond was re-elected, four years after he resigned the post, to reverse the party's decline. This he appeared to do, as in 2007 the SNP became the largest party in the Scottish parliament (by one, over Labour) and formed a minority government. It has proved popular and Salmond talks of a referendum on independence in the near future, though polls show only a minority support such a move. In May 2010 he declared his party willing to form a coalition with Labour, but not with the Conservatives.

Sampson, Anthony (1926–2004)

Journalist and author. He was educated Westminster School and Christ Church, Oxford. He served in the Royal Navy 1944–47 and then became a journalist, mostly with the *Observer* but also with *Newsweek* and other publications. He also made a number of radio and television programmes, for example *The Midas Touch* (BBC2, 1992). He is best known for his prolific output of books, especially *The Anatomy of Britain*, which first appeared in 1962 (and has been updated regularly since); he inspired many future journalists and students of British politics (including this author). His other books have addressed topics as varied as banking and the oil and arms industries; he also wrote biographies of Harold Macmillan and Nelson Mandela.

Sands, Bobby (1954–80)

IRA hunger striker. He was born in a loyalist area; the Catholic Sands family was twice intimidated into moving by loyalists, in 1962 and 1972. Bobby also was forced by loyalists to give up his job as a coach builder. He joined the IRA in 1972 and served time in Long Kesh Prison for possession of firearms. In 1976 he rejoined the IRA upon his release and became active in his community. In 1977 he was sentenced to 14 years for possession of a handgun. He led the 'dirty protest' in the H Block of Long Kesh and began his hunger strike against prison conditions in March 1980. He stood as a candidate on behalf of the strikers in the Fermanagh and Tyrone by-election that April and was elected but on 5 May died of hunger. Throughout, Margaret Thatcher refused to compromise with Sands and the hunger strikers, who undoubtedly won a significant propaganda victory by their actions.

Scanlon, Hugh (1913–2004), Lord

General secretary of the Amalgamated Union of Engineering Workers (AUEW). He was educated at Stretford Elementary School, Manchester, and the National Labour College. He worked as an instrument maker before becoming a shop steward and full-time union official. He became president of the AUEW 1968–78 and member of the General Council of the Trades Union Congress 1968–78. In the 1970s, during times of high inflation and the Social Contract, he was linked with

Jack Jones of the Transport and General Workers' Union as one of the 'two most powerful men in the country'.

> Of course liberty is not a licence. Liberty in my view is conforming to majority opinion. (1977)

Scargill, Arthur (1938–)

Union leader and founder of the Socialist Labour Party. He left school at 15 to work in the mines. He became president of the National Union of Mineworkers in 1982, though he had been a militant activist in the union long before that, especially as the organiser of flying pickets in the 1972 and 1974 miners' strikes. He is best known as the instigator of the doomed miners' strike 1984–85, when he sought to use his union as a political battering ram against the government of Margaret Thatcher. His strategic sense was much criticised during this strike but his predictions of pit closures and the plans to run down the industry proved prescient. As a fervent opponent of Blairism he formed the left-wing Socialist Labour Party in May 1996 but its electoral success was scant. He stood in Hartlepool, the constituency of Peter Mandelson, in the general election of June 2001 but mustered under 1,000 votes.

> The capitalist society belongs to the dustbin of history. The ideal of a socialist society belongs to the youth of today and to the future. I have seen the vision of the socialist tomorrow and it works. (1975 – he was not more specific as to where he had seen this socialist 'vision')

> Parliament itself would not exist in its present form had people not defied the law. (To the Select Committee on Employment, 1980)

> I wouldn't vote for Ken Livingstone if he were running for the mayor of Toytown. (May 2000)

Scarman, Leslie (1911–2004), Lord

High Court judge 1961–73, Appeal Court judge 1973–77 and lord of the appeal in ordinary 1975–86. He was reformist on divorce laws and called for a bill of rights in 1974. He is best known for his eponymous report on the Brixton riots in 1981.

> A government above the law is a menace to be defeated. (1992)

> The people as a source of sovereign power are in truth only occasional partners in the constitutional minuet danced for most of the time by Parliament and the political party in power. (1989)

Scott, Richard (1934–)

High Court judge. He was educated Michaelhouse College, Natal, and the University of Cape Town, South Africa, Trininty College, Cambridge, and Chicago University. He was called to the bar and became queen's counsel in 1975. He served as judge in the High Court of Justice, Chancery Division, and as lord justice of appeal 1991–94. He was the chairman of the arms to Iraq investigation 1992–96, which produced the Scott report (1996). He retired from the High Court in September 2009.

Seldon, Anthony

Political biographer, historian and master of Wellington College. Son of the economist Arthur Seldon, he was educated at Tonbridge School and Worcester College, Oxford. He also studied at the London School of Economics, King's College London and Westminster University. He was head of Brighton College before moving to Wellington. He has been astonishingly prolific, producing a much-praised two-volume study *Tony Blair* (2004, 2005) as well as works on history, education and political science. With Peter Hennessy, he founded the Institute of Contemporary British History.

Selwyn Lloyd, John (1904–78), Lord

Conservative cabinet minister. He was educated at Fettes and Cambridge, then became a barrister in Liverpool. He stood as a Liberal in 1930 but switched to the Conservatives. He rose to the rank of colonel in the Second World War. He was elected Conservative MP for Wirral 1945 and served as minister of supply

and defence 1954, foreign secretary 1955
(when he defended Anthony Eden's Suez
debacle), chancellor 1960 but was purged
by Macmillan in his 'Night of the Long
Knives'. He was later lord privy seal, leader
of the house 1963–64 and speaker of the
Commons 1971–76. He was made a life
peer in 1976.

Sheen, Michael (1969–)
Welsh actor best known for playing public
figures. Born in Newport, he was brought
up in Port Talbot, where he attended
Glan Afon comprehensive school. He then
went to the Royal Academy of Dramatic
Art (RADA). His father is a part-time
professional Jack Nicholson look-alike.
A talented footballer, Sheen decided to
pursue an acting career and has shone in
portrayals of public figures, including Tony
Blair in Channel 4's *The Deal* and in the
film *The Queen*, plus David Frost in the
film *Frost/Nixon*.

Shore, Peter (1924–2001), Lord
Leading Labour MP and cabinet minister.
He was educated at Quarrybank School,
Liverpool, and Cambridge University.
He served as a flying officer in the Royal
Air Force before he joined and then
headed Labour's Research Department in
Transport House. He was elected MP for
Stepney in 1964, served as parliamentary
private secretary to Harold Wilson and
then as junior minister for technology under
Tony Benn. In 1967 he was surprisingly
promoted into the cabinet as secretary of
state for economic affairs. His department
was weak, however, and he was shifted to
deputy leader of the house – Wilson is said
to have commented 'I over promoted him.
He's no good.' He polled only 39 votes
in the shadow cabinet elections in 1970.
During the 1970s he became associated
with opposition to the Common Market.
This helped his popularity in a party
shifting leftwards and he polled 105 votes
in the 1971 shadow cabinet elections. He
became environment secretary in 1976 and
in 1979 stood as a leadership candidate
of the left; he was eliminated after the first

ballot. In 1983 he mustered only 3 per cent
of the vote. For the rest of his life he was
seen as a principled elder statesman to the
right of the party with a powerful antipathy
to Europe. He became a life peer in 1997.

Short, Clare (1946–)
Labour MP and cabinet minister. She
was educated at St Paul's Grammar
School, Birmingham, and the Universities
of Birmingham and Keele. She was MP
for Birmingham Ladywood from 1983.
She was seen as something of a maverick
member of Labour's otherwise well
disciplined cabinet, as secretary of state
for international development, because
she was given to encouraging debate, for
example on the legalisation of certain
drugs, and she made disparaging remarks
about the islanders of Montserrat when
they demanded compensation following
the volcanic eruption in 1997. While given
to blunt speaking, she was regarded as an
excellent minister in her post and did much
to raise the profile of international development. She was known to be unenthusiastic
about the proposed war on Iraq in early
2003. In March 2003 she threatened to
resign but was persuaded to remain in the
government by Tony Blair, for whom the
resignation would have been embarrassing.
However, she resigned that May over the
minor role allowed for the United Nations
in the reconstruction of Iraq. She added
wider and quite bitter criticisms of Blair's
style of government in public statements
around this time. She stood down at the
2010 election.

> Having met all these ministers and MPs in
> the civil service, I knew they had feet of clay.
> If they could do it, I could do it.

Simpson, Wallis (1896–1986), Duchess of Windsor
Wife of King Edward VIII. She was
born into relative poverty in Pennsylvania
but her upbringing was assisted by rich
relatives, enabling her to attend the
exclusive Oldfields School in Maryland.
Her first husband, in 1916, was an air-force
pilot who drank. After several affairs

she divorced in 1927. She then married a shipping executive in 1928. In January 1931 a mutual friend introduced her to the Prince of Wales. Within three years he had become totally infatuated with her, taking apparent pleasure from her domineering manner. Having become king, Edward clearly intended to marry her, much to the alarm of the political class, as such an act would be incompatible with his role as head of the Church of England, because Wallis was a divorcee twice over. In the end the king abdicated, in favour of his brother 'Bertie', in order to live with his lover. Both were eventually cast out from the royal family with the title of Duke and Duchess of Windsor but with precious little else. Alarm was expressed in official circles when both appeared to be very friendly to Nazi Germany. It was rumoured that Wallis – who continued to have affairs – had a liaison with Von Ribbentrop, ambassador to Britain and later Hitler's foreign minister. Both were eventually exiled during the war to prevent their sympathies providing a possible foothold for the Nazis should they succeed in invading and establishing a pro-German regime by making Edward king again.

Skinner, Dennis (1932–)

Left-wing MP known as 'the Beast of Bolsover' for his fearless, uncompromising style. He was educated at Tupton Hall Grammar School and Ruskin College, Oxford. He worked as a miner in Parkhurst and Galpwell collieries before entering the House of Commons in 1970. He was a member of Labour's National Executive Committee 1978–96 and vice chair of the Labour Party 1987–88. Usually sitting in the front row of the Commons, he was well known for his direct and memorable interventions on the side of his unchanging socialist principles; he is therefore not a favourite with New Labour but, as with all such nationally known rebels, his effectiveness has tended to decline in inverse proportion to his popularity. He won an unlikely fan in Margaret Thatcher, who called him a 'marvellous

parliamentarian'. He retained his seat in 2010 by 11,162 votes.

> I thought you were taking Marquand with you. (Heckling Roy Jenkins in 1976 when, during his farewell speech before leaving for the European Commission, he said: 'I leave this party without rancour'. Jenkins, who famously pronounced his Rs like Ws, left the Commons at the same time as David Marquand, the MP for Ashfield and a close ally of Jenkins)

Smith, Adam (1723–90)

Scottish philosopher and economist. He was educated at Glasgow and Oxford. In the middle of the 18th century he became a member of the group surrounding the philosopher David Hume as professor of logic at Glasgow. He then moved to London, where he wrote *An Inquiry into the Nature and Causes of the Wealth of Nations* (1776), an analysis of successful economics and an attack on medieval mercantile protectionism and monopolies. Smith's work was hugely influential and provided the basis of classical liberalism; he is still acknowledged by modern neo-liberals as their inspiration.

> Little else is requisite to carry a state to the highest degree of opulence from the lowest barbarism, but peace, easy taxes and a tolerable administration of justice; all the rest being brought about by the natural course of things. (1795)

> It is not from the benevolence of the butcher, the brewer or the baker, that we expect our dinner, but from their regard to their own interest. We address ourselves not to their humanity but their self love, and never talk to them of our necessities but of their advantages. (1776)

> That insidious and crafty animal vulgarly called a statesman or politician, whose councils are directed by the momentary fluctuations of affairs. (*Wealth of Nations*, 1776)

Smith, Chris (1951–)

Labour MP and minister. He was educated at George Watson's College, Edinburgh, and Pembroke College, Cambridge, and Harvard University. He has a doctorate in English literature. He became MP for Islington South and Finsbury 1983. He came out in public in 1984 at a protest meeting in Rugby. He was Treasury and then environment spokesman in opposition, and the first openly gay cabinet minister when made secretary of state for culture, media and sport 1997–2001 (though was disappointed not to get health). He lost his job in the June 2001 cabinet reshuffle. In January 2005 he admitted he had been HIV positive for 17 years.

Smith, Godric (1965–)
Civil servant. He was educated at Perse School and the Universities of Oxford and Cambridge. He worked for the charity Sane 1988–91 before joining the Government Information Service, where he became a senior press officer 1995 and then a deputy press secretary in Downing Street 1998–2001. In 2001 he was made the prime minister's official spokesman. He went on to become director of communications for the Olympic Delivery Authority.

Smith, Jacqui (1962–)
Labour MP and first female home secretary. She was educated at Dyson Perrins High School in Malvern and took philosophy, politics and economics (PPE) at Oxford, followed by a teacher's certificate at Worcester College of Higher Education. With the advantage of an all-women short-list she was selected to stand for Redditch in 1996 and was elected the following year. She served as a junior minister at the Department of Education and then at Health after 2001. She was minister of state for schools after 2005 and was widely judged to be a better communicator than her boss, Ruth Kelly. She was made chief whip in 2006 and home secretary by Gordon Brown in 2007. After a confident start when she handled the terrorist attack on Glasgow airport she stumbled rather, suffering eventual defeat over the 42-day detention issue and receiving a bad press generally. Her insistence her 'second home' was a room in her sister's flat in London (to facilitate her claiming the extra allowance

as an MP's expense) made her seem grasping and deceitful but the revelation that her husband had caused her to claim for the rental of a blue movie caused fatal damage to her reputation. She resigned on 5 June 2009 and went on to lose her seat in the May 2010 general election.

> When I became home secretary I'd never run a major organization. I hope I did a good job but if I did it was more by luck than by any kind of development of skills. I think we should have been better trained. I think there should have been more induction. (Interview with *Total Politics*)

Smith, John (1938–94)
Labour MP and party leader. He was educated at Glasgow University and called to the bar in 1967; he became queen's counsel in 1970. From 1970 he was Labour MP for North Lanarkshire (renamed Monklands East in 1983) and held junior posts in Harold Wilson's governments. In 1978 he was appointed secretary of state for trade by James Callaghan. In 1979 he was made opposition spokesman on trade, energy and then industry before he became shadow chancellor in 1988. His shadow budget in 1992 proposed some tax increases and was dubbed by the Conservatives a 'tax and spend' extravaganza. This was clearly a misrepresentation but the voters were influenced and Labour lost the election. When Neil Kinnock then resigned as Labour leader John Smith took his place. Labour MPs were relieved to have a leader who always performed well in debates and at prime minister's questions. He was tragically struck down by a heart attack in 1994 and was succeeded by Tony Blair.

> I am a doer and I want to do things but there is always the terrible possibility in politics that you might never win. (1992)

Snowden, Philip (1864–1937)
Labour chancellor in the interwar years. He was educated at elementary school. He joined the civil service but was disabled in a cycling accident and forced to leave. He became an MP in 1906 and served

as chancellor in 1924 and 1929, when he pursued orthodox economic policies which did not alleviate the depression afflicting Britain. He resigned from the national government in 1932 over free trade. He was one of the genuinely talented early prophets of socialism, who found the world far less tractable once he was in power than when he was fighting for it.

> This is not socialism. It is Bolshevism run mad. (On Labour's election manifesto, 1931)

Spedding, David (1943–)
Head of MI6 1994–99. He was educated at Sherborne and Oxford and spent his whole career in the security service. He became head of MI6 in 1994. He had to face the embarrassment of the former MI6 man David Shaylor revealing secrets about the service. He also helped to adjust the service to a non-Cold War world.

Spelman, Caroline (1958–)
Conservative MP and minister. She was educated at the Herts and Essex High School for Girls and Queen Mary's College, London University, where she received a first in European studies. She was elected for Meriden in 1997. She was made secretary of state for environment, food and rural affairs in May 2010.

St John Stevas, Norman (1929–), Lord
Conservative MP and cabinet member. He was educated at Radcliffe School and Fitzwilliam College, Cambridge (where he was president of the Union), Christ Church, Oxford (where he was secretary of the Union) and Yale University. He qualified as a barrister and lectured at Southampton University and Merton College, Oxford, 1953–57. He worked for the *Economist* from 1959. He was MP for Chelmsford 1964–87. In shadow cabinet 1974–79 he served as education spokesman and shadow leader of the house. He was appointed chancellor of the Duchy of Lancaster, leader of the house and minister for the arts 1979–81 under Margaret

Thatcher. A witty and media-friendly politician, Norman St John Stevas was a favourite of Thatcher initially and was able to push through certain reforms of parliament under her aegis, especially the reform of the select committees. However, he was on the 'wet' side of the cabinet politically and compounded this disadvantage with his witty disloyalties to his leader, which, some say, contributed to his early political demise. He was considered to be a Conservative expert on the constitution. He was made a life peer in 1997 as Lord St John of Fawsley.

> It's a modern miracle. (On the House of Lords, quoted in the *Observer*, 30 May 2010)

Staines, Paul (1967–)
Leading political blogger, known as Guido Fawkes (http://order-order.com). Though Irish by nationality, he was educated at Salvatorian Catholic Grammar, near Harrow, and at the Humberside College of Higher Education. He flirted with right-wing libertarian ideas when younger, with the Federation of Conservative Students and other libertarian bodies. He worked for the Committee for a Free Britain, for the right-wing David Hart and in the City, as well as an organiser of raves and acid house parties. His blog, begun in 2004, was subversively named after the man who tried to blow up parliament in 1605. It attracts around 120,000 hits a month and concentrates on the gossip and trivia of politics, rather than more serious issues. He did manage a few 'coups', however, during the spring and summer of 2009, most notably being the recipient of emails from Damien McBride to his colleague Derek Draper which suggested that wholly untrue stories about Conservative politicians be disseminated via a Labour blog.

Steel, David (1938–), Lord
Liberal MP and party leader. He was educated in Kenya and Edinburgh. When he was first elected in 1965 he was the youngest MP. He sponsored the bill which made abortions legal in 1967. He became

Liberal chief whip in 1970 and succeeded Jeremy Thorpe as party leader in 1977. As leader he formed the Alliance with the Social Democratic Party in 1981. The two parties merged in 1988 but Steel did not seek its leadership. He became a life peer in 1997 and was presiding officer of the Scottish parliament 1998–2003.

> Go back to your constituencies and prepare for government. (To the Liberal Party conference, 1985)

Steen, Anthony (1939–), Sir

Conservative MP for Totnes in Devon. He was educated at Westminster School and London University, where he studied law. He has tended to be on the left of the party, supporting Kenneth Clarke, but is less enthusiastic than Ken over the European Union. He merits a mention in this collection of biographies only for summing up the attitude of MPs who 'did not get it' regarding voter disgust at MPs' exploitation of their expenses. He was revealed to have used a tree expert to tend to his 500-strong arboretum but reacted to criticism by constituents by accusing them of being 'jealous' of his big house and insisting they had no right to 'interfere' with his private life. David Cameron delivered a stern rebuke and Steen humbly backtracked in public. On 22 May 2009 he announced he would not contest the next election.

> But Steen is a lone voice in the Commons raising with a persistence bordering on the manic the plight of young children who disappear from local-authority care. He has single-handedly made into a Commons issue the hidden slavery of young girls trafficked as prostitutes to satiate the dirty old men in our community. When he goes, who will speak for these voiceless teenage victims of the sex trade? (Denis MacShane MP, seeking to redress some of the damage to Steen's reputation, *Observer*, 9 August 2009)

Strathclyde, Thomas (1960–), Lord

Conservative peer. He was educated at Wellington College and the University of East Anglia. He served as a junior minister in the Scottish Office and at

the Department of Trade and Industry during the early 1990s. He acquired a reputation as a *bon viveur* but was also a shrewd politician. He became Tory leader in the Lords in December 1998 when Conservative leader William Hague chose him to replace Viscount Cranbourne after the latter's secret deal with Tony Blair over Lords reform. He joined the cabinet in May 2010 as leader of the House of Lords and chancellor of the Duchy of Lancaster.

Straw, Jack (1946–)

Labour MP and minister. He was educated Leeds University and was president of the National Union of Students 1969–70. He was called to the bar in 1972 and served as a councillor for Islington 1971–78. He became MP for Blackburn 1979 and was Labour spokesman on Treasury and economic affairs. He was in the shadow cabinet for education 1987–92, environment 1992–93 and home affairs 1994–97. Not the most admired member of Tony Blair's cabinet initially, he was an outwardly tough home secretary 1997–2001 who maintained a more liberal agenda in practice. He gained credibility in 1997 when his son was tricked by a tabloid into supplying soft drugs and he took the matter and his son to the police. He was surprised, pleasantly, to be given the Foreign Office portfolio in June 2001, though he found himself overshadowed by Blair, especially after the events of 11 September 2001. He was disappointed to be reshuffled out of this job to be leader of the House of Commons in 2006. Gordon Brown made him lord chancellor and secretary for justice in June 2007. He ruled himself out of the party leadership contest in May 2010, after retaining his seat by 9,854 votes.

Summerskill, Ben (1961–)

Chief executive of Stonewall, the campaigning body for gays, lesbians and bisexual rights. He was educated at Sevenoaks School and Merton College, Oxford, and worked in the catering industry before becoming a journalist at the *Daily Express*, *Evening Standard* and *Observer*, where he became assistant editor. He moved to Stonewall in 2003 and led the campaign against section 28. In 2006 he was appointed a commissioner in the Equality and Human Rights Commission; he resigned in July 2006 in protest against Trevor Phillips' leadership.

> I still recall being struck dumb on being shown, as an undergraduate, a note from an Oxford tutor to a successful candidate's father: 'Many thanks for lunch, and the trip in the Rolls'. (Letter to the *Guardian* about his time in Oxford)

Sutch, 'Lord' (with its prefix 'Screaming'), David (1940–98)

Leader of the Monster Raving Loony Party. He was born in Kilburn, the son of a policeman. He became a plumber, rock singer (of questionable ability) and then political party leader, ending up as the longest-serving leader – albeit of a joke party – by the time of his death. He became a constant and colourful feature of television election and especially by-election broadcasts, often standing against party leaders to maximise the publicity gained. He stood 39 times for parliament, polled 15,000 votes and lost £10,000 in deposits. His high-point came in May 1994, when his party's candidate polled 554 votes in the Bootle by-election to the Social Democratic Party's 155, which persuaded David Owen that it was time to wind up his party. His other major achievement is probably to have been the reason for parliamentary deposits being raised from £150 to £500.

T

Tatchell, Peter (1952–)

Campaigner for homosexual and civil rights. He was born in Australia but was educated in Mount Waverley High School, London, and the Polytechnic of North London. He worked as a social worker. He stood unsuccessfully as Labour candidate for Bermondsey in a controversial by-election in which his sexuality was a major issue. He helped found Outrage in 1990 and led many high-profile demonstrations. He began to target Robert Mugabe for civil rights violations towards the end of the 1990s and bravely attempted to arrest him for torture in February 2003 during the African dictator's visit to Paris. The *Observer* named him Campaigner of the Year in 2009.

Tawney, R. H. (1880–1962)

Socialist philosopher and economist. He was born in Calcutta and was educated at Balliol College, Oxford, where he became a fellow in 1918 and wrote several volumes on economic history. He was active in the Workers' Educational Association (WEA), an active Christian and a passionate advocate of equality. He was a professor at the London School of Economics 1931–49. His works include *The Acquisitive Society* (1920), *Religion and the Rise of Capitalism* (1926) and *Equality* (1931). His influence in the Labour Party was considerable, especially his emphasis on equality.

> Freedom for the pike is death for the minnow. (*Equality*, 1931)

> Private property is a necessary institution, at least in a fallen world; men work more and dispute less when goods are private than when they are common. But it is to be tolerated as a concession to human frailty, not applauded as desirable in itself. (1926)

Taylor, Ann (1947–)

Labour MP, peer and minister. She was educated at Bolton School, and Bradford and Sheffield Universities. She was MP for Bolton West 1974–83 and Dewsbury after 1987. She shadowed various ministries in opposition before becoming chief whip 1998–2001, president of the Council and leader of the House of Commons 1997–98. She returned to the back benches in 2001. After being made a life peer in 2005, she served as minister for defence procurement

in 2007, and for international defence and
security 2008–10.

Taylor, Matthew (1961–)

Head of Number 10's Policy Directorate
from 2003, officially charged with policy
planning and strengthening policy links
between Number 10 and the Labour Party
and 'the wider policy community'. He was
educated at Emmanuel School, Clapham,
and Southampton University, where he followed in the footsteps of his father, Laurie,
in studying sociology. He became assistant
general secretary of the Labour Party and
then director of the Labour think-tank
Institute for Public Policy Research, a
post which he retained. He was also chief
executive of the Royal Society of Arts.

Tebbit, Kevin (1946–), Sir

Civil servant. He was educated at Cambridgeshire High School and Cambridge
University. Unlike his famous cousin
Norman, he took a politically neutral
career route by joining the civil service in
1969. He was assistant personal private
secretary to the secretary of state for
defence 1973–74, principal at the Ministry
of Defence 1974–79, a member of the UK
delegation to NATO 1979–82, counsellor
at the Washington embassy 1989–91, head
of economic relations at the Foreign Office
1992–94, under-secretary at the Foreign
Office 1997 and head of Government
Communications Headquarters 1998 and
permanent under-secretary for the Ministry
of Defence after 1998. He was questioned
by the Hutton inquiry, when he sought to
distance himself from the decision to allow
David Kelly's name to become public; the
Hutton report cleared him as well as Tony
Blair of any wrongdoing. He retired in
2005 to posts in business and academe.

Tebbit, Norman (1931–), Lord

Famously combative Conservative cabinet
minister. He left school at 16 to work as a
journalist and after national service became
an airline pilot. He went on to lead the
Airline Pilots' Association. He became
Conservative MP for Chingford in 1970.

Margaret Thatcher liked his clear mind
and unrelenting right-wing politics, as well
as his aggression as a debater – something
which did not appeal to older colleagues
like Edward Heath, who deplored Tebbit's
style. He was employment secretary
1981–83 and trade and industry secretary
1983–85 but his career was almost
ended by the bomb placed by the IRA in
Brighton in 1984, when he was injured
(and his wife, Margaret, more seriously).
In 1987 he became chancellor of the
Duchy of Lancaster and chairman of the
Conservative Party, but in the latter role
fell out with his prime minister over election
strategy. Some suggested she suspected
Tebbit was interested in taking over as
party leader and that this provoked her
enmity. He retired to the back benches
in 1987, where he established a strong
anti-Europe profile. He was made a life
peer in 1992. His (in)famous brutal rude-
ness served to conceal an infinitely subtle
political mind and an administrative ability
which won the admiration of his civil servants. A persistent champion of Thatcherite
ideas, especially over the European Union,
he criticised David Cameron's shifting of
the party to the centre-ground after 2005.

> He [Tebbit's unemployed father] did not
> riot. He got on his bike and looked for work.
> (Blackpool Conservative Party conference,
> 15 October 1981)

> The talk of the town is Norman Tebbit's
> vulgar grand-standing barn-storming
> performance on Europe. He savaged
> Maastricht, poured scorn on monetary
> union, patronised the PM ... and brought
> the conference (or a good part of it) to its
> feet roaring for more. He stood there, arms
> aloft, acknowledging the ovation, Norman
> the conqueror. (Gyles Brandreth's diaries,
> *Breaking the Code*, on Tebbit's intervention
> at the 1992 conference)

Thatcher, Margaret Hilda (1925–), Baroness

Leader of Conservative Party 1975–79
and prime minister 1979–90. She was
educated at Grantham Grammar School
and Oxford University, where she studied

chemistry (and became president of the Conservative Association). Her father was a local small shopkeeper and councillor – later mayor – and exerted substantial influence upon her. She worked in industry before studying for the bar and marrying wealthy businessman Dennis Thatcher. She was MP for Finchley 1959–92. She served as junior opposition spokesperson in the late 1960s. In 1970 she became education secretary in the cabinet. She stood against Edward Heath in the Conservative Party leadership contest in 1975 following his two election defeats in 1974. Those who supported her on the first ballot, which she won by 130 votes to 119, did not expect her to win but voted for her in protest against Heath's lofty style of leadership. She won on the second ballot. Initially she did not do well as leader of the opposition; she was, after all, an avowed free market enthusiast and the senior Tory MPs were still largely 'Heathite' supporters of the postwar consensus. And she was female. However, she concentrated, with some success, on changing policy and improving her performances in the house and the media. Her general election success in 1979 was greatly aided by the imploding Labour Party after the 'winter of discontent' of 1978–79. She won the election handsomely and set about leaving her mark on the country. Her insistence on letting inefficient businesses die a natural death, combined with high interest rates, produced high unemployment and social division but her heroic conduct of government during the Falklands war ensured she won the 1983 general election, aided by an economic recovery and a hopelessly divided Labour Party under Michael Foot. During her second ministry she won the battle of the extended miners' strike, 1984–85. She also pressed on with her discovered policy of privatisation, as the public flocked to buy shares they could later sell at a profit. She also worked her way through the establishment – the universities, the BBC, the Church, and many of the professions – doing her best to destroy protective practices and monopolies. She won her

third election in 1987 but overstepped herself by seeking to reform not only the welfare state but local government finance with the ill-fated community charge, or poll tax. From here she gradually lost touch with voters. Her second ill-fated mission was to attack what she believed as a creeping centralisation around the European Community – the 'Belgian empire' as she is alleged to have called it. Her bungled reshuffles in 1989 and 1990 alienated some of her closest colleagues and things came to a head in 1990 when she attacked the European Community and angered her long-suffering deputy prime minister, Geoffrey Howe. His devastating resignation speech, in which he attacked her style as much as her policies, triggered a challenge to her in the annual leadership election by the famously ambitious Michael Heseltine. She received 204 votes to his 152; she was just four short of the margin she required. She consulted with her cabinet, the majority of whom advised her to resign, which she did on 21 November 1990. She backed John Major in the resultant leadership election, though criticised him when things went wrong. She thereafter spent much of her time in retirement lecturing and raising money for her Margaret Thatcher Foundation. She said she had no remaining leadership ambitions but allowed the occasional hint that she was still available. Her effect on the politics of Britain was immense and her achievements unchallengeable though still controversial. She privatised nearly 20 per cent of the economy; she greatly reduced the power of trade unions; she abolished a tier of local government (the metropolitan counties); she won a tense war with Argentina against many predictions; she introduced market forces into much of the public sector, including the health and education services; and she restrained the progress towards European integration. In terms of government she demonstrated that determination and will and sheer ability can still fundamentally change this conservative and tradition-bound country. To be hated by many and regarded with distaste by even more, including members of their own party, is a price most politicians seem willing ultimately to pay.

> The Lady's not for turning. (Speech to Conservative Party conference, Brighton, 10 October 1980)

> Ladies and gentlemen, I stand before you in my green chiffon evening gown, my face softly made up, my fair hair gently waved.... The Iron Lady of the Western World. Me? A cold warrior? Well yes, if that is how they wish to interpret my defence of values and freedom fundamental to our way of life. (To Finchley constituency, 31 January 1976)

> The President of the Commission, M. Delors, said at this conference the other day that he wanted the European parliament to be the democratic body of the Community, he wanted the Commission to be the executive, and he wanted the Council of Ministers to be the Senate. No. No. No. (In the Commons on her return from the Rome summit, 3 January 1990)

> I don't mind how much my ministers talk as long as they do what I say.

> Let me make one thing absolutely clear. The NHS is safe with us. (Speech to Conservative Party conference, Brighton, 8 October 1982)

> I usually make my mind up about a man in ten seconds and I very rarely change it. (1970)

> If someone is confronting our essential liberties, if someone is inflicting injuries and harm – by God, I'll confront them! (1979)

> Most of us have stopped using silver every day. (1970)

Thorpe, Jeremy (1929–)
Leader of the Liberals 1967–76. He was educated at Oxford and became a barrister before entering the House of Commons for North Devon in 1959. Witty and articulate, he had his moment of glory in 1974, when the Liberal vote was the highest in 50 years and the party won 14 seats. Rumours began to circulate in the early 1970s that Thorpe had possibly had a relationship with a former male model, Norman Scott. It subsequently became clear that

Scott had been receiving money from the Liberal Party via one of its MPs, Peter Bessell. The allegations were repeated by an emotional Scott when he appeared in court in 1976, with the result that Thorpe stood down as leader. In May 1979 he lost his North Devon seat and in June stood trial for the attempted murder of Scott. It transpired that a former pilot, Andrew Newton, had been hired to shoot Scott but had bungled the attempt, shooting his dog, Rinka, instead. Thorpe and three other accused were acquitted. Thorpe's lawyer did not let Thorpe give evidence and in the wake of the trial there was some scepticism about the verdict. Thorpe's career was destroyed by the scandal and he left politics to live quietly in the south-west. Some time later he was diagnosed with Parkinson's disease.

Trevor, John (1637–1717), Sir
Speaker of the House of Commons who was forced from office. He was educated at Ruthin School in Wales. Beginning life as a clerk, he worked his way up to become a king's counsel under Charles II. In 1685 he was appointed speaker and master of the rolls by James II. The accession of William of Orange saw him lose his offices but he was reappointed to both in 1690. He remained in post until 1695, when he was found guilty of receiving £1,000 (equivalent to £1.6 million in the present day) from the City of London; this he did to assist the passage of a bill through the house. Speaker Trevor was famous for being exceptionally cross-eyed, so much so that he had difficulty in naming MPs who wished to speak, thus creating the convention by which the speaker calls out the name of the member concerned. It was over 300 years later that the next speaker – Michael Martin – was forced from office.

Trimble, David (1944–), Lord
Ulster Unionist MP and leader. He was educated Bangor Grammar School and Queen's University, Belfast, where he later lectured in law. He was MP for Upper Bann from 1990 and became leader of

PEOPLE

the Ulster Unionist Party in 1995. He worked hard to engineer the Good Friday agreement in 1998, when many of his party were suspicious and tended to take the line of Ian Paisley, though less raucously, that the agreement was a sell-out. He skilfully persuaded his party to support the process and the resultant agreement and won the Nobel Peace Prize in 1998, jointly with John Hume, leader of the Social Democratic and Labour Party, for his efforts. He resigned as Northern Ireland's first minister in July 2001 in response to the IRA's failure to disarm, though he maintained his position as party leader and the hope that moderation might triumph eventually. However, the delayed elections to the Northern Ireland assembly in November 2003 saw his party lose much ground to Paisley's Democratic Unionist Party. The defection of key members of his own party to the hard-line Protestants further weakened his position from 2004. He entered the Lords in 2006.

> Once we are agreed our only weapons will be our words, then there is nothing that cannot be said, there is nothing that cannot be achieved. (September 1998)

Turnbull, Andrew (1945–)
Cabinet secretary and head of home civil service 2002–05. He was educated at Enfield Grammar School and Cambridge University. He entered the civil service via the Treasury in 1970. He served as principal private secretary to Margaret Thatcher and was praised by Tony Blair for his work in developing the Office of Government Commerce and Partnership UK before being appointed as secretary to the cabinet in late 2002. He was seen by some commentators as the 'establishment' candidate. In 2005 he was succeeded by Gus O'Donnell.

Turner, Adair (1955–), Lord
Director general of the Confederation of British Industry 1995–99. He was educated at Cambridge University and was president of the Union in 1976. He worked for McKinsey and Co. and was

a director of Chase Manhattan Bank and of Merrill Lynch. He was a public figure associated with the centre-ground. He chaired an influential inquiry into pensions in 2007 and in 2008 chaired government's Committee on Climate Change.

Wakeham, John (1932–), Lord
Conservative MP and peer, minister, and chair of the Press Complaints Commission (PCC). He was educated at Charterhouse. He served as a cabinet minister under both Margaret Thatcher and John Major, as chief whip 1983–87 and as leader of the House of Commons 1987–88 and of the House of the Lords 1992–94. In 1984 his wife was killed by the Brighton bomb and he was trapped in rubble for several hours. He was made a life peer in 1992. He chaired the commission on reform of the Lords and produced a formula for a largely appointed new chamber. He was appointed chair of the PCC in 1995 but resigned in February 2002 when Enron, the energy conglomerate of which he was a director, collapsed.

Waldegrave, William (1946–), Lord
Famously clever Conservative cabinet minister whose reputation was damaged by his involvement in the arms to Iraq affair. He was educated at Eton, Corpus Christie College, Oxford, and Harvard University. He was a member of Central Policy Review Staff (a think-tank) 1971–73, and advisor to Number 10 Downing Street 1973–74 and to the leader of the opposition 1974–75; he then worked for GEC 1975–81. He was Bristol West MP 1979–97 and secretary of state for health 1990–92. Waldegrave was criticised by the Scott report for his role in the Matrix Churchill trial and the arms to Iraq affair. He was made provost of Eton College in 2009.

Walden, Brian (1932–)

Former Labour MP turned television presenter and interviewer. He was educated at West Bromwich Grammar School, and Queen's and Nuffield Colleges, Oxford (he was president of the Union 1957). He was MP for Birmingham All Saints 1964–74 and Ladywood 1974–77, then worked as a television presenter on *Weekend World* 1977–86, as well as a columnist for the *Evening Standard* and a number of broadsheets. He was a gifted young politician who was perceived by many Labour MPs as too self-seeking; he left to pursue a successful career in the media. He still does some occasional broadcasting.

> You come over as being someone who one of your backbenchers said is slightly off her trolley, authoritarian, domineering, refusing to listen to anybody else – why? Why cannot you publicly project what you have just told me is your private character? (Brian Walden interviewing Margaret Thatcher, November 1989, to which her rejoinder was 'Brian, if anyone's coming over as domineering in this interview, it's you. It's you.')

Wall, Stephen (1947–)

Civil servant. He was educated Douai School and Cambridge. He joined the Foreign Office in 1965, and served in Africa, Washington and at the European Union. He was press officer to Number 10 Downing Street 1971–77, ambassador to Portugal 1993–95 and to the European Union 1995–2000. He then became head of the European Secretariat in the Cabinet Office and the prime minister's advisor on European foreign policy. He was one of the most influential diplomats in the political system. In 2008 he became the chair of the University College London Council.

Walpole, Robert (1676–1745)

Usually reckoned to be the first British prime minister (1721–42). He was educated at Cambridge and became a Whig MP in 1701. He became secretary for war in 1708. He spent some time in prison on corruption charges in 1712 but was recalled by George I as chancellor

in 1715 and returned to the post in 1721. About this time he became known as the 'prime minister' – a sobriquet he resisted. Both George I and George II found him indispensable until policy misjudgements led him to resign in 1742.

> Madam, there are fifty thousand men slain this year in Europe and not one Englishman. (To Queen Caroline on the War of Polish Succession, in which England had refused to take part)

> All those men have their price. (On parliamentarians, 1798)

> They now ring their bells but will soon wring their hands. (On the declaration of war on Spain, 1739)

Walters, Alan (1926–2009), Sir

Economic advisor to Margaret Thatcher. He was educated at Alderman Newton's School, Leicester University College and University College London. He lectured at Birmingham University before he became a monetarist professor of economics at the London School of Economics and then Johns Hopkins University 1976–91. He served as a member of various commissions before serving as the prime minister's economic advisor 1981–84 and 1988–90. Walters was the cause of a long-running row between chancellor Nigel Lawson and Thatcher as he advised her against joining the European Exchange Rate Mechanism.

Warsi, Sayeeda Hussain (1972–), Baroness

Chair of the Conservative Party. She was born in Dewsbury to Pakistani parents and was educated at Birkdale High School, Dewsbury College, and the University of Leeds, where she studied law. She trained with the Crown Prosecution Service and the Home Office Immigration Department. She has married twice, her first (arranged) marriage having ended in divorce. She stood as a Conservative candidate in 2005 in Dewsbury but lost by 5,000 votes. In 2007 she was made a life peer and appointed as shadow minister for community cohesion and in May 2010 she entered the cabinet in her present post.

Webb, Sidney (1859–1947); Webb, Beatrice (1858–1943)

Social reformers and left-wing intellectuals. Sidney was educated privately, then at the Birkbeck Institute and the City of London College. Both husband and wife played a formative role in the Fabian Society and the early years of the Labour Party. Sidney helped to write its constitution in 1918 and its manifesto for the 1918 election. He entered the Commons in 1922 and, after becoming Lord Passfield in 1929, was secretary of state for the colonies 1929–31. Sidney was a prolific journalist and author, and was chair of the editorial board of the *New Statesman*. He married Beatrice (a wealthy heiress) in 1892 and they collaborated closely on research and writing, and both helped to set up the London School of Economics in 1895. They both visited the USSR in the 1930s and, like George Bernard Shaw, proved vulnerable to Soviet propaganda when they declared that Joseph Stalin's dictatorship represented a 'New Civilisation'.

> Old people are always absorbed in something, usually themselves. We prefer to be absorbed in the Soviet Union.

West, Alan Lord (1948–)

Former admiral appointed security minister, 2007. He was educated at Windsor Grammar School and Clydebank High School before joining Britannia Royal Naval College in 1965. He served on 14 different ships, commanding three of them. He received the DSO for being the last to leave HMS *Ardent* during the Falklands war. He became a rear admiral 1994 and first sea lord 2002. He was appointed as a minister as one of the four 'goats' (government of all the talents) appointed by Gordon Brown in 2007 and was the only one to serve until Brown lost office.

White, Michael (1945–)

Broadcaster and columnist. He was educated at Bodmin Grammar School and University College London. He was made political editor of the *Guardian* in 1990.

He has been rated by some as arguably the paper's most distinguished sketch writer; he is also a regular broadcaster.

Whitelaw, William ('Willie') (1918–99)

Veteran Conservative cabinet member. He was educated at Winchester and Cambridge. He served with distinction in the Second World War. He entered the House of Commons in 1955 and served as secretary of state for Northern Ireland 1972–73 and for employment 1973–74 and home secretary 1979–83. He stood for leadership of the party in 1975 when he was widely deemed to be the strongest candidate, but loyalty to Edward Heath prevented him from standing in the first ballot as Margaret Thatcher had, thereby establishing the momentum which saw her elected on the second ballot. He was deputy to Thatcher and displayed a similar loyalty, though he was one of the few advisors she allowed to be honestly critical of her policies. It was often said that once she lost him as her close advisor her policy judgement declined.

> It is never wise to appear more clever than you are. It is sometimes wise to appear slightly less so. (1975)

> The Labour Party is going around the country stirring up apathy. (May 1983)

Widdecombe, Ann (1947–)

Conservative MP and minister. She was educated at La Sainte Union Convent, Bath, Birmingham University and Lady Margaret Hall, Oxford. She worked as a university administrator before she entered parliament for Plymouth Devonport in 1983, then Maidstone 1987–97 and Maidstone and Weald from 1997. She served as a junior minister in employment and as minister of state in the Home Office, in charge of prisons. An unusual, combative politician, she clashed with Michael Howard, her boss at the Home Office, over prison management. During the contest for Conservative Party leader in May 1997 she made a speech in the House of Commons in which she attacked Howard with her observation that there was 'something of the night' about him; his bid for the leadership was effectively torpedoed. Her obvious ability combined with a forthrightness verging on aggression won her the health position in William Hague's shadow cabinet in 1998. She considered standing for the leadership in the wake of the party's 2001 general election defeat and Hague's resignation but lacked sufficient support in the parliamentary party. She has become something of a television celebrity as well as a published novelist since leaving government. She did not stand for re-election in 2010.

> As for Michael Portillo ... I can hardly believe that it has all worked out so perfectly. (On the defeat of Portillo's challenge for the leadership, which she hotly opposed, and his subsequent retirement from front-line politics, 2001)

Wilby, Peter (1944–)
Journalist and editor. He was educated at the Kibworth Beauchamp Grammar School in Leicestershire and then at the University of Sussex. He has written for the *Guardian, Observer, Independent* and *Sunday Times* and was editor of the *New Statesman* 1998–2005.

Wilkes, John (1727–97)
Archetypical political radical. He was educated at the University of Leiden, to avoid the Anglicanism of Oxford and Cambridge. He was elected to parliament in 1757 at a by-election. He was accused shortly afterwards of libelling the king's speech in number 45 of his weekly essay papers but argued successfully that he was protected by parliamentary privilege. Wilkes soon became a champion of liberty in the public view, especially after the king had him expelled from parliament. He was returned in 1768 for the seat of Middlesex. He then surrendered to the courts and was imprisoned for two years. He was released in 1770. He was elected an alderman of London and went on to become lord mayor in 1774, then once again was returned for Middlesex. He opposed the American

War of Independence and the mob in the anti-Catholic Gordon riots. His support for Pitt the Younger tended to lose him radical support. His colourful, rakish life and rebellious attitudes created an early template for flamboyant radicalism.

> Nothing has been so obnoxious to me through life, as dead calm.

> That will depend, my lord, on whether I embrace your principles or your mistresses. (To the Earl of Sandwich's comment, 'Egad sir, I do not know if you will die on the gallows or of the pox.')

Willets, David (1956–)
Clever Conservative minister and thinker, nicknamed, by friend and foe alike, 'two brains'. He was educated at King Edward's School, Birmingham, and Christ Church, Oxford. He worked as an assistant to Nigel Lawson in 1978 and in the Treasury 1978–84. He moved to the Policy Unit in Number 10 Downing Street and then was director of the Centre for Policy Studies 1987–92. He was MP for Havant from 1992; he served as a whip and in the Office of Public Services in the Cabinet Office. He was paymaster general 1996–97 and then shadow employment spokesman 1997. Under Michael Howard he was made shadow secretary of state for work and pensions and welfare reform. He went on to shadow the Department of Universities and Skills. He gained a majority of 12,160 in Havant in 2010 and, though he failed to become secretary of state for education, he was appointed minister of state for universities and science.

Williams, Gareth (1941–2003), Lord
Welsh barrister and Labour leader of the House of Lords. He was famously born in a taxi between Mostyn and Prestatyn. He was educated at Rhyl Grammar School and Cambridge. He was called to the bar in 1965 and became queen's counsel and then recorder from 1978. He became a Labour peer in 1992 and shadow spokesman for legal affairs from 1997. He served as a junior minister at the Home Office

1997 and minister of state 1998, deputy leader of the Lords and attorney general 1999, and leader of Lords from 2001.

> This almost irreplaceable figure was universally popular because the steel of his radicalism and the iron of his logic were covered with the velvet of his deft articulacy and the sheen of his sparkling wit. (*Guardian* obituary, 22 September 2003)

Williams, Marcia (Lady Falkender) (1932–)

Personal secretary to Harold Wilson when he was prime minister and rumoured to exercise great influence over him. She was educated at Queen Mary College, London University, then worked at Labour headquarters before she became Wilson's private and political secretary 1956–73. She was given a life peerage in 1974.

Williams, Shirley (1930–), Baroness

Labour secretary of state for education 1976–79 and member of the 'gang of four' who founded the Social Democratic Party (SDP). Born to political scientist George Catlin and writer Vera Brittain, she was likely to favour public life and an education at Oxford and Columbia Universities did not discourage her. She was MP for Hitchin 1964–74 and Hertford and Stevenage 1974–79. She was a steadfast supporter of the revisionist Labour line associated with Hugh Gaitskell. She was also fervently pro-Europe. She held junior posts in Harold Wilson's 1966 government and was elected to the shadow cabinet in 1971; she was secretary of state for prices and consumer affairs 1974–76, then education secretary 1976–79, as which she pressed on with the comprehensive project. In 1980 she stated she would leave the party if it committed itself to leaving the European Community, and thereupon formed the Social Democratic Party along with Bill Rodgers, Roy Jenkins and David Owen. She was elected president of the SDP in 1982, after she had won the Crosby by-election in 1981. She lost the seat in 1983 and went on to support the merger with the

Liberals to form the Liberal and Social Democratic Party (later renamed the Liberal Democrats). She joined the Lords in 1993 though she worked at Harvard University. She was the third member of the 'gang of four' to become leader of the Liberal Democrats in the Lords, in November 2001.

> The saddest illusion of revolutionary socialists is that revolution itself will transform the nature of human beings.

Wilson, Harold (1916–95)

Labour prime minister 1964–70 and 1974–76. He was educated at Wirral Grammar School and Oxford, where he shone and became secretary of the Liberal Association. He was director of economics and statistics in the wartime civil service for the Ministry of Fuel and Power. He was on the brink of choosing an academic career but chose Labour politics instead, being returned for Ormskirk 1945 and then for Huyton, Liverpool, 1950–83. By 1947, aged 31, he was already president of the Board of Trade and did much to remove wartime controls on economic activity. He resigned in 1951 with Aneurin Bevan in protest against health cuts. Some speculate he was establishing left-wing credentials for a future attempt on the leadership, though when younger he seemed unambitious. He fought Hugh Gaitskell for the leadership in 1960 but lost; he succeeded after the death of Gaitskell in 1963, in a party without the left-wing firebrand Bevan, who had died in 1960. He established himself as a dynamic Kennedy-type figure in the early 1960s and won the 1964 general election, though only by four seats. He succeeded brilliantly in managing his tiny majority and in 1966 won a landslide victory. Then his problems started, with devaluation and inflation plus relative economic decline and abortive attempts to reform the Lords and the trade unions, as well as join the Common Market. His administration's rather few achievements included the Open University, liberalisation of laws on homosexuals and the abolition of the death penalty. His defeat in the 1970 general election was unexpected, as his poll position had been promising. In opposition his party moved to the left, especially on Europe. He strove to maintain party unity and was rewarded by the victory over Edward Heath in February 1974, after the miners had weakened Heath's credibility, and the narrow victory in October 1974. He defused the split over Europe with a referendum, in which membership was endorsed by two to one. In 1976 he resigned dramatically. Perhaps the most astonishing thing about it was that there was no shocking scandal underlying it – the reason seemed to be mere boredom with public life; some have suggested he already knew he was suffering from Alzheimer's, the disease which eventually killed him. His final honours list, which rewarded businessmen, marred his reputation and it continued to decline for several years until new biographies by Ben Pimlott (1992) and Philip Zeigler (1993) revived it somewhat. One of the cleverest and most pragmatic of Labour politicians, he resembled David Lloyd George in trying to please too many people and ending up being distrusted by almost everyone.

> We are re-defining and we are re-stating our socialism in terms of the scientific revolution…. The Britain that is going to be forged in the white heat of this revolution will be no place for restrictive practices or out-dated methods on either side of industry. (Speech to the Labour Party conference, Scarborough, 1 October 1963)

> Smethwick Conservatives can have the satisfaction of having topped the poll, of having sent a member who, until another election returns him to oblivion, will serve his time here as a parliamentary leper. (Referring to Peter Griffiths, who defeated Patrick Gordon Walker in a racist campaign, 4 November 1964)

> It does not mean, of course, that the pound here in Britain in your pocket or your purse or your bank has been devalued. (Announcing the devaluation of the pound, 20 November 1967)

> A week is a long time in politics. (Probably used in a lobby briefing, 1964)

> Selsdon Man is designing a system of society for the ruthless and pushing, the uncaring…. His message to the rest of us is: you're out on your own. (Referring to the Tory policy meeting at Selsdon Park, Croydon, 1970)

> One man's wage rise is another man's price increase. (When opposition leader, 1970)

> If I had the choice between smoked salmon and tinned salmon, I'd have it tinned. With vinegar. (1962)

> If Harold Wilson ever went to school without boots, it was merely because he was too big for them. (Harold Macmillan on Wilson's much-vaunted poverty-stricken childhood)

Wilson, Richard (1942–), Sir

Civil servant. He was educated at Radley and Cambridge. He served as cabinet secretary and head of the home civil service 1998–2002. He subsequently became master of Emmanuel College, Cambridge. He was a self-effacing, urbane mandarin.

> There are occasions when you have to say 'bollocks' to ministers. (February 2000)

Wollstonecraft, Mary (1759–97)

One of the first feminist writers. She married one of the so-called English Jacobins, William Godwin. She wrote *A Vindication of Rights of Man* (1790) and *A Vindication of the Rights of Woman* (1792), which advocated equality of the sexes, especially in education.

Woodward, Shaun (1958–)

Labour MP for St Helens South from 2001 and Northern Ireland secretary 2007–10. He was educated at Bristol Grammar School and Cambridge and Harvard Universities. He worked as a lobbyist, a producer for the BBC and as Conservative director of communications, 1991–92. He was elected for Witney for the Tories in 1997 but defected to Labour in 2001, being 'parachuted', to use the term of his opponents, into a safe seat. He was re-elected in 2005 and given junior office by Tony Blair. Gordon Brown made him Northern Ireland secretary in June 2007 and he survived a couple of subsequent

reshuffles, suggesting he demonstrated
competence in post.

Woolf, Harry (1933–), Lord Justice
Lord chief justice of England and Wales
from 2000 and master of the rolls 1996–
2000. He was educated at Fettes and
University College London. He was called
to the bar in 1954, served as a captain in
the army from 1955 and practised law after
1956. He chaired an inquiry into prisons
in 1990, which attracted much publicity,
though only some of its recommendations
were implemented. His report into civil
justice when master of the rolls was more
successful and inaugurated profound
changes to civil litigation procedures.

Worcester, Bob (1933–)
Chairman of Market Opinion Research
International (MORI) from 1973. He
was educated at Kansas University before
he became a consultant with McKinsey
and Co. 1962–65. He joined MORI
in the late 1960s and quickly became
identified as the public face of the polling
organisation as well as pollsters in general.
In addition to being a visiting professor at
City University and the London School
of Economics, as well as Strathclyde
University, he has authored several books
and regularly writes in the broadsheet
press, and appears on television and radio
current affairs programmes.

Wright, Anthony (1948–)
Labour backbencher and political
scientist. He was educated at Kettering
Grammar School, the London School
of Economics, Harvard University and
Balliol College, Oxford. He lectured in
politics at Birmingham University, and
was MP for Cannock after 1992. He
has written several well received books on
political philosophy and British politics.
He was chair of the Public Administration
Committee from 1997. He was a (not
uncritical) Blairite 'moderniser' and
advocate for reform of parliament. He was
(deservedly) chosen Parliamentarian of the
Year in August 2009.

Yelland, David (1963–)
Editor of the *Sun* 1998–2003. He was
educated at grammar school in Yorkshire
and at Lancashire Polytechnic. He started
his career as a business reporter, and
proved hardworking and prescient. He was
a surprise choice as replacement for Stuart
Higgins as editor of the *Sun*. He followed
a pro-Labour line, though only up to a
point – he branded Tony Blair the 'most
dangerous man in Britain' in August 1998
for his pro-European stance.

> I don't think the Blairs are *Sun* readers.
> (July 2000)

Yeo, Tim (1945–)
Conservative MP and member of the
shadow cabinet. He was educated at
Charterhouse and Cambridge and worked
in business until he was elected MP for
South Suffolk in 1983. He served as
a junior minister under John Major but
resigned after a scandal involving an affair.
After 1997 he shadowed agriculture for a
while and then trade and industry under
Tory leader Iain Duncan Smith. He was
occasionally seen as a possible leadership
contender from the left of the party. He was
the party's spokesman for health and education after November 2003 – a wide area in
which he had responsibility for convincing
voters that his party cared deeply about
public services. In the summer of 2004
Michael Howard redistributed the health
and education portfolios and made Yeo
shadow spokesman for the environment.

Young, George (1941–), Sir
Conservative MP, leader of the House of
Commons and lord privy seal from May
2010. The 6th baronet was educated at
Eton and then Christ Church, Oxford,
where he read philosophy, politics and
economics (PPE). In the mid-1960s he
worked for a merchant bank for a while,
then for a year in the National Economic

Development Office before taking a postgraduate degree at the University of Surrey. From 1969 to 1974 he worked as an advisor to the Post Office, also becoming an elected councillor in the borough of Lambeth. In 1974 he was elected Conservative MP for Acton and served 23 years for this constituency before representing North West Hampshire from 1997 onwards. He served as a junior health minister 1981–86. His enthusiasm for cycling earned him the press nickname the 'Bicycling Baronet'. On the liberal wing of his party, Young had an uneasy relationship with Margaret Thatcher and led the revolt against the poll tax. When John Major became prime minister he was made successively: minister for housing and planning; financial secretary to the Treasury from 1994 to 1995; and in the cabinet as secretary of state for transport 1995–97. In opposition Young held a number of posts and was favourite to be elected speaker in 2000 when Michael Martin was preferred; he stood again in 2009 and lost out this time to John Bercow. This popular member of the party and the Commons generally was given his current posts by David Cameron upon the Tory victory in 2010.

Young, Hugo (1938–2003)
Leading political columnist. He was educated at Ampleforth and Balliol College, Oxford, where he studied law. He worked for the *Sunday Times* as political editor before moving to the *Guardian*, where he established a reputation as a profound analyst of British politics in his twice-weekly columns. His Radio 4 programmes (such as *The Thatcher Phenomenon* and *No, Minister*) were well received and his book *One of Us: Life of Margaret Thatcher* (1989) was widely regarded as the best biography of her. He died, lamented by colleagues and readers alike, in September 2003, having continued writing his column until the last week of his life.

Bibliography

General works of reference
Axford, B., *et al.*, *Politics: An Introduction*, Routledge, 1997.
Butler, D. and Butler, G., *British Political Facts 1900–1994*, Macmillan, 1994.
Crystal, D., *The Cambridge Biographical Encyclopaedia*, 2nd edition, Cambridge University Press, 1998.
Gardiner, J. (ed.), *Who's Who in British History*, Collins and Brown, 2000.
Heywood, A., *Politics*, Macmillan, 1997.
Hutchinson Encyclopedia of Britain, Helicon, 1999.
Hutchinson Softback Encyclopaedia, 3rd edition, Softback Preview, 1996.
Macmillan Encyclopaedia, Guild Publishing, 1981.
Magnusson, M., *Chambers Biographical Dictionary*, 1990.
Oxford Dictionary of Quotations, Oxford University Press, 1996.
Oxford World Encyclopaedia, Oxford University Press, 1998.
Parliamentary Yearbook and Diary, 2000, Blake Contracting Publishing, 2001.
Pritchard, J., *The Penguin Guide to the Law*, 2nd edition, Guild Publishing, 1986.
Urmson, J. O. and Ree, J., *The Concise Encyclopaedia of Western Philosophy and Philosophers*, Routledge, 1993.
Who's Who, A. and C. Black, 1998.

General politics sources
Day, A., *et al.*, *Political Parties of the World*, 4th edition, Cartermill, 1996.
Kavanagh, D. (ed.), *The Oxford Dictionary of Political Biography*, Oxford University Press, 1998.
McLean, I. (ed.), *The Concise Oxford Dictionary of Politics*, Oxford University Press, 1996.
Pilkington, C., *The Politics Today Companion to the British Constitution*, Manchester University Press, 1999.
Roberts, G. and Edwards, A., *A New Dictionary of Political Analysis*, Edward Arnold, 1991.
Robertson, D., *The Penguin Dictionary of Politics*, Penguin, 1993.

British history
Gardner, J. and Wenborn, N. (eds), *The History Today Companion to British History*, Collins, 1995.
Kenyon, J. P., *A Dictionary of British History*, Secker and Warburg, 1981.
Lee, C., *This Sceptred Isle*, BBC, 2000.
Schama, S., *A History of Britain*, BBC, Vol. I 2000, Vol. II 2001, Vol. III 2002.
Trevelyan, G. M., *English Social History*, Pelican, 1979.

General British politics
Budge, I., *et al.*, *The New British Politics*, Longman, 1998.

Coates, D. and Lawler, P. (eds), *New Labour in Power*, Manchester University Press, 2000.

Dunleavy, P., *et al.* (eds), *Developments in British Politics 6*, Macmillan, 2000.

Holliday, I., *et al.* (eds), *Fundamentals in British Politics*, Manchester University Press, 1999.

Jones, B. (ed.), *Political Issues in Britain Today*, 5th edition, Manchester University Press, 1999.

Jones, B., *British Politics Today: The Essentials*, Manchester University Press, 2010.

Jones, B. and Kavanagh, D., *British Politics Today*, Manchester University Press, 2003.

Jones, B., *et al.*, *Politics UK*, 7th edition, Pearson Education, 2010.

Kavanagh, D., Richards, D., Smith, M. and Geddes, A., *British Politics*, Oxford University Press, 2006.

Kingdom, J., *Government and Politics in Britain: An Introduction*, 3rd edition, Polity, 2003.

Leach, R., Coxall, B. and Robins, L., *Contemporary British Politics*, 4th edition, Palgrave, 2006.

McAnulla, S. D., *British Politics: A Critical Introduction*, Continuum, 2006.

Moran, Michael, *Politics and Governance in the UK*, Palgrave, 2005.

Roberts, D. (ed.), *British Politics in Focus*, Causeway Press, 2003.

Specific issues, policy areas and topics in British politics

Abercrombie, N., *et al.*, *Contemporary British Society*, Polity, 1988.

Adonis, A., *Parliament Today*, Manchester University Press, 1993.

Adonis, A. and Pollard, S., *A Class Act: The Myth of Britain's Classless Society*, Hamish Hamilton, 1997.

Alderdson, J., *A New Cromwell: The Centralisation of the Police*, Charter 88, 1994.

Almond, G. A. and Verba, S., *The Civic Culture*, Princeton University Press, 1963.

Almond, G. A. and Verba, S. (eds), *The Civic Culture Revisited*, Little, Brown, 1980.

Althusser, L., *For Marx* (transl. B. Brewster), Penguin, 1969.

Amery, L. S., *Thoughts on the Constitution*, Oxford University Press, 1947.

Arblaster, A., *The Rise and Decline of Western Liberalism*, Blackwell, 1984.

Armstrong, P., Glyn, A. and Harrison, J., *Capitalism Since World War II*, Fontana, 1984.

Armstrong, P., Glyn, A. and Harrison, J., *Capitalism Since 1945*, Blackwell, 1991.

Audit Commission, *We Can't Go On Meeting Like This*, Audit Commission Publications, 1990.

Audit Commission, *Passing the Buck: The Impact of Standard Spending Assessments on Economy, Efficiency and Effectiveness*, HMSO, 1993.

Audit Commission, *Realising the Benefits of Competition: The Client Role for Contracted Services*, HMSO, 1993.

Auerback, M. M., *The Conservatism Illusion*, Columbia University Press, 1959.

Bagehot, W., *The English Constitution*, Fontana, 1963 (first published 1867).

Baggott, R., *Pressure Groups Today*, Manchester University Press, 1995.

Bains, M. A. (chairman), *The New Local Authorities: Management and Structure*, HMSO, 1972.

Baker, K., *Turbulent Years: My Life In Politics*, Faber, 1993.

Baldwin, R. and Kinsey, R., *Police Powers and Politics*, Quartet, 1982.

Balogh, T., 'The apotheosis of the dilettante: the establishment of mandarins', in Thomas, H. (ed.), *Crisis in the Civil Service*, Anthony Blond, 1968.

Banton, M., *Promoting Racial Harmony*, Cambridge University Press, 1985.

Bar Council, *Quality of Justice: The Bar's Response*, Bar Council, 1989.

Barberis, P. (ed.), *The Whitehall Reader*, Open University Press, 1996.

Barker, R., *Politics, Peoples and Government*, Macmillan, 1994.

Barnett, A., *Iron Brittania*, Allion and Busby, 1982.

Barnett, A., Ellis, C. and Hirst, P., *Debating the Constitution*, Polity, 1993.

Barron, J., Crawley, G. and Wood, T., *Councillors in Crisis*, Macmillan, 1991.

Batty, K. and George, B., 'Finance and facilities for MPs', in Norton, P. (ed.), *Parliament in the 1980s*, Basil and Blackwell, 1985.

Baxter, J. and Koffman, L. (eds), *Police, the Constitution and the Community*, Professional Books, 1985.

Beard, H. and Cerf, C., *The Official Politically Correct Dictionary and Handbook*, Grafton, 1992.

Beer, S. H., *Modern British Politics*, Faber, 1965.

Beer, S. H., *Britain Against Itself*, Faber, 1982.

Bell, D., *The End of Ideology*, Free Press, 1960.

Benn, M., 'Policing women', in Baxter, J. and Koffman, L. (eds), *Police, the Constitution and the Community*, Professional Books, 1985.

Benn, M., *et al.*, *The Rape Controversy*, National Council for Civil Liberties, 1983.

Benn, T., *Arguments for Socialism*, Penguin, 1979.

Benn, T., 'Manifestos and mandarins', in *Policy and Practice: The Experience of Government*, Royal Institute of Public Administration, 1980.

Bentley, A. F., *The Process of Government*, Harvard University Press, 1967 (first published 1908).

Bentley, M., *Politics Without Democracy, 1815–1914*, Fontana, 1984.

Berlin, I., 'Two concepts of liberty', in Berlin, I., *Four Essays on Liberty*, Oxford University Press, 1970.

Beveridge, W. (chairman), *Social Insurance and Allied Services*, HMSO, 1942.

Birch, A. H., *Small Town Politics*, Oxford University Press, 1959.

Birkinshaw, P., *Freedom of Information: The Law, the Practice and the Ideal*, Weidenfeld and Nicolson, 1988.

Birkinshaw, P., *Reforming the Secret State*, Open University Press, 1991.

Bishop, M., Kay, J. and Mayer, C. (eds), *The Regulatory Challenge*, Oxford University Press, 1995.

Blake, R., *The Conservative Party from Peel to Thatcher*, Fontana, 1985.

Blunkett, D., *On a Clear Day*, Michael O'Mara, 1995.

Blunkett, D,. *The Blunkett Tapes*, Bloomsbury, 2006.

Boaden, N., *Urban Policy Making*, Cambridge University Press, 1971.

Boddy, M. and Fudge, C. (eds), *Local Socialism: The Way Ahead*, Macmillan, 1984.

Bogdanor, V., *The People and the Party System*, Cambridge University Press, 1981.

Bognador, V., *Politics and the Constitution: Essays on British Government*, Dartmouth, 1996.

Bognador, V., *The Monarchy and Constitution*, Oxford University Press, 1997.

Bogdanor, V., *The New British Constitution*, Hart, 2009.

Bottomore, T., *Elites in Society*, Penguin, 1964.

Bower, T., *Maxwell: The Outsider*, Aurum Press, 1988.

Bower, T., *Gordon Brown, Prime Minister*, Harper, 2007.

Box, S., *Deviance, Reality and Society*, Holt, Rinehart and Winston, 1971.

Brand, J., *British Parliamentary Parties: Policy and Power*, Oxford University Press, 1992.

Brendon, P., *Eminent Edwardians*, Pimlico, 2003.

Brett, E. A., *The World Economy Since the War: The Politics of Uneven Development*, Macmillan, 1985.

Bruce, B., *Images of Power*, Kogan Page, 1992.

Bruce-Gardyne, J., *Mrs Thatcher's First Administration*, Macmillan, 1984.

Bull, H., *The Anarchical Society*, Macmillan, 1977.

Bunyan, A., *The History and Practice of the Political Police in Britain*, Quartet, 1977.

Burch, M. and Holliday, I., *The British Cabinet System*, Prentice Hall/Harvester Wheatsheaf, 1996.

Burnham, J., *The Managerial Revolution*, Putnam, 1942.

Burnham, J. and Pyper, R., *Britain's Modernised Civil Service*, Palgrave, 2008.

Butler, D., *British General Elections Since 1945*, Blackwell, 1995.

Butler, D. and Butler, G., *British Political Facts, 1900–1994*, Macmillan, 1994.

Butler, D. and Kavanagh, D. (eds), *The British General Election of 1987*, Macmillan, 1987.

Butler, D. and Kavanagh, D. (eds), *The British General Election of 1992*, Macmillan, 1992.

Butler, D. and Kavanagh, D. (eds), *The British General Election of 1997*, Macmillan, 1997.

Butler, D. and Rose, R., *The British General Election of 1959*, Macmillan, 1960.

Butler, D. and Stokes, D., *Political Change in Britain*, Macmillan, 1969.

Butler, D. E., Adonis, A. and Travers, T., *Failure in British Government: The Politics of the Poll Tax*, Oxford University Press, 1994.

Butler, M., *Europe: More Than a Continent*, Heinemann, 1986.

Cabinet Office, *The Citizen's Charter: Raising the Standard*, Cm 1599, HMSO, 1991.

Cabinet Office, *Open Government*, Cm 2290, HMSO, 1993.

Cabinet Office, *Review of Fast Stream Recruitment*, HMSO, 1994.

Cabinet Office, *The Civil Service: Continuity and Change*, Cm 2627, HMSO, 1994.

Cabinet Office, *Development and Training for Civil Servants: A Framework for Action*, Cm 3321, Stationery Office, 1996.

Callaghan, J., *Time and Chance*, Collins, 1987.

Callaghan, J., *Great Power Complex*, Pluto, 1997.

Camilleri, J. A. and Falk, J., *The End of Sovereignty?*, Edward Elgar, 1992.

Cannadine, D., *The Decline and Fall of the British Aristocracy*, Picador, 1992.

Cannadine, D., *In Churchill's Shadow*, Penguin, 2003.

Castells, M., *The Urban Question*, Edward Arnold, 1977.

Castle, B., *The Castle Diaries, 1974–6*, Weidenfeld and Nicolson, 1980.

Cawson, A., *Corporatism and Political Theory*, Basil Blackwell, 1986.

Cecil, H., *Conservatism*, Thornton Butterworth, 1912.

Chandler, J. A., *Local Government Today*, 2nd edition, Manchester University Press, 1997.

Chandler, J. A., *Public Policy-Making for Local Government*, Croom Helm, 1998.

Clark, A., *The Tories: Conservatives and Nation State 1922–1997*, Weidenfeld and Nicolson, 1998.

Clark, A., *Diaries*, Phoenix, 2000.

Cockerell, M., *Live From Number 10: The Inside Story of Prime Ministers and Television*, Faber and Faber, 1988.

Cohen, N., *Pretty Straight Guys*, Faber and Faber, 2004.

Colley, L., *Britons*, Yale University Press, 2005.

Copus, C., *Leading the Localities: Executive Mayors in Local Governance*, Manchester University Press, 2007.

Crick, M., *Michael Heseltine*, Hamish Hamilton, 1997.

Crick, M., *In Search of Michael Howard*, Simon and Schuster, 2005.

Crossman, R., *Diaries of a Cabinet Minister*, Hamish Hamilton, Vol. I 1975, Vol. II 1976, Vol. III 1977.

Curran, J. and Seaton, J., *Power Without Responsibility*, Fontana, 1981.

Dale, I., *A Guide to Political Blogging in the UK, 2007–08*, Harriman House, 2007.

Day, R., *But With Respect*, Orion, 1993.

Dell, E., *A Strange Eventful History*, Harper Collins, 1999.

Denver, D., *Elections and Voting in Britain*, Palgrave, 2003.

Donoughue, B., *The Heat of the Kitchen*, Politico's, 2003.

Dorling, D., *Injustice: Why Social Inequality Persists*, Polity, 2010.

Dynes, M. and Walker, D., *The Times Guide to the New British State*, Times Books, 1995.

Ferguson, N., *Empire*, Allen Lane, 2003.

Franklin, B. (ed.), *Televising Democracies*, Routledge, 1992.

Garner, R. and Kelly, D., *British Political Parties Today*, 2nd edition, Manchester University Press, 1998.

Geddes, A. and Tonge, J., *Labour's Landslide*, Manchester University Press, 1997.

Geddes, A. and Tonge, J., *Labour's Second Landslide*, Manchester University Press, 2002.

Giddens, A., *The Third Way: The Renewal of Social Democracy*, Polity Press, 1998.

Hennessy, P., *Whitehall*, Secker and Warburg, 1988.

Hennessy, P., *Never Again, Britain 1945–51*, Cape, 1992.

Heseltine, M., *Life in the Jungle*, Coronet, 2000.

Heywood, A., *Key Concepts in Politics*, Palgrave, 2000.

Hogwood, P. and Roberts, G., *European Politics Today*, 2nd edition, Manchester University Press, 2003.

Howe, G., *Conflict of Loyalty*, Pan, 1994.

Hutton, W., *The State We're In*, Vintage, 1996.

Jenkins, R., *The Chancellors*, Macmillan, 1998.

Jenkins, R., *Churchill*, Pan, 2001.

Kavanagh, D. and Seldon, A., *The Powers of the Prime Minister*, Harper Collins, 1999.

Kelner, P., *Democracy*, Random House, 2009.

King, A. (ed.), *New Labour Triumphs at the Polls*, Chatham House, 1997.

Kochan, N., *Ann Widdicombe*, Politico's, 2000.

Lawson, N., *The View From Number 11: Memoirs of a Tory Radical*, Corgi Books, 1993.

Layard, R., *Happiness*, Penguin, 2005.

Little, R. and Whickam-Jones, M. (eds), *New Labour's Foreign Policy*, Manchester University Press, 2000.

Ludlam, S. and Smith, M. (eds), *New Labour in Government*, Macmillan, 2001.

Lyn, J. and Jay, A., *The Complete Yes Prime Minister*, BBC, 2003.

Marquand, D., *The Progressive Dilemma*, Phoenix, 1999.

McIlroy, J., *Trade Unions in Britain Today*, 2nd edition, Manchester University Press, 1996.

McNaughton, N., *Local and Regional Government in Britain*, Hodder and Stoughton, 1998.

McQuail, D., *McQuail's Mass Communication Theory*, 4th edition, Sage, 2000.

Mullin, C., *A View From the Foothills: Diaries of Chris Mullin*, Profile, 2009.

O'Brien, C. C., *Edmund Burke*, Vintage, 2002.

Peston, Robert, *Who Runs Britain?*, Hodder and Stoughton, 2008.

Paxman, J., *The English*, Michael Joseph, 1999.

Paxman, J., *The Political Animal*, Michael Joseph, 2002.

Perkins, A., *Red Queen*, Macmillan, 2003.

Pilkington, C., *Representative Democracy in Britain Today*, Manchester University Press, 1997.

Pilkington, C., *The Civil Service in Britain Today*, Manchester University Press, 1999.

Pilkington, C., *Britain in Europe Today*, Manchester University Press, 2001.

Pilkington, C., *Devolution in Britain Today*, Manchester University Press, 2002.

Pimlott, B., *Harold Wilson*, Harper Collins, 1992.

Price, L., *Where the Power Lies*, Simon and Schuster, 2010.

Rawnsley, A., *Servants of the People: The Inside Story of New Labour*, Hamish Hamilton, 2000.

Rawnsley, A., *The End of the Party*, Viking, 2009.

Reiner, R., *Law and Order*, Polity, 2008.

Rentoul, J., *Tony Blair: Prime Minister*, Time Warner, 2001.

Ridley, N., *My Style of Government: The Margaret Thatcher Years*, Huchinson, 1991.

Rivlin, G., *Understanding the Law*, Oxford University Press, 2004.

Routledge, P., *Gordon Brown: The Biography*, Pocket Books, 1998.

Rush, M., *Parliament Today*, Manchester University Press, 2005.

Sampson, A., *Who Runs This Place?*, John Murray, 2004.

Seldon, A., *Blair*, Pocket Books, 2005.

Seldon, A., *Blair Unbound*, Pocket Books, 2007.

Sevaldsen, J. and Vadmand, O., *Contemporary British Society*, Akedimisk Forlag, 1997.

Silk, P. and Walters, R., *How Parliament Works*, Longman, 1998.

Taylor, R., *The Trade Union Question in British Politics*, Blackwell, 1993.

Tebbitt, N., *Upwardly Mobile*, Futura, 1991.

Thatcher, M., *The Downing Street Years*, Harper Collins, 1995.

Thomas, G., *Government and the Economy Today*, Manchester University Press, 1993.

Thomas, G., *Prime Minister and Cabinet Today*, Manchester University Press, 1998.

Thompson, E. P., *The Making of the English Working Class*, Penguin, 1963.

Thorpe, J., *In My Own Time*, Politico's, 1999.

Toynbee, P., *David Walker: Did Things Get Better?*, Penguin, 2001.

Toynbee, P., *Hard Work*, Bloomsbury, 2003.

Toynbee, P., and Walker, D., *Unjust Rewards*, Granta, 2008.

Trench, A., *Devolution and Power in the United Kingdom*, Manchester University Press, 2007.

Watt, P., *Inside Out*, Biteback, 2009.

Watts, D., *Political Communication Today*, Manchester University Press, 1997.

Watts, D., *US/UK Government and Politics*, Manchester University Press, 2008.

Westlake, M., *Kinnock: The Biography*, Little, Brown, 2001.

Wilkinson, R., and Pickett, K., *The Spirit Level*, Allen Lane, 2009.

Williams, M., *Inside Number 10*, New English Library, 1972.

Winder, R., *Bloody Foreigners: The Story of Immigration to Britain*, Abacus, 2004.

Young, H., *One of Us: Life of Margaret Thatcher*, Macmillan, 1989.

Young, H., *Supping with the Devil*, Guardian Books, 2003.

Useful websites

Constitution
Constitution Unit at University College London
www.ucl.ac.uk/constitution-unit

House of Commons within the British constitution
www.leeds.ac.uk/law/teaching/law6cw/hc-1.htm

Elections and voting behaviour
UK Data Archive
www.data-archive.ac.uk

European Union
European Central Bank
www.ecb.int

European Commission
http://ec.europa.eu

European Court of Justice
http://curia.eu.int

European Parliament
www.europarl.eu.int

UK Office of the European Parliament
www.europarl.org.uk

University Association for Contemporary European Studies
www.uaces.org

Judiciary, police, crime
Crown Prosecution Service
www.cps.gov.uk

Home Office Research Development Statistics
http://rds.homeoffice.gov.uk/rds

Law Society
www.lawsociety.org.uk

Local government
Improvement and Development Agency for local government
www.idea.gov.uk

Local Government Information Unit
www.lgiu.gov.uk

Ministers, departments and civil servants
Civil service
www.civilservice.gov.uk

Directgov – public service information
www.direct.gov.uk